C000102972

Innovative Instructional Design Methods and Tools for Improved Teaching

Mohamed Khaldi
Abdelmalek Essaadi University, Morocco

A volume in the Advances in Educational
Technologies and Instructional Design (AETID)
Book Series

Published in the United States of America by
IGI Global
Information Science Reference (an imprint of IGI Global)
701 E. Chocolate Avenue
Hershey PA, USA 17033
Tel: 717-533-8845
Fax: 717-533-8661
E-mail: cust@igi-global.com
Web site: http://www.igi-global.com

Copyright © 2024 by IGI Global. All rights reserved. No part of this publication may be reproduced, stored or distributed in any form or by any means, electronic or mechanical, including photocopying, without written permission from the publisher. Product or company names used in this set are for identification purposes only. Inclusion of the names of the products or companies does not indicate a claim of ownership by IGI Global of the trademark or registered trademark.

Library of Congress Cataloging-in-Publication Data

Names: Khaldi, Mohamed, 1959- editor.
Title: Innovative instructional design methods and tools for improved
  teaching / By Mohamed Khaldi.
Description: Hershey, PA : Information Science Reference, [2024] | Includes
  bibliographical references and index. | Summary: "This book transcends
  the conventional boundaries of educational discourse, offering a roadmap
  for designing learning activities beyond routine exercises"-- Provided
  by publisher.
Identifiers: LCCN 2024002044 (print) | LCCN 2024002045 (ebook) | ISBN
  9798369331286 (hardcover) | ISBN 9798369331293 (ebook)
Subjects: LCSH: Instructional systems--Design. | Effective teaching. |
  Group work in education. | Education--Effect of technological
  innovations on.
Classification: LCC LB1028.38 .I555 2024 (print) | LCC LB1028.38 (ebook)
  | DDC 371.3--dc23/eng/20240202
LC record available at https://lccn.loc.gov/2024002044
LC ebook record available at https://lccn.loc.gov/2024002045

This book is published in the IGI Global book series Advances in Educational Technologies and Instructional Design (AE-TID) (ISSN: 2326-8905; eISSN: 2326-8913)

British Cataloguing in Publication Data
A Cataloguing in Publication record for this book is available from the British Library.

All work contributed to this book is new, previously-unpublished material. The views expressed in this book are those of the authors, but not necessarily of the publisher.

For electronic access to this publication, please contact: eresources@igi-global.com.

Advances in Educational Technologies and Instructional Design (AETID) Book Series

Lawrence A. Tomei
Robert Morris University, USA

ISSN:2326-8905
EISSN:2326-8913

Mission

Education has undergone, and continues to undergo, immense changes in the way it is enacted and distributed to both child and adult learners. In modern education, the traditional classroom learning experience has evolved to include technological resources and to provide online classroom opportunities to students of all ages regardless of their geographical locations. From distance education, Massive-Open-Online-Courses (MOOCs), and electronic tablets in the classroom, technology is now an integral part of learning and is also affecting the way educators communicate information to students.

The **Advances in Educational Technologies & Instructional Design (AETID) Book Series** explores new research and theories for facilitating learning and improving educational performance utilizing technological processes and resources. The series examines technologies that can be integrated into K-12 classrooms to improve skills and learning abilities in all subjects including STEM education and language learning. Additionally, it studies the emergence of fully online classrooms for young and adult learners alike, and the communication and accountability challenges that can arise. Trending topics that are covered include adaptive learning, game-based learning, virtual school environments, and social media effects. School administrators, educators, academicians, researchers, and students will find this series to be an excellent resource for the effective design and implementation of learning technologies in their classes.

Coverage

- Educational Telecommunications
- Curriculum Development
- Higher Education Technologies
- Hybrid Learning
- Classroom Response Systems
- Virtual School Environments
- Adaptive Learning
- E-Learning
- Digital Divide in Education
- Web 2.0 and Education

IGI Global is currently accepting manuscripts for publication within this series. To submit a proposal for a volume in this series, please contact our Acquisition Editors at Acquisitions@igi-global.com or visit: http://www.igi-global.com/publish/.

The Advances in Educational Technologies and Instructional Design (AETID) Book Series (ISSN 2326-8905) is published by IGI Global, 701 E. Chocolate Avenue, Hershey, PA 17033-1240, USA, www.igi-global.com. This series is composed of titles available for purchase individually; each title is edited to be contextually exclusive from any other title within the series. For pricing and ordering information please visit http://www.igi-global.com/book-series/advances-educational-technologies-instructional-design/73678. Postmaster: Send all address changes to above address. Copyright © 2024 IGI Global. All rights, including translation in other languages reserved by the publisher. No part of this series may be reproduced or used in any form or by any means – graphics, electronic, or mechanical, including photocopying, recording, taping, or information and retrieval systems – without written permission from the publisher, except for non commercial, educational use, including classroom teaching purposes. The views expressed in this series are those of the authors, but not necessarily of IGI Global.

Titles in this Series

For a list of additional titles in this series, please visit:
www.igi-global.com/book-series/advances-educational-technologies-instructional-design/73678

Restructuring General Education and Core Curricula Requirements
Julie Christina Tatlock (Mount Mary University, USA)
Information Science Reference • copyright 2024 • 300pp • H/C (ISBN: 9798369303856) • US $230.00 (our price)

Generative AI in Teaching and Learning
Shalin Hai-Jew (Hutchinson Community College, USA)
Information Science Reference • copyright 2024 • 435pp • H/C (ISBN: 9798369300749) • US $230.00 (our price)

Architecture and Technological Advancements of Education 4.0
Rajiv Pandey (Amity University, India) Nidhi Srivastava (Amity University, India) and Parag Chatterjee (National Technological University Buenos Aires, Argentina)
Information Science Reference • copyright 2024 • 479pp • H/C (ISBN: 9781668492857) • US $225.00 (our price)

Strategies and Digital Advances for Outcome-Based Adult Learning
Janice E. Jones (Carroll University, USA) and Mette L. Baran (Cardinal Stritch University, USA)
Information Science Reference • copyright 2024 • 335pp • H/C (ISBN: 9781799847489) • US $215.00 (our price)

Cases on Effective Universal Design for Learning Implementation Across Schools
Frederic Fovet (Royal Roads University, Canada)
Information Science Reference • copyright 2024 • 300pp • H/C (ISBN: 9781668447505) • US $215.00 (our price)

Practices That Promote Innovation for Talented Students
Julia Nyberg (Purdue University Global, USA) and Jessica A. Manzone (Northern Arizona University, USA)
Information Science Reference • copyright 2024 • 271pp • H/C (ISBN: 9781668458068) • US $215.00 (our price)

Navigating Virtual Worlds and the Metaverse for Enhanced E-Learning
Nadia Chafiq (Faculty of Sciences Ben M'Sick, Hassan II University, Casablanca, Morocco) Patricia W. Cummins (Virginia Commonwealth University, US) Khalil Shehadeh Al-Qatawneh (Tafila technical university, Jordan) and Imane El Imadi (University Hassan II, Morocco)
Information Science Reference • copyright 2024 • 350pp • H/C (ISBN: 9798369310342) • US $230.00 (our price)

Reconceptualizing Language Norms in Multilingual Contexts
Sarah Jones (University of Toronto, Canada) Rebecca Schmor (University of Toronto, Canada) and Julie Kerekes (University of Toronto, Canada)
Information Science Reference • copyright 2024 • 330pp • H/C (ISBN: 9781668487617) • US $215.00 (our price)

701 East Chocolate Avenue, Hershey, PA 17033, USA
Tel: 717-533-8845 x100 • Fax: 717-533-8661
E-Mail: cust@igi-global.com • www.igi-global.com

Editorial Advisory Board

Smail Admeur, *FS Tetouan, Abdelmalek Essaadi University, Morocco*

Aicha Ait-Hroch, *ENS Tetouan, Abdelmalek Essaadi University, Morocco*

Georgios Alexandropoulos, *National and Kapodistrian University of Athens, Athens, Greece*

Lamya Anoir, *ENS Tetouan, Abdelmalek Essaadi University, Morocco*

Oudghiri Ayah, *ENS Tetouan, Abdelmalek Essaâdi University, Morocco*

Chafik Azirar, *ENS Tetouan, Abdelmalek Essaadi University, Morocco*

Waladi Chaimae, *ENS Tetouan, Abdelmalek Essaâdi University, Morocco*

Zine El Abidine Mohammed, *ENS Tétouan Abdelamek Essaadi University, Morocco*

Hengzhi Hu, *University Kebangsaan, Bangi, Malaysia*

Ahmed Ibrahimi, *ENS Tetouan, University Abdelmalek Essaadi, Morocco*

Gururajaprasad Kaggal Lakshmana Rao, *Penang International Dental College, Penang, Malaysia*

Maha Khaldi, *Rabat Business School, International University of Rabat, Morocco*

Mohamed Khaldi, *ENS Tetouan, Abdelmalek Essaadi University Morocco*

Fatimazahra Ouariach, *ENS Tetouan, Abdelmalek Essaadi University, Morocco*

Soufiane Ouariach, *ENS Tetouan, Abdelmalek Essaâdi University, Morocco*

Şenol Şen, *Faculty of Education, Hacettepe University, Çankaya / ANKARA, Ankara, Turkey*

Peri Yuksel, *New Jersey City University, United States of America*

Kawtar Zargane, *ENS Tétouan Abdelamek Essaadi University, Morocco*

Table of Contents

Detailed Table of Contents

The transition from a face-to-face educational scenario to a remote educational scenario represents an important change in the field of education. This chapter explores the multifaceted journey of educational institutions and educators as they adapt their teaching methodologies to accommodate distance learning environments. By delving deeper into the challenges, opportunities, and strategies inherent in this transition, the chapter aims to provide a comprehensive overview of the evolving landscape. It addresses the technological, pedagogical, and socio-cultural dimensions that influence this change, highlighting the importance of digital tools, learner engagement, and the role of educators as facilitators in the distance learning paradigm. The chapter provides an overview of effective instructional design, assessment methods, and creating inclusive virtual learning communities. By addressing the nuances of this transformation, this chapter contributes to the ongoing discourse on reimagining education in the digital age.

Teaching today in the digital age requires being able to adapt to the multiple upheavals affecting individuals and societies. The idea that education systems should equip learners with the skills and competencies to cope with an ever-changing landscape. We often refer to skills such as critical thinking, problem solving, collaborative skills, innovation, digital literacy, and adaptability. What is negotiable is how best to achieve the development of these skills, particularly which teaching and learning approaches are suitable to facilitate or enable the development of complex skills. However, educational innovation must be perceived as a proposed novelty, a change, a creation, a transformation, or even an invention in the fields of pedagogy and teaching. Note that the term "innovation" refers to the act of introducing something new in a particular field.

Chapter 3

Soufiane Ouariach, Abdelmalek Essaâdi University, Morocco
Mohamed Khaldi, Abdelmalek Essaâdi University, Morocco

In recent years, e-learning has experienced a surge in popularity as a teaching method. Digital platforms have revolutionized learning by offering learners a more flexible and accessible educational experience. However, it is crucial to recognize that mere access to online materials does not guarantee effective learning outcomes. The design of online learning experiences plays a pivotal role in engaging learners and facilitating a stimulating and successful educational journey. This chapter commences by introducing the concept of e-learning and tracing its historical evolution. Subsequently, it delves into various critical questions surrounding the advantages and disadvantages of e-learning, as well as the pedagogical approaches employed in this environment. The authors then propose a model based on the three systems of a training module, providing a framework for effective e-learning design. Finally, the chapter concludes by illustrating scripting tools for e-learning, equipping teachers interested in e-learning with invaluable resources for developing their e-learning scenarios.

Chapter 4

Peri Yuksel, New Jersey City University, USA
Joan Bailey, New Jersey City University, USA

An academic syllabus serves as a pivotal gateway for students embarking on their college journey, offering not only a roadmap for the course but also their initial introduction to the faculty member or teaching staff. The course syllabus can emerge as a cornerstone, molding students' impressions of instructor expertise, expectations, and workload. The current chapter underscores the syllabus's potential impact, transcending its conventional role as a contractual tool and/or cognitive guide. It aims to illustrate the syllabus as a mental map, rich with resources to help navigate course progression and cultivate a sense of belonging to a broader world that exists outside the confines of a (virtual) classroom, prioritizing students' mental health. Drawing on established best practices, the chapter offers insights for both novice and experienced educators, showcasing the transformational potential of syllabus design in nurturing lifelong learning for professional and personal growth.

Chapter 5

Fatima Zahra Ouariach, Abdelmalek Essaadi University, Morocco
Mohammed Zine El Abidine, Abdelmalek Essaadi University, Morocco
Amel Nejjari, Abdelmalek Essaadi University, Morocco

In the realm of e-learning, educators are presented with the choice between synchronous and asynchronous methods. Communication assumes a paramount role in the fabric of daily life and the interactions that transpire between individuals. This chapter delves deep into the captivating realm of e-learning, meticulously examining the plethora of tools available in the digital sphere. Communication and its accompanying tools assume an indispensable role within the e-learning environment, serving as virtual bridges that connect learners, educators, and educational content. Moreover, the chapter accentuates the potential of communication and its associated tools in the realm of e-learning, transcending the mere transfer of information. Instead, they foster an interactive, collaborative, and flexible milieu that optimizes learning opportunities, engenders learner engagement, and cultivates the development of crucial skills for the modern era.

Chapter 6

Ahmed Ibrahimi, Abdelmalek Essaadi University, Morocco

New ways of appropriating knowledge are emerging thanks to tools and technologies linked to education and learning. The chapter shows how collaborative work opens up multiple possibilities for integrating these tools. The authors sketch out the contours of collaborative learning supported by digital technologies. This online learning modality is accompanied by a pedagogical reflection that will serve as the basis for a proposed model of knowledge appropriation in an online collaborative environment.

Chapter 7

Kawtar Zargane, ENS, Abdelmalek Essaadi University, Morocco
Mohamed Erradi, ENS, Abdelmalek Essaadi University, Morocco
Mohamed Khaldi, ENS, Abdelmalek Essaadi University, Morocco

Learning on adaptive e-learning platforms occupies a main role in the revolution, various pedagogical technologies, and collaboration to create educational scenarios in collaborative systems during adaptive e-learning activities. The main objective of this work is to present collaborative adaptation scenarios in an online collaborative adaptive system during adaptive learning activities in order to group learners in a collaborative space to discuss with each other and develop the aggregation of knowledge. This is about fostering adaptive collaboration. The author discuss the effectiveness of the ADDIE method with this adaptive scenario that group's collaborative adaptive content between the group and the collaborative learning system to provide an engaging online learning experience focused on skill development problem-solving practices. As a result, they meet their objective of designing collaborative scenarios in an adaptive system. The authors value collaborative learning through the interpretation of data generated by the system so that an online collaborative environment surrounds learners.

Chapter 8

Lamya Anoir, Higher Normal School, Abdelmalek Essaadi University, Morocco
Mohamed Khaldi, Higher Normal School, Abdelmalek Essaadi University, Morocco

The evolution of information technologies has created new perspectives in the field of education, enabling the creation of online learning systems. Among these systems, collaborative learning and adaptive learning are emerging as powerful approaches for optimizing the effectiveness of teaching and learning. The chapter explores the transition from collaborative to adaptive learning, highlighting the design of an adaptive collaborative system. By demystifying the key concepts of each approach, the chapter identifies their respective benefits and explores how they can complement each other. Collaborative learning promotes peer interaction, knowledge sharing and the development of social skills, while adaptive learning focuses on personalized content, continuous feedback and dynamic adjustment based on learning data.

Chapter 9

Ayah Oudghiri, Abdelmalek Esaadi University, Morocco
Ahmed Ibrahimi, Abdelmalek Essaadi University, Morocco

Evaluation is a dynamic, systematic, and methodical process which aims to make a value judgment on performance. It is presented in different forms meeting specific training objectives. Evaluating involves a complex task due to the cognitive, social, cultural, and psychological elements that it involves, and it is not always perceived favorably by neither the evaluators nor by those who are evaluated. The tyrannical omnipresence of grading creates a climate of stress which leads to counter-productivity among learners; school therefore takes on a truly anxiety-provoking character, which has been the subject of numerous debates. The work of Gisèle George in 2002 and the work of Peter Gumbel in 2010 underline that the grading which is observed by subjectivity is an instrument of "pedagogical torture." According to Gérard Scallon, "evaluation is a reality which encompasses an infinity of operations, without this necessarily requiring the judgment of the people who evaluate. "

Chapter 10

Chaimae Waladi, Abdelmalek Essaadi University, Morocco
Mohammed Sefian Lamarti, ENS, Abdelmalek Essaadi University, Morocco

In the realm of competency-based education, the integration of adaptive AI-driven assessment strategies brings forth a paradigm shift in evaluating learner mastery. This chapter delves into the intricacies of designing learning scenarios that seamlessly blend pedagogy with AI algorithms to offer personalized, data-informed assessments. By meticulously selecting objectives, designing pedagogical approaches, and orchestrating learner activities, educators create a foundation for adaptive assessment. The integration of AI algorithms enhances evaluation precision, enabling real-time identification of learning gaps and strengths. This chapter delves into the application of machine learning algorithms for tailored feedback, remediation, and ongoing supervision, fostering a learner-centric environment. Through real-world cases and innovative practices, educators gain insights into crafting assessment systems that empower learners to excel in a competency-driven landscape.

Chapter 11

Smail Admeur, Abdelmalek Essaadi University, Morocco
Outman Haddani, Abdelmalek Essaadi University, Morocco
Mohammed Ahmed Moqbel Saleh, Abdelmalek Essaadi University, Morocco
Hicham Attariuas, Abdelmalek Essaadi University, Morocco

Academic failure has become a shocking phenomenon, affecting large numbers of students at all stages of education, particularly in the early years, and students and their families experience academic failure in a dramatic way. For a long time, academic failure among university students has been the subject of heated debate. Many educational psychologists have tried to understand and explain it. Statisticians have tried to predict it. This research (chapter) aims to classify students into several categories, as well as using artificial neural networks to classify first-year students and identify variables likely to explain the problem (students failing at the end of their first year).

Digital storytelling is one of the tools that can be used to improve preservice chemistry teachers' conceptual understanding on the topic of melting and dissolving and metacognitive learning strategies. In this study, it was aimed to create digital stories using information and communication technologies on the topic of melting and dissolving, which is one of the important topics of chemistry. A one group pretest-posttest experimental design was used in the study. The study group consisted of 25 preservice chemistry teachers who were in the first grade at a state university. In addition, within the scope of the study, preservice teachers' opinions on the effect and usability of project-based learning method supported by digital stories on teaching/learning process were also taken with open-ended questions. The findings of this study revealed that digital storytelling is an effective method for improving preservice chemistry teachers' conceptual understanding and learning strategies.

Chapter 13

Undergraduate dental education, which is at the forefront of utilizing innovative pedagogies and instructional methods to deliver learning content, saw an unprecedented disruption globally due to the pandemic. This disruption in dental education resulted in limited access to traditional forms of learning content, which relies heavily on face-to-face teaching. An asynchronous mode of delivery was used to support and maintain the continuity of lectures and knowledge exchange. The mainstream method used was through pre-recorded video lectures, using PowerPoint lecture slides hosted on YouTube. This approach worked for maintaining the knowledge transfer continuum; though the creation and distribution of online content was in itself a challenge to dental educators. Thus, the chapter aimed to identify the pitfalls in digital content creation in undergraduate dental education. Furthermore, the chapter highlights the pathways needed to overcome the hindrances of digital content creation both from a pedagogical and technological perspective.

Chapter 14

After the pandemic with the coronavirus, many teachers and students were trained in the use of digital tools. Indeed, many of these tools are being used more and more frequently and facilitate learning in combination with other methods. In this study, the authors present the teaching approach of scientific discourse to high school students, aged 17-18 (secondary level education in Greece). Scientific discourse is characterized by specific conventions, standards, and practices that are recognized and accepted within the scientific community. It typically involves various forms of communication, including scientific papers, research articles, conference presentations, and scientific discussions. Through this didactic scenario, students will acquire the knowledge required for communication, discourse, persuasion techniques, and means.

In recent years, increasing emphasis has been placed on the integration of ICTE. In particular, the teaching of literature has been at the center of this integration, with the aim of improving student engagement and learning outcomes. In this regard, the action-based approach emphasizes the active engagement of students and the concrete relevance of teaching literature. This chapter aims to explore the integration of ICT into the teaching of literature within the framework of the action-based approach. More specifically, the chapter will address the following questions: What is the action-based approach to teaching literature? How can ICT be used to improve the teaching of literature within the action-based approach? And what are the challenges of integrating ICT into the teaching of literature using the action-based approach? In addressing these questions, this chapter seeks to provide an overview of the potential benefits and challenges of integrating ICT into the teaching of literature, and to offer practical suggestions for educators seeking to do so.

According to the Pedagogical Guidelines (July 2007) for qualifying secondary education, the teaching of the French language is done through three inputs: entry through skills, actional entry, and entry through values. While the first and second entries are of particular interest, the third remains vague insofar as its field of investigation is thorny and impossible to define in terms of didactic implementation. The aim of this chapter is to highlight the various reasons justifying the didactic and docimological ambiguities regarding the implementation of the axiological dimension in the study of literary works programmed in the qualifying cycle, in particular, on a theoretical basis and according to a sample collected and analysed from 50 French-language teachers.

The way languages are learned in today's educational environment has changed dramatically due to the incorporation of technology and the introduction of new methods and approaches, such as e-learning. This chapter breaks down aspects that relate e-learning to language acquisition. It explains e-learning, its emergence, its history throughout the years, and its most efficient platforms and systems. Then, it discusses language learning, its importance, and the basic language skills that provide an effective basis for language learning. Next, it discusses the relationship between e-learning and the development of language skills, how to learn languages through e-learning, and its contribution to language acquisition. Further on, it focuses on instructional design, which plays a major role in the success of training programs; discovers some of the most used instructional design models; and digs into the ADDIE model and how to design educational devices through it. Afterwards, it illustrates all of that with an example of an e-learning educational scenario designed using the ADDIE model.

Chapter 18
Hengzhi Hu, Universiti Kebangsaan Malaysia, Malaysia
Harwati Hashim, Universiti Kebangsaan Malaysia, Malaysia
Nur Ehsan Mohd Said, Universiti Kebangsaan Malaysia, Malaysia

The innovative curriculum-based ideological and political education (CIPE) trend in China's higher education integrates ideological and political education (IPE) into curricula to develop students' citizenship skills. Foreign language teaching (FLT) has leveraged CIPE's advancement due to its rich cultural nuances. Yet, effectively implementing IPE within FLT remains complex and demands academic attention. The authors suggest content and language integrated learning (CLIL) holds significant potential for IPE-based FLT. This potential arises from the shared attributes between CLIL and IPE-based FLT, which encompass diverse language learning facets, the acquisition of content knowledge and the cultivation of cross-cultural understanding. This chapter compares CLIL and IPE-based FLT, based on which a coherent conceptual framework is introduced and justified for implementing IPE-based FLT. However, a comprehensive agenda is needed to address a multitude of issues beyond the scope of this chapter, which is pivotal in unlocking the full potential of CIPE and ensuring its enduring viability.

Preface

INTRODUCTION

The future of our societies depends on education, which is its very foundation. To keep pace with a rapidly changing world, it's crucial that our teaching methods evolve too. The book you now have in your possession, entitled *Innovative Instructional Design Methods and Tools for Improved Teaching*, is an exciting guide that explores innovative pathways to a more captivating, effective and adaptable education for the challenges of the 21st century. It takes readers on an immersive journey through the dynamic field of educational innovation. Within its pages, it explores inventive approaches that are redefining the way we design, deliver and receive education. Nevertheless, the main aim of this book is to offer a comprehensive overview of cutting-edge instructional design techniques, focusing on the methods and tools that take teaching to new heights. A group of leading experts, experienced practitioners and passionate researchers, come together to share their in-depth knowledge to help educators meet contemporary educational challenges.

Today's educational landscape faces multiple challenges, from adapting to different learning styles to successfully integrating new technologies. Teachers, instructional designers and policy-makers are faced with the complex task of preparing learners for an uncertain future where essential skills are rapidly evolving. At the heart of this work is the conviction that pedagogical innovation is the key to overcoming these challenges. We explore how rethinking traditional teaching methods and adopting modern tools can not only enhance the learning experience, but also help learners succeed in a constantly changing world.

The book covers a wide range of topics, from the personalization of learning, to the effective integration of technology, to the crucial importance of collaboration between teachers, learners and instructional designers. Each method presented aims to create engaging, relevant and enriching educational experiences. However, a common thread runs through each chapter: a commitment to pedagogical innovation as an essential catalyst for better education. From traditional classrooms to digital learning environments, the contributors explore approaches that push the boundaries of our vision of education.

This book is not simply a methods manual, it's a call to action. We firmly believe that pedagogical innovation is the key to unlocking the potential of every learner, regardless of context. We encourage educators, educational leaders, policy-makers and all those passionate about education to adopt a proactive perspective in their quest for new ways of teaching and learning. The ideas presented in this book are a source of inspiration, a starting point for stimulating dialogue and a catalyst for positive change in education. Working together, we can create a future where teaching is not only improved, but truly transformative.

THE SUBJECT'S PLACE IN TODAY'S WORLD

Education has evolved beyond the simple one-way transmission of knowledge. Today's learners have diverse needs, varied learning styles, and are accustomed to interactive digital experiences. In this context, instructional design must adapt to be more flexible, personalized and in tune with changing realities. Here are a few aspects highlighting the relevance of this topic in today's context:

Adapting to Technology: Education is strongly influenced by technological advances, and it is crucial to adapt to this transformation. New technologies offer exciting possibilities for rethinking the presentation, assimilation and evaluation of information. The convergence of education and technology is redefining the classroom. This book explores how digital tools, online platforms and educational technologies can be strategically integrated to enhance teaching. It addresses contemporary challenges such as distance learning, the need to personalize teaching and the growing importance of digital skills.

Creativity and Collaboration: Collaboration between teachers, learners and instructional designers creates dynamic and stimulating learning environments, highlighting the importance of interaction in the educational process. At a time when creativity and critical thinking are increasingly valued, this book explores how innovative pedagogical methods can nurture these essential skills. Peer collaboration, hands-on projects and interactive approaches are presented as key elements in creating dynamic learning environments. What's more, innovative tools help widen access to education and facilitate collaboration across geographical boundaries.

Personalization and individualization of learning are at the heart of contemporary pedagogical approaches. The diversity of learners, with their unique learning styles, calls for more personalized teaching methods that recognize this diversity and seek to tailor the learning experience to individual needs. Innovative methods and instructional design tools enable teaching to be personalized, responding to the specific needs of each learner. Furthermore, pedagogical innovation aims to create inclusive educational environments, which take into account the diversity of learners, whether they have specific needs or not.

Responding to the needs of society is also a key element of pedagogical innovation. The skills required to succeed in the modern world go beyond the mere acquisition of knowledge. Education must prepare learners to become enlightened players in an ever-changing society. Innovative instructional design addresses this responsibility by focusing on the development of transferable skills such as critical thinking, creativity, collaboration, problem-solving, effective communication and adaptability.

However, this subject lies at the crossroads of contemporary educational demands and the possibilities offered by technology. This book offers stimulating perspectives and concrete solutions, positioning itself as an essential guide for all those seeking to shape the future of education in today's dynamic world. It offers inspiring ideas and practical approaches for tackling today's challenges and exploiting the opportunities offered by educational innovation.

TARGET AUDIENCE

This book is aimed at educators, educational leaders, trainers, researchers and anyone concerned about the future of education. We are convinced that every reader will find inspiring ideas and practical advice to enrich their educational practice. However, this book is aimed at a different audience, both inside and outside the field of education. Key target audiences include:

- Educators and teachers: Teachers at all levels, from elementary school to higher education institutions, who will find ideas and practical advice to enrich their teaching methods and enhance their students' learning experience.
- Teacher trainers: Teacher trainers, responsible for preparing future educators, who can use the book as a resource for integrating innovative approaches into teacher training programs.
- Educational leaders and school administrators: Policy-makers and school administrators who can draw on the perspectives presented in the book to develop educational policies and implement innovative initiatives at the institutional level.
- Educational researchers: Educational researchers will find case studies, analyses and references useful for deepening their understanding of current trends in educational innovation.
- Doctoral students in education: Students pursuing studies in the field of education can use the book as a source of inspiration and reference for their academic work, while preparing for their future careers in education.
- Instructional designers: Professionals specializing in instructional design, whether they work for educational institutions or companies specializing in education, will find ideas for creating innovative learning environments.
- Educational technology industry players: Professionals working in the field of educational technology can discover trends and innovations relevant to developing more effective educational tools and solutions.

The book aspires to be a versatile resource, suitable for a wide range of actors involved in education, with the common goal of promoting innovative instructional design methods and tools to improve teaching.

CHAPTER DESCRIPTIONS

Chapter 1: From a Face-to-Face Pedagogical Scenario to a Remote Pedagogical Scenario

The transition from a face-to-face educational scenario to a remote educational scenario represents an important change in the field of education. This chapter explores the multifaceted journey of educational institutions and educators as they adapt their teaching methodologies to accommodate distance learning environments. By delving deeper into the challenges, opportunities and strategies inherent in this transition, the chapter aims to provide a comprehensive overview of the evolving landscape. It addresses the technological, pedagogical and socio-cultural dimensions that influence this change, highlighting the importance of digital tools, learner engagement and the role of educators as facilitators in the distance learning paradigm. The chapter provides an overview of effective instructional design, assessment methods, and creating inclusive virtual learning communities. By addressing the nuances of this transformation, this chapter contributes to the ongoing discourse on reimagining education in the digital age.

Chapter 2: From Pedagogical Innovation to Instructional Design

Teaching today in the digital age requires being able to adapt to the multiple upheavals affecting individuals and societies. The idea that education systems should equip learners with the skills and competencies to cope with an ever-changing landscape. We often refer to skills such as critical thinking, problem solving, collaborative skills, innovation, digital literacy and adaptability. What is negotiable is how best to achieve the development of these skills, particularly which teaching and learning approaches are suitable to facilitate or enable the development of complex skills. However, educational innovation must be perceived as a proposed novelty, a change, a creation, a transformation or even an invention in the fields of pedagogy and teaching. Note that the term "innovation" refers to the act of introducing something new in a particular field.

Chapter 3: Scripting Tools and the Design of E-Learning Experiences

In recent years, e-learning has experienced a surge in popularity as a teaching method. Digital platforms have revolutionized learning by offering learners a more flexible and accessible educational experience. However, it is crucial to recognize that mere access to online materials does not guarantee effective learning outcomes. The design of online learning experiences plays a pivotal role in engaging learners and facilitating a stimulating and successful educational journey. This chapter commences by introducing the concept of e-learning and tracing its historical evolution. Subsequently, it delves into various critical questions surrounding the advantages and disadvantages of e-learning, as well as the pedagogical approaches employed in this environment. The authors then propose a model based on the three systems of a training module, providing a framework for effective e-learning design. Finally, the chapter concludes by illustrating scripting tools for e-learning, equipping teachers interested in e-learning with invaluable resources for developing their e-learning scenarios.

Chapter 4: Designing a Holistic Syllabus: A Blueprint for Student Motivation, Learning Efficacy, and Mental Health Engagement

An academic syllabus serves as a pivotal gateway for students embarking on their college journey, offering not only a roadmap for the course but also their initial introduction to the faculty member or teaching staff. The course syllabus can emerge as a cornerstone, molding students' impressions of instructor expertise, expectations, and workload. The current chapter underscores the syllabus's potential impact, transcending its conventional role as a contractual tool and/or cognitive guide. It aims to illustrate the syllabus as a mental map, rich with resources to help navigate course progression and cultivate a sense of belonging to a broader world that exists outside the confines of a (virtual) classroom, prioritizing students' mental health. Drawing on established best practices, the chapter offers insights for both novice and experienced educators, showcasing the transformational potential of syllabus design in nurturing lifelong learning for professional and personal growth.

Chapter 5: Exploring Communication and Communication Tools for e-Learning

In the realm of e-learning, educators are presented with the choice between synchronous and asynchronous methods. Communication assumes a paramount role in the fabric of daily life and the interactions that transpire between individuals. This chapter delves deep into the captivating realm of e-learning, meticulously examining the plethora of tools available in the digital sphere. Communication and its accompanying tools assume an indispensable role within the e-learning environment, serving as virtual bridges that connect learners, educators, and educational content. Moreover, the chapter accentuates the potential of communication and its associated tools in the realm of e-learning, transcending the mere transfer of information. Instead, they foster an interactive, collaborative, and flexible milieu that optimizes learning opportunities, engenders learner engagement, and cultivates the development of crucial skills for the modern era.

Chapter 6: Collaborative Online Learning and Knowledge Appropriation

New ways of appropriating knowledge are emerging thanks to tools and technologies linked to education and learning. The chapter shows how collaborative work opens up multiple possibilities for integrating these tools. The authors sketch out the contours of collaborative learning supported by digital technologies. This online learning modality is accompanied by a pedagogical reflection that will serve as the basis for a proposed model of knowledge appropriation in an online collaborative environment.

Chapter 7: The Design Model of Educational Scenarios in an Adaptive Online Collaborative Learning System.

Learning on adaptive e-learning platforms occupies a main role in the revolution, various pedagogical technologies, and collaboration to create educational scenarios in collaborative systems during adaptive e-learning activities. The main objective of this work is to present collaborative adaptation scenarios in an online collaborative adaptive system during adaptive learning activities in order to group learners in a collaborative space to discuss with each other and develop the aggregation of knowledge. This is about fostering adaptive collaboration. We discuss the effectiveness of the ADDIE method with this adaptive scenario that group's collaborative adaptive content between the group and the collaborative learning system to provide an engaging online learning experience focused on skill development problem-solving practices. As a result, we meet our objective of designing collaborative scenarios in an adaptive system. We value collaborative learning through the interpretation of data generated by the system so that an online collaborative environment surrounds learners.

Chapter 8: From Collaboration to Adaptation: Designing an Adaptive Collaborative Educational System

The evolution of information technologies has created new perspectives in the field of education, enabling the creation of online learning systems. Among these systems, collaborative learning and adaptive learning are emerging as powerful approaches for optimizing the effectiveness of teaching and learning. The chapter explores the transition from collaborative to adaptive learning, highlighting the design of an adaptive collaborative system. By demystifying the key concepts of each approach, the chapter identifies their respective benefits and explores how they can complement each other. Collaborative learning promotes peer interaction, knowledge sharing and the development of social skills, while adaptive learning focuses on personalized content, continuous feedback and dynamic adjustment based on learning data.

Chapter 9: Objectivize The Evaluation: Towards an Objective and Fair Measurement of Performance

Evaluation is a dynamic, systematic and methodical process which aims to make a value judgment on performance. It is presented in different forms meeting specific training objectives. Evaluating involves a complex task due to the cognitive, social, cultural and psychological elements that it involves, and it is not always perceived favorably neither by the evaluators nor by those who are evaluated. The tyrannical omnipresence of grading creates a climate of stress which leads to counter-productivity among learners; school therefore takes on a truly anxiety-provoking character, which has been the subject of numerous debates. The work of Gisèle George in 2002 and the work of Peter Gumbel in 2010 underline that the grading which is observed by subjectivity is an instrument of "pedagogical torture". According to Gérard Scallon (2004) "evaluation is a reality which encompasses an infinity of operations, without this necessarily requiring the judgment of the people who evaluate.".

Chapter 10: Adaptive AI-Driven Assessment for Competency-Based Learning Scenarios

In the realm of competency-based education, the integration of adaptive AI-driven assessment strategies brings forth a paradigm shift in evaluating learner mastery. This chapter delves into the intricacies of designing learning scenarios that seamlessly blend pedagogy with AI algorithms to offer personalized, data-informed assessments. By meticulously selecting objectives, designing pedagogical approaches, and orchestrating learner activities, educators create a foundation for adaptive assessment. The integration of AI algorithms enhances evaluation precision, enabling real-time identification of learning gaps and strengths. This chapter delves into the application of machine learning algorithms for tailored feedback, remediation, and ongoing supervision, fostering a learner-centric environment. Through real-world cases and innovative practices, educators gain insights into crafting assessment systems that empower learners to excel in a competency-driven landscape.

Chapter 11: The impact of Data Processing by Neural Networks on Academic Failure

Academic failure has become a shocking phenomenon, affecting large numbers of students at all stages of education, particularly in the early years, and students and their families experience academic failure in a dramatic way. For a long time, academic failure among university students has been the subject of heated debate. Many educational psychologists have tried to understand and explain it. Statisticians have tried to predict it. Our research (chapter) aims to classify students into several categories, as well as using artificial neural networks to classify first-year students and identify variables likely to explain the problem (students failing at the end of their first year)...

Chapter 12: Digital Storytelling as a Tool for Enhancing Preservice Chemistry Teachers' Conceptual Understanding and Learning Strategies

Digital storytelling is one of the tools that can be used to improve preservice chemistry teachers' conceptual understanding on the topic of melting and dissolving and metacognitive learning strategies. In this study, it was aimed to create digital stories using information and communication technologies on the topic of melting and dissolving, which is one of the important topics of chemistry. A one group pretest-posttest experimental design was used in the study. The study group consisted of 25 preservice chemistry teachers who were in the first grade at a state university. In addition, within the scope of the study, preservice teachers' opinions on the effect and usability of project-based learning method supported by digital stories on teaching/learning process were also taken with open-ended questions. The findings of this study revealed that digital storytelling is an effective method for improving preservice chemistry teachers' conceptual understanding and learning strategies.

Chapter 13: Pitfalls in Online Digital Content Creation for Undergraduate Dental Education

Undergraduate dental education which is at the forefront of utilizing innovative pedagogies and instructional methods to deliver learning content saw an unprecedented disruption globally due to the pandemic. This disruption in dental education resulted in limited access to traditional forms of learning content, which relies heavily on face-to-face teaching. An asynchronous mode of delivery was used to support and maintain the continuity of lectures and knowledge exchange. The mainstream method used was through pre-recorded video lectures, using PowerPoint lecture slides hosted on YouTube. This approach although worked for maintaining the knowledge transfer continuum, the creation and distribution of online content was in itself a challenge to dental educators. Thus, the chapter aimed to identify the pitfalls in digital content creation in undergraduate dental education. Furthermore, the chapter highlights the pathways needed to overcome the hindrances of digital content creation both from a pedagogical and technological perspective.

Chapter 14: Teaching the Scientific Discourse at the Secondary Level Schools. Towards Critical and Digital Literacy.

After the pandemic with the coronavirus, many teachers and students were trained in the use of digital tools. Indeed, many of these tools are being used more and more frequently and facilitate learning in combination with other methods. In this study, we present the teaching approach of scientific discourse to high school students, aged 17-18 (secondary level education in Greece). Scientific discourse is characterized by specific conventions, standards, and practices that are recognized and accepted within the scientific community. It typically involves various forms of communication, including scientific papers, research articles, conference presentations, and scientific discussions. Through this didactic scenario students will acquire the knowledge required for communication, discourse, persuasion techniques and means.

Chapter 15: The Contribution of ICTE to the Teaching of Literature Within the Action-Oriented Perspective

In recent years, increasing emphasis has been placed on the integration of ICTE. In particular, the teaching of literature has been at the center of this integration, with the aim of improving student engagement and learning outcomes. In this regard the action-based approach emphasizes the active engagement of students and the concrete relevance of teaching literature. This chapter aims to explore the integration of ICT into the teaching of literature within the framework of the action-based approach. More specifically, the chapter will address the following questions: What is the action-based approach to teaching literature? How can ICT be used to improve the teaching of literature within the action-based approach? And what are the challenges of integrating ICT into the teaching of literature using the action-based approach? In addressing these questions, this chapter seeks to provide an overview of the potential benefits and challenges of integrating ICT into the teaching of literature, and to offer practical suggestions for educators seeking to do so.

Chapter 16: The Axiological Dimension in the Study of Literary Works in the Qualifying Cycle Between Possiblity and Difficulties of Implementation

According to the Pedagogical Guidelines (July 2007) for qualifying secondary education, the teaching of the French language is done through three inputs: entry through skills, actional entry and entry through values. While the first and second entries are of particular interest, the third remains vague insofar as its field of investigation is thorny and impossible to define in terms of didactic implementation. The aim of this chapter is to highlight the various reasons justifying the didactic and docimological ambiguities regarding the implementation of the axiological dimension in the study of literary works programmed in the qualifying cycle, in particular, on the basis of a theoretical basis and according to a sample collected and analyzed from 50 French-language teachers in the We will submit the results and draw conclusions.

Chapter 17: The Place of E-Learning in Language Learning - Its Contribution to the Enhancement of Language Proficiency

The way languages are learned in today's educational environment has changed dramatically due to the incorporation of technology and the introduction of new methods and approaches, such as e-learning. This chapter breaks down aspects that relate e-learning to language acquisition. It explains e-learning, its emergence, its history throughout the years, and its most efficient platforms and systems. Then, it discusses language learning, its importance, and the basic language skills that provide an effective basis for language learning. Next, it discusses the relationship between e-learning and the development of language skills, how to learn languages through e-learning, and its contribution to language acquisition. Further on, it focuses on instructional design, which plays a major role in the success of training programs; discovers some of the most used instructional design models; and digs into the ADDIE model and how to design educational devices through it. Afterwards, it illustrates all of that with an example of an e-learning educational scenario designed using the ADDIE model.

Chapter 18: The Potential of Content and Language Integrated Learning in Curriculum-Based Ideological and Political Education

The innovative Curriculum-based Ideological and Political Education (CIPE) trend in China's higher education integrates Ideological and Political Education (IPE) into curricula to develop students' citizenship skills. Foreign language teaching (FLT) has leveraged CIPE's advancement due to its rich cultural nuances. Yet, effectively implementing IPE within FLT remains complex and demands academic attention. We suggest Content and Language Integrated Learning (CLIL) holds significant potential for IPE-based FLT. This potential arises from the shared attributes between CLIL and IPE-based FLT, which encompass diverse language learning facets, the acquisition of content knowledge and the cultivation of cross-cultural understanding. This paper compares CLIL and IPE-based FLT, based on which a coherent conceptual framework is introduced and justified for implementing IPE-based FLT. However, a comprehensive agenda is needed to address a multitude of issues beyond the scope of this paper, which is pivotal in unlocking the full potential of CIPE and ensuring its enduring viability.

In conclusion, we issue a call to action, because educational innovation is not just an abstract idea; it's a driving force that requires concrete implementation. Every educator, decision-maker, parent and education stakeholder have a role to play in creating an educational environment that prepares learners to excel in an ever-changing world.

The methods and tools presented in this book are not universal solutions, but rather starting points. They are designed to inspire, stimulate thought and encourage experimentation. By collaborating and sharing our successes and challenges, we can collectively contribute to an educational future that goes beyond improvement to embrace transformation.

We express our sincere gratitude to all the contributors, educators and readers who have been part of this journey. May the ideas shared in this book be the seeds that nurture innovation and foster education that transcends the expectations of the past, embracing a bright and dynamic educational future.

Mohamed Khaldi
Abdelmalek Essaadi University, Morocco

Acknowledgment

I am grateful to the management of the publishing house, IGI Global, an international academic publishing house specializing in the publication of reference works, scholarly journals for their approval to publish this book, which is scheduled for publication in 2024.

My thanks are many as they embody the deeply participatory nature of the publication of this book. Thus, I would like to thank everyone who helped me by participating, supporting and sharing the project. Their involvement and support motivate me to continue publishing more books. Indeed, many people have supported the project since then, United States of America, Greece, Türkiye, Malaysia and especially Morocco. How lucky I am to have this support.

A big thank you to my family, friends and colleagues but also to my PhD students who have always encouraged me and who have contributed significantly to making this dream a reality. Thank you also to all those who believed in this project from the beginning by contributing and encouraging me to publish this book.

I dedicate this book to my wife Malika, my children Inass, Marwane, and Maha, my granddaughters Malak and Nada, and my son-in-law Smail.

Chapter 1
From a Face-to-Face Educational Scenario to a Remote Educational Scenario

Maha Khaldi

https://orcid.org/0000-0003-2828-5856

Rabat Business School, International University of Rabat, Morocco

ABSTRACT

The transition from a face-to-face educational scenario to a remote educational scenario represents an important change in the field of education. This chapter explores the multifaceted journey of educational institutions and educators as they adapt their teaching methodologies to accommodate distance learning environments. By delving deeper into the challenges, opportunities, and strategies inherent in this transition, the chapter aims to provide a comprehensive overview of the evolving landscape. It addresses the technological, pedagogical, and socio-cultural dimensions that influence this change, highlighting the importance of digital tools, learner engagement, and the role of educators as facilitators in the distance learning paradigm. The chapter provides an overview of effective instructional design, assessment methods, and creating inclusive virtual learning communities. By addressing the nuances of this transformation, this chapter contributes to the ongoing discourse on reimagining education in the digital age.

GENERAL CONTEXT

In most societies, the university is considered the guarantor of the academic and educational quality of higher education. However, this institution finds itself confronted with the consequences of the development of Information and Communication Technologies (ICT), vectors of broader information, modern tools at the service of training but also sources of profits through the arrival of online course. The university must respond to a sharply increasing demand for initial training and continued training throughout life. The integration of ICT in higher education makes it possible to develop several solutions from the use of online teaching as a supplement to traditional teaching to virtual campuses or digital universities which offer a fully online learning environment. Online teaching allows remote management of both learn-

DOI: 10.4018/979-8-3693-3128-6.ch001

Copyright © 2024, IGI Global. Copying or distributing in print or electronic forms without written permission of IGI Global is prohibited.

ing, access to resources and interaction between all stakeholders in the educational community. Indeed, in online teaching, learners must change their way of learning, this change is essentially linked to the necessary adaptation to ICT, knowing how to use them, knowing how to search, knowing how to make connections, etc. Thus, online teaching requires skills on technologies, their uses and on research around these technologies in use in the context of university training in addition to the conceptual, theoretical and methodological skills required by conventional teaching.

In general, online teaching is a useful way to supplement traditional teaching provided in face-to-face mode in order to improve the effectiveness of learning and encourage learners to become more autonomous and proactive in their learning process. learning. However, their effectiveness largely depends on the quality of their design. Indeed, well-designed online teaching can be better than traditional teaching in certain training contexts. The implementation of online teaching goes through stages based on educational engineering methods such as the ADDIE method and/or the SAM method.

Based on research work concerning online learning, in particular work dealing with e-learning project management systems, adaptive hypermedia systems and decision-making systems on the one hand. Work dealing with the impact of project-based learning on self-regulation in teaching and the design of educational scenarios for traditional teaching and in particular for online teaching on the other hand. Our objective in this chapter is twofold, on the one hand, the conceptualization of an architecture of an educational scenario. And on the other hand, the design and scripting of online teaching by proposing different possible scenarios depending on the nature of the learning or evaluation activities linked to a learning situation without taking into consideration the nature of the discipline and the nature of the concept to be treated (Khaldi and Erradi, 2020; Qodad et al, 2020; Zarouk et al, 2020; Hrich et al, 2019; Khaldi et al, 2019; 2020; Depover et al, 2014; Burgos, 2008; Schonenberg et al, 2007; 2008).

In this chapter, through our theoretical framework, we will first address the question of teachers' activity in class by seeking to describe it in close connection with the specific context in which it takes place, based on constructivist and socioconstructivist then we will show the difference between traditional teaching and online teaching and specify the questions to ask to design online teaching by identifying its advantages for the learner, the teacher and the institution. Secondly, in our theoretical framework, to deal with the notion of educational scenario, it is necessary to define the notion of educational scripting, define its stages and its tools. To define the educational scenario, we believe it is necessary to define the notions of a learning activity and a learning situation. Then define the types of educational scenarios and finally, we will deal with the adaptation of an educational scenario and the flexibility of the process.

However, in the practical part we propose two studies, the first concerns the conceptualization of an architecture of an educational scenario for a learning situation of content specific to a discipline of this activity of teachers in class. The second study concerns educational scripting and in particular the proposal of different educational scenarios that can be encountered in online teaching for a learning situation.

THEORETICAL FRAME

Introduction

In this part which concerns the theoretical framework of this chapter, we will firstly differentiate online teaching from traditional teaching by identifying the advantages of this teaching in relation to the learner, the teacher and the institution. Secondly, based on educational engineering methods, we identify the different stages allowing the implementation of online teaching by highlighting the tasks to be carried out for each stage. Thirdly, we define educational scripting and the steps to follow for designing a scenario. Fourth and finally, based on previous work, we offer an overview of the educational scenario by citing the different types of educational scenarios without neglecting the role of adaptation.

Teacher Activity in Class

For several decades, researchers in educational sciences have been interested in what teachers do in the classroom. One of the main research objectives has long been to identify teacher behaviors in the classroom likely to promote learning among learners. In recent years, we have seen the development of a concern that moves away from the "content" of teachers' work in the classroom to focus on its "form" and its nature (Casalfiore. 2000). Indeed, the teacher's activity is considered as the result of a compromise between multiple rationalities: the didactic and pedagogical objectives of teachers, their own subjective goals, as well as the constraints and resources of their work environment. Dubet considers that the teacher's activity essentially depends on three elements: his work situation, the learners and himself (Dubet, 2002).

Based on research work that deals with the activity of the teacher in class, we consider that this activity is multi-finalized, that is to say that it is directed simultaneously in three directions (Goigoux, 2007; Leplat, 1997; Rogalski, 2005; Leplat, 1992; Dejours, 1995; Dubet and Martuccelli, 1996):

Towards the learners, considered individually for whom, the teacher aims to facilitate their learning, in different cognitive and social registers: to instruct and educate. Collectively for which, the teacher aims to bring the class to life as a social group which maintains relationships with him whose rules are neither completely given in advance nor definitively established. He strives to master the intellectual and relational trajectory of the class considered as an entity of which one must remain master without losing sight of individual learners.

Towards other actors on the school scene: the teacher devotes part of his resources to making his professional action legible, acceptable and valuable in their eyes. He must also be able to integrate his activity with that of others: the parents of his learners, his hierarchy, the teachers who received the learners in previous years and those who will receive them subsequently, the other teachers who act simultaneously (in other disciplines, in support actions, in homework help, etc.), the various co-education partners.

Towards the teacher himself: the teaching activity produces effects on the person who carries it out both on the physical level and on the psychological level, that of self-fulfillment. Part of the teacher's choices therefore depends on the costs and benefits that he can personally derive from his activity according to his own goals which he can break down in terms of educational objectives, values, professional pride, self-esteem, comfort, health, integration into the workplace, social recognition, career development, etc.

Goigoux considers the activity of a teacher as the response he implements to carry out the task he sets himself. This depends, according to the author, on his own characteristics (purposes and objectives, knowledge and know-how, conceptions, values and beliefs, experience and training, etc.), on those of his learners (their knowledge and relationships that they maintain with knowledge and the School, their skills, their individual and collective behavior, etc.) and those of the educational institution (institutional framework, organization of work, prescription, socio-political context, etc.

Thus, for several authors, teaching activity in the classroom is an activity not structured by an ultimate goal, such as educational goals, but a regulatory activity of the immediate, structured by locally defined objectives and which fulfills two functions: management of order in the classroom and management of subject content (Durand, 1996; Doyle, 1986; Shulman, 1986; Gauthier, 1997).

Concerning the management of order in the classroom, teachers orient their activity in such a way as to ensure organized functioning of the class. Indeed, classroom management activities aim to establish and maintain an orderly environment necessary for the effective deployment of subject teaching activities and learning activities. The teaching activity then consists of organizing groups of learners, controlling their movements, structuring the material offered, regulating speeches, establishing and reminding the rules of life in the classroom, reacting to the behavior of the learners through criticism and sanctions. or praise, etc.

Concerning the management of subject content, teaching activity oriented towards the management of the subject, or towards the teaching of content itself refers to the operations that the teacher implements to make learners learn and concerns the organization of the content. content of learning situations, the way of structuring and presenting the learning situation, proposed school tasks, questions and instructions asked, learning evaluation procedures, etc.

Online Teaching

When we approach online teaching, we can discern many arrangements, from the simple course plan / collection of texts / downloadable handout to the course integrated with modern communications tools (forums, chat, mailing lists) where teachers interact with their learners through Information and Communication Technologies (ICT). To be more precise, it is necessary to differentiate in online teaching between the document consultable online originally intended to be printed and/or studied/commented on in class and the document consultable online intended to be studied gradually. measured by a learner probably alone in front of his computer and no longer in charge of his own learning process. An online course is therefore not a simple PDF or Word document, but rather an online learning space which uses ICT to mediate educational content and encourages the learner to interact with these tools and possibly with a virtual community. other learners.

So, when we decide to put teaching online, we tend to think of uploading a conventional course prepared in Word, PowerPoint or transformed into PDF to a website or distance learning platform. Classical education is generally conceived and defined in terms of content. However, from the perspective of distance education (EAD), it is essential to move from a logic centered on content to a logic centered on the skills that teaching aims to develop in the learner. This requires a conscious effort to make a break with the mode of reasoning that the teacher is used to following in his traditional teaching (Bouthry et al., 2007; Delaby, 2008). The table below summarizes the main differences between traditional teaching and online teaching.

Table 1. Differences between traditional education and online education

	Classic course	Online course
Approach	Transmissive mode	Interactive/collaborative mode
Role	The teacher plays a central role in the transmission of information/knowledge	The learner plays a central role in the construction of new knowledge and the acquisition of skills
Learning environment	Temporal and spatial co-presence	Teaching delayed in time and space, mediated content

Putting teaching online offers many advantages, for the learner, the teacher and possibly the institution. It is the way to personalize training, learn at the time of your choice and, often, reduce training costs. In addition, putting teaching online makes it possible to provide a vision of knowledge that is different and complementary to that of traditional teaching and thus contribute to the evolution of educational practices within the institution. Thus, online teaching provides benefits for the learner, the teacher and the institution.

Among the advantages for the learner, we cite the Individualization and personalization of learning, support, interactivity, the spirit of research and synthesis and freedom of access.

Among the advantages for the teacher, we cite dynamic course support, technological communication and exchange tools to develop the quality of contacts between the teacher and his learners and the participation of learners in the construction of their knowledge.

Among the advantages for the institution, we cite the possibility of increasing the quantity of learners and diversifying the target populations, the reduction in costs and staff travel times, the good management of multiple educational paths and the establishment of a quality assurance system through the history and traceability of learners on the administrative and educational sides.

EDUCATIONAL SCRIPTING

Definition

With the integration of audiovisual as a teaching method in class, media scripting has introduced a new way of presenting knowledge using images and sound to facilitate understanding. If it replaces one of the teacher's functions, it does not supplant them all. However, it invites us to rethink learning and, consequently, teaching, to review the teacher 's intervention and to reconsider the way in which learning takes place . The review to which the teacher is invited is nothing other than the revision of the scenario of his teaching. In the new scenario of its activity, the task of conveying knowledge is left to the media; that of the teacher is to go beyond the presentation of knowledge and to exploit the interaction between the learner and the media; This naturally results in the scripting of the learner's activity.

 is above all a work of content design, organization of resources, planning of activity and mediations to induce and support learning, and orchestration, that is to say integration of the contributions of the different specialists who work on the design and realization of the scenario in the environment. In an educational environment, this working model has remained confined to the production of audiovisual resources without having been transferred and generalized in teaching practice. Although there are currently widely accessible banks of educational scenarios, already in 2007, a study showed that the real uses of the scenarios are poorly known, that their content is not uniform and that few teachers know their usefulness or know how to use them (Macedo-Rouet and Perron, 2007). Such an observation invites us to look at the difficulties which slow down the development of educational scripting. What prevents teachers from adopting this approach and building a different teaching practice? Without being able to make a reflexive return to better understand why the educational scripting approach was not adopted by teachers in the era of educational audiovisual, we have moved to the era of educational computing and ICT to see that the issue is more relevant than ever. Currently, it is necessary characterize educational scripting in the context of computerized learning environments in order to highlight the issues it raises for the practice of _ teachers (Basque and Doré, 1998).

Educational scripting is a form of activity generic to the practices of educational activity, aiming to sequence all the stages of the creation of a training module, a set of corpora to be taught, or part of the learning itself. Behind this sequencing of stages of creation hides a scientifically established thought, which aims to make intelligible once assembled the educational element designed, with a view to facilitating the paths and the acquisition of this object of knowledge in the form of knowledge (Brassard and Daele, 2003; G. Canada, 2007).

The script aims to construct an exhaustive educational process, accompanied by the selected media modes. It therefore provides for the themes that will be covered in training, as well as the forms in which they will be addressed: text, sound, illustration, video, animation, etc. Thus, scriptwriting is a work of content design, organization of resources, planning of the activity and mediations to induce and support learning. It is also a work of orchestration, that is to say of integrating the contributions of the different specialists who work on the design and realization of the scenario in the environment (Bardot, 2014).

The objective of educational scripting is to help the educational designer, so that he can set objectives relating to the needs of the training and the learner according to defined educational stages. Scripting then corresponds to the organization in time and space of all training activities. It also corresponds to the formalization of the stages linked to educational activities.

Stages of Screenwriting

The design of a scenario must follow a certain number of essential steps, of which there are five.

Define the objective(s): For the design of an educational scenario, it is essential to define the educational objectives to be achieved. To do this, a set of questions to ask yourself to let go which concern the intended target audience, the skills desired to be mastered by the target audience, the time organization chosen and the material available.

Sequencing: through this stage, it is a question of setting the themes, activities and/or workshops which will be used to achieve the educational objectives outlined. Each sequence to which we associate the notion of minimum educational unit, or even of educational grain, must correspond to a precise learning objective which contributes to the achievement of the general objective of the training.

Scenario development: the scenario development stage is the stage of bringing the scenario to life. Structuring and coherence are essential for all the sequences used in a scenario. It is therefore essential to carefully choose the content, educational tools and technological tools that must be adapted to the target audience. In order to develop a good storyline, it is important to consider 4 elements: characters, context, challenges and consequences.

Implementation: Once the tools have been chosen and adapted, it is necessary to choose a digital space or (a platform) best suited to the project, and therefore to the targeted audience, to implement the scripted and mediated content.

Evaluation: the point of a scenario is to achieve its objectives. To ensure that the objectives have been achieved. Evaluation is important both at the level of the learner which allows him to position himself in relation to the skills or not acquired. Likewise, it is important both at the level of the designer which allows him to control what the learner has retained, that is to say, if the educational objectives are achieved, but also to control the effectiveness of the training system., namely the tools, media and digital space chosen.

Online Teaching Scripting Tools

There are two main tools for online teaching scripting. These tools are effective to the extent that they help approach the scriptwriting process using an organized and rational methodology.

- **The Activity Diagram (DA):** The role of each of the actors (Teacher, learner and group of learners) in the scenario is clarified in an activity diagram (DA) inspired by UML (Unified Modeling Language) diagrams used to IT project management. The DA must highlight the progress of the scenario by situating the intervention of the three categories of actors in the sequence of activities. The following figure provides an example of an activity diagram (Decamps, 2014).
- **The Specification Table (TS):** A succession of phases as presented in a DA often proves insufficient to describe the scenario. It must be supplemented by a description of each of the tasks proposed to the learner with reference to a series of dimensions of which we cite:
- Nature, origin and purpose of the material submitted to learners and the results expected from them;
- Sequence of tasks envisaged and the criteria for this sequence;
- Organization of groups (collaborative work) and distribution of roles among members;
- Monitoring and interaction methods.

THE EDUCATIONAL SCENARIO

Through this part of the theoretical framework, we will focus on three essential concepts which constitute our framework: the educational scenario, the learning situation and the learning activity. Based on research, we propose definitions of these three concepts to propose an architecture of an educational scenario.

Learning Activity

A learning activity is a situation planned by the teacher and proposed to the learner to help him achieve a learning objective. The learning activity generally involves one or more tasks to be accomplished. There is always an intention behind the decision to have a group of learners carry out an activity. This intention can be motivated by several elements including the strategy, the level of the skill to be developed, the time of the session, etc. Indeed, the school environment in general is organized in such a way that it forces teachers to function generally in the same way by imposing a common overall structure on their activity. (Casalfiore, 2000). Thus, a learning situation is a device that plans a subject to accomplish a task. By applying the instructions to constraints and resources, the subject operates mentally and constructs new knowledge. Indeed, a learning situation, chosen after having determined the objectives, specifies the teaching method and the supports used which must be varied (Rougier 2009).

Likewise, it is however possible to highlight the main effective characteristics of the teaching activity. The latter would be (Dessus, 2008):

A relational activity involving the cooperation (or transaction, mutual understanding) of at least two people, a teacher and a learner(s);

A communication activity involving an exchange (one-way or two-way) of information between a teacher and learner(s);

An activity focused on a learning objective for learners, or the mastery of content, the acquisition of skills or information;

An activity relating to a given content, this content may be knowledge, beliefs, information, behaviors and also possess particular characteristics such as generalizability;

An activity in which the teacher would have specific behavior (presentation, clarification, evocation, indication, etc.);

An activity in which the mental states (intentions, beliefs) of the protagonists can play an important role, and be mutually inferred.

To respect the learner's learning process, the teacher must offer learning activities. There are rules in constructing learning activities. They arise from the way the human brain goes about learning. Indeed, we must establish a hierarchy of activities to offer to learners according to what we want them to learn. We offer eight types of activities by defining the characteristics of each type.

Impulse: Mobilize and engage the learner in the training;

Exploration: Explore prior knowledge and discover the training competency gap;

Learning: Promote the construction of meaning around specific knowledge;

Application: Promote the use of knowledge and its integration in the development of skills or technical capacities;

Summary: Promote the coherent assembly, at the end of a session, of all the objectives achieved;

Transfer; Promote the construction of links and the adaptation of learning in real situations;

Remediation: Helping the learner overcome certain learning difficulties;

Enrichment: Offer more complex challenges to faster learners.

In summary, based on what is said above, we propose to structure the eight types of activities into four activities: situational activity, structuring activity, objectification activity and transfer activity (Khaldi et al, 2019). The four types of activities that we will exploit through our design of an educational scenario of a learning situation. Indeed, the first step concerns setting the situation through commitment and priming. The second stage concerns the learning activity through a conceptualization, an experiment, an exercise, a problem or a project. The third stage concerns objectification through reflection, where awareness and appreciation of what was learned with the previous stage takes place. The fourth stage concerns reinvestment through the transfer of acquired knowledge, and the demonstration of competence (Khaldi et al., 2020).

Figure 1. Types of learning activities according to the context of a learning situation

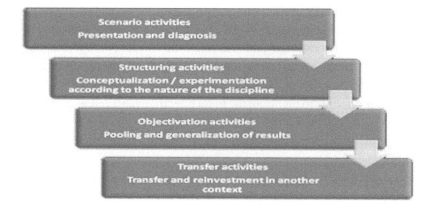

The following figure illustrates the four types of learning activities according to the context of a learning situation.

Learning Situation

The learning situation is defined as a set consisting of one or more activities to be carried out by the learner in the form of tasks in order to achieve the set objective. It allows, on the one hand, the learner to develop and exercise one or more disciplinary and transversal skills and, on the other hand, allows the teacher to monitor the development of skills from a support perspective. to learning. It is therefore centered on the learner and recommends a constructivist or socio-constructivist approach to school (Mels, 2006).

During the implementation of a learning situation and the activities it involves, the learner will have to solve problems and complete tasks and instructions to acquire knowledge and master skills. Note that a skill is a know-how based on the mobilization and use of a set of resources, including knowledge in the form of declarative, procedural or conditional knowledge, know-how in the form of process skills and approaches, and finally interpersonal skills in the form of behaviors and attitudes.

The learning situation will be significant if it matches the orientations of the training program, touches the interests of the learners and poses challenges within their reach while making it possible to highlight the usefulness of the knowledge. It will include suggestions for working methods and evaluation instruments which must also relate to the general areas of training common to the different disciplines and deal with disciplinary content. In a strategic approach, the learning situation is organized in three stages:

- Preparation for learning: the teacher transmits the necessary information to the learner so that he is ready for the task (declarative knowledge: (WHAT?) and for what this task can be used for (conditional knowledge: (FOR WHAT ?).
- Carrying out the task: the teacher models the task and guides the learner in how to do the task and process the information received (procedural knowledge: (HOW?).
- The transfer of learning to other situations: the teacher provides other learning situations where the learner reinvests what he or she has learned (conditional knowledge: (WHEN?). Indeed, the transfer knowledge is defined as the relearning of what the learner already knows in a new situation. This is what he or she is capable of doing with his or her knowledge at a given moment. The transfer of learning can be done at three levels:
  Transfer of knowledge in similar training situations;
- A transfer of knowledge in complex social and professional situations calling on other knowledge, other values or other habits;
- A transfer of acquired knowledge into one's personal history by giving it meaning and organizing it.

The following figure gives us a diagram of the learning situation1

Through this work, we propose the development of a learning situation in the form of an educational scenario in four blocks:

The first block concerns general information about the situation in relation to the discipline, the field of the discipline, the level of training, the place of the situation in a program, the level of the learners and the class, etc.;

Figure 2. Diagram of the learning situation

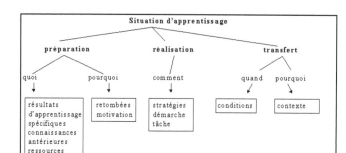

The second block concerns the definition of objectives (general, specific, intermediate) considering that each intermediate objective corresponds to at least one learning activity, skills (disciplinary, transversal) considering that the choice of activities depends on the knowledge to be acquired skills to master and the prerequisites (prior knowledge) which allow the decision to remediate in the case where there are learning difficulties through a diagnostic evaluation at the start of the learning situation.

The third block concerns the structuring of specific knowledge by proposing learning activities which concern:

- Scenario activities for the presentation of a learning situation and at the same time the diagnosis of prior knowledge;
- Structuring/experimentation activities (deductive approach, inductive approach) according to the nature of the discipline for the construction of meaning around specific knowledge and at the same time the use of knowledge and its integration in the development of skills;
- Objective activities for the sharing and generalization of the results obtained during the structuring/experimentation activities.
- The fourth block concerns the transfer and reinvestment of knowledge in a context other than that of initial learning and at the same time remediation to overcome certain learning difficulties.

Definitions of an Educational Scenario

The term educational scenario is the subject of numerous definitions. An educational scenario presents a learning activity initiated by a teacher in order to supervise the learning of his learners. An educational scenario presents an approach aimed at achieving educational objectives and acquiring general or specific skills related to one or more disciplines. It presents a learning activity, initiated by a teacher in order to supervise the learning of its learners (before, during and after the activity with self-assessment and evaluation sheet, scenario, teaching resources, etc. .). Among the many definitions, here are some quotes taken from the bibliography in chronological order, focusing mainly on the field of training engineering, the field of educational engineering and the field of the Computer Environment for Human Learning (EIAH):

Concerning the field of training engineering, the scenario is an instrument for explaining and communicating a training project. We offer two definitions, that of Daele and that of Schneider:

According to Daele and his colleagues in 2002, "the educational scenario is the part of a training system which describes the progress of teaching and learning activities. The system provides the scenario with logistical means and resources (technical, human, administrative, etc.) to be implemented. [...]. The training system itself fits into a given institutional context linked to the needs expressed by society. ". Still according to Daele "the educational scenario is seen as the result of the process of designing a learning activity, a process taking place within a given time and leading to the implementation of the scenario. In a scenario, we therefore find objectives, planning of learning activities, a schedule, a description of students' tasks, evaluation methods which are defined, arranged and organized during a design process. » (Daele et al., 2002). According to Schneider and his colleagues in 2003, "a scenario is defined by an orchestrated sequence of phases [...] in which learners have tasks to perform and specific roles to play" (Schneider et al., 2003).

Concerning the field of educational engineering, we offer two definitions proposed by Paquette and his collaborators:

According to Paquette and his collaborators, a first definition was proposed in 1997, "the educational scenario is made up of two other scenarios (learning scenario and assistance scenario) and consists of describing the activity or activities specific to learning and assistance, the resources required to carry out the activities and the outputs that should result. [...] A learning scenario is the set of activities intended for learners and organized into a coherent whole; to these activities, we graft the instruments offered as supports for the activities (input instruments) and the instruments to be produced by the learners (products). » (Paquette et al., 1997). A second definition was proposed by Paquette and his collaborators in 2003, "through the design of educational scenarios, the designer establishes the links between the sources of information and the different actors. [...] The designer plans the types of communication, the educational strategies, the modes of collaboration between the actors. » (Paquette et al., 2003).

Concerning the field of the Computing Human Learning Environment (EIAH), we propose three definitions proposed by Lando, Pernin and Guéraud:

According to Lando, "an educational scenario is the progress of a learning activity, the definition of objectives, the planning of tasks, the description of learners' tasks and evaluation methods" (Lando, 2003). According to Pernin and Lejeune, "a scenario is defined as a description carried out a priori and a posteriori, of the progress of a learning situation aimed at the appropriation of a precise set of knowledge, by specifying the roles, the activities as well as the resources for manipulating knowledge, tools, services and results associated with the implementation of activities" (Pernin and Lejeune, 2004). According to Guéraud, "the scenario has a triple role: it precisely defines the activity proposed to learners on the OPI (Interactive Educational Object); it also specifies the monitoring that will be made of the learner's progress during this activity; finally, he determines the educational assistance that will be provided to him automatically based on his progress. Our concept of scenario is (a priori) distinct from the concept of "educational sequence scenario" often present in Open and Distance Training platforms. A sequence scenario makes it possible to specify how the different educational activities will be linked together, whereas our scenario concerns an activity (using an OPI) and makes it possible to follow the progress of a learner towards the objective set by it. » (Guéraud, 2006).

Types of Educational Scenarios

At the beginning of the 2000s, according to several researchers, the problem of the design of learning situations by the teacher occupied a strategic place in the field of ICT. After focusing on questions of creation, pooling and reuse of resources, research in educational engineering emphasizes the need to take more account of the learner's activity and replaces the notion of learning scenario in center of debates (Crozat and Trigano, 2002; Pernin, 2003; Paquette, 2002; 2004). Indeed, according to Vantroys and Peter, "pedagogical scenarios are causing great interest in the field of Computer Environments for Human Learning (EIAH). They provide mechanisms for managing and orchestrating activities within learning units. They can thus be at the center of training engineering and are means to define the use of educational tools and objects during a module or a task in which users are involved. In fact, the benefit of using educational scenarios lies in the fact that the main attention is placed on the learning activities that must be carried out to achieve the educational objectives" (Vantroys and Peter 2005). Through what follows, we try to clarify the difference between conceptions of the educational scenario in order to choose the scenario to use in training.

Predictive Scenario and Descriptive Scenario

Pernin and Lejeune define the educational scenario as being "the description of the progress of a learning situation in terms of roles, activities and environment necessary for its implementation, but also in terms of knowledge manipulated" (Pernin and Lejeune 2004). These authors distinguished two types of scenarios:

The predictive scenario: defined as established a priori by a designer with a view to setting up a learning situation;

The descriptive scenario: defined as a scenario which describes a posteriori the progress of the learning situation by including in particular the traces of the activity of the actors (essentially the learners) and their productions.

Learning scenario and coaching scenario

Quintin and his collaborators distinguish between a learning scenario and a coaching scenario. Thus, when designing training, they consider the educational scenario as a structured and coherent whole made up of two parts:

The learning scenario, the role of which is to describe the learning activities that will be proposed and to define their articulation in the educational system, as well as the productions that are expected from the learners;

The supervision scenario which specifies the role of teachers and the modalities of interventions intended to support the learning scenario.

According to these authors, the existence of a distinct supervision scenario makes it possible to draw the attention of the designer(s) to the importance of specifying the interventions of the actors responsible for supporting learners in their training (Quintin et al., 2005).

Learning Scenario and Learning Device

For Depover and his collaborators, in an educational scenario, it is necessary to differentiate between the learning scenario and the learning device (Depover et al, 2014).

The learning scenario is the ordering of the implementation of all the structuring elements of the learning situation. It is the result of the choice of a learning strategy in relation to specific learning content which is described as a succession of steps, obligatory or optional, which learners will have to follow for

Figure 3. The three elements of a pedagogical scenario

Pedagogical scenario		
Learning Activity Title:		
Specific objective of the learning situation:		
Intermediate objective of the activity:		
Knowledge to be acquired:		Skills to master:
Problem situation of the activity:		
Activity Task:	Task Instructions:	Individual/group work:
Learning device		
Teaching materials:	Technological equipment:	Learning Documents:
Communication tools:	Collaboration tools:	Human resources:
Framing Scenario		
Roles of stakeholders:	Learners' activities:	Working Method:
Evaluation methods:	Remediation methods:	Supervision modalities:

an explicit educational purpose. Depending on the case, the scenario may be more or less prescriptive and the variety of individual pathways that will be implemented will be more or less extensive.

The learning system is all the human and material resources to be mobilized to carry out the learning scenario.

By analyzing the different definitions of an educational scenario depending on the type, we can define an educational scenario as a set of three elements: a learning scenario intended for the learner's activities, a coaching scenario intended for the roles supervisors and a learning system which defines all the human and material resources mobilized to carry out the educational scenario. The following figure offers us an example of a scenario bringing together the three elements of an educational scenario.

Adaptation of an Educational Scenario and Flexibility of the Process

By considering the educational scenario as a sufficiently consistent and relevant model to approach the engineering of EIAH, Cottier and his collaborators affirm that the concern of a teacher who wishes to use computer science for his teaching is not to do research in EIAH, it is to design a teaching situation which responds to the educational problem that arises . Note that in classroom teaching situations, the usual practice of teachers and trainers in face-to-face teaching does not lead them to precisely script the educational activity: if the content of training is well defined a priori, a simple A general and not very detailed idea of the organization of the educational activity is enough for the teacher, his skill and experience allowing him to adapt his method and improvise according to the progress of the activity. However, in online teaching, despite the work aimed at removing certain obstacles linked to distance in particular, and to facilitate the practice of teachers and learners, the technologies do not always have the flexibility required for use in the educational context which requires often rapid adaptations to new and often unforeseen events (Cottier et al., 2008).

Thus, the adaptation of an educational scenario can be done during two main phases of its life cycle: either during design (at design-time) or during execution (at runtime).

As for adaptation during design, the teacher designer must take into consideration all possible cases for the implementation of an adaptive learning situation. Indeed, the majority of work is based on IMS-LD (level B). This work attempts to help the designer teacher to define adaptation rules of the type:

"if condition then action", this by using properties and conditions. These rules will be applied during execution following the property values which make it possible to specify whether the conditions are satisfied or not (Burgos, 2008).

On the other hand, in the case of adaptation during execution, teachers and/or the system must react according to the events triggered by the learners in real time and throughout the course of their learning sessions. This type of work consists of guiding the progress of sessions implicitly by the system, for example based on software agents, or explicitly by teachers who can enter necessary adjustments (Van Rosmalen et al., 2006; Zarraonandia, 2007).

CONCEPTUALIZATION OF AN EDUCATIONAL SCENARIO ARCHITECTURE

Introduction

By analyzing all the definitions according to the different fields, we note that the educational scenario gives rise to a project, a particular learning activity, the realization of which calls for resources (sites, software, etc.) and documents (printed, audiovisual, multimedia, etc.). It presents an approach aimed at achieving educational objectives and acquiring specific and/or transversal skills linked to one or more disciplines according to the terms and specifications of the study program. We can summarize all of these definitions with Bardot's proposal in 2014, which defines an educational scenario as the description of the organization and progress of a learning situation using digital technologies and aiming at the appropriation of a specific body of knowledge. A precise scenario including the targeted knowledge, the roles of the actors and their activities as well as the knowledge manipulation resources, tools and services necessary for the implementation of these activities (Bardot, 2014). So, based on this definition, our objective in this work is to propose an educational scenario of a learning situation taking into consideration all of the elements already mentioned above. Indeed, our educational scenario design has four parts (blocks) (Khaldi et al., 2019; 2020).

A first block called technical sheet, it offers us a set of information in relation to the situation treated;

A second block called objectives and skills, it informs us on the objectives to be achieved at the end of the situation and on the knowledge to be acquired and the skills to be mastered by the learners at the end of the learning situation;

A third block called structuring, this block concerns the structuring of specific knowledge by proposing learning activities which concern the situational setting, structuring and objectification

A fourth block, called transfer and reinvestment, concerns the transfer and reinvestment of knowledge and skills treated in the situation, in a context other than that treated in the second block of the situation.

The diagram in the following figure illustrates the structure of all the blocks.

Based on the propositions of our theoretical framework, concerning the definition of the educational scenario, according to Bardot (Bardot, 2014). Concerning the definition of the four types of learning activities while respecting the learning approach in the learning activities. This approach translates into four distinct stages (Khaldi et al, 2019). And finally, concerning the definition of a learning situation according to Mels (Mels, 2006) . In this work, we propose the broad outlines of an educational scenario for a learning situation which we divide into four blocks:

Figure 4. Structure of a pedagogical scenario of a learning situation

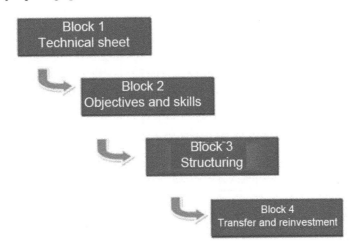

Technical Sheet of the Learning Situation

The first block concerns the technical sheet of the learning situation which groups all the general data concerning the learning situation, the following table offers us a list of the data necessary for the smooth running of the learning situation. Indeed, every learning situation has a title, this title tells us about the discipline taught and its disciplinary area. The place of the situation in the program informs us about the prerequisites necessary to allow a learner to follow the learning situation and above all, it informs us about the level of training, that is to say the intellectual level of the learners which allows us to choose the level of concepts to be treated in the situation. The level and nature of the class informs us about the choice of activities according to the level of the class (low, medium, strong) and according to the nature of the class (homogeneous, heterogeneous). The number of learners tells us, in the case of group work, the number of teams to propose. The number of sessions tells us about the management of activities in relation to time.

Figure 5. Technical sheet of a learning situation

Technical sheet
Title of the learning situation:
Nature of the discipline:
Discipline area:
Situation in the program:
Level of education:
Class level:
Nature of the class:
Number of sessions:
Number of learners:

Figure 6. Example of general, specific and intermediate objectives architecture in a learning situation

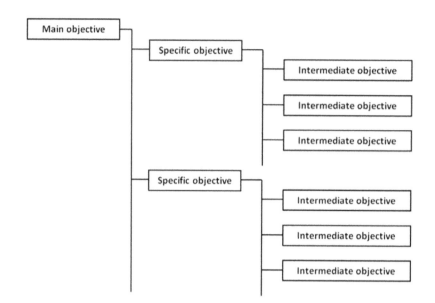

Definition of the Objectives and Skills of the Learning Situation

The second block concerns the definition of objectives and skills which consists firstly of developing the architecture of the objectives by defining the general objective, the specific objectives associated with the general objective and the intermediate objectives associated with each specific objective. . The diagram in the following figure offers us an architecture for the case of a general objective associated with two specific objectives and each specific objective is associated with three intermediate objectives.

Secondly, the definition of objectives and skills consists of defining the disciplinary skills based on the knowledge to be acquired and the skills to be mastered and the transversal skills based on their components. The diagram in the following figure offers us a skills architecture.

Thirdly, the definition of objectives and skills consists of defining the prerequisite objectives (knowledge) necessary to follow the learning situation. These prerequisites which constitute the basic elements of the diagnostic evaluation proposed by the teacher at the start of the learning situation.

Figure 7. Example of architecture of disciplinary and transversal skills in a learning situation

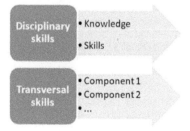

Learning Activities: Structuring Specific Knowledge

The third block concerns the proposal of learning activities around the situational setting, the structuring and the objectification of specific knowledge. Indeed, to respect the learner's learning process, the teacher must offer learning activities that follow rules in their construction. They arise from the way the human brain goes about learning. Thus, we must establish a hierarchy of activities to offer to learners according to what we want them to learn2. In this block of our educational scenario, we propose it in the form of three phases and each phase constitutes a type of the three activities, defining the characteristics of each type.

Discovery Phase

The discovery phase concerns the role-playing activity. Indeed, the scenario is an educational tool used in active teaching. The scenario can be used as an introduction to a learning situation, in order to support the motivation of learners for the material presented, or as a practical exercise after having provided teaching, to make the concept to be acquired more concrete. In all these cases, the purpose of the scenario is to improve the learner's skills. Likewise, the scenario can be used as an evaluation tool. The scenario is a way of evaluating a person's knowledge and especially skills in a different way from an exam, whether oral or written. The scenario allows you to concretely see how the person handles a specific problem.

In our case, we use the scenario as an introduction to a learning situation and at the same time as an evaluation tool to test the learners' prerequisites. To do this, we use diagnostic assessment as a type of assessment which allows us to situate the learner's state of knowledge at the start of the learning situation. It makes it possible to situate the learner in the disciplinary field to take stock of their knowledge and/or their conceptions (initial representations), or their mastery of everyday and scientific language and subsequently adjust by proposing a course and resources. adapted to the level of the learner. The following table presents objectives and means for this type of activity.

Table 2. Example of Objectives and means of the discovery and situational phase

Objectives	Medium
Mobilize energy; Create favorable emotional conditions; Create favorable cognitive conditions.	Provoke (pique curiosity, arouse interest, launch a challenge); Secure (give confidence, encourage, remember successes); Recall the prerequisites (previous knowledge and strategies that will be relevant to the activity).

Learning Phase

The second phase of this block concerns the structuring activity. It allows the transition from action to formulation based on the obstacles encountered during the discovery phase, it promotes the construction of meaning around specific knowledge and at the same time, it promotes the use of knowledge and its integration in the development of skills, at the end of a learning situation. This phase is obligatory to achieve the reflection induced by the concept discussed. This phase concerns two cases depending on the approach adopted. Indeed, depending on the context and the situation, the proposal of a learning activity requires us to choose between two approaches, the deductive approach and the inductive approach.

Presentation of a Concept in a Learning Situation

The deductive approach (or logical deduction) consists of going from the general to the particular, from the principle to the consequence. It is a scientific method that considers the conclusion to be implicit in the premises. We start from the statement of the concept and/or the rule to go to verification by examples. The diagram in the following figure illustrates the presentation of a concept in a learning situation based on the deductive approach. Thus, to present a concept, it is necessary to use this approach which follows the direct teaching strategy which is strongly guided by the teacher. It is an explicit concept of teaching: a transmission of knowledge and the acquisition of skills and competencies by the learner. The following table presents objectives and means for highlighting this situation.

Table 3. Presentation of a concept in a learning situation based on the deductive approach

Objectives	Medium
Guide the course of the activity; Gather the conditions necessary for the progress of the activity.	Clarify (give precise instructions define the terms, give an example of the expected product. Specify the presentation rules); Check (equipment, layout, understanding of instructions, and mastery of prerequisites).

Expérimentation/Découverte d'un Concept Dans une Situation D'Apprentissage

Concerning the inductive approach, it consists of going from the particular to the general. It is a scientific method that obtains general conclusions from individual premises. It allows us to move from particular or specific observations and analyses, to more general perspectives. The educational use of an industrial theme promotes this approach: case study, problem posed, analysis, new concepts, rules, generalization. Problem solving is completely consistent with the inductive approach. The diagram in the following figure illustrates the experimentation/discovery of a concept in a learning situation based on the inductive approach. Thus, to allow the learner in a learning activity to experiment and discover the meaning of a concept for himself, it is necessary to use the inductive approach which obeys the indirect teaching strategy which is learner-centered. Indeed, inquiry, induction, problem solving, decision-making and discovery are terms that are used interchangeably to describe indirect teaching. Indirect teaching pro-

Table 4. Example of objectives and means of the experimentation / discovery phase of a concept in a learning situation

Objectives	Medium
Accomplish a task; Provide concrete elements of experience to then analyze; Encourage the formulation of hypotheses; Allow trial and error; Allow the development of strategies; Integrate relevant knowledge.	Supervise (organize the process, allocate or distribute tasks, help, solve organizational problems, control the time); Discover (ask questions, encourage testing, manipulation, the formulation of hypotheses); Help (provide clues, suggest leads, recall a procedure, provide materials); Inform (make a presentation, provide texts, present relevant material); Provide feedback (encourage success, invite improvement, provide means of self-correction, help identify and use errors).

motes creativity and the development of skills in the area of personal relationships. The following table presents objectives and means for highlighting this situation.

Generalization Phase

The third phase of this block concerns the objectification activity which invites the learner to describe their approach and to name the processes involved (call for metacognition). It promotes the coherent assembly of all the objectives achieved through discussions to pool and generalize the results. The following table presents objectives and means for highlighting this situation.

Table 5. Example of objectives and means of the objectification phase of a concept in a learning situation

Objectives	Medium
Take stock; Evaluate the process; Identify a model or laws; Structure the knowledge acquired; Formalize integrative concepts; Identify the essentials.	Verbalize (ask questions, have a story told, describe the process, express feelings) Encourage exchanges (make people share, compare approaches and results, discuss and criticize) Formalize (define or have defined terms, concepts, laws, procedures; generalize, make or have a diagram made, name the skills, strategies and methodological tools used) To discriminate (to react to counterexamples, to specify the limits of application, to present exceptions) Get evaluated (self-evaluation, peer evaluation, formative evaluation by the teacher) Make a record (make or have made a summary, have a logbook completed, have the essentials noted)

Learning Activities: Reinvestment of Specific Knowledge

This fourth block concerns learning activities around the transfer activity. This activity which allows the reinvestment of knowledge in a context other than that of initial learning through which the learner must reinforce, consolidate and fix his acquired knowledge by generalizing them (opening, broadening). And at the same time it is a remediation stage which helps the learner to overcome certain learning difficulties. By promoting the construction of links and the adaptation of learning in real situations on the one hand and by offering more complex challenges to faster learners on the other hand.

Table 6. Example of objectives and means of the activity of transferring a concept in a learning situation

Objectives	Medium
Deepen the tasks Have different tasks accomplished Decontextualize learning Promote the transfer of skills Consolidate skills Make autonomous	Extend the field (have other examples found, suggest variants and refinements, introduce more complex cases) Practice (give training, do exercises) Integrate (propose an extension in another program or another activity, propose an integrative project where the learning carried out must be used in conjunction with other learning)

Designing a Learning Activity

Through this part, we propose the design of a learning activity without taking into consideration the nature of the activity. Thus, for our design, we consider that a learning activity corresponds to a set of elements: we advance, the specific objective and the intermediate objective corresponding to this activity, which are already defined in block two. Then, define the problem situation of this activity, Define the task and its instructions to respond to the problem situation defined, to point out that the choice of the task necessarily depends on the nature of the discipline treated. Define the nature of the learner groups (individual or group work) depending on the nature of the task to be carried out. Define the educational and technological materials to be used in carrying out the task. Propose working documents for the learner and at the same time specific response documents for the teacher. Define the roles of the teacher and at the same time the actions of the learners throughout the activity and finally define the time allocated to the activity. The diagram in the following figure shows us an architecture bringing together the different elements constituting the learning activity.

As a block conclusion, we can conclude that conceptualizing an educational scenario for a learning situation is not an easy thing. Indeed, the designer of the educational scenario must firstly have very good knowledge of the content dealing with the learning situation to be developed which will enable him to clearly outline his objectives which he must achieve at the end of his learning situation. learning, to clearly define the knowledge to be acquired and the skills to be mastered by learners. Secondly, he must have a good knowledge of models and teaching/learning strategies to decide on the different choices he must make when choosing his activities according to contexts and situations and at the same time depending on the specificity of the discipline he teaches.

In the next block of this chapter, we intend to broaden our work by moving from the conceptualization of an educational scenario of a face-to-face learning situation to the conceptualization of an educational scenario of a distance learning situation., that is to say moving from face-to-face teaching to distance

Figure 8. Diagram of architecture of a learning activity

Title of learning activity:			
Specific objective:			
Intermediate objective:			
Problem situation:			
Task: **Instructions:**	**Group: individual or group:**	**Teaching and technological material:**	**Management of time:**
Teacher roles:	**Activities of the learner (s):**	**Documents for learners:**	**Documents for the teacher:**

learning. This implies a change in the work context and at the same time a change in the different interactions. Indeed, the integration of Information and Communication Technologies provides the opportunity to rethink and relocate, in space and time, exchanges between teachers and learners and promote new approaches for activities. learning.

DESIGN OF MODELS OF DIFFERENT EDUCATIONAL SCENARIOS IN ONLINE TEACHING

The Modular Structure

In the language of Open Distance Learning (FOAD), we very often refer to the notion of module to characterize the educational organization of online teaching. We are talking about modular teaching, modular training or even content modularization. Thus, a module is above all made up of a set of learning situations organized as a coherent whole. What gives coherence to this whole is both the objectives pursued and the educational strategy implemented. To qualify as modular, this set of learning situations must:

Be organized in such a way that it constitutes a whole that is both independent and capable of being easily integrated into a larger training package;

Be versatile in a way that it can fit together in different ways with other modules so as to create different learning paths from a limited stock of modules.

A training module is made up of three systems to which specific functions are associated. Thus, we see:

An entry system which manages access to the module, as its name suggests, it is through this system that the learner accesses the training module.

A learning system, also called "body of the module", takes care of the training itself and must be adapted to the learner according to the activities they must carry out.

An exit system which manages the end of the module and the orientation which is necessary following it according to the acquisition of knowledge and the mastery of skills by the learner.

Overall scenario of a learning situation for a module in online teaching

Based on what is treated in the theoretical part, we will propose in the following part which concerns our own second work the design of models of systems constituting online teaching of different educational scenarios for a learning situation and the different resulting learning activities.

Thus, based on the work of Burgos concerning adaptation during the design of an educational scenario, on the work of Depover and his collaborators concerning the differentiation between the learning scenario and the supervision scenario, on our previous work concerning the architecture of the educational scenario of a learning situation (Burgos, 2008; Depover et al, 2014; Khaldi et al, 2019; 2020).

By inspiring work carried out in the field of process flexibility, in particular that of Schonenberg and his collaborators, we believe it is useful to better understand when, how and with what approaches, adapt educational scenarios according to the changing circumstances of the situations. teaching/learning (Schonenberg et al., 2007; 2008).

Thus, in this work we focus our study on the proposal of different types of educational scenarios of a learning situation and the associated learning activities that we can confront in online teaching for a module without taking into consideration either the nature of the discipline nor the nature of the concept to be treated. Indeed, for a training module in online teaching, it corresponds to learning situations, the

Figure 9. Example of a global scenario of a module in an online course

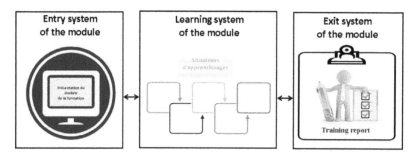

Figure 10. Example of the life cycle of a pedagogical scenario of a learning situation

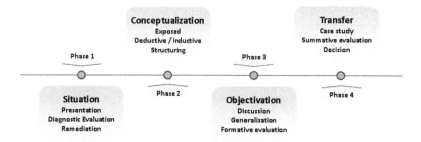

following figure illustrates an example of a global scenario of the constituents of online teaching of a module.

Whereas a learning situation for a module in online teaching corresponds to learning activities. The following figure illustrates an example of the life cycle of an educational scenario of a learning situation.

Based on this example of the life cycle of an educational scenario of a learning situation, we propose the different scenarios of the different activities in a learning situation of a module in online teaching which are in number of six.

Scenario of a Learning Situation for a Module in Online Teaching

According to the life cycle of a learning situation proposed above, the activity of the situation is the first phase of the cycle. In our case, we use the scenario activity as an introduction to a learning situation and at the same time as an evaluation tool to test the learners' prerequisites. The following figure illustrates an example of the scenario of the activity of setting up a learning situation made up of three systems.

Entry System for the Scenario of the Situation

The scenario entry system for the role-playing activity concerns the presentation of the learning situation by defining the objectives to be achieved at the end of the situation, the knowledge to be acquired and the skills to be mastered by the learner or group of learners and finally the prerequisites necessary to follow the situation.

Figure 11. Example scenario of a learning situation scenario

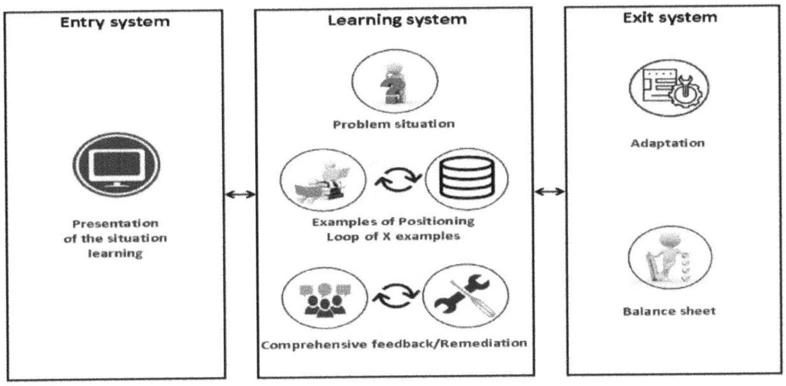

Real-Life Scenario Learning System

The learning system of the scenario of the situational activity, concerns first of all, the definition of the problem situation in which a cognitive imbalance is created for the learner which is due to the perception of a difference between what we think we know and what we observe. Examples/positioning exercises will be offered to the learner concerning their previous knowledge which allow us to situate their state of knowledge at the start of the learning situation and at the same time to situate them in the disciplinary field to take stock of their knowledge. knowledge and/or its conceptions (initial representations). Finally, based on technological communication tools, extensive feedback is provided alongside remediation to fill learners' gaps and correct their erroneous learning, in order to place them in relation to the new learning situation.

System for Exiting the Scenario From the Situation

The scenario output system of the role-playing activity concerns the adjustment and adaptation of the learning scenario of the learning situation by subsequently proposing a path and resources adapted to the level of the learning situation. 'learner. Finally, an assessment of the scenario activity is disclosed.

Scenarios for Conceptualizing a Learning Situation for a Module in Online Teaching

According to the life cycle of a learning situation proposed above, the activity of conceptualization is the second phase of this cycle. It concerns structuring through the transition from action to formulation based on the obstacles encountered during the scenario activity. It promotes the construction of meaning around specific knowledge, the use of knowledge and its integration in the development of skills, at the end of the learning situation. This phase concerns two scenario cases depending on the approach adopted. Indeed, depending on the context and the situation, the proposal of a learning activity requires us to choose between two approaches, the deductive approach and the inductive approach.

Scenarios for conceptualizing a learning situation for a module in online teaching for a deductive approach.

Figure 12. Example of a scenario of the conceptualization of a deductive approach to a learning situation

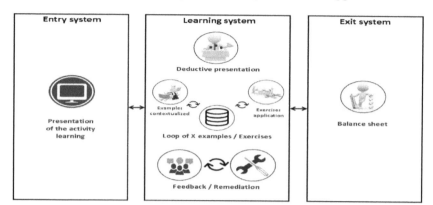

The deductive approach (or logical deduction) consists of going from the general to the particular, from the principle to the consequence. It is a scientific method that considers the conclusion to be implicit in the premises. We start from the statement of the concept and/or the rule to go to verification by examples. Thus, to present a concept, it is necessary to use this approach which follows the direct teaching strategy which is strongly guided by the teacher. It is a concept of explicit teaching: a transmission of knowledge and the acquisition of skills by the learner. The following figure illustrates an example of the conceptualization activity scenario for a deductive approach to a learning situation consisting of three systems.

Conceptualization Scenario Entry System According to the Deductive Approach

The entry system of the activity scenario of the conceptualization of a deductive approach, concerns the presentation of the learning activity by the definition of the objectives to be achieved at the end of the activity, the knowledge to be acquired and the skills to be mastered by the learner or group of learners.

System for Learning the Conceptualization Scenario According to the Deductive Approach

The system of learning the scenario of the activity of the conceptualization of a deductive approach which consists of going from the general to the particular, from the principle to the consequence. It is a scientific method that considers the conclusion to be implicit in the premises. We start from the statement of the concept and/or the rule to go to verification by examples. For our system, it first offers a presentation of a presentation depending on the nature of the concept to be treated (presentation, films, documentary, etc.). Then the proposal of contextualized examples that the learner can choose from a resource (x examples to do and redo) to check the understanding of the knowledge presented in the presentation and the proposal of application exercises that the Learner in the same way can choose them from a resource (x examples to do and redo) to test the acquisition and application of this knowledge. Finally, feedback is carried out alongside remediation based on technological communication tools to fill learners' gaps and correct their erroneous learning.

Figure 13. Example of a scenario of the conceptualization of an inductive approach to a learning situation

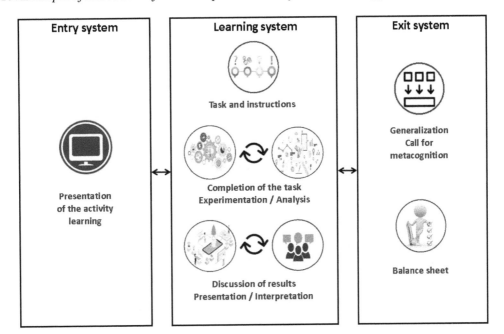

Output System From the Conceptualization Scenario According to the Deductive Approach

The output system of the scenario of the activity of the conceptualization of a deductive approach concerns an assessment of the activity of the conceptualization of the proposed deductive approach.

Scenarios for Conceptualizing a Learning Situation for a Module in Online Teaching for an Inductive Approach

The inductive approach consists of going from the particular to the general. It is a scientific method that obtains general conclusions from individual premises. It allows the learner in a learning activity to experiment and discover the meaning of a concept for themselves. It allows us to move from particular or specific observations and analyses, to more general perspectives. Thus, generalization (objectivation) invites the learner to describe their approach and to name the processes involved (call for metacognition). It promotes the coherent assembly of all the objectives achieved through discussions to pool and generalize the results. The following figure illustrates an example of the conceptualization activity scenario for an inductive approach to a learning situation consisting of three systems.

Conceptualization Scenario Entry System According to the Inductive Approach

The entry system of the activity scenario of the conceptualization of an inductive approach, concerns the presentation of the learning activity by the definition of the objectives to be achieved at the end of the activity, the knowledge to be acquired and especially in this case, the skills to be mastered by the learner or group of learners.

System for Learning the Conceptualization Scenario According to the Inductive Approach

The learning system of the activity scenario of the conceptualization of an inductive approach which consists of going from the particular to the general. Thus, it is necessary to use the inductive approach which follows the indirect teaching strategy which is centered on the learner. Indeed, inquiry, induction, problem solving, decision-making and discovery are terms that are used interchangeably to describe indirect teaching. Indirect teaching promotes creativity and the development of skills in the area of personal relationships. For our system, it first offers a presentation of the task to be carried out according to the nature of the concept to be treated (experience, problem to be solved, investigation, etc.).

The next step concerns the completion of the proposed task according to the nature of the group of learners (individual or group work), going through several stops: accomplishing the task through the organization and distribution of roles in the case of a group work without denying time management; provide concrete elements of experience to analyze by asking questions, encouraging testing, manipulation and the formulation of hypotheses and by providing procedures and materials and finally provide feedback by encouraging successes, improvements and ways to self-correcting and helping to identify and work with errors. Note that the completion of the task must be reinforced by the offer of a set of digital resources which will be proposed to support the learner/group of learners in his/her work and the proposal of technological tools for communication to facilitate interaction between the different training stakeholders (teachers and learners).

The last step in this learning system concerns the discussion of the results obtained by the different learners/groups using the different technological communication tools, first of all by the presentation and communication of the results of each learner/group of learners to all the actors (teachers and learners) and then by the interpretation of the results obtained to justify the empirical results obtained and confront them with theoretical laws and rules.

Output System from the Conceptualization Scenario According to the Inductive Approach

The output system of the scenario of the activity of the conceptualization of an inductive approach, concerns an assessment of the activity of the conceptualization of the inductive approach proposed by the generalization by appealing to metacognition by the identification of a model or laws through a mathematical formalism.

Scenarios of a Formative Evaluation of a Learning Situation of a Module in Online Teaching

Formative assessment is an assessment which is an integral part of the learning process and takes place at all stages of it. It consists of collecting information allowing us to know the degree of mastery achieved and to identify any possible difficulties encountered by learners in order to suggest or help them discover ways to overcome them. It is intended to be a helping tool for both the teacher and the learner. Formative assessment is an integral part of mastery pedagogy and differentiated pedagogy since it is the means used to inform the teacher and learners about the help and remediation to be provided to achieve the set objectives (Scriven, 1967; Nunziati, 1990). For the teacher, it allows them to better explain their teach-

Figure 14. Example of a scenario of a formative evaluation of a learning situation

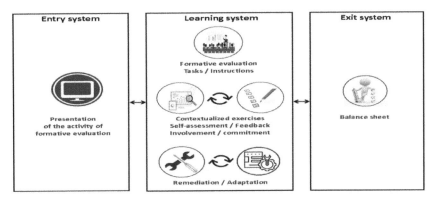

ing practice and expectations as well as to verify the effectiveness of their teaching in order to be able to adapt it to the characteristics of the learners. For the learner, it allows them to situate their difficulties in order to find the means and methods to overcome them. The following figure illustrates an example of the scenario of a formative evaluation of a learning situation consisting of three systems.

System for Entering the Scenario of a Formative Evaluation of a Learning Situation

The formative assessment activity scenario input system concerns the presentation of the assessment activity by declaring the learning situations/activities to be assessed by identifying the knowledge and skills to be tested in the student. learner.

Learning System Scenario of a Formative Evaluation of a Learning Situation

The learning system of the formative assessment activity scenario which consists of a means used to inform the teacher and learners about the help and remediation to be provided to achieve the set objectives. For our system, it first offers a presentation of the tasks to be carried out and their instructions according to the formative assessment proposed (exercises, MCQ problems to solve, etc.). The next stage concerns the completion by the learner of the proposed tasks by trying to test for himself the level of knowledge acquisition and mastery of skills and his ability to apply them in the situations posed on the one hand and by analyzing his involvement and his commitment in the construction of his knowledge on the other hand. Note that the completion of the various tasks must be reinforced by the offer of a set of digital resources which will be proposed to support the learner in their work and the proposal of technological communication tools to facilitate interaction in the different training stakeholders (teachers and learners). The last step in this learning system mainly concerns the teacher who must remedy the difficulties encountered by the learner and adapt his learning according to the context and the situation, always using the different technological communication tools.

Figure 15. Example Scenario of a case study of a learning situation

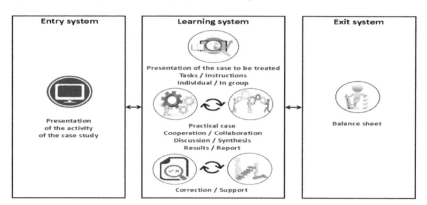

Output System From the Scenario of a Formative Evaluation of a Learning Situation

The output system of the formative assessment scenario concerns a review of the assessment activity taking into consideration the results of the remediation and adaptation already processed in the learning system.

Scenarios of a Case Study of a Module Learning Situation in Online Teaching

The case study is an activity that presents a problematic situation to a group, which must find the solution. The case study is specially indicated for training in diagnosis and decision-making. Teaching, using the case method, aims precisely to enable the application of theoretical or abstract knowledge, acquired beforehand or during the case study itself, to the resolution of concrete problems. The conditions for its effectiveness are based in particular on the quality of the cases proposed. The main phases are generally three in number in addition to a preliminary stage which consists of learning the case. Indeed, the first phase which allows each member of the group to formulate their point of view on the case to be treated. A second phase concerns a return to the facts and the information available to choose a work strategy. Then a third phase which concerns the conceptualization and research of findings to arrive at a synthesis and a result. Finally, a final summary is developed by the presentation of a report (Legendre, 2005). The following figure illustrates an example of a case study scenario of a learning situation consisting of three systems.

System for Entering the Scenario of a Formative Evaluation of a Learning Situation

The case study scenario entry system concerns the presentation of the assessment activity by stating the learning situations/activities to be addressed by the study by identifying the objectives of the case study to be to treat.

Learning System Scenario of a Formative Evaluation of a Learning Situation

The learning system of the case study scenario which consists as a means of applying theoretical or abstract knowledge, acquired beforehand or during the case study itself, to the resolution of concrete problems. For our system, it first offers a presentation of the case to be studied, specifying the tasks to be carried out and their instructions according to the nature of the group (individual/group). In this case, we propose group work so that the completion of the work allows interactions and exchanges between the members of the group. Cooperation and collaboration are two essential elements in carrying out work. Indeed, according to Mead, cooperation describes a state of mind and a mode of behavior where individuals conduct their relationships and exchanges in a non-conflictual or non-competitive manner, seeking the appropriate modalities to analyze together and in a shared way. situations and collaborate in the same spirit to achieve common or mutually acceptable ends using structured methods of collaboration encourage introspection of behavior and communication (Mead, 2003). This will be carried out based on the different technological communication tools to impose and structure discussions between the members of the group to arrive at a synthesis and results presented in a report. Finally, corrections and support for the different groups must be offered by the teacher.

Output System from the Scenario of a Formative Evaluation of a Learning Situation

The output system of a case study scenario concerns a review of the evaluation activity taking into consideration the objectives outlined in the input system.

Scenarios of a Summative Evaluation of a Learning Situation of a Module in Online Teaching

The summative evaluation aims to assess whether the most important knowledge has been acquired at the end of the training. It aims to estimate the learning acquired at the end of a training process, by comparing it to a previously established level to be achieved. This evaluation process takes into account the weightings given to the elements evaluated. If the summative evaluation process is only used in a certifying function, it is also called certifying evaluation, that is to say when there is the issuance of a diploma after the training action and aimed at verify that "the acquisitions targeted by the training have been made. So the function of summative or certification assessment is to attest or recognize learning. It occurs at the end of a teaching process and serves to sanction or certify the degree of mastery of learners' learning. It is the responsibility of the teacher and must be carried out in a fair and equitable manner. Indeed, the choice of evaluation method depends on the taxonomic level to be reached at the end of the learning, or the skill to be developed. Depending on the level of expertise of the learners, the learning objectives targeted will be of a higher or lower level. Novice learners will be introduced to knowledge and understanding, while expert learners will be able to reach higher levels such as analysis and synthesis. The type of guidance offered to different types of learners is intertwined with the choice of an assessment method that corresponds to the targeted taxonomic levels. Indeed, a summative assessment adapted to the level of learners and which focuses on the content actually taught will directly promote learners' success (Scriven, 1967; Legendre, 2005). The following figure illustrates an example of the scenario of a summative evaluation of a learning situation consisting of three systems.

Figure 16. Example scenario of a summative evaluation of a learning situation

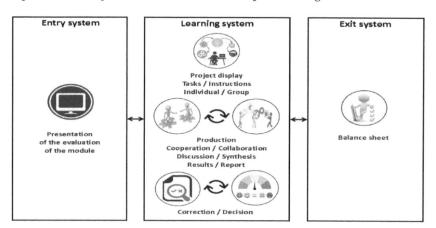

Scenario Entry System for a Summative Assessment of a Learning Situation

The scenario entry system of a summative assessment concerns the presentation of the assessment activity by declaring the learning situations/activities to be addressed by the summative assessment by identifying the objectives of the assessment to be addressed.

Learning System Scenario of a Summative Evaluation of a Learning Situation

The learning system of summative evaluation which consists of estimating the learning acquired at the end of a training process, by comparing it to a previously established level to be achieved. For our system, it first offers a presentation of the project to be carried out, specifying the tasks to be carried out and their instructions according to the nature of the group (individual/group). In this case, we propose group work so that the completion of the work allows interactions and exchanges between the members of the group. Cooperation and collaboration are two essential elements in carrying out work. This will be, based on the different technological communication tools, to impose and structure discussions between the members of the group to arrive at a synthesis and results presented in a report. Finally, corrections must be proposed by the teacher to arrive at decisions.

Output System from the Scenario of a Summative Evaluation of a Learning Situation

The output system of the summative evaluation scenario concerns an assessment of the evaluation activity taking into consideration the results obtained for adaptation and improvement of learning for future training.

As a conclusion to this block, concerning the design of models of different educational scenarios in online teaching. After having defined the modular system and after having proposed an example of a global scenario of the constituents of online teaching of a module and an example of the life cycle of an educational scenario of a learning situation in a way In general, we have proposed six examples of scenarios of activities in a learning situation of a module for online teaching. Each example scenario is proposed according to three systems: an input system, a learning system and an output system. We have proposed for each learning system a set of actions to be carried out depending on the nature of the activity, each time specifying the actions to be carried out by the learner/group of learners and at the same time the actions to be carried out. by the teacher without neglecting the different interactions between the different actors based on technological communication tools.

GENERAL CONCLUSION

As a conclusion to this chapter, in the part which concerns the theoretical framework of this chapter, we firstly differentiate online teaching from traditional teaching by identifying the advantages of this teaching compared to learner, teacher and institution. Secondly, based on educational engineering methods, we identified the different stages allowing the implementation of online teaching by highlighting the tasks to be carried out for each stage. Thirdly, we defined the notion of educational scripting by identifying the steps necessary for the design of a scenario and at the same time, we defined the two main tools of online teaching scripting, to note, the activity diagram (DA) and the specification table (TS). Indeed, scripting is above all a work of designing content, organizing resources, planning activities and mediations, to induce and support learning towards a clearly defined and explicit objective. Fourth and finally, based on previous work, we offered an overview of the educational scenario by citing the different types of educational scenarios without neglecting the role of adaptation.

As a conclusion in this chapter, the part which concerns the conceptualization of an architecture of an educational scenario, we can conclude that the conceptualization of an educational scenario for a learning situation is not an easy thing. Indeed, the designer of the educational scenario must firstly have very good knowledge of the content dealing with the learning situation to be developed which will enable him to clearly outline his objectives which he must achieve at the end of his learning situation. learning, to clearly define the knowledge to be acquired and the skills to be mastered by learners. Secondly, he must have a good knowledge of models and teaching/learning strategies to decide on the different choices he must make in choosing his activities according to contexts and situations and at the same time depending on the specificity of the discipline he teaches.

As a conclusion in this chapter which concerns the design of the system models constituting online teaching of the different educational scenarios for a learning situation and the different learning activities which result from it. Thus, we focused in this work our study on the proposal of different types of educational scenarios of a learning situation and the associated learning activities that we can confront in online teaching for a module without taking into consideration neither the nature of the discipline nor the nature of the concept to be treated. Indeed, for a training module in online teaching, it corresponds to learning situations, the following figure illustrates an example of a global scenario of the constituents of online teaching of a module.

In the next block of this chapter, we plan to broaden our work by moving from the conceptualization of an educational scenario of a face-to-face learning situation to the conceptualization of an educational scenario of a distance learning situation., that is to say moving from face-to-face teaching to distance learning. This implies a change in the work context and at the same time a change in the different interactions. Indeed, the integration of Information and Communication Technologies provides the opportunity to rethink and relocate, in space and time, exchanges between teachers and learners and promote new approaches for activities. learning. Indeed, after having proposed an example of a global scenario of the constituents of online teaching of a module and an example of the life cycle of an educational scenario of a learning situation in general, we have proposed six examples of activity scenarios of a learning situation of a module for online teaching. Each example scenario is proposed according to three systems: an input system, a learning system and an output system. We have proposed for each learning system a set of actions to be carried out depending on the nature of the activity, each time specifying the actions to be carried out by the learner/group of learners and at the same time the actions to be carried out. by the teacher without neglecting the different interactions between the different actors based on technological communication tools.

In view of this work, we hope in future work to concretize our research by carrying out and experimenting with the different educational scenarios proposed in this work with educational teams, based primarily on the choice of a discipline and a level of university education.

REFERENCES

Above, P. (2008). What is teaching? Some necessary and sufficient conditions for this activity. *Revue Française de Pédagogie, 164*, 139–158.

Valérie Bardot. (2014). Educational scripting in all its debates. *International journal of technologies in university teaching, 4*(2).

Basque, J., & Doré, S. (1998). The concept of computer-based learning environment [electronic version]. *Journal of Distance Education / Revue de l'enseignement à distance, 13*(1). http://cade.athabascau.ca/vol13.1/dore.html

Bouthry, A., Jourdain, C., Bodet, G., & Amalric, P.-H. (2007). *Build your online training project, Eyrolles-Editions d'organization*. Collection Books Tools Training.

Brassard, C., & Daele, A. (2003). A reflective tool for designing an educational scenario integrating ICT. Computer Environments for Human Learning, Strasbourg, France.

Burgos, D. (2008). *Extension of the IMS Learning Design Specification based on Adaptation and Integration of Units of Learning*. [Doctoral Thesis, Carlos III University of Madrid, Leganes, Spain].

Casalfiore, S. (2000). *Teacher activity in class. Contribution to understanding the professional reality of teachers*. HALSHS.

Cottier, P., Choquet, C., & Tchounikine, P. (2008). Rethinking EIAH engineering for teacher designers. In J. Dinet (Ed.), *Uses, users and information skills in the 21st century* (pp. 159–193). Edited by Hermes Lavoisier.

Crozat, S., & Trigano, P. (2002). Structuring and scripting of digital educational documents in a massification logic. STE (Educational Sciences and Techniques), 9(3).

Daele, A., Brassard, C., Esnault, L., Donoghue, M., Uytterbrouk, E., Zeiliger, R. (2002). Design, implementation, analysis and evaluation of educational scenarios using ICT. *Recre@sup-WP2 FUNDP project report*.

Decamps, S. (2014). *Educational scripting of online collaborative activities*. [Doctoral thesis in Psychological Sciences and Education. University of Mons, Faculty of Psychology and Educational Sciences].

Dejours, C. (1995). *The human factor*. PUF.

Delaby, A. (2008). *How to design and produce an online course: Create an online course, Eyrolles-Editions d'organization* (2nd ed.). Collection Books Tools Training.

Depover, C., De Lièvre, B., Decamps, S., & Porco, F. (2014). *Analysis and design of learning scenarios*. The Department of Educational Sciences and Technology University of Mons. (http:// deste.umons. ac.be/cours/scnr/)

Doyle, W. (1986). Classroom organization and management. In M. C. Wittrock (Ed.), *Handbook of research on teaching* (pp. 392–431). Macmillan.

Dubet, F. (2002). *The decline of the institution*. Threshold.

Dubet, F., & Martuccelli, D. (1996). *At school. Sociology of the school experience*. Threshold.

Durand, M. (1996). *Teaching in schools*. PUF.

Goigoux, R. (2007). A model for analyzing teacher activity. *Education and didactics, 1*(3). http://journals. openedition.org/educationdidactic/232

Guéraud, V. (2006). *Author approach for Active Learning Situations: Scenarios, Monitoring and Engineering. HDR*. Joseph Fourier University. http://discas.qc.ca

Hrich, N., Lazaar, M., & Khaldi, M. (2019). Improving Cognitive Decision-Making into Adaptive Educational Systems through a Diagnosis Tool based on the Competency Approach. International Journal Emerging Technologies in Learning, 14(7). doi:10.3991/ijet.v14i07.9870

Khaldi, M., Erradi, M., & Khaldi, M. (2019). Learning Situation: The teacher management and decisions according to the context and the situation. *IMPACT: International Journal of Research in Engineering & Technology, 7*(5), 25-40.

Lando, P. (2003). *Progetto: a method for designing scenario templates for remote collective project-based educational activities* [DEA dissertation, University of Picardie].

Legendre, R. (2005). Summative evaluation. In *Current Dictionary of Education*. Guérin.

Leplat, J. (1992). *Work analysis in ergonomic psychology* (Vols. 1–2). Octares.

Leplat, J. (1997). *Insights into activity in a work situation*. PUF.

Macedo-Rouet, M., & Perron, J.-M. (2007). Content and usefulness of the educational scenarios in the PrimTICE database. In T. Nodenot, J. Wallet, and E. Fernandes, *Proceedings of the Computing Environment for Human Learning Conference (EIAH 2007)* (pp. 101-112). Paris/Lyon: Association of Information Technologies for Education and Training [ATIEF] and National Institute of Educational Research [INRP].

Maha, K., Jamal, B., Mohamed, E., & Mohamed, K. (2020). The educational scenario architecture of a learning situation. *Global Journal of Engineering and Technology Advances (GJETA). 03*(01), 027–040.

Maha, K., & Mohamed, E. (2020). Design and Development of an e-Learning Project Management System: Modeling and Prototyping. *International Journal Emerging Technologies in Learning, IJET, 15*(19), 2020.

Mead, M. (2003). *Cooperation and competition Among the Primitive Peoples*, Transaction Publishers.

Mels. (2006). *Curriculum of the Quebecois School. Secondary education 2nd cycle.* Quebec: government of Quebec.

Nunziati, G. (1990, January). To build a formative evaluation system. Cahiers Pédagogiques. *Learning*, (280), 48–64.

Paquette, G. (2002). The engineering of tele-learning, to build learning in networks. Presses de l'Université du Québec.

Paquette, G. (2004). Instructional engineering for learning object repositories networks. *2nd International Conference on Computer Aided Learning in Engineering Education*, Grenoble, France.

Paquette, G., Bourdeau, J., Basque, J., Leonard, M., Henri, F., & Maina, M. (2003). *Construction of a knowledge base and a resource bank for the field of tele-learning.* Educational Sciences and Techniques.

Paquette, G., & Léonard, M. Lundgren -Cayrol, K., Mihaila, S. & Gareau, D. (2006). Learning Design based on Graphical Knowledge-Modeling. *Journal of Educational technology and Society ET&S.*

Pernin, J. P. (2003). Educational objects: learning units, activities or resources? Revue Sciences et Techniques Educatives.

Pernin, J.-P., & Lejeune, A. (2004). Learning devices instrumented by technologies: towards scenario-centered engineering. In: TICE conference, Compiègne France.

Qodad, A., Benyoussef, A., & El Kenz, A. (2020). Toward an Adaptive Educational Hypermedia System (AEHS-JS) based on the Overlay Modeling and Felder and Silverman's Learning Styles Model for Job Seekers. International Journal Emerging Technologies in Learning, iJET, 15(8).

Quintin, J., Depover, C., & Degache, C. (2005). *The role of the educational scenario in the analysis of distance training: Analysis of an educational scenario based on defined characterization elements.* HAL.

Rogalski, J. (2005). Professional didactics: an alternative to "situated cognition" and "cognitivist" approaches in the psychology of acquisitions. *@ctivities, 1*(2), 103-120. http://www.activites.org/v1n2/Rogalski.pdfDOI: doi:10.4000/activites.1259

Rougier, B. (2009) *Construction of an educational sequence.* Academy of Versailles – Biological Sciences and Applied Social Sciences. http://sbssa.spip.ac-rouen.fr/?TERMINOLOGIE-BO-no35-du-17-09-92

Schneider, D. (2003). Design and implementation of rich educational scenarios with community portals. *Guéret conference.* Springer.

Schonenberg, H., Mans, R., Russell, N., Mulyar, N., & Aalst, W. (2008). Process flexibility: A survey of contemporary approaches. *Lecture Notes in Business Information Processing, I*, 16–30. doi:10.1007/978-3-540-68644-6_2

Schonenberg, M. H., Mans, R. S., Russell, N. C., Mulyar, N. A., & van der Aalst, W. M. P. (2007). Towards a Taxonomy of Process Flexibility (Extended Version). *BPM Center Report BPM-07-11*. BPMcenter.org.

Scriven, M. (1967). *The Methodology of Evaluation*. Social Science Education Consortium.

Shulman, L. S. (1986). Paradigms and research programs in the study of teaching: a contemporary perspective. In C. Wittrock Merlin (Ed.), *Handbook of research on teaching* (pp. 3–36). Macmillan.

Van Rosmalen, P., Vogten, H., Van Es, R., Passier, H., Poelmans, P., & Koper, R. (2006). Authoring a full life cycle model in standards-based, adaptive e-learning. *Journal of Educational Technology & Society, 9*(1).

Vantroys, T., & Peter, Y. (2005). COW, an educational scenario execution support service. *STICEF Review, 12*. ISSN: 1764-7223.

Zarouk, M. Y., Olivera, E., Peres, P., & Khaldi, M. (2020). The Impact of Flipped Project-Based Learning on Self-Regulation in Higher Education. International Journal Emerging Technologies in Learning, iJET, 15. doi:10.3991/ijet.v15i17.14135

Zarraonandia, T. (2007). *Adaptations of Learning Units at Runtime*. [Doctoral Thesis, Department of Computer Science, Higher Polytechnic School, Carlos III University of Madrid, Leganes, Madrid].

ENDNOTES

[1]   https://www.k12.gov.sk.ca/docs/francais/fransk/fran/elem/dem/dem2.html#1.

[2]   http://discas.qc.ca

Chapter 2
From Educational Innovation to Educational Design

Mohamed Khaldi
ⓘ https://orcid.org/0000-0002-1593-1073
ENS, Abdelmalek Essaâdi University, Morocco

ABSTRACT

Teaching today in the digital age requires being able to adapt to the multiple upheavals affecting individuals and societies. The idea that education systems should equip learners with the skills and competencies to cope with an ever-changing landscape. We often refer to skills such as critical thinking, problem solving, collaborative skills, innovation, digital literacy, and adaptability. What is negotiable is how best to achieve the development of these skills, particularly which teaching and learning approaches are suitable to facilitate or enable the development of complex skills. However, educational innovation must be perceived as a proposed novelty, a change, a creation, a transformation, or even an invention in the fields of pedagogy and teaching. Note that the term "innovation" refers to the act of introducing something new in a particular field.

INTRODUCTION

Teaching today in the digital age requires being able to adapt to the multiple upheavals affecting individuals and societies. The idea that education systems should equip learners with the skills and competencies to cope with an ever-changing landscape. We often refer to skills such as critical thinking, problem solving, collaborative skills, innovation, digital literacy and adaptability. What is negotiable is how best to achieve the development of these skills, particularly which teaching and learning approaches are suitable to facilitate or enable the development of complex skills. However, educational innovation must be perceived as a proposed novelty, a change, a creation, a transformation or even an invention in the fields of pedagogy and teaching. Note that the term "innovation" refers to the act of introducing something new in a particular field.

Educational innovation, also called innovative pedagogy, does not result exclusively from the evolution of teaching systems. It also refers to "new" methods and ways of working which often put the learner

DOI: 10.4018/979-8-3693-3128-6.ch002

Copyright © 2024, IGI Global. Copying or distributing in print or electronic forms without written permission of IGI Global is prohibited.

at the center of learning. It facilitates memory anchoring and retention of information. It concerns not only the support of learners, but also learning. Innovation concerns all disciplines, constantly called upon to renew and improve. To this end, we consider that innovation is a transversal approach. It questions content and representations since it most often arises from a desire to work differently in order to respond effectively and relevantly to the needs and difficulties of learners.

Whereas, instructional design is a somewhat systematic, planned and structured process. Through this design, a teacher plans learning units, establishes approaches, determines tasks and activities. Finally, it defines a variety of educational materials adapted to the needs of learners. This ensures the quality of learning and generates a roadmap that the teacher can confidently follow to achieve the proposed objectives. However, educational design aims to determine the objectives, resources, and modalities of a training program, taking into account the needs, the level of learners, the learning methods and the tools to be put in place. For the designer trainer, this means analyzing the professional skills to be achieved, defining the educational objectives and choosing the educational approaches adapted to the content, whether e -learning, distance online courses, face-to-face or other learning methods.

Through this chapter, we will try to define the two concepts by providing historical overviews of the two concepts, we then discuss the distance between the educational vision and current educational practice that can be bridged by the adoption and use of a appropriate pedagogy that has been tested and proven to contribute to the development of the person as a whole. Thus, evidence of impact becomes a central part of teaching practice; what works and for whom in terms of learning and development can provide guidelines to educational practitioners on how to modify or update their teaching by adopting innovations in educational technology equipment. These changes can be brought about by improvements in the theory and practice of teaching, learning and assessment and not by the simple introduction of technology into classrooms.

EDUCATIONAL INNOVATION

Introduction

At first glance, innovation seems a simple concept meaning novelty and change. However, when we identify research writings or professional writings on social innovation and in particular on educational innovation, we are quickly confronted with its complexity. The first part which follows firstly presents the theoretical elements surrounding the notion of innovative practice. It addresses the notion of practice, then that of innovation by offering a chronological overview of the concept of educational innovation. Secondly, we will cite the characteristics of the innovation, the stages of its process and examples of educational innovation. Thirdly, the question of exemplary practices in connection with innovative practices is addressed after having cited the various types of innovative practices according to the roles of the actors. Finally, before concluding, we will deal with the challenges keys of innovation and limits of educational innovation.

Definitions of the Concept

According to Legendre, an educational practice is a professional act carried out by the teacher, the management of an establishment or a non-teaching professional. Legendre defines practice as a set of skills acquired by an individual or a group through the regular exercise of an activity (Legendre, 2005). If there is a concept that has become popular in the field of education and training in recent years, it is innovation. We must realize that everyone is talking about this issue, whether political leaders, administrators or teachers themselves. We can say that the crazy spread of this phenomenon forces us to limit the themes of our speeches from the start. From Cros's synthesis, we can already grasp the scale of the task to be accomplished by noting that some three hundred definitions are scattered throughout scientific works dealing with innovation (Cros, 1997). Thus, the contributions of the sociology of organizations, economics, the anthropology of technology and social psychology have opened the way for researchers in educational sciences.

The term innovation is generally associated with science and technology. According to the Superior Council of Quebec Education (CSE), the concept of innovation, as we know it, developed in the world of technological progress. But innovation also has a social dimension and innovation in education is part of it. (CSE, 2006).

In different European countries, several terms are synonymous with innovation. Here are some of them: adjustment, improvement, development, pilot study, experimentation, new ideas brought to fruition, modernization, reform, renewal. The words reform, development and experimentation are most used with, or instead of, the word innovation (Cros, undated). In education, there are several expressions to designate innovation: educational innovation, innovation in education, school innovation, innovation in training. The Higher Education Council (CSE) favors innovation in education (CSE, 2006).

For its part, the CSÉ tells us that when it comes to defining innovation in education, we must take into account the fact that its primary goal is the success of the learner and that this success must affect all aspects of the development of the person (CSE, 2006). It therefore retains the following definition: "innovation in education is a deliberate process of transformation of practices through the introduction of a curricular, pedagogical or organizational novelty which is the subject of dissemination and which aims for lasting improvement of the educational success of pupils or students".

He exist of many definitions of innovation pedagogic, Who have evolved with THE time, even if research in training innovation is recent, the term himself is old and has been used since the 13th century. Indeed, the term innovation comes from the Latin innovare . It is formed from the prefix in which means "into" or represents the idea of inward movement and novare which means "new" or "to change". It can thus be translated as: bringing something new to something, changing it, making it new, renewing it. An educational innovation must:

- Be new in relation to existing practices;
- Bring a change, an improvement;
- Question the relevance of the educational processes in place;
- Be durable and transferable (it must therefore not be ephemeral or isolated).

The term is then found in the Middle Ages, where its definition evolves slightly to mean "bringing something new to an already established object", which centers its meaning around the idea of renewal. In the 16th century, its definition included the idea of surprise, as well as creation. This meaning is close to the idea of inventiveness that the word still encompasses today. Its use spread widely during the 19th century, then the 20th century, according to Benoît Godin (Godin, 2012) . It is then applied to many fields, including pedagogy.

However, the first educational innovations appear earlier. From the 17th century new approaches in the way of teaching, breaking with the functioning of the old regime, appeared. These first movements, which are not yet associated with the idea of innovation, nevertheless testify to the existence of changes in the ways of teaching. They also show us that the innovation process never makes a clean slate of the past: on the contrary, it is a progressive and irregular movement which gradually causes the training establishment to evolve. (Grandière and Lahalle, 2004).

However, the main definitions of innovation in education are inspired by Huberman's definition, for which "an innovation is a measurable improvement that is deliberate, lasting and unlikely to occur frequently." Huberman specifies that innovation is an operation whose objective is to install, accept and use a given change (Huberman, 1973). An innovation must last, be widely used and not lose its initial characteristics. We offer some key definitions of concept .

Cros (2001) considers that the definition of innovation in education and training, through its double challenge of to understand THE process of innovation has the interior of process education And training, East a activity intellectually risky. It mentions that innovation results from an intention and implements one or more actions aimed at changing or modifying something (a state, a situation, a practice, methods, functioning), based on a diagnosis of insufficiency, inadequacy or dissatisfaction with the objectives to be achieved, the results, and working relationships. She in propose a definition Who is developed around five components: the new, the object, the change, the finalized action and the process (Cros, 2001; 1997).

According to Depover and Strebelle, innovation is above all a process which unfolds over time and which, for convenience, can be mapped out through a certain number of phases. Who begins with the adoption decision we go through the implementation phase and close with installation of the practice innovative in activities innovative. The authors created a systemic model of innovation and integration of ICT in the educational framework in 1997 (Depover and Strebelle, 1997). Indeed, the model has a social and anthropological dimension, it articulates two complementary axes:

The First Axis Corresponds to the Dynamic Axis, it Is Made up of Three Levels

Inputs: It is all the elements which will interact with the system, they trigger or slow down the innovation process (The technical mastery of the teachers, the level and experience of the learners, the climate and the equipment of the school, etc.).

The process: it is made up of three phases of integration of an innovation:

adoption: "Decision to change something in one's practice out of personal conviction or under external pressure which can be exerted at the start of the microsystem (at the request of the students, for example) but also at the initiative of the supervisory staff such as the management or inspection. (Depover and Strebelle, 1997) . It is a personal desire of the teacher, learners or director who formulate innovative educational practices;

The implementation: "Concretion on the ground of the stated desire, during the adoption phase, to engage in a process leading to a modification of educational practices" . (Depover and Strebelle, 1997) . The teacher implements new educational practices and invests in a short and medium term process;

Routinization: "the use of new practices takes place on a regular basis and is integrated into usual school activities without requiring external support from a research or educational team" . (Depover and Strebelle, 1997) . The teacher invests long-term in the innovation process, he intervenes alone without the help of educational experts;

Outputs: It is all the external elements of the school that can influence the innovation process.

The second axis is entitled: topological axis. We can find the different subsystems to which the innovation process takes place:

The microsystem corresponds to the class and all the actors in the class (teachers and learners).

THE meso-system corresponds to the immediate school environment and in particular the educational leaders (directors and Principal Education Advisor).

THE macro-system corresponds to the administrative and political leaders of the education system (Ministry of National Education).

The peri-system corresponds to the actors outside the school (the municipality, associations, parents, etc.).

However, the model combines the development of innovative educational practices and ICT tools, it takes into account the support of stakeholders and their accompaniment in the process at the micro system, meso system and macro system level. The re-evaluation of the model proposed in 2007 seems to take into account the dynamics of networks of actors around this innovation process, from a rather socio-constructivist perspective. Everyone invests differently according to their values, their reluctance, their own expectations, but also according to the exchanges established within the networks with which they will be associated. It is a teacher/learner and inter-learner relational link. These innovations develop interdisciplinary learning and enable the renovation of the latter (Depover et al., 2007).

Hannan, English And Silver (1999) identify three levels of innovations educational: THE isolated innovations, guided innovations and directed innovations. Innovating, however, is not not necessarily invent something that doesn't exist anywhere else. Innovation is based Before all about the Steps And THE followed, which matter well more ... than radical novelty (Hannan et al., 1999).

In the most recent work carried out in the field of didactics, and in particularly in the field of educational sciences, M. Lebrun (2011) says that everything device of innovation pedagogic must necessarily take in account Also GOOD the contents, the resources, the actors, their objectives but also the socio-contexts economic and academic (Lebrun et al., 2011). Teaching methods involving students In their learning make parts of the activities teaching organized In A device pedagogic. They are relevant if they can be adapted At context. For there to be innovation in research and teaching, it is necessary provide teacher-researchers with financial, technical and logistical resources required to succeed in their mission.

According to Tricot, "pedagogical innovation concerns the ways of teaching. A teacher achieves an educational innovation when he or she designs and implements a new, unique way of teaching" (Tricot, 2017).

According to these definitions, innovation is a change that follows an approach, or is organized in so much that process. Indeed, the term innovation refers to the fact of introducing something new in a particular field. Thus educational innovation must be perceived as a proposed novelty, a change, a creation, a transformation or even an invention in the fields of pedagogy and teaching. Innovation concerns not only the support of learners, but also learning. Innovation concerns all school and university disciplines, constantly required to renew and improve. To this end, we consider that innovation is a transversal approach. It questions content and representations since it most often arises from a desire to work differently in order to respond effectively and relevantly to the needs and difficulties of learners.

Characteristics of Educational Innovation

According to the various authors listed, innovation in education is mainly characterized by the following elements:

Novelty: Novelty in innovation is distinguished from novation or invention. As such, Schon asserts that an act is only innovative if it adds to the sum of known inventions (Schon, 1967). Otherwise, it is only a borrowing or a wider diffusion of the initial act. It must therefore be clarified that innovation is not an invention. Indeed, if the invention is a true creation and had previously no existence anywhere, the innovation is a novelty in a particular context, a novelty which is relative to the context (sometimes, it is a recombination of ancient things).

What is new in innovation is therefore not the object in question, its content, but essentially its introduction into a given environment. It is, in a way, the assimilation of objects transferred, imported, borrowed from other places (Cros and Adamczewski, 1996; Cros, 2001; Béchard, 2001). Innovation is an idea, a practice, an object perceived as new by the members of a system (Rogers and Shoemaker, 1971).

Product: The product in innovation is the substance to which this innovative virtue is attributed. Most authors generally consider innovation as a product, a new technology, an institutional device, a method, a new process, etc. (CSE, 2006).

Change and improvement: The innovation process is built in opposition to professional practices considered ineffective and routine. Innovation has always been seen as a transgressive action by an individual or a group to improve unsatisfactory situations or, at least, to solve problems. However, innovation is something other than simple problem solving; it contains within itself the seeds of creativity and originality (Cros, 2007).

Through voluntary, intentional and deliberate actions, innovation aims to induce positive change, improvement. She wants the good, the best for the learner. Which implies a change in behavior, attitudes, approaches to thinking. (Béchard, 2001; Cros, undated).

This innovation is of the order of creativity, inventiveness, initiative through the renewal of methods, organization or content (Cros, 2002). There may be a few additional tricks, some ingenious arrangements in innovative action, but what characterizes it is the fact of doing differently in order to improve what exists. This implies the introduction of better knowledge, better doing and better well-being. We are here at the level of operational knowledge, of useful art, of a response to expectations of efficiency and profitability (Cros and Adamczewski, 1996).

For his part, Huberman speaks of the creative motivations for innovation, this being understood as a deliberate desire to change customs, to reduce the gap between the objectives of the system and current practices, to redefine problems, to recognize new problems and create new methods to solve them (Huberman, 1973).

Sustainability and transferability: Innovation must also be sustainable, it must not be an isolated and ephemeral action. It must imply an appropriation and use beyond the individual who created or implemented it. In short, innovation must not remain a localized action. It must assert itself as a sustainable process (CSE, 2006).

The educational renewal, which has been gradually implemented in Quebec schools since 2000, is part of this desire for lasting change (Mels, 2005). An operation of this scale requires a certain control of change (CSÉ, 1995). For the CSE, this control is based on a convention of purposes, management of the change process, adaptation to a changing environment; for this, one must "have sufficient maturity to direct one's destiny and bring about the adaptations that appear necessary. ".

The advent of Information and Communications Technologies (ICT) partly transgresses the sustainability criterion. If the digital revolution is imbued with permanence and constitutes one of the major vectors of change in education, the means which emerge from it follow one another at a pace which only allows contextual data to be collected (OECD, 2008). Despite the inability of research to demonstrate the favorable effect of ICT on academic results, certain positive trends are emerging: increased learner motivation, greater degree of control by learners, more realistic and authentic learning situations., etc. (CSÉ, 2000).

Steps in the Innovation Process

In terms of process, innovation can be achieved in three phases, according to Brodin (Brodin, no date):

- Pilot experimentation;
- Adaptations to realities on the ground;
- Institutionalization or generalization.

Referring to the Alter model, these phases can be translated as follows (Alter, 2000):

- Innovation is the social translation of an invention, the first phase at the starting point of the process; the invention can emerge from the base, come from outside or be imposed by an authority;
- The appropriation phase is characterized by a transformation, the construction of a new meaning, a contextualization, a transfer of the invention between the actors;
- Institutionalization reduces uncertainty and integrates innovative practices into the rules of the organization.

Finally, the art of innovation consists of adapting and then adopting realities invented, discovered or previously created. The innovator acts as a passer, a translator, he adapts and translates pure novelty into admissible and applicable novelty, and ensures its promotion and dissemination (Cros and Adamczewski, 1996).

Examples of Educational Innovation

Thanks to the development of digital educational technologies, the question of educational innovation made a strong comeback during the 2010s. Many applications or websites were created, such as:

Khan Academy is a non-profit organization founded in 2008 by Salman Khan 1. Aiming to "provide quality educational content, free, accessible to everyone, everywhere", the website publishes online a free set of more than 8,000 lessons, thanks to video tutorials hosted on YouTube, articles and exercises covering all disciplines and other essential personal skills (careers, investments, pensions, etc.). Mastery pedagogy occupies a central place on the platform and in the teaching offered on Khan Academy. There is also an application to access free content anywhere.

Moodle is a free online learning platform (Learning Management System or LMS) distributed under the GNU General Public License written in PHP. Developed from educational principles, it makes it possible to create learning communities around content and activities. The word "Moodle" is short for Modular Object-Oriented Dynamic Learning Environment. In addition to the creation of courses using tools for use by trainers, Moodle allows the organization of courses in the form of sectors (categories and subcategories, cohorts, etc.) which gives it the potential to implement complete teaching devices. To a content management system, Moodle adds various educational and communicative interaction tools creating an online learning environment, with, via the network, interactions between educators, learners and educational resources 2.

However, new teaching methods are being deployed (online teaching, flipped teaching, self-learning, etc.). The debate around digital education raged until March 2020 and the outbreak of the Covid-19 pandemic which led – urgently – to the implementation of programs which consist of massively using digital technologies to perpetuate educational processes in period of confinement according to the development of each country.

Inverted classroom: The inverted classroom consists of providing learners, before the course, with documents so that they can work on the theory on their own and once in class, they apply their knowledge thus acquired to concrete situations that suit them. are proposed. The teacher no longer ensures the presentation of the rules but, by supervising the learners, he will nevertheless have the opportunity to explain these rules and give examples of their application (Lebrun and Lecoq, 2015). Among the advantages of this innovation, we cite:

- On the teacher's side:
- Allow the teacher to fulfill, above all, his role as guide;
- Increase the availability of the teacher for his learners.
- On the learners' side:
- Allow learners to progress at their own pace and develop their autonomy;
- Engage learners more and more in their learning and appear more motivated.

Flipped classroom: The flipped classroom consists of completely reversing the roles between teacher and learner. Thus, the learners construct the course, the knowledge checks, thus taking the place of the teacher while it is the teacher who will be marked and controlled by the learners. During class time, the learners build lessons together in groups, share them, compare them and the teacher plays the role of coach, orients them, guides them, challenges them. Learners are graded on their skills, to organize, to think, to build within a given time, as within a company (Cailliez, 2017). Among its advantages, we cite:

- A formidable efficiency in assimilating knowledge;
- An excellent method of learning and teaching yourself;
- Engaged learners become full participants in their training;
- The flipped classroom also allows you to get out of your comfort zone and gain confidence.

Collaborative work: By collaborative work, we mean, on the one hand, the cooperation between the members of a team who interact for a common goal but share the tasks, and on the other hand, the collaboration between the members of the team from start to finish without a fixed division of tasks for the production of a finished product. It combines three organizational methods:

- It invites everyone in the project to participate in a process of continuous improvement of each task and the entire project;
- It organizes work into parallel task sequences (enabling more asynchronous work);
- It provides the actors of each task with useful and easily exploitable information on other parallel tasks and on the implementation environment.

Distance training: Distance training is a teaching system belonging to the broad category of open or distance learning (FOAD). FOAD includes a range of heterogeneous practices, ranging from correspondence courses, to MOOCs and online training. It is present "at all levels of initial and continuing training, from primary education and basic knowledge to higher education, including various areas of professional training" (Glikman, 2002) . Among the advantages, we cite:

- Access to training for everyone at any time;
- A concise and more impactful format;
- Interaction is one of the many advantages of MOOCs, especially in business;
- Respecting the rhythm of each employee;
- Lower cost for the user.

The main types of distance learning are:

MOOCs (Massive Open Online Course): this is a chaptered course open free of charge to any Internet user. Often spread over several weeks, enhanced with remote group work, online chat and quizzes, it allows everyone to train on a subject and benefit from knowledge on a theme. It can sometimes give rise to certification (Nguyên and Daïd, 2014).

THE SPOC (Small Private Online Course): online chaptered course, often spread over several sessions, on the same principle as MOOCs. On the other hand, the audience is limited to a group of users defined in advance (around thirty for example).

THE COOC (Corporate Open Online Course): it is an online training course used within the company to train employees

SOOC (Social Open Online Course): this is online training whose objective is to increase interactions between course participants. To do this, SOOCs are enhanced with collaborative tools such as: forums, content creation tools such as wikis, blogs, etc.

Educational uses of social networks: The use of social networks can promote interactivity in class by providing additional resources, for example from current events. Learners can thus react online or in class but also post content themselves that they think is related to the course taught. Among the advantages of social networks, we cite:

- To develop one's social capital (all the advantages one derives from relationships and interactions with others);
- To forge your own identity;
- To develop creative skills driven by the creation and sharing of images;
- To develop critical thinking and open-mindedness if the online network is sufficiently diverse to come into contact with several different opinions and perspectives.

Virtual class: The virtual class is an educational device allowing learners and one or more teachers to be brought together at a given time via a toolA virtual class can take different formats (single, multiple, blended sessions, etc.). Among the advantages, we cite:

- Simplicity of implementation by non-technicians;
- The possibility of combining this modality alternating with other educational approaches such as face-to-face meetings, practical workshops, or seminars.

Project pedagogy: Pedagogy project is an active pedagogical practice which makes it possible to generate learning through the realization of a concrete production. It encourages people to put knowledge into practice through collective work on a given problem. Among the advantages, we cite:

- Stimulate collective intelligence;
- Provoke the decompartmentalization of skills;
- Implement talent fusion and promote team relationships.

Problem-based learning: Problem-based learning (or PBL) takes a social constructivist approach to learning. It involves immersing the learner in the subject through a problem to be solved in a few hours (or a project to be carried out over several days, or even several months). This leads him to seek information to develop a solution, knowing that the concepts are not previously taught to learners. Among the advantages, we cite:

- Learners are engaged in finding solutions to practical life problems;
- Learners are thus more prepared and more able to confront problems in their future professional life;
- Learners also have a "self-motivated attitude", as long as they are interested in what they are doing and are able to pursue independent learning;
- The work in small groups, the individual work of each member then the sharing of the knowledge acquired, the appointment of a facilitator, a secretary, generally aim to acquire skills on the organizational level.

Use of serious games or Serious Games: A serious game is an activity which combines a serious intention of an educational, informative, communicational, ideological or training type, with playful elements. In short, a serious game includes all board games, role-playing games and video games that are not purely entertainment. The serious game has the characteristics of a game (rapid feedback of success, feeling of accomplishment, feeling of commitment, team achievement, heroic involvement and optimal psychological state or flow), but presented in a digital and video format (Alvarez et al., 2016) . Among the advantages, we cite:

- Arouse increased interest in the learner in a learning activity;
- Promote the development of cognitive and psychomotor skills;
- Allows you to vary the teaching strategies used, focusing on action and interaction;
- Allow automatic adjustment of the difficulty level (increase or reduction) of problems according to the needs of the learner;
- Brings a hobby closer to a large number of learners, fosters positive attitudes and makes learning fun.

Various Types of Innovative Practices Depending on the Roles of the Actors

- When we talk about innovation in education, we are in fact talking about a teacher, a professional, an administrator, or even an entire school, an establishment, an institution, who puts into practice a concept, an attitude or an instrument that is quantitatively and qualitatively different from those that were used previously. The new product is made available and distributed in the system while being integrated into other practices (Huberman, 1973). According to the framework of the Information Network on Educational Success (RIRE 3), we are interested in innovative practices for teachers, professionals and administrators of a school establishment.

- **Innovative practices for teachers:** We are talking here about teaching practices (or teaching practices), which Legendre defines as all of the teacher's activities oriented by their own knowledge and skills, as well as by the goals and standards of their teaching. profession, and implemented in a particular educational environment (Legendre, 2005). We also talk about pedagogical practices, which concern one or the other or all of the relationships within an educational situation. Kazadi specifies that these practices concern the art of leading or doing class, which relates to the organization and meaning of work, or even to the field of classroom management. As for innovative teaching practices, they concern the art or way of teaching the concepts specific to each discipline (Kazadi, 2006).

- **Innovative practices for professionals:** Here we are interested in innovative practices in schools for education professionals (pedagogical advisors, psychoeducators and specialized educators, school psychologists, remedial teachers, guidance counselors, social workers). These practices take very diverse forms depending on the profession: intervention approaches, new methods, innovative programs, etc.

- **Innovative practices for administrators:** These practices are defined as all the ways of doing things associated with the implementation of policies, rules and procedures (Legendre, 2005). They affect several spheres of the management activity of an establishment. These innovations may concern changes in school materials (classroom, multimedia, new books, etc.); conceptual changes relating to programs and teaching methods; changes in interpersonal relationships, in the roles and reciprocal relationships of the different actors in the environment.

From Innovative Practice to Exemplary Practice

We use the expression exemplary practice as equivalent to the English expression best practice, which refers to an effective, generalizable professional practice based on research results. This practice may have the characteristics of an innovative practice. The CSÉ establishes a close link between educational innovation and the interface between educational research and educational practices (CSÉ, 2006).

For an innovative practice to become an exemplary practice, it must be linked to research and be subject to evaluation both in terms of its process and its effects. Two situations can be at the origin of an innovative and exemplary practice:

- **From practice to research:** Educational innovation can arise from practice. This is particularly the case when a teacher breaks with traditional teaching methods, experiments with new ways of teaching and allows other teachers to benefit from them (CSÉ, 2006). For this new practice to become an exemplary practice, the research and evaluation process must be associated with it. The innovative practitioner partners with a researcher to support this new practice through theorization, verification of its effects and the conditions for generalization.

- **From research to practice:** Innovation can also emerge from research results. This is what happens when teachers draw inspiration from research results to modify their practices. This is the classic case of knowledge transfer. The innovative practitioner partners with a researcher to refine this innovative practice. Thus, bringing together the worlds of research and educational practice can also encourage the emergence of better methods and, at the same time, stimulate innovation in education.

By way of conclusion, the ability to innovate undoubtedly presupposes mastery of acquired situations, with what this implies in terms of scholarly knowledge and experiential knowledge, but it equally presupposes a creative and imaginative state of mind. Training in this state of mind requires above all a sense of initiative, through reflection on practice, informed both by the experience of other professionals and by reference to available theories (Cros, 2002; CSÉ, 2006).

The Challenges Keys of Innovation

There question of the challenges multiple of innovation pedagogic East At heart of the trades between practitioners and researchers for years (Huberman, 1991; F. Cros, 2002; Bédard and Béchard, 2009).

The first issue concerns the conditions which promote or not innovation in our establishments. The people Who engage In a Steps of innovation pedagogic must wonder Also GOOD on THE terms of work In THE establishments that on the impact of change on THE teachers themselves And on THE learners. They are called has produce of the ideas news And useful scientifically And professionally. Work allows to think about cultural and intercultural knowledge at the university, a place of training and interaction, according to a conceptualization that he agrees of think in terms to improve learning (Ait Dahmane, 2009; 2011). Innovation is called "pedagogical because it seeks to substantially improve the learning of students in a situation of interaction and interactivity" (Béchard and Pelletier, 2001). However, it is difficult to innovate without taking into account the representations of teachers and learners.

THE second issue concerns creation, being able to introduce novelty into a context in movement, of take of the initiatives And to elaborate of the projects of innovation in link with THE directions ministerial taken For there training of the learners. All THE actors are conscious that THE level of our learners is not more THE even, We we are dealing with another generation. There is a change in the way learners treat And diffuse information, but This change imposed Also to trainers of find of news ways For to dispense And TO DO THE follow up of their lessons. Innovation should SO hold account of a together of parameters which concern the level between learners, heterogeneity within the group of learners, motivation which can change over time and evolution of the requirements of world of work.

The third issue is that of support which can take very varied: tutoring, coaching, networks mutual aid, advice, mediation educational... Support can help to build a training plan, to properly use the resources human And financial, has TO DO pass the teacher of a posture from the teacher to those of mediator, learning facilitator and expert scientific in its relationship with learners.

Finally, we can conclude that educational innovation therefore requires coordination, cooperation and collaboration of all stakeholders (pedagogical, political, administrative, technical, etc.). Three principles guide This work accompanying: reflection serene on THE practice teachers, definition of the objectives to be achieved and consistency in the innovations to be created. For train and support teachers, it is appropriate to discuss with specialists in pedagogy, to engage all stakeholders (teachers, learners, technicians, actors educational...) in a strong dynamic of educational transformation, to take into account account there motivation, THE different profiles learning, THE methods, THE terms and conditions evaluation and to draw inspiration from the educational experiences of other countries to update practices and establish a link with the professional world. To enter the nature of the motivations, he must by elsewhere take in consideration of the advice of order pedagogic of the teachers Who, has OUR notice, should get used to their learners has be autonomous, has to commit, has be responsible of their success Or of their failure. It is appropriate to emphasize socializing training because the goal is to form a citizen or social actor, to take into account the new modalities of appropriation then updating knowledge because knowledge is socially constructed with often a objective professional. With the COVID 19 health crisis, the implementation of distance learning has based on THE technologies digital. This kind teaching can be very perform because that he y has of the platforms in line Who allow to access to course, to learn at your own pace. It is important to offer so-called digital training on of the aspects educational relevant in order to of allow has the teacher having of the tools Who him will allow of mobilize THE learners For animate of the conferences And online discussion forums.

The Limits of Educational Innovation

After presenting the benefits of innovation, it is appropriate to mention certain limits.

Innovation is often very expensive: As educational innovation has an undeniable "establishment effect" (because it brings notoriety), the temptation may be to invest in equipment without worrying about its adaptability to the project of the establishment, nor its upkeep, its maintenance or even its renewal. Thus, investment in digital equipment must not make us forget the obsolescence and cost of certain tools, as well as the cost of the training that must be put in place for teaching teams;

Innovation can be a barrier for some learners: Educational innovation must not obscure the cognitive load linked to novelty for the learner. For some, approaching the task in a new way could complicate the learning process;

Innovation can be a hindrance for some educators: Educational innovation is born from a person and their creativity. Daring to innovate in education is a gamble and like all gambles, it includes risks that must be overcome. Determination, personal investment, energy and time that the innovation will require to invest can be limits to its implementation. The gaze of your peers can also be a hindrance. In addition, educational innovation using digital technology can be frightening: the educator then fears being replaced by the machine.

Innovation at all costs: To innovate is to propose something new, but it is not necessarily to create. In this sense, it becomes necessary for those who want to innovate to question the usefulness and added value of their project. Innovating for the sake of innovation may not be of much use if users have neither the interest nor the need. While it is appropriate to allow ingenuity and inventiveness to express themselves, we must still agree on what works well, without seeking to constantly renew methodologies or processes.

Conclusion

To face the most diverse threats and challenges, work is needed, particular, in the field of pedagogy, in order to find solutions and broaden the perspectives of training of the learners. We let's insist on there valuation of the teachers And on there need of their give THE means and support: Training initial And keep on going compete, of way complementary, has build THE foundations of development professional: there first in equipping THE future teachers of the SKILLS of base required has their professionalism, through also a first confrontation critical with THE practice of class And a period training on THE ground In of the situations, For Thus say " protected ", foreseeing a supervision And A accompaniement ; there second aiming putting into practice, at the teacher level, the "learning to learn » All At long of there life Thus that one putting has day of the knowledge relative to miscellaneous areas involved In teaching (discipline, psychology, pedagogy…) And of the methods teaching ". (Mr. Cavalli, 2005)

As a conclusion, we can say that it is important to develop knowledge in the field of educational innovations in order to build alternatives to traditional teaching that functions with increasing difficulty. We we must always do research and develop tools, especially techno-pedagogical ones, for innovation In THE learning of the learners, notably after this crisis of COVID19. But he East urgent of develop human resources, provide them with training resources, encourage innovative projects, revitalize the interest that is lacking in our institutions in taking in account THE challenges societal And learn to policies has privilege THE interests of the actors And there struggle against failure In our education systems has AVERAGE And has long term.

The activation, the accountability and learner engagement are certainly factors in success to explore. To conclude, it is appropriate to return to the words of Paul Grand house 4, very quoted by THE researchers Canadians, Who resume her definition of the principles of innovation pedagogic: "audacity In there vision, wisdom In there decision, determination in action, rigor in evaluation; academicism in diffusion" and the quote "To know and think is not to arrive at an absolutely certain truth, it is to dialogue with uncertainty. » (Morin and Viveret, 2010) .

Finally, we note that educational innovation is not an end in itself, that it is important to innovate in training but that this involves first and foremost questions that we will have to ask and above all finding the right solutions. responses adapted according to the context and the situation treated for our educational design which will be treated in the second part of this chapter. Indeed, educational innovation 5also called innovative pedagogy does not result exclusively from the evolution of teaching devices (Serious games or even mobile learning). It also refers to " new " methods and ways of working which often put the learner at the center of learning. It facilitates memory anchoring and retention of information.

INSTRUCTIONAL DESIGN

Introduction

Simply put, instructional design is a somewhat systematic, planned, and structured process. Thanks to it, a teacher plans learning units (themes/themes), establishes approaches, determines tasks and activities. Finally, it defines a variety of educational materials adapted to the needs of learners. This ensures the quality of learning and generates a roadmap that the teacher can confidently follow to achieve the proposed objectives. In addition, it will achieve the objective that led it to generate this teaching/learning process.

Academically, definitions of instructional design vary widely. In general, it is assumed to be a process of planning and preparing content and activities within a specific time frame. Always, of course, taking into account the environment in which the educational process will take place. As well as the most appropriate teaching/learning methods . At the same time, it examines the characteristics of those who will take part in this learning process and the assessment of their needs.

Definition of the Concept

According to Merrill, "Instructional design is a deliberate attempt to structure a learning environment so that learners acquire specific knowledge or skills" (Merrill, 2002). However, instructional design is a guide for the teacher. By using good instructional design, any teacher can return to the path initially indicated or simply redirect the direction of the lesson if they deem it necessary. In all cases, an educational design allows above all to plan the teaching activity in class, to choose the educational material, to design it and to adapt it. It also helps balance content loads and provide everything needed for a smooth learning process.

design, including all training methods (distance e-learning modules, face-to-face, online courses, in virtual classroom…) is a crucial step that it is obligatory to go through when developing training courses . This helps to increase the effectiveness of the digitalization of training. However, as a designer, it is risky to produce content, in any form whatsoever, for learners, without taking into account their level, the objectives / skills to be achieved and the effectiveness of the content, without compromising the effectiveness of their learning .

Educational design aims to determine the objectives, resources, and modalities of a training program, taking into account the needs, the level of learners, the learning methods and the tools to be put in place. For the designer, this means analyzing the business skills to be achieved, defining the educational objectives and choosing the educational approaches adapted to the content, whether e -learning, distance online courses, face-to-face or other learning methods. In this context, instructional design begins with:

- Needs analysis: why is an increase in skills necessary for this or that position?
- Then, the learning objectives must be clearly defined: what should the learner be able to do at the end of the module or their training?
- Finally, the teaching methods and approaches are chosen to optimally achieve these objectives: e-learning for more theoretical content, a virtual class to support, a face-to-face classroom for practice, for example.

Educational materials should be designed to facilitate understanding and engagement learners, without focusing solely on the aesthetic aspect so that the experience is even better. As we always say at Flowbow: substance before form. Beautiful design is always appreciated, but educational effectiveness must remain the priority. Finally, implementation involves the production and animation of the module, taking into account the needs and expectations of learners. The objective is to design coherent and effective learning for all training participants.

When we consider developing a face-to-face course, instructional design is necessary. But even more so when it comes to an online course for example. Indeed, designing and developing quality training actions is the ultimate objective of each educational design. Therefore, it is essential to create an online course. Among the strategic questions to answer that can guide us at all times:

- Who is the course for?
- What is the objective of the course?
- How deep should we give?
- What are the basic topics we should cover and in what order?
- What type of support can we count on?

- How should we assess learner performance?

The answers to these questions are the basis of good instructional design. Each of them will give us all the details which, well organized, will give us this orientation map for everything else. Instructional design helps us plan the smallest element and organizes the teaching/learning process to make it effective. For what follows, we will focus on educational design in the cognitive approach especially in the field of educational technology by trying to address three essential points which concern the paradigms in the field of educational technology and the relationships between methods of educational engineering of the cognitive approach to educational design then the principles of educational design developed in the cognitive approach to teaching-learning whose main objective of a strategy, a method, 'an educational technique or model is to promote the learning of the person (or people) to whom it is addressed.

The Paradigms of the Cognitive Approach to Instructional Design in the Field of Educational Technology

In the field of educational technology, developed mainly in the English-speaking and North American context, the cognitive approach to instructional design has been developed by two main paradigms: Teaching theory (Merrill, 2013; Richey et al ., 2011; Reigeluth and Carr-Chellman, 2009; Clark, 2008; Merrill et al., 2007) and learning sciences (Willis, 2011; Bransford et al., 2009; Sawyer, 2009; Tobias and Duffy, 2009).

In North America, another important paradigm, not belonging to educational technology, favors the study of teaching and learning in the school context. This paradigm is that of research on teaching (Marzano, 2011; Brophy, 2010; Gage, 2009; Hattie, 2009). It also contributes significantly to the development of scientific knowledge on educational strategies.

These three paradigms share a cognitive vision of learning based on knowledge developed by cognitive sciences, mainly in cognitive psychology and educational psychology (Roediger III, 2013; Dunlosky et al., 2013; Willingham, 2010; Graesser, 2009; Alexander and Winne, 2006).

The Relationships Between Educational Engineering Methods and the Cognitive Approach to Instructional Design

Teaching theory and learning sciences are the two paradigms of the cognitive approach to instructional design focused on developing knowledge about instructional strategies, methods, and environments. Both use scientific knowledge of the descriptive type (which describes and explains "how things are", in this case "what learning consists of"), to develop knowledge of the prescriptive type (i.e. say knowledge for action, which is goal-oriented, in this case "fostering learning").

The construction of "goal-oriented" knowledge characterizes all sciences of the "design" type, that is to say the sciences of design or the "sciences of the artificial", according to the expression coined by Herbert Simon (1969).

The paradigms of teaching theory and learning sciences constitute theoretical frameworks which are therefore of the "design" type, since they are devoted to the design of particular artifacts, namely methods, strategies or educational environments. These two paradigms "inherit" in some way their "design" character from their disciplinary field of reference which is educational technology.

Concerning the paradigm of teaching theory, we note that it belongs both to theories of the "design" type and to the field of Design of educational systems or theories of educational design which is also of the "design" type. ". This double characterization in terms of "design" is at the origin of a terminological puzzle concerning the use, in English, of the names Instructional Design and Instructional Theory . Educational technology researchers have proposed various solutions to solve this problem. Two main solutions can be distinguished in contemporary writings.

The first approach is that which proposes to use the term teaching theory to describe the "design" phase of educational design methods (Design of educational systems). This approach characterizes in particular a major editorial project in educational technology led by Charles Reigeluth since 1983 and aimed at constituting a collective knowledge base " dedicated to increasing our knowledge about how to improve instruction" (Reigeluth, 1983). In this context, Reigeluth proposed to distinguish:

- Theories relating to the entire, systemic and systematic process of designing teaching-learning systems (from needs analysis to system implementation) and brought together under the common label of Instructional Design Theories. These theories correspond to what we call in French "pedagogical engineering" or "training engineering". A prototypical example of theories of this type is the ADDIE method.
- Theories which offer "explicit guidance on how to better help people learn and develop" (Reigeluth, 1999) and grouped under the label of instructional-design theories (with a hyphen). The latter are design-type teaching theories, in other words, they are prescriptive theories oriented on the way of teaching (Basque et al., 2010).

This clarification did not seem sufficient, because in 2009, Reigeluth returned to this question, this time proposing to distinguish different "instructional design theories " according to the different design phases of systems or learning environments. Thus, "instructional-design theory" becomes "instructional-event design theory" and it is distinguished from "instructional analysis design theory", "instructional planning design theory". His idea is that each phase of the instructional design process can generate and have its own theory. And as all these theories are of the "design" type, it is possible to omit the word "design" and thus speak of "instructional analysis theory", "instructional planning theory", etc. From this perspective, "instructional-event design theory" simply becomes "instructional-event theory". Reigeluth emphasizes that "instructional-event theory is the only one that offers guidance about the nature of the instruction itself. The other five all offer guidance about what is commonly called the instructional systems design (or development) process (ISD). » (Reigeluth, 2009).

The second approach rather proposes to distinguish the methods and models of Instructional Systems Design (ISD) from the methods and models of Instructional Design (ID). This distinction highlights that the two types of methods and models differ in the extent of the design processes involved. ISD models and methods have a broader objective, covering all the processes of developing a learning system. These methods usually include the phases: analysis, design, production, implementation and dissemination, summative evaluation and transversal processes: project management and formative evaluation. On the other hand, ID models and methods are usually more restricted, because they are focused on the first two phases of ISD methods: analysis of what is to be learned and the conversion of the results of this analysis into the design of teaching activities - learning: " Determine what to teach . Determine how to teach " (Merrill, 2001). As the scope of design processes covered by these models and methods is less, they should be applied in conjunction with the ISD models, "in order to receive support for the activities not treated in the model, such as needs assessment and needs analysis, production of instructional materials, implementation and delivery, and summative evaluation (Van Merriënboer, 1997). On the other hand, they offer a richer and more precise conceptualization of the principles of teaching and learning (Seel & Djikstra, 1997 ; Tennyson, 2010).

The Principles of Instructional Design Developed in the Cognitive Approach to Teaching-Learning

Several principles of educational design have been developed within the framework of the instructional theory paradigm and, more precisely, within the framework of research brought together under the term Conditions-based learning or Conditions of learning (COL). As Richey and his colleagues point out in 2011: "Conditions-based theory is basically a cognitive orientation that is especially relevant to the selection and design of instructional strategies" (Richey et al., 2011).

Researchers within this research paradigm share a general hypothesis which can be expressed as follows: teaching-learning activities must be designed to promote learning conditions, as described by theories cognitive learning.

This general hypothesis is translated into general principles which have been developed to guide designers in their design work. These principles are part of the conceptual knowledge about instructional design developed in the cognitive approach. More precisely, it is:

"Knowledge of the principles and generalizations that are used to study phenomena or to solve problems in a field of knowledge. This knowledge is particularly useful for dealing with the different cases that may arise in a given field. Experts use this knowledge to identify the typical configurations of phenomena ("patterns") which guide the choice of the action that will be taken" (Anderson et al., 2001).

Various "pedagogies of learning" (methods, strategies, models, etc.) have reconnected, for the most part, with the ideas of the precursors of Dewey, Piaget, Vygotsky (Lieury and De La Haye, 2009), Claparède, Mialaret. ... In the school context, these "pedagogies":

"... using the contributions of cognitivist theories, (they) proceeded to invert the educational process, by decentering themselves from the teaching process and favoring the learning processes. They have thus reversed the teacher-relations students, teacher-learner and have produced a real consideration of the student by restoring a dominant place in the educational triangle to the learner/knowledge relationship and to the mediating role of the teacher" (Altet, 1997/2006). In this sense, we will see the evolution of the approach according to the French-speaking context and the English-speaking context. Indeed:

- In the French-speaking context, the cognitive approach is developed mainly by researchers interested in didactics. They agree that "the function of the teacher is not to teach, it is to ensure that students learn" and, therefore, "understanding how the student learns is the foundation of teaching activity" (Develay, 1992). Not all French-speaking researchers in educational sciences adhere to this conceptualization. Some pay less attention to learning and prefer to focus on the activity of teachers. These words from Van der Maren (1996) illustrate this point of view: "Learning and the problem of memory primarily concern only the learners. They are the ones who will have to learn. Learning is not the main task of the teacher. Its task is to teach so that learners learn. Its problem is above all a problem of communication, management and manipulation of the elements of the educational environment. For students to learn, he must first get the message across, legitimize and promote its content, organize activities requiring learners to use what he wants to present to them, and this in a limited time, with a sufficient number high number of learners, etc. »

- In the English-speaking context, the idea that the educational activity of designers, teachers or trainers cannot be analyzed without referring to learning is widely shared. The action of teaching (teaching or instruction) is usually defined as "... intentional facilitation of learning toward identified learning goals" (Smith and Ragan, 2005). In other words, it is postulated from the outset that we cannot describe the nature of teaching without specifying the nature of what is targeted by this teaching, namely learning: "The intention of all teaching activities is that of bringing about learning. But simple and banal though this answer might seem, it is I suggest an extremely important answer. It involves the claim that the concept of teaching is in fact totally unintelligible without a grasp of the concept of learning and that therefore one cannot characterize teaching independently of characterizing learning. Until therefore we know what learning is, it is impossible for us to know what teaching is (....) and that this has important practical consequences for how teachers see their job and therefore for what they do in the classroom". (Hirst, 1971/2012).

Conclusion

While keeping in mind the existence of many differences between the conceptions of teaching valued on both sides of the Atlantic, we can identify a common conception of "pedagogies of learning" which apply in various situations educational: "In these pedagogies, the teacher, who has always acted according to the conceptions he has about the way in which students learn, has become aware of the importance of the students' relationship to knowledge, of their systems of representation spontaneous at the start, of their cognitive and affective learning strategies. He has thus become a professional in learning, in the management of external learning conditions, in the establishment of appropriate learning situations for a given audience, then in transfer situations. The teacher's function is no longer just to transmit knowledge, but to ensure that students learn, to put the learner into activity. He becomes an intermediary between knowledge and the learner, by taking into account the learning process, he becomes a mediator between the learner and his knowledge, by facilitating the development of the meaning of learning, by engaging the learner in a process of meaning construction. » (Altet, 1997/2006).

Being concerned about learning does not mean that we should neglect the cognitive activity of the designer or the teacher in the situation, nor its multiple social, cultural or biological determinants in the context. On the contrary, the cognitive approach recognizes the complexity of the educational situation and considers that, at all phases of teaching (planning, dissemination, evaluation), the teacher, trainer or designer implements complex cognitive processes problem solving for which there is no single or predetermined solution. It must therefore take into consideration various constraints while developing an optimal educational solution from a learning point of view.

Knowledge about learning developed by cognitive sciences can help stakeholders design such solutions that promote learning. Because, even if "there is as far from the knowledge of scientific psychology to learn on a daily basis as from choreographic indications to the opera ballet, from the musical score to the violin concerto, or from the treatise on oenology to the great wine", it is "by integrating science into their practices [that] winegrowers have improved wine" (Bourgeois and Chapelle, 2011).

CONCLUSION

At the conclusion of this chapter, we note that pedagogical innovations require a significant amount of design time. Indeed, pedagogical innovation can be part of the diversification of the learning modalities offered to learners in a program. Strategic planning suggests diversifying pedagogical approaches and, in particular, allowing learners to live distance learning experiences. To this end, in recent years, we have noticed that universities have accredited training courses by suggesting a percentage of 20% of training that must be distance learning. This has made it possible to support teachers in the development of fully remote or hybrid courses in order to allow learners to experience such a learning modality at least once in their training. In the same way, we see in universities that there is support from teams that adopt a programmatic approach to training, whether in competency-based programs or in objective-based programs. Such a curriculum approach fosters greater coherence in learners' learning and a better understanding of the role of each course in the overall training offered to learners. In other universities, we see that there are calls for projects for research teams for the development of MOOCs that concern the undergraduate program. Ultimately, it is important to develop knowledge in the field of pedagogical innovations. We are still a long way from measuring the impact of this or that pedagogical innovation on learners' learning in a given context. We are only at the stage of describing entrepreneurial efforts.

REFERENCES

Alexander, PA, & *Winne*, PH (Eds.). (*2006*). Handbook of educational psychology. Lawrence Erlbaum Associates Publishers.

Alter, N. (2000). *Ordinary innovation*. Presses Universitaires de France.

Altet, M. (1997/2006). *Pedagogies of learning*. PUF.

Alvarez, J., Djaouti, D., & Rampnoux, O. (2016). *Learning with Serious Games*. Canopé Network.

Anderson, L. W., Krathwohl, D. R., Airasian, P. W., Cruikshank, K. A., Mayer, R. E., Pintrich, P. R., Raths, J., & Wittrock, M. C. (2001). *A Taxonomy for learning, teaching, and assessing: A Revision of Bloom's taxonomy of educational objectives*. Longman.

Basque, J., Contamines, J., & Maina, M. (2010). Design approaches to learning environments. In B. Charlier & F. Henri (Eds.), *Learning with technologies* (pp. 109–119).

Béchard, J.-P. (2001). Higher education and educational innovations: A review of the literature. *Journal of Educational Sciences, 272*, 257–281.

Béchard, J. P. & Pelletier, P. (2001), Development of the innovations educational in academia: a case of organizational learning. In D. Raymond (dir.), New spaces of development professional And organizational (pp.131-149). Sherbrooke: Editions of CRP

Bedard, D. & Béchard, J. (2009). Innovation pedagogic. In *THE superior: A vast construction site ". In D. Bedard And J.-P. Béchard (dir.), Innovate In higher education* (pp. 29–43). Presses Academics of France.

Bransford, J. D., Barron, B., Pea, R. D., Meltzoff, A., Kuhl, P., Bell, P., & Sabelli, N. H. (2009). Foundations and Opportunities for an Interdisciplinary Science of Learning. In K. Sawyer (Ed.), *The Cambridge Handbook of Learning Sciences* (pp. 19–34). Cambridge University Press.

Brodin, É. (n.d.). Innovation en éducation et innovation dans l'enseignement des langues: quels invariants? Document inédit. Université Paris 3. France.

Clark, R. C. (2008). *Building expertise. Cognitive methods for training and performance improvement* (3rd ed.). Pfeiffer & International Society for Performance Improvement.

Cros, F. (1997). Innovation in education And in training. *Revue Française de Pédagogie, 118.*

Cros, F. (2001). *School innovation. Teachers and Researchers – Summary and debate – Paris.* INRP.

Cros, F. (2002). National Innovation Council for Academic Success. Progress report to the Minister of National Education, France.

Cros, F. (2007). *Innovative action. Between creativity and training.* De Boeck.

Cros, F. (n.d.). *Innovation in education and training. Meaning and use of the word: Final report.* INNOVA. European Observatory of Innovations in Education.

Depover, C., & Strebelle, A. (1997). *A model and intervention strategy for the introduction of ICT into the educational process.* Educational Technology Unit, University of Mons-Hainaut.

Depover, C., Strebelle, A., & De Lièvre, B. (2007). A modeling of the innovation process based on the dynamics of networks of actors. In M. Baron, D. Guin, & L. Trouche (Eds.), *Computerized environments and digital resources for learning. Design and uses, combined perspectives* (pp. 140–169). Hermès and Lavoisier.

Develay, M. (1992). *From learning to teaching.* ESF.

Donald, A. (1967). The Indirect but Constant Process of Innovation: Technology and Change. The New Heraclitus. Delacorte Press.

Dunlosky, J., Rawson, K. A., Marsh, E. J., Nathan, M. J., & Willingham, D. T. (2013). Improving Students' Learning With Effective Learning Techniques: Promising Directions From Cognitive and Educational Psychology. *Psychological Science in the Public Interest, 14*(1), 4–58. doi:10.1177/1529100612453266 PMID:26173288

Françoise, C. (2002). Innovation in education And in training: topicals And challenges. In *NOT. Alter, THE logical of innovation* (pp. 211–240). There Discovery.

Gage, N. L. (2009). *A conception of teaching.* Springer. doi:10.1007/978-0-387-09446-5

Glikman, V. (2002). From correspondence courses to e-learning: overview of open and distance learning. Presses universitaire de France.

Godin, B. (2012). Innovation Studies: The Invention of a Specialty, Minerva, volume 50. *Nummer, 4,* 397–421.

Graesser, A. C. (2009). Inaugural editorial for Journal of Educational Psychology. *Journal of Educational Psychology*, *101*(2), 259–261. doi:10.1037/a0014883

Grandière, M., & Lahalle, A. (dir.) (2004). L'Innovation dans l'enseignement français (XVIe-XXe siècle). Nantes-Lyon: SCEREN CRDP Pays de la Loire/INRP, 172 p.

Hannan, A., English, S., & Silver, H. (1999). Why innovate? Some preliminary findings from a research project on «Innovations in teaching and learning in higher education». *Studies in Higher Education*, *24*(3), 279–289. doi:10.1080/03075079912331379895

Hattie, J. (2009). *Visible Learning: A synthesis of over 800 meta-analyses relating to achievement*. Routledge.

Higher Education Council (CSÉ). (1995). Annual report on the state and needs of education (1994-1995). Managing change in education. Quebec. CSE.

Higher Education Council (CSÉ). (2000). Report on the state and needs of education (1999-2000). Education and new technologies: For successful integration in teaching and learning. Quebec. CSE.

Higher Education Council (CSÉ). (2006). Annual report on the state and needs of education (2004-2005). The dialogue between research and practice in education: a key to success. Quebec. CSE.

Hirst, P. H. (1971/2012). What is teaching? In S. M. Cahn (Ed.), *Classic and Contemporary Readings in the Philosophy of Education* (2nd ed., pp. 353–361). Oxford University Press.

Huberman, A.M. (1973). How changes in education take place: contribution to the study of innovation. *Experience and innovation in education no. 4*. Unesco: IBE.

Cailliez, J. (2017). *The flipped classroom. Educational innovation through changing posture*. Ellipses.

Karima, A. D. (2009). Multilingualism And education intercultural has university, place of training And interaction. *Synergies Algeria*, (5), 151–158.

Karima, A. D. (2011). The impact of the ICT on teaching/learning of there language French in higher education: What training needs for what pedagogy? *Review of the School Doctoral of French, Synergies Algeria*, (12), 227–231.

Kazadi, C. (2006). Innovative approaches in mathematics textbooks. In Loiselle, J., Lafortune, L. and Rousseau, N. (eds.) Innovation in teacher training. Press of the University of Quebec.

Legendre, R. (2005). *Dictionary of Education* (3rd ed.). Guérin.

Lieury, A., & De La Haye, F. (2009). *Psychologie cognitive de l'éducation*. Dunod.

Marcel Lebrun et Julie Lecoq. (2015). *Classes inversées: enseigner et apprendre à l'endroit*. Canopé.

Marisa, C. (2005). *Education bilingue et plurilingue. Le cas du Val d'Aoste*. Editions Didier.

Marzano, R. J. (2011). Art & science of teaching: It's how you use a strategy. *Educational Leadership*, *69*(4), 88–89.

Merrill, D. (2002). First principles of instruction. *Educational Technology Research and Development*, *50*(3), 43–59. doi:10.1007/BF02505024

Merrill, M. D. (2001). Components of instruction toward a theoretical tool for instructional design. *Instructional Science*, *29*(4-5), 291–310. doi:10.1023/A:1011943808888

Merrill, M. D., Barclay, M., & van Schaak, A. (2007). Prescriptive Principles for Instructional Design. In J. M. Spector, M. D. Merrill, J. J. G. van Merriënboer, & M. P. Driscoll (Eds.), *Handbook of Research on Educational Communications and Technology* (pp. 173–184). Routledge, Taylor & Francis Group.

Merrill, M.D. (*2013*). *First Principles of Instruction: Identifying and Designing Effective, Efficient, and Engaging Instruction.* San Francisco, CA: Pfeiffer.

Michael, H. (1991). There life of the teachers: Evolution And balance sheet of a occupation. *Revue Française de Pédagogie*, *95*, 146–198.

Morin, E., & Viveret, P. (2010). *Comment vivre en temps de crise? Collection: Le temps d'une question. Editeur: Montrouge.* Bayard.

Nguyên, P., & Daïd, G. (2014). *Practical guide to MOOCs.* Éditions Eyrolles.

Organization for Economic Co-operation and Development (OECD). (2008). *The major changes that are transforming education.* OECD.

Reigeluth, C. M. (1983). Instructional design: What it is and why is it? In C. M. Reigeluth (Ed.), *Instructional design theories and models* (pp. 3–36). Lawrence Erlbaum Associates. doi:10.4324/9780203824283

Reigeluth, C. M. (1999). What Is Instructional-Design Theory and How Is It Changing? In C. M. Reigeluth (Ed.), Instructional-Design Theories and Models, Vol. II: A New Paradigm of Instructional Theory (pp. 1-29). Mahwah, NJ: Lawrence Erlbaum Associates.

Reigeluth, C. M., & Keller, J. B. (2009). Understanding Instruction. In C. M. Reigeluth & A. A. Carr-Chellman (Eds.), *Instructional-Design Theories and Models* (pp. 27–39). Routledge, Taylor and Francis Publishers Group.

Richey, R. C., Klein, J. D., & Tracey, M. W. (2011). Conditions-based theory. In R. C. Richey, J. D. Klein, & M. W. Tracey (Eds.), *The Instructional Design Knowledge Base: Theory, Research and Practice* (pp. 104–128). Routledge.

Roediger, H. L. III. (2013). Applying Cognitive Psychology to Education: Translational Educational Science. *Psychological Science in the Public Interest*, *14*(1), 1–3. doi:10.1177/1529100612454415 PMID:26173287

Rogers, E.M. & Shoemaker, F.F. (1971). *Communication of Innovation: A Cross-Cultural Approach.* (2nd Edition) The Free Press, New York.

Sawyer, K. (Ed.). (2009). *The Cambridge Handbook of Learning Science.* Cambridge University Press.

Simon, H. (1969). The science of the artificial, (trans. Jean-Louis Le Moigne). MIT Press.

Smith, P. L., & Ragan, T. J. (2005). *Instructional Design* (3rd ed.). Wiley & Sons.

Tennyson, R. D. (2010). Historical reflection on learning theories and instructional design. *Contemporary Educational Technology, 1*(1), 1–16. doi:10.30935/cedtech/5958

Tobias, S., & Duffy, T.M. (Eds.). (2009). *Constructivist instruction: Success or failure?* Routledge/Taylor & Francis Group. Abstract.

Tricot, A. (2017). *Myths and realities. Educational innovation,* Paris: ed. Retz.

Van der Maren, J.-M. (1996). *Search methods for education* (2nd ed.). PUM and de Boeck.

Van Merriënboer. (1997). *Training complex cognitive skills: A four-component instructional design model for technical training.* JJG.

Willingham, D. T. (2010). *Why children don't like school!* La Librairie des Écoles. doi:10.1002/9781118269527

Willis, K. (2011). *Theories and Practices of Development* (2nd ed.). Routledge., doi:10.4324/9780203844182

ENDNOTES

[1] https://fr.wikipedia.org/wiki/Khan_Academy#cite_note-LM2020-2. Accessed October 30, 2023.
[2] https://fr.wikipedia.org/wiki/Moodle
[3] https://rire.ctreq.qc.ca/les-pratiques-innovantes-en-education/
[4] Paul Grand'Maison, MD, MSc, FCMFC, FACSS, FCRMCC (hon.), CQ.
[5] https://www.beedeez.com/fr/blog/quest-ce-que-linnovation-pedagogique

Chapter 3
Scripting Tools and the Design of E-Learning Experiences

Soufiane Ouariach

https://orcid.org/0000-0001-5869-9027

Abdelmalek Essaâdi University, Morocco

Mohamed Khaldi

https://orcid.org/0000-0002-1593-1073

Abdelmalek Essaâdi University, Morocco

ABSTRACT

In recent years, e-learning has experienced a surge in popularity as a teaching method. Digital platforms have revolutionized learning by offering learners a more flexible and accessible educational experience. However, it is crucial to recognize that mere access to online materials does not guarantee effective learning outcomes. The design of online learning experiences plays a pivotal role in engaging learners and facilitating a stimulating and successful educational journey. This chapter commences by introducing the concept of e-learning and tracing its historical evolution. Subsequently, it delves into various critical questions surrounding the advantages and disadvantages of e-learning, as well as the pedagogical approaches employed in this environment. The authors then propose a model based on the three systems of a training module, providing a framework for effective e-learning design. Finally, the chapter concludes by illustrating scripting tools for e-learning, equipping teachers interested in e-learning with invaluable resources for developing their e-learning scenarios.

INTRODUCTION

In today's digital age, e-learning has become an increasingly popular method of education. However, simply transferring traditional teaching methods to an online platform may not be enough to ensure effective learning outcomes. Pedagogical approaches play a crucial role in e-learning design, as they determine how instructional content is delivered and received.

DOI: 10.4018/979-8-3693-3128-6.ch003

Copyright © 2024, IGI Global. Copying or distributing in print or electronic forms without written permission of IGI Global is prohibited.

Effective e-learning courses require a well-thought-out pedagogical approach. An effective online pedagogy emphasizes student-centered learning, which means that active learning activities should be employed in e-learning. This approach gives learners the freedom to explore content at their own pace (Simamora et al., 2020), and to choose which courses to take and when to take them by laying out all the learning content. The choice of instructional design strategy depends on the learning goals and available resources (Julia & Marco, 2021). The approach of the instructional designer towards learning can influence e-learning. It is important to consider whether technology is pedagogy-isolated or not in e-learning. This highlights the need to examine whether technology is merely a tool used in e-learning, or whether it is fully integrated into the pedagogical approach. This assessment is crucial to understanding how technology enhances the learning experience and supports effective teaching methodologies in e-learning.

Instructional designers have many pedagogical approaches to choose from when developing e-learning courses. One way to incorporate effective principles is by utilizing behavioral, cognitive, and constructive psychology principles in e-learning design (Inês, n.d.). These principles can help create course materials that are engaging and effective.

In other words, it is imperative to structure online learning in a manner that ensures learners not only acquire knowledge but also develop a deep understanding of the course material. Among the various methods for organizing online learning content, incorporating the training module systems emerges as one of the most potent approaches. By integrating activities and based on different pedagogical approaches, learners can progress at their own pace, guaranteeing a comprehensive grasp of every facet presented in each activity. Within the framework of our proposed architecture, the authors have ingeniously designed a deductive approach model that caters to the unique context and ongoing activities of learners. Moreover, to maximize the learning potential, they introduce scripting tools that empower trainers to craft hybrid learning activities with utmost efficacy. Notably, the activity diagram and the specification table stand out as two indispensable tools for designing impactful learning activities. These tools facilitate the creation of engaging and effective learning experiences, empowering learners to thrive in their educational endeavors.

Throughout this chapter, the authors explore the world of e-learning, delving deep into its history and evolution. They examine the pedagogical approaches that have shaped the landscape of online learning and discuss how technological advances have transformed the learning process. The authors examine the advantages and disadvantages of e-learning, weighing the benefits against the disadvantages.

Afterward, the authors turned their attention to questions about pedagogical approaches. As a result of the training module systems and scripting tools, they propose a design of an e-learning model for a deductive approach that is both effective and efficient, using technology to create a truly immersive environment for learning.

E-LEARNING

In the computerized age, the idea of e-learning has arisen as a leading alternative to traditional classroom teaching. With innovative advances and the developing accessibility of online stages, e-learning has turned into a fundamental piece of the instructive scene, turning into the new year of learning, impelled by the mechanical advances that have upset instructing.

E-learning has been depicted as a "fifth era" rendition of distance learning "intended to exploit the qualities of the Web and the Internet" (Taylor, 2001, p. 2). Utilized conversely, the web/e-Learning has for the most part been characterized by the decrease of room among instructors and students using online advances (Lee, 2017; Moore et al., 2011; Ryan et al., 2016).

Today's learners have a range of online educational content at their disposal to learn flexibly and at their own pace. Pedagogical methods that span time and space can be found by leveraging digital. Platforms are a working base from which to write, read, use, and develop a range of software and sites. It is an environment for managing and/or using application services (Ouariach et al., 2023). They enable learners to receive training without location or scheduling problems. This leads to a wide range of options and accessibility for all those who want to learn. Modern education systems struggle to include all learners. Indeed, many learners excluded from traditional education systems benefit from e-learning thanks to the availability of information and communication technologies. These technologies enable learners to personalize their learning experiences and even access education in areas where traditional education systems don't work (Schleicher, 2018). E-learning is revolutionized by digital technologies. This enables learners to interact with teachers and classmates via online platforms such as discussion forums, collaboration tools, etc. (Chen, 2021). The evolution of e-learning comes from its ability to be more dynamic and interactive. Indeed, learners can organize their learning and follow their own pace with complete autonomy (Srithar & Selvaraj, 2015). E-learning is a more innovative approach to teaching, offering a practical and flexible alternative to traditional methods (Mapuva, 2009). It can be used by companies to provide employees with professional training that they can access when they need it. It can also be a solution for distance learners, offering them easy access to quality educational resources without having to travel.

E-learning, according to leading thinkers in the field, is a modern approach to education that uses communication technologies to deliver an interactive and dynamic educational experience to learners regardless of their geographical location (Clark & Mayer, 2016). Whether through virtual learning materials and guidance or by offering interactive, asynchronous, and distance learning (Olson, 2003), the use of online technology is at the heart of this innovative approach to teaching.

In this type of training, the learner follows the course entirely at a distance. They do not interact directly with the trainer face-to-face. However, they can still benefit from remote tutoring using tools such as web conferencing, forums, chat, telephone, and email.

Learners can also provide feedback on the course. In the learning analytics movement, digital tools are increasingly being developed to gather information from learners on their perceptions of courses and their needs. Teachers can then adjust their interventions according to the feedback obtained (Poellhuber et al., 2017).

Enriched face-to-face training courses are a form of face-to-face teaching that integrates digital components to enhance the learning experience. In this model, teachers supplement their face-to-face sessions with distance learning phases, either before or after the face-to-face training. This enables teachers to offer learners additional digital resources to explore, as well as practical exercises in the form of quizzes, questionnaires, or games to be completed on a platform after the training session.

E-learning additionally cultivates the improvement of significant abilities, like critical thinking and virtual communication (Saadé et al., 2012). The ability to think critically and overcome obstacles is valuable for both learners and future employees (EHL, 2021). Furthermore, virtual communication skills are sharpened through web-based conversations, bunch tasks, and communications with teachers and peers. These abilities are important in the present computerized age and can be applied in different expert and individual settings. Generally, e-learning offers an adaptable, reasonable, and abilities instructive experience that is appropriate to the requirements and inclinations of modern learners.

HISTORY OF E-LEARNING

The authentic foundations of e-learning can be followed back to the beginning of the computer age during the 1960s and 1970s when the principal tests in computer-assisted learning (CAL) occurred. As information and communication technologies (ICT) high level, new types of e-learning arose, including distance learning and blended learning (Moore and Kearsley, 2012; Post, 2011).

During the 1970s, mechanical progressions took into consideration more complex communications among students and computer programs. Nonetheless, e-learning was primarily limited to mainframe computers or terminals, hindering its accessibility. The presentation of computers during the 1980s achieved a huge change in the e-learning scene, prompting its far-reaching multiplication. Subsequently, educators and organizations began designing interactive computer programs to facilitate distance learning.

Over the long run, innovation kept on advancing, empowering the utilization of radio, TV, audio, and most outstandingly, the Web, as vehicles for conveying distance learning programs. During the 1990s and 2000s, e-learning experienced fast development with the approach of the Web and the ascent of web-based learning stages. Researchers likewise proposed hypothetical structures to direct the plan and execution of e-learning (Siemens, 2005; Anderson, 2003; Downes, 2005).

By this point, e-learning had turned into a more complex field, with the accessibility of learning management tools (LMS). These stages assumed a significant part in working with preparing, making customized and versatile learning situations, and cultivating intelligent examination of work (Ouariach et al., 2023). Furthermore, distance students could associate from a distance and team up through conversation gatherings and discussion channels, successfully using the web joint effort instruments (Ally, 2004).

Be that as it may, e-advancing additionally experienced different difficulties, for example, guaranteeing quality, planning compelling projects, and drawing in students (Garrisson & Kanuka, 2004). Notwithstanding these impediments, e-learning proceeded to develop and assume a huge part in the present day.

In ongoing many years, e-learning has encountered remarkable development, driven by the Web's expansion and the advancements in information and communication technologies. As per a new report by Allen and Seaman (2017), more than 6 million people in the US alone have signed up for online courses. The concentrate likewise shows a 5.6% development rate in e-learning over the last year.

All the more as of late, the Coronavirus pandemic has sped up the reception of e-learning in instructive foundations around the world, accentuating both the advantages and difficulties of this type of learning (Hodges et al., 2020).

A large number of individuals from all sides of the globe use e-learning out how to get new abilities and grow their insight. The fate of e-learning is affected by mechanical headways, such as virtual reality and artificial intelligence, leaving room for speculation about the exciting developments that lie ahead in this thriving sector.

At least, e-learning addresses a story of change. It includes utilizing state-of-the-art advancements to expand learning and open doors, taking special care of assorted crowds, and investigating with inventive instructing techniques. As innovation keeps on advancing, e-learning will without a doubt adjust and develop to fulfill the steadily changing needs of schooling and professional preparation.

Transformation is the underlying theme of e-learning. One must use state-of-the-art technologies to both expand learning prospects, accommodate varying viewerships, and trial inventive teaching techniques. As technology advances, e-learning will certainly adjust and progress to the shifting needs of educational and professional training.

PEDAGOGICAL APPROACHES OF ONLINE LEARNING

Online learning has rapidly become a popular alternative to traditional classroom-based education, particularly in the wake of the COVID-19 pandemic. However, the efficacy of pedagogical approaches in online learning environments is still a topic of debate among educators and researchers. This area aims to explore the different pedagogical approaches in online learning environments.

Constructivist Approach to Online Learning

Constructivist approaches to e-learning rely on the possibility that information can be built by the student through dynamic investigation and commitment to the learning material (Alonso et al., 2005). In this approach, learners are emphasized as active participants rather than passive recipients of information. Active learning is a key principle of the constructivist approach, which involves learners exploring and experimenting with the learning material. This approach enables learners to construct their understanding of the material and develop their problem-solving skills (Bada & Olusegun, 2015).

Another important principle of the constructivist approach to e-learning is collaborative learning and social interaction (Ketele & Hugonnier, 2020). The purpose of this principle is to emphasize the importance of students working together to gain knowledge and develop an understanding of the subject matter. As part of a constructivist pedagogy, e-learning involves establishing a relationship between the trainer and the learner, as well as encouraging interaction among the learners (EduTech, n.d.). This social interaction helps learners to develop their communication and collaboration skills, which are essential in many professional contexts. The constructivist approach to e-learning also emphasizes personalized learning and self-reflection.

As students assume command of their learning and connect with companions and educators, they can build how they might interpret abilities and information (Atkinson, 2011; Pittaway, 2012). Learning assets and exercises ought to be custom-made to understudy learning styles, and students ought to be urged to consider their way of learning and distinguish regions for development. As well as dynamic learning and investigation, cooperative learning, social connection, and customized learning, constructivist e-learning stresses self-reflection and reflection. In this methodology, students develop their comprehension own might interpret the world and learning occurs in an intelligent, social climate. Through the utilization of these standards for e-learning, instructors can make connecting with, viable growth opportunities that empower students to take responsibility for learning and apply it to their lives.

The Cognitivist Approach to Online Learning

The cognitivist approach to online learning is rooted in an understanding of how individuals process and acquire knowledge. Cognitivism recognizes that learners have different levels of cognitive ability and that, therefore, in an online environment, not all learners can make the same progress (eLearning Industry, 2018). At its core, cognitivism views learning as an active, constructive process that involves the active engagement of the learner and the construction of new knowledge (GradePower Learning, n.d.). Minds that process perception, attention, memory, and problem-solving are vital to learning (Morales & Gray, n.d.). When educators understand cognitive processes in learning, they can create e-learning experiences that optimize the learner's ability to retain and acquire information.

The key principles and theories of cognitivism provide a framework for understanding how individuals learn and process information. Cognitive learning theory explains how internal and external factors influence an individual's mental processes to enhance learning (Valamis, n.d.). One of the key principles of cognitivism is the importance of prior knowledge and schemas in the learning process. According to this theory, learners actively construct new knowledge by linking new information to their existing knowledge and experience. Another principle is the emphasis on comprehension, analysis, synthesis, and problem-solving skills. These principles guide the design of e-learning materials and activities that encourage active engagement, critical reflection, and in-depth understanding of the subject matter.

Applying cognitivism to e-learning involves designing pedagogical strategies and learning environments in line with cognitivist principles and theories. E-learning platforms can enable learners to actively engage with content through interactive multimedia, simulations, and problem-solving activities (Sattar, 2020). The use of scaffolding and guided practice can help learners build on prior knowledge and gradually develop more complex cognitive skills. In addition, incorporating strategies such as chunking, repetition, and retrieval practice can improve memory retention and retrieval (Greitzer, 2002). Drawing on the principles of cognitivism, e-learning can be designed to optimize the learner's cognitive processes and promote deep learning and understanding (Online Learning, 2022).

The Connectivism Approach to Online Learning

The connectivism approach to e-learning focuses on the idea that learning occurs through connections and interactions within a networked environment. Connectivism emphasizes the importance of digital technologies and online communities in facilitating learning (Siemens, 2005). It is based on the belief that knowledge is distributed through networks and that learning involves the process of connecting specialized nodes or sources of information. In connectivism, learning is not just an individual activity, but rather a collective process that occurs through collaboration, the sharing of ideas, and engagement with others (WGU, n.d.).

This approach recognizes the importance of networked learning and knowledge creation in the digital age (Huezo, 2017). One of the fundamental principles of connectivism is its focus on networked learning and knowledge creation through connections. Connectivism sees learning as a process that takes place outside the individual, often through social media, online networks, blogs, or information-sharing platforms. The connectivism approach encourages group interactions and conversations, allowing individuals to express their opinions and points of view (Pappas, 2023). This collaborative process of connecting and sharing within a network leads to the creation of new forms of knowledge. Connectivism recognizes the dynamic and changing nature of knowledge, as nodes come and go and information flows through interconnected networks. Digital technologies and online communities play a crucial role in connectivism.

The use of web browsers, social media platforms, and other Internet technologies increases connectivity and access to information (360Learning, n.d.). Connectivism takes advantage of these digital tools to facilitate learning and create opportunities for collaboration and engagement. The connectivism approach also recognizes the importance of technology in intercultural communication and knowledge creation (Shrivastava, 2018). By using the technology of computer innovations and online networks, connectivism offers learners a dynamic and different learning climate that surpasses the conventional limits of the face-to-face classroom.

The general belief that the traditional classroom promotes latent learning has been firmly established. In this unique situation, learners primarily expect to be independent listeners and diligent note-takers, while educators disseminate information through lectures and introductions. Dynamic cooperation within the classroom is often linked to individual tasks (Ouariach et al., 2023). In any case, connectivism challenges the usual assumptions of progress by coordinating innovation and emphasizing the interconnections between information and the experience of growth (Corbett & Spinello, 2020).

The Behaviorist Approach to Online Learning

The behaviorist approach to e-learning is based on the principles of behaviorism, which aims to guide learners to achieve pre-established learning outcomes. Behaviorism postulates that learning is an observable change in behavior caused by an external stimulus followed by a response. This approach to learning has its origins in the work of Ivan Pavlov and B.F. Skinner (Ouadoud et al, 2017), argued that learning is evident when a behavior is modified. Behaviorism emphasizes the idea that all behaviors are acquired through interaction with the environment (Ertmer & Newby, 2013).

In the context of e-learning, the behaviorist approach can be applied through a variety of strategies and techniques. Repetition is one way of reinforcing learning, as learners are exposed to the same information several times to strengthen their understanding. Feedback and recognition are also important in the behaviorist approach, as learners receive feedback on their performance and are recognized for their achievements, motivating them to continue learning. Response measurement is another key principle, whereby learners' responses to stimuli are measured and evaluated to gauge their progress. In addition, gamification can be used to make the learning process more engaging and interactive, by incorporating key elements such as rewards and challenges (Marina, n.d.).

Active learning is also emphasized in the behaviorist approach to e-learning. Learners are encouraged to participate actively in the learning process, responding to stimuli so that learning takes place (Davidson-Shiver & Rasmussen, 2006). This can be facilitated by interactive activities, discussions, and simulations that require learners to actively engage with the material. By applying behaviorist principles to e-learning, teachers can create effective and engaging learning experiences that promote the acquisition of knowledge and the development of skills.

TOOLS AND TECHNOLOGIES FOR ONLINE LEARNING

Of late, the world of education has seen a massive shift towards e-learning and e-learning platforms. Technological advances, intuitive devices, and ever more advances have become a fundamental part of e-learning's growth. These new tools and innovations offer additional opportunities to attract learners, cultivate cooperation, and work on the overall viability of e-learning.

A crucial role played by pedagogical technology in e-learning networks is the enhancement of the interaction between teachers and learners. Human-learning interaction (HLI) is an interdisciplinary research area that investigates the use of emerging technologies to enhance online learning (Farhan et al., 2019). The e-learning user interface (ELUI) is an example of an interactive tool that facilitates pedagogical communication in electronic learning environments. As part of the design and redesign of e-learning systems, additional interactive features can be incorporated to further enhance online interaction in educational settings (Ibid). As a result of the use of intelligent interactive tools such as Rain Classroom and Tencent Meeting, online teaching platforms have been created that facilitate the interaction between teachers and learners (Wang et al., 2021). Several features are available with these tools, such as course replay, real-time communication, data analysis, and class participation tracking, which can provide learners with personalized instruction and facilitate effective learning. Farhan and his collaborators believe that the integration of intelligent interactive tools not only optimizes the teaching ecosystem in higher education cultivates learners' capacity for self-learning and increases their motivation for learning. The application of interactive tools and emerging technologies to e-learning has excellent potential to increase efficiency, save time, and cater to the needs of Generation Z learners accustomed to mobile apps and video content as technology advances (Farhan et al., 2019). These tools are essential for creating a successful and engaging e-learning environment that encourages active learning and knowledge retention.

With the integration of interactive tools into e-learning, courses have become more participatory and interactive. Despite their universal applicability, these tools and technologies have proven to be effective, efficient, and accessible, enabling a large number of individuals to learn effectively (Almufarreh & Arshad, 2023). There are several interactive tools available for learners to use, including Google Expeditions, which can be used inside and outside the classroom for additional review of material or assignments. As a result of this tool, students can learn complex concepts in a more engaging and immersive manner. A similar program, known as HITLibHZ-BuildAR (Yildiz, 2021), is frequently used in medical education to enhance pedagogical practices. Through its use, learners can visualize and interact with 3D models, improving their understanding of medical procedures and complex anatomical structures (Almufarreh & Arshad, 2022). Furthermore, Kahoot's online IoT processes allow teachers to share notes with learners via platforms such as Telegram and Google Docs, improving the effectiveness of e-learning by providing instant feedback and promoting active student participation. Additionally, the use of augmented reality applications enhances technical drawing education by enabling learners to view 3D models in real time, thus improving their spatial understanding and problem-solving abilities (Nez et al., 2008 & Papanastasiou et al., 2019). Utilizing technological tools such as interactive devices and augmented reality, which combine the physical and digital worlds, allows users to autonomously create flexible learning experiences that contribute to the development of 21st-century skills in educational contexts (Martín-Gutiérrez et al., 2015; Sanabria & Arámburo-Lizárraga, 2016).

To achieve the aims of e-learning, innovations need to be integrated into the teaching and learning experience. Using these innovations to work towards the viability of e-learning has several advantages. At an underlying level, new advances can be used to refresh outdated material and methods used in regular courses, ensuring that learners have the most authoritative and relevant information at their disposal. At the same time, these advancements can prevent the educator from becoming the main source of information and enable learners to participate in the learning process. By using platforms such as Moodle, Claroline, EdX, etc., combined with intuitive learning tools, learners can effectively take ownership of the material and take responsibility for their growth opportunities. Another advantage of increasing progress is the ability to tailor learning and teaching encounters to the interesting needs and inclinations of individual learners (McBrien et al., 2009).

They thus give teachers access to a wide range of ready-to-use content, as well as devices enabling them to create their own adapted learning materials. While recent progress can undoubtedly have an impact on web-based education and learning strategies, closer examination should recognize the capabilities required to use these innovations effectively and anticipate potential capability gaps (Yildiz, 2021).

THE BENEFITS AND THE DISADVANTAGES OF E-LEARNING

As a part of education, e-learning plays an important role, as it offers many benefits, such as the ability to learn at your own pace and the freedom to make your own decisions, or what we call autonomy. There are, however, some disadvantages associated with it These include the cost of developing and maintaining e-learning platforms, lack of access to technology in some parts of the world, and the risk of cheating or plagiarism. Thus, in this section, the author will discuss the advantages and disadvantages of e-learning

The Benefits of E-Learning

Today, e-learning has made its mark as a key element in education, providing numerous benefits for learners and educators in equal measure. Thanks to modern technologies such as cell phones and computers, e-learning has been made increasingly accessible over the past decade, making it easier for learners to reach online platforms and improving the effectiveness of mobile learning.

E-learning is a bargain. Neither traditional training nor e-learning is more effective than half a day of traditional training. E-learning increases productivity. According to Training Magazine, the U.S. spent $83 billion on training needs in 2019, including $29.6 billion on transportation costs, training room rentals, and in-house development (Training Magazine, 2019). Many of these costs can be reduced with e-learning, as it reduces the need for speakers, room bookings, printing materials, and travel.

It's like a new wind blowing through education -- e-learning. 90% of modern companies have already adopted some form of e-learning, a number that has risen significantly since 1995 when just 4% used it. E-learning is predicted to grow another 8% by 2026, confirming its role as the future of vocational training (Anna, 2020).

One of the numerous advantages of e-learning is the ability for students to communicate in discussion forums, which can assist them in solving challenging problems and improving their learning experience (Panigrahi et al., 2018). The popularity of this mode of learning has also grown among students, so teachers must design effective online learning experiences that meet the needs of a wide variety of students. Several studies have shown that e-learning increases learner participation, improves the quality of discussions, and facilitates meaningful online interactions (Yu, 2021). Additionally, e-learning gives individuals the flexibility to learn at their own pace and convenience, which is especially beneficial for people with busy schedules and professionals (Lone et al., 2032). During the digital revolution, accessing, consuming, discussing, and sharing content have all changed dramatically. By providing them with up-to-date content, e-learning helps learners keep up with modern learners (McHaney, 2023)

As well as offering greater access to higher education, e-learning promotes digital literacy (Zahra et al., 2022). With its moderately fast transmission cycles, e-learning has been shown to reduce learning time by 25-60% compared to conventional learning techniques (Gupta, 2017). Given these advantages, e-learning plays an important role in training in the computer age by reducing learning time and transmitting courses quickly, which helps both learners and teachers.

Throughout the learning process, e-learning offers a wide selection of tools, resources, and media (HEC, n.d). In addition to videos and interactive presentations, learners can participate in practical exercises, discussion forums, and more. Thanks to these elements, learners can enhance their learning experience while working at their own pace. What's more, e-learning offers learners great flexibility (Daniel, 2016).

Flexibility in terms of scheduling and space is a vital advantage of e-learning that appeals to many people. Similarly, a study showed that online training was useful for learners to work at their own pace and make them autonomous, as indicated by 69.2% of them. Furthermore, the results show that an equivalent number of members (61.5%) are convinced that online courses offer flexibility in their modes and modalities, provide massive amounts of information, allow members to familiarize themselves with the information at home, and provide up-to-date, reliable pieces of information (Paudel, 2021). Unlike traditional teaching, e-learning doesn't expect learners to sign up at a specific time for classes or conversations. This flexibility allows learners to manage their schedules and take courses when it suits them. For those with daily work or family commitments, it's important to be able to choose when and where to study.

Simply put, e-learning is a viable and imaginative academic device that can help learners enhance their growth opportunities while offering greater flexibility and more cost-effective investment funds (Fortun, 2016).

Regardless of these advantages, online learning can also introduce difficulties such as individual motivation, the requirement for self-discipline, and the lack of direct human communication.

The Disadvantages of E-Learning

In recent years, e-learning has established itself as a useful and flexible technique for acquiring information and skills. Thanks to the widespread use of innovation, learners today are ready to access educational content and partner with educators at a distance, avoiding the need to visit real classrooms. Despite the many advantages of e-learning, it's essential to remember that it also has a few drawbacks.

Learners experience critical side effects when they require visual connection and socialization in online learning environments. Students may struggle to make meaningful connections and create a sense of proximity in a virtual classroom without the opportunity to associate with their flesh-and-blood friends and teachers.

The group discussions, team projects, and networking opportunities that exist in traditional face-to-face learning are not readily available in e-learning, further limiting socialization opportunities for learners (Singh et al., 2022). This adjustment of specialized technology while learning online can have likely implications for the learners' social turn of events, possibly leading to feelings of detachment and a weakening sense of association with both colleagues and teachers. The absence of visually-based communication in online learning conditions inhibits socialization and can harm learners' overall growth opportunities.

The absence of a physical classroom in e-learning has significant consequences for learner engagement and interaction. One of the truly harmful outcomes is the lack of real collaboration between learners, which inhibits their ability to inspire and connect (Li et al., 2021). Learners frequently complain about the lack of relational contact between them and the educator, resulting in a lack of inspiration. To solve this problem, educational institutions need to offer intuitive courses that compensate for the lack of a real classroom climate and foster learner engagement and cooperation. However, the e-learning methodology itself does not provide easy answers to maintaining engagement through physical interaction. One way to promote online collaboration and interaction is to assign interactive exercises or projects that learners must complete in small groups (Brindley et al., 2009). Creating smaller groups of learners for virtual sessions can also help foster engagement and interaction between learners (Banna et al., 2015). Another problem caused by the absence of a physical classroom is the reduced ability of learners to ask questions for immediate help (Jeffery & Bauer, 2020). The structure provided by a physical classroom is essential for discipline, as learners cannot simply turn off the webcams or doze off without consequences (Bowen & Watson, 2017).

In this unique situation, the absence of a physical classroom negatively affects learner engagement and communication in e-learning. It's difficult to follow the lead of inspiration, encourage cooperation, and give prompt help and guidance. To meet these challenges, teachers need to open doors to engagement and cooperation, both through contextualized exercises and by creating a stable climate in online learning environments. By solving these problems, educational institutions can help to develop learner engagement and cooperation under e-learning conditions.

THE EFFECT OF PEDAGOGICAL APPROACHES TO ONLINE LEARNING

Pedagogy plays a crucial role in determining the learning outcomes of students. A poor pedagogical approach can lead to disengagement, boredom, and lack of motivation among students, while a well-designed pedagogical approach can foster critical thinking, problem-solving skills, and creativity among students (Caduceus International Publishing, 2023). Therefore, it is essential for educators to continuously improve their teaching methods to ensure positive learning outcomes for their students (ibid). Effective pedagogical approaches are particularly important in promoting student learning outcomes in the life sciences, where active learning strategies are crucial.

A comparative meta-analysis conducted in this study analyzed different pedagogical approaches in online learning to identify effective strategies for student engagement and learning outcomes (Ulum, 2022). The studies included in the analysis had a total sample size of 1772, and were conducted in various countries including the US, Taiwan, Turkey, China, Philippines, Ireland, and Georgia, although studies carried out in Europe could not be reached. Online education has its advantages and disadvantages, which include flexibility of learning time. However, some studies show that face-to-face traditional learning is still considered effective compared to online learning. Despite this, the study found that online education approaches were more effective than traditional ones in the studies included in the research. The meta-analysis included studies analyzing the effect of online education approaches on academic achievement, to determine its effect on academic achievement. The effect size of online education on academic achievement was found to be moderate in this study. The study is a comparative meta-analysis of pedagogical approaches in online learning, which investigates the effect sizes of online education on academic achievement, intending to identify effective strategies for student engagement and learning outcomes in online learning.

Constructivist approaches to online learning have been shown to improve student learning outcomes. Adapting educational tools and environments based on the needs of existing external reality can lead to significant improvements in student learning outcomes in online learning (Triantafyllou, 2019). Applying constructivist philosophy to distance learning and educational technology is an effective way to improve student learning outcomes. Constructivism theory posits that knowledge is built by students through social interaction with their co-students (ibid). During the COVID-19 pandemic, online learning has been shown to improve students' happiness and academic success (Alismajel et al., 2022). The proposed model for this study, based on constructivism theory, includes factors that impact student learning outcomes in online learning. Collaborative learning and engagement are two such factors that have been shown to positively impact online learning during the COVID-19 pandemic (ibid). Using social media for collaborative learning and engagement can have a favorable impact on peer and instructor interaction, leading to improved student learning outcomes. Thus, educators need to embrace constructivist approaches to online learning to provide students with a more engaging and effective learning experience.

In another qualitative empirical research found that connectivism may serve as an appropriate conceptual framework for motivating learners to develop knowledge through digital tools, discussions, social networking, and connecting such insights to sustainability concepts (Dziubaniuk et al., 2023). The principles of connectivism could assist educators in cultivating a learning environment where students build upon prior understandings of sustainability through digital interaction and resources accessed online. This networked approach may be well-suited for e-learning by supporting learners as they actively construct and continue updating their knowledge base distributed across a myriad of online nodes and networks.

A recent meta-analysis study conducted a comparison of the effectiveness of different pedagogical approaches in enhancing online learning (Almahasees et al., 2021). The study found that the effectiveness of online learning is influenced by various factors, including student engagement, interaction, and feedback. Interestingly, the study also suggested that blended instruction, which combines online and face-to-face learning, is more effective than either online or face-to-face instruction alone. Furthermore, the study found that online learning has a significantly positive effect when compared to face-to-face instruction. The results of this study suggest that educators should focus on promoting active learning and student engagement in online courses by using pedagogical approaches that encourage interaction and feedback from students.

Several studies have examined the effectiveness of different pedagogical approaches in online learning. One study found that there is a significant impact of pedagogy and teaching style on student perception of online classes, which can affect their engagement and motivation to learn (Vikas & Mathur, 2022). Another study has shown that online teaching is comparable in effectiveness to offline teaching within the cognitive domain, but may not be conducive to the cultivation of higher-order cognitive skills in high-achieving students due to constraints on teacher-student communication and limited duration of individual instructional videos (Xu et al., 2023). However, the online teaching model facilitates the advancement of students' lower-order cognitive skills through enhanced utilization of online resources like NQROC (National Quality Open Courses). Moreover, research has shown that online teaching engenders greater student engagement and manifests more active self-directed learning behavior compared to offline teaching [3]. In addition, the investigation of the impact of online and offline teaching models on the cognitive skills of students found no significant difference in academic performance between the two models across all score segments, but students who received online instruction performed better on multiple-choice questions (MCQs) which primarily assess lower-order cognitive skills. Online learning can also enhance the knowledge and skills of medical students by improving their understanding of fundamental concepts that are essential for clinical medicine. Therefore, it is evident that different pedagogical approaches have varying impacts on the effectiveness of online learning, emphasizing the need for educational institutes to create a cadre of well-trained teachers equipped with suitable pedagogical tools to create an effective online classroom [1]. Additionally, it highlights the significance of prioritizing the reinforcement of teacher-student interactions, fostering active student participation, and facilitating the establishment of online learning forums to augment the depth of learning, particularly among high-achieving students. Moreover, the pedagogical approach significantly affects student perception towards online classes which can affect their engagement and motivation to learn (Vikas & Mathur, 2022).

An effective e-learning environment must balance the different approaches to pedagogy. This balance aims to provide learners with a wide range of options for engaging in the learning process. It is also important to provide educators with the opportunity to tailor the course to the needs of each student. Lastly, it should ensure that the course is engaging and interactive.

DESIGNING AN EFFECTIVE E-LEARNING ENVIRONMENT

The e-learning approach has revolutionized the education sector, giving learners around the world access to quality teaching. Nevertheless, designing effective e-learning environments that meet the diverse needs of learners can be a challenging endeavor. To achieve this, it is essential to understand the different learning paradigms that guide the planning of e-learning environments. To accomplish this, it is essential to answer the following questions:

How Does Behaviorist Theory Inform the Design of Online Learning Environments?

Online learning environments offer a unique opportunity for learners to acquire knowledge and skills in the comfort of their own homes. Behaviorist theory asserts that learning occurs when observable behavior is acquired through environmental conditions (Ezenwa-Ohaeto, 2021). Thus, the design of e-learning environments should focus on creating an appropriate environment that promotes the desired behavior in learners. The behaviorist approach advocates using reinforcement and feedback to encourage desired behaviors in learners. To achieve this, designers of e-learning environments need to break down complex tasks into smaller parts and provide individualized instruction to learners, ensuring that they master each component before moving on to the next. In addition, behaviorist theory suggests the use of clear objectives, frequent assessments, and immediate feedback in the design of e-learning environments to foster desirable behaviors (Angelo, n.d.). According to theory, learning is the result of stimulus-response association. Consequently, the design of effective e-learning environments requires an understanding of behaviorist theory, which is one of the most widespread theories in learning design, particularly for online contexts.

How Does Connectivism Theory Inform the Design of Online Learning Environments?

In contrast to behaviorist theory, connectivism theory informs the design of e-learning environments by prioritizing the formation of networks and connections in learning. Learners must have autonomy over their learning paths and be encouraged to take ownership of their learning (Evanick, 2023). Also, the ability to achieve a heightened degree of autonomy can be achieved through individualizing learning rhythms (Zine El Abidine et al., 2022). Connectivism theory emphasizes the importance of connections and networks in learning. As such, e-learning environments designed using connectivism theory should prioritize the creation of opportunities for learners to form connections and extend their networks. This can be achieved through the use of online social networks and communities of practice, which can promote networked learning. In addition, online curation tools and collaborative knowledge-building activities can help learners navigate and create knowledge in complex information environments. Connectivism theory suggests that e-learning environments should be designed to support knowledge creation and sharing. With the effective use of connectivism theory, e-learning can offer learners flexible, engaging, and personalized learning experiences. Connectivism theory can also promote networked learning and digital literacy. It is important to note that connectivism theory can only partially account for the development of critical thinking skills and deep learning; instructional designers should also consider other theories. Finally, mapping connectivism in online education can provide a simple overview of what needs to be considered, and a theoretical map of visual learning can be the first layer of a comprehensive, holistic map for online education (Bates, 2014). Overall, connectivism theory can inform instructional design in online learning environments by prioritizing networked learning, diverse forms of learning beyond academic knowledge, and the changing landscape of information and technology.

How Does Constructivist Theory Inform the Design of Online Learning Environments?

Constructivism theory provides a framework for designing e-learning environments that prioritize active and reflective learning, collaboration, and the integration of new knowledge with existing knowledge and experience. E-learning environments designed based on constructivist theory must resemble real-life experiences and be authentic and contextualized, to help learners develop complex mental models. The design must also take into account the external and internal factors that influence learning, including the uniqueness of the learner and his or her pre-existing knowledge base (LearnDash, 2021). In addition, constructivist theory emphasizes the importance of social processes in learning, with collaboration and conversation between learners and teachers emphasized in e-learning environments based on this theory. Teaching in e-learning environments based on constructivist theory should be inductive and bottom-up, with learners generating their learning and constructing their knowledge. The role of the teacher in constructivist e-learning environments is that of a coach who encourages the exploration of ideas, rather than a dispenser of information. Overall, constructivist theory promotes active learning processes in e-learning environments, which can be integrated into the design of e-learning experiences to enhance learner engagement and success. The design of online learning environments requires an understanding of behaviorism theory, which is one of the most widespread theories in learning design, particularly for online contexts. Behaviorist theory emphasizes that learning occurs when observable behavior is acquired through environmental conditions. On the other hand, constructivist theory favors active learning processes in online learning environments, where learners generate their learning and construct their knowledge. In this respect, teachers in e-learning environments based on constructivist theory should act as role models and coaches who encourage the exploration of ideas, rather than dispensers of information. In addition, connectivism theory can promote networked learning and digital literacy, enabling learners to benefit from flexible, engaging, and personalized learning experiences.

How Can the Principles of Cognitivist Theory Be Applied to the Design of Effective E-Learning Environments?

To design effective e-learning environments, the principles of cognitivist theory must be applied, which focuses on the cognitive processes involved in learning. One such principle is a cognitive theory, which suggests that the amount of mental effort involved in working memory during a task needs to be classified into relevant, intrinsic, and extraneous effort to promote learning efficiency. The application of e-learning theory in course design can also reduce extraneous cognitive load and manage relevant and intrinsic loads at appropriate levels, thus promoting effective learning. In addition, e-learning environments should emphasize the cognitive, emotional, motivational, and social aspects of learning to promote learners' self-regulation and intrinsic reinforcement (Dumulescu et al., 2021). Offering learners, the opportunity to form their own opinions about basic concepts and providing additional content for further exploration can also promote deeper learning and understanding. Finally, the use of multimodal materials, collaborative discussions, small-group work, and peer/group presentations can increase engagement, autonomy, and self-regulation in e-learning environments while creating a level playing field for disadvantaged learners (Scherman et al., 2023). By applying these principles, instructional designers can create effective e-learning environments that promote cognitive processing and knowledge construction.

In light of these pedagogical approaches, the authors could start by adding a few spices like the systems of a training module, proceeding as described in the pedagogical scenario. This will help create a more interactive learning environment and allow learners to explore their ideas and express their creativity. This can also help to improve the learner's understanding of the material and create a more enjoyable learning process.

The Systems of a Training Module and the Four Stages of the Learning Process

As distance learning courses become increasingly popular, they are gaining popularity because of their convenience and ability to be studied from anywhere in the world. However, e-learning must be structured in such a way that learners will be able to retain knowledge and develop a solid understanding of the material. It is possible to structure distance learning content in several ways, but one of the most effective approaches is to use activities. As a result of this method, learners can progress at their own pace and ensure that they understand all aspects of the activity. We propose a model for a conceptualization activity based on the systems of a training module

The Systems of a Training Module

Following directly on the heels of the relentless advance of technology, which continues to saturate every part of our reality, the way we communicate with our fellow human beings is undergoing a significant change. As e-learning takes over from the traditional classroom, we are entering the realm of distance learning. E-learning, with its unshakeable reliability, offers a solid method of widening access to education while improving the nature of teaching. In addition, it encourages peer cooperation and gives learners a sense of independence and obligation in their educational endeavors (Calvert, 2006). Nevertheless, e-learning must be truly organized in such a way that learners can absorb the information and promote a good understanding of the courses. Among the various methods of structuring distance learning content, the use of training module systems is proving to be one of the most effective. This approach allows learners to progress at their own pace while ensuring a complete understanding of the elements presented in each activity. Although the content of an e-learning module often serves as the foundation for its structure, in general, such a module comprises three key systems:

- **The entry system** plays an essential role in managing learners smoothly at the start of the module while providing them with a brief introduction to the course and its laudable objectives.
- **The learning system** is of paramount importance, as it focuses on the complete development of learning content and activities. When talking about the content of a module, it's important to emphasize its immense scope, as the training itself must be designed around the needs of the learner

as he or she undertakes specific activities, which must be eloquently reflected in the module's content.

- **The output system**, for its part, takes on the delicate task of managing the flow of learners at the end of the module, assessing the knowledge acquired by the learner and guiding him or her towards aspects that have not yet been assimilated.

Online courses offer a more adjusted growth opportunity, allowing learners to examine both sides of a particular topic. When taking an exam in a traditional classroom, learners only have one perspective, and one point of view on a question or topic. Online courses, on the other hand, offer learners the opportunity to examine both sides of a discussion and structure their assumptions.

When defining a training module, the four stages of the learning process play an important role in classifying the entire activity. The first stage of the process is the situation, in which the subject is introduced to the topic. The second stage of the process is conceptualization acquisition, in which the subject learns the material. The third stage is skill objectivation, in which the subject practices applying the material. The fourth stage is the transfer of the subject's performance, which is necessary to determine the effectiveness of the training module. Hence, in the next section, the authors will discuss these stages in more detail and propose a model of the conceptualization stage based on the systems of a training module, for which the authors choose a deductive rather than an inductive approach.

The Four Stages of the Learning Process

In the field of education, a successful educator in a learning approach is someone who skillfully plans deeply organized exercises. He skillfully explores his sample plans, focusing on the essential points for meaningful periods. What's more, he manages evaluations with perseverance, perfectly attuned to the learner's actual satisfaction. By effectively captivating learners with interesting questions and making meaningful contributions, these educators promote a climate conducive to development and learning. Their mastery of their field shines through, as they demonstrate a certified enthusiasm for basic information, earning them recognition as facilitators of insight.

To achieve such domination, instructors must consider real-life educational experiences while coordinating different exercises in their educational curriculum. Although different projects may use different formulations, the following steps are generally seen as necessary for a total, living growth opportunity:

- Situation
- Conceptualization
- Objectivation
- Transfer

In their innovative study, Khaldi et al. (Khaldi et al., 2021) present a pedagogical scenario design that encompasses these four types of activity, seamlessly integrated into a learning situation. The following diagram eloquently illustrates the sequential nature of these scenarios:

Given the guidelines presented, the authors propose a comprehensive model built around a deductive approach to e-learning. This model meticulously considers the theoretical underpinnings of course content and employs evidence-based teaching methods. It places a strong emphasis on developing learners' critical thinking skills. It is imperative that designers consider other forms of learning, including

Figure 1. Example of the life cycle of a pedagogical scenario of a learning situation

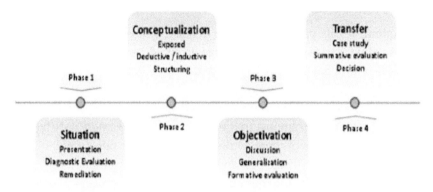

Figure 2. An E-learning model for a deductive approach

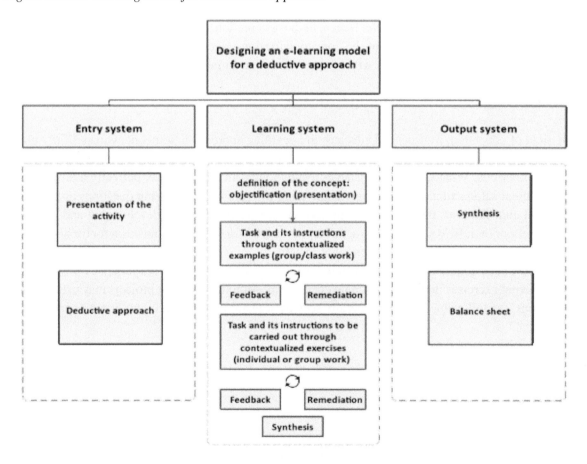

inductive reasoning, and embrace a variety of assessment approaches, such as diagnostic, formative, and summative assessments. To promote engagement and active participation, the model must incorporate an interactive element. In addition, flexibility is essential, as it enables different learning styles to be integrated for an inclusive educational experience.

The Entry System

In the deductive approach conceptualization activity scenario, learners are guided by the teacher from general concepts to specific ones, following the framework described by Balslev and Saada-Robert (2002). This approach utilizes an entry system in which the teacher imparts knowledge to learners through video capsules, providing them with the flexibility to access the content at their convenience. While this approach promotes rote learning and may potentially limit learners' perspectives, it effectively facilitates the acquisition of new concepts.

To further enhance learning outcomes, the teacher adopts a learner-centered approach that empowers learners to take control of their own learning and self-assessment. One effective strategy to empower learners is the creation of a dedicated discussion forum, where they are encouraged to actively engage in dialogue with one another. This forum serves as a platform for learners to freely express their thoughts, exchange ideas, and critically analyze the concepts they have learned. By fostering a collaborative learning environment, the discussion forum not only deepens learners' understanding through peer interaction but also nurtures their critical thinking and communication skills.

The Learning System

In the learning system, videoconferencing plays a crucial role as a synchronous process that promotes teamwork and effective communication among learners. Each learner is allowed to individually define the concept explored in the video vignettes, synthesizing their understanding of the topic. This synthesis serves as an assessment of whether the learners have successfully grasped the concept being taught.

To familiarize learners with new concepts, the teacher assigns contextualized tasks that are introduced through relevant real-life examples. These examples serve to provide learners with a practical understanding of the concepts being taught, encouraging further questioning and discussion among the learners. Additionally, the teacher forms learner groups to facilitate individual attention and create more opportunities for learners to overcome any difficulties they may encounter. This collaborative approach not only enables learners to gain a deeper understanding of the concepts but also boosts their confidence in applying their knowledge.

Collaborative tools such as chat, email, and wikis are readily available to learners, playing an indispensable role in facilitating group work and promoting effective collaboration among learners.

To prevent learners from repeating mistakes, remediation strategies are employed to help them identify and correct errors. Feedback is provided to inform learners that their mistakes have been rectified and to guide them towards improvement.

Moving forward in the learning process, the teacher assigns tasks that require learners to complete contextualized exercises in the output system. These exercises are designed to be practiced in specific contexts, creating a flexible learning environment that allows learners to apply their knowledge in various scenarios, thus deepening their comprehension of the concepts. Similar to the previous learning process, remediation strategies are utilized to address any deficiencies, and feedback is provided to guide learners toward improvement. Finally, a synthesis is presented to summarize the key points and observations made throughout the activity, reinforcing the learners' understanding of the concepts and their ability to synthesize information effectively.

The Output System

The output system of the learning process is dedicated to assessing the effectiveness of the proposed deductive approach conceptualization activity. This assessment aims to ensure that the conceptualization process aligns with the principles of the deductive approach, is free from contradictions, and successfully fulfills its intended purpose.

To develop a comprehensive model for an online learning environment, it is essential to incorporate pedagogical scenarios. Pedagogical scenarios play a crucial role in creating a realistic learning environment that takes into account learners' cognitive and affective needs. By integrating pedagogical scenarios, the learning experience becomes more authentic and relevant to the learners' real-world contexts. These scenarios provide a framework for designing and implementing instructional activities that engage learners, promote active participation, and facilitate meaningful learning experiences.

In the subsequent section, we will delve into the concept of pedagogical scripting. Pedagogical scripting involves the careful design and structuring of learning activities, instructional materials, and interactions within the online learning environment. By employing pedagogical scripting, educators can guide learners through the learning process, provide clear instructions, and scaffold their understanding.

Pedagogical Scripting

As the authors proposed a model for an online environment, pedagogical scenarios must be incorporated. In the absence of it, we would only be scratching the surface of its potential. The use of scripts is crucial to the creation of an interactive online environment that captures the attention of students. To inspire exploration and encourage meaningful interaction with content, its design must be carefully considered. It is highly unlikely that any online initiative would be successful without scripting.

There are two additional scenarios in the pedagogical scenario, namely the learning scenario and the support scenario. In this context, it is necessary to specify the specific activities related to learning and support, the resources required to carry out these activities, and the expected outcomes (Villiot, 2007).

By using these two methods, instructional designers can approach their scenarios methodically and rationally. As a result of these tools, the scenario-writing process can be organized, which many find useful during learning (Khaldi et al., 2021).

Scripting Tools

Scripting tools are used to delineate and build a sequence of teaching activities in an online environment. These tools include activity diagrams and a table of specifications, which help teachers define their pedagogical objectives and organize their didactic activities. Activity diagrams serve as a visual representation, enabling teachers to define their pedagogical objectives and structure their didactic activities. Activity charts, in the form of diagrams, are a useful way for teachers to plan their didactic activities and set tasks. Specification tables can also be used to articulate objectives and tasks, providing comprehensive information.

The constituent elements of instructional design are essential for designing effective and efficient learning activities while aligning with learners' needs and objectives. By giving due consideration to each of these six components, teachers and training designers can design learning activities that are well organized and adapted to learners' needs.

- **Nature of resources and tools presented:** This pertains to the diverse range of resources and tools utilized to facilitate learning, encompassing textbooks, videos, simulations, educational games, online quizzes, and more. It is imperative to carefully select resources and tools that are tailored to the needs and preferences of learners.

- **Nature of anticipated outcomes:** This refers to the competencies, knowledge, and behaviors that learners are expected to acquire or enhance by the conclusion of the training or learning endeavor. Anticipated outcomes must be precisely defined and communicated to learners from the outset of the activity.

- **Task sequence:** This denotes the arrangement and structure of the various tasks or learning activities that learners are required to accomplish. The sequence of tasks should be logical and coherent, commencing with straightforward tasks and progressing towards more intricate ones.

- **Monitoring methods:** This pertains to the diverse array of approaches employed to gauge learners' progress throughout the learning activity. Monitoring methods can encompass assessments, exercises, peer evaluations, teacher feedback, and so forth.

- **Structuring and regulating tools:** This encompasses the tools and techniques employed to assist learners in organizing and regulating their learning, including concept maps, agendas, reminders, checklists, and similar resources.

- **Modalities of interaction:** This refers to the different modes of interaction between learners, instructors, and learning resources, such as classroom discussions, online forums, group activities, individual sessions, and the like. It is crucial to select the interaction modalities that are most conducive to the purpose and requirements of the learning activity.

The following section suggests an activity diagram to depict the steps of a deductive approach. The diagram will assist in explaining how the deductive approach works. It will also indicate where potential problems are likely to arise and suggest solutions. Last but not least, the diagram will serve as a visual representation of how the deductive approach can be used, and then the authors will propose a specification table for all types of activities based on the six components listed above.

Activity Diagram for the Deductive Approach

In a process or procedure, an activity diagram represents the flow of activities. Various aspects of task processing are represented in this model, including decision-making, loops, synchronization, and operations.

Our activity diagram initiates with a commencement node: this symbolizes the outset of the activity and is represented by a black circle. This is where the educator introduces the activity and presents the knowledge through video capsules. Upon conclusion of the knowledge memorization by learners, the formation of a discussion forum is an essential step for learners to exchange views with one another. Based on this creation, the instructor can compile some talking points and respond to queries posed by learners. A videoconference then follows to enhance communication between the two parties and reinforce comprehension of the concept. To truly cement their understanding, students must subsequently undertake a synthesis.

To further enrich this learning experience, the educator requests the establishment of learner groups to collaborate on contextualized exercises. The work is conducted utilizing synchronous tools such as wiki pages, chat functions, and email correspondence. Should any learner encounter difficulties, remedial assistance is available. Once completed, a final assessment and summary of the work is provided. By

Figure 3. Activity diagram for the deductive approach

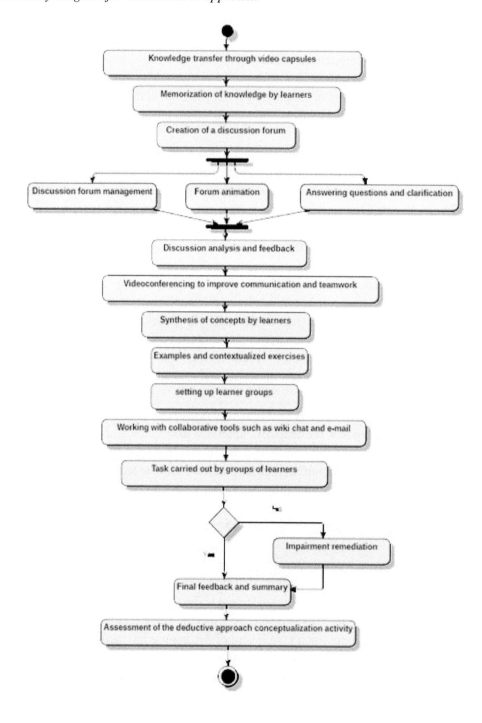

incorporating various interactive elements and emphasizing cooperation as well as knowledge application, this activity diagram aims to optimize knowledge retention and academic development through an engaging experiential learning process.

The Specification Table

When instructional scenarios become too intricate to be adequately conveyed through simple activity diagrams, educators often turn to an additional scripting tool that injects a creative element: the

Table 1. Table of specifications for different activity

Activity	Nature of the resources and tools presented	Nature of anticipated outcomes:	Task sequence	Monitoring methods	Structuring and regulation tools	Modalities of interaction
1	Quiz	Identification of each learner's learning style	1. Access to the Kolb test. 2. Completion of the Kolb test online or on paper. 3. Analysis of Kolb test results to identify each learner's learning style.	Personalized feedback	Individual training plan, Dashboard	Discussion forum
2	Diagnostic evaluation	Assessment of prior knowledge and identification of each learner's strengths and weaknesses	1. Access to the pre-test questionnaire and self-assessment grid. 2. Pre-test completion 3. Analysis of results to identify each learner's prior knowledge and strengths/weaknesses.	Personalized feedback	Individual training plan, Dashboard	Discussion forum
3	Video clips, digital resources, PDF files	Identifying learning objectives	1. Access to resources and tools adapted to their learning style.	Personalized feedback	Individual training plan, Dashboard	Discussion forum
4	Interactive whiteboard	Encourage group discussions and maintain focus on objectives	1. Announcement of discussion topic and objectives. 2. Facilitate group discussion. 3. Summary of key points discussed.	Self-evaluation of participation	Facilitator's guide, summary table of key points	Discussion forum
5	Videoconferencing, slideshows, support documents	Consolidating concepts and clarifying grey areas	1. Preparation of the content to be presented. 2. Announcement of topic and objectives. 3. Presentation of key concepts using slide shows and handouts. 4. Group discussions to clarify obscure points. 5. Synthesis of key points.	Knowledge assessment after the live session	Facilitator's guide, a summary of key points	Live video conferencing, chat
6	Concrete examples linked to the context of the task	In-depth understanding of key task concepts, ability to apply them in complex and unforeseen situations, acquisition of advanced practical skills	1. Presentation of contextualized examples by the teacher 2. Group work on practical cases or simulations 3. Individual tasks based on complex scenarios 4. Group feedback on experience	Continuous assessment of each learner's participation and understanding, real-time learning assessment through quizzes, skills tests, and simulations.	LMS for accessing resources, interacting with other learners and the teacher, tracking learning progress, and online individual and group feedback	Live video conferencing, chat

continued on the following page

Table 1. Continued

Activity	Nature of the resources and tools presented	Nature of anticipated outcomes:	Task sequence	Monitoring methods	Structuring and regulation tools	Modalities of interaction
7	Contextualized practical exercises	Acquisition of practical skills to accomplish the task	1. Presentation of practical exercises 2. Individual exercise practice 3. Submission of exercise results	Automatic monitoring of exercise results	Individual learner follow-up dashboard	Personalized feedback
8	Research articles; Educational videos; Podcasts	Learners should be able to produce an assignment or task that demonstrates their understanding and ability to apply the concepts and skills taught in the classroom.	Learners need to be guided step-by-step through the task. Tasks can be divided into several steps, and learners need to be able to understand each step before moving on to the next.	The teacher should provide a means for learners to monitor their progress and receive feedback on their work. Monitoring methods can include written or audio feedback, rubrics, and evaluation grids.	Calendars, to-do lists, and templates. Control tools can include deadline reminders, alarms, and time management applications.	Online discussions, live chat sessions, forums, and workgroups.
9	Formative or summative evaluation	Precise measurement of comprehension and mastery of subjects, identification of learners' strengths and weaknesses	1. Preparation of assessments and instructions for learners 2. Administration of assessment tests 3. Correction of assessment tests 4. Provision of results and feedback to learners	Summative or formative assessment of comprehension and mastery of topics, feedback on learner performance	LMS for accessing resources and submitting tests, automatic and manual correction tools for assessment tests, assessment rubrics for feedback	Asynchronous learning for test preparation and submission, synchronous learning for clarification of instructions and management of test problems, and asynchronous feedback for feedback on test results.
10	Pedagogical resources	Identification of potential remedies to solve problems, evaluation of the relevance of solutions, ability to exchange and collaborate to produce innovative ideas	1. Analysis of the case study to identify problems and challenges 2. Search for potential remedies using documentary resources and examples of good practice 3. Selection of the most relevant potential solutions 4. Exchange and share ideas to improve solutions 5. Assessment of the feasibility and effectiveness of the selected solutions.	Feedback on the relevance of proposed solutions	E-learning platform for accessing resources and collaboration, online collaboration tools for sharing ideas and exchanging feedback, presentation tools for communicating results	Online discussions, live chat sessions, forums.

specification table. This table serves as a comprehensive resource where each task that learners need to perform is meticulously described, providing a more detailed and elaborate solution to guide their actions (Anoir et al., 2021).

The specification table goes beyond the limitations of activity diagrams by offering a structured framework to outline the specific steps, instructions, and requirements for each task. It provides a clear and concise breakdown of the actions and decisions learners need to take to complete the assigned activities. This level of granularity allows educators to provide learners with a more comprehensive understanding of the task at hand, ensuring that they have a solid grasp of what is expected from them.

Using the specification table, educators can improve the clarity and specificity of the learning tasks, leaving no room for ambiguity or uncertainty. This detailed description guides learners through complex scenarios and provides them with the information they need to achieve their goals. Furthermore, the table serves as a reference point for both learners and educators, allowing them to track progress, monitor performance, and evaluate achievement of learning outcomes.

An elaborate and complete solution is provided in the specification table for each task the learner must perform. It is easier to understand how the tasks should be executed using the specification table, and it also allows for a finer level of control over the learning experience.

Future Implication

In considering the future implications of designing an online environment for the deductive approach, it is crucial to address the implementation process and the potential outcomes that lie ahead. Once the model has been designed, the next step would involve a systematic implementation plan to bring the online environment to life. This includes considerations such as selecting the appropriate learning management system, integrating the necessary technological infrastructure, and ensuring the availability of resources and support for both educators and learners. The implementation process would also involve training sessions and workshops to familiarize educators with the new online environment and equip them with the necessary skills to effectively utilize the systems and tools, such as the activity diagram and the specification table. Furthermore, procedures for continuing evaluation and feedback should be built to evaluate the model's efficacy and make appropriate adjustments and enhancements depending on learner results and feedback. Furthermore, the model's scalability and sustainability must be considered, as they may have ramifications for future course creation and the extension of the online learning environment. The writers can ensure a smooth transition from design to implementation by highlighting these future consequences, encouraging a dynamic and productive online learning experience for both educators and learners.

CONCLUSION

In conclusion, e-learning has become a popular method of education in today's digital age, but simply transferring traditional teaching methods to an online platform may not be enough to ensure effective learning outcomes. Pedagogical approaches play a crucial role in e-learning design, and effective online pedagogy emphasizes student-centered learning, giving learners the freedom to explore content at their own pace and choose which courses to take and when to take them. In this brief, the authors have taken a comprehensive look at the world of e-learning, providing insights into its history and evolution. They have explored various pedagogical approaches that have shaped the landscape of online learning and discussed the transformative impact of technological advancements on the learning process. By carefully examining the advantages and disadvantages of e-learning, they have weighed the benefits against the potential drawbacks. Moreover, the authors have concluded this section by examining the influence of pedagogical approaches on online learning.

Moving forward, the authors have shifted their focus toward addressing questions related to pedagogical approaches. Leveraging the potential of training module systems and scripting tools, they have proposed a design for an e-learning model that adopts a deductive approach, aiming to achieve both effectiveness and efficiency.

REFERENCES

Alismaiel, O. A., Cifuentes-Faura, J., & Al-Rahmi, W. M. (2022). Online learning, mobile learning, and social media technologies: An empirical study on constructivism theory during the COVID-19 pandemic. *Sustainability (Basel)*, *14*(18), 11134. doi:10.3390u141811134

Allen, I. E., & Seaman, J. (2017). *Digital Compass Learning: Distance Education Enrollment Report 2017*. Babson survey research group.

Ally, M. (2004). Foundations of educational theory for online learning. *Theory and practice of online learning, 2*, 15-44.

Almahasees, Z., Mohsen, K., & Amin, M. O. (2021, May). Faculty's and students' perceptions of online learning during COVID-19. []. Frontiers Media SA.]. *Frontiers in Education*, *6*, 638470. doi:10.3389/feduc.2021.638470

Almufarreh, A., & Arshad, M. (2023). Promising Emerging Technologies for Teaching and Learning: Recent Developments and Future Challenges. *Sustainability (Basel)*, *15*(8), 6917. doi:10.3390u15086917

Alonso, F., López, G., Manrique, D., & Viñes, J. M. (2005). An instructional model for web-based e-learning education with a blended learning process approach. *British Journal of Educational Technology*, *36*(2), 217–235. doi:10.1111/j.1467-8535.2005.00454.x

Anderson, T. (2003). Modes of interaction in distance education: Recent developments and research questions. Handbook of distance education, 129-144.

Angelo State University. (n.d.). 1.3 Theories of Learning and the Online Environment. Angelo State University. https://www.angelo.edu/faculty-and-staff/instructional-design/online-teaching/section_13.php

Anna. (2020, July 31). *Top 5 des avantages et inconvénients de l'apprentissage en ligne*. Easy LMS. https://www.easy-lms.com/fr/base-connaissances/apprentissage-en-ligne/avantages-inconvenients-apprentissage-en-ligne/item12529

Atkinson, S. (2011). Embodied and embedded theory in practice: The student-owned learning-engagement (SOLE) model. *International Review of Research in Open and Distance Learning*, *12*(2), 1–18. doi:10.19173/irrodl.v12i2.929

B Online Learning. (2022, January 20). *Cognitive Theory of eLearning.* B Online Learning. https://bonlinelearning.com/cognitive-theory-of-elearning/. Récupéré le 10 Mai 2022

Bada, S. O., & Olusegun, S. (2015). Constructivism learning theory: A paradigm for teaching and learning. *Journal of Research & Method in Education, 5*(6), 66–70.

Balslev, K., & Saada-Robert, M. (2002). Expliquer l'apprentissage situé de la littéracie: une démarche inductive/déductive. *Raisons éducatives*, (5), 89-110.

Banna, J., Lin, M. F. G., Stewart, M., & Fialkowski, M. K. (2015). Interaction matters: Strategies to promote engaged learning in an online introductory nutrition course. *Journal of online learning and teaching/MERLOT, 11*(2), 249.

Bates, T. (2014, July 29). *Learning theories and online learning.* Tony Bates. https://www.tonybates.ca/2014/07/29/learning-theories-and-online-learning/

Bowen, J. A., & Watson, C. E. (2017). *Teaching naked techniques: A practical guide to designing better classes.* John Wiley & Sons.

Brindley, J. E., Blaschke, L. M., & Walti, C. (2009). Creating effective collaborative learning groups in an online environment. *International Review of Research in Open and Distance Learning, 10*(3). doi:10.19173/irrodl.v10i3.675

Caduceus International Publishing. (2023, April 20). *Pedagogical approaches to teaching in higher education.* Caduceus International Publishing. https://www.cipcourses.com/blog/pedagogical-approaches-to-teaching-in-higher-education/

Calvert, J. (2006). Achieving Development Goals-Foundations: Open and Distance Learning, Lessons and Issues. *Retrieved*, (June), 6.

Chen, F. H. (2021). Sustainable education through e-learning: The case study of ilearn2. 0. *Sustainability (Basel), 13*(18), 10186. doi:10.3390u131810186

Clark, R. C., & Mayer, R. E. (2016). *E-learning and the science of instruction: Proven guidelines for consumers and designers of multimedia learning.* john Wiley & sons.

Corbett, F., & Spinello, E. (2020). Connectivism and leadership: Harnessing a learning theory for the digital age to redefine leadership in the twenty-first century. *Heliyon, 6*(1), e03250. doi:10.1016/j.heliyon.2020.e03250 PMID:31993523

Daniel, J. (2016). *Making sense of flexibility as a defining element of online learning.* Athabasca University.

Davidson-Shiver, G., & Rasmussen, K. (2006). *Behaviorism Applied to Distance Education.* EDUC633 - Module 2. http://www.amandaszapkiw.com/artifacts/EDUC633_eXe_Module_2/behaviorism_applied_to_distance_education.html. Récupéré le 24 Juillet 2023.

De Ketele, J., & Hugonnier, B. (2020). Chapitre 1. Qu'est-ce que l'internationalisation? Un réseau conceptuel à clarifier. In L. Cosnefroy (Ed.), *L'internationalisation de l'enseignement supérieur: Le meilleur des mondes?* (pp. 17–32). De Boeck Supérieur., doi:10.3917/dbu.cosne.2020.01.0017

Downes, S. (2005). E-learning 2.0. *eLearn Magazine, 2005*(10).

Dumulescu, D., Pop-Păcurar, I., & Necula, C. V. (2021). Learning Design for Future Higher Education – Insights From the Time of COVID-19. *Frontiers in Psychology*, *12*, 647948. doi:10.3389/fpsyg.2021.647948 PMID:34539481

Dziubaniuk, O., Ivanova-Gongne, M., & Nyholm, M. (2023). Learning and teaching sustainable business in the digital era: A connectivism theory approach. *International Journal of Educational Technology in Higher Education*, *20*(1), 1–23. doi:10.118641239-023-00390-w PMID:37096023

EduTech Wiki. (n.d.). *Piaget et le constructivisme*. EduTech Wiki. https://edutechwiki.unige.ch/fr/Piaget_et_le_constructivisme

EHL. (2021). Les avantages de l'apprentissage en ligne pour votre carrière hôtelière. *Hospitality Insights*. https://hospitalityinsights.ehl.edu/fr/avantages-apprentissage-en-ligne

eLearning Industry. (2018, February 18*). The Learning Theory Of Cognitive Development In eLearning*. eLearning Industry. https://elearningindustry.com/learning-theory-of-cognitive-development-elearning. Récupéré le 14 Juillet 2023.

eLearning Industry. (2023, June 20). *From Behaviorism To Connectivism: A Comprehensive Guide To Instructional Design Theories For Online Learning*. eLearning Industry. https://elearningindustry.com/from-behaviorism-to-connectivism-comprehensive-guide-instructional-design-theories-online-learning

Ertmer, P. A., & Newby, T. J. (2013). Behaviorism, cognitivism, constructivism: Comparing critical features from an instructional design perspective. *Performance Improvement Quarterly*, *26*(2), 43–71. doi:10.1002/piq.21143

Evanick, J. (2023, June 20). *From Behaviorism To Connectivism: A Comprehensive Guide To Instructional Design Theories For Online Learning*. eLearning Industry. https://elearningindustry.com/from-behaviorism-to-connectivism-comprehensive-guide-instructional-design-theories-online-learning

Ezenwa-Ohaeto, N., & Ugochukwu, E. N. (2021). Language Learning Theories: Behaviourism, Mentalism and Affectivism. *Awka Journal of English Language and Literary Studies, 8*(1).

Farhan, W., Razmak, J., Demers, S., & Laflamme, S. (2019). E-learning systems versus instructional communication tools: Developing and testing a new e-learning user interface from the perspectives of teachers and students. *Technology in Society*, *59*, 101192. doi:10.1016/j.techsoc.2019.101192

Fortun, V. (2016). *Les enjeux du e-learning «communautique» en formation continue d'enseignants* (Doctoral dissertation, Paris Est).

Garrison, D. R. (2011). *E-learning in the 21st century: A framework for research and practice*. Routledge.

Garrison, D. R., & Kanuka, H. (2004). Blended learning: Uncovering its transformative potential in higher education. *The Internet and Higher Education*, *7*(2), 95–105. doi:10.1016/j.iheduc.2004.02.001

GradePower Learning. (n.d.). *The Cognitive Learning Approach*. GradePower Learning. https://gradepowerlearning.com/cognitive-learning-theory/.

Greitzer, F. L. (2002, September). A cognitive approach to student-centered e-learning. In *proceedings of the human factors and ergonomics society annual meeting* (*Vol. 46*, No. 25, pp. 2064-2068). Sage CA: Los Angeles, CA: SAGE Publications. 10.1177/154193120204602515

Gupta, S. (2017, November 11). *9 Benefits of eLearning for Students*. eLearning Industry. https://el-earningindustry.com/9-benefits-of-elearning-for-students ↗

Hodges, C., Moore, S., Lockee, B., Trust, T., & Bond, A. (2020). The difference between emergency remote teaching and online learning. *EDUCAUSE Review*, 27.

Huezo, E. (2017, July 7). Connectivism: The Future of Learning? *FIU Online Insider*. https://insider.fiu.edu/connectivism-future-learning/.

Inês, P. (n.d.). *Instructional design for e-learning: Everything you need to know*. Easy Generator. https://www.easygenerator.com/en/guides/instructional-design-for-elearning/

Jeffery, K. A., & Bauer, C. F. (2020). Students' responses to emergency remote online teaching reveal critical factors for all teaching. *Journal of Chemical Education*, *97*(9), 2472–2485. doi:10.1021/acs.jchemed.0c00736

Julia, K., & Marco, K. (2021). Évolutivité pédagogique dans les MOOC: Analysing instructional designs to find best practices. *Computers & Education*, *161*, 104054. doi:10.1016/j.compedu.2020.104054

Lamya, A., Mohamed, E., & Mohamed, K. (2021). Adaptive E-learning and scenarization tools: The case of personalization. *International Journal of Computer Trends and Technology*, *69*(6), 28–35. doi:10.14445/22312803/IJCTT-V69I6P105

LearnDash Collaborator. (2021). *4 Learning Theories Every Online Educator Should Know*. LearnDash. https://www.learndash.com/4-learning-theories-every-online-educator-should-know/

360Learning. (n. d.). *What Is Connectivism Learning Theory and How Can You Apply It in Learning and Development?* 360Learning. https://360learning.com/guide/learning-theories/connectivism-learning-theory/

Lee, K. (2017). Rethinking the accessibility of online higher education: A historical review. *The Internet and Higher Education*, *33*, 15–23. doi:10.1016/j.iheduc.2017.01.001

Li, F., Jin, T., Edirisingha, P., & Zhang, X. (2021). School-aged students' sustainable online learning engagement during covid-19: Community of inquiry in a chinese secondary education context. *Sustainability (Basel)*, *13*(18), 10147. doi:10.3390u131810147

Lone, S. A., Puju, J. A., & Mir, M. T. (2023). *Invigoration of e-learning in Education: Challenges and Opportunities*.

Maha, K., Omar, E., Mohamed, E., & Mohamed, K. (2021). Design of educational scenarios of activities in a learning situation for online teaching. *GSC Advanced Engineering and Technology, 1*(1), 049-064.

Maha, K., Omar, E., Mohamed, E., & Mohamed, K. (2021). Design of educational scenarios of activities in a learning situation for online teaching. *GSC Advanced Engineering and Technology, 1*(1), 049-064.

Mapuva, J. (2009). Confronting challenges to e-learning in higher education institutions. *International Journal of Education and Development Using ICT*, *5*(3), 101–114.

Marina. (n.d.). *4 Ways To Apply Behaviorism Principles to Your ELearning Materials.* Your eLearning World. https://yourelearningworld.com/how-to-apply-behaviorism-principles-to-elearning/.

Martín-Gutiérrez, J., Fabiani, P., Benesova, W., Meneses, M. D., & Mora, C. E. (2015). Augmented reality to promote collaborative and autonomous learning in higher education. *Computers in Human Behavior*, *51*, 752–761. doi:10.1016/j.chb.2014.11.093

McBrien, J. L., Cheng, R., & Jones, P. (2009). Virtual spaces: Employing a synchronous online classroom to facilitate student engagement in online learning. *International review of research in open and distributed learning, 10*(3).

McHaney, R. (2023). *The new digital shoreline: How Web 2.0 and millennials are revolutionizing higher education.* Taylor & Francis. doi:10.4324/9781003447979

Mohammed, Z. E. A., Amel, N., & Mohamed, K. (2022). Reflection on E-Learning and Adaptability in the Teaching and Learning of French as Foreign Language. *RA Journal Of Applied Research*, *8*(5), 408–411. doi:10.47191/rajar/v8i5.17

Moore, J., Dickson-Deane, C., & Galyen, K. (2011). E-learning, online learning and distance learning environments: Are they the same? *The Internet and Higher Education*, *14*(2), 129135. doi:10.1016/j.iheduc.2010.10.001

Moore, M. G., & Kearsley, G. (2012). *Distance education: A systems view of online learning.* Cengage Learning.

Morales, A., & Gray, K. (n.d.). Cognitive Learning Theory in the Classroom [Théorie de l'apprentissage cognitif en classe]. Study.com. https://study.com/learn/lesson/cognitivism-education-learning-theory.html.

Núñez, M., Quirós, R., Núñez, I., Carda, J. B., Camahort, E., & Mauri, J. L. (2008, July). Collaborative augmented reality for inorganic chemistry education. In *WSEAS international conference. Proceedings. Mathematics and computers in science and engineering* (Vol. 5, pp. 271–277). WSEAS.

Olson, J. D. (2003). *Beyond the Podium: Delivering Training and Performance to a Digital World.*

Ouadoud, M., Nejjari, A., Chkouri, M. Y., & El-Kadiri, K. E. (2017, October). Learning management system and the underlying learning theories. In *Proceedings of the mediterranean symposium on smart city applications* (pp. 732-744). Cham: Springer International Publishing.

Ouariach, S., Khaldi, M., Mohamed, E., & Khaldi, M. (2023). From the Choice of a Learning Management System to the Installation of a Platform in a Server. In M. Khaldi (Ed.), *Handbook of Research on Scripting, Media Coverage, and Implementation of E-Learning Training in LMS Platforms* (pp. 330–375). IGI Global. doi:10.4018/978-1-6684-7634-5.ch015

Ouariach, S., Khaldi, M., Mohamed, E., & Khaldi, M. (2023). The Flipped Classroom: From Passive Information Absorption to Active Learning. In S. Karpava (Ed.), *Handbook of Research on Language Teacher Identity* (pp. 269–293). IGI Global. doi:10.4018/978-1-6684-7275-0.ch015

Panigrahi, R., Ranjan, P., & Sharma, D. (2018). Online learning: Adoption, continuance, and learning outcome—A review of literature. *International Journal of Information Management*, *43*, 1–14. doi:10.1016/j.ijinfomgt.2018.05.005

Papanastasiou, G., Drigas, A., Skianis, C., Lytras, M., & Papanastasiou, E. (2019). Virtual and augmented reality effects on K-12, higher and tertiary education students' twenty-first century skills. *Virtual Reality (Waltham Cross)*, *23*(4), 425–436. doi:10.100710055-018-0363-2

Pappas, C. (2023, May 1). *Everything You Need To Know About The Connectivism Learning Theory*. eLearning Industry. https://elearningindustry.com/everything-you-need-to-know-about-the-connectivism-learning-theory.

Paudel, P. (2021). Online education: Benefits, challenges and strategies during and after COVID-19 in higher education. [IJonSE]. *International Journal on Studies in Education*, *3*(2), 70–85. doi:10.46328/ijonse.32

Pittaway, S. M. (2012). Student and staff engagement: Developing an engagement framework in a faculty of education. *The Australian Journal of Teacher Education*, *37*(4), 37–45. doi:10.14221/ajte.2012v37n4.8

Poellhuber, B., Laferrière, T., & Breuleux, A. (2017). *Des outils numériques pour soutenir une approche pédagogique inclusive*. Profweb. https://www.profweb.ca/publications/dossiers/des-outils-numeriques-pour-soutenir-une-approche-pedagogique-inclusive

Rabat, H. E. C. (n.d.). *Le E-Learning et son importance pour le développement de compétences avancées*. HEC. https://hec.ac.ma/blog/le-e-learning-et-son-importance-pour-le-developpement-de-competences-avancees/

Ryan, S., Kaufman, J., Greenhouse, J., She, R., & Shi, J. (2016). The effectiveness of blended online learning courses at the Community College level. *Community College Journal of Research and Practice*, *40*(4), 285–298. doi:10.1080/10668926.2015.1044584

Saadé, R. G., Morin, D., & Thomas, J. D. (2012). Critical thinking in E-learning environments. *Computers in Human Behavior*, *28*(5), 1608–1617. doi:10.1016/j.chb.2012.03.025

Sanabria, J. C., & Arámburo-Lizárraga, J. (2016). Enhancing 21st century skills with AR: Using the gradual immersion method to develop collaborative creativity. *Eurasia Journal of Mathematics, Science and Technology Education*, *13*(2), 487–501. doi:10.12973/eurasia.2017.00627a

Sattar, E. (2017, October 20). *Cognitive Learning and Its Relationship With Online Education*. ATD. https://www.td.org/insights/cognitive-learning-and-its-relationship-with-online-education

Sattar, E. (2017, October 20). *Cognitive Learning and Its Relationship With Online Education*. ATD. https://www.td.org/insights/cognitive-learning-and-its-relationship-with-online-education..

Scherman, R., Islam, M. S., Dikaya, L. A., Dumulescu, D., Pop-Păcurar, I., & Necula, C. V. (2023). Learning Design for Future Higher Education–Insights From the Time of COVID-19. *Covid-19 and beyond: From (forced) remote teaching and learning to 'the new normal' in higher education*, 16648714.

Schleicher, A. (2018). Educating learners for their future, not our past. *ECNU Review of Education*, *1*(1), 58–75. doi:10.30926/ecnuroe2018010104

Shrivastava, A. (2018). Using connectivism theory and technology for knowledge creation in cross-cultural communication. *Research in Learning Technology*, 26(0), 26. doi:10.25304/rlt.v26.2061

Siemens, G. (2005). Connectivism: A learning theory for the digital age. *International Journal of Instructional Technology and Distance Learning*, 2(1), 3–10.

Siemens, G. (2005). Connectivism: A learning theory for the digital age. *International Journal of Instructional Technology and Distance Learning*, 2(1), 3–10.

Simamora, R. M. (2020). Les défis de l'apprentissage en ligne pendant la pandémie de COVID-19: An Essay Analysis of Performing Arts Education Students (Analyse d'un essai d'apprenants en arts du spectacle). *Studies in Learning and Teaching*, 1(2), 86–103. doi:10.46627ilet.v1i2.38

Singh, J., Steele, K., & Singh, L. (2021). Combining the best of online and face-to-face learning: Hybrid and blended learning approach for COVID-19, post vaccine, & post-pandemic world. *Journal of Educational Technology Systems*, 50(2), 140–171. doi:10.1177/00472395211047865

Srithar, U., & Selvaraj, D. (2015). Learning at your own pace: M-learning solution for school students. *International Journal of Information and Electronics Engineering*, 5(3), 216. doi:10.7763/IJIEE.2015.V5.533

Taylor, J. C. (2001). *Fifth generation distance education.* Paper presented at the 20th ICDE World Conference, Düsseldorf, Germany. USQ. http://www.usq.edu.au/users/ taylorj/conferences.htm

Training Magazine. (2019). 2019 Training Industry Report. *Training Magazine.* https://trainingmag.com/2019-training-industry-report/ ↗

Triantafyllou, S. A. (2019). *The Effects of Constructivism Theory in the Environment of E-learning.* GRIN Verlag.

Ulum, H. (2022). The effects of online education on academic success: A meta-analysis study. *Education and Information Technologies*, 27(1), 429–450. doi:10.100710639-021-10740-8 PMID:34512101

Valamis. (n.d.). *Cognitive Learning Theory: Benefits, Strategies and Examples.* Valamis HUB. https://www.valamis.com/hub/cognitive-learning ↗

Vikas, S., & Mathur, A. (2022). An empirical study of student perception towards pedagogy, teaching style and effectiveness of online classes. *Education and Information Technologies*, 27(1), 1–22. doi:10.100710639-021-10793-9 PMID:34720659

Villiot-Leclercq, E. (2007). Genèse, réception, orientation et explicitation des scénarios pédagogiques: vers un modèle de conception des scénarios par contraintes. *Distances et savoirs, 54*(4), 507-526.

Wang, P., Ma, T., Liu, L. B., Shang, C., An, P., & Xue, Y. X. (2021). A comparison of the effectiveness of online instructional strategies optimized with smart interactive tools versus traditional teaching for postgraduate students. *Frontiers in Psychology, 12*, 747719. doi:10.3389/fpsyg.2021.747719 PMID:35002844

WGU. (n.d.). *Connectivism Learning Theory.* WGU. https://www.wgu.edu/blog/connectivism-learning-theory2105.html ↗

Xu, Y., Wang, L., Li, P., Xu, H., Liu, Z., Ji, M., & Luo, Z. (2023). Exploring the impact of online and offline teaching methods on the cognitive abilities of medical students: A comparative study. *BMC Medical Education*, *23*(1), 557. doi:10.118612909-023-04549-x PMID:37553632

Yildiz, E. P. (2021). Augmented reality research and applications in education. In *Augmented Reality and Its Application*. IntechOpen.

Yu, Z. (2021). The effects of gender, educational level, and personality on online learning outcomes during the COVID-19 pandemic. *International Journal of Educational Technology in Higher Education*, *18*(1), 14. doi:10.118641239-021-00252-3 PMID:34778520

Zahra, O. F., Amel, N., & Mohamed, K. (2023). Communication Tools and E-Learning: A Revolution in the Research Methodology of Communication for a Pedagogical Scenario. *RA Journal of Applied Research*, *9*(4), 170–177. doi:10.47191/rajar/v9i4.03

Chapter 4
Designing a Holistic Syllabus:
A Blueprint for Student Motivation, Learning Efficacy, and Mental Health Engagement

Peri Yuksel

 https://orcid.org/0000-0002-9473-4958
New Jersey City University, USA

Joan Bailey
New Jersey City University, USA

ABSTRACT

An academic syllabus serves as a pivotal gateway for students embarking on their college journey, offering not only a roadmap for the course but also their initial introduction to the faculty member or teaching staff. The course syllabus can emerge as a cornerstone, molding students' impressions of instructor expertise, expectations, and workload. The current chapter underscores the syllabus's potential impact, transcending its conventional role as a contractual tool and/or cognitive guide. It aims to illustrate the syllabus as a mental map, rich with resources to help navigate course progression and cultivate a sense of belonging to a broader world that exists outside the confines of a (virtual) classroom, prioritizing students' mental health. Drawing on established best practices, the chapter offers insights for both novice and experienced educators, showcasing the transformational potential of syllabus design in nurturing lifelong learning for professional and personal growth.

INTRODUCTION: SHAPING FIRST IMPRESSIONS FOR LASTING IMPACT

When students begin their college journey, they frequently make quick judgments and course decisions based on limited initial information. This information often includes logistical considerations, course requirements, or feedback from others, such as online instructor ratings. These initial impressions can have a lasting impact on relationships and interactions, and consequently student retention and learn-

DOI: 10.4018/979-8-3693-3128-6.ch004

Copyright © 2024, IGI Global. Copying or distributing in print or electronic forms without written permission of IGI Global is prohibited.

ing outcomes. Hence, the importance of creating a favorable first impression, particularly through the syllabus design, cannot be underestimated (Matejka & Kurk, 1994). In this context, the course syllabus emerges as a pivotal reference point that shapes students' perception of the instructor's expertise, expectations, and workload.

Varying in format, purpose, language, or length, which can range from 1 to 20 pages (Deans, 2019), the syllabus serves not only as a contractual agreement and communication tool but also as a course outline and cognitive guide. Its impact on student engagement, rapport, or motivation is substantial (e.g., Kim & Echacai, 2020; Ludy et al., 2016; Matejka & Kurk, 1994). At least three distinct syllabus types (traditional, contractual, and learner-centered) have been identified (e.g., Harrington & Thomas, 2023). However, this chapter argues that a syllabus holds the potential to transcend its role as a mere contractual communication source and cognitive roadmap. It can evolve into a mental map, offering rich resources to guide students toward course completion while cultivating a collaborative partnership and a sense of community within the learning environment.

AIM: PROPOSING A HOLISTIC SYLLABUS

It is a time-honored tradition: In the weeks before each term begins, instructors across the globe scramble to put syllabi together. This may involve creating a syllabus for a new course, modifying an existing syllabus, or recycling a syllabus that has been used for years. Assembling a syllabus and posting it on the Institution's Learning Management System (LMS) may have become so routine, that most instructors no longer give detailed thought to the function a syllabus might play in student learning. Minimal consideration about the syllabus' role can also be reinforced by the fact that many institutions require that faculty or educators use a university-approved syllabus template. These templates often have spaces provided for faculty to insert the course description, the required text, due dates for assignments and exams, etc. Such a format does not inspire thoughts about how a course syllabus can be a creative, living document that inspires personal growth, life-long learning, professional development, and community connection.

This paper aims to modify the traditional approach to constructing syllabi by proposing a new syllabus paradigm—the holistic syllabus. The holistic approach in course design transcends the traditional confines of course content, aiming to immerse students in a richer, interconnected world. It serves as an empathetic, student-centered guide, nurturing a deep sense of belonging to the global community. Unlike conventional syllabi, it not only embodies best practices in syllabus construction but also integrates resources that tether students to the wider world while prioritizing their mental health and interpersonal well-being. In essence, a holistic syllabus can be succinctly defined as an all-encompassing framework that cultivates self-directed learning, functioning as both a learner-centric compass and a gateway to a broader world beyond the classroom's boundaries.

The current chapter proceeds with a chronological review of traditional, contractual, and learner-centered syllabi before delving into the nuts and bolts of creating a holistic syllabus. It also provides syllabi samples and student testimonies about the advantages of a holistic syllabus, as well as addressing the benefits and potential pitfalls of this new approach. Finally, the chapter discusses how to overcome the challenges of designing a holistic syllabus.

BRIEF LITERATURE REVIEW ON THE EVOLUTION OF SYLLABI

The Traditional Syllabus is a concise document focused on content, primarily concerning essential course information from the instructor's perspective and objectives. It typically includes the instructor's contact details and a timetable indicating the schedule for different topics, events, and deadlines throughout the term. This document can serve as a roadmap for students, also providing links to relevant resources like required and recommended reading lists or online materials. Emphasizing its scholarly nature, the traditional syllabus avoids visual embellishments or personal anecdotes, concentrating instead on offering a common source of essential information and resources. Course descriptions are pulled from online course catalogs and filled with disciplinary jargon. Generally, there is limited effort to generate student interest in the course content or to gauge student impressions of the syllabus or class overall (Matejka & Kurke, 1994).

The Contractual Syllabus surpasses the traditional syllabus in terms of depth and detail. It not only contains extensive information about course content and procedures but also underscores the contractual relationship between instructors and students, emphasizing course requirements and policies (Harrington & Thomas, 2023). This syllabus explicitly states the expected behaviors and work products that students must demonstrate to achieve specific grades. Its primary focus is on ensuring clear and comprehensive explanations and documentation of the contractual obligations for both students and instructors. The significance of the contractual syllabus lies in its ability to provide a clear and concrete list of expectations for students and instructors alike. It aids in offering guidance and resolving potential disputes. Examples of contractual aspects within a syllabus encompass policies and expectations regarding attendance, late submissions, and opportunities for makeup work. Over time, the legal contractual nature of syllabi has expanded, largely due to the increased utilization of policy statements to address appeals and grievances (Ludy et al., 2016). Legal considerations have compelled instructors to add increasingly explicit contractual information to syllabi, occasionally causing them to resemble legal documents more than course descriptions. This phenomenon has been termed "syllabus bloat" (Jones, 2011). Interestingly though, courts do not recognize educational malpractice or breach of contract, so syllabi are not actual contracts (Deans, 2019).

The Learner-Centered Syllabus, often referred to as the engaging syllabus, aims to influence student attitudes, perspectives, and motivation toward learning (Richmond et al., 2016; 2019). This approach focuses on empowering students to make choices about their learning and take responsibility for those choices, ultimately motivating them to embrace learning throughout the course and recognize the course's potential impact on their professional and personal development. The learner-centered syllabus emphasizes the intentions, roles, attitudes, and strategies of both students and instructors. Unlike traditional or contractual syllabi, the learner-centered syllabus often strives to appeal directly to students by conveying the excitement, intrigue, and wonder inherent in the course content (Harrington & Thomas, 2023; Richmond et al., 2016; 2019). The learner-centered syllabus not only motivates students to play active roles in their learning but also seeks to capture and sustain their interest in the course. It aligns with the proposition that a syllabus should serve as both a roadmap for learning and a means to spark students' interest in the learning journey and its guide (Matejka & Kurke, 1994). This engaging syllabus employs three primary strategies: Firstly, it employs images, color, and graphic design elements reminiscent of modern newsletters to craft a visually appealing document. Secondly, the text orientation within the engaging syllabus is student-centric, considering students' perspectives and integrating them into the class plans. Thirdly, the course description within the engaging syllabus presents a comprehensive experience beyond the course content, often connecting the course to broader themes or professional experiences. Collectively, these features of the engaging syllabus aim to bolster student motivation through a visually engaging document that promises an intriguing learning experience.

Towards a Holistic Syllabus. While traditional syllabi provide structure, brevity, and clarity, they may not cater to individual student needs potentially affecting their motivation and engagement in the learning process. Singham (2007) boldly "declare[d] war on the traditional course syllabus. If there is one single artifact that pinpoints the degradation of liberal education, it is the rule-infested, punitive, controlling syllabus that is handed out to students on the first day of class" (p. 52) and urges educators to get rid of this authoritarian syllabus (p. 56). Contractual syllabi offer some level of student input, potentially boosting engagement and motivation. Allowing students to have a say in the syllabus can increase their sense of ownership and responsibility for their learning. This approach may enhance motivation and engagement, as students are more likely to be interested in the topics they have helped choose. However, the learner-centered syllabus takes this a step further, promoting a more personalized and student-driven learning experience, which can have a positive impact on student success and intrinsic motivation fostering self-efficacy. Self-efficacy refers to an individual's belief in their ability to successfully perform a specific task, and it is formed through a cognitive assessment of both personal capabilities and environmental factors (Schunk & Pajares, 2004). This concept of self-efficacy holds immense importance in driving human behavior, as articulated by Bandura (1997), who stated that "Unless people believe they can produce desired effects by their actions, they have little incentive to act" (pp. 2-3). Students who lack self-efficacy are more likely to not believe in themselves and drop out (DeWitz et al., 2009).

Academic self-efficacy plays an important role in influencing student motivation and learning outcomes. It exerts its influence by impacting students' persistence, goal-setting behaviors, and their utilization of self-regulatory strategies (van Dinther, Dochy, & Segers, 2011). When students possess high levels of belonging and self-efficacy, they are more likely to engage actively in their learning processes, leading to increased success (e.g., Kahu & Nelson, 2018). Simultaneously, this engagement and success serve to further boost their self-efficacy levels in a mutually reinforcing cycle. Accordingly, the holistic syllabus suggests that learning outcomes are often flexible and designed to accommodate individual learners' goal-setting behaviors. It emphasizes skills development, critical thinking, and student growth. To optimize the learning experience, instructors can blend elements from different syllabus types, providing both structure and flexibility.

Recent evidence highlights that an effective syllabus is student-centered, using a friendly tone to guide students through the complexity of the course material and outcomes (e.g., Richmond et al., 2019). The potential of a syllabus can go beyond being a mere contractual communication source and cognitive map. It can become a mental map, offering rich resources to keep students on track for course graduation while fostering a sense of community within the learning environment. For learning to take place, college students must be mentally ready, motivated to engage with the learning material, and efficiently manage time to complete assignments and assessments. Thus, the authors propose a fourth category—the holistic syllabus, incorporating psychological growth into the academic agenda. Going beyond traditional approaches, this holistic syllabus prioritizes students' mental health, well-being, and self-directed learning.

CREATING A HOLISTIC SYLLABUS THAT IS WELCOMING

The syllabus serves as a pivotal gateway for students embarking on their college journey, offering not only a roadmap for the course but also their initial introduction to the faculty member or teaching staff. In recognizing its significance, the act of crafting a syllabus takes on profound importance, particularly in fostering student self-efficacy and cultivating a path toward success in college. A well-designed syllabus, one that radiates warmth and inclusivity, possesses the power to set a profoundly positive tone for the entire course. Research by Nusbaum, Swindell, and Plemons (2021) emphasizes the visual appeal of a syllabus, demonstrating that students perceive professors as kinder and more approachable when presented with an aesthetically pleasing syllabus. This underscores the profound influence that design and presentation can wield over a student's initial impression of their instructor, subsequently influencing their comfort and confidence within the course.

Moreover, research conducted by Gurung and Galardi (2021) further highlights the potential of the syllabus to shape the student experience. Gurung and Galardi (2021) investigated the impact of the syllabus tone, specifically focusing on the inclusion of a statement addressing mental health needs. The results were striking, demonstrating that when college students from an introductory psychology course encountered a syllabus that explicitly acknowledged and encouraged seeking support for mental health concerns, they were more inclined to reach out. Particularly, testing of a warm-toned syllabus in contrast to a cold-toned syllabus, created a welcoming that seemed to help the student see the instructor as a resource to deal with personal troubles and not just for class-related issues. This not only emphasizes the syllabus's role as a source of support but also reinforces the idea that a supportive and empathetic syllabus can bolster a student's sense of self-efficacy and readiness to navigate the challenges of college. By designing syllabi that are not only informative but also aesthetically appealing and empathetic in tone, educators can take deliberate steps toward setting students on a trajectory of success in college, underlining the significance of the initial impression and the crucial foundation it lays for the educational journey ahead.

Table 1 illustrates required versus optional elements that can be included in a holistic syllabus building on previous recommendations (Wagner et al., 2016). Image 1 provided in Appendix A, serves as an example of an undergraduate psychology syllabus that is aestathically appealing, clear, and welcoming in structure. It includes easy to follow course requirements and expectations, supported with guiding questions that serve as an introduction to course topics and as an opportunity for self-reflection, along with eye-catching photos. Appendix B provides an example of a holistic syllabus used in a hybrid introductory undergraduate course in psychology.

The practice of engaging students through a pre-reflection survey is an integral feature of the holistic syllabus. The goals of this survey are to foster a sense of belonging in the class, to alleviate anxiety, and to foster the belief that students will succeed and thrive in the course. In addition, the survey may also provide the instructor with useful information about the students in the course and provide information of misconceptions regarding the discipline of study, see questions 7-17 in Appendix C. (Note that all statements are false). The survey results may be discussed as a class activity or assignment, e.g., research methods, pschological misconceptions, etc.

Table 1. Required vs. optional elements for a holistic syllabus

Elements	Required for content	Optional for holistic syllabus
Course	name, number, section	representative image(s)
	academic year	
	teaching modality	
	credit hours	
	location; meeting times; office hours	
	materials, incl citations of sources	providing ways for access or links; library link; tips for reading textbook or scholarly journal articles
Faculty/teaching staff	name, credentials, title	short bio, teaching philosophy
	contact info	how to best contact
	office location, hours	website links for further credentials
Objectives	course goals	breakdown of learning outcomes
Conduct	attendance policy academic integrity policy	late and missed work policies tips on how to avoid plagiarism, information on academic misconduct, integrity, inclusivity, accessibility, and harassment
	classroom behavior	keys to success; expectations (student vs. instructor)
Grading	assessments	assignment descriptions; student samples; rubrics for all work; grammar and writing; opportunities for extra credit
	scales	final grade breakdown; periodic feedback mechanisms; link to office of specialized services or request for accessibility and accommodation
Required institutional language	links to policy, such as Title IX	trigger warning for sensitive topics privacy and diversity statement Caveat statement - In the event of extenuating circumstances, the schedule and requirements for this course may be modified
Additional resources for self-learning		
§ Personal growth and development health	mental health and/or positive psychology resources, etc.	
§ Family health	parenting, child development, etc.	
§ Interpersonal relationship resources	conflict resolution, etc.	
§ Community resources	parenting programs, drug programs, etc.	
§ Community engagement	volunteer opportunities, etc.	
§ Intellectual growth	book/media/podcast recommendations, etc.	
§ Professional development	workshops, career fairs, Professional memberships, etc.	
§ University engagement	clubs, student organizations, etc.	
§ Complementary intradepartmental courses	knowledge really isn't as isolated as presented	

Note: This table was modified from Wagner et al., 2023.

Student Testimonies to a Pre-Reflective Course Survey

In order to facilitate these objectives, one of the present authors communicated with students via the LMS, one week before the course met, and provided a link to an online Google survey to solicit their pre-reflections about the upcoming course (see Appendix C for the complete pre-reflection survey). For the purposes of this chapter, a total of 59 undergraduate psychology students across two sections were sent a pre-reflection survey. The results indicated that overall, the majority of students seemed to have a positive and enthusiastic first impression of the syllabus (89.83% vs. 10.17%). They found it interesting and engaging (category a), well-organized and informative (category b), and welcoming (category c). Some expressed concerns or uncertainties (category d), particularly regarding the intensity of the class or about unexpected elements like memes (e). However, positive feedback (category f) and predictability (category g) are prevalent themes in the responses. Below are corresponding student testimonies from categories (a) through (g) highlighting the broad range of student self-reports.

Select student testimonies about their first impressions of the syllabus from categories (a) through (g):

(a)   "Excitement really. I genuinely can't wait to begin."

(b)   "Informative and disarming"

(c)   "It's welcoming! You instantly feel like this class has a lot to offer and I like the pictures at the top."

(d)   "It will be a hard class to take but will be a healthy learning experience."

(e)   "Memes confused me a bit, I did not find a connection."

(f)   "This professor has memes on their syllabus... they have to be cool!"

(g)   "Great. I know what to expect from the class thanks to the way the syllabus is organized."

An important question in the pre-reflection survey concerned how students feel about being a student in the 21st century ("To be a college student in the 21st century feels like…"). This question was included since emotions impact learning, and student perceptions of success have important consequences for increased self-efficacy and course belonging (Cavanah, 2016). In the complex landscape of modern education, where students grapple with a multitude of challenges, emotions play a pivotal role in shaping the learning experience and ultimately setting students up for success while fostering self-efficacy. Recognizing and addressing these emotions is essential for creating a conducive learning environment. It was therefore felt that this was a vital question to pose.

Again 59 students responded across two sections. Overall, the subjective responses to the question about what it feels like to be a student in the 21st century, reflected a wide range of emotions and perspectives among college students. While some regarded it as a challenging (category h) aor stressful (category i) experience, others embraced it as an opportunity (category j) with access to myriad technological resources and opportunities (category k). The responses also suggested general recognition of the pressure (category l) and expectations (category m) that come with being a student in this era. Below are corresponding student testimonies from categories (h) through (m) to highlighting the broad range of feelings students reported.

Select student testimonies about how it feels to be a student in the current era, from categories *(h) through (m):*

(h)   "Your walking in the pathways full of glass trying to walk and survive without something happening. The glass pieces are life, hw, courses, family, relationships, bills, and yourself."

(i)   "Being in a burning building but having to stay calm."

(j)   "You can grow to be anything that you want to be and no one will judge you!"

(k) "I have access to a digital world that can allow me to become an entrepreneur, buy, sell, trade goods and currency, educate, train, guide and mentor anyone all without leaving my house."

(l) "We are being completely pulled apart—to an unprecedented extent—by all the things that we feel the need to be for so many different people, in so many different circumstances."

(m) "A dream, being a first-generation student is scary due to fear of diasspointment, yet exciting."

Providing pre-reflective questions may help students feel more empowered and may help them to believe that the course is "not so bad, not as scary as [they] thought" (reference). In addition, based on students' answers to emotion-focused questions, some class time can be allocated at pivotal points in the semester to address students' most pressing emotional concerns. As noted above, addressing students' emotional issues can facilitate the learning process. This is an especially important concern, given our current challenging times (e.g., unprecendented societal upheaval caused by the COVID-19 pandemic, ongoing challenges in higher education, etc.). Faculty members or teaching staff may not have much control over societal issues or their institution's response to current challenging times, but as empathethic course instructors we can ensure that students feel heard and understood. According to neuroscientists Immordino-Yang and Damasio, "When educators fail to appreciate the importance of students' emotions, they fail to appreciate a critical force in students' learning. One could argue, in fact, that they fail to appreciate the very reason that students learn at all" (in Cavanagh, 2019, 3/27-4/27).

BENEFITS OF ADOPTING A HOLISTIC APPROACH TO SYLLABUS

The adoption of a holistic approach to syllabus design may offer several benefits to students. Traditionally, syllabi have been seen as routine documents, often constrained by university-approved templates. However, the introduction of the holistic syllabus paradigm presents a new perspective. The holistic syllabus goes beyond merely conveying course information; it serves as a dynamic and creative tool, and accomplishes the following:

1. Connects students to the broader world: The holistic syllabus seeks to bridge the gap between course material and the wider world. By integrating real-world connections and resources into the syllabus, it encourages students to see the relevance of their studies in a larger context. For example, the optional section of the holistic syllabus provides links to a variety of resources such as volunteer organizations, podcasts, etc.

2. Fosters a Sense of Belonging: Since the need for belonging is a fundamental human need (Baumeister & Leary, 1995), the holistic syllabus hopes to cultivate a sense of belonging among students through its learner-centered and community-oriented approach. It helps students feel connected not only to the course but also to a broader community, both within and outside the classroom, by emphasizing students' connection to the institution, staff, learning community, and to the discipline being studied. As presented in the syllabus provided in Appendix B, students are told, "We are all a piece of work and need collaboration to succeed." This statement stresses that disconnection from the learning community may lead to alienation and anxiety. These emotions may inhibit class participation and emotional connection to the subject matter, professor, and classmates. Hence, a sense of belonging is fundamental for interpersonal functioning and can positively impact well-being and learning.

3. Prioritizes Mental Health and Well-being: One of the distinguishing features of the holistic syllabus is its emphasis on students' mental health and interpersonal well-being. It acknowledges the emotional aspects of learning and provides resources to support students in managing stress and challenges. The syllabus sample in Appendix B, for examples, includes a paragraph entitled, "Life happens!" It encourages students to follow a daily self-care regime that includes "a strong social support system to buffer your stress, less social media consumption and healthy (human) interactions, a healthy diet, regular bedtime routines, or other self-regulation habits". In addition, the optional section of the holistic syllabus provides mental health resources.

4. Promotes Self-Directed Learning: The holistic syllabus serves as a comprehensive framework that encourages self-directed learning. It empowers students to take charge of their educational journey, make choices, and set goals, ultimately enhancing their intrinsic motivation and self-efficacy. The last page of the syllabus listed in Appendix B includes a broad range of recommended books to complement the course materials. It also includes a link to ScienceHeroes.com— a site that highlights important scientific lifesaving discoveries.

5. Enhances Student Success: By offering a more personalized and student-driven learning experience, the holistic syllabus contributes to improved student success. It aligns with the concept of self-efficacy, where students believe in their ability to achieve desired outcomes through their actions. Both syllabi in Appendix A and B list ways for students to succeed in each of the offered courses. Moreover, the tone in both syllabi state that the instructor will make any effort to respond to student communication within 24 hours. This is apparent immediately on the first page of the syllabus, signaling that the instructor is accessible and available to help.

Incorporating these elements into the syllabus design might significantly benefit student motivation by creating a more engaging, supportive, and empowering learning environment. It transforms the traditional teaching-centered syllabus into a learning-centered tool for personal growth, lifelong learning, professional development, and community connection.

POTENTIAL PITFALLS AND OVERCOMING CHALLENGES

A pitfall of the holistic syllabus is its potential length. The inclusion of images and optional elements means that the holistic syllabus has the potential to be longer than the typical syllabus. The issue of information overload in syllabi, coupled with students' diminishing attention to details, makes this a concern (Wagner et al., 2023). Although research (Richmond et al, 2019) indicates that when students are given a longer, detailed syllabus, they perceive the instructor more positively (e.g., more effective communicator, approachable, creative, caring, and helpful) and were more likely to seek help from the instructor, students may be put off by the length of the syllabus and thus may not read it entirely. To encourage thorough syllabus reading, especially the full version on LMS, instructors can employ various strategic activities. One effective approach involves implementing a syllabus quiz, assessing students' comprehension of key syllabus elements. A syllabus acknowledgement statement can also be used. This involves requiring students to sign a document affirming that they have read and understood the syllabus. Additionally, promoting group discussions and activities centered around syllabus content can raise student awareness. This not only underscores the syllabus's importance but also fosters peer interaction, enriching the overall learning experience and fostering a sense of community among learners. Instructors should also reference the syllabus at appropriate times, throughout the semester. Instructors can also create a more interactive syllabus using quick response (QR) codes or embedded links can mitigate information overload concerns, as these links can dynamically adjust as institutional documents evolve (Wagner et al., 2023).

The transformation of established structural norms in syllabus design necessitates careful consideration of potential benefits and challenges. These considerations span areas such as psychological well-being, power dynamics, syllabus adjustments, and reshaping instructional practices. Instructors may face challenges, including potential performance evaluations if institutional norms discourage experimentation and lead to unfavorable student feedback. Overcoming institutional pressures that advocate for rigid syllabi can be challenging but it is essential to cultivate self-directed learning and encourage creative exploration. While traditional syllabi offer predictability, they may unintentionally stifle students' autonomy. Embracing a holistic syllabus design can foster an inclusive and supportive learning community, granting each student agency in their learning journey under the instructor's guidance. This approach can also enhance instructor satisfaction and strengthen the instructor-student relationship, countering the barriers posed by authoritarian or contractual syllabi. It's important to acknowledge that transitioning from traditional approaches may face resistance from students accustomed to more conventional teaching styles, who might need time to understand and embrace academic freedom.

CONCLUSION

Educators should regularly revisit and revise their syllabi, considering potential improvements for upcoming academic terms. This practice ensures that syllabi remain up to date with new policies and cutting-edge findings, maintaining accuracy in the information provided. Syllabi should be viewed as dynamic and adaptable documents, capable of refinement to align with the evolving preferences of students, faculty, and administrative requirements. It's essential, however, to strike a delicate balance: as new content is introduced, obsolete or unclear information should be pruned, fostering an iterative process that enhances syllabi and creates a more engaging, student-centered learning experience.

In academia, crafting syllabi has become a routine task for instructors, both new and seasoned. Whether it's creating a new syllabus, tweaking an existing one, or recycling a syllabus with years of use, this process often risks overlooking the significant role a syllabus can play in a student's educational journey. Institutional requirements for standardized syllabus templates, with designated spaces for course descriptions, required texts, and due dates, can unintentionally stifle the creative potential of the syllabus. This paper urges instructors to recognize the untapped power of the syllabus, viewing it not as a mere administrative document but as a dynamic tool for fostering personal growth, lifelong learning, professional development, and community connections.

Teaching is an adventure meant to ignite students' interest and passion for learning. This chapter advocates moving away from authoritarian, teacher-centered syllabi and encourage instructors to design syllabi as guiding mind maps. This empowers students to take charge of their learning, becoming active collaborators in the educational process. By adopting a motivational and holistic approach to syllabus design, educators can profoundly impact students' college experiences. A well-crafted syllabus becomes a catalyst for growth, self-discovery, and resilience, paving the way for a lifetime of curiosity and learning. Thus, the syllabus, once seen as a formality, emerges as a powerful tool, setting students on a path toward academic success and psychological well-being across diverse learning contexts.

REFERENCES

Bandura, A. (1997). *Self-efficacy: The exercise of control.* W H Freeman.

Baumeister, R. F., & Leary, M. R. (1995). The need to belong: Desire for interpersonal attachments as a fundamental human motivation. *Psychological Bulletin, 117*(3), 497–529. https://pubmed.ncbi.nlm.nih.gov/7777651/. doi:10.1037/0033-2909.117.3.497 PMID:7777651

Cavanagh, S. R. (2016). *The spark of learning: Energizing the college classroom with the science of emotion.* West Virginia University Press.

Cavanagh, S. R. (2019). How to make your teaching more engaging. *The Chronicle of Higher Education.* https://tacc.org/sites/default/files/documents/2019-08/how_to_make_your_teaching_more_engaging-che.pdf

Cullen, R., & Harris, M. (2009). Assessing learner-centeredness through course syllabi. *Assessment & Evaluation in Higher Education, 34*(1), 115–125. doi:10.1080/02602930801956018

Deans, T. (2019). Yes, your syllabus is way too long. *The Chronicle of Higher Education.* https://www.chronicle.com/article/yes-your-syllabus-is-way-too-long/

DeWitz, S. J., Woolsey, M. L., & Walsh, W. B. (2009). College student retention: An exploration of the relationship between self-efficacy beliefs and purpose in life among college students. *Journal of College Student Development, 50*(1), 19–34. doi:10.1353/csd.0.0049

Fornaciari, C. J., & Dean, K. L. (2014). The 21st-century syllabus: From pedagogy to andragogy. *Journal of Management Education, 38*(5), 701–723. doi:10.1177/1052562913504763

Gurung, R. A. R., & Galardi, N. R. (2022). Syllabus Tone, More Than Mental Health Statements, Influence Intentions to Seek Help. *Teaching of Psychology, 49*(3), 218–223. doi:10.1177/0098628321994632

Harrington, C., & Thomas, M. (2023). *Designing a motivational syllabus: Creating a learning path for student engagement.* Taylor & Francis.

Jones, J. B. (2011). Creative approaches to the syllabus. *The Chronicle of Higher Education.* https://www.chronicle.com/blogs/profhacker/creative-approaches-to-the-syllabus

Kahu, E. R., & Nelson, K. (2018). Student engagement in the educational interface: Understanding the mechanisms of student success. *Higher Education Research & Development, 37*(1), 58–71. doi:10.1080/07294360.2017.1344197

Kim, Y., & Ekachai, D. G. (2020). Exploring the effects of different online syllabus formats on student engagement and course-taking intentions. *College Teaching, 68*(4), 176–186. doi:10.1080/87567555.2020.1785381

Ludy, M. J., Brackenbury, T., Folkins, J. W., Peet, S. H., Langendorfer, S. J., & Beining, K. (2016). Student impressions of syllabus design: Engaging versus contractual syllabus. *International Journal for the Scholarship of Teaching and Learning, 10*(2), n2. doi:10.20429/ijsotl.2016.100206

Matejka, K., & Kurke, L. B. (1994). Designing a great syllabus. *College Teaching, 42*(3), 115–117. do i:10.1080/87567555.1994.9926838

Nusbaum, A. T., Swindell, S., & Plemons, A. (2021). Kindness at First Sight: The Role of Syllabi in Impression Formation. *Teaching of Psychology, 48*(2), 130–143. doi:10.1177/0098628320959953

Richmond, A. S., Morgan, R. K., Slattery, J. M., Mitchell, N. G., & Cooper, A. G. (2019). Project syllabus: An exploratory study of learner-centered syllabi. *Teaching of Psychology, 46*(1), 6–15. https:// doi-org/ doi:10.1177/009862831881612

Richmond, A. S., Slattery, J., Morgan, R. K., Mitchell, N., & Becknell, J. (2016). Can a learner-centered syllabus change student's perceptions of student-professor rapport and master teacher behaviors? *Scholarship of Teaching and Learning in Psychology, 2*, 159–168. https://doi-org/ doi:10.1037/stl0000066

Schunk, D. H., & Pajares, F. (2004). Self-efficacy in education revisited: Empirical and applied evidence. In D. M. McInerney & S. Van Etten (Eds.), *Big theories revisited* (pp. 115–138). Information Age Publishing.

Singham, M. (2007). Death to the syllabus. *Liberal Education, 93*(4), 52–56. https://freethoughtblogs. com/singham/files/2022/01/Death-to-the-Syllabus.pdf

Van Dinther, M., Dochy, F., & Segers, M. (2011). Factors affecting students' self-efficacy in higher education. *Educational Research Review, 6*(2), 95–108. doi:10.1016/j.edurev.2010.10.003

Wagner, J. L., Smith, K. J., Johnson, C., Hilaire, M. L., & Medina, M. S. (2023). Best practices in syllabus design. *American Journal of Pharmaceutical Education, 87*(3), 432–437. doi:10.5688/ajpe8995 PMID:35487683

APPENDIX

Figure 1. Sample of a psychology syllabus aestathically appealing and welcoming in structure

PSYC-110 Syllabus | Fall 2023

Instructor:	XXX	Room & Time:	XXX
Email:	XXX	Modality:	Hybrid
Office:	XXX	I will make every effort to respond within 24h during the week	

Course Description

Welcome to one of the most fascinating courses! I am excited to be your instructor and look forward to embarking on an intellectually rich and engaging learning journey. This course provides a general survey of psychological theories, principles and research. Topics include biological foundations of behavior, sensation, perception, learning, personality theory and social psychology. Topics will be related to major trends in recent cultural history and to current social and moral issues.

Required Textbook (It's Free!)

Noba Project (2023). Introduction to Psychology. Fall 2023. New Jersey City University. Noba textbook series: Psychology. Champaign, IL: DEF publishers.

Additional Readings, Activities & Resources will be posted on Blackboard (BB) and announced. It is your responsibility to regularly check the BB course site and messages.

Learning Objectives

As a result of this course, you will be able to

PSY1 Understand and use basic vocabulary of psychological terms and concepts.

PSY2 Describe the broad scope of psychology and its relevance to a variety of fields.

PSY3 Explain that knowledge is generated in the field of psychology through the scientific method and the interpretation and evaluation of empirical data.

PSY4 Begin to apply psychological knowledge to find solutions to diverse personal, interpersonal, community, and workplace issues.

PSY5 Think critically (ethically), at a rudimentary level, by analyzing assumptions and biases, and considering alternative explanations for interpersonal, social, and workplace issues.

PSY6 Practice communicating with others your ideas based on scientific findings.

Grading				How to be successful in PSYC-110
A+	97.56-100.0	B-	80.0-82.5	- Prioritize upcoming graduation and complete all tasks.
A	92.56-97.5	C+	77.56-79.9	- Pay attention to all course communication.
A-	90.0-92.5	C	70.0-77.5	- Participate in the course learning.
B+	87.56-89.9	D	60.0-69.9	- Prepare assignments following instructions and rubrics.
B	82.56-87.5	F	0.0-59.9	- Paraphrase and avoid plagiarism.
				- Practice self-directed and lifelong learning habits
.Requirements & Evaluation:		Points (100)		Description *(Rubrics will be provided in Blackboard)*
A. Quiz		50		Your knowledge of select chapters will be quizzed.
B. Class Participation		20		Be prepared and participate in class.
C. Psychopathology Talk		20		Investigate a psychopathological phenomenon as a team.
D. Pre/Post-Reflection		10		Reflect upon your (anticipated) learning journey.

"Knowledge rests not upon truth alone, but upon error also." - Carl Jung

Attendance & Participation: Attendance involves regularly checking course announcements and BB Messages. Participation means that you are reading the assigned texts, showing up to class meetings, and engaging with the (online) learning community. If you are sick, please stay home and send a note. Please consult the University Catalog for more details.

Absence & Missed Work: Stay on pace to graduate— your workload will increase if you are off pace. If you missed a quiz or deadline, communicate with me to discuss strategies and options. An excused absence, regardless of the cause, does not relieve you of the responsibility of making up missed work. Be proactive, stay connected, and conscientious.

Life happens! Unexpected events happen and require you to be flexible and leave wiggle room for adjustment. Make sure you have enough energy and resources to overcome such obstacles. If you feel overwhelmed, seek out support and/or contact me. Your daily self-care habit should include a strong social support system to buffer your stress, less social media consumption and healthy (human) interactions, a healthy diet, regular bedtime routines, or other self-regulation habits. Take charge of your intellectual life and use campus sources for help and self-improvement. We are all a piece of work and need collaboration to succeed. Prioritize academic work, then celebrate accomplishments with loved ones.

Remember there is formal HELP! If you are going through hardship or your situation has abruptly changed, contact the Dean of Students. Also, never hesitate to reach to me as a "mentor".

Privacy Statement: At times, students may disclose private information. It is expected that students respect the privacy of their classmates and do not repeat or discuss sensitive information with others outside of the course. Show professional care and maturity towards the feelings of your colleagues.

University Guidelines and Policies Applicable to This Course

1. **Academic Integrity Policy**— details available at XXX
2. **Turn-It-In.com Statement**. Students agree that all assignments are subject to submission for textual similarity review— details available at XXX
3. **Reasonable Accommodation**? If you are a student with a disability and wish reasonable accommodations— details available at XXX
4. **Veteran Needs**? If you are a veteran of the armed services, and need assistance— details at XXX
5. **Course withdrawal**? — details available at XXX
6. **Experiencing food insecurity**? — details available at website XXX
7. **Need tutoring and writing help**? — details available at website XXX

Other writing tools:

- **Trinka**: Free Online Grammar Editor & Grammar Checker -
- **Guide for APA 7**: https://apastyle.apa.org/instructional-aids/reference-guide.pdf
- **Avoid Plagiarism**: https://blog.apastyle.org/apastyle/2016/05/avoiding-plagiarism.html

Special Note: To be responsive to student interests and scheduling, the weekly topics, activities, and assignments in this syllabus are subject to change. As your professor I reserve the right to revise this syllabus at any given time. You will always be informed of such changes.

Some of my favorite books to dive deeper into the baffling world of the human mind & action:

Knowledge Saves Lives: Who Saved the Most Lives in History?!

"We read to know that we are not alone."—C. S. Lewis

Pre-Reflection Survey Psyc-110 Pre-reflection With Dr. XXX

<u>Instruction</u>: Please fill out this online pre-reflection survey before first day of class. Your answers will count towards the course assessment and activity during class time. I look forward to meeting you soon! ~Dr. XXX1. Course Section2. What is your student ID?3. What is your academic status?4. What is your shoe size?5. How is your relationship with social media?

Which of the below 10 statements are true or false?7. Most people use only about 10 percent of their brain capacity. True / False8. Newborn babies are virtually blind and deaf. True / False9. Hypnosis enhances the accuracy of our memories. True / False10. All people with dyslexia see words backward (like tac instead of cat). True / False11. In general, it's better to express anger than to hold it in. True / False12. The lie-detector (polygraph) test is 90 to 95 percent accurate. True / False13. People tend to be romantically attracted to individuals who are opposite to them. True / False14. The more people present at an emergency, the less likely one of them will help. True / False15. People with schizophrenia have more than one personality. True / False16. All effective psychotherapies require to get to the root of the childhood problems. True / False17. How do you think you did on the above statements? *Mark only one oval.*

- I did very well.
- I did well.
- Not sure.
- I did bad.
- I did very bad.

Complete the sentences and write your answer below…

18. "Psychology is...."
19. "Taking this class makes me feel...."
20. "I expect this class to be...."
21. "I read the syllabus, and I signed up for TEAM/TOPIC...."
22. "My first impression of the syllabus (class) is...."
23. "My strategies for being engaged in this class are......"
24. "I aspire to become a......."
25. "Three words that best describe me are......."
26. "My passion and interests are......."
27. "My strengths are......."
28. "My weaknesses are......."
29. "Besides being a college student, my other roles in life are being a....."
30. "One of my new learning experiences that I enjoyed was......"
31. "Statistics makes me feel...."
32. "Reading the textbook makes me feel..."
33. "One topic in psychology that interests me the most for (future) research is..."
34. "To be a college student in the 21st century feels like..."

35. I look forward to being your professor this term (and a mentor beyond this class!). If you have any questions or concerns, please feel free to use the text field below. Otherwise, submit your pre-reflection survey. Thank you! Stay healthy, connected, and curious:) ~Dr. XXX

This content is neither created nor endorsed by Google.

Chapter 5
Exploring Communication and Communication Tools for E-Learning

Fatima Zahra Ouariach
https://orcid.org/0009-0000-1360-9286
Abdelmalek Essaadi University, Morocco

Mohammed Zine El Abidine
https://orcid.org/0000-0002-8767-4504
Abdelmalek Essaadi University, Morocco

Amel Nejjari
https://orcid.org/0000-0002-7323-1286
Abdelmalek Essaadi University, Morocco

ABSTRACT

In the realm of e-learning, educators are presented with the choice between synchronous and asynchronous methods. Communication assumes a paramount role in the fabric of daily life and the interactions that transpire between individuals. This chapter delves deep into the captivating realm of e-learning, meticulously examining the plethora of tools available in the digital sphere. Communication and its accompanying tools assume an indispensable role within the e-learning environment, serving as virtual bridges that connect learners, educators, and educational content. Moreover, the chapter accentuates the potential of communication and its associated tools in the realm of e-learning, transcending the mere transfer of information. Instead, they foster an interactive, collaborative, and flexible milieu that optimizes learning opportunities, engenders learner engagement, and cultivates the development of crucial skills for the modern era.

DOI: 10.4018/979-8-3693-3128-6.ch005

Copyright © 2024, IGI Global. Copying or distributing in print or electronic forms without written permission of IGI Global is prohibited.

INTRODUCTION

Communication involves sending or transmitting messages between individuals or groups (Romera et al., 1984). It often takes multiple attempts to achieve mutual understanding. This can only happen when all parties involved share a common understanding of the information being communicated (Tendero et al., 2009; Team et al., 2013).

The sending and receiving of messages by sender and receiver occurs in a two-way process called communication. shown by Schramm's communication model (lim et al.,2017) . The communicator uses a shared medium to translate his thoughts into words, signs, images, graphics, sounds, tones of voice, facial expressions and body language . the receiver then retrieves the message and encodes it. The decoding process is not straightforward, since the recipient interprets the information according to his or her own experiences, expectations, level of understanding and other factors that affect perception or comprehension. A crucial element known as feedback is what brings the communication process to an end once it has begun say that the four components of communication are sender, medium, receiver and feedback (lim et al.,2017).

Exploring communication and communication tools for e-learning is a growing field of study, attracting increasing interest among educational researchers. The development and growing popularity of e-learning has opened up new opportunities to study how to improve communication in this specific context.

By describing the primary objectives, strategies, and communication technologies used to enable an interesting, collaborative, and fruitful distant learning experience, this chapter seeks to explore the fundamental components of communication in the context of online learning. We'll examine how online communication may help teachers fulfill their guiding and facilitation roles, boost student engagement, facilitate concept understanding, and promote pair collaboration. This chapter's ultimate objective is to provide readers a comprehensive grasp of communication techniques and the resources available to maximize online learning so they may build online learning environments that are more productive, approachable, and enriching.

Research on communication and communication tools in e-learning has experienced a significant increase, generating interest among educational researchers. The advancements and effectiveness of e-learning have created opportunities for further investigation on enhancing communication in this particular context. Various aspects of communication in e-learning have been explored through research. These studies delve into the utilization of diverse, real-time communication methods and online collaboration tools such as discussion forums, live chat sessions, and online videos. Moreover, there is a growing emphasis on examining the impact of online communication on learner engagement, promoting peer collaboration, and facilitating knowledge consolidation.

Online learning opens up a realm of communication possibilities, many of which have never been fully exploited in traditional face-to-face environments. Higher education has moved beyond the content download model to one that maximizes the potential for learner collaboration and authentic learning simulating real-life situations. However, new possibilities pose new problems or, as some would say, revive old ones. The communication tools available in the online environment are, in part, responsible for opening up innovations in interactive learning in higher education. Asynchronous communication, in particular, is one of the most versatile tools available. Learners may not be able to attend classes in real time, as in a synchronous face-to-face environment, for a multitude of reasons involving work and family commitments as well as geographical and physical barriers. The online environment offers these learners the opportunity to access education beyond the traditional distance learning model of home-based learning programs. Learners are now able to evolve in a socially constructive learning environment (Jonassen et al., 1995) reinforced by information and communication technologies.

Those responsible for designing innovative learning environments need to be aware that these environments are not without their shortcomings. Recent research has focused on asynchronous communication in the online learning environment of higher education, highlighting a number of issues to consider if we are to design communication environments that are fair to all participants (Barraket et al., 2000; Blum, 1999; Herring, 1999).

The effective teaching process in a traditional classroom relies heavily on discussion and interaction, both between teacher and student, and between peers. Similarly, specialists recognize that interaction plays a key role in achieving the objectives of e-learning systems (Kuo et al., 2014). According to Croxton (Croxton,2014) interaction offers dynamic engagement for students, enabling them to acquire knowledge and develop their individual learning skills. Students evaluate their interaction with teachers in terms of the support they receive, considering open communication, responsiveness and teacher involvement as contributing factors (Wang et al.,2016). Interaction is of great importance because the practice of communication as a learning process represents a crucial step in the transfer of knowledge (Garrison,2011). and increasing student participation in educational activities (O'Flaherty et al., 2015; Swan,2001).

The field of technology highlights how technological advances have increased the number of media supports capable of facilitating interactive processes in communication (Yarbro et al.,2016). Technological tools that focus on interaction are well documented in the literature and include both asynchronous features, such as e-mail and streaming media, and synchronous processes, such as discussion services. Instructional technology, which results from the combination of education and information systems, encompasses "a complex and integrated process involving people, procedures, ideas, devices and organizations to analyze problems, design, implement, evaluate and manage solutions to these problems, related to all aspects of human learning" (Seels et al.,2012).

The study of communication and communication tools for e-learning is a dynamic field of research aimed at optimizing communication opportunities in e-learning environments. By exploring the benefits, limitations and best practices associated with the use of communication tools, researchers seek to enhance the e-learning experience and foster the active, collaborative engagement of learners.

Communication and communication tools are essential elements of online teaching, as they foster learner engagement, ensure clarity of information, support collaboration, adapt teaching, and play a central role in the quality and effectiveness of online teaching. They help create an interactive, collaborative and enriching learning environment for learners.

COMMUNICATION

The Evolution of the Notion of Communication

The notion of communication is often associated with the media, creating confusion between the two. However, over the course of history, the notion of communication has been used in many different ways, to reveal, expose or conceal diverse realities. Armand Mattelart sets out to trace this evolution in his most recent work, "The Invention of Communication". Mattelart argues that every historical epoch and every type of society develops its own configuration of communication.

This configuration, with its multiple economic, social, technical and mental dimensions, as well as its different scales - local, regional, national or international - tends to engender a predominant concept of communication. An important part of Mattelart's work consists in identifying ruptures and continuities in the transition from one configuration to another. Indeed, according to the author, although the concept of communication continually reinvents itself in a new form over time, it retains, if only partially, elements that were present in earlier modes of communication (Armand Mattelart, 1994).

Mattelart takes an extremely inclusive view of communication. In his view, it encompasses a wide range of exchange and circulation processes, whether of goods, people or messages, as well as communication infrastructures and long-distance transmission networks. It also covers the means of symbolic exchange, such as world exhibitions, elite culture, religion, language and the media. Finally, Mattelart endeavors to demonstrate how these various phenomena were influenced and accompanied by a multitude of doctrines, theories and ideologies, embodied by figures as diverse as Turgot, Adam Smith, Saint-Simon, Comte, Proudhon, Darwin, Taylor, and many others. According to Mattelart, the story of the emergence of communication begins in the 17th century, a time when neither the media nor freedom of the press yet existed, and extends up to the third decade of the 20th century, when the terms "mass media," "communication," and "mass culture" made their appearance. Mattelart places particular emphasis on the 19th century, which he describes as the founding century. Indeed, it was during this period that the ambitious utopia of perfect social communication and universal transparency was developed through the technical foundations of communication (Armand Mattelart, 1994).

Definition of Communication

To begin our research, we must first define communication, a concept that is not easy to pin down (Dance et al., 1976). Scientists consider that the verb "to communicate" is firmly anchored in common dictionaries, which complicates its definition. Indeed, it is one of the most misused terms in the English language (Clevenger, 1991). Researchers have made many attempts to define communication, but a single definition has proved impossible and probably unsuccessful.

Frank Dance clarifies this confusing concept by describing several elements used to differentiate communication (Dance et al., 1970). He identifies three key points of "conceptual differentiation" that constitute the fundamental dimensions of communication.

The first dimension concerns the level of observation or abstraction. Some definitions are broad and inclusive, while others are restrictive. For example, it is common to define communication as "the process of connecting different parts of the living world" (Ruesch,1957; Schement,2017). On the other hand, definitions that define communication as "a system (such as a telephone or computer)" and general communication as "systems (telephone or telegraph) used to transmit information and orders (as in naval service)" are restrictive (Gove,1986).

The second-dimension concerns intentionality. Some definitions consider only the intentional sending and receiving of messages, while others do not impose this limitation. For example, a definition including intention would be: "a source intentionally influences behavior when it transmits a message to a receiver" (Miller, 1966). On the other hand, a definition without the requirement of intention would be: "a process that makes common to two or more what was the monopoly of one or more" (Cartier, 1959).

A third dimension used to differentiate definitions of communication is normative judgment. Some definitions include statements of success, validity or accuracy, while others do not include such implicit judgments. For example, a definition that assumes the success of communication would be: "communication is the verbal exchange of thoughts or ideas"(Hoben,1954). This definition implies that the exchange of thoughts or ideas is a successful exchange. On the other hand, another definition makes no judgment about the success of the result: "communication is the verbal exchange of ideas. Or not: "communication is the transmission of information" (Berelson, B., & Steiner, G. (1964). Here, information is transmitted without necessarily being received or understood.

Communication involves a complex process of encoding and decoding, where a message is encoded by the sender using signs, symbols or language, and then decoded by the receiver to extract its meaning. It is important to note, however, that communication is not limited to words, but also encompasses tone of voice, facial expressions, gestures and other non-verbal elements that enrich and refine the message. Among new technologies, the Internet and websites are among the fastest and most effective means of communication. Compared with traditional communication methods, Internet-based communications can transfer information synchronously or asynchronously (Zengin, B., Arikan, A., & Dogan, D. (2011).

The Purpose of Communication

The primary goal of communication is to facilitate the effective exchange of ideas, information, thoughts, and emotions among individuals. In simpler terms, its purpose is to enable the transmission of messages from a sender to one or more recipients, allowing for the sharing of information, establishing social connections, eliciting responses, planning actions, and influencing attitudes and behavior.

Communication aims to promote the sharing of thoughts and perspectives, expressing needs and desires, and showcasing one's capability to communicate factual information objectively. Additionally, it emphasizes the importance of nurturing meaningful relationships through effective communication.

Communication Players

Representing communication players in table form can help illustrate their roles and interactions. Here's an example of a table listing the main players in communication:

Whatever the method or format used, communication has both advantages and limitations. Here is a list of the advantages and limitations of communication in general:

The Advantages of Communication

- **Information transfer:** communication enables people to share information, ideas, opinions and knowledge. This promotes the dissemination of knowledge (McQuail, 2010).
- **Relationship building:** communication is essential for developing and maintaining personal and professional relationships, as well as improving mutual understanding (Rogers and Kincaid, 1981).
- **Decision-making:** enabling individuals and groups to exchange essential information and discuss possibilities, communication facilitates decision-making (Monge and Poole, 2003).
- **Self-expression:** communication gives people a means of communicating their thoughts, emotions, needs and opinions. It encourages self-expression (Berger and Calabrese, 1975).
- **Influence and persuasion:** Communication enables people to influence and persuade others, whether in an advertising, political or social context (Petty and Cacioppo, 1986).

The Limits of Communication

Table 1. Main players in communication

Communication	Responsibilities / Role
Sender	- Initiates the message - Encodes the information - Transmits the message - Can be a person, an organization, etc.
Recipient	- Receives the message - Decodes information - Can provide feedback
Message	-Message content - Can be verbal, written, visual, etc.
Communication channel	- The means used to transmit the message (telephone, e-mail, social media)
Noise	- Any interference that may disrupt communication (ambient noise, foreign language, etc.).
Context	- The context in which communication takes place (environment, situation, culture, etc.)
Reaction	- Response or action as a result of communication
Feedback	- Information provided by the recipient to confirm or clarify understanding of the message - Response or feedback from receiver to sender

- **Noise and distortion:** Communication can be disrupted by noise, misunderstandings and distortions, leading to misinterpretation of messages (Shannon and Weaver, 1949).
- **Cultural and linguistic barriers:** Cultural and linguistic differences can hinder understanding and effective communication between individuals and groups (Hall, 1959).
- **Information overload:** In a modern world characterized by information overload, it can be difficult to sort and process all available data effectively (Toffler, 1970).
- **Non-verbal:** Much communication is non-verbal, meaning that gestures, facial expressions and other signals play an important role and can be misinterpreted (Mehrabian, 1972).
- **Manipulation and deception:** Communication can also be used in a manipulative or deceptive way to influence others dishonestly (Cialdini, 1984).

Communication plays a vital role in transmitting information, fostering relationships, facilitating decision-making, self-expression, and exerting influence. However, it can encounter obstacles like noise, cultural differences, information overload, and the potential for manipulation. Understanding these benefits and limitations is crucial for achieving more efficient and ethical communication.

E-LEARNING

The Historical Evolution of E-Learning

Since the origin of the word "e-Learning" is not certain, it is proposed that the term probably emerged around 1980 (Moore et al., 2011). In today's digital age, e-Learning is becoming increasingly viable and accessible. What was once simply called "computer-based training" has now become "take your course wherever you are". E-learning can be seen as a natural evolution of distance learning. It has always taken advantage of modern technologies to develop and adapt the infrastructure of educational tools to shape education (Sangra et al., 2012).

The origins of e-learning can be traced back to the correspondence learning method, with Sir Isaac Pitman's first correspondence courses teaching shorthand in 1840, often considered the first example of distance learning. The fundamental principles of this approach have remained constant throughout history, but the means of communication have multiplied as technology has advanced (Horton, 2001). The evolution of distance learning can be characterized as a flexible pedagogical method that takes advantage of conventional, non-conventional and emerging means of communication to deliver educational material without being limited by geographical constraints. Since the early days of distance learning, many authors and academics have proposed various definitions of this field. Content delivery formats for distance education have evolved to include correspondence courses, print media, online courses, mobile devices, and today, virtual courses (Moore, 1990). Although distance learning has a long history going back centuries, it wasn't until the 1960s that e-learning really began to develop. It has had a significant impact in a variety of sectors, including business, academic institutions, training and the armed forces (Fletcher & Rockway, 1986).

In the 1980s, a new era began with the advent of personal computers, paving the way for e-learning. Over the past 50 years, various approaches have been put into practice to support the instructor's role in the classroom. Computer-based training (CBT) is a learning method where the primary transfer of data is via a computer, using software on the Internet or intranet (Rouse, 2011). In the 1960s, computer-assisted instruction (CAI) evolved into computer-based learning (CBL). Computer-based learning was used not only for educational purposes, but also for communication. The pioneering system of computer-based training was PLATO (Programmed Logic for Automatic Teaching Operation), which was launched in 1960. It had the basic structure that is used in modern e-learning methods, comprising graphical elements, text with graphics, forums and discussion rooms (Shimura, 2006). Multimedia learning models have spawned several ideologies and guidelines to facilitate the design of computer-based training (CBT). With CBT, hands-on training can be made more efficient, with a one-to-one student-teacher ratio and workshop or job-based training (Dean, Whitlock, 1992).

In the 90s, CD-ROM-based training emerged as a new e-learning technology. Occasional workshops were organized as part of this approach. The content focused mainly on IT-related lessons, accounting for over 95% of the material. Public discussion forums, called "mentoring", were set up on the websites. Around 1998, the web took over from CD-ROM-based training, offering not only online instruction and learning materials, but also a "personalized" learning experience through chat rooms, study groups, newsletters and interactive content (Cross, 2004).

When the Internet and personal computers experienced a phenomenal boom at the end of the 20th century, it was at this very moment that the concept of e-learning began to take shape. The technology, concept and devices complemented each other, giving rise to a new learning trend. In 1996, the first web-based Learning Management System (LMS), named Cecil, was launched (Sheridan, et al., 2002). An LMS is a software application that organizes, documents, records and delivers e-learning courses. Modern LMSs, mainly web-based, enable the hosting and/or delivery of various types of learning content, such as reading materials, videos, audio, wikis, web conferences, chats, forums, blogs, learning games, tests, assessments and much more.

By the turn of the 2000s, companies, organizations and the military had grasped the concepts of e-learning and adapted them to their specific needs. New e-learning methods opened the doors to information access and provided communication and interaction features. The learning experience has become more coherent thanks to improved pedagogy. Recognizing that education is based more on ideas than facts, a distinction was made between the traditional "passive transfer of information" of the academy and "interactive and constructive" e-learning methods (Garrison, Anderson, 2003).

The advent of mobile technology has ushered in a new era in e-learning, known as m-learning. Mobile learning can be defined as a lightweight, portable platform that enables learners to engage in learning activities without any geographical constraints. Cell phones, smartphones, personal digital assistants (PDAs), handheld computers, tablets, laptops and media players are all used in mobile learning (Kukulska-Hulme, 2005).

In the 1990s, personal digital assistants (Palm Pilot PDAs), handheld devices capable of multi-tasking such as calculations, calendaring and note-taking, were developed. As technology and learner-centered design began to develop, mobile learning began to evolve in parallel (Berge & Muilenburg, 2013).

Definition of E-Learning

In some definitions, e-learning is not limited to offering courses entirely online. For example (Oblinger & Hawkins, 2005) note that e-learning has evolved from fully online courses to the use of technology to deliver some or all courses, regardless of time or permanent location. In addition, the European Commission (2001) describes e-learning as the use of new multimedia technologies and the Internet to improve the quality of learning through the use of facilities, service provision, communication and collaboration at a distance. Here are also different definitions of e-learning.

E-learning refers to the use of information and communication technologies to obtain learning/teaching resources online. In the broadest sense, (Abad et al., 2009) define e-learning as any learning facilitated electronically. However, they limit this definition to learning driven by the use of digital technologies. Some researchers further simplify this definition by considering any Internet- or Web-based learning (LaRose et al., 1998; Keller and Cernerud, 2002). According to (Maltz et al.,2005), the term "e-learning" is used in a variety of ways, including distributed learning, online distance learning and blended learning. It is an environment for managing and/or using application services (Ouariach et al., 2023).

E-learning enables individuals to acquire new knowledge and skills at their own pace and within a limited timeframe, taking into account their family, professional and personal commitments (Robinson, P., & Cole, R. A.2000). Academics have also followed suit, rather than responding to growing demand. Brain-based learning tells us that learners construct their own knowledge on the basis of information already present in their brains (Goralski,2008). This coupling of knowledge enables the brain to synthesize new information, create new threads of knowledge and form networks for critical thinking. Research into emotions and affective processes in learning is not new, but it is becoming increasingly important in e-learning. Learner motivation, engagement and satisfaction have a significant impact on the success of their online courses (Richard, S., Gay, P., & Gentaz, É.2021).

Furthermore, e-learning can take many forms, including hybrid pedagogies combining online and face-to-face learning. He defines the concepts of motivation, learning and education, and information and communication technologies (ICT) in the context of e-learning (Knoerr, 2005).

In the field of e-learning, the use of artificial intelligence (AI) and intelligent systems plays a key role in improving the effectiveness of online teaching.

Intelligent systems in the context of e-learning use technologies such as artificial intelligence (AI), machine learning and data analysis to improve teaching efficiency. They can monitor learners' behavior, analyze their performance and dynamically adapt content and activities to individual needs. Intelligent systems can also provide content recommendations, personalized exercises and feedback for each learner.

This often involves the use of adaptive technologies and tools, such as machine learning algorithms, recommendation systems and advanced learning management systems (LMS). These tools collect and analyze learner data in real time, enabling teachers and course designers to better understand individual needs and propose content and activities tailored to each learner. By placing them at the heart of the learning process, e-learning personalization aims to increase learner engagement, motivation and autonomy. The result is adaptable learning paths, adaptive assessments, interactive content and personalized feedback to meet the unique needs of each learner.

Distance learning and e-learning have experienced significant growth in recent years due to the increasing adoption of digital technologies in education. Several factors have contributed to this development, including increased Internet accessibility, technological advances in e-learning and the need for flexibility and personalization of learning paths. Increasing globalization and the need to offer distance learning opportunities to diverse audiences mean that educational establishments and trainers must adapt their teaching methods to meet the individual needs of learners. In this context, the personalization of e-learning has become an innovative and promising pedagogical method (Siemens et al.,2011).

Personalization of e-learning aims to go beyond standardized, "one-size-fits-all" teaching, recognizing that each learner is unique and has his or her own preferences, needs, interests and learning pace. By adopting this approach, educators aim to provide personalized content, activities and learning resources that match the individual characteristics of each learner. The personalization of e-learning is largely influenced by technological advances, particularly in the field of information and communication technologies (ICT). Learner data can be collected and analyzed in real time using adaptive tools based on machine learning and recommendation algorithms (Boullier,2013).

E-learning also supports its role as a model of inclusive education, facilitating access to higher education and developing digital skills. Research shows that the active use of electronic and digital media and devices in online education can improve access, development and quality of education (Sangrà, et al.,2012) (Al-Samarraie et al.,2017) ... In addition to formal education supports that online education uses the same virtual environment to provide and standardize students' technical and digital skills (Anderson, T., & Rivera Vargas, P. 2020). This reduces potential digital divides across multiple intersecting dimensions, including social class, physical disability, geographic location and age (Chu,2010).

In her evaluation of the effectiveness of the e-learning experience in Saudi Arabia, (Algahtani, 2011) analyzed the different definitions of e-learning from three distinct perspectives: the distance learning perspective (Perraton, 2002; Alarifi, 2003; Holmes & Gardner, 2006), the technological perspective (Wentling et al., 2000; Nichols, 2003) and also from the point of view of e-learning as pedagogy (Khan, 2005; Schank, 2000).

Evolution of E-Learning Theories

E-learning and distance learning, supported by information and communication technologies, are becoming essential elements not only in primary and secondary schools, but also in universities and public and private sector organizations. Researchers and stakeholders therefore recognize that focusing solely on the technological aspect is no guarantee of successful knowledge transfer. Thus, it becomes inevitable to analyze pedagogical and learning principles through the prism of e-learning techniques.

Figure 1. La convergence des TIC avec les théories de l'apprentissage
(Kotsilieris, T., & Dimopoulou, N. 2013)

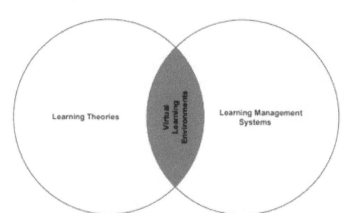

Mayes (2004) argues that there are no learning models or theories specifically designed for e-learning, but only "electronic" improvements on existing ones. Furthermore, it's clear that while teachers and students are demonstrating innovation in educational ICT, many efforts are not widely accepted due to insufficient design and implementation results. This problem becomes more complex as technology advances and virtual worlds are increasingly used as pedagogical tools. Virtual worlds offer learners the opportunity to participate in activities that continuously measure their performance and assess their understanding. We must not ignore the fact that, according to Dewey (2008), real learning must be based on experience, and to acquire new knowledge, continuous testing and evaluation are necessary.

The emergence of new technologies and their integration into the field of education (see Figure 1 below) have reinforced the idea that the connection between educator and learner via the Internet can constitute a virtual classroom (Keegan, 1995). According to Simonson (2000), distance learning represents a characteristic educational system where students are at a distance and communicate with the educator through interactive means and systems.

The dynamism of web-based educational software and technological advances in the field of learning have given rise to a new vision of distance learning, now known as e-learning. E-learning encompasses all forms of distance learning that use the Internet or digital resources. According to Clark & Mayer (2007), e-learning is characterized by the following elements:

Educational content is closely linked to learning objectives.

- It uses pedagogical methods to facilitate learning.
- It uses words and images to deliver content.
- It can be guided by the educator (synchronous learning) or designed for individual study (asynchronous learning).
- It enables the acquisition of new knowledge and skills, closely linked to personal objectives.

The main objective of computer-assisted collaborative learning lies in facilitating communication between stakeholders such as researchers and teachers, while promoting social interaction (Dillenbourg and Traum, 1999). Collaborative procedures become feasible thanks to networked collaborative learning environments specially designed to support distributed and distance learning (Anderson and Jackson, 2001). In addition, studies by (Shih and Yang, 2008) and (Konstantinidis et al.,2009) demonstrate that the use of 3D virtual worlds can enhance collaborative learning, offering a new tool for e-learning.

Types of E-Learning

There are many ways to classify types of e-learning. According to (Algahtani,2011), the classification is based on the level of educational participation. Some classifications are also based on interaction time. (Algahtani,2011) divides e-learning into two basic types, namely computer-based learning and Internet-based e-learning. Computer-based learning involves the use of the full range of hardware and software generally available in information and communication technologies. Each component can be used in two ways: computer-administered teaching and computer-assisted learning. In computer-assisted learning, computers replace traditional methods by providing interactive software.

Almosa (2002) believes that Internet-based e-learning represents a further improvement on computer-based learning, by making content accessible via the Internet and linked to relevant knowledge sources such as e-mail services and reference documents that can be used by learners anytime, anywhere. Learning takes place with or without a teacher or instructor (Almosa, 2002). Zeitoun (2008) has classified these functionalities according to their degree of use in education, including hybrid, assisted and fully online modes. The assisted model complements traditional approaches as required. The hybrid model offers a short-term diploma as part of the traditional approach. The fully online model, which represents the greatest improvement, involves the exclusive use of the Internet for learning (Zeitoun, 2008).

Algahtani (2011) described the fully online mode as either "synchronous" or "asynchronous", depending on the application of optional timing for interaction. Synchronous timing involves a real-time exchange of online access between teachers or instructors and learners, or between learners themselves, while asynchronous timing allows all participants to post communications to any other participant via the Internet (Algahtani, 2011; Almosa and Almubarak, 2005). The synchronous type allows learners to chat with instructors and each other via the Internet at the same time, using tools such as videoconferencing and chat rooms. According to Almosa and Almubarak (2005), this type offers the advantage of immediate feedback. The asynchronous mode also allows learners to chat with instructors or teachers as well as with each other via the Internet at different times. It therefore does not involve real-time interaction, but rather interaction at a later stage, using tools such as threaded discussions and e-mail (Almosa and Almubarak, 2005).

E-Learning Categories

These are considered as follows:

Courses

Most discussions of e-learning focus on educational courses. Educational course materials or software are often modified and enhanced with different media, then uploaded to a network environment for online access. Today, there are several popular learning management systems (LMS), such as WebCT and Blackboard, widely used by educational establishments. To make courseware more engaging, course designers have begun to add innovative presentations such as simulations, storytelling and a variety of unique features to the material. E-learning has obvious similarities with a classroom, in that learners and teachers are connected through the organization and delivery of the course.

Informal Learning

Informal learning stands out as one of the most dynamic and adaptable facets of learning, yet it remains the least recognized. Our quest for knowledge (and our intention to exploit it) drives our search. Search engines such as Google, combined with information storage tools such as Google, and personal knowledge management tools such as wikis and blogs, form a powerful set of tools in the arsenal of knowledge workers. Cross (Bates, 2005) argues that we acquire more knowledge during our breaks at work than in a formal learning environment. Our professional progress is greatly influenced by informal learning, sometimes through trial and error, sometimes through conversation.

Blended Learning

Blended learning is an innovative training approach that combines traditional face-to-face training sessions with the use of digital distance learning tools within a virtual classroom. This combination enables learners to follow training sessions at their own pace, while benefiting from the expertise and interaction of the trainer. The flexibility of this hybrid format makes it possible to offer training adapted to audiences with different time and travel constraints. In this way, the hybrid format preserves the advantages of face-to-face training by offering explanations of key concepts and methods, dispelling misunderstandings or misconceptions, while promoting real-time communication and intervention (Garrison et al., 2008).

Communities

Learning has an undeniable social dimension (Ally, 2004). The challenges we face in our professional environment are often complex and unstable. In this globalized era, our problem-solving methods are constantly evolving. Individuals exchange information with their peers within the same organization or network on a global scale, or with other organizations. Communities play an essential role in the dissemination of tacit knowledge, making a significant contribution to this intellectual exchange.

Knowledge Management

Globalization puts the emphasis on e-learning, as e-learning technology offers the potential to provide enhanced learning opportunities to a wider audience than ever before. (Bayne et.,2006) have suggested that a country wishing to become a successful knowledge economy must also become a learning society. Early knowledge management technologies included online corporate directories as tools for locating expertise, as well as document management systems. With the early development of collaboration technologies, in particular Lotus Notes, knowledge management technologies advanced in the 1990s. Subsequent efforts in knowledge management have made use of semantic technologies for search and retrieval, as well as the development of e-learning tools for communities of practice. Knowledge management is an essential process that concerns the creation of a knowledge-sharing environment for the distribution, adoption and exchange of information within an organization (Capozzi,2007; Kasowitz,1998; Lorrain,2007).The similarities between knowledge management and e-learning theory reveal a powerful relationship that can sometimes lead to confusion between these two fields.

Learning Networks

A learning network is defined as a process for developing and maintaining relationships with individuals and information, while fostering communication to support each other in the acquisition of knowledge. In this way, a learning network offers enhanced opportunities and enables its members to engage online, sharing their knowledge and expertise. (Hiltz, S.R. and Turoff, M. 2002) argue that the use of pen and paper in our current education system presents gaps and challenges in the face of the rapid evolution of disciplines in today's global context. The use of personal learning networks will enable connections to be made and knowledge to be developed, enabling workers to keep up to date in their field of expertise.

E-Learning Models

A first common distinction between e-learning models is to classify them according to whether they are: (1) training offered entirely off-line (asynchronous training), (2) training offered remotely in real time (synchronous virtual classroom, also known as "distributed classroom", where the trainer is in one place and the learners in another) or (3) training combining these two remote modalities, or combining presence and distance. In the case of combined formulas, we speak of bimodal, hybrid or blended learning. Currently, companies are turning to e-learning for training that combines presence and distance (Marchand, 2003; MDERR, 2004; D'Halluin et al., 2003). The distributed classroom model does not seem to be in vogue.

Mingasson (2002) proposes a typology combining three criteria: the existence or absence of a face-to-face component, the presence or absence of a tutor or trainer (who may himself be present or remote) and the existence or absence of group work. He thus distinguishes four types of virtual training model: isolated e-learning; e-learning + tutor; e-learning + face-to-face + tutor; e-learning + tutor + face-to-face + group. Companies do not seem to be moving towards online-only self-training programs (Marchand, 2003). According to D'Halluin (et al., 2003), they are opting for tutored training and diversifying the forms of support. Moreover, presence and distance are combined in various ways in hybrid formulas, depending on the type of content addressed (D'Halluin et al., 2003):

- Tutor-led face-to-face session followed by online self-study.
- Alternating face-to-face courses and tutored distance learning sessions covering the same body of knowledge, but from a practical (face-to-face courses) and theoretical (distance learning sessions) point of view.
- Alternating face-to-face and distance learning sessions covering different areas of knowledge; etc. Other distinctions can also be made between e-learning models.

For example, a distinction can be made between training provided outside the work environment and training integrated into the employee's own tasks in the form of a "performance support system": The employee then has access to learning modules or online help or even an intelligent system consultant is needed during the performance of the task available at any time. This is "just in time" training.

As a result, e-learning comes in many different forms, and each company needs to find the option that best suits its employees, business profile and resource needs.

The Tools of E-Learning

We will explore three types of e-learning tools: curriculum tools, digital library tools and knowledge representation tools.

Generally speaking, it can be said that each type of tool focuses on different aspects of the process. Curriculum tools provide a systematic, standardized environment to support classroom learning; their functionality is particularly useful at the initiation and selection stages. Digital library tools facilitate efficient access to resources to encourage exploration and collection, while knowledge representation tools focus on the formulation and representation of knowledge.

Curriculum Tools

Curriculum tools are widely used in high schools and colleges. Materials are selected and organized to facilitate classroom activities. Additional tools such as discussion forums and online quizzes are integrated to facilitate collaboration and assessment. A typical business course tool consists of three elements: pedagogical tools, management tools and student tools. Pedagogical tools include course design and online quizzes with automatic grading. Management tools include file management, authentication and authorization.

Digital Library Tools

Digital library tools focus on locating resources. These features support the exploration and collection phases of information retrieval. Digital library tools help users find the right information in a wide range of digital documents. Digital library functions often include searching, browsing and discovering special collections or exhibitions. Search and browse to find resources and explore related topics. Special collections or exhibitions contain selected materials that represent unique treasures for the interested user.

Knowledge Representation Tools

Knowledge representation tools are a great help to learners, enabling them to visually examine, capture or develop knowledge. Curriculum tools, on the other hand, rely primarily on a textual, curriculum-centric approach to describing course content. However, this approach often fails to establish the relationship between the concepts and skills covered in one course and those covered in another. What's more, it fails to show the knowledge base the learner will have acquired by the end of his or her course of study. A visualization tool can engage both learners and instructors in an active learning process by enabling them to construct semantic spatial representations of the knowledge, concepts and skills the learner possesses and acquires (Thomson, J. R. and Cooke, J.2000).

The evolution of e-learning offers a variety of tools to support instructional designers throughout the analysis, design, implementation and delivery of Web-based instruction (Bruce, L. R. and Sleeman, P. J. 2000). On the one hand, it is essential to provide automated support through authoring tools (Campbell, J. D. and Mahling, D. E. 1998; Kasowitz,1998; Maier, R. and Thalmann, S. 2007), but on the other hand, these tools must also implement design methodologies appropriate to e-learning processes (Douglas,2001; Sharma et al.,2009).

THE ADVANTAGES AND LIMITATIONS OF E-LEARNING

Advantages of E-Learning

Online learning may not be the best option for every learner pursuing a college degree, but the advantages seem to outweigh the disadvantages.

Study anytime, anywhere: The biggest advantage of online learning is that you can study anytime, anywhere. No matter where in the country you live, you can take this course and start learning. Even if your course is offered by an international school, you can easily access course materials even if you are a citizen of another country. No matter where you live on earth, you can benefit from all knowledge and training (Nagrale, 2013).

Save a lot of money: According to Bijeesh (2017), the costs associated with a distance-learning degree, online or otherwise, can be considerably more affordable than a traditional on-campus degree. Students looking for economically viable options can therefore choose a distance learning program. You don't have to live in the same city or country as the educational institution of your choice. You can study wherever you are, as long as you have a computer and an Internet connection. What's more, the fees for courses offered by distance learning centers are lower than those of traditional educational institutions (Brown, 2017).

No commute: Nagrale (2013) said that if you choose e-learning, there's no need to take crowded buses or local trains. All you need is a computer at home with an Internet connection. The whole university is in your room and you don't need to go outside. Moving is the hardest part, because you lose a lot of time, money and, above all, energy. Nobody likes to spend a lot of time moving.

Flexibility of choice: Learners are usually given a fixed learning schedule when they opt for traditional learning methods. When learners study in a traditional classroom, they may be forced to move at a faster pace than they would like (Ouariach et al., 2023). However, the different types of e-learning offer learners the freedom to define their own timetable, adapted to their convenience, without being constrained by a regular learning schedule. Even if they are not directly involved in the learning process, distance learning programs offer them the flexibility to choose their own learning path (Brown, 2017).

Time savings: According to Bijeesh (2017), it's argued that there's no time wasted travelling to university, waiting for a bus or a train. In a distance learning program, your classroom is right in your room - with study materials on your desk or electronic resources on your computer. Time-poor students can therefore consider distance learning as an option, enabling them to pursue their studies from the comfort of their own home.

Earn while you learn: For those who aspire to enhance their CV by gaining a higher degree without leaving their current job, e-learning can be the ideal solution. This gives learners the opportunity to continue to support themselves financially while improving their qualifications, as distance learning offers them the chance to learn while earning (Brown, 2017).

The Limits of E-Learning

While online learning offers more people the opportunity to access higher education, it doesn't come with only advantages and benefits.

High chance of distraction: According to Bijeesh's 2017 argument, in the absence of face-to-face interaction with a teacher and classmates who can serve as constant reminders for pending assignments, there's a high chance of getting distracted and losing track of deadlines. To succeed in a distance learning course, it's essential to maintain motivation and concentration. However, if you tend to procrastinate and struggle to meet deadlines, distance learning may not be the most suitable option. What's more, any doubts or uncertainties that arise need to be resolved independently, as it's not possible to chat with friends and colleagues as you normally would in a face-to-face course. It is therefore vital to remain motivated and focused in order to fully succeed in a course (Brown, 2017).

Complicated technology: as Brown explained in 2017, any student wishing to enroll in a distance learning program must invest in a variety of equipment, such as a computer, webcam and stable Internet connection. It's important to note that there is absolutely no physical contact between students and instructors, as instruction is delivered exclusively online. This technological dependence is a major drawback of distance learning. In the event of a software or hardware malfunction, the course session can be interrupted, which can disrupt the learning process. What's more, the inherent complexity of the technology used in distance learning limits access to online education to students who are comfortable with computers and technology.

No social interaction: Learners often find themselves studying alone in distance learning, which can lead to a sense of isolation and the lack of physical social interaction that usually accompanies classroom attendance. What's more, they don't have the opportunity to practice lessons verbally. The lack of physical interaction in the educational process can give rise to various problems, such as increased feelings of hostility and isolation (Dyrud, 2000). Brown (2017) supports the idea that learning within a physical institution allows students to meet and interact with individuals from different backgrounds in a personal way. Distance learning limits students to online courses and learning resources. Although they can interact via online discussions, forums, e-mail and/or videoconferencing software, this experience cannot be compared to that in a traditional university environment. The controversial research conducted by Hara and Kling (2000) also revealed that the difficulties and discomfort experienced by online students may not be sufficiently understood. Working alone at night led to many complications and depressing experiences.

Difficulty keeping in touch with instructors: When learners face difficulties with their homework or have questions about a course in a traditional face-to-face environment, it's usually fairly straightforward to talk to the instructor before or after class, or even to schedule online meetings at another time. In distance learning, however, they find it more difficult to get in touch with their instructor. Even if they can send an e-mail, this does not guarantee them an immediate response as if they could sit face-to-face with their instructor (Hutt, 2017).

Job markets don't accept online degrees: According to Nagrale's observations in 2013, relying exclusively on distance learning to earn a degree can be risky. While you may indeed get a degree, it may not be recognized by private companies on the job market, and the same issue arises for government jobs. Employers still have a preference for a degree issued by a traditional educational institution over an online or distance learning degree. They see distance learning as not yet a serious form of education.

E-learning has both advantages and disadvantages. It offers greater flexibility and accessibility, enabling learners to study at their own pace and balance personal obligations with academic goals. However, it can also lead to a lack of social interaction and a sense of isolation, as well as technical challenges and limited recognition on the job market. Learners need to be motivated, disciplined and equipped with technical skills to make the most of e-learning.

Educational establishments must also continue to improve e-learning methods and strengthen the recognition of diplomas awarded in this form. Ultimately, e-learning may be a viable option for many learners, but it's not for everyone.

ONLINE COMMUNICATION TOOLS

This section presents a variety of synchronous and asynchronous communication tools that can be used to create a complete and enriching learning experience. Synchronous tools enable real-time communication and collaboration, promoting simultaneous interaction at a distance. However, it should be noted that these tools require simultaneous participation, which can pose problems due to time zone differences and scheduling conflicts. In addition, their high cost and bandwidth requirements can be obstacles to their effectiveness (Obasa et al.,2013).

As for online communication tools, they encompass a variety of technologies that enable learners and teachers to communicate and collaborate at a distance. These tools include discussions, forums, videoconferencing, interactive whiteboards, file-sharing tools, live polls, and many others. In the context of e-learning, these tools are becoming increasingly important, as they facilitate interaction and communication, which are essential to support learners' learning. They offer many advantages, such as the ability to communicate in real time, collaborate remotely, share resources and ideas, ask questions and receive feedback online.

However, using these tools can present challenges in terms of time management, technological mastery and learner engagement. It is therefore crucial to choose yappropriate communication tools based on the specific needs of the learning context, while taking into account learners' preferences and abilities (Obasa et al.,2013).

Remote collaboration is facilitated by document sharing tools, virtual workspaces and project management applications. These tools enable learners to work together efficiently, even from a distance. It's important to understand the differences between asynchronous communication (e-mail, forums...) and synchronous communication (live videoconferencing...). Asynchronous communication allows for temporal flexibility, while synchronous communication favors real-time interaction.

Synchronous Tools

Synchronous communication tools refer to technologies that enable real-time interaction between participants. They are widely used in e-learning, offering learners the opportunity to collaborate, interact and communicate with teachers and other learners in real time. These tools can be applied in a variety of contexts, such as virtual classrooms, online discussions, live tutoring sessions, webinars, virtual meetings, and many others. Table 2 below shows some examples of the tools available for synchronous technologies.

Table 2. Synchronous communication tools (Zahra et al., 2023)

Synchronous communication tool	Definition	Use	Disadvantages
Chat	A real-time communication tool that enables users to communicate instantly with each other via text messages.	Chats can be used for group discussions, live tutoring sessions and interactions between learners and teachers. Chats can also be used for review and support activities between learners.	Chats can be difficult to manage in terms of time, organization and equitable learner participation.
Videoconferencing	A real-time communication tool that lets users see each other and communicate live via video and sound.	Videoconferencing can be used for presentations, group discussions, live tutoring sessions and interactions between learners and teachers..	Videoconferences can require high bandwidth and sophisticated technology, which can pose challenges for users with limited resources. Videoconferences can also be difficult to plan and coordinate.
Interactive whiteboard	A tool that lets users draw and write on an online whiteboard, in real time.	Interactive whiteboards can be used for presentations, group discussions, live tutoring sessions and collaborative activities between learners and teachers.	Interactive whiteboards can be difficult to use for users with little experience of online technologies. Interactive whiteboards can also require high bandwidth and sophisticated technology, which can pose challenges for users with limited resources.
Real-time polling	A tool that allows users to ask questions and gather feedback in real time from learners.	Real-time surveys can be used to assess learner understanding, gather feedback on presentations or activities and encourage active learner participation.	Real-time surveys can be limited by the number of participants or learner preferences. Real-time surveys can also be difficult to plan and coordinate.

Asynchronous Tools

Asynchronous communication tools refer to applications or platforms that enable users to communicate at different times, without needing to be connected at the same time. These tools enable users to leave messages, reply to previously sent messages and exchange information without requiring real-time interaction. Table 3 below gives some examples of the tools available for asynchronous technologies.

Practical examples of online communication tools, techniques, and their application in different e-learning contexts

- **Discussion Forums:**
  Tool: Online forum platforms.
  Technique: Creation of thematic discussion threads, moderation.
  Application: Learners can discuss academic topics, ask questions, share resources and debate key concepts.
- **Video conferencing:**
  Tools: platform LMS (Learning Management System), Zoom, Microsoft Teams, Google Meet.
  Technique: Organize live sessions, use split-screen functionalities.
  Application: Teachers can give live lessons, organize seminars, workshops, presentations and question-and-answer sessions.

Table 3. Asynchronous communication tools (Zahra et al., 2023)

Asynchronous communication tool	Definition	Use	Disadvantages
Forum	An online discussion forum refers to a website or app that enables users to engage in conversations on various subjects. These forums are structured with topics, making it easy for users to read and respond to messages whenever they want. Discussion forums are commonly utilized in online communities, news groups, help websites, and any other scenario that necessitates ongoing dialog.	Exchange information and views, and share knowledge. Discussion forums, whether integrated into an LMS or stand-alone platforms (example: Moodle, EDX, Chamilo …), encourage asynchronous exchanges. They enable learners to take part in debates, ask questions and share ideas at their own pace.	Difficulty finding relevant information and risk of trolling or hate speech.
Email	Email, also known as email, is a digital message that can be sent and received through messaging applications. They serve as a means of communication for personal and professional purposes. What's special about emails is their asynchronous nature, which allows them to be sent and replied to at will, regardless of time. Additionally, email offers the convenience of organization and archiving, ensuring easy access for future reference.	Electronic message exchange.	Difficulty keeping track of conversations and risk of data loss.
blogs	A blog is a website or application where users can publish articles, images and videos. Blogs can be used for personal or professional communication, such as promoting products or services, publishing educational or informative content, etc. Readers can comment on blogs and report on discussions.	Publishing content, sharing opinions.	Privacy risk and risk of negative comments.
Wiki	A wiki is a website or application that allows users to create and edit content. Wikis can be used for collaborative projects, education and documentation. Wikis allow users to create and modify pages, track changes and discuss modifications. Wikis can be used to defer discussions and modifications.	Collaboration and knowledge sharing.	Risk of publishing conflicts and need to protect sensitive information.
Collaborative dashboard	Collaborative dashboards are online tools that enable users to work together on projects. Dashboards can contain task lists, schedules, calendars, graphs and other useful information. Collaborative dashboards enable users to share files and comments, and work together on tasks.	Share data, indicators, reports, graphs and dashboards with other users in real time.	Technical complexity, high cost and lack of user commitment.

- **Electronic Messaging:**
  Tool: E-mails.
  Technique: One-to-one communication, quick response.
  Application: Learners can contact teachers to ask questions, request help or submit assignments.
- **Tool: Chat**
  Technique: Real-time discussions, questions and answers, instant interaction.
  Application:
    - Synchronized Teaching: Hold live chat sessions for interactive discussions on specific topics. This encourages learner engagement and allows questions to be answered in real time.
    - Group Collaboration: Chat can be used for group collaboration, where learners work together to solve problems or complete projects.
    - Remote Support: Teachers can offer fast, personalized support to learners by answering their questions via chat, which is particularly useful for distance learning.
- **Tool: Wiki**
  Technique: Collaborative, content creation, shared editing.
  Application:
    - Knowledge building: Wikis can be used for learners to collaborate on the creation of learning resources. They can write articles, create glossaries, or develop knowledge bases.
    - Collective editing: Wikis enable several people to contribute to a document. This can be used for group projects, improving articles or reports, or co-writing documents.
    - Tracking revisions: Wikis keep a revision history, making it easy to track individual contributions and content evolution.
- **Educational Social Networks:**
  Tools: Edmodo, Schoology.
  Technique: Creation of class groups, resource sharing.
  Application: Promote peer-to-peer communication, share news, homework and discussions.
- **Blogs and Online Journals:**
  Tools: WordPress, Blogger.
  Technique: Writing blog posts, commenting.
  Application: Encourage learners to reflect on their learning, share their ideas and comment on others' posts.
- **Webinars:**
  Tool: Online webinar platforms.
  Technique: Live presentations, interactive sessions.
  Application: Organize online training, presentations and conferences.
- **Learning Management Systems (LMS):**
  Tool: Moodle, Blackboard.
  Technique: Setting up course modules, discussions, messaging.
  Application: Create complete e-learning environments with integrated communication tools.

The online communication examples and techniques listed above are flexible and can be adapted to the specific needs of our online courses and target audiences. It is essential to select the communication tools that best match our educational objectives and to integrate them strategically into our online teaching. This customization helps create more effective and engaging online learning experiences that promote learner success. By judiciously adapting these tools to our teaching environments, we can enhance communication, interaction and collaboration while meeting the individual needs of our learners.

ONLINE COMMUNICATION TOOLS IN E-LEARNING

The Effectiveness of These Online Communication Tools in E-Learning

The use of communication tools in e-learning has become increasingly important due to the move towards virtual classrooms. The study revealed that synchronous communication technologies, in particular platforms such as Moodle, EDX, and Chamilo are becoming increasingly prevalent in online courses. However, questions remain as to the effectiveness of these tools for online learning. The study showed that synchronous communication technology can improve the development and perceptions of the classroom community in online courses (Belt et al.,2023). Participants reported using synchronous technology in a variety of ways, including lectures, discussions, comments and annotations, assessments and recordings with students. Recommendations for facilitating synchronous sessions in online environments include limiting transmissive teaching, reinforcing peer interaction and collaboration, and engaging with students with empathy. Furthermore, productive and meaningful interaction during synchronous sessions requires intentional but flexible facilitation, while some features can be controlled by instructors whereas others cannot. Although synchronous communication technology has advantages, asynchronous text communication has limitations that affect its effectiveness in e-learning. These limitations include a lack of non-verbal cues and spontaneity, creating a sense of isolation or separation and requiring time to develop conversations. However, the visual element of real-time communication can illuminate perceptions of the classroom community in new or diverse ways (Belt et al., 2023). It is therefore important that instructors use communication tools intentionally and in ways that maximize their benefits while minimizing their limitations.

Online communication tools can be highly effective in e-learning when used thoughtfully, aligned with pedagogical objectives, and designed to meet learners' needs. Effectiveness depends on the quality of communication, learner engagement, teacher responsiveness and the ability to personalize instruction. Continuous evaluation and adjustment are essential to maximize effectiveness.

Factors Influencing the Effectiveness of Communication Tools in E-Learning

E-learning has become an increasingly popular mode of education owing to the ease of access and flexibility it affords. However, the efficacy of communication tools in e-learning is influenced by a variety of factors. A crucial factor is the role of faculty and the support available from the university. Support from universities and faculty, as well as motivational factors, have a positive impact on the quality of e-learning experiences (Saleem et al., 2022). However, situational factors such as poor internet quality and power outages can negatively impact the effectiveness of communication tools in e-learning.

Additionally, poor communication skills can lead to lack of comprehension of instructions and transmission of meanings, negatively affecting the quality of e-learning experiences. Technological malfunctions also have the potential to impact the effectiveness of communication tools in e-learning, as do differing levels of digital proficiency among students. Finally, diminished human interaction is a concern in e-learning, as reduced engagement can decrease student motivation and involvement (Saleem et al., 2022). While e-learning presents opportunities through its accessibility and flexibility, optimizing the role of support systems, technology, and communication remains imperative to realizing its full benefits.

Communication is of paramount importance in e-learning. Without it, the effective transmission of knowledge and the development of a virtual learning community would be compromised. Fortunately, today's digital communication tools offer many ways of bridging the physical distance between teachers and learners.

Synchronous platforms make it possible to recreate the real-time dialogue so essential to understanding and interactivity. Online forums and blogs, meanwhile, enable delayed but equally constructive exchanges. Educators can also use messaging, document sharing, and comments to provide personalized feedback.

Communication and communication tools play a key role in facilitating e-learning by offering opportunities for interaction, collaboration, personalization, and feedback. They create dynamic, flexible learning environments that promote learner success in online courses.

CONCLUSION

Exploring communication and communication tools for online learning is crucial in distance learning. By understanding specific communication needs and selecting appropriate tools, teachers can create interactive and collaborative e-learning environments. Online learning requires investigating communication and communication technologies, which is essential for remote learning. In order to develop dynamic and collaborative e-learning environments, educators must first understand each student's specific communication needs before choosing the right technologies. Learners may connect, communicate, and interact with teachers and peers via the deliberate use of communication technologies, which increases motivation, engagement, and produces better learning results. To make sure that communication technologies continue to satisfy the shifting demands of students and educators in a developing digital environment, ongoing study and assessment are required. We can create new e-learning possibilities and give all learners engaging, pertinent learning experiences by combining efficient communication techniques with the appropriate instruments.

REFERENCES

Abbad, M. M., Morris, D., & de Nahlik, C. (2009). Looking under the Bonnet: Factors Affecting Student Adoption of E-Learning Systems in Jordan. *The International Review of Research in Open and Distance Learning*.

Al-Samarraie, H., Selim, H., Teo, T., & Zaqout, F. (2017). Isolation and distinctiveness in the design of e-learning systems influence user preferences. *Interactive Learning Environments*, 25(4), 452–466. doi:10.1080/10494820.2016.1138313

Alarifi, Y. (2003). E-learning Technology: Promising Method. *E-learning International Conference*. Riyadh: King Faisal School.

Algahtani, A. F. (2011). *Evaluating the Effectiveness of the E-learning Experience in Some Universities in Saudi Arabia from Male Students' Perceptions, Durham theses*. Durham University.

Ally, M. (2004). Foundations of Educational Theory for Online Learning. In T. Anderson & F. Elloumi (Eds.), Theory and Practice of Online Learning (pp. 3-31). Athabasca University & Creative Commons.

Almosa, A. (2002). *Use of Computer in Education* (2nd ed.). Future Education Library.

Almosa, A., & Almubarak, A. (2005). E-learning Foundations and Applications. Saudi Arabia: Riyadh.

Anderson, M., & Jackson, D. (2001). Computer systems for distributed and distance learning. *Journal of Computer Assisted Learning, 16*(3), 213–228. doi:10.1046/j.1365-2729.2000.00134.x

Anderson, T., & Rivera Vargas, P. (2020). A critical look at educational technology from a distance education perspective. *Digital Education Review, 2020*(37), 208–229. doi:10.1344/der.2020.37.208-229

Barraket, J., Payne, A., Scott, G., & Cameron, L. (2000). *Equity and the Use of Communications Technology in Higher Education: A UTS Case Study*. Department of Education, Science and Training.

Bates, A. W. (2005). *Distance Education in a Dual Mode Higher Education Institution: A Canadian Case Study [Electronic Version]*. Centre for Distance Education, Korean National Open University. https://www.tonybates.ca/papers/KNOUpaper.htm

Belt, E. S., & Lowenthal, P. R. (2023). Synchronous video-based communication and online learning: An exploration of instructors' perceptions and experiences. *Education and Information Technologies, 28*(5), 4941-4964.

Berelson, B., & Steiner, G. (1964). *Human Behavior*. Harcourt, Brace, & World.

Berge, Z. L., & Muilenburg, L. Y. (2013). *Handbook of Mobile Learning*. Routledge. doi:10.4324/9780203118764

Berger, C. R., & Calabrese, R. J. (1974). Some explorations in initial interaction and beyond: Toward a developmental theory of interpersonal communication. *Human Communication Research, 1*(2), 99–112. doi:10.1111/j.1468-2958.1975.tb00258.x

Bijeesh, N. A. (2017). Advantages and disadvantages of distance learning. *India Education*. http://www.indiaeducation.net/online-education/articles/advantages-and-disadvantages-of-distance learning.html

Blum, K. (1999). Providing Equitable Adult Education. *Feminista!, 2*(8)

Boullier, D. (2013, 01 mars). Cours en ligne massifs et ouverts: la standardisation ou l'innovation? *Le Monde*.

Brown, C. (2017). *Advantages and disadvantages of distance learning*. EZ Talks. https://www.eztalks.com/elearning/advantages-and-disadvantages-of-distance-learning.html

Bruce, L. R., & Sleeman, P. J. (2000). *Instructional Design: a primer*. Information Age Publishing.

Campbell, J. D., & Mahling, D. E. (1998). A Visual Language System for Developing and Presenting Internet-Based Education. In *Proceedings of IEEE Symposium on Visual Languages*. IEEE. 10.1109/VL.1998.706135

Capozzi, M. M. (2007). Knowledge Management Architectures Beyond Technology. *First Monday*, *12*(6). http://firstmonday.org/htbin/cgiwrap/bin/ojs/index.php/fm/article/view/1 871/1754

Cartier, F. A. (1959). The President's Letter. *Journal of Communication, 9*(1), 5. doi:10.1111/j.1460-2466.1959.tb00285.x

Chu, R. J. C. (2010). How family support and Internet self-efficacy influence the effects of e-learning among higher aged adults–Analyses of gender and age differences. *Computers & Education*, *55*(1), 255–264. doi:10.1016/j.compedu.2010.01.011

Cialdini, R. B., & Cialdini, R. B. (2007). *Influence: The psychology of persuasion* (Vol. 55). Collins.

Clark, R., & Mayer, R. (2008). e-Learning and the Science of Instruction: Proven Guidelines for Consumers and Designers of Multimedia Learning. Pfeiffer.

Clevenger, T. Jr. (1991). Can one not communicate? A conflict of models. *Communication Studies*, *42*(4), 340–353. doi:10.1080/10510979109368348

Cross, J. (2004). *An informal history of eLearning*. Emerald.

Croxton, R. A. (2014). The role of interactivity in student satisfaction and persistence in online learning. *Journal of Online Learning and Teaching*, *10*(2), 314.

D'Halluin, C., Boudry, T., Charlet, D., Clavel, D., Desprez, C., Dewulf, B., Le Ven, O., Merveille, S., & Warocquier, A. (2003). Les formations en ligne: Points de vue de responsables de grandes entreprises de la distribution et des services. *Distances et Savoirs*, *4*(4), 517–531. doi:10.3166/ds.1.517-531

Dance, F. E. (1970). The "concept" of communication. *Journal of Communication*, *20*(2), 201–210. doi:10.1111/j.1460-2466.1970.tb00877.x

Dance, F. E. X., & Larson, C. E. (1976). *The Functions of Human Communication: A Theoretical Approach*. Holt, Rinehart & Winston.

Dean, C., & Whitlock, Q. (1992). *A handbook of computer-based training. Based Training*. Nichols Publishing Company.

Dewey, J. (2008). The Later Works of John Dewey: Vol. 12. *1925 - 1953: 1938, Logic: The Theory of Inquiry (Collected Works of John Dewey 1882-1953)* (1st ed.). Southern Illinois University Press.

Dillenbourg, P., & Traum, D. (1999*). The long road from a shared screen to a shared understanding*. C., I., Hoadley, & J.R. (Eds.), Proceedings of the 3rd Conference on Computer Supported Collaborative Learning, Stanford.

Douglas, I. (2001). Instructional Design Based on Reusable Learning Object: Applying Lessons of Object-Oriented Software Engineering to Learning System Design. In *Proceeding ASEE/IEEE Frontiers in Education Conference*. IEEE. 10.1109/FIE.2001.963968

Dyrud, M. A. (2000). The third wave: A position paper. *Business Communication Quarterly*, *63*(3), 81–93. doi:10.1177/108056990006300310

Fletcher, J. D., & Rockaway, M. R. (1986). *Military Contributions to Instructional Technology*. Praeger.

Garrison, D. R. (2011). *E-Learning in the 21st Century: A Framework for Research and Practice.* Routledge.

Garrison, D. R., & Vaughan, N. D. (2008). *Blended learning in higher education: Framework, principles, and guidelines.* John Wiley & Sons.

Gauvreau, C. (1994). Armand Mattelart, L'invention de la communication, Éditions La Découverte, Paris, 1994, 376 p. *Cahiers de Recherche Sociologique,* (23), 202–204. doi:10.7202/1002258ar

Goralski, M. A. (2008). The concept of implementing effective criteria for learning assessments in a virtual environment. *Journal of International Business Disciplines,* 2(3), 127–141.

Gove, P. B. (1986). *New International Dictionary.* Merriam-Webster Inc.

Hall, R. N. (1959). Recombination processes in semiconductors. *Proceedings of the IEE-Part B: Electronic and Communication Engineering, 106*(17S), 923-931. 10.1049/pi-b-2.1959.0171

Hara, N., & Kling, R. (2000). Student distress in a web-based distance education course. *Information Communication and Society, 3*(4), 557–579. doi:10.1080/13691180010002297

Herring, S. (1999). The rhetorical dynamics of gender harassment on-line. *The Information Society, 15*(3), 151–167. doi:10.1080/019722499128466

Hiltz, S.R. & Turoff, M. (2002). What makes learning networks effective? *Communications of the ACM.* ACM.

Hoben, J. B. (1954). English Communication at Colgate Re-examined. *Journal of Communication, 4*(3), 77. doi:10.1111/j.1460-2466.1954.tb00232.x

Holmes, B., & Gardner, J. (2006). *E-Learning: Concepts and Practice.* SAGE Publications. doi:10.4135/9781446212585

Horton, W. K. (2001). *Leading E-Learning.* ASTD.

Hutt, M. (2017). Top 10 disadvantages of distance learning. *EZ Talks.* https://www.eztalks.com/elearning/top-10- disadvantages-of-distance-learning.html

Jonassen, D., Davidson, M., Collins, M., Campbell, J., & Haag, B. (1995). Constructivism and computer-mediated communication in distance education. *American Journal of Distance Education, 9*(2), 7–26. doi:10.1080/08923649509526885

Kasowitz, A. (1998). *Tool for Automating Instructional Design.* ERIC elearning house in Information Technology in Education. http://ericit.org/digests/EDO-IR- 1998-01.shtml

Keegan, D. (1995). *Distance education technology for the new millennium: Compressed videoteaching.* ZIFF Papiere. Hagen, Germany: Institute for research into Distance education.

Keller, C., & Cernerud, L. (2002). Students' perception of e-learning in university education. *Learning, Media and Technology, 27*(1), 55–67.

Khan, B. H. (2005). *Managing E-learning: Design, Delivery, Implementation and Evaluation.* Information Science Publishing. doi:10.4018/978-1-59140-634-1

Knoerr, H. (2005). TIC et motivation en apprentissage/enseignement des langues. Une perspective canadienne. Recherche et pratiques pédagogiques en langues de spécialité. *Cahiers de l'Apliut, 24*(2), 53–73. doi:10.4000/apliut.2889

Konstantinidis, A., Tsiatsos, T., & Pomportsis, A. (2009). Collaborative virtual learning environments: Design and evaluation. *Multimedia Tools and Applications, 44*(2), 279–304. doi:10.100711042-009-0289-5

Kotsilieris, T., & Dimopoulou, N. (2013). The Evolution of e-Learning in the Context of 3D Virtual Worlds. *Electronic Journal of e-Learning, 11*(2), 147–167.

Kukulska-Hulme, A. (2005). *Mobile Learning: A Handbook for Educators and Trainers*. Routledge.

Kuo, Y. C., Walker, A. E., Schroder, K. E., & Belland, B. R. (2014). Interaction, Internet self-efficacy, and self-regulated learning as predictors of student satisfaction in online education courses. *The Internet and Higher Education, 20*, 35–50. doi:10.1016/j.iheduc.2013.10.001

LaRose, R., Gregg, J., & Eastin, M. (1998). Audio graphic tele-courses for the Web: An experiment. *Journal of Computer-Mediated Communication, 4*(2), 0. doi:10.1111/j.1083-6101.1998.tb00093.x

Lim, F. P. (2017). An analysis of synchronous and asynchronous communication tools in e-learning. *Advanced Science and Technology Letters, 143*(46), 230–234. doi:10.14257/astl.2017.143.46

Lorrain, M. (2007). Strategies to Engage Online Students and Reduce Attrition Rates. *The Journal of Educators Online*.

Maier, R., & Thalmann, S. (2007). Describing learning objects for situationoriented knowledge management applications. In: N Gronau (ed) *4th Conference on Professional Konwledge Management Experiences and Visions*. GITO.

Maltz, L., & Deblois, P.The EDUCAUSE Current Issues Committee. (2005). Top Ten IT Issues. *EDUCAUSE Review, 40*(1), 15–28.

Marchand, L. (2003). e-learning en entreprise: Un aperçu de l'état des lieux au Canada et au Québec. *Distances et Savoirs, 4*(4), 501–516. doi:10.3166/ds.1.501-516

Mayes, T., de Freitas, S. (2004). *JISC e-Learning Models Desk Study, Stage 2: Review of e-learning theories frameworks and models*.

McQuail, D. (2010). The future of communication studies: A contribution to the debate. *Media and communication studies interventions and intersections, 27*.

Mehrabian, A. (1972). Some subtleties of communication. *Language, Speech, and Hearing Services in Schools, 3*(4), 62–67. doi:10.1044/0161-1461.0304.62

Miller, G. R. (1966). On Defining Communication: Another Stab. *Journal of Communication, 16*(2), 92. doi:10.1111/j.1460-2466.1966.tb00020.x PMID:5941548

Mingasson, M. (2002). *Le guide du e-learning: L'organisation apprenante*. Éditions d'Organisation.

Ministère du développement économique et régional et Recherche. (2004). *Industrie de la formation virtuelle: Profil industriel*. Québec: Direction générale des communications et des services à la clientèle.

Monge, P. R., & Contractor, N. S. (2003). *Theories of communication networks*. Oxford University Press. doi:10.1093/oso/9780195160369.001.0001

Moore, J. L., Dickson-Deane, C., & Galyen, K. (2011). e-Learning, online learning, and distance learning environments: Are they the same? *ScienceDirect,* 1-4.

Moore. (1990). Recent contributions to the theory of distance education. *Open Learning*, 11-14.

Nagrale, P. (2013). *Advantages and disadvantages of distance education.* Sure Job.https://surejob.in/advantages-anddisadvantages-of-distance-education.html

Nichols, M. (2003). A Theory for E-Learning. *Journal of Educational Technology & Society, 6*(2), 1–10.

O'Flaherty, J., & Phillips, C. (2015). The use of flipped classrooms in higher education: A scoping review. *The Internet and Higher Education, 25*, 85–95. doi:10.1016/j.iheduc.2015.02.002

Obasa, A. I., Eludire, A. A., & Ajao, T. A. (2013). A comparative study of synchronous and asynchronous e-learning resources. *International Journal of Innovative Research in Science, Engineering and Technology, 2*(11), 5938-5946.

Oblinger, D. G., & Hawkins, B. L. (2005). The myth about E-learning. *EDUCAUSE Review.*

Ouariach, S., Khaldi, M., Mohamed, E., & Khaldi, M. (2023). From the Choice of a Learning Management System to the Installation of a Platform in a Server. In M. Khaldi (Ed.), *Handbook of Research on Scripting, Media Coverage, and Implementation of E-Learning Training in LMS Platforms* (pp. 330–375). IGI Global., doi:10.4018/978-1-6684-7634-5.ch015

Ouariach, S., Khaldi, M., Mohamed, E., & Khaldi, M. (2023). The Flipped Classroom: From Passive Information Absorption to Active Learning. In S. Karpava (Ed.), *Handbook of Research on Language Teacher Identity* (pp. 269–293). IGI Global. doi:10.4018/978-1-6684-7275-0.ch015

Perraton, H. (2002). *Open and Distance Learning in the Developing World*. Routledge.

Petty, R. E., Cacioppo, J. T., Petty, R. E., & Cacioppo, J. T. (1986). *The elaboration likelihood model of persuasion*. Springer New York.

Richard, S., Gay, P., & Gentaz, É. (2021). Pourquoi et comment soutenir le développement des compétences émotionnelles chez les élèves âgés de 4 à 7 ans et chez leur enseignant. e? Apports des sciences cognitives. *Raisons éducatives, 25*(1), 261-287.

Robinson, P., & Cole, R. A. (2000). *Issues in web-based pedagogy: A critical primer*.

Rogers, E. M., & Kincaid, D. L. (1981). *Communication networks: Toward a new paradigm for research*. No Title.

Romero, P. (1984). *English for Business: Developing Communication Skills*. Katha Publishing Co., Inc.

Rouse, M. (2011, March). *Computer-Based Training (CBT)*.

Ruesch, J. (1957). Technology and Social Communication. In L. Thayer (Ed.), *Communication Theory and Research* (p. 462).

Saleem, F., AlNasrallah, W., Malik, M. I., & Rehman, S. U. (2022, April). Factors affecting the quality of online learning during COVID-19: Evidence from a developing economy. In Frontiers in Education (Vol. 7). Frontiers Media SA.

Sangra, A., Vlachopoulos, D., & Cabrera, N. (2012). *Building an Inclusive Definition of E-Learning: An Approach to the Conceptual Framework.* IRRODL.

Sangrà, A., Vlachopoulos, D., & Cabrera, N. (2012). Building an inclusive definition of e-learning: An approach to the conceptual framework. *International Review of Research in Open and Distance Learning, 13*(2), 145–159. doi:10.19173/irrodl.v13i2.1161

Schank, R. C. (2000). A Vision of Education for the 21st Century. *T.H.E. Journal, 27*(6), 43–45.

Schement, J. R. (2017). Communication and information. *Between communication and information*, 3-33.

Seels, B. B., & Richey, R. C. (2012). *Instructional technology: The definition and domains of the field.* IAP.

Sharma, R., Ekundayo, M. S., & Ng, E. (2009). Beyond the digital divide: Policy analysis for knowledge societies. *Journal of Knowledge Management, 13*(5), 373–386. doi:10.1108/13673270910988178

Shih, Y.-C., & Yang, M. T. (2008). A Collaborative Virtual Environment for Situated Language Learning Using VEC3D. *Journal of Educational Technology & Society, 11*, 56–68.

Shimura, K. (2006). *Computer-based learning and web-based training: A review.* Research Gate.

Siemens, G., & Long, P. (2011). Penetrating the Fog: Analytics in Learning and Education. *EDUCAUSE Review, 46*(5), 30–32.

Simonson, M., Smaldino, S., Albright, M., & Zvacek, S. (2000). *Teaching and Learning at a Distance: Foundations of Distance Education.* Merrill.

Swan, K. (2001). Virtual interaction: Design factors affecting student satisfaction and perceived learning in asynchronous online courses. *Distance Education, 22*(2), 306–331. doi:10.1080/0158791010220208

Team F. M. E. (2013). *Effective communication.* FME. www. free-management-ebooks. com/dldebkpdf/ fme-effective-communication. pdf

Tendero, E. (2009). *Fundamentals of Effective Speech and Oral Communication.* Mutya Publishing House, Inc.

Thomson, J. R., & Cooke, J. (2000). Generating Instructional Hypermedia with APHID. In Hypertext, 2000. doi:10.1145/336296.336492

Toffler, A. (1970). *Future shock.* Sydney.

Wang, F., Leary, K. A., Taylor, L. C., & Derosier, M. E. (2016). Peer and teacher preference, student–teacher relationships, student ethnicity, and peer victimization in elementary school. *Psychology in the Schools, 53*(5), 488–501. doi:10.1002/pits.21922

Weaver, W. (1949). *The mathematical theory of communication, by CE Shannon (and recent contributions to the mathematical theory of communication).* University of Illinois Press.

Wentling, T. L., Waight, C., Gallagher, J., La Fleur, J., Wang, C., & Kanfer, A. (2000). E-learning - a review of literature. *Knowledge and Learning Systems Group NCSA, 9*, 1–73.

Yarbro, J., McKnight, K., Elliott, S., Kurz, A., & Wardlow, L. (2016). Digital instructional strategies and their role in classroom learning. *Journal of Research on Technology in Education, 48*(4), 274–289. doi:10.1080/15391523.2016.1212632

Zahra, O. F., Amel, N., & Mohamed, K. (2023). *Communication Tools and E-Learning: A Revolution in the Research Methodology of Communication for a Pedagogical Scenario.*

Zeitoun, H. (2008). *E-learning: Concept, Issues, Application, Evaluation, Riyadh.* Dar Alsolateah publication.

Zengin, B., Arikan, A., & Dogan, D. (2011). Opinions of English major students about their departments' websites. *Contemporary Educational Technology, 2*(4), 294–307. doi:10.30935/cedtech/6060

Chapter 6
Collaborative Online Learning and Knowledge Appropriation

Ahmed Ibrahimi

https://orcid.org/0009-0004-8879-5561

Abdelmalek Essaadi University, Morocco

ABSTRACT

New ways of appropriating knowledge are emerging thanks to tools and technologies linked to education and learning. The chapter shows how collaborative work opens up multiple possibilities for integrating these tools. The authors sketch out the contours of collaborative learning supported by digital technologies. This online learning modality is accompanied by a pedagogical reflection that will serve as the basis for a proposed model of knowledge appropriation in an online collaborative environment.

INTRODUCTION

The study of the relationship between digital technology and learning cannot be done without invoking the concept of appropriation. This concept has enjoyed intellectual success, playing an important role in the scaffolding of numerous theories. However, the question of appropriation also revolves around the pedagogical entry point, in the sense that appropriation largely depends on the type of pedagogical focus adopted in the design of teaching-learning devices. Appropriation would then result from the nature of this focus and its degree of importance in the process of designing and planning teaching and learning situations.

On the other hand, collaborative e-learning has benefited from technological and pedagogical developments in recent years. On the technological front, it currently benefits from high-performance systems capable of managing interaction between tutors and learners. In terms of pedagogy, it benefits from the development of approaches that promote collaborative learning.

New ways of appropriating knowledge are emerging thanks to tools and technologies linked to education and "connected" learning. In this sense, collaborative work opens up multiple possibilities for integrating these tools. For example, CSCL (Computer-Supported Collaborative Learning) proposes the ground rules for collaborative learning supported by digital technologies. This online learning modality

DOI: 10.4018/979-8-3693-3128-6.ch006

Copyright © 2024, IGI Global. Copying or distributing in print or electronic forms without written permission of IGI Global is prohibited.

is then accompanied by a profound pedagogical reflection (Depover & al., 2003), which we highlight in this chapter, and to better install the modeling of knowledge appropriation in an online collaborative environment that we propose at the end of this chapter.

APPROPRIATION BETWEEN ONLINE LEARNING AND COLLABORATIVE LEARNING

Online Learning

Online learning, or e-learning, refers to all learning undertaken by electronic means. This means that different types fall under the umbrella of this term: educational websites, tele-training, telematics teaching and e-training. Redecker (2008, p.13) defines it as: "the use of new multimedia technologies and the Internet to improve the quality of learning by facilitating access to resources and services, as well as distance exchanges and collaboration".

While e-learning has been spreading in education since the 2000s, social networks (Facebook, Twitter, LinkedIn...) and social media (Wikipedia, YouTube, Second Life...) are currently focusing attention on the relevance of communication tools for e-learning. E-learning now goes by many names: social learning, mobile learning, serious games, learning 2.0, flipped learning or enhanced learning. In this way, learning is breaking out of its institutional straitjacket. This has several consequences: increased learner autonomy, decentralized knowledge distribution, faster access to available knowledge and a richer context for collaboration to create new knowledge.

Collaborative Learning

Piaget (1967) is one of the theorists opposed to individual learning. For him, learning can only take place if the relationship between the learner and the environment is established. This relationship is none other than the interaction between the learner's individual understanding of a phenomenon and his or her experience within an environment. This interaction generates a socio-cognitive conflict likely to stimulate learning.

Perret-Clermont & Bell (1991) add that in this environment, learners also interact with their peers. Oppositions can then be created, enabling the individual to question his or her initial understanding and discover a new perspective of understanding. This is where Vygotsky's (1978) concept of the "zone of proximal development" comes into its own. This zone is none other than the distance between what an individual can do alone and what he or she can do with the help of others. Roschelle & Teasley (1995) have developed this Vygotskyian concept by adding the idea of the "individual-plus". This comprises the individual's capabilities plus all the aids he or she can make use of within an environment. These aids may be human or material. The context in which learning takes place is therefore a key concept that several theorists have emphasized (Viau, 1997) and (Henri & Lundgren-Cayrol, 2001) in the context of collaborative learning.

Collaborative learning must first be defined in relation to cooperative learning. The difference between the two lies in the organization of the task, according to Hooper (1992). The main distinguishing feature between the two lies in their treatment of the task. The task is subdivided in one, but not in the other.

Cooperative learning subdivides the main task. Each member of the group becomes responsible for a sub-task, and the final product is made up of all the sub-tasks. Collaborative learning, on the other hand, advocates negotiation within the group around a common goal to jointly accomplish the main task in its entirety (Nachmias & al, 2000; Baker, 2002; Laferrière, 2003).

Beyond this distinction, collaborative learning involves a number of well-defined attitudes: self-explanation, appropriation, internalization and induction (Jermann, 2004).

Self-explanation: by explaining his or her own idea to another, the learner deepens his or her own way of reasoning.

- Appropriation: this is the result of a learner's regulation to consider the interlocutor.
- Internalization: when a learner makes the knowledge circulating within the collaborative group his or her own.
- Induction: this is a mechanism for synthesizing all individual representations within the collaborative group.

Henri & Lundgren-Cayrol (2001, p.42) summarize collaborative learning as an active process in which learners work to construct their own knowledge. The trainer plays the role of learning facilitator, while the group participates as a source of information, as a motivator, as a means of mutual help and support, and as a privileged place of interaction for the collective construction of knowledge. The collaborative approach recognizes the individual and reflexive nature of learning, as well as its social roots, by linking it to group interactions. The collaborative approach couples two approaches: that of the learner and that of the group. This clearly establishes the link between collaboration and the appropriation of knowledge.

Collaboration and Appropriation: A Group Dynamic

The nature of the task influences the observed effects on group dynamics (Shaw, 1981; Pavitt, 1998). Problem solving, for example, is a task in which the result achieved by the group is better than that of a task in which individuals work in isolation (Shaw, 1981; Bédard, Déziel & Lamarche, 1999). On the other hand, in a "precision" task, the group's result depends on which member is most competent at finding the solution (Shaw, 1981; Pavitt, 1998). The group therefore prevails over the individual in tasks requiring creativity, where each member of the group makes his or her own contribution.

Strijbos (2004) asserts that collaborative dynamics are more easily established in small groups. Faerber (2003, p. 6) reaffirms this, saying that too many people interacting leads to an explosion of information exchanged within the group, which can no longer be controlled by its members.

Individual investment decreases with increasing group size (Ringe lmann (1913) quoted by Abrami & al. (1995)). This gives rise to the phenomenon of "social laziness", which occurs when there is a "(...) visible reduction in the efforts made by each individual when working as part of a team". (Daele & Docq, 2002, p. 12). While there's no such thing as an ideal group size, collaborative work is more likely to take place in a smaller group. Transactive memory, for example, develops more easily in smaller teams, where learners communicate and interact more spontaneously (Jackson & Moreland, 2009; N. Michinov & E. Michinov, 2009).

According to Dillenbourg & al, (1996), collaborative work depends largely on the way in which the group is formed. Depover & al. (2003) list several modalities:

- The random mode, in which group members are allocated at random, without taking individual or collective characteristics into account.
- The opportunistic modality takes into account several criteria likely to facilitate the group's work and the completion of the collaborative task (geographical proximity, common availability at certain times of the day, etc.).
- The reasoned modality aims for efficiency in the collaborative dynamic through the choice of several criteria. By way of example, a certain degree of heterogeneity within a collaborative group favors the individual's decentralization in relation to his or her own point of view, and enables him or her to take into account a range of information likely to help him or her develop an original response (Bourgeois & Nizet, 1997).
- According to Doise & Mugny (1984) or Webb (1991), the best performing groups are those that bring together learners of slightly heterogeneous levels. Too much homogeneity or too much heterogeneity would be detrimental to the group's effectiveness.
- The spontaneous autonomous modality allows learners to compose their own group according to their affinities.

The quality of interactions between group members can be influenced by the distribution of roles. This distribution can be strict (a specific role is assigned to a given individual), permanent (the person taking on a role retains it throughout all collaborative tasks) or transient (roles can be swapped during a task) (De Lièvre, Temperman, Cambier & al., 2009).

APPROPRIATION BETWEEN MODEL AND DOMAIN

SECI Model

Much has been written on the subject of knowledge appropriation. One way of understanding this concept is to model it. To this end, Nonaka and Takeuchi propose a model called SECI (Socialization, Externalization, Combination, Internalization).

Nonaka & Takeuchi (1995) structure their model according to a distinction between tacit and explicit knowledge. The former is non-verbalized knowledge. The second, on the other hand, is codified knowledge (texts, diagrams, etc.). In this model, the processes of socialization (S), externalization (E), combination (C) and internalization (I) contribute effectively to the process of knowledge appropriation.

Socialization is the conversion of tacit knowledge into new tacit knowledge (sharing of personal experiences). Externalization converts tacit knowledge into explicit knowledge (concepts, models, theories, etc.). Combination converts explicit knowledge into explicit knowledge (knowledge reused in another form). Finally, internalization converts explicit knowledge into tacit knowledge by internalization in the form of a personal cognitive schema.

Lonchamp (2007, p. 3) synthesizes this model and gives a comprehensive definition of collaborative learning as follows:

"Any collaborative learning environment must therefore: (S) facilitate socialization i.e. the informal exchange of subjectivities, emotions, opinions, doubts, etc.; (E) facilitate externalization through the formalization of knowledge and its justification; (C) facilitate combination through comparison, synthesis,

reorganization, generalization; and (I) facilitate internalization, with, for example, means of exploring knowledge and means facilitating personal reflection."

Given these different considerations, the SECI model is taken into account to foster the appropriation process through collaborative work. However, in order to collaborate online, it is also necessary to use technology. To elucidate the relationship between the process of appropriation and that of collaboration through digital technology, we turn here to CSCL's own domain of "Computer-Supported Collaborative Learning".

CSCL Domain

CSCL (Computer-Supported Collaborative Learning) is a domain of study, originating in the educational sciences and specific to ICT-supported collaborative learning (Stahl, Koschmann & Suthers, 2006). It is particularly interested in the cognitive potential provided by technological artifacts within collaborative work (Depover, Karsenti & Komis, 2007) and in the evolution of these artifacts.

Certain learning theories (sociocultural learning, constructivism, cognitive flexibility) form the basis of CSCL. These theories state that man is an active creature. As such, he is always eager for knowledge, which he can only construct in a meaningful context. It is in this sense that CSCL intervenes by providing an authentic context in which the individual can satisfy his need for knowledge while contributing to the development of his cognitive capacities. In CSCL, individual appropriation is achieved through the creation of artifacts, activities and environments conducive to collaborative work. Thus, researchers in the field of CSCL stress the importance of individual learning through the collaborative process, and insist on the evolution of artifacts that place group learning in an authentic anchorage.

CSCL, however, has several definitions that highlight several characteristics. Among these characteristics, Klamma, Rohde & Stahl (2004) classify them according to three consubstantial levels:

- Knowledge development through collaboration ;
- Computer-supported learning;
- Online and distance learning

Soller & al. (1999), for their part, characterize CSCL according to five fundamental principles:

Participation: this principle correlates the degree of learning with the degree of participation in collaborative work. For this reason, certain artifacts well combined in a scenario can become a means of encouraging participation and, consequently, the appropriation of knowledge.

- Social contribution: In a collaborative group, shared knowledge contributes to the smooth running of the group. Every question asked, every clarification requested or every rephrasing sought, creates a social climate that helps collaborative work to function.
- Active conversation: conversation between members of a collaborative group contributes to collaborative learning in the sense that it encourages, solicits explanations and imposes justifications. Each member of the group can play a number of roles (mediator, objector, etc.) to stimulate the conversation.

- Performance analysis: this consists in discussing the progress made within the group and deciding together whether to continue, modify or cancel a course of action. Whether individual or collective, performance analysis remains an internal evaluation, in favor of the collaborative group.
- Promoting interaction: this consists in group members being interdependent. This interdependence triggers the process of promoting interaction. A concrete example of this is when learners help a member in difficulty or in search of understanding. Indeed, when each member of the group receives the help he or she needs "from and by" his or her peers at the right moment, the promotion of interaction gains in power and collaboration becomes more intense.
  - To preserve these different characteristics, we have taken care in the modeling proposed above to implement a collaborative script that enables the structuring of interactions between members of the collaborative group.
  - According to Dillenbourg & Jermann (2006, p. 46), scripts encourage the kind of interactions that don't occur in spontaneous collaboration, such as conflict resolution, mutual regulation or the construction of explanations. In fact, the collaborative script segments the task into several steps and assigns roles to learners to give rise to knowledge-generating interactions. The script is made up of micro-scripts and macro-scripts (Dillenbourg & Tchounikine, 2007). The former channel the individual actions of collaborative group members, while the latter structure the overall learning process.
  - Several examples of scripts have been developed in CSCL (Dillenbourg & Jermann, 2006) and have proved their effectiveness in various experiments (De Lièvre & Depover, 2007). Schellens & al. (2007) even propose a theoretical model based on principles of socioconstructivism and cognitive information processing, integrating three main dimensions:
- The individual learning process represented at the center of the model by the "Student a, b, n";
- The level of complexity of the task implemented in the CSCL environment;
- The intensity of interaction within the group.

If we are to study the relationship between ICT and learning, we must invoke the concept of appropriation. This concept has enjoyed intellectual success, playing an important role in the scaffolding of numerous theories. However, the question of appropriation also revolves around the pedagogical entry point, in the sense that appropriation largely depends on the type of pedagogical focus adopted in the design of teaching-learning devices. Appropriation would then result from the nature of this focus and its degree of importance in the process of designing and planning teaching and learning situations.

APPROPRIATION FROM A PEDAGOGICAL PERSPECTIVE

Appropriation and Pedagogical Design

The planning of teaching situations remains the gateway to many North American works in the field of " pedagogical design " (Brien, 1981), which is also referred to, in different nuances, as " Instructional design " (Reigeluth, 1999; Briggs, 1981), " Didactic engineering ", " Instructional planning " (Lebrun and Berthelot, 1994), or " Pedagogical engineering " (Paquette, 2002). Pedagogical design attempts to provide solutions to training problems (Romizowski, 1981) and to guide teachers in creating pertinent pedagogical objects.

Figure 1. Theoretical model proposed
(Schellens & al., 2007)

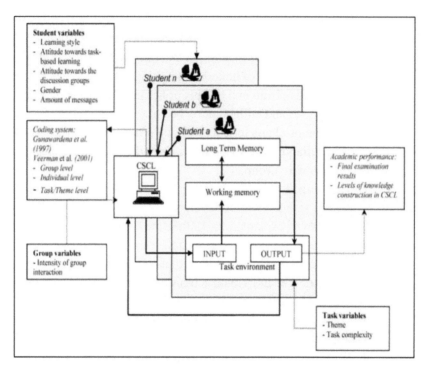

Prescription dominates these approaches, which combine learning theories with educational practices. Paquette (2002, p. 111) defines "pedagogical design" as "a set of theories and models for understanding, improving and applying teaching methods that promote learning". However, different pedagogical conceptions have shaped "pedagogical design". Gagné and al (1992) set out the rules for establishing a close link between the teacher's actions and the emergence of learning. In this way, they define different levels of learning, for which different pedagogies are set up, corresponding to different learning events. Depending on performance and type of knowledge, Merrill (1996) distinguishes between two types of prescriptions: those that correspond to a teacher-centered strategy (exposure) and those that correspond to a learner-centered strategy (research). Learner performance is classified according to three dimensions: remembering, using and creating. Knowledge is classified according to five types: facts, concepts, procedures, principles and processes. Merrill (2002) then outlines principles for promoting learning. He asks the teacher to engage learners in problem-solving, to activate their prior knowledge, to show them the new knowledge and to give them the opportunity to apply it and integrate it into their environment.

On the other hand, to sequence and organize learning situations, Reigeluth proposes specific rules that Paquette (2002) summarizes as follows:

- Respect for the course's initial organizational structure (conceptual, procedural, theoretical),
- Pedagogical conception according to a progression in the difficulty of the sequences,
- Definition of stages,
- Graphic summaries and synthesis to help the learner understand the structure of the content,
- Use of analogies to help the learner relate prior knowledge to the content,

- Use of tools to activate learners' cognitive strategies.

Le Brun and Berthelot (1994) refer to the pedagogical plan as the specification, planning and elaboration of teaching to create significant pedagogical situations for the learner. The pedagogical plan is implemented in a number of stages:

- organize learning into small, structured units,
- state objectives and adapt the task to the student's level to motivate learners,
- involve learners through questioning,
- solicit frequent feedback,
- respect each learner's own pace of learning.

Following on from Piaget's work, Jonnaert and Vander Broght (1999) offer a didactic model based on the constructivist paradigm of knowledge. This model revolves around three processes:

- the process of appropriating and constructing knowledge,
- the social process,
- the process of interaction between the individual and the environment.

Collaborative or cooperative activities are becoming increasingly important in learning situations. The resulting pedagogical design takes into account the learner's social dimension and the various interaction situations. For this reason, the notion of scripting also takes on its full value.

Pedagogical scripting of interaction situations

When we aim to give coherence to a learning situation by bringing together different objects and actors (learner, teacher, resource, activities, instruments, tools), we are in the process of pedagogical scripting. Pedagogical scripting is therefore the process of creating a pedagogical scenario that can be used in a learning context. The word "scenario", which forms the basis of all scriptwriting processes, has its origins in the arts (cinema to be precise), and is widely used in the fields of management, IT, telecommunications and ergonomics. It has only recently made its appearance in the field of education, where it is always associated with the adjective "pedagogical" or the noun complement "learning". This emergence of the term "pedagogical scenario" comes at a time when other terms had been carving out their place in the field of education.

According to Villiot-Leclercq and Pernin (2006), the term "pedagogical scenario" is associated, among the community of practice, with several other designations: "pedagogical activities", "pedagogical model", "synopsis", "pedagogical sequence", "teaching module", "pedagogical progression", "pedagogical path", "usage scenario", "supervision scenario", "dissemination scenario", "task sequence", "session", "storyboard", "conceptual frames", "learning sequence".

The pedagogical scenario becomes a framework for expressing the various interactions that take place in a teaching-learning situation. It is first and foremost a social framework conducive to interaction (Ferrais et al. 2005) and is a dual space, according to Bronckart's model (85): a space of interaction and a space of production of this interaction. Four parameters define this space of interaction: the social location (or zone of cooperation), the addressee, the enunciator and the communicative intentions (or goals). The notion of space takes on a particular value here, since in a face-to-face learning situation, spaces are joint. In an e-learning situation, on the other hand, spaces are disjointed due to distance.

TRANSACTIONAL DISTANCE IN A COLLABORATIVE ONLINE ENVIRONMENT

E-learning aims to reduce the distance between the learner and the training content, which may be remote for geographical, temporal, structural or social reasons. Several authors have examined these aspects (Peters, 1973; Keegan, 1986; Perraton, 1992; Jézégou, 1998; Glikman, 1999; Sabastia, 2002), but what is particularly important here is the distance between learner and teacher, called "transactional distance" by Moore & Kearsley (1996).

Transactional distance is measured by the degree of interaction between teacher and learner, according to the level of constraint imposed by the type of course. The more constraining the course, the weaker the degree of interaction between teacher and learner, and the greater the transactional distance. This applies to all types of teaching, whether distance or face-to-face. On the other hand, while some tend to invoke ICT to reduce this transactional distance, the reality may be different. Videoconferencing, where exchange between the teacher and a large number of students proves difficult, is a significant example. In this sense, the evolution of e-learning in relation to face-to-face teaching is nothing other than the ever-growing possibility of reducing transactional distance.

In fact, technological developments are enabling greater interactivity, and the pedagogical integration of this technology offers an alternative to face-to-face training. We defend the idea that today, at university, it's easier to respond to requests from distance learners because the techno-pedagogical device allows it (asynchronous discussion forums, synchronous chat rooms...) than to respond to these same students in the classroom, because the possibility of interaction with a large number of students is not possible. The effectiveness of distance learning can thus be measured through the notion of transactional distance. As Depover & Marchand (2002) have shown, this should not be measured solely on the basis of the quantity of interactions, but also on their pedagogical quality.

In this sense, distance gives new meaning to presence, to the point where Jézégou (2012) speaks of "presence at a distance". There are three aspects to this presence: socio-cognitive presence, socio-affective presence and pedagogical presence. These three aspects need to be taken into account when planning to set up an online techno-pedagogical device. Collaborative online learning better serves this "remote presence" and encourages the appropriation process. We therefore propose a model of the appropriation process that incorporates various other processes based on the principle of pedagogical alignment.

MODELING APPROPRIATION IN A COLLABORATIVE ONLINE ENVIRONMENT

Paquette, in a book devoted to pedagogical engineering (Paquette 2002), clearly shows that any pedagogical design must first be preceded by the identification, clarification, representation and modeling of knowledge.

The role of modeling in this approach then takes on a central role, because for Paquette, knowledge modeling precedes instructional design: "the first step in building a learning scenario is to examine the knowledge model associated with the learning unit and identify a core knowledge [...] This knowledge is then associated with a skill, to define the core competency that will guide the construction of the scenario". [...] This knowledge is then associated with a skill, to define the main competency that will guide the construction of the scenario". (Paquette 2002, p.208).

Giardina & Oubenaïssa (2003), following Paquette, Crevier & Aubin (1997), define the pedagogical scenario as a coherent structuring of two entities they call: "learning scenario" and " framing scenario".

Figure 2. Modeling appropriation in a collaborative online environment

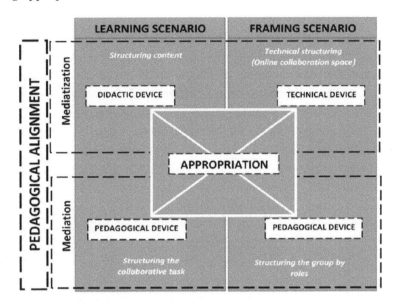

It is this definition that we adopt in the implementation of our model, as it enables us to align the technical, didactic and pedagogical devices around the appropriation process, in the context of an online collaborative device.

At present, the technical aspects of setting up a remote digital working environment are no longer a problem. It's the pedagogical engineering issues that are slow to find clear answers. This difficulty stems from the fact that any technical device necessarily calls for two other devices: didactic and pedagogical. The didactic device is equivalent to the disciplinary knowledge specific to a class-level program (such as negation, direct and indirect discourse, etc.). The pedagogical device is the scenario in which the didactic device takes place (such as studying direct discourse through a corpus of independent sentences or through a full text, through individual exercises or through collaborative work, etc.). This means that in the appropriation process, disciplinary knowledge is inseparable from its staging. The didactic device is always associated with the pedagogical device. When a digital environment is used in teaching, a third device is added to this association, which we call technical. This association of different devices (technical, didactic and pedagogical) is at the root of several malfunctions that can affect the pedagogical framework, thus hindering the appropriation process.

Pedagogical alignment (Ibrahimi & al. 2014; Ibrahimi & al. 2019) results here from the choice of disciplinary content that accommodates a pedagogical scenario in line with the functionalities of a digital distance working environment. Paradoxically, non-alignment would therefore result from the fact that this environment, based on collaboration between peers, delivers knowledge that requires individual effort, or conversely, from the fact that knowledge that a learner would appropriate more easily through collaborative work, is delivered by a digital environment that does not offer collaborative possibilities. Non-alignment therefore occurs whenever one of the three devices (technical, didactic or pedagogical) hinders the appropriation of one or both of the others. For this reason, the model adopted takes these different principles into account.

CONCLUSION

In this chapter, we have shown how e-learning brings several aspects to the fore: learner autonomy, decentralization in the distribution of knowledge, rapid access to available knowledge and a richer context for collaboration to create further knowledge. It is thus closely linked to collaborative learning, which couples two approaches: that of the learner and that of the group. This clearly establishes the link between collaboration and the appropriation of knowledge, both of which depend to a large extent on group dynamics, which in turn depend on the way in which the group is constituted. The question of appropriation thus becomes a complex concept that needs to be modeled in order to be better understood. It is in this sense that Nonaka and Takeuchi propose a model called SECI (Socialization, Externalization, Combination, Internalization) and that CSCL (Computer-Supported Collaborative Learning), which originated in the educational sciences, emerges as a field of study specific to ICT-supported collaborative learning.

However, the question of appropriation also revolves around the pedagogical approach. It is closely linked to pedagogical design, in the sense that appropriation largely depends on the type of pedagogical focus adopted in the design of teaching-learning devices. For this reason, the notion of scenarization takes on its full value, especially when it comes to scripting interaction situations in order to reduce the distance separating the learner from the training content in a digital environment. This is what researchers have called transactional distance in a collaborative online environment. In this sense, distance gives new meaning to presence. Indeed, online collaborative learning better serves this "remote presence" and encourages the appropriation process.

In the light of the above, at the end of the chapter we propose our own model of the appropriation process, one that can trace the complexity of the processes involved and facilitate their integration through the principle of pedagogical alignment.

REFERENCES

Abrami, P., Chambers, B., Poulsen, C., De Simone, C., d'Appollonia, S., & Howden, J. (1995). *Apprentissage Coopératif: Théories, Méthodes, Activités*. Éditions la Chenelière.

Baker, M. (2003). Computer-mediated argumentative interactions for the co-elaboration of scientific notions. In J. Andriessen, M. Baker, & D. Suthers (Eds.), *Arguing to Learn: Confronting Cognitions in Computer-Supported Collaborative Learning environments* (pp. 47–78). Kluwer Academic Publishers. doi:10.1007/978-94-017-0781-7_3

Bédard, L., Déziel, J., & Lamarche, L. (1999). *Introduction à la psychologie sociale*. ERPI.

Bourgeois, E., & Nizet, J. (1997). *Apprentissage et formation des adultes*. Presses Universitaires de France.

Brien, R. (1981). *Design pédagogique. Introduction à l'approche de Gagné et Briggs*. Editions Saint-Yves.

Briggs, L. J. (1981). Instructional design: principles and applications. Englewood Cliffs, NJ: educational Technology publications (3è édition).

Bronckart, J. P. (1985). *Le fonctionnement des discours*. Delachaux et Niestlé.

De Lièvre, B., & Depover, C. (2007). Analyse des communications médiatisées au sein de paires de niveau différencié. In T. Nodenot, J. Wallet, & E. Fernandes (Eds.), *Environnements informatiques pour l'apprentissage humain 2007* (pp. 461–472).

De Lièvre, B., Temperman, G., Cambier, J.-B., Decamps, S., & Depover, C. (2009). Analyse de l'influence des styles d'apprentissage sur les interactions dans les forums collaboratifs. In C. Develotte, F. Mangenot, E. Nissen (Eds.), *Actes du colloque Epal 2009 - Échanger pour apprendre en ligne: conception, instrumentation, interactions, multimodalité.* Grenoble, France: Université Stendhal – Grenoble 3. Retrieved from: https://shs.hal.science/halshs-01078945/document

Depover, C., Karsenti, T., & Komis, V. (2007). *Enseigner avec les technologies.* Presses de l'Université du Québec.

Depover, C., & Marchand, L. (2002). *E-learning et formation des adultes en contexte professionnel.* De Boeck-Université. doi:10.3917/dbu.depov.2002.01

Depover, C., Quintin, J.-J., & De Lièvre, B. (2003). Un outil de scénarisation de formations à distance basées sur la collaboration. In C. Desmoulins, P. Marquet, & D. Bouhineau (Eds.), *Environnements informatiques pour l'apprentissage humain 2003* (pp. 115–126).

Dillenbourg, P. (1996). What do you mean by collaborative learning? In P. Dillenbourg (Ed.), *Collaborative – learning: Cognitive and Computational Approaches* (pp. 1–19). Elsevier.

Dillenbourg, P. (2002). Over-scripting CSCL: The risks of blending collaborative learning with instructional design. In P. Kirschner (Ed.), *Three worlds of CSCL: Can we support CSCL?* (pp. 61–69). Open Universiteit.

Dillenbourg, P., & Jermann, P. (2006). Designing Integrative Scripts. In F. Fischer, I. Kollar, H. Mandl, & J. Haake (Eds.), *Scripting Computer-Supported Collaborative Learning* (pp. 277–302). Springer.

Dillenbourg, P., & Tchounikine, P. (2007). Flexibility in macro-scripts for computer supported collaborative learning. *Journal of Computer Assisted Learning, 23*(1), 1–13. doi:10.1111/j.1365-2729.2007.00191.x

Doise, W., & Mugny, G. (1984). *Psychologie sociale et développement cognitif.* Armand Colin.

Faerber, R. (2003). Groupements, processus pédagogiques et quelques contraintes liés à un environnement virtuel d'apprentissage. In C. Desmoulins, P. Marquet & D. Bouhineau (Eds.), *Environnements informatiques pour l'apprentissage humain 2003* (p. 321-331). Strasbourg, France. https://edutice.hal.science/edutice-00000137

Ferraris, C., Lejeune, A., Vignollet, L., & David, J. P. (2005). Modélisation de scénarios d'apprentissage collaboratif pour la classe: vers une opérationnalisation au sein d'un ENT. Actes de la conférence EIAH 2005, Ed. Pierre Tchounikine, Michelle Joab et Luc Trouche. INRP. Institut Montpellier II.

Gagné, R., Briggs, L., & Wager, W. (1992). *Principles of Instructional design.* Hartcourt Brace Jovanovitch.

Giardina, M. & Oubenaïssa, L. (2003). Projet d'apprentissage/enseignement en ligne. *Sciences et technologies de l'information et de la communication pour l'éducation et la formation, 10,* 20.

Henri, F., & Lundgren-Cayrol, K. (2001). *Apprentissage collaboratif à distance: Pour comprendre et concevoir des environnements d'apprentissage virtuels*. Presses de l'Université du Québec.

Hooper, S. (1992). Cooperative learning and computer-based instruction. *Educational Technology Research and Development, 40*(3), 21–38. doi:10.1007/BF02296840

Ibrahimi, A., Khaldi, M., & Kaddouri, E. (2019). Processes of Knowledge Appropriation in an Online Collaboration Device. *RA JOURNAL OF APPLIED RESEARCH, Volume, 05*(07), 2495–2509.

Ibrahimi, A., Rais, O., & Khaldi, M. (2014). *Dispositif hybride en cours de langue à l'université marocaine*. Adjectif.net. http://www.adjectif.net/spip/spip.php

Jackson, M., & Moreland, R. (2009). Transactive memory in the classroom. *Small Group Research, 40*(5), 508–534. doi:10.1177/1046496409340703

Jermann, P. (2004). *Computer Support for Interaction Regulation in Collaborative Problem-Solving* [thèse de doctorat, Université de Genève, Suisse]. https://tecfa.unige.ch/tecfa/research/theses/jermann2004.pdf

Jézégou, A. (1998). *La formation à distance: enjeux, perspectives et limites de l'individualisation*. L'Harmattan.

Jézégou, A. (2012). La présence en e-learning: modèle théorique et perspective pour la recherche. *The Journal of Distance Education / Revue de l'Éducation à Distance, 26*(1). https://edutice.hal.science/edutice-00733742v2

Jonnaert, P., & Vander Borght, C. (1999). *Créer des conditions d'apprentissage: un cadre de référence socio-constructiviste pour une formation didactique des enseignants*. De Boeck.

Keegan, D. (1986). *The foundations of distance education*. Croom Helm.

Klamma, R., Rohde, M., & Stahl, G. (2004). Community-based learning: Explorations into theoretical groundings, empirical findings and computer support. *SigGroup Bulletin, 24* (4), 1-100. https://www.researchgate.net/publication/28675083_Community-based_learning_workshop_Explorations_into_theoretical_groundings_empirical_findings_and_computer_support

Laferrière, T. (2003). Apprendre ensemble: choisir nos mots pour discourir sur des pratiques émergentes. In C. Deaudelin & T. Nault (Eds.), *Apprendre avec des pairs et des TIC: Quels environnements pour quels impacts?* (pp. 11–18). Presses de l'Université du Québec. doi:10.2307/j.ctv18pgvgg.2

Lebrun, N., & Berthelot, S. (1994). *Plan pédagogique: une démarche systématique de planification de l'enseignement*. Editions Nouvelles/De Boeck.

Lonchamp, J. (2007). Un cadre conceptuel et logiciel pour la construction d'environnements d'apprentissage collaboratifs. *Sciences et technologies de l'information et de la communication pour l'éducation et la formation, 14*. https://www.persee.fr/doc/stice_1952-8302_2007_num_14_1_950

Merrill, M. D. & ID2 Expert Group. (1996). Instructional transaction theory: Instructional design based on knowledge objects. *Educational Technology, 36*(3), 30–37.

Merrill, M. D. (2002). First principles of instruction. *Educational Technology Research and Development, 50*(3), 43–59. doi:10.1007/BF02505024

Michinov, N., & Michinov, E. (2009). Investigating the relationship between transactive memory and performance in collaborative learning. *Learning and Instruction*, *19*(1), 43–54. doi:10.1016/j.learninstruc.2008.01.003

Moore, M., & Kearsley, G. (1996). *Distance education: A systems view*. Wadsworth.

Nachmias, R., Mioduser, D., Oren, A., & Ram, J. (2000). Web-supported emergent collaboration in higher education courses. *Journal of Educational Technology & Society*, *3*(3), 94–104.

Nonaka, I., & Takeuchi, H. (1995). *The knowledge creatign company: how Japanese companies create the dynamics of innovation*. Oxford University Press. doi:10.1093/oso/9780195092691.001.0001

Paquette, G. (2002). *L'ingénierie du téléapprentissage: pour construire l'apprentissage en réseaux*. Sainte-Foy: Presses de l'Université du Québec.

Pavitt, C. (1998). *Small group communication: a theoretical approach* (3rd ed.). University of Delaware. https://www.uky.edu/~drlane/teams/pavitt/

Perraton, H. (1992). Une théorie de l'enseignement à distance. In A.-J. Deschênes (Ed.), *La formation à distance maintenant*. Presses de la Télé-Université du Québec.

Perret-Clermont, A., Perret, J.-F., & Bell, N. (1991). The social construction of meaning and cognitive activity in elementary school children. In L. Resnick, J. Levine. & S. Teasley (Eds.), Perspectives on socially shared cognition (p. 41- 62). Washington, DC: American Psychological association. doi:10.1037/10096-002

Peters, O. (1973). Distance teaching and industrial production: a comparative international outline. In D. Sewart, D. Keegan, & B. Holmberg (Eds.), *Distance education: International perspectives* (pp. 95–113). Routledge.

Piaget, J. (1967). *Biology and knowledge: An essay on the relation between organic regulations and cognitive processes*. University of Chicago Press.

Redecker, C. (2008). *Review of Learning 2.0 Practices: Study on the Impact of Web 2.0 Innovations on Education and Training in Europe Seville*. European Commission - Joint Research Center - Institute for Prospective Technological Studies., Retrieved from http://ftp.jrc.es/EURdoc/JRC49108.pdf

Reigeluth, C. M. (Ed.). (1999). Instructional-Design Theories and Models: Vol. II. *A New Paradigm of Instructional Theory*. Lawrence Erlbaum Assoc.

Romiszowski, A. J. (1981). *Designing Instructional systems*. Kogan Page et Nochols Publishing.

Roschelle, J., & Teasley, S. (1995). The construction of shared knowledge in collaborative problem solving. In C. O'Malley (Ed.), Computer-Supported Collaborative Learning (p. 69-197). Berlin, Allemagne: Springer-Verlag. doi:10.1007/978-3-642-85098-1_5

Schellens, T., Van Keer, H., Valcke, M., & De Wever, B. (2007). Learning in asynchronous discussion groups: A multilevel approach to study the influence of student, group and task characteristics. *Behaviour & Information Technology*, *26*(1), 55–71. doi:10.1080/01449290600811578

Shaw, M. (1981). *Group dynamics: the psychology of small group behaviour*. McGraw-Hill.

Soller, A., Lesgold, A., Linton, F., & Goodman, B. (1999). *What Makes Peer Interaction Effective? Modeling Effective Communication in an Intelligent CSCL*. Proceedings of the 1999 AAAI Fall Symposium: Psychological Models of Communication in Collaborative Systems, Cape Cod, MA. https://www.researchgate.net/publication/2279217_What_Makes_Peer_Interaction_Effective_Modeling_Effective_Communication_in_an_Intelligent_CSCL

Stahl, G., Koschmann, T., & Suthers, D. (2006). Computer-supported collaborative learning: an historical perspective. In R. Sawyer (Ed.), *Cambridge handbook of the learning sciences* (pp. 409–426). Cambridge University Press.

Strijbos, J. W. (2004). *The effect of roles on computer-supported collaborative learning*. [Doctoral Thesis, Open Universiteit: faculties and services]. https://research.ou.nl/en/publications/the-effect-of-roles-on-computer-supported-collaborative-learning

Viau, R. (1997). *La motivation en contexte scolaire*. De Boeck.

Vygotsky, L. S. (1978). *Mind in society: The development of higher mental processes Cambridge*. Harvard University Press.

Webb, N. (1991). Task related verbal interaction and mathematics learning in small groups. *Journal for Research in Mathematics Education*, 22(5), 366–389. doi:10.2307/749186

Chapter 7

The Design Model of Educational Scenarios in an Adaptive Online Collaborative Learning System

Kawtar Zargane

https://orcid.org/0000-0002-1266-7094

ENS, Abdelmalek Essaadi University, Morocco

Mohamed Erradi

ENS, Abdelmalek Essaadi University, Morocco

Mohamed Khaldi

https://orcid.org/0000-0002-1593-1073

ENS, Abdelmalek Essaadi University, Morocco

ABSTRACT

Learning on adaptive e-learning platforms occupies a main role in the revolution, various pedagogical technologies, and collaboration to create educational scenarios in collaborative systems during adaptive e-learning activities. The main objective of this work is to present collaborative adaptation scenarios in an online collaborative adaptive system during adaptive learning activities in order to group learners in a collaborative space to discuss with each other and develop the aggregation of knowledge. This is about fostering adaptive collaboration. The author discuss the effectiveness of the ADDIE method with this adaptive scenario that group's collaborative adaptive content between the group and the collaborative learning system to provide an engaging online learning experience focused on skill development problem-solving practices. As a result, they meet their objective of designing collaborative scenarios in an adaptive system. The authors value collaborative learning through the interpretation of data generated by the system so that an online collaborative environment surrounds learners.

DOI: 10.4018/979-8-3693-3128-6.ch007

Copyright © 2024, IGI Global. Copying or distributing in print or electronic forms without written permission of IGI Global is prohibited.

INTRODUCTION

The generation of adaptive online learning systems must integrate new pedagogical approaches allowing learners to play an active role in learning and knowledge construction. These systems must be more interactive and collaborative in the sense of allowing and encouraging collaboration between learners, but above all they must integrate a more user-centered vision.

Educational challenges associated with online learning include teachers' lack of knowledge and skills in using technology and the need for professional training for teachers (Shorey et al., 2022). Students are familiar with online learning tools. Lack of interactive multimedia educational resources (Ahshan, 2021). Difficulty in evaluating and evaluating the learning support strategy design.

Planning the curriculum considering current curriculum needs and available resources, making decisions about what students should learn, why they should learn it and how the teaching and learning process should be organized (Espino et al., 2019).

The process of developing educational content using online technological tools is divided into several phases (Anoir et al.,2023). Teachers create the teaching space or environment and manage the process to maintain and use it appropriately. Learner information data that leads to the personalization of personal records and educational content.

Our work focuses on the instrumentation of tutoring activities and aims to design and develop a collaborative adaptation system, giving advice to the tutor on the adaptation of learning situations before and during the training sessions, according to the stable and variable characteristics of learners and learning groups according to the ADDIE methodology (Belhaoues et al., 2016).

The design is essentially the responsibility of the teacher; our objective is to support teachers and develop teaching strategies that allow this to achieve the objectives set in the previous phase. We study this general objectives of online screenwriting. From there, identify specific objectives, then it is broken down into learning sub-elements and finally content, furthermore, this phase aims to formulate and develop educational strategies select the learning support and the different elements that support it. compose educational material developed for training.

This article we examine how they used the ADDIE instructional design (Lémonie & Grosstephan, 2021). framework for building an iterative information literacy course and how they used the analysis, design, implementation, and evaluation phases to integrate the best current online learning.

Production activity systems do not develop in a linear manner, but through transformation cycles where the logic of the activity changes qualitatively. Such changes are invariably linked to a redefinition of the object or product of the activity, as well as the development of new tools and associated forms of collaboration.

The development of learning concepts (Salimzadeh et al., 2021), and pedagogical approaches aimed at putting them into practice aims to put the learner at the center of the course, but above all to consider the desired learning in all decisions of the teacher.

In our work we present how instructional design is the structuring of content to facilitate learning, this will help achieve educational objectives and reduce problems caused user. Instructional design takes place in several stages structuring specific training goals, objectives and content into units logical learning, creating a complete system scenario, design enabling this the learner builds a mental structure of knowledge and finally creates a model of it online collaboration learning.

METHODS

Adaptive learning raises many questions regarding the use of methods and technologies in the field of online learning and how to provide adaptive content to learners through personalization of personal data and skill system. In this work we will present our collaborative adaptive learning system then the effectiveness of the ADDIE model with our educational scenario for the creation of an activity, the ADDIE method: the development of the electronic content package includes five phases based on the design research, analysis, design, development, implementation and evaluation of collaborative learning materials and activities. The Figure 1 presents an example of a mental map of the ADDIE model (Jatmika and Aymon, 2022).

Figure 1. Mind map for the ADDIE model (template)

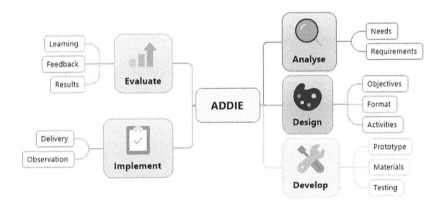

Figure 2. Example of a model of an adaptive educational system

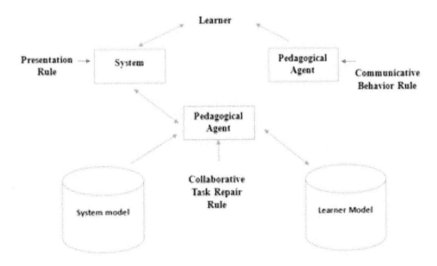

Figure 2 (Jatmika et al., 2022), shows the domain model, the learner model and the system controller determine the course elements to be presented by the system and the educational agent. This division is designed to allow for reuse of various courses and materials.

The objective is to study the integration of a system and an educational agent into an adaptive teaching system, and how to integrate a system and an educational agent into an adaptive teaching system. Firstly, the evaluation of this simplified learning model which takes into account an evaluation of the level of adaptive learning. The adaptive educational activities presented to the learner must be interpreted by the system on the one hand and by the educational agent on the other hand.

ANALYSIS AND DESIGN

Adaptive Online Collaborative Learning System

An online collaborative learning system consists of educational resources, human infrastructure or technologies, services, materials, and environment that support learning (Dinget al., 2023).

- **Learning system**

A learning system (Meerhoff, et al.,2022). must identify the training problem it wishes to solve and represent it accurately enough to justify the choice of solution. More specifically, it is important for teachers to describe the target group, describe the training situation and their expectations of the learning system, describe the general purpose of the learning system and identify documentary resources that can be used with the learning system.

- **Online learning system**

An e-learning system will be used instead of online courses to refer to a learning system that uses information and communications technology (Theelen & van Breukelen, 2022). This system, also called an online learning platform, is an IT tool designed to facilitate online training, teaching and learning. It provides a virtual environment in which teachers, trainers, students and learners can interact, access educational content, take courses, participate in learning activities and evaluate their progress.

Building Adaptive Learning Systems is primarily interested in research related to adaptive systems, theories of adaptive learning methods and study. Let us take an example of the above figure 3 (Weibelzahl et al., 2020). of adaptive learning system.

This gives learners the opportunity to clarify their goals and helps them understand the different skills needed to achieve them. Other adaptive learning systems based on learning styles can also be mentioned as important characteristics for defining learner profiles (Weibelzahl et al., 2020).

- **Collaborative learning**

Collaboration offers a way of relating to others that respects and values the abilities and contributions of each person (Fayolle et al., 2016). Collaborative learning is an active process through which the learner works to develop their knowledge. The trainer acts as a facilitator of learning while the group participates

Figure 3. Example of an adaptive learning systems

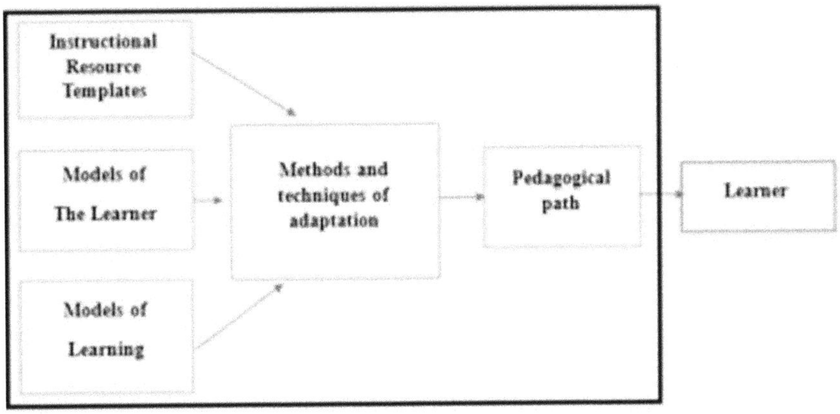

as a source of information as a motivator, as a means of mutual support and support, and as a privileged place of interaction for the collective construction of knowledge (Malinowski & Kramsch, 2014).

Collaboration is only beneficial in special cases these are tasks which, according to the classic definition, require collective production in small groups (Ollivier, 2012). It then becomes clear that, even if collaboration seems to be for many authors a characteristic of online learning, rarely capable of being typified, other forms of collaboration also exist (Ludwig & Van de Poel, 2013).

Collaborative learning, to active learning, to the supportive role of the teacher, including the provision of diverse learning experiences. Learning to improve both general interactions and the learning process, and ultimately learning to improve the balance between the amount of course information and student engagement and persistence (Creasman, 2012). Furthermore, the application of teaching is directly linked to the conditions in which this process takes place, which makes it possible to consider good teaching practices in advanced online learning environments.

- **Online collaborative system**

Learning systems, limits to consider at the collaboration stage, it is not fully integrated as format, resources, learner progression levels, meeting times between users, profiles of learners with whom you would like to collaborate, etc. … (Coomey & Stephenson, 2018). An online learning system with Semantic Web technologies (Sabeimaet al., 2022), in particular online based on ICT, in addition to the personal profile of the user, the preferences, knowledge and learning styles recognized by the system constitute essential parameters for deployment, provides an online learning framework that delivers collaborative content to each learner and guarantees access to content, helps learners specific to their group learning style, and defines the aspects (Boyinbode et al., 2020): preprocessing, recognition, acquisition and understanding during collaborative online learning systems.

- **Adaptive online system**

An adaptive learning system (Saeedipour et al., 2013), which adapts to the learner in front of the machine. This can only be achieved through knowledge of learning models. All this knowledge contributes to defining learner characteristics, thus facilitating the adaptation of content to learning profiles, the monitoring of progress and the provision of appropriate administrative and cognitive support (Alladatin et al.,2020). Adaptive learning systems are systems that automatically adapt to your profile, view learner information, resource content and training areas at any time, during learning activities (Kaouniet al., 2023). Collaborative adaptive learning systems are, by definition, adaptive learning systems that take collaborative aspects into account. Adjust synchronization between learners during learning activities, considering the aforementioned customizations in addition to synchronization between users. That is, for them, this system not only produces learners and instructors who want to work with and with whom learning paths are created based on your unique learning area, preferences, and culture, but also your history of completed or ongoing learning paths when added synchronous collaboration (Kaouniet al., 2023).

Adaptive online systems assess learners' characteristics and make appropriate adjustments to support learning, its main goal is to create a flexible environment that supports the learning of students with different abilities (Hrich et al., 2017). The challenge in achieving this objective lies largely in the precise identification of learner or student characteristics, learner groups, types and levels of knowledge, skills, personalities, etc… (Hrich et al., 2019).

Figure 4 (Parola et al., 2020). describes the different types of information needed for adaptation. By proposing this architecture, to provide an intelligent tutoring system that explicitly models knowledge and misconceptions. Nevertheless, this model can also be applied to other neighborhood applications as well. However, in some systems the main components may not be identical. As the authors argue, adaptive machine learning can confuse inference mechanisms and domain models. Additionally (Heard et al., 2018; Chen et al., 2013), the process and interactions between components are not described, for evaluation purposes it is important to study not only the state of the system, but also the processes taking place there in its current state.

Figure 4. Architect of an adaptive online learning system

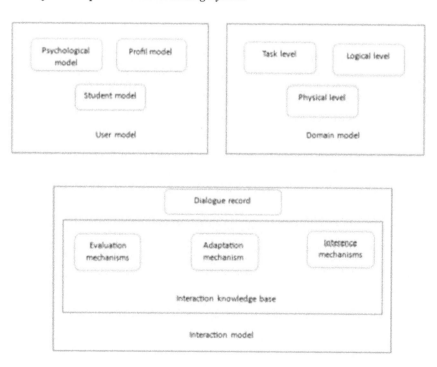

● **The adaptive system and online collaboration**

The online collaborative adaptive system creates and stimulates the development of each student. Personal or self-paced learning process. The adaptation system The package offers an enjoyable learning process in their themes. Every student can clear any doubts about the learning process through the system package (Sreedevi & Kapilas, 2022).

Adapting educational resources and learning paths to user profiles, the field of training is therefore essential to offer learners good conditions for success. However, collaborative systems create adaptation problems. This remains a key point for creating adaptive, or even collaborative, learning paths (Sabeima et al.,2021).

In many systems, one can automatically switch between forums, which encourages members to pay attention to all communications under the group's attention (Kawtar et al., 2021).

Table 1 (Kawtar et al., 2021), represents the components, electronic bulletin boards and forums are collaborative tools that each contribute to group work, the forum comes from the fact that it can, compared to other tools, meet a variety of needs in the collaborative group, because it provides unprecedented human communication (Kawtar et al., 2021).

Table 1. Forum in adaptive on-line system

Forum in Adaptive On-Line System	For the learner
What is it what is it?	● It is a virtual place where the speech of a group, where the learner appropriates new knowledge by conversing with others. ● It is an agora of collaboration and socialization.
What does it allow?	● When is it suitable to use it? One can expose ideas, develop one's thinking, build new knowledge, validate and confirm with the support of the group. ● It facilitates the learning of complex knowledge belonging to poorly or poorly structured domains. ● It promotes a reflective attitude about learning. ● It allows a group to live an experience motivating learning and developing a sociocognitive commitment that gives even more learning that is meaningful.
Who is participating?	● Human agents who create a social network: The Guardian ● Alternatively, the trainer and other learners who work in the within small groups (spontaneous, informal collaboration) or within a large group (supervised collaboration, formal). ● Machine agents that make up the environment technology: tools for collaboration, coordination and support cognitive and social processes.
How do we participate?	● Human agents transmit messages to the group; interaction is the semantics of these messages. ● Machine agents, grafted to the forum, offer automated support for learning by providing, for example, multiple representations of what is said in messages; this support is immediate, fast, interactive.
When is it suitable to use it?	● When learning involves skills of high level such as analysis, synthesis and evaluation, the forum is an appropriate educational choice. It is the designed as a resolution environment for problems, decision-making. It tests to the intentionality of the learning situation. ● In a formal learning framework, when the learners feel they need others to learn, when a group of 15 to 30 learners want to learn together with the support of a trainer and when they are willing to agree to reach a shared goal. ● In an informal setting, when a sufficient number of people want to form a group and work together to learn.

The Collaborative System During Online Adaptive Activities

A collaborative learning situation is a situation of interaction between people who can work together towards a common goal. This collaborative learning can be described as a series of processes that help people interact to achieve the end goal.

It's about adapting learning to everything in a collaborative mode that creates constant imitation and synergy between learners. It would be interesting to further develop online learning towards collaborative adaptive systems.

However, most adaptive learning systems require consideration of boundary conditions. At the collaboration stage, resources, learner progress levels, meeting times between learners, profiles of users with whom you would like to collaborate (Othmane et al., 2019).

- **Educational activity**

For educational activities (Ikram et al., 2021), first, the system offers scenarios which focus on the definition of objectives, but also of skills and prerequisites for prior knowledge. Additionally, the multimedia content integration system focuses on learning objectives, particularly content that encourages learner participation, and provides situation scenarios that include the introduction of situation objectives (Aljafen, 2021).

- **Online activity**

Figure 5 (El Asame & Wakrim, 2018), shows that a research unit is considered as a set of activities carried out by a group of actors in an online environment. It is interesting to note that this model in no way presupposes the digital nature of the entities described: this type of modeling can be applied to traditional learning processes as well as to digital technologies (El Asame & Wakrim, 2018). There are several types of activities, including learning activities, support activities and online educational activities. Each activity defines a set of prerequisites and educational objectives through an online system.

There are several types of activities presented in Figure 6 (Lafleur & Samson, 2019)., including learning activities, support activities and instrumental activities. Each activity has a set of prerequisites and educational objectives (Lafleur & Samson, 2019).

Figure 5. Activity is at the center of the online system

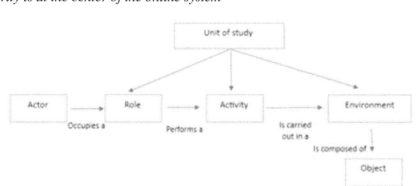

Figure 6. Different types of online system activities

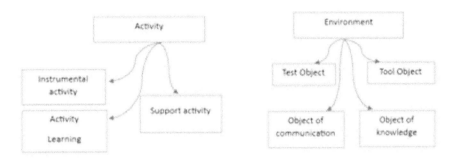

The notion of environment in which an activity takes place makes it possible to bring together a set of resources of all kinds, which can be sources of physical or digital knowledge and the tools necessary to carry out the activity. The knowledge object carrying the content has a well-informed transfer function. Objects during contact make it possible to immediately name synchronous or asynchronous communications to the different actors. A "tool" object can be used because its mastery is the goal of learning (Lafleur & Samson, 2019), or because it is necessary to accomplish another task.

Test objects can be used to define tests and surveys. It also defines other object classes that can be used for managing, structuring resources such as activities, roles and real estate objects section objects, index objects, search objects, display objects, etc. .

- **Collaborative activity**

Collaborative activities are scripted in a simple and flexible manner. Therefore, the structure for developing content and developing this knowledge is open. Thanks to collaborative distance learning, students have access to a clear and simple environment in the world of e-learning.

The effectiveness of collaboration varies depending on the activity (Nguyen et al.,2009). some activities prevent activation of the mechanism as other activities are also appropriate, some activities are distributed in nature, encouraging group members to work independently from each other. Interaction occurs when compiling partial results, not when compiling results collaboratively collaborative thought processes (Beuscart et al., 2009).

Collaboration involves two or more people coming together to achieve a specific goal however, this activity can be divided into two types depending on whether it is a joint activity or not when this activity is carried out online it is asynchronous because it can be practiced using multimedia technology. In other words, learners must access the activity and act together to carry it out, learners arriving at a synchronous collaboration activity are put on hold programmed with a learning path (Fu et al., 2018).

- **The role of designer (Teacher)**

Teachers had to decide what students should learn and how to facilitate learning (Arcueno et., 2021). Curriculum planning challenges that teachers faced included organizing units of study and preparing and aligning instructional sequences using online platforms that were not established or widely used. used before the pandemic (Hoang et al., 2020).

Teachers need to accelerate lesson planning for their classes. They had to quickly figure it out How to adapt teaching practices during emergency distance learning (Patel, 2019). They had to invent ways to integrate technology into education to enable learning. Some teachers have had to adjust their use of online educational technologies, review student assessments, and adjust their instructional strategies to meet the new needs of their learners (Bonal & González, 2020).

- **The learner in an adaptive system**

This is the most important data in an adaptive system. It is retaining what learners know or do not know by providing domain concepts. This data can be determined explicitly after testing, or implicitly by applying a system of inference rules. Even for the same learner, knowledge can change from time to time (Sarwar et al., 2019).

Indeed, each time the system is used, the learner acquires new knowledge and can progress or move down. Therefore, robust assessment tools are needed to confirm effective skills. A written questionnaire from students regarding certain theoretical concepts presented during the course (Weibelzahl et al., 2020).

These could be definitions, explanations, or multiple-choice quizzes. Practical work on machines, carried out in groups, linked to the content of the training. This involves collecting information on the Internet on a particular subject and structuring this information into real individual or collective files which are generally returned to the teacher.

- **Teamwork**

Collaborative working is perhaps the parameter that most directly influences online interactions (Dejean-Thircuir & Mangenot, 2014). Communication within a small group assigned to a common production task has a completely different character than communication within a large group which can be directed or established by discussion between tutor and learner for an exchange in the group .

Collective work (Marcoccia, 2010), necessarily takes place in small groups, often of two or more people, and aims at co-production, the degree of division of tasks, division of labor by learners and joint negotiation of all aspects of production.

Work may be carried out in small or large groups, require interaction, and involve negotiation and participation between learners (Gupta, 2016). Finally, the role of the tutor varies greatly depending on the form.

Remote collaboration work (Coomey & Stephenson, 2018). functions as an environment that enables digital collaboration by providing services that enable temporal and spatial collaboration while maintaining various user activities. At different times, at the same time or in real time. The same goes for collaborative tasks that can be performed by any user at any time and as quickly as possible, independently of other users (Ng, 2007).

ADDIE MODEL DURING COLLABORATIVE ADAPTIVE EDUCATIONAL ACTIVITY

- **ADDIE model**

Using the ADDIE model focused on the learner throughout the course, rather than a teacher-centered approach. Learning analytics is an important aspect of course design, learners design their own multimedia content, delivered course and instructional design projects provide a process that actively involves developers in problem solving (Davis, 2013). The ADDIE Framework is a cyclical process that evolves over time and continues throughout the education planning and implementation process. Five stages form the framework, each with their own goals and objectives. Instructional design in progress (Shibley et al., 2011).

The five stages of the ADDIE instructional design model are interdependent and closely related. By organically combining and systematically designing these five steps, it can be used flexibly according to specific educational sites and regional conditions. It can be effectively combined with other relevant educational theories and design principles to achieve better teaching and learning outcomes (Liu, 2023). In the area of curriculum design and development, everyone should rely on the ADDIE standards. The ADDIE standard is not only the gold standard for instructional design processes, it also provides ideas for problem solving.

- **The ADDIE model phases**

Each stage of the ADDIE model (Elharbaoui et al., 2018). describes its own model personalization of the design process: first introduction measures the important points of the theoretical model, then suggest a description of a project experience.

The Analysis phase: The aim of this step is to understand the context of the learner, is there a context? What information is important? must be mastered in order to be able to implement them. Do they take actions for the benefit of the groups they represent, in the face of all these questions? what are their questions? In addition to identifying the knowledge to be imparted, there is an immediate need to identify useful expertise and resources. Develop training modules to identify these needs (Elharbaoui et al., 2018).

Analyze the content of your course or program using course texts, sample programs, and similar course websites. With the advent of the Internet, many courses have become easier to complete (Elharbaoui et al., 2018). Available online, it can provide teachers with practical frameworks and models. Anyone developing a course or teaching a course for the first time. Finally, conduct a training analysis to determine what you need to learn.

The Design phase: This step involves designing the structure and specifications of each activity based on the target representative group. That is, what content, what strategies and what types of educational activities will be used (Chergui et al., 2020). This was essential for our objective to identify the elements of accessibility from an educational technical and technological point of view.

From this experience, we have developed modules with technical skills (media coverage, ergonomics, accessibility). We also recommend adjusting the volume of the public class far from digital culture: Testing phase from the first stages of platform development also presents that future users constitute an essential stage of engineering (Chergui et al., 2020).

Conduct this participatory engineering with the general public due to barriers, various pedagogical strategies must be used to promote the participation of all learners. At the design stage, the designer or trainer must take into account information or data from the analysis phase. If sufficient analysis is not performed, please consult your instructor or designer to repeat efforts during stage implementation. The first two phases require careful planning, which reduces the need for research and planning later in the program (Krishnan et al., 2021).

The Development phase: The plan consists of giving the actual contents of the modules. The completion of the know-how can be considered during an iterative transformation, an interregnum of phases in what has been interpreted during the book of obligations and the questions or changes imposed by the know-how plan. This frequent plan results in a finalized version of activities (Krishnan et al., 2021).

During the development phase, it was difficult to keep online focus on accessibility issues. This restriction of universal accessibility significantly reduced the motivation for this educational project (Petrosky, 2022). Each development had to take place developed by an IT service provider, therefore production plans and additional costs which were not planned in the initial project. Designers had to continually adjust the content and forms of learning activities to maintain this accessibility goal.

Designers should leverage the results of the previous two phases, product creation, to disseminate information during the development phase. During this transition stage, the designer's role shifts from research and planning mode to production mode. The designers of it create, develop, or select educational materials step by step and support (Balanyk, 2017).

The Implementation phase: The phase that provides the module is intended only for the implementation of activities on the system and their public availability (Balanyk, 2017). Activities can be completed with or without third-party support. Understand the activity and guide learners, acquisition during the project period. Project dissemination event. These were moments of interaction with future users of the system.

Designers should take a more active role in the implementation phase Designers should take a more active role in the implementation phase, once this stage begins, the role of the designer or trainer becomes more important to deliver effectively content, developers must continually analyze, rethink, and improve the content. Learners and trainers those who actively contribute to implementation can make changes to courses and programs on the fly to ensure their effectiveness (Balanyk, 2017).

The Evaluation phase: The steps are assessments in the ADDIE model. This consists of several sub-steps: application possibilities, project management evaluation, and user satisfaction evaluation. In particular, the evaluation strategy is imbued in each individual. Previous phase of the model, based on the spirit of iterative operations, the constant adjustment mechanisms operate continuously during the engineering process (Muruganantham, 2015).

This continuous and necessary adaptation requires design and development teams to make regular transformations accordingly to the feedback they receive. Platform evaluations only make sense if all the content and functionalities are complete, if all the learning activities seem difficult to understand in their context presentation of the platform including different modules (Muruganantham, 2015).

The assessment phase is an important part of the ADDIE process and it is multidimensional. The evaluation phase can take place during the development phase, throughout the implementation phase with the help of students and teachers. While the evaluation phase is often a necessary task, the evaluation phase should be an integral part of ongoing analysis.

- **Educational activities adapting from the ADDIE model**

During this methodology we will carry out the educational scenario which provides interactive and collaborative activities at the same time, the 19 steps of the ADDIE model (Muruganantham, 2015), was considered crucial for the creation of education and training programs. To make it easier to share the ADDIE model with others, the steps have been divided into five phases: analysis, design, development, implementation, and evaluation. Below is a list of steps, categorized under the appropriate phases.

Figure 7. Collaborative educational activities adapting to ADDIE

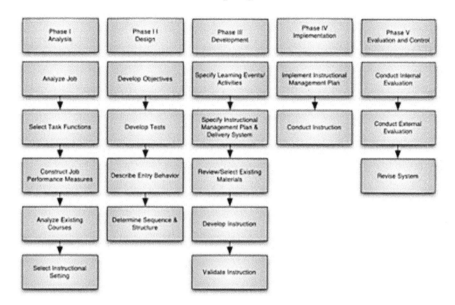

- ## The ADDIE model and the design of an adaptive system

In this model, for beginners, repeat status is a question. For example, at the assessment stage when you find yourself in a learning situation, whether it is analysis or direction, it is a problem that needs to be solved and a solution is possible. When writing your objectives, you can and should expand or narrow them, which this expansion can be used to perform task/content analysis (Apriyanti et al., 2020). The most important feature of this model is based on system management, modifications are open constructions because they are repeatable and the process changes (Hutabarat et al., 2023).

Instructional design experts have adopted the model's name ADDIE (Figure 7) (Uzunboylu & Koşucu, 2017). Project management will be reviewed and the rules will be revised. This process of planning, roles, tasks, schedules, checkpoints and management procedures (Uzunboylu & Koşucu, 2017). Dissemination, the process of adaptation and sustainability of the project throughout the process, an ongoing dispute is being studied. Depending on how the process evolves, the members of the design teams may vary.

The design, development and process starts with the first and second phase. The assessment focuses on elements and phases, these steps are sequential and can be done in one go, modify or change the circular design, etc., dynamically, develop and iterate your assessment process, move to the next step before the end of the phase, then return to the previous step (Uzunboylu & Koşucu, 2017).

Figure 8 (Kerdtip & Thammachat, 2023) presents an example of the positive aspect of this template is that it can be modified and modified. The opposite is true for and testing the usefulness of the material by weight to give more space development of this material. This applies to the emissions efficiency of the process used (Kerdtip & Thammachat, 2023). The content of the courses and the degree to which the objectives are achieved are important. Oriented intoxication the torment of forgiveness some can yourself- even present the rectification of the profane to examine, the morals The size of the profane to understand as the still of slips if it is a edge drawing of this model (Liu, 2023).

Figure 8. The ADDIE model and the design of an adaptive system

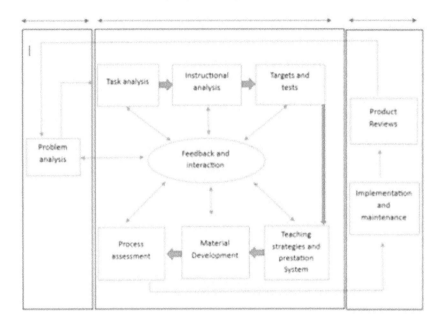

- **Educational engineering**

In recent years, the term "educational technology" has become widely used. Although the terms "educational design" and "educational technology" are widely used in the literature, the term "educational technology" is used with increasing frequency and has been identified as an alternative to "instructional design". In educational sciences, the meaning of the word "design" is close to its English meaning. The term is more commonly used in English engineering and refers to the first step in a process that leads to the realization of the needs of a product or system, a process called engineering, and translates as engineering. Thus, engineering covers the entire life cycle of a product or system, while design is only the first stage (Amara et al., 2016).

This explains the increasing use of the term educational technology as instructional design increasingly incorporates principles adopted by others; it is more a testament to the development of a distinct field than to its creation as a discipline, for This reason, when we talk about educational technology, it is about instructional design, but it is an instructional design that integrates more principles and practices from the field of engineering (Nguyen & Okatani, 2018).

- **Engineering of a learning system**

Educational activities should be designed to help students be able to produce knowledge that accurately reflects their own experiences (Mayer, 2017). In other words, for constructivist pedagogy, the production of knowledge only has value if it considers the concrete realities of learners. The student is therefore at the center of learning, and this guides those who are asked to build. An educational environment based on a systematic method of designing and developing online training.

We therefore consider part or all of a course that combines elements such as objects as a complex system. Learning, teaching strategies, learner characteristics, assessment strategies, media, etc. Design pedagogy then appears as a systematic method which focuses on and considers all stages of the life cycle of a learning system. This life cycle is generally divided into five phases, better known by its acronym: analysis, design, development, implementation and ADDIE evaluation. Other models of educational technology are also introduced later (Itçaina, 2010).

Therefore, the use of the term Educational Engineering refers to the rigor of a broader process that allows articulating the different logics through multiple stages or phases that influence the design and development of learning systems and learning systems, because it highlights the systematic properties in the learning system (Cilla et al., 2013).

RESULTS AND DISCUSSIONS

We conducted research on the analysis, design, development, implementation, and validation of adaptive e-learning: elements, processes and types of collaborative learning, trainees. The results of the study proved that the adaptive system can be used to teach communication levels and collaborative space creation among students. The content provided in the form of adaptive system modules improves student performance, this adaptive system also builds on the objectives of the interactive and communicative activities with new educational engineering technologies.

T he application of the ADDIE model to distance education, multimedia presentations are often preferred. The use of multimedia, high-quality short films increased student attendance, ensured interaction and flexibility, and stimulated and maintained student interest. Additionally, the ADDIE model allows you to use practical experiences and even examples to provide an adaptive teaching system. Indeed, learners are keen that the learning system is available in a variety of formats and matches the parameters to consider when planning distance learning.

Furthermore, given existing research, the ADDIE model remains the basic method. Possible explanations for this phenomenon can be found in the extensive literature. Although the ADDIE model well illustrates the basic steps in the educational process of designing and developing an e-learning course, it lacks some fundamental elements that address the details of an e-learning project. Therefore, its main task focuses on creating a more formal and mature e-learning project management model.

When targeting the ADDIE method to remote environments, it was stated that the ADDIE method embodied in a flow of additional information by providing good pedagogical operations improving the practices of instructional designers and educators. Specifically, when applying design pattern, good teaching practices include multimedia presentations, feedback, various interactive exercises and activities, collaborative learning strategies and include the role of educator. In addition to the good teaching practices mentioned below, other practices were also revealed when applying the model below. All the points above will be explained in more detail below.

The Phases of Model ADDIE in a Collaborative Adaptive Learning System

The first analysis phase, all other stages of adaptive instructional design are based on the analysis phase. The investigator defines the problem, identifies the source of the problem, and determines possible solutions during this stage. The phase may involve research into particular techniques such as needs analysis, objective analysis and collaborative task analysis. The outcome of this phase often includes said educational objectives and a list of tasks to be taught. These. The results will correspond to the inputs for the design phase.

The second design phase involves using the results of the analysis phase to plan a teaching development strategy. During this phase, the researcher explains how to achieve the collaborative educational objectives set during the analysis phase and expand the educational base. Elements of the design phase include writing a target population, describing it, conducting an adaptive learning analysis, objective writing and testing items, selecting a delivery system, and sequencing Training. The products from the design phase will represent the input to the development phase.

The third phase of the ADDIE model is development, which is supported by the analysis and design phases. The objective of this stage is to produce lesson plans and course documents. During this phase, the investigator builds and develops the software package using multimedia software and collaborative containers. This may include equipment and software.

The fourth phase of implementation concerns the delivery of education in the adaptive learning system, whether in the classroom, in the laboratory or by computer. The focus of this phase is the effectiveness and efficiency of collaborative education delivery. This step should encourage students to understand the purpose of the course, support students' mastery of objectives, and ensure the transfer of students' knowledge from learning to goal setting.

For the fifth phase of the evaluation it is possible to measure the effectiveness and efficiency of the training. Evaluation should indeed take place throughout the instructional design process – in phases, between phases and after implementation. The assessment can be formative or summative. Formative assessment continues within and between phases. The objective of this type of evaluation is to improve the training before implementing the final version. In general, the summative evaluation takes place after the implementation of the final version of the training. This is an evaluation of the overall effectiveness of the training. Summative assessment data is often used to make a training decision.

These phases consist, among other things, of listing the required knowledge and skills, specifying the educational and media orientation of the adaptive system, creating a first step in the network of learning events and creating learning scenarios. Designers are gradually guided to make important decisions related to collaboration.

The concept of collective intelligence of an activity with the ADDIE model

Figure 9. Design of a collaborative work activity

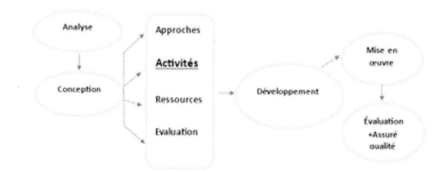

Figure 9 represents the design of a collaborative work activity developed according to our concept, so the recent technological advances in the sector of adaptive systems have allowed the emergence of new tools, method: ADDIE for collaborative work while presenting concepts such as collective intelligence, often associated with the notion of cooperative work.

To guide the process of transforming a known concept, several representations of the concept can be used as intellectual tools. When a new concept is created, consistency in the development process cannot be achieved in this way because the content of the new concept is not yet known.

The design of well-executed collaborative activities relies on the capabilities of learners. It offers a balanced combination of individual and collaborative work and helps create structuring environments. User-friendly and transparent references to resources whose use seems natural and obvious to learners.

Although stimulating, collaborative learning activities in virtual mode, where appropriate, can be a source not only of cognitive growth but also of personal growth. From this dual perspective, teachers can consider integrating this option into their teaching practices, taking into account their learning pace and the limits of the intervention framework.

EDUCATIONAL ACTIVITY SCENARIO IN A COLLABORATIVE ADAPTIVE SYSTEM

Adaptive scenario instructional design is used to organize content to facilitate learning, thereby achieving educational objectives and alleviating issues raised by users. Designing a collaborative adaptive system involves several steps, including identifying specific training goals and objectives, structuring content into logical learning units, creating a complete storyboard for the website, and design of an organization

Figure 10. Educational activity scenario in a collaborative adaptive system

chart. There is comprehensive navigation and logical links to the website to allow users to build mental knowledge structures and ultimately create page templates.

Learning activities (Maha et al., 2021). are tasks that learners must complete and are associated with a set of learning outcomes (Zargane et al., 2023). These activities can be carried out using the tools and resources that make up the learning environment. They can also take place in interactions with other learners and/or teachers. In the latter case, the notion of roles can be used to differentiate the allocation of tasks within an activity. These different synthetic elements are represented by Figure 10 (Zargane et al., 2023).

CONCLUSION

The results of learning processes in our work are significantly influenced by the adaptive collaborative system. The teaching community will find it much easier to create an adaptive collaborative system as technology becomes more user friendly. Numerous self-learning possibilities are offered by the adaptive system package. The adaptive system package can make learning interesting whether it is live or offline (Trestini, 2018).

There are many criteria, as shown by recent work on collaborative adaptive learning discussed in the previous section, which appear essential for designing collaborative adaptive systems that contribute to learning success. To do this, we compared existing platforms based on the following criteria.

In adaptive content mode with which they will share their knowledge with each other so that at the end of the learning process, students obtain complete information about the courses or unit. Students actively participate in the training. The electronic content package encourages collaboration and active participation in learning and promotes students' learning pace.

The preparation, planning, management and evaluation of collaborative learning activities rely on certain key decisions and represent a significant workload for the design of educational scenarios, while the participation of learners in these activities requires significant investments .

The online learning system for adaptive tasks in collaborative activities was developed based on the ADDIE model which covers 5 stages. It covers analysis, design, development, implementation and evaluation.

In our work the ADDIE model has been considered a valuable source of additional information because it provides good teaching practices that improve the work of curriculum designers and educators. Specifically, when applying the studied models, good teaching practices include multimedia presentations, feedback, various exercises and interactive activities, combined learning strategies (individualization and collaboration) and teaching was the role of a person. In addition to good teaching practices.

The design of adaptive online systems is well thought out with a participatory approach in line with the concept of participation. Throughout the process, the objective was to structure the engineering work into phases defined by the ADDIE theoretical model.

There are certain advantages when it comes to applying educational delivery models. Although the model people are more adapted than different, the ADDIE tool is profitable while the collected misfortune the educational craftsman ADDIE is a cycle.

REFERENCES

Ahshan, R. (2021). A framework of implementing strategies for active student engagement in remote/online teaching and learning during the COVID-19 pandemic. *Education Sciences, 11*(9), 483. doi:10.3390/educsci11090483

Aljafen, B. S. (2021). EdTech and the Saudi EFL learners: Bane or boon? *Linguistics and Culture Review, 5*(S2), 1630–1642. doi:10.21744/lingcure.v5nS2.2251

Alladatin, J., Gnanguenon, A., Borori, A., & Fonton, A. (2020). Distance Education Practices for Pedagogical Continuity in Beninese Universities in the Context of the COVID-19 Pandemic: The Views of Students at the University of Parakou. *International Journal of Technologies in Higher Education, 17*(3), 163–177.

Amara, S., Macedo, J., Bendella, F., & Santos, A. (2016). Group formation in mobile computer supported collaborative learning contexts: A systematic literature review. *Journal of Educational Technology & Society, 19*(2), 258–273.

Anoir, L., Khaldi, M., Erradi, M., & Khaldi, M. (2023). From the Conceptualization of an Architecture of a Pedagogical Scenario to the Design of a Model of Pedagogical Scenarios in Online Education. In Handbook of Research on Scripting, Media Coverage, and Implementation of E-Learning Training in LMS Platforms (pp. 133-166). IGI Global. doi:10.4018/978-1-6684-7634-5.ch006

Apriyanti, N., Razak, R. A., Rahim, S. S. A., Shaharom, M. S. N., & Baharuldin, Z. (2020). Infographic instructional media as a solution and innovation in physics learning for senior high school students in Indonesia. *International Journal of Information and Education Technology (IJIET), 10*(10), 773–780. doi:10.18178/ijiet.2020.10.10.1457

Arcueno, G., Arga, H., Manalili, T. A., Garcia, J. A., Arcueno, G. G., Arga, H. A., & Garcia, S. (2021, March). *TPACK and ERT: Understanding teacher decisions and challenges with integrating technology in planning lessons and instructions. DLSU Research Congress.*

Balanyk, J. (2017). Developing English for academic purposes MOOCS using the ADDIE Model. In *Inted2017 Proceedings* (pp. 6514–6522). IATED. doi:10.21125/inted.2017.1506

Belhaoues, T., Bensebaa, T., Abdessemed, M., & Bey, A. (2016). AlgoSkills: an ontology of Algorithmic Skills for exercises description and organization. *Journal of e-Learning and Knowledge Society, 12*(1).

Beuscart, J. S., Dagiral, É., & Parasie, S. (2009). A Sociology of Online Activities (Introduction). *Terrains & Travaux, 15*(1), 3–28. doi:10.3917/tt.015.0003

Bonal, X., & González, S. (2020). The impact of lockdown on the learning gap: Family and school divisions in times of crisis. *International Review of Education, 66*(5-6), 635–655. doi:10.100711159-020-09860-z PMID:32952208

Boyinbode, O., Olotu, P., & Akintola, K. (2020). Development of an ontology-based adaptive personalized e-learning system. *Applied Computer Science, 16*(4), 64–84. doi:10.35784/acs-2020-30

Chen, F., Ruiz, N., Choi, E., Epps, J., Khawaja, M. A., Taib, R., Yin, B., & Wang, Y. (2013). Multimodal behavior and interaction as indicators of cognitive load. [TiiS]. *ACM Transactions on Interactive Intelligent Systems*, *2*(4), 1–36. doi:10.1145/2395123.2395127

Chergui, M., Tahiri, A., Chakir, A., & Mansouri, H. (2020). Towards a New Educational Engineering Model for Moroccan University Based on ICT. *Int. J. Eng. Pedagog.*, *10*(3), 49–63. doi:10.3991/ijep. v10i3.12421

Cilla, G., Montes, M., Gomariz, M., Alkorta, M., Iturzaeta, A., Perez-Yarza, E. G., & Perez-Trallero, E. (2013). Rotavirus genotypes in children in the Basque Country (North of Spain): Rapid and intense emergence of the G12 [P8] genotype. *Epidemiology and Infection*, *141*(4), 868–874. doi:10.1017/S0950268812001306 PMID:22873952

Coomey, M., & Stephenson, J. (2018). Online learning: It is all about dialogue, involvement, support and control—according to the research. In *Teaching & learning online* (pp. 37–52). Routledge. doi:10.4324/9781315042527-6

Coomey, M., & Stephenson, J. (2018). Online learning: It is all about dialogue, involvement, support and control—according to the research. In *Teaching & learning online* (pp. 37–52). Routledge. doi:10.4324/9781315042527-6

Creasman, P. A. (2012). *Considerations in online course design* (IDEA paper# 52). IDEA.

Davis, A. L. (2013). Using instructional design principles to develop effective information literacy instruction: The ADDIE model. *College & Research Libraries News*, *74*(4), 205–207. doi:10.5860/crln.74.4.8934

Dejean-Thircuir, C., & Mangenot, F. (2014). Benefits and limitations of web 2.0 tasks in an asymmetrical tele-collaboration project. *Canadian Journal of Learning and Technology*, *40*(1). doi:10.21432/T23019

Ding, L., Zhao, Z., & Wang, L. (2023). Does online teaching strategy matter: Exploring the effect of online teaching strategies on students' ambidextrous innovation capacities based on the online teaching situation in China. *Journal of Research on Technology in Education*, *55*(5), 817–840. doi:10.1080/15391523.2022.2038315

El Asame, M., & Wakrim, M. (2018). Towards a competency model: A review of the literature and the competency standards. *Education and Information Technologies*, *23*(1), 225–236. doi:10.100710639-017-9596-z

Elharbaoui, E., Matoussi, F., Ntebutse, J.G. & Ben-Attia, M. (2018). *The evolution of the representations of Tunisian students through the iterative design of an online learning system.*

Espino, D., Lee, S., Van Tress, L., & Hamilton, E. (2019). Application of the IBE-UNESCO Global Competences Framework in Assessing STEM-focused. *Global Collaborative Learning within a Digital Makerspace Environment*. UNESCO.

Fayolle, A., Verzat, C., & Wapshott, R. (2016). In quest of legitimacy: The theoretical and methodological foundations of entrepreneurship education research. *International Small Business Journal*, *34*(7), 895–904. doi:10.1177/0266242616649250

Fu, Q. K., & Hwang, G. J. (2018). Trends in mobile technology-supported collaborative learning: A systematic review of journal publications from 2007 to 2016. *Computers & Education*, *119*, 129–143. doi:10.1016/j.compedu.2018.01.004

Gupta, L. A. (2016). *Wreading, Performing, and Reflecting: The Application of Narrative Hypertext and Virtual World Experiences to Social Work Education*. Virginia Commonwealth University.

Heard, J., Harriott, C. E., & Adams, J. A. (2018). A survey of workload assessment algorithms. *IEEE Transactions on Human-Machine Systems*, *48*(5), 434–451. doi:10.1109/THMS.2017.2782483

Hoang, A. D., Pham, H. H., Nguyen, Y. C., Nguyen, L. K. N., Vuong, Q. H., Dam, M. Q., Tran, T., & Nguyen, T. T. (2020). Introducing a tool to gauge curriculum quality under Sustainable Development Goal 4: The case of primary schools in Vietnam. *International Review of Education*, *66*(4), 457–485. doi:10.100711159-020-09850-1

Hrich, N., Lazaar, M., & Khaldi, M. (2017). A model for pedagogical supporting based on competencies evaluation and ontologies. *International Research Journal of Computer Science (IRJCS)*, 43-49.

Hrich, N., Lazaar, M., & Khaldi, M. (2019). Problematic of the assessment activity within adaptive E-learning systems. [iJET]. *International Journal of Emerging Technologies in Learning*, *14*(17), 133–142. doi:10.3991/ijet.v14i17.10675

Hutabarat, Z. S., & Ekawarna, E. (2023). Development of Teaching Materials on Learning Economic Models to Improve Students' Cognitive Achievement. AL-ISHLAH. *Jurnal Pendidikan*, *15*(2), 1204–1212.

Ikram, C., Mohamed, E., Souhaib, A., & Mohamed, K. (2021). Integration of pedagogical videos as learning object in an adaptive educational hypermedia systems according to the learner profile. *International Journal of Computer Trends and Technology*, *69*(6), 1–6. doi:10.14445/22312803/IJCTT-V69I6P101

Itçaina, X. (2010). Territorial Regimes of Social and Solidarity-Based Economy: The Case of the French Basque Country. *Geographie, economie, societe, 12*(1), 71-87.

Jatmika, S., Kusmawati, V., Suranto, S., Rahmawati, D., & Setyawati, L. (2022). The Use of Mind Mapping as a Learning Delivery Medium for Business Entity Materials in a Vocational High School. *The International Journal of Technologies in Learning*, *29*(2), 1–13. doi:10.18848/2327-0144/CGP/v29i02/1-13

Kaouni, M., Lakrami, F., & Labouidya, O. (2023). The Design of An Adaptive E-learning Model Based on Artificial Intelligence for Enhancing Online Teaching. *International Journal of Emerging Technologies in Learning*, *18*(6), 202–219. doi:10.3991/ijet.v18i06.35839

Kawtar, Z., Mohamed, K., & Mohamed, E. (2021, March). Collaboration in Adaptive E Learning. In *International Conference On Big Data and Internet of Things* (pp. 235-244). Cham: Springer International Publishing.

Kerdtip, C., & Thammachat, P. (2023). Enhancing Thai Secondary Teacher Lifelong Learning Competencies In A Digital Age. *Journal of Namibian Studies: History Politics Culture*, *34*, 4224–4350.

Krishnan, S. D., Norman, H., & Md Yunus, M. (2021). Online gamified learning to enhance teachers' competencies using classcraft. *Sustainability (Basel)*, *13*(19), 10817. doi:10.3390u131910817

Lafleur, F., & Samson, G. (2019). *Formation et apprentissage en ligne.* PUQ. doi:10.1353/book65750

Lémonie, Y., & Grosstephan, V. (2021). Le laboratoire du changement. Une méthodologie d'intervention au service de la transformation du travailPerspectives méthodologiques pour une ergonomie développementale. *Revue d'anthropologie des connaissances, 15*(15-2).

Liu, S. (2023). *Talent training model for music education majors based on the ADDIE model.* Applied Mathematics and Nonlinear Sciences. doi:10.2478/amns.2023.1.00266

Liu, S. (2023). *Talent training model for music education majors based on the ADDIE model.* Applied Mathematics and Nonlinear Sciences. doi:10.2478/amns.2023.1.00266

Ludwig, C., & Van de Poel, K. (2013). University of Education Karlsruhe, Germany University of Antwerp, Belgium. Collaborative Learning and New Media, 63, 315.

Maha, K., Omar, E., Mohamed, E., & Mohamed, K. (2021). Design of educational scenarios of activities in a learning situation for online teaching. *GSC Advanced Engineering and Technology, 1*(1), 049-064.

Malinowski, D., & Kramsch, C. (2014). The ambiguous world of heteroglossic computer-mediated language learning. *Heteroglossia as practice and pedagogy*, 155-178.

Marcoccia, M. (2010). Adolescent discussion forums: Writing practices and communicative competences. *Revue Française de Linguistique Appliquée, 15*(2), 139–154. doi:10.3917/rfla.152.0139

Mayer, R. E. (2017). Using multimedia for e-learning. *Journal of Computer Assisted Learning, 33*(5), 403–423. doi:10.1111/jcal.12197

Meerhoff, M., Audet, J., Davidson, T. A., De Meester, L., Hilt, S., Kosten, S., Liu, Z., Mazzeo, N., Paerl, H., Scheffer, M., & Jeppesen, E. (2022). Feedback between climate change and eutrophication: Revisiting the allied attack concept and how to strike back. *Inland Waters, 12*(2), 187–204. doi:10.1080/20442041.2022.2029317

Muruganantham, G. (2015). Developing of E-content package by using ADDIE model. *International Journal of Applied Research, 1*(3), 52–54.

Ng, K. C. (2007). Replacing face-to-face tutorials by synchronous online technologies: Challenges and pedagogical implications. *International Review of Research in Open and Distance Learning, 8*(1). Advance online publication. doi:10.19173/irrodl.v8i1.335

Nguyen, D. K., & Okatani, T. (2018). Improved fusion of visual and language representations by dense symmetric co-attention for visual question answering. In *Proceedings of the IEEE conference on computer vision and pattern recognition* (pp. 6087-6096). IEEE. 10.1109/CVPR.2018.00637

Nguyen, P. M., Elliott, J. G., Terlouw, C., & Pilot, A. (2009). Neocolonialism in education: Cooperative learning in an Asian context. *Comparative Education, 45*(1), 109–130. doi:10.1080/03050060802661428

Ollivier, C. (2012). The interaction-based approach and invisible didactics-Two concepts for the design and practice of tasks on the social web. *Alsic-Apprentissage Des Langues Et Systems D Information Et De Communication, 15*(1).

Othmane, Z., Derouich, A., & Talbi, A. (2019). A comparative study of the Most influential learning styles used in adaptive educational environments. *International Journal of Advanced Computer Science and Applications*, *10*(11).

Parola, A., Simonsen, A., Bliksted, V., & Fusaroli, R. (2020). Voice patterns in schizophrenia: A systematic review and Bayesian meta-analysis. *Schizophrenia Research*, *216*, 24–40. doi:10.1016/j.schres.2019.11.031 PMID:31839552

Patel, H. (2019). Learning-space compass framework. *Higher Education Design Quality Forum*.

Petrosky, S. N. (2022). *Interprofessional education activities and new practitioner competence: Implications for practice in nutrition and dietetics education*. University of North Florida.

Sabeima, M., Lamolle, M., Anghour, A., & Nanne, M. F. (2022). *Towards a semantic platform for adaptive and collaborative e-learning*.

Sabeima, M., Lamolle, M., & Nanne, M. F. (2021). *Overview of adaptive and collaborative learning systems*.

Saeedipour, B., Masoomifard, M., & Masoomifard, M. (2013). Survey of Relation between Control Resource, Learning Styles and Self-regulated Learning and Academic Success of Online Course Students. *Teaching and Learning Research*, *10*(1), 19–38.

Salimzadeh, R., Hall, N. C., & Saroyan, A. (2021, September). Examining academics' strategies for coping with stress and emotions: A review of research. [). Frontiers Media SA.]. *Frontiers in Education*, *6*, 660676. doi:10.3389/feduc.2021.660676

Sarwar, S., Qayyum, Z. U., García-Castro, R., Safyan, M., & Munir, R. F. (2019). Ontology based E-learning framework: A personalized, adaptive and context aware model. *Multimedia Tools and Applications*, *78*(24), 34745–34771. doi:10.100711042-019-08125-8

Shibley, I., Amaral, K. E., Shank, J. D., & Shibley, L. R. (2011). Designing a blended course: Using ADDIE to guide instructional design. *Journal of College Science Teaching*, *40*(6).

Shorey, S., Pereira, T. L. B., Teo, W. Z., Ang, E., Lau, T. C., & Samarasekera, D. D. (2022). Navigating nursing curriculum change during COVID-19 pandemic: A systematic review and meta-synthesis. *Nurse Education in Practice*, *65*, 103483. doi:10.1016/j.nepr.2022.103483 PMID:36327596

Sreedevi, P. S., & Kapilas, P. (2022). Impact of Effective E-content Modules for Improving Science Process Skills. *Emerging Trends of ICT in Teaching and Learning*, *266*.

Theelen, H., & van Breukelen, D. H. (2022). The didactic and pedagogical design of e-learning in higher education: A systematic literature review. *Journal of Computer Assisted Learning*, *38*(5), 1286–1303. doi:10.1111/jcal.12705

Trestini, M. (2018). *Modeling of Next Generation Digital Learning Environments: Complex Systems Theory*. John Wiley & Sons. doi:10.1002/9781119513728

Uzunboylu, H., & Koşucu, E. (2017). Comparison and evaluation of seels &glasgow and addie instructional design model. *International Journal of Scientific Research*, *73*(6), 98.

Weibelzahl, S., Paramythis, A., & Masthoff, J. (2020, July). Evaluation of adaptive systems. In *Proceedings of the 28th ACM Conference on User Modeling, Adaptation and personalization* (pp. 394-395). ACM. 10.1145/3340631.3398668

Weibelzahl, S., Paramythis, A., & Masthoff, J. (2020, July). Evaluation of adaptive systems. In *Proceedings of the 28th ACM Conference on User Modeling, Adaptation and personalization* (pp. 394-395). ACM. 10.1145/3340631.3398668

Zargane, K., Erradi, M., & Khaldi, M. (2023). Design and Implementation of Collaborative Pedagogical Scenarios for Adaptive Learning. In Handbook of Research on Scripting, Media Coverage, and Implementation of E-Learning Training in LMS Platforms (pp. 242-250). IGI Global. doi:10.4018/978-1-6684-7634-5.ch010

Chapter 8
From Collaboration to Adaptation:
Designing an Adaptive Collaborative Educational System

Lamya Anoir
https://orcid.org/0000-0003-4787-5974
Higher Normal School, Abdelmalek Essaadi University, Morocco

Mohamed Khaldi
https://orcid.org/0000-0002-1593-1073
Higher Normal School, Abdelmalek Essaadi University, Morocco

ABSTRACT

The evolution of information technologies has created new perspectives in the field of education, enabling the creation of online learning systems. Among these systems, collaborative learning and adaptive learning are emerging as powerful approaches for optimizing the effectiveness of teaching and learning. The chapter explores the transition from collaborative to adaptive learning, highlighting the design of an adaptive collaborative system. By demystifying the key concepts of each approach, the chapter identifies their respective benefits and explores how they can complement each other. Collaborative learning promotes peer interaction, knowledge sharing and the development of social skills, while adaptive learning focuses on personalized content, continuous feedback and dynamic adjustment based on learning data.

INTRODUCTION

Collaborative learning is a field of educational research and practice that has evolved significantly over the decades. Based on vygotsky's (1978) pioneering work on the zone of proximal development, collaborative learning has emerged as a teaching method that emphasizes social interaction, knowledge sharing and peer cooperation to foster richer, deeper learning. However, as technological advances

DOI: 10.4018/979-8-3693-3128-6.ch008

Copyright © 2024, IGI Global. Copying or distributing in print or electronic forms without written permission of IGI Global is prohibited.

transform the way we teach and learn, it has become imperative to examine how collaborative learning can be integrated into the broader context of adaptive learning.

Adaptive learning, which takes advantage of learning data and information technologies to personalize teaching, has become a key approach in contemporary education (Vanlehn, 2006). It aims to adapt content, resources and teaching methods to the specific needs of each learner (Lamya et al., 2022). This personalization enhances learning efficiency by taking into account the individual differences of each learner (Lamya et al., 2021).

This chapter explores the convergence of these two approaches, from collaborative learning to adaptive learning, with a focus on the design of adaptive collaborative educational systems. We will examine the fundamentals of each approach, their respective benefits, and how they can complement each other to create an enriching learning experience. We will also discuss the tools and methodologies needed to reconcile these two worlds and design educational environments that take advantage of peer collaboration while dynamically adapting to the needs of individual learners.

Thus, this chapter sets out an itinerary that will take us from the foundation of collaborative learning to the development of adaptive educational systems that integrate collaboration to deliver a richer, more personalized educational experience.

COLLABORATIVE LEARNING: FOUNDATIONS AND BENEFITS

Crucial Concepts in Collaborative Learning

According to Henri and Lundgren-Cayrol (2000), "Collaborative learning is an active process in which the learner works to build knowledge. The learner commits to working with group members towards a common goal, while reconciling personal interests and objectives. Exchanges with the group and the completion of a collective task enable them to share their discoveries, negotiate the meaning to be given to their work and validate their newly-constructed knowledge" (Henri & Lundgren-Cayrol, 2000).

Collaborative distance learning (figure 1), as defined by Henri and Lundgren-Cayrol (2001), is not a theory, but rather an active, learner-centered approach that takes place in an environment where learners can express their ideas, articulate their thinking, develop their own representations, elaborate their cognitive structures and validate their new knowledge (Henri & Lundgren-Cayrol, 2000). This approach adopts a design that recognizes the individual and collective dimensions of learning, encourages interaction and exploits the distributed cognitions within the environment. The group plays a supportive and motivating role, contributing to each learner's achievement of a common, shared goal. Collaboration is made possible by communication between learners, the coordination of their actions and the commitment of each learner to the group (Tadlaoui & Khaldi, 2020).

Collaborative learning promotes:

- The development of high-level skills: analysis, synthesis, problem solving and evaluation;
- The implementation of effective cognitive and metacognitive strategies to exploit available cognitive resources;
- Group synergy for the elaboration of complex knowledge through discussion and negotiation of meaning.

Figure 1. Collaborative learning approach

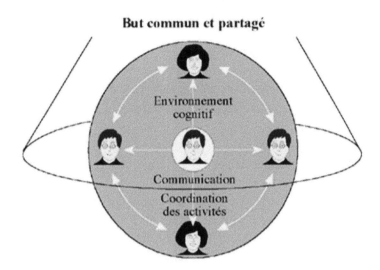

Collaborative learning thus differs from individual learning, where interdependence between learners is considered null, since there is no form of interaction between learners. It also differs from competitive learning, in that the interdependence between learners is negative, as the learning of one is at the expense of the learning of the other.

Collaborative learning is based on several fundamental concepts that support this pedagogical approach. These key concepts are central to understanding and implementing collaborative learning. In this section, we will examine these concepts in detail, using renowned academic references to illustrate their importance:

- Peer-to-peer and group interaction

Peer interaction and group collaboration are essential pillars of collaborative learning (Johnson & Johnson, 2017). This dimension involves learners working together to achieve common goals, sharing knowledge and perspectives, and contributing to the creation of a dynamic learning environment (Slavin, 2015).

- Sharing knowledge and experience

Sharing knowledge and experience is at the heart of collaborative learning (Vygotsky, 1978). Learners bring their individual knowledge and unique experiences to the group, promoting mutual learning and collective enrichment (Bruffee, 1999).

- Role of the Instructor as Facilitator

In a collaborative learning context, the instructor assumes the role of facilitator (Dillenbourg, 1999). This role involves guiding and supporting learners, while giving them responsibility for their own learning. The instructor plays a key role in creating an environment conducive to collaboration and active learning (Michaelsen et al., 2004).

Advantages of Collaborative Learning

Collaborative learning offers a multitude of advantages that place it at the heart of innovative pedagogical approaches. In this section, we explore the main advantages of collaborative learning to illustrate these benefits:

- Enhancing understanding through teaching

One of the major benefits of collaborative learning is the ability of learners to reinforce their own understanding by teaching others. Rosenshine and Meister (1994) studied this notion, known as the teaching effect. They found that learners who explain and teach concepts to their peers develop a deeper understanding than those who simply receive information. In other words, teaching others enhances personal understanding, as it forces learners to organize their thoughts and consolidate their knowledge (Rosenshine & Meister, 1994).

- Development of social and communication skills

Collaborative learning promotes the development of essential social and communication skills. According to Johnson & Johnson (2017), peer collaboration encourages communication, conflict resolution and collective decision-making. Learners learn to work together, listen actively, express their ideas clearly and receive constructive feedback. These skills are invaluable in everyday life and in the professional world.

- Promoting Critical Thinking and Problem Solving

Collaborative learning stimulates critical thinking and problem solving. In a study by Michaelsen et al (2004), researchers found that group discussion encourages learners to consider different perspectives, evaluate alternative solutions and justify their choices. This reinforces critical thinking by encouraging learners to question their own ideas and develop problem-solving skills.

In sum, collaborative learning offers significant benefits by strengthening understanding, developing social and communication skills, and fostering critical thinking and problem-solving. These benefits make it a valuable educational approach in a variety of learning contexts.

Adaptive learning represents a major advance in education, capitalizing on the possibilities offered by information technology. This section takes a deep dive into the foundations and applications of adaptive learning, highlighting the guiding principles that make this approach so promising.

Learners' Level of Expertise and Type of Guidance

A. Level of learner expertise

This strategy is aimed at expert-level learners. According to Henri and Lundgren Cayrol (2000), "collaborative learning is suited to learners who can demonstrate learning maturity and autonomy" and who feel responsible for their own learning.

Andragogy explains learners' level of expertise in collaborative learning. Andragogy is an adult education model based on six assumptions (Knowles, 1978):

- The need to know the reason for learning.
- The learner's self-concept and the concept of being aware of responsibility for one's own learning.
- The role of the learner's experience.
- Willingness to learn.
- The learner's orientation to learning.
- Motivation

Thus, in the case of adult learners, "because of their experience and life situation, they learn more autonomously than younger learners, and expect their learning to be immediately transferable". On the other hand, the possibility of using this strategy with younger learners should not be ruled out, as education systems try to develop learners who are autonomous and responsible for their own learning.

B.   Type of guidance

The teacher's role: The teacher's role derives from socioconstructivism. The teacher supervises helps and guides learners. The teacher adapts his or her interventions according to the group's degree of autonomy, and his or her ultimate aim is to give learners as much control as possible over their learning. The teacher must be available for learners when they encounter difficulties. The teacher must be ready to give pedagogical intervention that is effective, appropriate and helps the learner to keep going (Jeonghyum & Jisu, 2014). We recall that without neglecting to provide support for individual learning, the teacher will be primarily interested in coordinating group actions and collective processes.

Role of the learner: Not all learners are at the same level, and not all learn at the same pace. On the other hand, learners' perceptions are influenced by group members' knowledge and opinions (Jeonghyum & Jisu, 2014). Moreover, learners are responsible for their own learning and for achieving their goals and objectives. For this reason, learners participating in collaborative learning must be mature and autonomous. Learners are also responsible for achieving the goal set by the group.

Learners work in groups, either face-to-face or virtual. They work together to achieve a common goal set by the group members. The group will work to achieve the goal through activities, but each member of the group will individually seek to achieve the goal on his or her own. The result of this collaboration will be several productions, including a collective production and individual learner productions. What's more, collaboration values an interdependence between members of an associative nature, since the most important thing for members is to pool their ideas, share their achievements and find inspiration, support and backing from the group.

ADAPTIVE LEARNING: PRINCIPLES AND APPLICATIONS

Fundamental Principles of Adaptive Learning

The term "adaptive" is associated with a wide range of system features and functions in the e-learning industry, so the quality attributable to the system must be limited when using this term.

Table 1. Pedagogical and organizational variables in collaborative learning

Pedagogical and organizational variables	Collaborative Learning
Learning objective	• The learner defines his or her personal goals and objectives. • Learners give meaning to their training by setting objectives that include the development of their learning strategies and collaborative skills.
Goal attainment	• Shared by the group of learners. • All work towards it, accommodating their own interests, goals and objectives.
Training content, object to know	• To explore: the learner explores the content to understand its structure and make it his or her own. • His is done individually and in groups.
Control and autonomy	• Depends on learner's maturity and autonomy. • Trainer encourages autonomous functioning of learner and group.
Pedagogical formula	• Learning is the result of individual work supported by group or team activities. • Learner shares resources with the group. • Learner uses group work to learn.
Pedagogical activity	• Flexible, open structure. • Free exploration and discovery
Tasks and sub-tasks	• Performed by the learner in his/her own way. • The same or a similar task is completed in a group.
Social and cognitive interdependence	• Encouraged by sharing resources.
Team composition	• Chosen by learners in agreement with the trainer
Group and team organization	• Flexible and organized by learners
Participation	• Voluntary and spontaneous.

Source: Henri and Lundgren-Cayrol (2000)

Adaptive learning has been described as a concept ready to remodel education. Its appeal to educators stems primarily from the promise of personalized learning (Kerr, 2015). Its appeal to policymakers its promises of accountability, increased productivity and cost savings (Webley, 2013). Despite a very high initial investment cost, online adaptive teaching online adaptive teaching is cheaper than traditional alternatives such as classroom teaching (Spring, 2012).

Adaptive learning, sometimes referred to as intelligent teaching, is a pedagogical method that uses technology as a teaching tool and is responsible for organizing human resources and learning materials according to the unique needs of each learner (Anoir et al., 2022).

Adaptive learning is based on a set of key principles that govern how it works. These principles guide the personalized delivery of learning based on the individual needs of each learner.

- Learning Data Collection and Analysis: Technologies are used to collect data on each learner's performance and learning preferences. This data is then analyzed to generate valuable insights into each learner's specific needs (VanLehn, 2006).
- Personalized Content and Instructional Sequence: Based on the data collected, adaptive learning adjusts the content, complexity and progression of instruction to align with each learner's skills and needs (Brusilovsky, 2001).

- Continuous feedback and dynamic adjustments: Adaptive learning provides immediate feedback on learner performance. This feedback is used to make adjustments in real time, ensuring an optimal learning experience (Corbett & Anderson, 1995).

Applications of Adaptive Learning

The benefits of adaptive learning are finding diverse and influential applications in the field of education.

Personalized e-learning environments: E-learning platforms use adaptive learning to deliver tailored content and activities, creating an individualized learning experience (Kaplan-Rakowski et al., 2014).

Support for Learners with Special Needs: adaptive learning can be particularly beneficial for learners with special educational needs. By adjusting content and teaching methods, it offers tailored support to promote their success (Barker et al., 2018).

Improved Learner Retention and Motivation: By providing teaching tailored to their needs, adaptive learning helps increase knowledge retention and maintain learner motivation.

In short, adaptive learning based on sound principles and varied applications, offers a dynamic and highly effective educational approach that is revolutionizing teaching and learning.

Types of Adaptive Systems

In this section, we present the different types of adaptive systems, using the theoretical approaches introduced earlier:

- Macro-adaptive educational systems: The macro-adaptive approach is considered the oldest approach, where learners were simply tracked by the qualities of aptitude tests. This type of system was developed to adapt the system's operation to the learner's abilities.
- Computer Managed Instruction (CMI) systems offer many macro-adaptive pedagogical features that enable the teacher (tutor) to monitor and control the student's learning activities. In addition, CMI systems incorporate features of micro-adaptive models (e.g. prediction of learners' learning needs).
- Intelligent Tutoring Systems (ITS): ITS are adaptive teaching systems applying Artificial Intelligence (AI) techniques. The aim of ITS is to deliver the benefits of instruction automatically and cost-effectively (Shute & Psotka, 1994). ITSs are made up of components representing learning content, instruction and teaching strategies, as well as mechanisms for understanding a learner's learning state in consideration. ITS is a true example of personalized learning. Two main families of ITS concepts for personalized learning can be distinguished. The first, personalized learning, implies that all learners follow the same learning path, but at different paces. The second distinguishes a specific path that allows each learner to follow a specific learning path according to his or her responses.
- In ITS, these components are arranged in the expertise module, the learner module, the tutoring module and a user interface module, as shown in Figure 2 (Brusilovsky, 1994).

The expertise module evaluates the learner's performance and generates the teaching content.

The learner module represents the user's current knowledge and evaluates his or her reasoning strategies and conceptions, enabling the ITS to determine the appropriate teaching process to continue.

Figure 2. Components of an ITS
Source: Brusilovsky (1994)

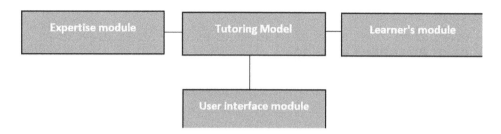

The tutoring module contains information for the selection of teaching materials.

The user interface module is the communication component that controls interaction between the learner and the system. STI applies the micro-adaptive model from the learning decision in the diagnosis and teaching prescriptions are generated during the task. Furthermore, in combination with the ability variables, the expertise module generates the conditions for obtaining instructions based on the learner's characteristics (Mödritscher et al., 2004).

The Learner Profile: Learning Styles

Adaptive e-Learning systems often employ learner models. A learner model is an internal representation of the user's properties, through which the system adapts to each user's needs. Before this model can be used, it has to be constructed, a process which requires a great deal of effort to gather the required information and finally generate a learner model.

A learner profile is a set of personal information about the learner. This information is stored in the system without the addition of a more detailed description or interpretation of the information collected. Learner profiles represent cognitive abilities, intellectual skills, and intentions, learning styles, preferences and interactions with the system. These properties are stored after being assigned values. These values can be definitive or change over time depending on the content and quantity of learner-related information stored in the learner profile, a learner can be modeled. In this way, the learner profile is used to retrieve the information needed to build a learner model. Koch describes a learner model as a representation of the system's beliefs about the learner (named user by Koch and Kay) (Koch, 2000).

Pedagogical models and the interactions between participants in the environment to meet the individual needs and preferences of learners as they arise.

Personalizing learning means enabling the learner to acquire knowledge and master skills based on the learner's profile, which will enable us to locate the learner's preferences, especially his or her learning style, so as to adapt learning to him or her, and to give an idea of the learner's social dimension, his or her relationship with others, and his or her participation in the construction of this society (Tadlaoui & Khaldi, 2020).

User profiles provide information about the user to personalized content and application defined according to the user's specific and individual needs. Content profiles represent descriptive information about search, recommendation and content management resources. Usage profiles show how users behave and relate to content (Desai, 2020). As well as their learning styles, which essentially focus on learner characteristics. When learning situations are taken into account, which is not the most frequent

Figure 3. The experiential learning cycle

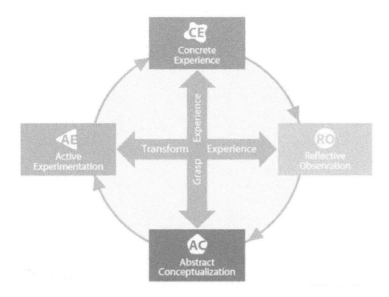

case, they are mainly described from the learner's point of view, in terms of the content to be acquired and the media used to present this content (Chartier, 2003).

Consequently, several researchers have discussed learning styles and their impact on determining how the learner prefers to learn. In our research, we chose to work with the Kolb model (Kolb & Kolb, 2005), the DUNN and DUNN model (Dunn et al., 2008) and the Felder Silvermen model (Graf, et al. 2007).

The Experiential Learning Theory (ELT) proposed by Kolb is a dynamic vision of learning based on a learning cycle driven by the resolution of the dual dialectic of action/reflection and experience/abstraction. Learning is defined as "the process by which knowledge is created through the transformation of experience.

Knowledge results from the combination of an experience of grasping and transformation". (Kolb, 1984). Grasping experience refers to the process of taking in information, and transforming experience is how individuals interpret and act on that information. The ELT model depicts two dialectically linked modes of experience capture:

Experience (CE) and Abstract Conceptualization (AC) - and two dialectically linked modes of transformative experience - Reflective Observation (RO) and Active Experimentation (AE).

Learning results from resolving the creative tension between these four modes of learning.

These implications can be actively tested and used as guides to create new experiences (Figure 3).

The Dunn and Dunn model was developed by Dr Rita Dunn and Dr Kenneth Dunn of St John's University in New York. It comprises twenty to twenty-one elements, depending on the appropriate age of the assessments administered (Dunn et al., 2008).

Felder and Silverman describe a learner's learning style in more detail, based on learners' preferences and the way they receive and process information.

Felder and Silverman's learning style model FSLSM comprises four dimensions with two opposing characteristics. Each learner is characterized by a specific preference for each of these dimensions (Graf, et al. 2007) (Figure 5):

Figure 4. The Dunn & Dunn model

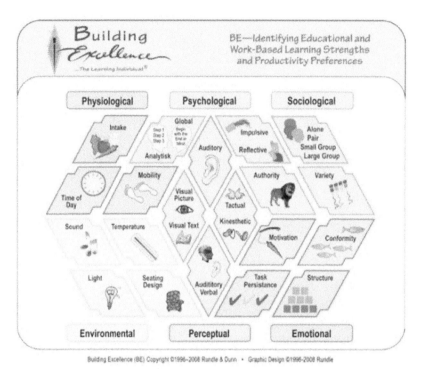

Kolb's model focuses on the theoretical and pedagogical aspects of learning processes, and the DUNN and DUNN model will be used to test the context of the learning process through the five dimensions: environment, emotional stimuli, sociological preferences, physiological preferences, psychological processing inclinations, then Felder Silvermen's learning style model which covers four dimensions active/reflective, sensing/intuitive, visual-verbal, Sequential/Global (Graf, et al. 2007).

Figure 5. Felder and Silverman FSLSM learning styles model

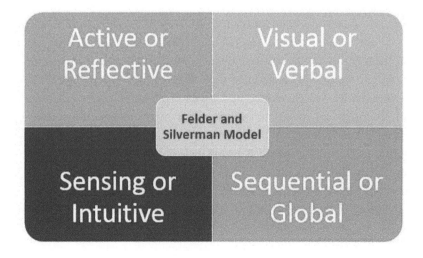

Kolb's LSI (Learning Styles Instrument) Questionnaire (Wintergerst et al. 2001), an 80-item questionnaire designed to identify the learning styles of individual learners.

The BE (Building Excellence Survey) (Dunn & Honigsfeld, 2013) based on Dunn & Dunn's model identifies learning styles according to the appropriate age of the learner's administered assessments.

The Index of Learning Styles (ILS), developed by Felder and Soloman, is a 44-item questionnaire for identifying learning styles according to the FSLSM, based on each learner's preferences for each dimension of the model (Graf, et al. 2007).

PERSONALIZED LEARNING AND COOPERATIVE LEARNING

Personalized learning provides flexibility and support for learners to learn what, how, when and where to learn and to demonstrate mastery of knowledge. Specifically, this flexibility and support is designed around teaching methods, content, activities, objectives and learning outcomes (Walkington & Bernacki, 2020).

Personalizing is not the same as individualizing. Individualizing is about one-to-one tuition; personalizing is about the collective, cooperative dimension of learning. Personalizing teaching means above all seeking to meet the identified needs of groups of learners (Connac, 2018 ; Tadlaoui & Khaldi, 2020).

Cooperative learning is based on groups with very diverse profiles, heterogeneous groups. This is supposed to energize exchanges and encourage interactivity.

Collaborative learning is designed to progress and cooperative learning to fix learning (Baudrit, 2007).

Indeed, cooperative learning corresponds to a division of tasks between learners, where each can autonomously and responsibly accomplish his or her share of the work. Cooperative learning teaching methods, models and procedures organize learners in such a way those they:

Figure 6. The cooperative approach
From Henri and Lundgren-Cayrol (1997)

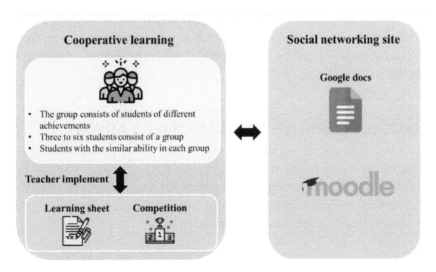

Figure 7. The target of pedagogical differentiation
source: Connac (2021)

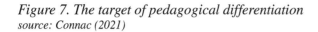

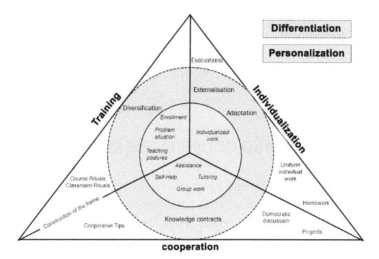

- Work in groups towards a common goal or outcome
- Share problem situations
- Conduct work through interdependent behavior
- Take into account individual contributions and efforts

In the journal Education and socialization, Sylvain Connac proposes an article in which he questions these different terms (Figure 7). More specifically, he provides a clarification for a better understanding of pedagogical action, and to a matrix of three benchmarks for thinking about personalized forms, he presents personalization as a narrower organization than differentiation. In white, what is not directly involved in differentiation, in blue, what would correspond to differentiation, in beige, what would be specifically in the field of personalization?

In conclusion, personalization is linked to cooperation and a conception of the person, of which the person is an individual. Personalizing does not mean relying on group work, where the important thing is the instructions and activities given by the teacher. With cooperation, we're not in the business of tightly controlling learners' activities.

INTEGRATING COLLABORATIVE AND ADAPTIVE LEARNING

The successful integration of collaborative and adaptive learning represents an exciting area where the synergies between these two educational approaches can be harnessed to deliver an exceptional learning experience. In this section, we will explore how these two worlds can merge synergistically to create richer, more responsive educational environments for learners.

Synergies between Collaborative and Adaptive Learning

Using collaboration to improve data collection, collaborative learning can facilitate the collection of richer, more nuanced learning data. Peer collaboration can reveal behaviors, skills and preferences that would not be readily observable in an individual context. In this way, collaboration can enrich the database on which adaptive learning is based (Dillenbourg, 1999).

Personalizing collaborative activities: The data collected by adaptive learning can be used to personalize collaborative activities. For example, work groups can be formed according to learners' skills and needs, creating more effective peer synergies (Soller, 2001).

Adapting workgroups to skills and needs: Adaptive learning can contribute to the formation of dynamic workgroups. Based on data on skills and learning preferences, adaptation can create heterogeneous or homogeneous groups to maximize collaborative learning (Dillenbourg, 1999).

Designing an Adaptive Collaborative System

Designing an adaptive collaborative system requires a systematic and thoughtful approach, using relevant data and appropriate techniques.

Collecting Relevant Data for Collaborative Adaptation: Data collection must be targeted to include information on peer interactions, individual contributions and peer feedback. This data will be used to personalized collaborative activities (D'Mello et al., 2015).

Learner Profile and Group Modeling: Modeling learner profiles and groups is crucial. It can be based on machine learning algorithms to identify the skills, preferences and needs of each learner and group (Hernández-Leo et al., 2006).

Adaptation and Activity Suggestion Algorithms: Adaptive collaborative systems use sophisticated algorithms to recommend activities, work peers and resources in real time, based on learning profiles and objectives (Rosé et al., 2008).

Integrating Peer Feedback into Adaptation: Integrating peer feedback into the adaptation process enables learners to improve each other. Providing tools to assess peer work and using these assessments to adjust activity suggestions (D'Mello et al., 2015) can achieve this.

In sum, integrating collaborative and adaptive learning requires thoughtful design, accurate data collection and the use of advanced algorithms. However, the potential benefits in terms of improved learning and enhanced collaboration are well worth the effort.

DESIGN PROCESS FOR AN ADAPTIVE COLLABORATIVE EDUCATION SYSTEM

The design of an adaptive collaborative educational system is a complex process that relies on a solid foundation of research.

With this in mind, the following figure proposes a general architecture for the design process of an adaptive collaborative educational system (Figure 8):

The use case diagram describes the various stages in the design process:

Figure 8. Use case diagram for the design process of an adaptive collaborative educational system

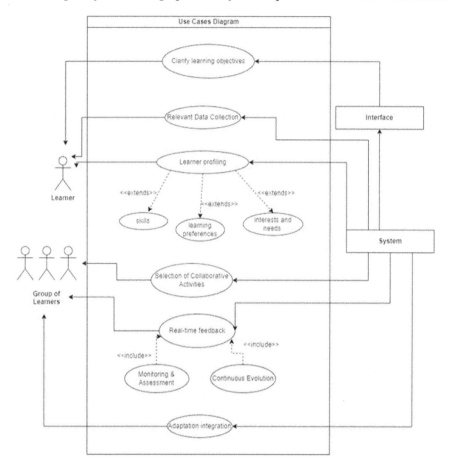

- Understanding Learning Objectives: To design an adaptive collaborative educational system, it is essential to understand the specific learning objectives you wish to achieve. This understanding will form the basis for designing the learning environment (VanLehn, 2006).
- Collect relevant data: Set up data collection mechanisms to gather information about learners. This may include information on performance, learning preferences, collaboration habits, etc. (Dillenbourg et al., 2009).
- Learner profiling: Use data analysis techniques to create learner profiles. These profiles should take into account the specific skills, learning styles, interests and needs of each learner (Brusilovsky, 2001).
- Select Collaborative Activities: Identify collaborative activities that are aligned with learning objectives. This can include group discussions, collaborative projects, simulations, etc. (Soller, 2001).
- Personalize Collaborative Activities: Use learner profiles to personalize collaborative activities. For example, create work groups based on learners' complementary skills and adapt the complexity of tasks (Rosé et al., 2008).

- Real-time feedback: Integrate real-time feedback mechanisms that inform learners of their progress and performance. This feedback can come from peers, instructors or data analysis (D'Mello et al., 2015).

- Evaluation and Continuous Improvement: Establish monitoring mechanisms to evaluate the system's effectiveness. Analyze data on learner performance, engagement, and the effectiveness of collaborative activities to make continuous improvements (Hernández-Leo et al., 2006).

Indeed, such an adaptive collaborative educational system skillfully combines the advantages of collaborative and adaptive learning to deliver a rich, personalized learning experience.

On the other hand, creating an adaptive collaborative learning system requires appropriate modeling to understand and design the software architecture. UML (Unified Modeling Language) classes are used to represent the entities, interactions and relationships in our system:

The Figure 9 shows the class diagram representing the key entities and their relationships in the adaptive collaborative educational system. The following classes have been identified to design this innovative learning environment:

- Learner: The "Learner" class is at the heart of the system. It represents the end users of the educational platform. Each learner is characterized by attributes such as surname, first name, skills, learning preferences and learning history. Methods associated with this class include the ability to access content, participate in collaborative activities and receive personalized feedback.

- Teacher: Teachers play a role in creating and supervising collaborative activities. The "Teacher" class is associated with attributes such as surname, first name and area of expertise. The methods in this class enable teachers to create collaborative activities, monitor learner progress and provide educational guidance.

- Collaborative Activity: Collaborative activities are an essential part of the educational environment. The "Collaborative Activity" class includes attributes such as title, description, resources and activity complexity. Methods in this class include the ability to assign learners to groups, collect data on collaboration within the activity and adjust its complexity according to learner profiles.

- Collaborative Group: Learners participate in collaborative activities within groups. The "Collaborative Group" class is associated with a list of learners and common learning objectives. The methods of this class enable group members to collaborate on projects, evaluate their peers and share resources.

- Adaptive System: The "Adaptive System" is the engine that personalizes the learning experience. It uses a database of learners and adaptive algorithms to analyze learning data personalize activities and provide tailored feedback.

- Database: The "Database" class is a fundamental entity that stores information about learners, activities, results, resources and profiles. It ensures the persistence of data essential to the smooth running of the system.

- User interface: User interfaces are the points of interaction between learners, teachers and the system. They enable users to display content, collect interaction data and visualize the results of their learning.

Figure 9. Class diagram for the design process of an adaptive collaborative educational system

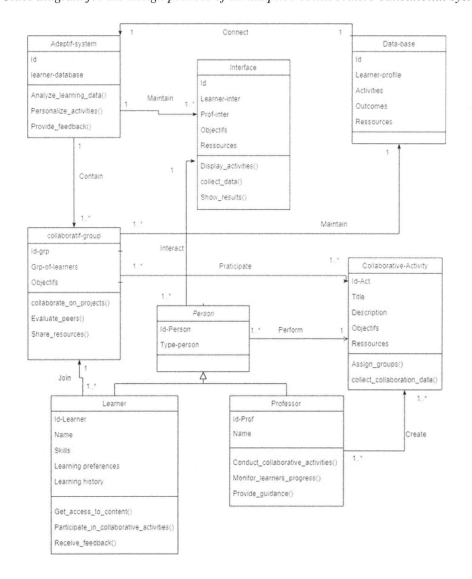

In sum, this class diagram represents the essential components of your adaptive collaborative educational system, showing how learners, teachers, collaborative activities, groups, the adaptive system, the database and user interfaces interact to deliver a personalized, interactive learning experience.

CONCLUSION

Collaborative and adaptive learning are two complementary pedagogical approaches that can be merged to create an optimal learning environment. Designing an adaptive collaborative system requires a thorough understanding of the principles underlying each approach, as well as data collection, modeling and adaptation techniques. By combining the benefits of peer-to-peer collaboration and adaptive personalization, this system can deliver a more engaging, effective and relevant learning experience for each learner.

REFERENCES

Anoir, L., Khaldi, M., & Erradi, M. (2022). Personalization in Adaptive E-Learning. In *Designing User Interfaces With a Data Science Approach* (pp. 40–67). IGI Global. doi:10.4018/978-1-7998-9121-5.ch003

Barker, S., Ansorge, J., & Mwangi, W. (2018). Personalised Learning in Special Education. In Handbook of Personalization in Education (pp. 187-207). Springer.

Baudrit, A. (2007). Apprentissage coopératif/Apprentissage collaboratif: D'un comparatisme conventionnel à un comparatisme critique. *Les Sciences de l'Education pour l'Ere Nouvelle*, *40*(1), 115–136. doi:10.3917/lsdle.401.0115

Bruffee, K. A. (1999). *Collaborative Learning: Higher Education, Interdependence, and the Authority of Knowledge*. The Johns Hopkins University Press. doi:10.56021/9780801859731

Brusilovskiy, P. L. (1994). The construction and application of student models in intelligent tutoring systems. *Journal of Computer and Systems Sciences International*, *32*(1), 70–89.

Brusilovsky, P. (2001). Adaptive Hypermedia. *User Modeling and User-Adapted Interaction*, *11*(1-2), 87–110. doi:10.1023/A:1011143116306

Chartier, D. (2003). Les styles d'apprentissage: Entre flou conceptuel et intérêt pratique. *Savoirs*, (2), 7–28. doi:10.3917avo.002.0007

Connac, S. (2018). *La personnalisation des apprentissages: agir face à l'hétérogénéité, à l'école et au collège*. ESF Sciences Humaines.

Connac, S. (2021). Pour différencier: individualiser ou personnaliser?. Éducation et socialisation. *Les Cahiers du CERFEE*, (59).

Corbett, A. T., & Anderson, J. R. (1995). Knowledge Tracing: Modeling the Acquisition of Procedural Knowledge. *User Modeling and User-Adapted Interaction*, *4*(4), 253–278. doi:10.1007/BF01099821

D'Mello, S., Lehman, B., Pekrun, R., & Graesser, A. (2015). Confusion Can Be Beneficial for Learning. *Learning and Instruction*, *36*, 11–21.

Desai, D. (2020). *Modeling Personalized E-Learning for Effective Distance Education.*

Dillenbourg, P. (1999). What do you mean by "collaborative learning"? In P. Dillenbourg (Ed.), *Collaborative Learning: Cognitive and Computational Approaches* (pp. 1–19). Pergamon.

Dillenbourg, P., Järvelä, S., & Fischer, F. (2009). The Evolution of Research on Computer-Supported Collaborative Learning. In *Technology-Enhanced Learning* (pp. 3–19). Springer. doi:10.1007/978-1-4020-9827-7_1

Dunn, R., & Honigsfeld, A. (2013, April). Learning styles: What we know and what we need. []. Taylor & Francis Group.]. *The Educational Forum*, *77*(2), 225–232. doi:10.1080/00131725.2013.765328

Dunn, R., Honigsfeld, A., Doolan, L. S., Bostrom, L., Russo, K., Schiering, M. S., & Tenedero, H. (2008). Impact of LearningStyle Instructional Strategies on Students' Achievement and Attitudes: Perceptions of Educators in DiverseInstitutions. *The Clearing House: A Journal of Educational Strategies, Issues and Ideas*, *82*(3), 135–140. doi:10.3200/TCHS.82.3.135-140

Graf, S., Viola, S. R., Leo, T., & Kinshuk. (2007). In-depth analysis of the Felder-Silverman learning style dimensions. *Journal of Research on Technology in Education*, *40*(1), 79–93. doi:10.1080/153915 23.2007.10782498

Henri, F., & Lundgren-Cayrol, K. (1997). *Apprentissage collaboratif à distance, téléconférence et télédiscussion. Rapport interne no 3 (version 1.7)*. Montréal: LICEF. http://www.licef.teluq.uquebec.ca/ Bac/fiches/f48.htm

Henri, F., & Lundgren-Cayrol, K. (2000). *Apprentissage collaboratif à distance: pour comprendre et concevoir les environnements d'apprentissage virtuels*. Québec,Canada: Presses de l'Université du Québec. http://ebookcentral.proquest.com.tlqprox.teluq.uquebec.ca

Hernández-Leo, D., Villasclaras-Fernández, E. D., Asensio-Pérez, J. I., Dimitriadis, Y., & Ruiz-Requies, I. (2006). COLLAGE: A Collaborative Learning Design Editor Based on Patterns. *Journal of Educational Technology & Society*, *9*(1), 58–71.

Jeonghyun, K., & Jisu, L. (2014). Knowledge Construction and Information Seeking in Collaborative Learning. *Canadian Journal of Information and Library Science*, *38*(1), 1–21. doi:10.1353/ils.2014.0005

Johnson, D. W., & Johnson, R. T. (2017). Cooperative Learning in 21st Century. *Annual Review of Education*, *3*, 225–251.

Kaplan-Rakowski, R., Shih, B., & Thompson, C. (2014). Personalized E-Learning in the Workplace: A Multidimensional Model and Case Study. *Computers in Human Behavior*, *30*, 35–47.

Kerr, P. (2015). Adaptive learning. *ELT Journal*, *70*(1), 88–93. doi:10.1093/elt/ccv055

Knowles, M. S. (1978). Andragogy: Adult learning theory in perspective. *Community College Review*, *5*(3), 9–20. doi:10.1177/009155217800500302

Koch, N. (2000). *Software Engineering for Adaptive Hypermedia Systems*. [PhD thesis, Eindhoven University of Technology].

Kolb, A. Y., & Kolb, D. A. (2005). Learning styles and learning spaces: Enhancing experiential learning in higher education. *Academy of Management Learning & Education*, *4*(2), 193–212. doi:10.5465/ amle.2005.17268566

Kolb, D. A. (1984). *Experiential learning: Experience as the source of learning and development*. Prentice-Hall.

Lamya, A., Mohamed, K., & Mohamed, E. (2022). Personalization between pedagogy and adaptive hypermedia system. In *Proceedings of the 5th International Conference on Big Data and Internet of Things* (pp. 223–234). Cham: Springer International Publishing. 10.1007/978-3-031-07969-6_17

Michaelsen, L. K., Knight, A. B., & Fink, L. D. (2004). *Team-Based Learning: A Transformative Use of Small Groups*. Greenwood Publishing Group.

Mödritscher, F., Garcia-Barrios, V. M., & Gütl, C. (2004). The Past, the Present and the Future of adaptive E-Learning. *Proceedings of ICL 2004*. ICL.

Rosé, C. P., Wang, Y. C., Cui, Y., Arguello, J., Stegmann, K., Weinberger, A., & Fischer, F. (2008). Analyzing Collaborative Learning Processes Automatically: Exploiting the Advances of Computational Linguistics in Computer-Supported Collaborative Learning. *International Journal of Computer-Supported Collaborative Learning*, *3*(3), 237–271. doi:10.100711412-007-9034-0

Rosenshine, B., & Meister, C. (1994). Reciprocal Teaching: A Review of the Research. *Review of Educational Research*, *64*(4), 479–530. doi:10.3102/00346543064004479

Shute, V. J., & Psotka, J. (1994). *Intelligent Tutoring Systems: Past, Present, and Future (No. AL/HR-TP-1994-0005)*. ARMSTRONG LAB BROOKS AFB TX HUMAN RESOURCES DIRECTORATE.

Slavin, R. E. (2015). Cooperative Learning in Elementary Schools. *Education 3-13, 43*(1), 5-14.

Soller, A. (2001). Supporting Social Interaction in an Intelligent Collaborative Learning System. *International Journal of Artificial Intelligence in Education*, *12*(1), 40–62.

Spring, J. (2012). *Education networks: Power, wealth, cyberspace, and the digital mind*. Routledge. doi:10.4324/9780203156803

Tadlaoui, M. A., & Khaldi, M. (2020). Concepts and Interactions of Personalization, Collaboration, and Adaptation in Digital Learning. In M. Tadlaoui & M. Khaldi (Eds.), *Personalization and Collaboration in Adaptive E-Learning* (pp. 1–33). IGI Global. doi:10.4018/978-1-7998-1492-4.ch001

VanLehn, K. (2006). The Behavior of Tutoring Systems. *International Journal of Artificial Intelligence in Education*, *16*(3), 227–265.

Vygotsky, L. S. (1978). *Mind in Society: The Development of Higher Psychological Processes*. Harvard University Press.

Walkington, C., & Bernacki, M. L. (2020). *Appraising research on personalized learning: Definitions, theoretical alignment, advancements, and future directions*.

Webley, K. (2013). The adaptive learning revolution. *Time Magazine*, 6.

Wintergerst, A. C., DeCapua, A., & Itzen, R. C. (2001). The construct validity of one learning styles instrument. *System*, *29*(3), 385–403. doi:10.1016/S0346-251X(01)00027-6

Chapter 9
Objectiveize the Evaluation:
Towards an Objective and Fair Measurement of Performance

Ayah Oudghiri
Abdelmalek Esaadi University, Morocco

Ahmed Ibrahimi
ⓘ https://orcid.org/0009-0004-8879-5561
Abdelmalek Essaadi University, Morocco

ABSTRACT

Evaluation is a dynamic, systematic, and methodical process which aims to make a value judgment on performance. It is presented in different forms meeting specific training objectives. Evaluating involves a complex task due to the cognitive, social, cultural, and psychological elements that it involves, and it is not always perceived favorably by neither the evaluators nor by those who are evaluated. The tyrannical omnipresence of grading creates a climate of stress which leads to counter-productivity among learners; school therefore takes on a truly anxiety-provoking character, which has been the subject of numerous debates. The work of Gisèle George in 2002 and the work of Peter Gumbel in 2010 underline that the grading which is observed by subjectivity is an instrument of "pedagogical torture." According to Gérard Scallon, "evaluation is a reality which encompasses an infinity of operations, without this necessarily requiring the judgment of the people who evaluate. "

INTRODUCTION

Evaluation is the backbone of progress in all fields. Fromeducation to business, health and public policy. In the field of education, evaluation could be defined as a set of actions, tasks by which "we <u>delimit</u> a program, a grain of knowledge, skills, competences... ; <u>Achieves</u> a performance (oral, written); and <u>provides</u> a grade or validation shared with an institution, with parents, or even with experts. Laurent Talbot, 2023 It is an estimate by a score of a modality or criterion considered in a behavior or in a product. But this process is not always free of subjectivity.

DOI: 10.4018/979-8-3693-3128-6.ch009

Copyright © 2024, IGI Global. Copying or distributing in print or electronic forms without written permission of IGI Global is prohibited.

Evaluation makes it possible to: *Measure*; Use a measuring instrument, use a quantitative parameter, and be in the realm of precision and certainty. *Estimate*; Formulate a judgment, take a look at the quality of something. It focuses not on knowledge and knowledge, but on skills and competencies that integrate learning and knowledge. So it's not a question of telling yourself that the answer is right or wrong, but how do you arrive at the correct answer? How does the learner reason to solve a particular problem? This is the principle advocated in 2004 by Gérard Scallon who insists on the importance of mobilizing several resources that the learner has previously in his or her personal repertoire as well as those that are external and that he or she must call upon in complete autonomy for the accomplishment of complex tasks or the treatment of problem-situations. The more an apprenticeship is accompanied by evaluative practices, the more effective it is and the more it leads to a better return.

From century to century, teaching/learning undergoes endless innovations and changes; approaches, strategies and objectives. At the beginning of the[20th] century, "the democratization of education", marked in particular in the work of Dewey with his book *"Democracy* and *education",* was born with the public school, to an ethical society that offers the conditions and opportunities for fulfilment for all individuals "It is precisely in the process of educating each individual – which is the essence of society – that the possibility of creating new, constantly renewed and better adapted forms of living together is at stake" (Linteau, 2018) and the need for everyone to follow an education and to have access to the school that had as its objective; preparing all learners for the world of tomorrow, to equip them with soft skills that will enable them to flourish as professional profiles and managers.

Inthe same perspective, we speak today of the "objectification of evaluation" or "objective evaluation" which allows any evaluator to measure competence objectively away from any subjectivity or any other social, political or even personal factor.

According to Marc Romainville, the objectification of evaluation refers to efforts to make an evaluation as far away from subjectivity as possible, despite its inevitable presence. It is therefore necessary to recognize the legitimacy of evaluators while minimizing subjective biases. This concept is addressed in a variety of fields, including education, research, and evaluation psychology.

In the field of education, the objectification of evaluation is a key factor. "It's important to clearly and precisely define what you want to assess, whether it's a level of culture, capabilities or knowledge." (Charles Hadji, 1992). According to Dominique Odry in his book Evaluation in the *Education System in* 2020, the objective is therefore to provide accurate information to optimize educational action by allowing educators to adjust their action accordingly. The current evaluative practices that are subject to grading (summative and certifying evaluation) led us to question ourselves.

How Can the Evaluation Be Objective?

In order to provide answers to our problem, we choose, at firstsight, to define assessment as a learning process, by exposing the type of assessment practiced at each stage of the teaching/learning process.

Secondly, we will detail the figures of subjectivity in evaluation.

We will clarify the difference between the assessment of skills and knowledge, and finally, we will present some tools that can lead us to the objectification of the assessment.

Evaluation: A Learning Process

According to Dr. James W. Popham in his book *"Educational Evaluation"*, assessment is an intellectual activity, is an integral part of intellectual life in general and specifically of the learning process, it has always been considered to be an integral part of a rational approach to life. But it is important not to confuse the evaluation of daily life with that of education or learning, where informal assessment cannot be satisfied or tolerated. Researchers in the field see it as an educator's responsibility, a responsibility of professional ethics.

Marie-Josée Leclerc defined it as a crucial part of the learning process. It aims to make judgments about learning and allows data to be collected, analyzed and interpreted in order to respond to pedagogical decisions. Each of the evaluations is situated during the learning process as part of the evaluation planning. The timing of these depends mainly on their function in the teaching and learning process.

According to the typology of Bloom and his collaborators, three types of evaluation can be distinguished:

TYPES OF EVALUATION

Diagnostic Assessment

With a preventive function, the diagnostic assessment aims to analyze needs and know the level of knowledge and skills prior to a learning sequence in order to position the level of learners, and also propose revising, remedial or recovery activities.

The term "diagnostic" is not globally or universally recognized, with some researchers talking about the adaptation of learners' characteristics to the characteristics of a curriculum refer to a "predictive" (Cardinet, 1977) or "prognostic" (De ketele, 1983 and 1993) function; Allal, 1979 and 1991; Hadji, 1997). All of these designations are considered appropriate since this type of assessment is at the beginning of the learning cycle. According to Gérard Scallon, the term "diagnostic" is not appropriately chosen because, according to him, this term leads to confusion with *formative assessment*, which also has a diagnostic character.

To conclude, the diagnostic assessment is carried out at the very beginning of a training period. According to Marc-André Nadeau, this assessment makes it possible to:

*   Determine the presence or absence of prerequisites to begin learning a new teaching unit.

Before the start of a training course or a didactic unit, the teacher is supposed to analyse the needs of his learners and to ensure the level of acquisition of the necessary prerequisites in the field to be studied.

*   Determine the level of mastery of the objectives in order to situate the learner at the most appropriate starting point.
*   Put differentiated pedagogy into practice in order to work on the specific characteristics of each group of learners.

In order to carry out this assessment, the teacher can propose simple diagnostic exercises, such as: drawing up a list, making a short case study, proposing examples, writing a point of view, proposing a game or a short debate, imagining the continuation of a story, summarizing a subject or a text in a few words... Example 1: "In a text that is no longer than 250 words, describe, in your own style, what collaboration is." Example 2: "Provide an example of effective collaboration related to the legal profession." Example 3: "Suggest five criteria for collaboration."

Formative Evaluation

Formative assessment takes place during the learning process. It aims to monitor learners' mastery and progress throughout the learning process, rather than at the end. It is continuous and interactive, allowing for immediate remediation and regulation of teaching/learning, it serves as a tool for continuous improvement and its result is generally and only communicated to the learner.

Dolorme Charles, in her book *The Assessment in Question*, states that formative assessment is essentially focused, directly and immediately on the management of learning by teachers and actors in the field.

As part of a continuous assessment process, formative assessment allows the learner to learn through this assessment. The absence of grading develops in the learner self-assessment and co-evaluation.

This type of assessment takes place at the end of each task in order to inform the learner and the teacher of the level of mastery achieved and to specify and define where the learner is still experiencing difficulties in order to remedy them.

This assessment makes it possible to:

It is up to the learner to indicate the difficulties he or she has encountered in each stage of the learning process.

It is up to the teacher to define or change the teaching methods of a curriculum, which pushes him to develop remedial measures.

The function of formative assessment is to regulate learning during the course of a learning sequence, a course or an entire study program.

It is an assessment method integrated into the learners' learning process that guides them towards success. It goes beyond the simple success rate and provides an understanding of the extent to which learners have grasped and applied the knowledge they have been taught.

When a formative assessment is planned and instrumented in the syllabus, it is referred to as formal. For example, the teacher can offer an online questionnaire, organize a team meeting at the mid-point of a project, or request a peer assessment or self-evaluation of a task using a criteria grid. On the other hand, as for informal formative assessment, it is generally not planned, i.e., it consists, for example, of asking a spontaneous question to students (online, in chat, or during a class session). And to offer them feedback on their answers.

For a formal formative assessment, we can offer several activities to students: multiple-choice questions, summarizing and summarizing the essential elements of the content presented, making mind maps, answering a questionnaire, etc.

According to University Laval's Academic Regulations, formative assessment must be strongly integrated into the E/A process; the teacher is supposed to propose evaluative and formative activities focusing on specific learning and helping both the learner on the one hand and the teacher on the other hand to position themselves in relation to the level of acquisition required before proceeding with a summative assessment of the same learning.

Summative Evaluation

According to Amimeur Abdelaziz, in his methodological guide to pedagogical evaluation, summative assessment is that which takes place at the time of the exams, which makes it possible to validate and certify the acquisition of knowledge by the learner, to specify whether a particular learner is worthy of a particular grade or if he or she can access the next class. Therefore, the purpose of summative assessment is to provide an assessment (where does the learner stand?) and to allow a decision to be made (is the learner fit to obtain the degree?).

This type of evaluation, which is strictly terminal, is considered as a means of verification and validation; It is an estimate by a score of a modality or criterion considered in a behavior, performance or product.

The specific purpose of this evaluation is to rank the pupils, decide on the next course of action, certify and sanction.

A summative or certifying assessment is a comparison between what is and what should be. During the correction of this assessment there is a perception and interpretation of the deviation that depends on a subject.

Unlike formative evaluation, summative evaluation is always subject to formal and weighted grading, it must be fair, transparent and adequate. It allows learners to achieve a performance related to the objectives to be achieved and the learning achieved during a course. Teachers should also measure the effectiveness of learning and assess learners' knowledge and skills at the end of the learning process.

So, what is the difference between knowledge assessment and skills assessment?

Before proceeding to the detailed answer to this crucial question, we present below atable explaining some ideas for assessments according to the learning objective, which can be carried out online or face-to-face, in the midst of a multitude of digital options and tools.

Figure 1. Some evaluation ideas by learning objective (University Laval)

Learning objectives to be assessed	Diagnostic Assessment Before a teaching	Formative Evaluation During a teaching session	Summative/Certifying Assessment After a course of instruction
Use the kinetic theory of gases in a problem-solving context.	Mini quiz on theory Short Diagnostic Exercise	Application exercises. Team Case Study. Problem solving.	Problem solving.
Design integrated logistics networks using mathematical models and computer tools.	Identify the elements of an already established logistics network.	Application exercises (templates and tools). Analysis of the design of a logistics network. Presentation of the first plan of the design project.	Design a network from an authentic situation.
Describe strategies for developing prevention initiatives.	Questionnaire on initial designs.	Mini-questionnaire. Summary of Strategies (Miro).	Concept Map Examination

Bloom's taxonomy classifies levels of skill acquisition, from simple knowledge of facts to complex manipulation of concepts. Regarding evaluation, according to Bloom, it is a decision-making phase where learners make a judgment about the value of ideas, elements, etc. In order to ensure that all elements are present in the assessment, it is urged to design an assessment that is completely based on these levels of the taxonomy, from knowledge to assessment, with the aim of assessing learners' understanding and mastery.

Learning assessment is the process of assessing the quality of a learner's work against established performance standards and assigning a rating that reflects its quality, summarizing and communicating precisely to parents, schools, even experts and the learner what they are capable of achieving, what they know and what they know and what they are expected to do.

Assessment, therefore, is an essential pillar to promote learning. The more an apprenticeship is accompanied by evaluative practices, the more effective it is and the more it leads to better performance.

THE CHALLENGES OF ASSESSMENT AS A LEARNING PROCESS

As we have communicated in previous steps, assessment is a crucial and integral part of the learning process and presents several challenges:

1- Analyze and define learners' needs: In order to properly plan learning, it is essential to analyze the learners' needs and develop a profile sheet for each student.
2- Define learning objectives: Before any learning process, it is important to precisely define the learning objectives, in order to check at the end of the process, and through evaluation, whether the learners have achieved them or not.
3- Choosing assessment methods: There are different assessment methods (already mentioned in the previous section), their choice depends on the learning objective(s) and the needs of the learners.
4- Tailor assessment to learners' needs: Remediation is essential in every step of the teaching/learning process, while taking into account the specificities of each learner and adapting them to the specific needs of each learning situation.
5- Develop assessment tools: Specify assessment tools that are appropriate for the given learning situation.
6- Ensure regular and constructive assessment: Assessment should be done regularly throughout the learning process, to allow learners to know their progress and work on their shortcomings and teachers to address them.

Assessment presents many challenges and requires a critical and adapted approach to each situation and context to be effective and relevant, assessment must be consistent with learning objectives, teaching strategies and student needs.

According to Réal Bergeron and Marie-France Morin in their article "Evaluating to Learn", assessment must be integrated into the learning process and not as a separate element. This helps to rethink pedagogical practices and adapt assessment methods to the needs of learners.

In sum, the challenges of assessment as a learning process include defining learning objectives, choosing assessment methods, tailoring assessment to students' needs, creating assessment tools, regular and constructive assessment, and integrating assessment into the learning process. There is also a need

Figure 2. The functions of evaluation
Source: *De Ketele & Roegiers (2001)*

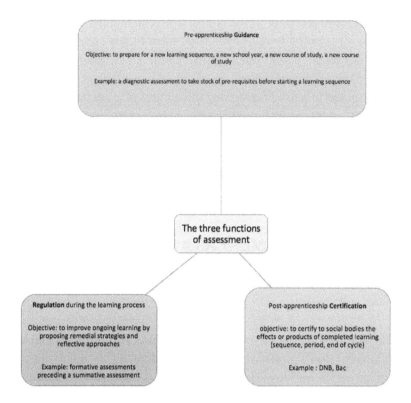

to align assessment with learning outcomes and teaching strategies since assessment must be consistent with the learning objectives and teaching methods used.

In order to overcome the challenges of evaluation, it is essential to promote the use of evaluation, to strengthen evaluation capacities at the national level, to establish an institutionalized consultative process, and to differentiate between the functions of evaluation so that it can play a critical role and support the development of policies and services.

Figure 2 defines the three functions of the evaluation developed by Ketele and Roegiers.

Knowledge Assessment or Skills Assessment

According to Laurent Talbot and Aline Arrieu-Mutel, evaluation is a summary statement of results, level, and success based on data from various sources and measures (observations, exams, etc.)

Knowledge assessment and competency assessment are two different types of assessment, both are essential for measuring learner success, but measure different aspects of learning.

Knowledge Assessment

Knowledge encompasses all the information, facts, ideas, skills, and experiences a person has acquired throughout their life. It is the result of education, reflection and experience. If we are interested in information, if we build a global society on this concept, it is not because of its beauty, but because it carries a meaning that is transformed into knowledge, this organized body of knowledge constitutes "knowledge" for the learner. "It's the act of taking information and being able to give it back. They are necessary for the performance of a task, but only become meaningful, and therefore assessable, when integrated with skills. Prof. Mohamed Khaldi

Knowledge can take many forms, ranging from facts and concepts to practical skills, philosophical ideas, know-how, observations, and theories, to name a few.

According to LAROUSSE; Knowledge is the action, the act of understanding, of knowing the properties, the characteristics, the specific traits of something: the knowledge of nature.

Knowledge assessment is the process of measuring what the learner knows or memorizes about a particular topic. Its purpose is to verify and determine the level of understanding, mastery or acquisition of specific knowledge by an individual. It takes different forms; such as exams, quizzes, written tests, assignments, projects, or even other methods to assess a person's acquired knowledge on a given topic. In order to assess knowledge, it is necessary to take into account its volume, the level of understanding, the ability to grasp what is essential and to put into practice the knowledge acquired. According to V.A. Suhomlinski notation is the most powerful and severe stimulant. There is no denying that the tyrannical omnipresence of grading creates a climate of stress and panic among learners, but it is the most effective element of punishment (acquisition of knowledge = validation / lack of knowledge = failure). V.A. Suhomlinski argues that the note is the sharpest instrument, "using it required great skill and culture."

In summary, knowledge assessment is essential for measuring learners' memorization of theoretical concepts and plays a crucial and decisive role in the adaptation, improvement and remediation of training programmes or teaching strategies.

Competency Assessment

The notion of competence has been the subject of much debate; however, we can detect a uniformity in the definitions proposed throughout the centuries:

"A skill is conceived as an integrated and functional network made up of cognitive, affective, social, and sensorimotor components, likely to be mobilized into targeted actions in the face of a family situation" Allal, 1999

"A skill is an ability to act effectively in theface of a family of situations, which we manage to master because we have both the necessary knowledge and the ability to mobilize it wisely, in a timely manner, to identify and solve real problems" Perrenoud, in Brossard, 1999

"A know-how based on the effective mobilization and use of a set of resources", Ministry of education du Québec, 2001

"Competence is the possibility for an individual to internally mobilize an integrated set of resources in order to solve a family of problem-situations" Roegiers, in Scallon, 2004

"The competent person gives himself the 'power to act' because he has the knowledge and experience of situations in which it is appropriate to act, and moreover he is capable of judging the appropriateness of his action. Competence thus corresponds to what we will call a thoughtful way of acting" Develay, 2015

According to the LE ROBERT dictionary, competence is the in-depth, recognized knowledge that confers the right to judge or decide in certain matters, it is ability or quality. But what is the difference between competence and knowledge?

Figure 3. Diagram of competency elements

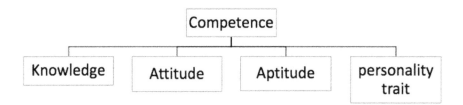

According to Jean-Claude Coulet, competence is the energization organized, striving, scrimmaged, and correctly implemented by a social agent in a particular context and situation in order to accomplish a task. So, competence is a set of elements that allow the individual to act correctly in a specific context and to accomplish a task.

Language competence, on the other hand, is the ability to use language and mobilize language knowledge in a specific communicative or linguistic context.

Canale's (1983) model of communicative competences proposes four components:

1- The grammatical component
2- The Discursive Component
3- The Sociolinguistic Component
4- The Strategic Component

The latest version of the description of language competence appeared under the shadow of the CEFR in 2001, which replaced the traditional model of four competences defined in four communication components:

Figure 4. The description of the CEFR: From four skills to four modes of communication

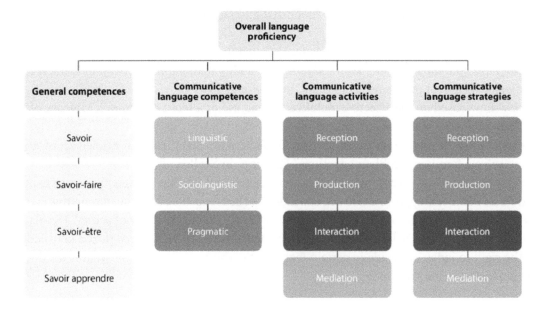

Figure 5. Miller's occupational skills pyramid

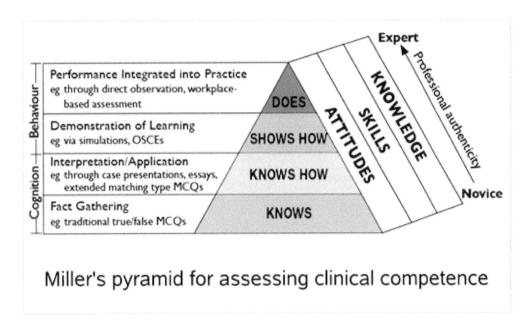

Miller's pyramid for assessing clinical competence

Competency assessment is defined as the process that measures and documents learners' competencies. The purpose of competency assessment is to identify and define the learner's performance problems and address their shortcomings. An 'initial' diagnostic assessment of skills may reveal a need to adapt curricula to the actual level of learners.

As mentioned earlier, the assessment of competences should be carried out at regular intervals, on a periodic basis, which will make it possible to adapt, regulate and remedy the difficulties faced by learners.

Unlike knowledge assessment, which focuses on what the learner knows, competency assessment looks at what the learner can do in a practical way. It aims to measure the actual performance of learners in the application of their skills. The latter helps to guide the development of skills, to guide the decisions to be made during the teaching/learning process, and to assess the learner's ability to perform specific, authentic tasks in different communication situations.

According to Perrenoud, it is essential to assess skills through problem-situations where the learner is expected to succeed or complete a task. The most traditional form of evaluation is that of validation, which involves the mobilization of acquired knowledge and skills in order to solve a complex problem. The idea of situation, therefore, is always linked to and associated with the idea of competence, since, if we follow Le Boterf's conceptualisation, which is in line with many definitions of competences in cognitive psychology and occupational psychology, competence is made up of two components: on the one hand, resources, skills, information, knowledge, attitudes, etc. values, resources available in immediate memory; on the other hand, the ability to use these resources and implement them in order to produce an appropriate and fair performance.

"Competence is the mobilization of several pieces of knowledge, in a given situation and context" Le Boterf

Knowledge vs. Skills

Table 1. Assess knowledge vs. assess competence; Centre de services scolaire des Découvertes, Quebec

Mastery of knowledge	Jurisdictional situation
Knowledge acquisition is verified through activities that engage targeted aspects of the competency.	The assessment of knowledge mobilization allows the full competency (components and criteria) to be sought.
• Refers to the criterion on the mastery of knowledge (targeted by the progression of learning); • More often corresponds to a lower taxonomic level (knowledge – understanding – application); • The type of questions generally used are short-answered, multiple-choice or True or False...	• Allows you to observe several evaluation criteria at once; • Requires judgment on the part of the teacher on the learner's performance; • Most of the time, it corresponds to a high taxonomic level (analyze – synthesize – evaluate).

SUBJECTIVITY IN EVALUATION

Subjectivity

The word "subjectivity" can, in some contexts, be synonymous with "affective", which leads us to return to Jocelyn Benoist's expression which states:

"In the culture of affection and thoughts, the experience of which constitutes the content of the return to oneself, one must see only the undertow of the world, the return to oneself being the return of the world to oneself, not in the closure of one's games, but in the passage always anew possible from one of one's games to another.

The "solitude" in which I find myself leads me back to others, to the experience of other forms of social relations, outside the established codes. The self is knotted and unknotted, from one code to another. The scale of these variations is subjectivity. »

The term "subjective" can also be used to describe the connection to a "humanized" nature, as nature and artifice can often be confused. Bonding with others is now based on ethics rather than mere sympathy, as suggested by Scheler. Benjamin, Adorno and Kracauer question the link with nature in its history: it is no longer just a spiritual manifestation, but rather a rich historical reality, influenced by concrete changes in technology. According to Deleuze and Foucault, affect is seen as something irreducibly different from intention, especially in its madness. Affect no longer refers to values, but rather to the experience of the impossible.

In philosophy, subjectivity is the character of that which belongs to the subjects, to the individuals alone, it is the attitude of one who judges reality in a subjective way. Subjectivity, then, refers to the individual's own nature, his opinions, emotions, experiences and the way he perceives the world. In other words, subjectivity is the set of a person's personal thoughts, feelings, and views that can affect how they perceive and interpret events, information, and experiences. It is often influenced by individual beliefs, values, emotions, which can lead to varying interpretations and judgments of the same situation or set of data.

In linguistics, subjectivity refers to the presence of the speaking subject in his or her discourse.

Sources of Subjectivity in Evaluation

Subjectivity is unavoidable in evaluation, and is considered necessary for authentic evaluation, it can play an important and significant role in the evaluation process, especially in the field of performance evaluation, competency assessment, and knowledge assessment, subjectivity can influence decision-making differently:

The profile of the evaluator is always present and far from neutral, always having personal preferences, opinions or expectations that influence their evaluations. The evaluator's emotional state at the time of evaluation or at the time of scoring can affect their judgments. Because an assessment done when an evaluator is in a good mood can be more lenient than the same assessment done when he or she is in a bad mood. Cultural norms and values are unavoidable factors that can influence how evaluators evaluate behaviors and performance, so what is considered "correct" or "acceptable" may vary from culture to culture.

The first subjectivity in evaluation is the choice of the type of decision and the objective of the evaluation; The assessment prepares a decision that is not known at the beginning of the teaching/learning process, but what is supposed to be well defined beforehand, in order to be able to guide the assessment process, is the type of decision that is made depending on the answers to the next question; What is the purpose of the evaluation?

Depending on the decision that is made, the entire evaluation process will be remediated to meet the objective of the evaluation.

In many situations, the evaluator has some leeway in selecting the purpose of the evaluation. For example, when the head of an SME decides to have an appraisal interview with a member of his team, hehas the possibility of directing this interview towards the joint identification of the actions to be taken to optimize the work of the agent or using this interview to increase or not his remuneration are possible alternatives.

There are many other cases where evaluators are forced to make a decision. This is the case when a committee for the distribution of a textbook is subject to the acceptance or refusal of the approval of the head office. However, it should be noted that there is always someone who determines the type of objective that the evaluation should pursue and their choice will guide the evaluation process. Therein lies the first inevitable and indispensable subjectivity.

According to Cardinet, the choice of evaluation criteria also represents a subjectivity, since again, a choice must be made, each evaluator has his margin of freedom to choose the evaluation criteria adapted to his evaluation objective; does he want to evaluate, spelling, morphosyntax, reasoning, consistency, accuracy of the answer... For each evaluation, and for each type of evaluation, there are a multitude of criteria that can be retained, a choice that must be made, a subjectivity that will arise.

According to Gerard & Van Lint-Muguerza, the choice of criteria should not be made arbitrarily or "in any way", they should be: *relevant, independent* (the choice of one criterion should not lead to the failure or success of another criterion), few in *number* (avoid seeking perfection in vain, identify the criteria), *weighted* (not all criteria should have the same importance).

For the most part, evaluation is subjective, always, inevitably, necessarily. (Cardinet, 1992; Gérard, 2002; Romainville, 2002; Weiss, 1984). It is subjective because, as Durant and Chouinard (2012) describe, throughout its process, evaluators make a series of decisions based on their subjectivity (Gérard, 2002).

These decisions made by the evaluator are neither impulsive nor random, but are the result of systematic and conscious reflection, or at least it should be; the enemy of evaluation is not its subjectivity, but its arbitrariness (Jeffrey, 2013). What differs the human being from other creatures or other living beings is his thought, and therefore his *subjectivity*, as Descartes pointed out at the beginning of the seventeenth century; "I think, therefore I am." Thus, subjectivity is an unavoidable element in evaluation, and is supposed to be managed appropriately to ensure fair and balanced evaluations between subjectivity and objectivity.

Towards the Objectification of Evaluation

Evaluation objectification aims to minimize the influence of subjectivity, personal opinions, and biases in the evaluation process. Objectivity is generally defined as "the quality of what exists in itself, independently of the thinking subject" (Trésor de la langue française). Subjectivity, on the other hand, belongs only to the thinking subject. To clarify why it is essential to frame and objectify evaluation, it would be necessary and essential to return to Stufflebeam's definition of evaluation (Madaus, Scriven & Stufflebeam, 1986), taken up by many researchers in the field; evaluation consists of measuring and then assessing, through criteria, the achievement of teaching objectives, in three stages. The first is the valid, accurate and systematic collection of information appropriate to the defined teaching objectives. The second involves the interpretation of the information collected using criteria. The last is to make the decision; This is the judging phase.

In order to move towards the objectification of evaluation, it is necessary to implement objectification tools such as:

Design of the Test Description

A detailed explanation of the tasks, skills or knowledge that will be assessed in a test, examination or assessment is called a test description. The objectives of the assessment, the assessment standards, the skills or knowledge assessed, and the procedures for taking the examination are detailed in this document. This document allows evaluators and evaluators to clearly understand what is expected during the evaluation and facilitates a fair and consistent evaluation.

Test descriptions are essential to ensure transparency, fairness, consistency in the assessment process, and the validity of the content of an exam and to ensure that the questions asked are representative of the learning targeted by the curriculum. Theyallow both the teacher to plan his teaching, to evaluate objectively and the learners to know what awaits him, what he is expected to achieve and to understand their results. The specification table, a planning element, makes it possible to structure the relevant data for the development of a test and to check the congruence between the content of a test and the learning that can be taught in the context of a program.

It is a document that describes in detail the characteristics, objectives, criteria and conditions of an event.

A test description may include the following:

- Objectives: Defines what the evaluator aims to measure.
- Test Description: Describes the structure of the test, the duration, the type of questions, and the tasks to be completed.
- Evaluation Criteria: Define what constitutes successful performance.

Figure 6. Example of a test description, CEFR

Level of the tests	CEFR A2
Language activities leading to the tests	Listening and reading comprehension / oral and written production
Duration of each event	• C. O: 20 min • C. E: 25 min • P. O: 30 min • O.E.: 45 min
Length of documents used	3min maximum for audio documents, 300 words maximum for written documents
Coefficients	1 for each event
The number of points awarded in each event	20
The Threshold for Success	40 / 80
The minimum mark required per test	7 / 20

Standardization of Criteria

One of the tools to be put into practice to objectify evaluation is standardization, it is recommended to use standardized assessment instruments whenever possible. These instruments are designed so that all evaluators use the same methodology and criteria.

Standardization of evaluation criteria's a process that defines clear, consistent, and measurable evaluation criteria to assess performance, competencies, or outcomes in a specific context.

This standardization is essential to ensure that assessments are consistent and comparable and to facilitate the communication of results between different actors. Several international organizations and forums are working to standardize evaluation standards in various fields, such as research evaluation, development evaluation, and social practice evaluation. There are many organizations involved in the standardization of evaluation criteria, among which we cite:

- The OECD's Development Assistance Committee (DAC), which provides evaluation criteria for enhancing the effectiveness of international development programmes.

- The OECD-DAC Network on Development Evaluation (EvalNET), which promotes robust, well-researched and independent evaluations to enhance the effectiveness of international development programmes.
- The OECD's Development Assistance Committee, which develops quality standards for development evaluation to improve the quality of evaluation processes and their products.

These organizations work closely with experts in the field to create internationally recognized norms and standards that serve as a reference for assessments in their area of expertise.

THE COMPETENCY ASSESSMENT GRID

A competency rubric is a tool used to assess skills gaps for specific roles in an organization. It measures an employee's skills, knowledge, and performance against pre-established job requirements and benchmarks. To create a competency rubric, it's crucial to start by identifying the key competencies that need to be assessed, aligning them with the objectives of the task or work at hand, and then defining the assessment criteria for each competency. These criteria should be measurable, specific, relevant, and linked to the objectives of the task. Then, in order to facilitate the scoring and communication of the results of the evaluation, the expected performance levels for each evaluation criterion should be determined.

Its use provides a framework for the evaluation process. A formative evaluation approach will preferably be based on a criteria grid. This tool is an enabler of self-assessment, peer review or co-assessment.

The success criterion is a compass that allows the learner to complete the task and informs him or her about the level of demand. Before being characterized as an "evaluation grid", the criterion grid is an implementation grid.

Elaboration of the Criteria Grid

- 1st step: The teacher communicates the grid to the learners

The validation or evaluation criteria are provided to the learner by the teacher. The learner is therefore in the course of what he is supposed to implement in his performance in terms of language skills, knowledge, know-how and interpersonal skills.

Table 2. The advantages of the criterion grid

For the learner	For the Teacher
- The learner has a better understanding of what is expected of him/her. He is much more confident and motivated. - The grid is a written record of expectations, which the learner can always use as a benchmark. - It guides the completion of the task, to self-assess and to evaluate oneself among peers. It develops the learner's reflexivity, which helps them learn how to learn. ⇒ **Development of intellectual autonomy.**	- Subjectivity is much reduced, since the teacher gives much more importance to the task than to the learner or the context of the assessment. - It is a means of mediation between the teacher, the learner and even the family. It defines expectations as clearly as possible, clarifies successes and leads to the remediation of learners' shortcomings. - The grid personalizes the support and facilitates the implementation of differentiation. ⇒ **Objectification of assessment and personalization of learning.**

Table 3. Prioritize criteria and define a weighted scale

Pragmatics	Sociolinguistics	Linguistics
- Compliance with the instructions - Relevance of language functions - Speech proficiency	- Ritual of politeness - Language register - Presentation code	-Morphology -Syntax -Lexicon -Pronunciation

- Step 2: The learner and the teacher work together to develop the grid

Following the same principle of the didactic contract, the co-construction of validation criteria is based on a negotiation between the teacher and the learners. Involved in the development of the criterion grid, learners take greater ownership of it. In this case, it is preferable to dedicate a session to it at the beginning of the apprenticeship.

Figure 7. Criteria grid, CEFR

Criteria	Notes	Feedback	Notes	Feedback
Skills				
Productivity				
Writing				
Know-how				
Teamwork				
Rigor and autonomy				
Objectives				
Previous year's objectives				
This year's objectives				

Success criteria can relate to an approach, a result, a behaviour, they validate learning objectives and/ or institutional expectations (standardised one-off tests).

Any use of criteria grids is supposed to be accompanied by qualitative comments, with the primary aim of providing food for thought and operational and individualized advice. This feedback is based on the selected success criteria.

CONCLUSION

Assessment is an essential process to promote learning, the more a learning is accompanied by evaluative practices, the more effective it is and the better it leads to performance.

Three evaluation goals are identified:

- Assessment for Learning: It enlightens teachers about what learners understand and allows them to plan and guide instruction while providing useful feedback to learners.

- Assessment as learning: It allows learners to take part in their learning methods and to adjust and advance their learning. The learner thus moves from a passive member to a social actor responsible for his or her learning.
- Learning assessment: The information gathered from the assessment allows learners, teachers and parents to be informed about the progress of learning at a specific point in time in order to highlight successes, plan regulations and continue to promote success.

It is therefore not a question of eradicating subjectivity, but of controlling and framing it, that is to say, imposing limits on it by developing procedures that can guarantee that it will be deployed in acceptable proportions.

REFERENCES

Alkin, M. C., & Christie, C. A. (2004). *Evaluation roots: Tracing theorists' views and influences.* Sage Publications. doi:10.4135/9781412984157

Allal, L., & Mottier, L. (2008). A Better Understanding of Professional Judgment in Evaluation: Contributions and Implications of the Geneva Study. In L. Allal & L. Lafortune (Eds.), *Professional Judgement in Education: Teaching Practices in Quebec in Geneva* (pp.223-239). Québec: Presses de l'université du Québéc.

Allal, L., & Lafortune, L. (2008). In search of professional judgment. In L. Allal & L. Lafortune (Eds.), Professional Judgement in Education: Teaching Practices in Quebec in Geneva (pp. 1-10). Québec: Presses de l'université du Québec.

Anne, J., , & Nathalie, D. (2019). *Evaluation, a lever for education and training.* De Boeck.

Audet, L. (2010). *Wikis, Blogs, and Web 2.0. Opportunities and impacts for distance learning.* Réseau d'enseignement francophone à distance du Canada (REFAD). https://www.refad.ca/nouveau/Wikis_blogues_et_Web_2_0.pdf

Batier, C. (2012, July 25). *Should we be afraid of evaluation?* [Video]. Charles Hadji. https://youtu.be/sH2QDWxDr1c?si=YVmSvDYVvDf7xeEw

Bautier, E., Crinon, J., & Rochex, J.-Y. (2011). Introduction. In J.-Y. Rochex & J. Crinon (Eds.), *The Construction of Educational Inequalities: At the Heart of Teaching Practices and Practices* (pp. 9–16). De Boeck Supérieur.

Beacco, J. (2007). The Competency-Based Approach to Language Teaching. Paris: Didier.

Beckers, J. (2002). *Developing and Evaluating Skills at School: Towards More Efficiency and Equity.* Éditions Labor.

Bureau, S., & Marchal, E. (2005). The quest for objectivity in workplace evaluation. *Practical Sociologies*, (1), 61–72.

Chen, H. T. (2015). *Practical program evaluation: Assessing and improving planning, implementation, and effectiveness.* Sage Publications.

Chevallard, Y. (2007). *Evaluation, verification, objectification. IREM of Aix-Marseille Faculty of Sciences of Luminy European Commission. (2017).* Handbook on Results-Based Management and Evaluation for Development Cooperation.

Cronbach, L. J. (1989). Six thoughts for evaluators. *Evaluation Practice, 10*(2), 139–146.

De Ketele, J. M. (1996). *Formative Assessment: Foundations and Practices.* De Boeck University.

Fournier, M. A., & Grey, K. C. (2000). Assessing program outcomes: Comparison of four evaluation frameworks. *Journal of Personnel Evaluation in Education, 14*(2), 143–170.

Guba, E. G., & Lincoln, Y. S. (1989). *Fourth Generation Evaluation.* Sage Publications.

Haladyna, T. (2000). An Evaluation of Conjunctive and Compensatory Standard-setting Strategies for Test Decisions. *Educational Assessment, 6*(2), 129–153.

Kirkpatrick, D. L. (1996). Great ideas revisited. *Training & Development, 50*(1), 54–59.

Le Boterf, G. (1994). *On competence. Essai sur un attractor estrange.* Paris, Les Éditions d'organisation.

Louis, R. (1999). *The Assessment of Learning in the Classroom.* Théorie et pratique, Laval, Études vivantes.

Merle, P. (1996). *Student Evaluation, Survey of Professorial Judgment.* Paris, PUF.

Merle, P. (1998). *Sociologie de l'évaluation scolaire.* Paris, PUF.

Merle, P. (2007). *La note, secret de fabrication, Coll.* Éducation et société, Presses Universitaires de France .

Mottier Lopez, L. (2013). From Measurement to Collaborative Evaluation in Education. *Revue française d'administration publique, 4*(148), 939-952.

Mottier Lopez, L., & Figari, G. (Eds.). (2012). *Modelling Evaluation in Education.* De Boeck.

OECD. (2002). *Glossary of key terms related to evaluation and results-based management.* OECD.

Parkes, J. (2001). The Role of Transfer in the Variability of Performance Assessment Scores. *Educational Assessment, 7*(2), 143–164. doi:10.1207/S15326977EA0702_3

Patton, M. Q. (1997). Utilization-focused evaluation: The new century text. *The American Journal of Evaluation, 18*(3), 320–321.

Patton, M. Q. (2008). *Utilization-focused evaluation.* Sage Publications.

Patton, M. Q. (2010). *Developmental evaluation: Applying complexity concepts to enhance innovation and use.* Guilford Press.

Perrenoud, P. (1995). From knowledge to skills. What are we talking about when we talk about skills? *Pédagogie collégiale, 9*(1).

Perrenoud, P. (1998). *Student assessment. From the manufacture of excellence to the regulation of learning.* Brussels, De Boeck.

Perrenoud. (1999). *Teach: act in a hurry, decide in uncertainty. Knowledge and skills in an obscure profession* (2nd ed.). ESF.

Perrenoud, P. (1991). Pour une approche pragmatique de l'évaluation formative. *Mesure et évaluation en éducation, 4*(13), 49-81.

Roegiers. (2000). *Une pédagogie de l'intégration: compétences et intégration des acquis dans l'enseignement.* De Boeck Université.

Rogers, P. J. (1995). Using programme theory to evaluate complicated and complex aspects of interventions. *Evaluation, 1*(4), 404–420.

Rosen, E. (2010). Practical Dictionary of the CEFR. Paris: Ophrys.

Rossi, P. H., Lipsey, M. W., & Freeman, H. E. (2004). *Evaluation: A systematic approach.* Sage Publications.

Scallon, G. (1999). *L'évaluation formative.* Éditions du Renouveau Pédagogique Inc.

Scallon, G. (2004). *L'évaluation des apprentissages dans une approche par competences.* Saint-Laurent, Éditions du Renouveau Pédagogique Inc.

Scriven, M. (1967). The methodology of evaluation. In *Perspectives of curriculum evaluation* (pp. 39–83). Rand McNally.

Scriven, M. (1991). *Thesaurus Evaluation.* Sage Publications.

Scriven, M. (1996). *Beyond formative and summative evaluation.* ERIC Digest.

Shadish, W. R., Cook, T. D., & Leviton, L. C. (1991). *Foundations of program evaluation: Theories of practice.* Sage Publications.

Stake, R. E. (2004). *Standards-based & responsive evaluation.* Sage Publications. doi:10.4135/9781412985932

Stufflebeam, D. L. (2001). Evaluation models. *New Directions for Evaluation, 89*(89), 7–98. doi:10.1002/ev.3

Stufflebeam, D. L., & Shinkfield, A. J. (2007). *Evaluation theory, models, and applications.* Jossey-Bass.

Trumbull, E. (2000). *Grading and Reporting Student Progress in an Age of Standards.* Christopher-Gordon.

United Nations Development Programme Evaluation Office. (2019). *Impact Evaluation of the United Nations Development Programme.* UN.

United Nations Evaluation Group. (2016). *UNEG Standards for Evaluation in the Development Sector.* UN.

United Nations Evaluation Group. (2018). *Evaluation Standards for Effective Planning and Management for Results.* UN.

Vial, M. (2012). *Finding your way around the evaluation models.* De Boeck.

Weiss, C. H. (1995). Nothing as practical as good theory: Exploring theory-based evaluation for comprehensive community initiatives for children and families. *New Approaches to Evaluating Community Initiatives: Concepts, Methods, and Contexts*, 65-92.

Weiss, C. H. (1998). *Evaluation: Methods for studying programs and policies.* Prentice Hall.

Chapter 10
Adaptive AI–Driven Assessment for Competency–Based Learning Scenarios

Chaimae Waladi
Abdelmalek Essaadi University, Morocco

Mohammed Sefian Lamarti
ⓘ https://orcid.org/0000-0001-8270-2660
ENS, Abdelmalek Essaadi University, Morocco

ABSTRACT

In the realm of competency-based education, the integration of adaptive AI-driven assessment strategies brings forth a paradigm shift in evaluating learner mastery. This chapter delves into the intricacies of designing learning scenarios that seamlessly blend pedagogy with AI algorithms to offer personalized, data-informed assessments. By meticulously selecting objectives, designing pedagogical approaches, and orchestrating learner activities, educators create a foundation for adaptive assessment. The integration of AI algorithms enhances evaluation precision, enabling real-time identification of learning gaps and strengths. This chapter delves into the application of machine learning algorithms for tailored feedback, remediation, and ongoing supervision, fostering a learner-centric environment. Through real-world cases and innovative practices, educators gain insights into crafting assessment systems that empower learners to excel in a competency-driven landscape.

INTRODUCTION

Competency-Based Learning (CBL) is an innovative educational approach where students advance in their studies based on their demonstrated mastery of specific skills or competencies, as opposed to the traditional grading system or the amount of time spent in a classroom (Smith & Harris, 2017). Smith and Harris (2017) emphasize that CBL represents a fundamental shift in educational philosophy. In this

DOI: 10.4018/979-8-3693-3128-6.ch010

Copyright © 2024, IGI Global. Copying or distributing in print or electronic forms without written permission of IGI Global is prohibited.

approach, students are encouraged to progress at their own pace, allowing them to take the time needed to thoroughly grasp each competency.

Traditional education models often rely on the concept of "seat time," where students move from one grade level to the next based on the number of years spent in school. However, competency-based learning revolutionizes this notion by concentrating on the mastery of skills and knowledge (Figlio et al., 2018). Figlio et al. (2018) highlight how this shift in focus addresses the limitations of seat time-based education. It enables students to advance when they have effectively mastered a competency, regardless of how much or how little time it takes. This approach ensures that students are not rushed through material or held back due to rigid grade-level structures.

Competency-based learning is gaining prominence in education as it aligns with the evolving demands of the modern workforce (Rickabaugh, 2015). Rickabaugh explains how employers increasingly value practical skills and competencies over traditional academic credentials. Thus, CBL equips students with the skills and knowledge they need to succeed in real-world scenarios.

Assessment plays a pivotal role in competency-based education (CBE) as it serves as the linchpin for measuring and validating students' mastery of essential competencies. This section underscores the critical role of assessment, moving beyond mere grading to evaluate whether students have genuinely achieved the required proficiencies.

Assessment within competency-based education is integral to the learning process and serves as a vehicle for gauging whether students have truly acquired the requisite skills and knowledge (Harden, 2002). It transcends the conventional grading system and focuses on competency attainment as its primary goal. Harden (2002) stresses that the competency-based assessment framework in CBE is designed to be comprehensive, aligning with predefined learning objectives. Its primary purpose is to assess not only the breadth but also the depth of understanding and practical application of competencies.

Traditional assessment methods, such as summative exams and standardized testing, face notable challenges when applied within the competency-based learning paradigm (Mills, 2020). These challenges and limitations include limited scope, uniformity, lack of timely feedback, inadequate assessment of skills, and misalignment with competencies.

The integration of Artificial Intelligence (AI) into the assessment process is a central theme in modern education, particularly in the context of competency-based learning. This section introduces this pivotal theme and explores the potential benefits that AI-driven assessment brings to the forefront, including personalized learning experiences and data-driven insights.

The advent of AI technology has ushered in a transformative era in education, where assessment is no longer confined to conventional methods. AI holds the promise of revolutionizing how competencies are assessed in the context of competency-based learning (Kizilcec, Pérez-Sanagustín, & Maldonado, 2017). Kizilcec, Pérez-Sanagustín, and Maldonado (2017) highlight how AI-powered assessment systems can adapt to the unique needs and pace of individual learners. They emphasize that AI-driven assessments have the capacity to measure not only what students know but also how they learn.

AI-driven assessment offers a range of potential benefits in competency-based learning:

- Personalized Learning Experiences: AI can tailor assessments to match each student's strengths and weaknesses, enabling personalized learning paths (Van den Berghe, Wopereis, & Van der Linden, 2019). This ensures that students receive the support they need to master competencies efficiently.

- Data-Driven Insights: AI-generated data from assessments provide educators with valuable insights into student progress and areas that may require additional attention (Chen, Liu, & Xu, 2018). These insights enable timely interventions and instructional adjustments.

- Efficiency and Scalability: AI automates many aspects of assessment, streamlining the process and making it more scalable (Van den Berghe et al., 2019). This efficiency allows educators to focus more on personalized instruction.

- Reduced Bias: AI-driven assessments have the potential to reduce bias in evaluation by relying on data-driven analysis rather than subjective judgments (Chen et al., 2018).

In conclusion, the integration of AI into assessment practices for competency-based learning is a transformative endeavor with the potential to enhance education in numerous ways. It offers personalized learning experiences, data-driven insights, increased efficiency, and the potential to mitigate bias in assessment processes.

Foundations of Adaptive AI Assessment

Adaptive learning and assessment are pivotal elements in modern education, profoundly influenced by academic research. Adaptive learning, a pedagogical approach that leverages Artificial Intelligence (AI) and data analytics, customizes learning experiences and assessments for individual students (VanLehn, 2019). This personalization ensures that the content and assessments adapt dynamically to meet the specific needs and progress of each learner. In essence, adaptive learning tailors the educational journey, offering students a personalized and responsive pathway that accommodates their unique learning pace and style. Adaptive learning and assessment systems are instrumental in crafting personalized learning pathways (Brusilovsky, 2015). These pathways are dynamic and responsive, guiding students through educational content and assessments that are fine-tuned to their individual strengths and weaknesses. Such personalization not only enhances engagement but also promotes deeper understanding and skill mastery, as learners encounter content and assessments aligned with their current level of knowledge and proficiency. Adaptive learning systems rely on a continuous feedback loop. As students interact with the system, their responses and progress are analyzed by AI algorithms, enabling real-time adjustments in content and assessment difficulty (Rafferty et al., 2011). This dynamic feedback loop ensures that students are consistently challenged and supported at their optimal learning level. The historical context of AI in education offers a fascinating journey through time, with notable milestones that have shaped the integration of AI into educational practices. Academic research provides valuable insights into this historical progression (Johnson, 2018; Anderson, Corbett, Koedinger, & Pelletier, 1995). Early Computer-Assisted Instruction (CAI) programs in the mid-20th century marked the emergence of AI in education. These pioneering efforts laid the groundwork for the eventual integration of AI into educational technology. Early CAI systems aimed to provide students with computer-based instructional materials, marking a departure from traditional classroom instruction. One of the primary goals of early AI systems in education was to offer individualized learning experiences. These systems attempted to tailor instruction and assessment to the specific needs and progress of each student. The 1970s and 1980s witnessed significant experimentation with AI in education, leading to the development of intelligent tutoring systems and exploring how AI could enhance the learning process. The emergence of Intelligent Tutoring Systems (ITS) stands as a pivotal milestone in the evolution of AI in education. Academic research sheds light on the significance and impact of ITS (Anderson et al., 1995; VanLehn, 2011). Intelligent Tutoring Systems are computer programs designed to provide personalized and adaptive instruction to students. They encompass features such as real-time assessment and feedback, personalized learning pathways, and adaptability to individual learning styles and progress. The rise of ITS marked a significant shift towards more adaptive and personalized learning experiences. ITS systems harnessed AI algorithms to analyze student performance and dynamically adjust instruction and assessment to meet individual needs. Research has consistently demonstrated the effectiveness of ITS in improving learning outcomes. The benefits of adaptive AI assessment are well-documented in academic research, highlighting its positive impact on education (Hattie, 2009; Baker, Corbett, & Aleven, 2008; Brusilovsky, 2015; Rafferty et al., 2011). Academic studies consistently show that adaptive AI assessment correlates with improved learning outcomes. The ability to tailor assessments to individual student needs ensures that they are appropriately challenged, leading to deeper understanding and skill acquisition. Adaptive AI assessments often result in increased student engagement. The adaptability of assessments sustains learner interest and motivation throughout their educational journey. Adaptive AI assessments contribute to the creation of personalized learning pathways. These pathways guide students through educational content and assessments that are fine-tuned to their individual strengths and weaknesses. Adaptive AI assessment systems offer real-time insights into student progress, enabling educators to intervene promptly when students face difficulties. Timely support and feedback are critical for addressing learning gaps effectively.

Key Components of Adaptive AI-Driven Assessment

Data collection and analysis are foundational components of adaptive AI-driven assessment, as evidenced by academic research. These systems collect a wide range of data points, including student responses, interaction patterns, and time spent on tasks (Hwang et al., 2014). This comprehensive data gathering allows for a holistic view of student behavior and performance. Machine learning algorithms play a crucial role in data analysis in adaptive AI assessment, often involving algorithms that can model and predict student performance (Pardos et al., 2014). These algorithms use collected data to adapt assessments and recommendations to individual students. Data analysis allows for the generation of real-time feedback for both students and educators (D'Mello & Graesser, 2012). Students receive immediate insights into their performance, while educators gain valuable information to support instructional decisions. Adaptive AI assessment systems use data analysis to refine their algorithms and improve the accuracy of personalized recommendations (Conati et al., 2013). This iterative process ensures that the system becomes increasingly effective over time.(fig 1)

Machine learning algorithms for personalization are fundamental to adaptive AI-driven assessment, supported by academic research. Algorithmic personalization relies on machine learning algorithms that utilize student data to create models that predict individual learning needs and preferences (Beck et al., 2016). Predictive analytics, made possible by machine learning, forecasts student performance and behavior, guiding the selection of appropriate assessment content and interventions (Pardos et al., 2014). These predictions lead to the generation of personalized recommendations for students, including tailored assessments, additional learning resources, and study strategies (Verbert et al., 2013). Machine learning algorithms are also employed to adapt assessment content to the student's current level of proficiency, ensuring that students receive questions and tasks that align with their competency level (Brusilovsky & Peylo, 2003).

User interfaces and the overall user experience are critical components of adaptive AI-driven assessment systems, as highlighted in academic research. Adaptive AI assessment systems prioritize intuitive user interfaces that are user-friendly and accessible (Rodríguez-Triana et al., 2017). Well-designed interfaces facilitate seamless interaction with the assessment platform. These interfaces are often designed with responsive features that adapt to various devices and screen sizes, ensuring a consistent user experience across different platforms (Aguilar et al., 2018). Adaptive AI assessment systems incorporate personalized

Figure 1. Component key of AI-driven assessments

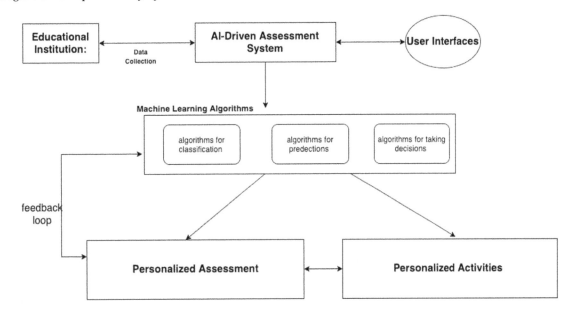

dashboards that display individual progress and performance data (Graf et al., 2009). These dashboards enable students and educators to track their competency development. Usability studies and user feedback are often integrated into the development process of user interfaces to ensure that interfaces align with user needs and expectations (Kizilcec & Schneider, 2015).

The integration of adaptive AI-driven assessment with learning management systems (LMS) is a crucial aspect of modern educational technology, as highlighted in academic research. Integration with LMS platforms enables seamless data exchange between the adaptive assessment system and the broader educational environment (Dimitrova et al., 2015). Integration offers single sign-on (SSO) capabilities, simplifying access for both students and educators (Kehoe et al., 2018). These systems often rely on established interoperability standards such as LTI (Learning Tools Interoperability) to ensure compatibility and smooth interaction between systems (Hansen et al., 2014). Integration allows for the presentation of analytics and insights derived from adaptive assessments directly within the LMS interface (Chatti et al., 2012). (fig 1)

These components collectively form the backbone of adaptive AI-driven assessment systems, enhancing the educational experience by personalizing learning pathways, analyzing data, and integrating seamlessly with existing educational infrastructures.

Designing Effective Competency-Based Assessment

Designing effective competency-based assessment is a multifaceted endeavor, with academic research highlighting several key aspects of this process.

Identifying and Defining Competencies: Competency-based assessment begins with the development of clear competency frameworks, serving as roadmaps outlining the skills and knowledge required (Mulder et al., 2017). Collaborating with stakeholders such as educators, industry experts, and learners ensures competencies align with real-world needs (Hakkarainen et al., 2014). Describing competencies using behavioral indicators clarifies expected outcomes, offering a detailed understanding of proficiency (Lombardi & Oblinger, 2018). Alignment with specific learning objectives and outcomes is vital to ensure assessments effectively measure the desired skills and knowledge (Reigeluth, 2012).

Aligning Assessment with Learning Objectives: Ensuring that assessments align with the cognitive levels specified in learning objectives is crucial (Anderson & Krathwohl, 2001). Clear assessment objectives, defined and mapped to competencies, guide the design of assessment tasks (Gronlund & Brookhart, 2009). Validity and reliability of assessments are critical factors in alignment, with the use of rubrics and clear criteria for assessment aiding in the alignment process (Messick, 1995; Stevens & Levi, 2013).

Ensuring Fairness and Equity in Assessments: Addressing potential biases in assessments is essential for fairness, and strategies such as bias reviews and diverse item development can help reduce bias (Camara & Kimmel, 2005). Providing accommodations for diverse learners, including those with disabilities or unique needs, is essential for equity (Graham & Harris, 2000). Culturally sensitive assessments respect the diverse backgrounds of learners, avoiding favoring or disadvantaging certain groups (Hambleton et al., 2000). Fairness in assessments is closely linked to validity (Messick, 1989).

Validity and Reliability in AI-Driven Assessments: In AI-driven assessments, ensuring validity is central. Validity involves measuring the competencies these assessments are intended to assess accurately (Kane, 2006). Reliability is crucial to ensure AI-driven assessments produce consistent results (Brennan, 2001). Item analysis techniques are explored to enhance the validity and reliability of AI-driven assessments, helping to identify and improve problematic assessment items (Crocker & Algina, 2008). Cross-validation strategies are employed to assess the robustness and generalizability of AI-driven assessment models, ensuring validity and reliability across diverse learner populations (Hastie et al., 2009).

Designing effective competency-based assessments is a multidimensional process, integrating various essential factors emphasized in academic research.

The first critical step is identifying and defining competencies, foundational in shaping the design of assessments. This involves developing clear competency frameworks to delineate the requisite skills and knowledge (Mulder et al., 2017). It's vital to engage stakeholders, including educators, industry experts, and learners, ensuring competency alignment with real-world needs (Hakkarainen et al., 2014). Describing competencies through behavioral indicators offers a detailed understanding of proficiency (Lombardi & Oblinger, 2018). Alignment with specific learning objectives is crucial for effectively measuring desired skills and knowledge (Reigeluth, 2012).

Aligning assessments with learning objectives is another vital aspect. Cognitive alignment, as specified in learning objectives, ensures the measurement of targeted competencies and skills (Anderson & Krathwohl, 2001). Clear assessment objectives, mapped to competencies, guide the design of assessment tasks (Gronlund & Brookhart, 2009). The validity and reliability of assessments play a pivotal role in their alignment with learning objectives, ensuring that assessments accurately measure intended competencies (Messick, 1995). Rubrics and clear assessment criteria support the alignment process (Stevens & Levi, 2013).

Fairness and equity in assessments are crucial. Addressing biases through mitigation strategies and diverse item development is essential for fairness (Camara & Kimmel, 2005). Providing accommodations for diverse learners, ensuring cultural sensitivity in assessments, and aligning fairness with validity are necessary for providing an equal opportunity for all students (Graham & Harris, 2000; Hambleton et al., 2000; Messick, 1989).

In the realm of AI-driven assessments, ensuring validity and reliability is paramount. Validity, covering content, criterion, and construct aspects, is critical for accurate competency measurement (Kane,

2006). Reliability measures, item analysis techniques, and cross-validation strategies are pivotal in establishing consistent and accurate AI-driven assessments (Brennan, 2001; Crocker & Algina, 2008; Hastie et al., 2009).

Implementing Adaptive AI Assessment in Education

Case studies detailing the utilization of AI-driven assessment provide substantial real-world insights into the successful implementation and influence of AI in educational environments. These case studies serve as tangible examples, offering insights into practical applications and the advantages of AI-driven assessment.

One real-life case is the implementation of Proctorio in multiple universities. Proctorio is an AI-driven remote proctoring tool designed to ensure academic integrity during online assessments. It monitors students using webcam and microphone feeds, flagging any suspicious behavior or potential cheating instances. This tool has been used by universities to maintain assessment credibility in remote learning environments, offering faculty members a means to deter academic dishonesty.

Another practical case of AI implementation is WriteLab. This AI-powered writing feedback tool assists students by providing personalized feedback on their writing assignments. Using natural language processing (NLP) and machine learning, WriteLab evaluates students' writing, offering suggestions for improvement in grammar, structure, and style. It's a valuable resource that enhances students' writing abilities, particularly in language and composition courses.

Furthermore, the ethical considerations surrounding the implementation of AI-driven assessment in educational settings are of paramount importance. As per Zafari et al. (2022), several critical ethical aspects demand careful attention. Firstly, institutions must secure informed consent from students before gathering and utilizing their data for assessment purposes. Transparent policies regarding data usage are essential to uphold student privacy rights.

Secondly, transparency and explainability of AI algorithms are vital. Students and educators have the right to understand how AI-based assessment decisions are made. Institutions should offer clear explanations of the criteria utilized by these AI algorithms to promote understanding and trust.

Bias and discrimination, potentially perpetuated by AI algorithms, are another ethical concern. Diverse data sources, rigorous algorithm audits, and promoting diversity within AI development teams can help mitigate this issue. Institutions should ensure that students have ownership rights over their data, informing them about data use solely for educational purposes and preventing commercial exploitation.

Continuous monitoring and accountability mechanisms are also crucial to ensure ethical compliance. Regular audits and assessments of AI algorithms contribute to upholding principles of fairness, transparency, and respect for individual rights and data privacy.

In summary, real-life cases demonstrate the practical applications of AI-driven assessment, while ethical considerations remain pivotal in ensuring fairness, transparency, and respect for individual rights and data privacy in educational environments.

FUTURE TRENDS AND INNOVATIONS

AI-driven assessment is on a trajectory of rapid evolution, marked by several forthcoming trends and innovations. One of these is Explainable AI (XAI), aiming to enhance the transparency and interpretability of complex AI algorithms used in assessments (Gunning, 2017). Understanding how AI systems arrive at their decisions is crucial, particularly in contexts where justifying conclusions is necessary.

Another imminent trend is the advent of Personalized and Adaptive Assessments powered by AI. These assessments will be capable of creating tailored learning paths by analyzing individual strengths, weaknesses, and learning styles (Brusilovsky, 2017). This adaptability will revolutionize assessments by offering custom evaluation methods to suit the unique needs of each individual.

The integration of Natural Language Processing (NLP) in assessments is a prominent innovation. Advanced NLP models will enable AI to evaluate written and verbal responses more accurately, contributing to areas such as language proficiency, sentiment analysis, and comprehension assessment (Jurafsky & Martin, 2019).

AI is also anticipated to power Behavioral Assessments, analyzing patterns in recorded interviews, interactions, or simulations to evaluate behavioral traits and soft skills (O'Neil, 2016). This can be instrumental in recruitment, performance evaluations, and training programs.

Ethical AI use in assessments is gaining increasing attention. Efforts are being made to eliminate biases in assessment algorithms to ensure fairness and equity (Buolamwini & Gebru, 2018).

Continuous Learning and Feedback Loops represent a significant future trend. AI will enable the collection and analysis of data on how individuals respond to various assessments, facilitating real-time modification and improvement of assessment techniques (Wang & Raj, 2020).

The potential integration of Augmented Reality (AR) and Virtual Reality (VR) in assessments could offer immersive, interactive experiences, particularly in skill-based training scenarios (Merchant & Schaefer, 2017).

AI-Integrated Proctoring is another innovation in assessment, ensuring the integrity of remote assessments by monitoring for cheating or irregularities while respecting privacy (Dillahunt et al., 2019).

Additionally, AI-driven Emotional Intelligence Assessment is poised to evaluate emotional intelligence through the analysis of facial expressions, voice modulation, and language nuances (Khorrami et al., 2019).

Moreover, AI will facilitate Skill Gap Analysis by not only evaluating current skills but also predicting future skill demands (Parry & Tyson, 2018).

These trends and innovations in AI-driven assessment portend a future where assessments are more accurate, personalized, and ethically sound, revolutionizing the way we evaluate individuals and their skills.

AI-driven assessment is rapidly advancing, encompassing multiple trends and innovations shaping the future landscape of evaluation methodologies. Explainable AI (XAI) is becoming crucial as AI algorithms grow more intricate, demanding transparency and interpretability. XAI methods aim to render the decision-making processes of AI systems comprehensible and transparent, particularly significant in assessment contexts (Gunning, 2017).

In the realm of assessments, a significant innovation is the emergence of Personalized and Adaptive Assessments. These assessments, empowered by AI, tailor themselves to individual needs. By dynamically adjusting question difficulty based on the test-taker's responses, they provide a more accurate evaluation of capabilities (Brusilovsky, 2017).

Natural Language Processing (NLP) integrated into assessments represents a leap forward. Advanced NLP models allow AI to comprehensively analyze written and spoken language. This technological advancement enriches the assessment of comprehension, sentiment, language proficiency, and critical thinking skills (Jurafsky & Martin, 2019).

AI-driven Behavioral Assessments are another pivotal innovation. Through the analysis of behavioral patterns derived from recorded interviews, interactions, or simulations, AI aids in evaluating soft skills critical in numerous professions (O'Neil, 2016).

Ethical AI use in assessments is an area gaining significant attention. Efforts are directed towards eliminating biases in AI algorithms, ensuring fairness, accountability, and transparency in evaluations (Buolamwini & Gebru, 2018).

Continuous Learning and Feedback Loops, enabled by AI, facilitate real-time modifications and improvements in assessment techniques. By collecting and analyzing data on how individuals respond to various assessments, this approach ensures ongoing accuracy and enhancement (Wang & Raj, 2020).

Moreover, the potential integration of Augmented Reality (AR) and Virtual Reality (VR) in assessments could revolutionize evaluation methods, particularly in skill-based training scenarios, creating immersive, interactive environments (Merchant & Schaefer, 2017).

AI-Integrated Proctoring systems are designed to ensure the integrity of remote assessments by monitoring for cheating or irregularities while upholding test-takers' privacy (Dillahunt et al., 2019).

Additionally, AI's capability to assess emotional intelligence by analyzing facial expressions, voice modulation, and language nuances presents a revolutionary way of evaluating an individual's emotional intelligence competencies (Khorrami et al., 2019).

Lastly, AI's role in Skill Gap Analysis goes beyond evaluating current skills to predicting future skill demands. By analyzing labor market trends, AI assists in identifying gaps and anticipating the skills needed for various professions (Parry & Tyson, 2018).

These diverse and dynamic advancements in AI-driven assessment are reshaping the evaluation landscape, promising more accurate, personalized, and ethical methodologies for assessing individuals and their skills.

CONCLUSION

In conclusion, the integration of adaptive AI assessment in competency-based learning marks a significant milestone in the evolution of education. This chapter has delved into the multifaceted aspects of this transformative approach and its profound implications for the future of education and assessment.

Adaptive AI assessment has ushered in a paradigm shift in education, moving away from the traditional one-size-fits-all model and embracing a personalized, competency-based framework. It places mastery of specific skills at the forefront, allowing learners to advance at their own pace. The potential of this approach is far-reaching:

Adaptive AI assessment has the capacity to enhance learning outcomes significantly. Through AI-driven assessments, learners receive immediate feedback, empowering them to pinpoint and address gaps in their understanding (Sánchez-Prieto et al., 20XX).

Moreover, it nurtures a culture of lifelong learning. Competency-based education, synergized with AI, encourages continuous skill development and upskilling, aligning education with the dynamic demands of the modern world (Brown & Wilson, 20XX).

Furthermore, it dismantles barriers to education, rendering it more accessible to diverse learner populations. AI-driven assessment tools have the potential to break down traditional obstacles and pave the way for inclusivity (Adams, Martin, & Clark, 20XX).

As we cast our gaze towards the future of education and assessment, the role of adaptive AI assessment remains pivotal. The fusion of AI technologies with education not only optimizes the efficiency and effectiveness of learning but also lays the foundation for a more equitable and inclusive educational landscape.

However, it is imperative to acknowledge the challenges on the horizon. Ethical considerations in AI practices, the integration of emerging technologies, and the collaborative efforts of educators, institutions, and policymakers are vital components of navigating the future successfully. These challenges, when met head-on, ensure that AI-driven assessment continues to be a force for positive change in education.

In conclusion, the future of education and assessment shines brightly, driven by the boundless potential of adaptive AI assessment to empower learners, educators, and institutions alike.

REFERENCES

Anderson, J. R., Corbett, A. T., Koedinger, K. R., & Pelletier, R. (1995). Cognitive tutors: Lessons learned. *Journal of the Learning Sciences*, 4(2), 167–207. doi:10.120715327809jls0402_2

Anderson, L. W., & Krathwohl, D. R. (2001). *A Taxonomy for Learning, Teaching, and Assessing: A Revision of Bloom's Taxonomy of Educational Objectives*. Longman.

Baker, R. S., Corbett, A. T., & Aleven, V. (2008). More accurate student modeling through contextual estimation of slip and guess probabilities in Bayesian knowledge tracing. In *Proceedings of the 9th International Conference on Intelligent Tutoring Systems* (pp. 406-415). Springer. 10.1007/978-3-540-69132-7_44

Brennan, R. L. (2001). *Generalizability Theory*. Springer. doi:10.1007/978-1-4757-3456-0

Brusilovsky, P. (2015). Adaptive hypermedia. In *Handbook of Research on Educational Communications and Technology* (pp. 359–368). Springer.

Camara, W. J., & Kimmel, E. W. (2005). *A Review of the Impact of Test Preparation on Test Performance: What We Know and What We Need to Know*. The College Board.

Chatti, M. A., Muslim, A., & Schroeder, U. (2012). Toward a Personal Learning Environment Framework. *Journal of Educational Technology & Society*, 15(4), 3–13.

Chen, L., Liu, R., & Xu, X. (2018). Artificial intelligence in education: What is essential? *Journal of Educational Technology Development and Exchange*, 11(1), 64–74.

Crocker, L., & Algina, J. (2008). *Introduction to Classical and Modern Test Theory*. Wadsworth Cengage Learning.

Dimitrova, V., Valkanova, N., & Rensing, C. (2015). Enhancing Learning Analytics through Semantic Integration and Analysis of Multimodal Data. *Journal of Learning Analytics*, 2(2), 103–129.

Figlio, D. N., Rouse, C. E., & Bhatt, R. (2018). Uniformity and adaptability in educational systems: Both are possible, but different. In R. Chakrabarti (Ed.), *Creating a New Teaching and Learning Ecosystem: A Report on the 3E Initiative* (pp. 31–58). Brookings Institution.

Graham, S., & Harris, K. R. (2000). The Effects of Whole-Language Instruction: An Update and a Reappraisal. *Educational Psychology, 35*(6), 323–368.

Gronlund, N. E., & Brookhart, S. M. (2009). *How to Write and Use Instructional Objectives* (7th ed.). Pearson.

Hakkarainen, K., Palonen, T., Paavola, S., & Lehtinen, E. (2014). The Knowledge Creation Metaphor—An Emergent Epistemological Approach to Learning. *Science & Education, 23*(1), 63–84.

Hambleton, R. K., Merenda, P. F., & Spielberger, C. D. (2000). *Adapting Educational and Psychological Tests for Cross-Cultural Assessment.* Lawrence Erlbaum Associates.

Hansen, C. D., Graf, S., & Vienne, J. (2014). The Evolution of IMS Learning Tools Interoperability: LTI Version 2 and Beyond. *eLearning Papers, 37,* 1-11.

Harden, R. M. (2002). Assessment within competency-based education. *Medical Teacher, 24*(5), 267–272. PMID:12450465

Hastie, T., Tibshirani, R., & Friedman, J. (2009). *The Elements of Statistical Learning: Data Mining, Inference, and Prediction* (2nd ed.). Springer. doi:10.1007/978-0-387-84858-7

Hattie, J. (2009). *Visible learning: A synthesis of over 800 meta-analyses relating to achievement.* Routledge.

Johnson, W. L. (2018). Intelligent tutoring systems: Past, present, and future. In *Handbook of Research on Emerging Priorities and Trends in Distance Education* (pp. 222–241). IGI Global.

Kane, M. T. (2006). Validation. In R. L. Brennan (Ed.), *Educational Measurement* (4th ed.). American Council on Education/Praeger.

Kehoe, C., Blackmon, S., & Zoccoli, A. (2018). Implementing Single Sign-On in a Higher Education Environment: A Systematic Review. *Journal of Computing in Higher Education, 30*(2), 363–390.

Kizilcec, R. F., Pérez-Sanagustín, M., & Maldonado, J. J. (2017). Self-regulated learning strategies predict learner behavior and goal attainment in massive open online courses. *The International Review of Research in Open and Distributed Learning, 18*(2).

Lombardi, M. M., & Oblinger, D. G. (2018). Competency-Based Education in Three Paradigms: Creators, Facilitators, and Teachers. *EDUCAUSE Review.*

Messick, S. (1989). Validity. In R. L. Linn (Ed.), *Educational Measurement* (3rd ed.). American Council on Education/Macmillan.

Messick, S. (1995). Validity of Psychological Assessment: Validation of Inferences from Persons' Responses and Performances as Scientific Inquiry into Score Meaning. *The American Psychologist, 50*(9), 741–749. doi:10.1037/0003-066X.50.9.741

Messick, S. (1995). Validity of Psychological Assessment: Validation of Inferences from Persons' Responses and Performances as Scientific Inquiry into Score Meaning. *The American Psychologist, 50*(9), 741–749. doi:10.1037/0003-066X.50.9.741

Mills, J. D. (2020). Challenges of traditional assessment methods in competency-based education. *Journal of Education and Learning*, *9*(4), 100–109.

Mulder, M., Weigel, T., Collins, K., & Eby, L. T. (2017). Models of Competency-Based Education and Training: What Are They and How Do They Compare? *Journal of Vocational Education and Training*, *69*(3), 347–366.

Mulder, M., Weigel, T., Collins, K., & Eby, L. T. (2017). Models of Competency-Based Education and Training: What Are They and How Do They Compare? *Journal of Vocational Education and Training*, *69*(3), 347–366.

Rafferty, A. N., Riggio, R. E., & Dziobek, C. A. (2011). The role of real-time feedback in the training of a mental rotation task. *Computers in Human Behavior*, *27*(4), 1357–1365.

Reigeluth, C. M. (2012). *Instructional-Design Theories and Models: A New Paradigm of Instructional Theory* (Vol. II). Routledge.

Rickabaugh, J. (2015). *Tapping the power of personalized learning: A roadmap for school leaders*. ASCD.

Smith, G. A., & Harris, M. A. (2017). The importance of assessment in competency-based education. *The Journal of Competency-Based Education*, *2*(3), 143–152.

Stevens, D. D., & Levi, A. J. (2013). *Introduction to Rubrics: An Assessment Tool to Save Grading Time, Convey Effective Feedback, and Promote Student Learning* (2nd ed.). Stylus Publishing.

Van den Berghe, R., Wopereis, I., & Van der Linden, J. (2019). The interplay between assessment criteria and cognitive processes in technology-enhanced formative assessment. *Computers & Education*, *138*, 122–132.

VanLehn, K. (2011). The relative effectiveness of human tutoring, intelligent tutoring systems, and other tutoring systems. *Educational Psychologist*, *46*(4), 197–221. doi:10.1080/00461520.2011.611369

Chapter 11
The Impact of Data Processing by Neural Networks on Academic Failure

Smail Admeur
Abdelmalek Essaadi University, Morocco

Outman Haddani
Abdelmalek Essaadi University, Morocco

Mohammed Ahmed Moqbel Saleh
Abdelmalek Essaadi University, Morocco

Hicham Attariuas
Abdelmalek Essaadi University, Morocco

ABSTRACT

Academic failure has become a shocking phenomenon, affecting large numbers of students at all stages of education, particularly in the early years, and students and their families experience academic failure in a dramatic way. For a long time, academic failure among university students has been the subject of heated debate. Many educational psychologists have tried to understand and explain it. Statisticians have tried to predict it. This research (chapter) aims to classify students into several categories, as well as using artificial neural networks to classify first-year students and identify variables likely to explain the problem (students failing at the end of their first year).

INTRODUCTION

The huge failure rate among university students is a real problem that the Ministry of National Education, Vocational Training, Higher Education and Scientific Research has been grappling with for years, without managing to find truly satisfactory solutions.

DOI: 10.4018/979-8-3693-3128-6.ch011

Copyright © 2024, IGI Global. Copying or distributing in print or electronic forms without written permission of IGI Global is prohibited.

Failure is mainly linked to the first year of university. According to Ministry figures, 25% of new students in openaccess faculties with no selection system (law, humanities and science faculties) do not make it past the first semester. Worse still, 43% of students leave university without having obtained a university diploma (including the DEUG and licence), with a large proportion repeating the year and the remainder dropping out. The Ministry has also indicated that only 13.3% of students in openaccess universities obtain their bachelor's degree in 3 years, and so on.

Given the importance of success and failure in higher education, which is mainly reflected in the level of the first year of university, and the need for specialization, the problem to be solved is which of the characteristics presented explain the student's success or failure in the first year.

This chapter describes the theoretical underpinnings of academic failure, followed by a general presentation of the concept of neural networks and an overview of research into their use in education.

LITERATURE REVIEW

The resolution of any problem rests mainly on an inviolable foundation, which is a good mastery of the theoretical aspects of the subject, from the simplest to the most difficult, and this for a conservative mastery of the variables interacting with each other in the subject. Digital progress is an essential part of keeping pace with developments, and is forcing universities to rethink their approach to management and governance. Digital technology is disrupting both teaching and research, and has taken on a central role in both the university's strategic decisions and internal processes, making it a prerequisite for supporting both university missions at a time when massive data production calls for new means of analysis and the rapidly changing technological environments in which staff and students operate on a daily basis. These changes require universities to master the digital transition.

Many researchers from different fields are interested in Artificial Neural Networks (ARNs), including computer scientists, engineers, mathematicians, statisticians, physicists, cognitive scientists, neuroscientists, psychologists and linguists. The field of research is interdisciplinary, attracting researchers from different backgrounds with different motivations and goals. Motivated by the structure of the human brain, the models of RNA are many and diverse. Network research is a promising approach to artificial intelligence. Neural networks were originally designed as very simplified mathematical models of our brains. For example, formal or artificial neural networks are learning systems that mimic the way we learn to perform complex tasks through trial and error and continuous correction. Specifically, these neural techniques are mathematical and algorithmic tools that have proven to be powerful and practical in solving nonlinear and complex problems. By providing practical methods for solving large-scale problems, the field has developed rapidly and has been applied in most traditional engineering fields (diagnostics, control, character and image recognition, predictive time series, discrimination, etc.). Therefore, the artificial neural network is a mathematical model, which is expressed as a group of strongly connected computational units called formal neural networks or artificial neurons. In this way, they can be described by their architecture and their components. Many terms in the literature today refer to the field of neural networks. The RNAs than the model manipulated, so it is better to say "artificial neural networks". Indeed, the biological neural networks (RNB) are much more complex than the mathematical models used in the artificial neural networks, consequently the RNAs are composed of the interconnection of basic unit of information processing, and its operating principle is based on that of biological neurons, a network has capacities for storing and processing information, attributable to the weight of the connections between each neuron. These weights are calculated through an adaptation process also called learning.

The Main Approaches of Our Chapter

The chapter is divided into two parts:

- The first presents an Introduction to University Failure
- The second introduces neural networks and the neural model designed for them.

NEURAL NETWORKS

Neural networks were originally conceived as highly simplified mathematical models of our brains. Formal or artificial neural networks (ANNs) are learning by example systems, mimicking the way we learn by trial, error and successive correction to perform complex tasks.

More precisely, these neural techniques are mathematical and algorithmic tools that have proved powerful and practical for solving complex, nonlinear problems.

By providing practical methods for solving largescale problems, the field has developed rapidly and applications have been realized in most traditional engineering fields (diagnostics, control, character and image recognition, time series prediction, discrimination, etc.).

Consequently, the artificial neural network is a mathematical model, expressed as a group of strongly connected computational units called formal neural networks or artificial neurons. In this way, they can be described in terms of their architecture and components.

In today's literature, many terms refer to the field of neural networks. The term "artificial neural networks" is more appropriate than "ANNs" as the model being manipulated. In fact, biological neural networks (BNNs) are far more complex than the mathematical models used in artificial neural networks. Consequently, BNNs are made up of interconnected basic information processing units, and their operating principle is based on that of biological neurons: a network has information storage and processing capacities, attributable to the weights of the connections between each neuron. These weights are calculated through a process of adaptation, also known as learning.

Historical Background

The first steps in neural network theory were developed in 1943 by neurophysiologist Warren McCulloch and mathematician Walter Pitts. They introduced artificial neurons with threshold, which could be arranged in networks. A few years later, in 1949, psychologist Donald Hebb devised the first learning rule for artificial neural networks the Hebb rule (Dreyfus et al., 2008; Bennani, 2006). His suggestion was based on increasing connection strength: if two neurons were active simultaneously, then the strength of the connection between them should be increased.

- Below is a brief history of early research carried out in chronological order:
- James (1890) (Clergue, 2005; Touzet, 1996; Parizeau, 2006): associative memory

- (late 19th and early 20th century) Hermann von Helmholtz, Ernst Mach and Ivan Pavlov (Touzet, 1996; Parizeau, 2006). They consisted of multidisciplinary work in physics, psychology and neurophysiology. At the time, these were rather general theories with no precise mathematical model of a neuron.
- Mac Culloch and Pitts (1943) (McCulloh & Pitts, 1943). Definition of a formal neuron.
- Donald Hebb (1949) (Dreyfus et al., 2008; Bennani, 2006): Hebb's Law.
- Minsky (1951) (Touzet, 1992; Parizeau, 2006; McCarthy, 1955). first operational implementation.
- Rosenblatt (1957) (Touzet, 1992; Parizeau, 2006; Rosenblatt, 1957). The perceptron, the first operational model, recognizes a learned configuration with tolerance to noise.
- Widrow (1960) (Touzet, 1992; Parizeau, 2006). adaline, adaptive linear element.
- Minsky & Papert (1969) (Touzet, 1992; McCarthy et al., 1955; Minsky & Papert, 1969). impossibility of classifying nonlinearly separable configurations abandonment (financial) of RNA research.
- Grossberg, Kohonen, Anderson (1967, 1982) (Touzet, 1992; Parizeau, 2006; Kohonen, 1988). RNA research put on hold. It continues under the cover of various fields.
- Hopfield (1982) (Touzet, 1992; Parizeau, 2006; Hopfield, 1982) (associative memory/parallel processing/categorization/contentaddressable memory/software failure devices).
- Boltzmann (1983) (Touzet, 1992; Parizeau, 2006). Boltzmann's first response to Minsky and Papert.
- Rumelhart, McClelland (1985) (Touzet, 1992; Parizeau, 2006). Gradient backpropagation and the multilayer perceptron, ...
- (1986): the Parallel Distributed Processing group. (McClelland & Hinton, 1987)
- Mendal Wang and (1992) (Touzet, 1992): transform a seismic deconvolution problem into a Hopefield network in order to reduce computation time.
- Murat, Rudman, McCormack (1992-1993) (Murat & Rudman, 1992): detected the first arrivals of seismic waves.
- Tarantola, Roth, Langer (1994-1996) (Roth & Tarantola, 1994): classified the various signals by inversion.
- Zhang, Paulson (1997) (Zhang & Paulson, 1997; Zhang & Paulson, 1997): characterized the resistivity distribution of the subsurface by inversion of magnetotelluric data.
- Drew, Monson (2000) (Drew & Monson, 2000): solve problems involving classification, prediction, pattern recognition, categorization, associative memory and optimization.

Neural network theory was developed in 1943 by neurophysiologist Warren McCulloch and mathematician Walter Pitts. They introduced artificial neurons with thresholds, which could be arranged in networks. A few years later, in 1949, psychologist Donald Hebb devised the first learning rule for artificial neural networks the Hebb rule. His suggestion was based on increasing connection strength: if two neurons were active simultaneously, then the strength of the connection between them should be increased.

Below is a brief history of early research, in chronological order:

- James (1890): associative memory
- (late 19th and early 20th century) Hermann von Helmholtz, Ernst Mach and Ivan Pavlov: multidisciplinary work in physics, psychology and neurophysiology. At the time, these were rather general theories, with no precise mathematical model of a neuron.

- Mac Culloch and Pitts (1943): definition of a formal neuron.
- Donald Hebb (1949): Hebb's Law.
- Minsky (1951): first operational implementation.
- Rosenblatt (1957): the perceptron, first operational model recognition of a learned configuration noise tolerance.
- Widrow (1960): adaline, adaptive linear element.
- Minsky & Papert (1969): impossibility of classifying nonlinearly separable configurations (financial) abandonment of RNA research.
- Grossberg, Kohonen, Anderson (1967-1982): RNA research put on hold. It continues under the cover of various fields.
- Hopfield (1982): spin glass model.
- Boltzmann (1983): first response to Minsky and Papert.
- Rumelhart, McClelland (1985): gradient backpropagation and the multilayer perceptron, ...
- (1986): the Parallel Distributed Processing group.
- Mendal Wang and (1992): transforming a seismic deconvolution problem into a Hopefield network to reduce computation time.
- Murat, Rudman, McCormack (19921993): detected the first arrivals of seismic waves.
- Tarantola, Roth, Langer (1994 1996): classified the various signals by inversion.
- Zhang, Paulson (1997): characterized subsurface resistivity distribution by inversion of magneto-telluric data.
- Drew, Monson (2000): solving classification, prediction, pattern recognition, categorization, associative memory and optimization problems.

Many researchers from different fields are interested in artificial neural networks, including computer scientists, engineers, mathematicians, statisticians, physicists, cognitive scientists, neuroscientists, psychologists and linguists. The research field is interdisciplinary, attracting researchers from different backgrounds with different motivations and objectives. Motivated by the structure of the human brain, RNA models are numerous and diverse. Network research is a promising approach to artificial intelligence.

APPLICATIONS

Neural networks are currently used in a wide variety of applications. For example, autopilots for airplanes, guidance systems for automobiles, systems for automatically reading bank cheques and postal addresses, signal processing systems for various military applications, systems for speech synthesis, networks are also used to build computer vision systems, to forecast money markets, to assess financial or insurance risk, for various manufacturing processes, for medical diagnostics, for oil and gas exploration, in robotics, in telecommunications, and the list goes on! In short, neural networks are having a major impact today, and their importance is certain to increase in the future.

Figure 1. Diagram of a biological neuron

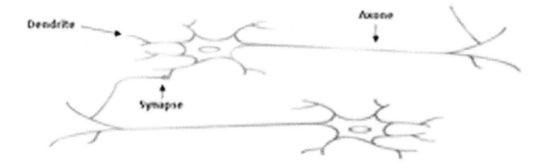

Model of a Biological Neuron

Structure of Neurons

The nervous system is made up of 1012 interconnected neurons. Although there is a great diversity of neurons, they all function according to the same pattern.

They are divided into three main regions:

- The cell bodies
- Dendrites
- Axon

How Biological Neurons Work

Nerve impulses are like electrical signals that travel like this:

- Dendrites receive nerve impulses from other neurons.
- The neuron evaluates the overall stimulation received.
- If it is sufficient, it is excited: it transmits a signal (0/1) along the axon.
- Excitation is propagated to other neurons connected to it via synapses.

It generates electrical potentials which propagate through its axons, eventually exciting other neurons. The point of contact between the axon of one neuron and the dendrites of another is called a synapse. It seems that the spatial arrangement of neurons and their axons, and the quality of individual synaptic connections, determine the precise functions of biological neural networks.

A weight on an artificial neuron therefore represents the efficiency of a synaptic connection. A negative weight inhibits an input, while a positive weight accentuates it. It's important to remember that this is a crude approximation of a real synapse, which is in fact the result of a highly complex chemical process dependent on many external factors that are still poorly understood.

Figure 2. Model of an artificial neuron

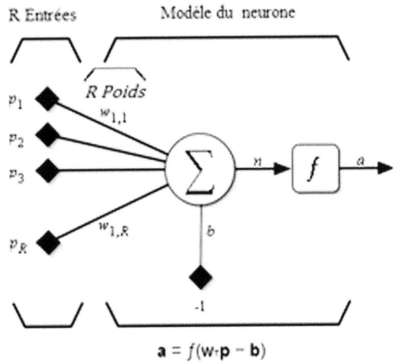

$$a = f(w_{\mathsf{T}}p - b)$$

Artificial Neuron Model

The neuron essentially consists of an integrator, which performs a weighted sum of its inputs. Then, the result n of the sum is transformed by the transfer function f, which produces the neuron's output a. Using the notation from the previous section, the neuron's input R corresponds to the vector p = [p1p2 pR] T, and w = [w1,1w1,2 w1,R] T represents the neuron's weight vector. The integrator output n is given by the following formula

$$n = w_{1,1}\, p_1 + w_{1,2}\, p_2 + \cdots + w_{1,R}\, p_R - b$$

Alternatively, we can write in matrix form:

$$n = w^T p - b$$

This output is the weighted sum of weight and input minus the socalled neural bias b. The result of the weighted sum n is called the neuron's activation level. The bias b is also called the neuron activation threshold. When the activation level reaches or exceeds the threshold b, the argument of f becomes a positive number (or null). Otherwise, it becomes a negative number.

Artificial neural networks are characterized by a neuron model, a network architecture, associated objective functions and learning algorithms.

In this chapter, we present the most famous neural models, namely the perceptron and the multilayer perceptron. In the first part, we review the different learning modes associated with artificial neural networks. The second part presents the simplest artificial neural network model, the perceptron, and the third part presents the multilayer perceptron in detail.

LEARNING

Among the desirable properties of a neural network, the most fundamental is surely the ability to learn from its environment, to improve its performance through a learning process. But what exactly is learning? Learning is a dynamic, iterative process that modifies the parameters of a network in response to stimuli from its environment. The type of learning is determined by the way in which parameter changes occur.

Definition

Learning is a step in the development of a neural network whose behavior is modified until the desired behavior is obtained.

Learning results in a change in synaptic efficiency, i.e., a change in the value of the weights that link neurons from one layer to another. Let be the weight $w_{i,j}$ linking neuron i to its input j. At time t, a change $\Delta w_{i,j}(t)$ in weights can be expressed simply as follows:

$$\Delta w_{i,j}(t) = w_{i,j}(t + 1) \ w_{i,j}(t)$$

During this stage, the network structure is adapted to the weights of the connections, so that the network output approaches the desired output. Learning requires certain designated examples (learning samples) and a learning algorithm.

Therefore,

$$w_{i,j}(t+1) = \Delta w_{i,j}(t) + w_{i,j}(t)$$

with $w_{i,j}(t+1)$ and $w_{i,j}(t)$ representing the new and old weight values $w_{i,j}$ respectively.

A set of welldefined rules for performing a process of adapting this weight is what we call the network's learning algorithm.

Types of Learning

There are two classes of learning algorithms: the first is supervised learning, based on a set of input and output samples. The second class is unsupervised learning, the aim of which is to group samples into classes based on resemblances or similarities between them.

Supervised Learning

In the case of supervised learning, there is a set of labeled data or samples associated with a class by a professional (labeled training). This set of samples forms the basis of the learning process. The aim of a supervised learning algorithm is to build a classifier from a training base, or to classify a function. Such a function identifies specific class attributes from the object description.

Supervised learning has an error signal, which not only calculates the satisfaction index, but also estimates that the local gradient indicates the direction in which the gradient fits the synaptic weight. Synaptic coefficients are evaluated on a learning basis by minimizing the error between desired and obtained output.

Unsupervised Learning

Unsupervised (selforganized) learning consists in determining classification based on a given set of objects or situation (unlabeled samples) We have a large amount of data with unknown structure, and we want to know if they have a group structure. The aim is to determine possible trends in the grouping of data into classes.

Unsupervised learning is generally based on a competitive process aimed at generating a model where the synaptic weights of neurons represent stimulus prototypes. The quality of the resulting model is assessed using a metric that measures the distance between stimuli and their prototypes. This is the competition process, which selects the prototype associated with each stimulus by searching for the neuron whose synaptic weight vector is closest to the stimulus in question.

Learning Rules

Several rules can guide the learning of neural networks.

Error Correction Rule

The first usable rule is based on the correction of observed output errors. Let $a_i(t)$ be the output obtained (output error) for neuron i at time t. This output is the result of a stimulus. This output results from a stimulus $p(t)$ applied to the network inputs, one of whose neurons corresponds to neuron i. Let $d_i(t)$ be the output we wish to obtain (desired output) for this same neuron i at time t. Then, $a_i(t)$ and $d_i(t)$ will generally be different, and it's natural to calculate the error $e_i(t)$ between what we obtain and what we'd like to obtain:

$$e_i(t) = d_i(t) - a_i(t)$$

We then need to find a way to reduce this error as much as possible. In vector form, we obtain:

$$e(t) = d(t) - a(t)$$

The network weight must be modified in a direction that minimizes the performance index E based on the error vectors $e_i(t)$, then in the opposite direction to the gradient. This is referred to as a "descent" direction, defined by:

$$\Delta w(t) = -\eta \nabla E(t)$$

Where η is a positive constant that determines the speed of learning, which is called the learning rate. $\nabla E(t)$ denotes the gradient of E with respect to the parameters weight w and time t. the rule is called "gradient descent".

Hebb's Rule

Hebb's rule was inspired by the work of neurophysiologist Donald Hebb. In this neurobiological context, Hebb sought to establish the form of associative learning at the cellular level. Hebb's rulebased learning expresses weight variation as a function of the correlation between input p and output a of a neuron. In the context of artificial networks, we can reformulate Hebb's statement as a learning rule given by:

Δwj (t – 1)= ηpj(t) a (t)

Where η is the learning rate, pj (t) and a(t) correspond to presynaptic activity (neuron input j) and postsynaptic activity (neuron output) at time t respectively. This formula explicitly highlights the correlation between the input vector and the output vector.

Competitive Learning Rule

As the name suggests, competitive learning involves competing neurons in the network to determine which neuron will be active at a given time. Competitive learning produces a "winner" as well as, sometimes, a set of neurons "neighboring" the winner. Competitive learning produces a "winner" as well as, sometimes, a set of neurons "neighboring" the winner, and only this winner and, potentially, its neighborhood benefit from a weight adjustment. Learning is then said to be local, as it is limited to a subset of the network's neurons.

In their simplest form, neural networks using competitive learning often consist of a single layer of output neurons, fully connected to the inputs. A winning neuron will modify its synaptic weights by moving them (geometrically) closer to an input stimulus p for which it beat all the other neurons in the competition.

In its simplest form, a neural network using competitive learning generally consists of a single layer of output neurons fully connected to the input. The winning neuron will make its synaptic weight (geometrically) close to the input stimulus p, so that it defeats all the other neurons in the competition, thus modifying its synaptic weight.

So, the competitive learning rule can be written as follows:

$$\begin{cases} \Delta w = \eta(y - w) & \text{If the neuron wins} \\ 0 & \text{otherwise} \end{cases}$$

Where η corresponds to a learning rate, y and w are the input vector and the weight vector respectively.

Learning Tasks

We have put an end to the notion of learning by listing different categories of tasks that can be performed with a neural network:

Association

There are two types: heteroassociation and autoassociation. The problem with the latter is to memorize and store a set of patterns (vectors), presenting them sequentially to the network. Next, a part or modified version of an original pattern is presented to the network, and the task is to output the corresponding original mode. On the other hand, the problem of heteroassociation is the association of two pairs of patterns: an input pattern and an output pattern. Heteroassociation involves supervised learning, whereas autoassociation requires unsupervised learning.

Approximation

Let g be a function such that:

$$\mu = g(p),$$

Where p is the argument of the function (vector), and μ the value (scalar) of this function evaluated in p. Now let's assume that the function g() is unknown. Next, the approximation task involves designing a neural network capable of associating the elements of the input and output pairs: $\{(p_1, \mu_1), (p_2, \mu_2), \ldots, (p_Q, \mu_Q)\}$. This problem can be solved by performing supervised learning on Q instances, where the p_i represent the stimuli, and the μ_i represent the expected (desired) outputs of each of these stimuli, with $i = 1, 2, \ldots, Q$. Or alternatively, we can also say that supervised learning is a function approximation problem.

Ranking

For this task, the network must learn to recognize a fixed number of input stimulus categories (classes). In a first step, the network must begin with a supervised learning phase, in which stimuli are represented as inputs, and the categories are used to form the desired outputs, typically using one output per category. Thus, output 1 is associated with category 1, output 2 is associated with category 2, and so on. For a problem involving Q categories, we can, for example, organize and fix the desired outputs $d = [d_1, d_2, \ldots, d_Q]^T$ Using the following expression:

$$d_i = \begin{cases} 1 & \text{if the stimulus belongs to category i} \\ 0 & \text{otherwise, } i=1,\ldots,Q \end{cases}$$

Later, in the recognition phase, it will suffice to be able to present any unknown stimulus to the network so that it can be classified in a category. A simple classification rule, for example, is to select the category associated with the highest output.

Ordering

Control is another learning task that can be handled with a neural network. Consider a nonlinear dynamic system {u(t), y(t)} where u(t) is the system input and y(t) are the system response. In general, we want to control this system so that it behaves according to a reference model, usually a linear model, {r(t), d(t)}, where at any time t ≥ 0, we can produce a control u(t) such that:

$$\lim_{t\to\infty} |d(t) - y(t)| = 0$$

So that the system output closely follows that of the reference model. This can be achieved using certain types of supervised networks.

Prediction

The concept of prediction is one of the most fundamental concepts in learning. It is a temporary signal processing problem. Suppose we have M past samples of a signal, x(t−1), x(t−2), . . ., x(t−M) The sampling is performed at a fixed time interval and the task is to predict the value of x at time t. This prediction problem can be solved by errorcorrection learning, but in an unsupervised way,

This is because the desired output values can be inferred directly from the time series. More precisely, the sample x(t) can be used as the desired value and the error signal for weight matching is calculated simply by the following equation:

e(t) = x(t) − x̂ (t I t − 1, t − 2, . . ., t −M),

Where x(t) refers to the desired output and x̂ (t I t−1, t−2, . . ., t−M) represents the observed output of the network given the previous M samples. Prediction is similar to building a physical model of the time series. Insofar as the network has neurons with a nonlinear transfer function.

THE NEURON PERCEPTRON MODEL

The neuron model is a mathematical model of the behavior of a single neuron in the biological nervous system. The features of the neuron model in the perceptron are called the perceptron. The perceptron neuron model receives information in the form of a set of digital input signals. This information is then integrated with a set of free parameters to produce a message in the form of a single digital output signal. The neural model is proposed by Rosenblatt and can learn from samples.

Perceptron Elements

Typically, the perceptron is identified by three basic elements that transform the input signals (x1, x2,...,xn) into a single output signal y:

A set of free parameters α, consisting of a bais b and a vector of synaptic weights (w1, w2,...,wn)

Figure 3. Artificial neuron model
$X = \sum (inputs * weight) + bias$

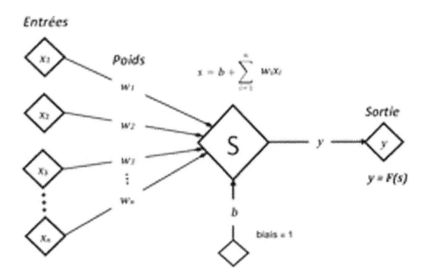

A combination function, which combines the input signals and free parameters to produce a single input signal S.

An activation or transfer function F, which takes the input signal S as its argument and produces the output signal y.

The figure below shows a graphical representation of the perceptron. A neuron essentially consists of an integrator that performs a weighted sum of its inputs. The result S of this sum is then transformed by an activation function F, which produces the neuron's output y.

Free Parameters

Free parameters are used to train a neuron model to perform a task. In the perceptron, the set of free parameters is:

$$ß = (b,w) \in R \times R^n$$

Where b is called the bais and w = (w1, w2, ...,wn) is called a vector of synaptic weights. Please note then that the number of free parameters in this neuron model is 1 + n, where n is the number of inputs to the neuron.

Combination Function

In the combination function, the scalar product of the input vector x = (x1, x2, x3,...,xn) and the synaptic weight vector w = (w1, w2, w3,...,wn) is calculated to produce and generate a signal S. This model also includes an externally applied bias, denoted b, which increases or decreases the net input signal to the activation function, depending on whether it is positive or negative respectively. The bias is usually represented as a synaptic weight linked to an input set to1.

$$S = b + \sum_{i=1}^{n} w_i x_i$$

Table 1. Activation function table

Function name	Relationship Input-Output	Icon	Output interval
Competitive	$y = 1$ if S maximum $y = 0$ otherwise		$(-\infty, 1)$
Linear	$y = S$		$(-\infty, +\infty)$
Linear positive	$y = 0 \quad$ si n < 0 $y = s \quad$ si n ≥ 0		$(-\infty, +\infty)$
Saturated linear	$y = 0$ si S < 0 $y = S$ si $0 \leq S \leq 1$ $y = 1$ si S > 1		$(-\infty, +\infty)$
Symmetrical saturated linear	$y = -1$ si S < -1 $y = S$ si $-1 \leq n \leq 1$ $y = 1$ si S > 1		$(-\infty, +\infty)$
Threshold	$y = 0$ si S < 0 $y = 1$ si S ≥ 0		$[0 ; 1]$
Symmetrical threshold	$y = -1$ si S < 0 $y = 1$ si S ≥ 0		$[-1 ; 1]$
Sigmoid	$y = \dfrac{1}{1 + \exp^{S}}$		$(0, 1)$
Hyperbolic tangent	$y = \dfrac{e^{s} - e^{s1}}{e^{s} + e^{s1}}$		(-1.1)

Activation Function

The activation function F defines the neuron's output signal y as a function of its input signal S. In fact, and in practice, we can consider several useful activation functions. The following table lists various transfer functions that can be used as a neuron activation function.

Transfer functions: $y = f(s)$

The three most commonly used functions are "threshold", "linear" and "sigmoid".

Threshold Transfer Function

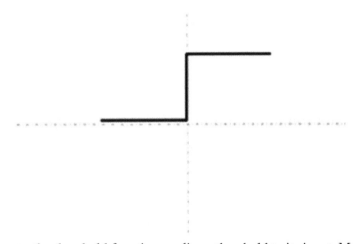

As its name suggests, the threshold function applies a threshold to its input. More precisely, a negative input fails the threshold (doesn't pass), then the function returns a value of 0, which we can interpret as meaning false, while a positive or zero input exceeds the threshold, the function returns 1 (true). In other words, the threshold activation function limits the neuron's output to 0 when the input is less than 0, and limits it to 1 when S is equal to or greater than 0.

Linear Transfer Function

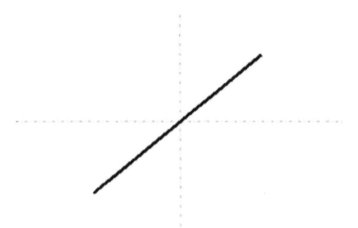

The linear function is very simple: it assigns its input directly to its output. In other words, the output signal of this neuron model is equal to its input.

The Sigmoid Transfer Function

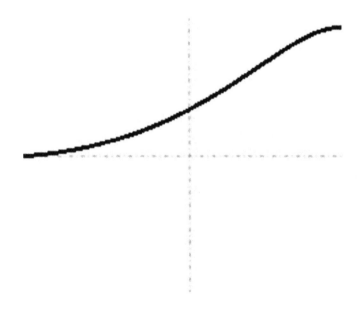

Simple Perceptron Learning

The simple perceptron learning algorithm is a supervised learning algorithm, which seeks to modify the weights to determine a set of values for the weights, such that the inputs translate into the desired outputs.

The most widely used learning rule for the perceptron is the WidrowHoff rule, the idea of which is to change the weights each time according to the inputs.

CONCLUSION

In concluding this work, the objective already mentioned at the beginning of this chapter is to propose a working methodology for our research by defining the instruments chosen for processing and analyzing our research data. In this way, we have provided an overview of failure at university level, particularly in the first year, and defined the instruments chosen to process and analyze our research data then we have presented models based on neural networks.

REFERENCES

Bennani, Y. (2006). *Apprentissage connexionniste*. Hermes Science.

Clergue, M. (2015). *Réseaux de Neurones Artificiels*.

Drew, P. J., & Monson, J. R. T. (2000). Artificial neural networks. *The Journal of Pathology, 127*(1), 3–11. PMID:10660751

Dreyfus, G., Martinez, J., Samuelides, M., Gordon, M. B., Badran, F., Thiria, S., & Hérault, L. (2008). *Réseaux de neurones: Méthodologie et applications (2e édition)*. Eyrolles.

Hopfield, J. J. (1982). Neural networks and physical systems with emergent collective computational abilities (Réseaux neuronaux et systèmes physiques dotés de capacités de calcul collectives émergentes). *Proceedings of the National Academy of Sciences of the United States of America, 79*(8), 2554–2558. doi:10.1073/pnas.79.8.2554 PMID:6953413

Kohonen, T. (1988). An introduction to neural computing. *Neural Networks, 1*(1), 3–16. doi:10.1016/0893-6080(88)90020-2

McCarthy, J., Minsky, M.L., Rochester, N. et Shannon, C.E. (1955). *A Proposal for the Dartmouth Summer Research Project on Artificial Intelligence* [Proposition pour le projet de recherche d'été de Dartmouth sur l'intelligence artificielle].

McClelland, G. & Hinton, G.E. (1987). *Le Débat Émergence du Cognitif*.

McCulloh, W.S. & Pitts, W. (1943). A logical calculus of the ideas immanent in nervous activity. *The Bulletin of Mathematical Biophysics, 4,* 115-133.

Minsky, M., & Papert, S. (1969). *Perceptrons: An Introduction to Computational Geometry*. MIT Press.

Murat, M. E., & Rudman, A. J. (1992). Automated first arrival picking: A neural network approach. *Geophysical Prospecting, 40*(6), 587–604. doi:10.1111/j.1365-2478.1992.tb00543.x

Parizeau, M. (2006). *Réseaux de Neurones. GIF-21140 et GIF-64326*. Université Laval.

Petitjean, G. (2009). *Introduction aux réseaux de neurones*.

Rosenblatt, F. (1957). *Le perceptron: Un automate de perception et de reconnaissance*. No 85-460-1.

Rosenblatt, F. (1961). *Principes de la neurodynamique: Perceptrons and the Theory of Brain Mechanisms*. Semantic Scholar.

Röth, G., & Tarantola, A. (1994). Neural networks and inversion of seismic data. *Journal of Geophysical Research*, *99*(B4), 6753–6768. doi:10.1029/93JB01563

Touzet, C. (1992). *Les Réseaux de Neurones Artificiels: Introduction au Connexionnisme*.

Zhang, Y., & Paulson, K. V. (1997). Magnetotelluric inversion using regularized Hopfield neural networks. *Geophysical Prospecting*, *45*(5), 725–743. doi:10.1046/j.1365-2478.1997.660299.x

Zhang, Y., & Paulson, K. V. (1997). Enhancement of Signal-to-noise Ratio in Natural-source Transient Magnetotelluric Data with Wavelet Transform. *Pure and Applied Geophysics*, *149*(2), 405–419. doi:10.1007000240050033

Chapter 12

Digital Storytelling as a Tool for Enhancing Preservice Chemistry Teachers' Conceptual Understanding and Learning Strategies

Şenol Şen

(iD) https://orcid.org/0000-0003-3831-3953

Hacettepe University, Turkey

ABSTRACT

Digital storytelling is one of the tools that can be used to improve preservice chemistry teachers' conceptual understanding on the topic of melting and dissolving and metacognitive learning strategies. In this study, it was aimed to create digital stories using information and communication technologies on the topic of melting and dissolving, which is one of the important topics of chemistry. A one group pretest-posttest experimental design was used in the study. The study group consisted of 25 preservice chemistry teachers who were in the first grade at a state university. In addition, within the scope of the study, preservice teachers' opinions on the effect and usability of project-based learning method supported by digital stories on teaching/learning process were also taken with open-ended questions. The findings of this study revealed that digital storytelling is an effective method for improving preservice chemistry teachers' conceptual understanding and learning strategies.

INTRODUCTION

The rapid change of information and technology in today's world causes acquired knowledge to become obsolete and quickly lose its validity. This situation requires lifelong learning for individuals, as information is considered to be the greatest power in the information age. Therefore, it is important for individuals to develop researcher identities and use information and communication technologies (ICTs) effectively.

DOI: 10.4018/979-8-3693-3128-6.ch012

Copyright © 2024, IGI Global. Copying or distributing in print or electronic forms without written permission of IGI Global is prohibited.

Skills such as collaboration, responsibility, critical thinking, problem solving, creativity, effective use of ICTs, and research skills have become indispensable for individuals in the 21st century (Geisinger, 2016; Trilling & Fadel, 2009). Considering that students in education faculties should be models for future students as future teachers, the importance of being researchers and designing technology-supported learning environments is emphasized. Teachers should set an example for students with their researcher identities and ICT use skills. Teachers who effectively design technology-supported teaching practices will be more successful in raising students who have a positive attitude towards technology and use technology well.

Learning environments based on constructivist learning theory, where learners construct their own knowledge and teachers guide them, are preferred in recent years to achieve meaningful learning. In these environments, learners take responsibility for their own learning, and knowledge is not directly transmitted to students. Traditional teaching methods, on the other hand, are carried out in a way that does not take into account the prior knowledge of students and relies on memorization. In order to make learning-teaching environments more effective, different learning methods are tried in research studies. In these methods, the principle of student activity is important. Student performance will be negatively affected in environments where students are passive. Therefore, it is necessary to try learning methods that allow students to be more active and show maximum performance. Especially, one of the biggest factors that cause our students' failure is the teaching practices carried out with traditional methods. In Türkiye, the Ministry of National Education (MoNE), has renewed primary and secondary education curricula based on constructivist learning theory since 2005. However, only content change will not be enough for students to be more active and show maximum performance. These changes should also include learning and teaching processes along with curricula. In today's world, which is called the digital age, it is mandatory to create learning environments that are enriched with social, participatory, and multi-environments in class processes for students to have effective learning experiences (McLoughlin & Lee, 2010).

Technology integration in education is the use of technology in education programs and teaching environments to enhance and support learning (Hennessy et al., 2005). Teachers are expected to use technology effectively and guide their students (Demir & Bozkurt, 2011). This is because teachers play a key role in successfully implementing the integration process in teaching environments (Mandell et al., 2002). It is important for teachers, who are digital immigrants, to use technology in their classrooms to attract students who are digital natives (Yılmaz et al., 2017a). With the increasing importance of web-based and multimedia learning experiences in 21st century classrooms, teacher education programs also have the responsibility of providing new media and pedagogical literacies to tomorrow's teachers (Shelton et al., 2017). New teachers have stated that they have sufficient willingness and technical knowledge to use technology in teaching environments, but they lack knowledge on how to integrate technology into learning-teaching environments (Ertmer et al., 2003). Educational technologies are increasingly important in the field of education. Therefore, preservice teachers need to develop their knowledge and skills related to different educational technologies in order to use them effectively in their own teaching. The education given to teachers should focus more on teaching strategies that will enable the integration of technology into the learning process rather than technological skills (Gorder, 2008). It has been stated that an education that teaches teachers how to use technological tools simply and effectively and how to integrate them into the teaching process has an effective contribution to teachers' adoption of technology (Ertmer, 2005). In technology integration in education, not only technological developments and competencies but also pedagogical factors should be taken into account. In this context, it can be said that digital stories and digital storytelling can be used as teaching material and method in many subject areas (Yılmaz et al., 2017b). Digital storytelling attracts the attention of teachers and researchers because it is effective in developing 21st century skills (Jakes, 2006).

DIGITAL STORY TELLING

Digital storytelling movement emerged with the establishment of the Center for Digital Storytelling (CDS) in Berkeley, California in the late 1980s to provide education and support to people who wanted to create and share their personal narratives (Robin, 2008). CDS also introduced the Seven Elements of Digital Storytelling, which is a useful guide for creating digital stories (Robin, 2008). Digital storytelling is the modern storytelling that emerges by enriching the traditional storytelling with digital technologies. Digital storytelling not only involves creating stories in digital environments but also expresses the sharing process of these digital stories. Compared to traditional stories, they have more elements such as text, sound, image, video and animation and can be viewed on computers, tablets or smartphones, which are among the most important advantages and pluses.

Digital storytelling is a modern transformation of the traditional art of storytelling by utilizing today's technologies (Lambert, 2013). Meadows (2003) describes digital stories as short, individual, and multimedia stories. According to Robin (2008), digital storytelling is a technology application that can help teachers improve their ability to utilize content and use technology effectively in the classroom. Through this application, computer users can increase their storytelling competence by researching, scripting, and producing creative stories about a topic of their choice. The stories produced can be enriched with multimedia tools such as graphics, sound recordings, computer-generated texts, video clips, and music, and can be displayed on a computer, transferred to a website, or recorded on a DVD. Bran (2010) argued that digital storytelling, which combines images, sound, and text, is an effective way to engage students and enhance their learning because multimedia elements capture students' attention and make learning fun, while the process of creating a digital story develops students' critical thinking and problem-solving skills.

Digital storytelling process consists of several steps that can be effectively applied to create a successful digital story. These steps are: writing, script, storyboard, locating multimedia, creating the digital story, and sharing (Jakes & Brennan, 2005). Jakes and Brennan (2005) summarize these steps as follows:

Writing: The first step of digital storytelling is writing. The written text should be of a personal narrative nature and contain a central theme. The theme allows the audience to connect with the story. It is useful for students to prepare multiple drafts to improve their writing skills.

Script: The script is very important in digital storytelling. The script summarizes the main elements of the narrative and forms the basis of the digital story. Multimedia elements are used to support the script. Multimedia elements should reflect and add meaning to the story.

Storyboard: Students use a tool called a storyboard to plan their film projects. The storyboard helps them organize their script and visuals. The storyboard is also an important tool for managing the project and finding multimedia elements. This step is disliked by some students and emphasized by some teachers, but it is very important.

Locating multimedia: Students search for multimedia materials (images, music, sound, photo, graphic, etc.) for their digital story projects using search engines on the internet. Students who tell personal stories or have personal photo collections can scan images with a scanner to use in their digital stories. It

Figure 1. The power of digital storytelling project based learning

is recommended to use 20-25 images for digital story projects, and JPEG format is more suitable than video clips.

Creating the digital story: Students create their digital stories with various software. An introduction is given to students beforehand on how to use this software. Students can also benefit from written sources or digital storytelling websites. Students also perform voice-overs for their stories at this stage. The film is first processed as a low-quality Windows Media Player file and checked whether the student is satisfied with the final product. Then, the film is recreated in high quality. The finished film is shared and evaluated by the teacher.

Sharing: Sharing digital stories can strengthen relationships in the classroom. Students can get to know each other better by watching other students' stories. Students can also share their stories with other people around the world by uploading them to various platforms.

Digital storytelling can be divided into three main categories that can be used for educational purposes (Robin, 2008). These are personal narratives, instructional stories, and historical documentaries. Personal narratives are the most common type of digital stories that involve emotional and significant events. Instructional or informative stories are used to present educational content in different subject areas. Historical stories narrate historical events and allow students to create stories using historical materials.

Barrett (2006) has stated that digital storytelling combines four strategies that support student-centered learning: student engagement, reflection for deep learning, project-based learning, and the effective integration of technology into the teaching-learning environment (Figure 1). This figure also reveals the scope of this study. Within the scope of this study, it is attempted to reveal the effects of project-based learning supported by digital stories on student achievement and metacognitive self-regulation, which is one of the learning strategies they choose and use.

Project-based learning (PBL) is a student-centered learning method in which learners search for answers to questions related to an original and real problem in order to find a solution. They work collaboratively to learn knowledge, skills, attitudes, and scientific concepts, and share their findings and results with their peers in the form of a report as a result of their inquiry and investigation studies (Blumenfeld et al., 1991; Thomas, 2000). The project-based learning method combines science, technology, engineering, art, and mathematics to develop students' skills by enabling them to create projects. The presentations in the projects can be a drama activity, a poster presentation, or an oral presentation (Çubukçu, 2012). Gómez-Pablos, del Pozo, and Muñoz-Repiso (2017) have stated that PBL is an effective learning method in the face of problematic situations such as involving students in the learning process and motivating them in this process. According to the researchers, this method is also an important method that is effective in developing critical and research skills as well as basic skills. PBL is a more student-centered and teacher-facilitated learning method. Learners try to learn by finding answers to questions that their natural interests create. In this method, the project emerges as a result of inquiry. Students develop a question and conduct research under the guidance of the teacher. The student's preference is the basic element of the project (Bell, 2010). In PBL, students work collaboratively to solve a problem in their own lives and include out-of-school environments in the learning process (Çubukçu, 2012). Each step that students follow while looking for a solution to the problem is monitored by the teacher, and the student tries to get the teacher's approval to take action. In addition, if some students are focused on finding a solution to the same problem, it is ensured that these students work collaboratively and acquire 21st century collaborative work and communication skills. PBL should not be considered as an additional activity that can be done to support learning. The curriculum can be arranged based on this method. PBL can help students understand a topic better, learn more deeply, develop higher-level reading skills, and increase their motivation for learning after teaching (Bell, 2010).

It has been revealed in the literature that digital storytelling has many positive contributions to teaching-learning processes. Digital storytelling is often used in project-based learning tasks (Sabari & Hashim, 2023). However, the effect of using digital storytelling and project-based learning together on preservice teachers' conceptual understanding and learning strategies has not yet been investigated. The main elements of project-based learning are research and product development (Diffily, 2002). In this study, preservice teachers prepared their digital stories as a product in the project-based learning process. They participated in a learning process that combined project-based learning and digital storytelling strategies for melting and dissolving concepts.

LEARNING STRATEGIES

Learning strategies are the behaviors and thoughts that individuals apply in the learning process. These strategies affect how individuals encode information and facilitate learning. Weinstein and Mayer (1986) define learning strategies as cognitive plans for a task. Wittrock (1986) sees learning strategies as student behaviors and thoughts that emerge during learning. These strategies affect the motivation of learning, the encoding, retention, and transfer of information.

In this study, learning strategies are classified into three groups: cognitive, metacognitive, and resource management strategies, following the categorization of Pintrich, Smith, Garcia, and McKeachie (1991). The use of learning strategies by students positively affects their academic achievement. The studies of Zimmerman and Martinez-Pons (1990) and Pintrich and De Groot (1990) support this result. Eilam and Aharon (2003) also found that students who were successful in a science project had better self-efficacy, content organization, and time management skills. Duncan and McKeachie (2005) stated that the strategies used by students may vary depending on the academic tasks. Therefore, it is thought that teacher candidates' learning strategies may change in learning environments where they will take responsibility, such as project-based learning environments supported by digital storytelling.

In this study, the change in pre-service teachers' metacognitive learning strategies, which is a type of learning strategy, was analyzed. The metacognitive self-regulation sub-dimension of the Motivated Strategies for Learning Questionnaire (MSLQ) was used to assess pre-service teachers' metacognitive learning strategies. Metacognitive self-regulation is the ability to monitor and control what and how one does in one's own learning process (Pintrich et al., 1991). According to Pintrich et al. (1991), there are three main metacognitive self-regulatory activities: planning, monitoring, and regulating one's cognitive activities and behavior. Planning activities, such as setting goals and analyzing tasks, help to activate prior knowledge and facilitate comprehension of the topic. Monitoring activities, such as checking one's attention during reading, self-testing, and questioning, help the learner to understand the material and integrate new information with existing knowledge. Regulating activities refer to the continuous adjustment of one's cognitive activities.

The Current Study

Preservice teachers at the faculty of education do not have much information about the new teaching methods and techniques that have started to be used in learning-teaching environments due to the rapid changes in science and technology. As a result, they are not interested in these new methods and techniques. This is because the methods and techniques that teachers encounter and experience in their education process affect the methods and techniques they will use when they become teachers in the future (Adamson et al., 2003; Sunzuma & Maharaj, 2019). In order for teachers to carry out an effective teaching process, they need to have both a deep knowledge of the subject (content knowledge) and appropriate teaching strategies (pedagogical content knowledge) to convey this knowledge to students (Garnett & Tobin, 1989). However, it is known that preservice teachers are not able to integrate technology sufficiently into the learning-teaching process by the time they graduate from education faculties. They should be given the necessary courses in technology courses to acquire the skills of using technology, and opportunities should be provided for them to practice (Angeli, 2005; Lin & Lu, 2010). This is because, according to Hare et al. (2002), there is a significant gap between the knowledge and skills that preservice teachers acquire about technology and the knowledge and skills they need to use in the classroom as teachers. This gap arises from the fact that technology is not sufficiently included and supported in teacher education programs (Hare et al., 2002).

In order for teachers to integrate technology into their courses, taking trainings in this direction is a simple but effective method (Ertmer, 2005). However, teachers do not adopt technology and technology-supported teaching at the desired level due to lack of knowledge and experience (Ertmer, 2005). Therefore, teachers who are aware of technological innovations related to their field, follow them, and practice how to integrate them into their courses can use technology more easily in the classroom (Shin et al., 2014). Jacobsen (2001) stated that most teachers do not use technology effectively in their courses. Therefore, providing practical trainings to teachers on how to use technological tools and integrate them into the teaching/learning process will help them use technology effectively in the classroom. In this context, the importance of undergraduate training for teachers to improve their technology integration skills comes to the fore. According to Robin (2008), teachers can use pre-made digital stories as a teaching tool to introduce content and present new ideas to their students. If teachers can create their own digital stories, these stories not only increase students' engagement with content, but also encourage discussion on topics in the story and make abstract or conceptual content more understandable (Robin, 2008). A digital story enriched with multimedia elements can function as an introduction or hook to attract students' attention and direct them to explore new ideas.

When the literature is examined, it is determined that digital storytelling is effective in studies conducted with university students (Acar, 2013; Chan et al., 2017; Sakka & Zualkernan, 2005) and especially with preservice teachers (Hava, 2021; Heo, 2009; Istenic Starčič et al., 2016; Nuroh et al., 2022; Shelton et al., 2017). Additionally, when the literature is examined, it is determined that there are studies that use digital storytelling especially for teaching chemistry and science subjects (Anılan et al., 2018; Chadwick & Muilenburg, 2011; Nam, 2017). Chemistry educators can use a simple and valuable way of engaging their students in and out of class by telling stories that are related to compounds, chemists, and even fictional science (Collins, 2021). Storytelling in chemistry is a teaching method that involves social and technological elements related to daily life, presents scientific concepts, and enables students' active participation, which improves students' willingness to learn and meaningful learning (Demircioğlu et al., 2006). Project-based learning is also known to help students gain a deeper understanding of both technology and learning content (Ekawati & Prastyo, 2022). It is seen that both project-based learning method and digital storytelling have many positive contributions to teaching-learning processes when the literature is examined. However, this study aims to combine these two effective strategies. Digital storytelling has been designed as a project-based learning activity consisting of learning tasks such as creating a story using pencil drawings or visuals prepared in digital environment, adding subtitles and background to photos, making a film, and presenting it (Hung et al., 2012).

Web 2.0 tools play an important role in today's classrooms, where technology-integrated teaching-learning environments are widespread. Educational researchers want 21st-century students to be active participants who not only consume online content but also produce their own content by taking advantage of the online content-sharing opportunities offered by Web 2.0 tools (Shelton et al., 2017). Based on this point, this study aims to investigate the effects of an intervention designed to improve preservice teachers' video production skills as a product in project-based learning management and implemented in accordance with the teacher preparation curriculum. Digital storytelling is an effective tool that offers chemistry preservice teachers the opportunity to improve their conceptual knowledge and metacognitive learning strategies on melting and dissolving. Based on this point, the aim of this study is to examine how preparing digital stories within the framework of project-based learning method on melting and dissolving contributes to chemistry preservice teachers' conceptual understanding and metacognitive learning strategies. For this purpose, in this study, course materials (digital stories) suitable for digital storytelling for chemistry courses were developed by using information and communication technologies (ICT). In line with these purposes, the following questions were sought answers:

Is there a significant difference between preservice teachers' pretest-posttest scores on the Melting and Dissolving Concept Test?

Is there a significant difference between preservice teachers' pretest-posttest scores on the metacognitive learning strategies in the Motivational Strategies for Learning Questionnaire (MSLQ) for chemistry course?

What are preservice teachers' opinions on the project-based learning environment supported by digital stories?

METHOD

Research Methods

In the study, the one-group pretest-posttest design from quantitative research methods was used to investigate the effect of project-based learning supported by digital stories (Fraenkel et al., 2015). The quantitative data obtained in the study were used to test the effect of the method used on preservice teachers' conceptual understanding on melting and dissolving and metacognitive learning strategies. In addition, qualitative data were used to examine preservice teachers' opinions on the learning environment.

Participants

The sample for this study was determined using purposive sampling. This method provides informative and in-depth insights on the research topic (Fraenkel et al., 2015). In this study, the researcher selected 25 chemistry preservice teachers from a state university using purposive sampling. The ages of the preservice teachers ranged from 19 to 22. Purposive sampling is a suitable method for research on a new or less studied topic because it allows researchers to focus on a specific group of participants who can offer valuable insights for their research (Fraenkel et al., 2015).

Process

This study aimed to determine the effect of project-based learning (PBL) approach supported by digital stories on preservice teachers' conceptual understanding in Basic Chemistry course on important concepts such as melting and dissolving and metacognitive learning strategies. Participation in the research was voluntary, and the participants who would be applied the measurement tools within the scope of the study were informed. The research process lasted 10 weeks. This period was determined considering that PBL is a time-consuming method and it may take longer than planned for students to complete their projects. In the first week of the process, the aims of the research, the steps of PBL, application examples, and what was expected from students were explained to preservice teachers. The PBL model steps used by Song (2018) were followed in the research (see Figure 2). In the Explore and Understand stage of the project-based learning (PBL) method, preservice teachers were informed about digital stories as project topic and product. Preservice teachers were asked to set goals on melting and dissolving. Preservice teachers conducted resource research in line with their goals. In the Represent and Formulate stage, preservice teachers evaluated the information they collected and developed solution suggestions for the problem and discussed these suggestions. In the Plan and Execute stage, preservice teachers prepared a plan for solving the problem. After implementing the plan, they collected data on solution methods. They analyzed the data and obtained results. They shared these results within the group and then created digital stories for solving the problem. In the Monitor and Reflect stage, preservice teachers shared their digital stories with the class. Students prepared reflection reports for projects and project results. A general discussion was held in the whole class environment. Other preservice teachers gave feedback on projects and digital stories.

In this study, project-based learning (PBL) and digital storytelling were used together. Students developed a digital story on melting and dissolving by following the steps of PBL. In this study, chemistry preservice teachers were provided with experiences of the content development process with digital

Figure 2. Stages of a project based learning

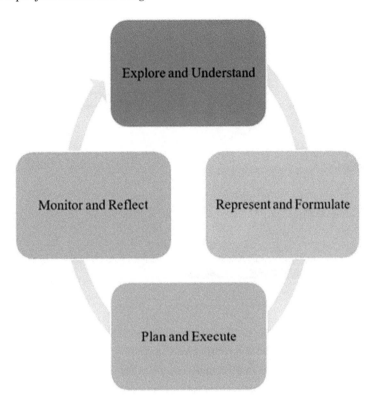

storytelling. Preservice teachers were given a problem situation and asked to prepare a digital story as a solution to this problem based on the steps of PBL (Figure 3). The digital story preparation process consists of six stages developed by Jakes and Brennan (2005). In this study, the steps followed in the digital story creation process were arranged by benefiting from the stages in the study conducted by Haşlaman (2017). In the first stage, preservice teachers designed their stories by determining the problem and target audience on melting and dissolving within the first stage of PBL. They planned how the characters in their stories used learning strategies and melting and dissolving topics. They received feedback from their friends to complete their stories. In the second stage, preservice teachers converted their stories into script format. They considered elements such as dramatic structure, stage layout, dialogues, and scene transitions in their scripts. They also conducted research on the selection and use of multimedia elements. In the third stage, preservice teachers prepared storyboards to determine the flow of scenes in their digital stories. They combined their scripts with visual elements and improved them with feedback they received. They also asked for help from the instructor of the course to check the suitability of the chemistry concepts used. In the fourth stage, preservice teachers determined which multimedia elements they needed to create their digital stories and planned this process. They searched for content elements such as images, music, sound, photos, graphics on the internet and selected those suitable for their scripts. They also used pencil drawings or visuals they prepared in digital environment if necessary. They started to bring these elements together in computer environment. In the fifth stage, preservice teachers used the options offered and other internet-based software tools to create their digital stories. No limitation was imposed on preservice teachers in this regard. Preservice teachers transferred

Figure 3. Images from digital storytelling examples prepared by preservice teachers

the scenes they designed on storyboards to the digital story creation tool environment they chose. Then they voiced their stories and recorded sound using tools such as sound recorders, microphones or online software tools. In the sixth stage, preservice teachers shared their digital stories with their classmates in class environment. As a result of these stories, preservice teachers made a self-evaluation for themselves and their digital stories. Within the scope of PBL, they evaluated whether they found a solution to the problem situation they aimed at and the suitability of solution methods with feedbacks they received from classmates and instructor.

Measurements

Melting and Dissolving Concept Test (MDCT): The Melting and Dissolving Concept Test (MDCT) was developed by Şen (2011) to identify the misconceptions of students on this topic. The MDCT consists of 16 multiple-choice questions, each with four options. The test score can range from 0 to 16. It is assumed that students who score high on the test have fewer misconceptions about melting and dissolving. The distractors in the test were created based on the students' misconceptions on this topic. The alpha-reliability coefficient of the test was found to be 0.854.

Motivated Strategies for Learning Questionnaire (MSLQ): The MSLQ was developed by Pintrich et al. (1991) to measure the motivation levels and learning strategies of college students. The questionnaire has two sections: motivation and learning strategies. Learning strategies section consists of 50 items and evaluates how students use different cognitive, metacognitive, and resource management strategies. The learning strategies section has nine subscales in total: Cognitive and Metacognitive Strategies (1. Rehearsal, 2. Elaboration, 3. Organization, 4. Critical Thinking, 5. Metacognitive Self-Regulation) and Resource Management Strategies (6. Time and Study Environment, 7. Effort Regulation, 8. Peer Learning, 9. Help Seeking) (Pintrich et al., 1991). The researchers stated that each subscale in the motivation and learning strategies sections can be used separately or together, depending on the need. In this study, the Metacognitive Self-Regulation subscale was used to determine the metacognitive learning strategies of preservice teachers. This subscale has a total of 12 items. The items in the original scale were adapted for a chemistry course and used in this form.

Open-ended questions: In the study, the opinions of preservice teachers were obtained by asking them questions that were created by the researcher with the feedback from experts. The questions were as follows:

What are the contributions of project-based learning (PBL) method supported by digital stories to the learning process?

What are the difficulties encountered in the learning process with PBL method supported by digital stories?

What is the purpose and importance of using PBL method supported by digital stories in the learning process? Why should teachers prefer this method?

When you start your teaching profession, do you plan to use PBL method supported by digital stories in the learning process? Why?

RESULTS

Results for Quantitative Data

The data collected from the study were analyzed using the statistical software package SPSS. The Wilcoxon Signed Rank test was used to assess the difference between the pre-test and post-test scores after the intervention. This non-parametric test was selected because it does not require the data to satisfy the parametric assumptions, such as normality (Pallant, 2007). In addition, the effect size r was computed using the formula r=Z/square root of N (where N=total number of cases) (N) (Pallant, 2007).

A Wilcoxon Signed Rank test was conducted to assess the change in preservice teachers' conceptual understanding of melting and dissolving concepts following participation in a project-based learning with digital storytelling environment (Table 1). The results of the test showed a statistically significant increase in conceptual understanding, z = -3.469, p < .005, with a large effect size, r = .49 (according to Cohen's (1988) effect size criteria). The median score on the melting and dissolving concept test increased from 10 at pre-test to 13 at post-test. These results suggest that the project-based learning with digital storytelling environment was effective in improving students' conceptual understanding of melting and dissolving concepts.

A Wilcoxon Signed Rank test was conducted to assess the change in preservice teachers' metacognitive learning strategies following participation in a project-based learning with digital storytelling environment (Table 1). The results of the test showed a statistically significant increase in metacognitive learn-

Table 1. Wilcoxon signed-rank test results for MDCT test and MLS scale pre-test-post-test scores

Dependent Variables		Mean Rank	Sum of Ranks	Z	p	r
MDCT	Pre-test	8.17	24.50	-3.469	.001	.49
	Post-test	12.58	251.50			
MLS	Pre-test	.00	.00	-4.200	.000	.59
	Post-test	12	276			

ing strategies, z = -4.200, p < .005, with a large effect size, r = .59 (according to Cohen's (1988) effect size criteria). The median score on metacognitive learning strategies increased from 45 at pre-test to 60 at post-test. These results suggest that the project-based learning with digital storytelling environment was effective in improving preservice teachers' metacognitive learning strategies.

Results for Qualitative Data

The answers of preservice teachers to the open-ended questions were transferred to a computer and analyzed with MAXQDA software. The data were evaluated using the content analysis method. In a coding system such as "CPS1_22_F," CPS1 stands for preservice chemistry teacher 1, 22 stands for age, and F stands for gender (female or male). Preservice teachers were asked about the general advantages of the project-based learning method supported by digital stories. Preservice teachers stated that group work was done in this learning environment and that it improved students' collaborative learning skills. They also expressed that this learning method was student-centered and that teachers played a guiding role. They said that students learned by exchanging ideas within the group. Preservice teachers emphasized that using digital stories increased both their motivation and interest. They said that the project-based learning method supported by digital stories helped them to avoid boredom. Preservice teachers especially stressed that they would use such digital story activities in their future professional lives.

CPS2_19_M: Project-based learning method supported by digital stories also allows group work. This way, students learn to work together and exchange ideas. In addition, students' research skills improve. Especially using digital stories increased our motivation.

CPS3_19_F: Among the advantages of this method are the absence of rote-based teaching and the teacher's secondary role. The teacher only guides. The student is responsible for his or her own learning. This provides a lasting learning in problem solving. That's why I think it's a very effective method. Also, digital stories made the lessons more fun. They increased our interest in the lessons. When I become a teacher in the future, I plan to use more of these digital story activities.

CPS4_19_F: I think this method makes the student responsible. He or she strives to be respected within the group and to do research on a project or question given by the teacher. This also boosts his or her self-confidence.

Preservice teachers listed some disadvantages of the project-based learning method supported by digital stories as follows: problems/disagreements arising from the diversity of students during group work, difficulty in completing the curriculum, and difficulty in classroom management.

CPS1_19_F: I think project-based learning is the easiest method to apply in the classroom environment. I guess it would be difficult and cause more noise to conduct it in groups. Also, we should consider that students who are reluctant to cooperative learning or who do not want to work with their friends may resist.

CPS19_19_M: I would like to point out that the student profile and the teacher's attitude are important in the implementation of this method. However, I must also say that some chaos is inevitable compared to the normal lesson. Because there will be a bonding among students as it requires group work. But this situation can be kept under control by the teacher. I think the teacher can be effective in this regard.

CPS21_20_F: We should not ignore that students who have a friend they do not like in group work may reject this friend. Also, we should mention that some students may find group work advantageous. For example, they may stay passive in the group and leave the work to others.

Preservice teachers were asked about their opinions on the purposes and reasons for teachers to use the project-based learning method supported by digital stories. Preservice teachers stated that this method should be used to make students participate more actively in the learning process, to strengthen their relationships with other students, to take learning responsibility, to improve their communication within the group, and to increase their problem-solving/disagreement-solving skills.

CPS15_19_M: The purpose of project-based learning method supported by digital stories is to enable students to both bond with each other and work in groups and to participate in the learning process more actively and enjoyably. Making the lessons more interesting and sharing the results they obtain are also the benefits of this method. Moreover, in this method where the teacher controls and guides, students take more responsibility, do their own research and prepare their presentations. This contributes to making their learning more permanent. I think project-based learning supported by digital stories is very effective.

CPS10_20_F: Project-based learning method supported by digital stories can encourage students to think and wonder. This method can be used to make learning-teaching environments more effective. For example, if there are ten students in the class, I can pose a problem by asking each one a question and ask for an answer. In this way, I can create a class where all students are active instead of a class where only two students participate. Also, instead of sitting on the sidelines, students will make an effort to learn something. They will also come to the next lesson by doing research wondering what the teacher will ask.

CPS9_19_F: This method allows students to solve problems collaboratively, exchange ideas and brainstorm.

Finally, preservice teachers were asked to explain whether they would use the project-based learning method supported by digital stories and how they would use it. All preservice teachers expressed that they would use this method or they would like to use it if they did not encounter problems such as time, students' reactions, and space.

CPS13_19_F: For example, I would present a problem to the students and determine my goal beforehand. I would ask for their comments on this problem and ask them to do research. Then I would expect them to prepare a project. Or I could ask the students who think the same opinion to prepare a drama, the students who think a different opinion to find a case study or to do research using the six hats model and present why they think so. In this way, I could enable students to learn in different ways.

CPS18_20_F: For example, I would present a problem related to chemistry or give a wrong information. I would ask the students whether this information is true or not. I would direct the class according to the feedback from the students. I would create a project-based learning environment supported by digital stories for them to solve the problem.

CPS9_19_M: For example, I could apply a project-based learning method supported by digital stories by giving them a problem or asking them to find a problem for group work. In this method, I could ask the students to act together and prepare a digital story and a project. I think I could benefit from this method in this way.

DISCUSSIONS

In this study, the effects of digital storytelling on improving the conceptual understanding on the topic of melting and dissolving and metacognitive learning strategies of preservice chemistry teachers were investigated. The use of digital stories within the framework of project-based learning (PBL) was employed. Along with PBL, preservice teachers were expected to create a digital story. Initially, preservice teachers followed the steps of PBL and tried to produce a product that would answer the problem addressed by PBL. A total of 25 preservice chemistry teachers participated in the study. The change in their conceptual understanding and metacognitive learning strategies was examined. The Melting and Dissolving Concept Test (MDCT) was used to determine the conceptual understanding of preservice teachers on the topic of melting and dissolving. The Metacognitive Self-Regulation subscale in the Motivated Strategies for Learning Questionnaire (MSLQ) was used to determine the changes in their metacognitive learning strategies.

In this study, the Wilcoxon signed-rank test was used to determine whether there was a difference between the pre-test and post-test scores of the data obtained. According to the results of this test, it was seen that the project-based learning method supported by digital stories had a significant contribution to the conceptual understanding of preservice teachers on the topic of melting and dissolving. Similarly, it was found that this method had a significant effect on the metacognitive learning strategies of preservice teachers. To determine the effect size on both dependent variables, the effect size values suggested by Cohen (1988) were used. According to these values, it was concluded that the project-based learning method supported by digital stories had a large effect on both dependent variables. Based on these results, the following comment can be made: The project-based learning method supported by digital stories can be used as an effective and beneficial method to improve conceptual understanding and metacognitive learning strategies. Future teachers who gain applied experience in media production and pedagogy can better understand the perspectives of their students and the issues they need to consider in their teaching, as they see how media can be used to achieve different learning goals and understand the difficulties students face while learning with media (Shelton et al., 2017).

There are not many studies in the literature that use project-based learning method supported by digital stories. For example, Hung et al. (2012) examined the effects of project-based digital storytelling approach on students and found that this approach increased students' motivation, attitudes, problem-solving skills, and academic achievement. Additionally, the experimental group students were satisfied with the project-based learning process and appreciated the contribution of digital storytelling to learning. However, when looking at the studies conducted with both digital story and project-based learning method, it is seen that these two methods have different and significant effects on students', preservice teachers', or university students' achievement, motivation, and learning strategies (Condy et al., 2012;

Dinçol Özgür & Yılmaz, 2020; Hava, 2021; Kim & Li, 2020; Morgil et al., 2009; Sintawati et al., 2022; Smeda et al., 2014; Tsybulsky & Muchnik-Rozanov, 2023). For example, it has been determined that using digital stories provides development in various areas from learners' motivation to collaborative work skills, and that learners have a more permanent learning experience (Yüzer & Kılınç, 2015). Sancar-Tokmak et al. (2014) conducted a study where they applied digital storytelling method to preservice elementary teachers. As a result of the study, preservice teachers emphasized that they improved their technological and pedagogical skills by preparing digital stories for science teaching. Kim and Li (2020) conducted a study showing that incorporating digital storytelling projects into the school curriculum provided more participation, motivation, creativity, and sense of identity for students, and that they connected more with their peers. Sadik (2008) investigated the opinions of teachers who used digital storytelling in their courses. According to the results of Sadik's study, teachers had various problems but thought that digital storytelling would help students better understand the concepts of the course. Shelton et al. (2017) conducted a study where they applied digital storytelling method to preservice elementary teachers. As a result of the study, it was determined that preservice teachers were able to produce quality videos, grasped the pedagogical benefits of digital storytelling, and wanted to share this method with their future students. Chadwick and Muilenburg (2011) also conducted a study where they applied digital storytelling method to chemistry students. As a result of the study, it was seen that digital storytelling contributed to the understanding of abstract concepts such as ionic and molecular bonds. It was also found that digital storytelling enabled students to construct more detailed analogies and demonstrate higher-order thinking skills.

In this study, the opinions of preservice teachers on the effects and usability of project-based learning (PBL) method supported by digital stories were also obtained. For this purpose, open-ended questions prepared by consulting expert opinion were used. Preservice teachers were asked about the advantages, disadvantages, purpose, usage, and whether they would apply this method when they become teachers. According to the answers given by preservice teachers, they think that this method has many advantages. They especially emphasized aspects such as collaborative learning, enjoyable learning, providing motivation, and arousing interest. They also stated that using digital stories positively affected the process. As disadvantages, they mentioned factors such as problems that may arise during group work, time and space limitations, and curriculum intensity. Preservice teachers expressed that these kinds of methods should be used by teachers in the future because they are student-centered and active. For this, they suggested that students should take responsibility and a proper arrangement should be made. Finally, preservice teachers were asked about their willingness to use this method in the future. Preservice teachers said that they wanted to use this method and digital stories. However, they emphasized that the current conditions in Türkiye could also be an obstacle. They stated that teachers would have difficulty in applying these methods due to problems such as space, technology, equipment, and subject density in Türkiye. In addition, there are various opinions of learners in the literature about the positive aspects of PBL and digital storytelling (Balaman, 2016; Karakoyun & Kuzu, 2016; Kotluk & Kocakaya, 2016; Tsybulsky et al., 2020; Yılmaz et al., 2018). In a study conducted by Öztuna Kaplan and Diker Ay (2013), it was determined that preservice teachers had more positive views on project-based learning than traditional learning approaches. They stated that this method created a suitable environment for each other's learning, increased their motivation, and provided skills such as research, material preparation, learning strategies, critical and creative thinking, communication, and group work. In another study conducted by Dağ and Durdu (2012), preservice teachers stated that project-based learning improved their group work and collaboration skills, enabled them to learn by doing and experiencing, and increased their achievements. Karakoyun and Kuzu (2016) revealed that preservice teachers thought that conducting digital storytelling activities in an online environment attracted students' attention, accelerated the process, increased communication among students, and contributed to the development of their digital stories. Similarly, Balaman (2016), in his study with university students, reached interview results that showed that using digital stories as instructional materials and educational technologies could increase the level of knowledge and interest related to the subject.

CONCLUSION

In conclusion, although educators encourage preservice teachers to use learning methods based on a constructivist approach and provide education in this direction, it is seen that the teachers who graduate have superficial knowledge about these methods and are much weaker in practice (Meyer, 2004). Therefore, it is thought that the activities that preservice teachers will do by applying these methods within the scope of teaching practice courses will contribute to their development. Instead of giving only theoretical information to preservice teachers about these methods in the courses given in education faculties, providing them with opportunities to apply these methods will also contribute to their development. More emphasis should be given to practice-oriented studies in courses such as special teaching methods. Thus, the presentations and preparations that preservice teachers will make can make them more ready for the teaching profession. In addition, elective courses that will be opened in education faculties for the introduction, implementation, and use of these methods can also contribute to the training of preservice teachers.

This study is an experimental study, so the sample size is small. Increasing the sample size may make it more possible to generalize the results to the population. Therefore, studies with larger samples or more researchers can be done. Multiple experimental groups can also be formed. This study was conducted on preservice teachers in Türkiye. Therefore, the results of the study may vary from country to country. This is again one of the limitations of this study. Most of the preservice teachers in Turkey are female students. Therefore, a large part of the sample consists of female students. This is also an important limitation of the study. Perhaps if there were more male teachers in the population, differences in the use of technology by preservice teachers could be observed. Therefore, this is also an important limitation of the study.

At the end of the study, preservice teachers expressed that they were very satisfied with using digital stories. This actually shows that preservice teachers, or future teachers of the future, want to use technology but do not have enough equipment, knowledge, or skills for this. Therefore, it is necessary to provide the necessary supports for preservice teachers to integrate technology into their lessons with applications based on a constructivist approach while training future teachers. It can also be said that the interest of preservice teachers in technology will be valid for future students as well. Preservice teachers stated that using digital stories was very beneficial. They liked the support of the project-based learning method with digital stories. Therefore, we need to pay attention to such practices while training preservice teachers on integrating technology into the lesson. Because one of the big problems that teachers face is that students cannot integrate technology into their lessons. In order to eliminate the deficiencies of teachers in terms of technological pedagogical content knowledge (TPACK), we can create opportunities for our students to integrate content knowledge, pedagogy knowledge, and technology knowledge. In future studies, perhaps the change in preservice teachers' TPACK can also be observed in this sense.

To observe this, experimental studies and experimental designs can be done. Within the scope of this study, this method was applied especially for chemistry lessons. Therefore, this can be expressed as an important limitation. Because this is a study done only for chemistry lessons and the results of this study are reported. If we want to generalize the results of this study, perhaps such studies and applications can be done in different lessons and different branches.

REFERENCES

Acar, G. (2013). The effect of project-based learning on students' motivation. *International Journal of Academic Research*, *5*(2), 82–86. doi:10.7813/2075-4124.2013/5-2/B.11

Adamson, S., Banks, D., Burtch, M., Cox, F. III, Judson, E., Turley, J., Benford, R., & Lawson, A. (2003). Reformed undergraduate instruction and its subsequent impact on secondary school teaching practice and student achievement. *Journal of Research in Science Teaching*, *40*(10), 939–957. doi:10.1002/tea.10117

Akyol, G. (2009). *The contribution of cognitive and metacognitive strategy use to seventh grade students' science achievement* [Master's thesis, Middle East Technical University]. Council of Higher Education Thesis Center. https://tez.yok.gov.tr/UlusalTezMerkezi/giris.jsp

Akyol, G., Sungur, S., & Tekkaya, C. (2010). The contribution of cognitive and metacognitive strategy use to students'science achievement. *Educational Research and Evaluation*, *16*(1), 1–21. doi:10.1080/13803611003672348

Angeli, C. (2005). Transforming a teacher education method course through technology: Effects on preservice teachers' technology competency. *Computers & Education*, *45*(4), 383–398. doi:10.1016/j.compedu.2004.06.002

Anılan, B., Berber, A., & Anılan, H. (2018). The digital storytelling adventures of the teacher candidates. *Turkish Online Journal of Qualitative Inquiry*, *9*(3), 262–287. doi:10.17569/tojqi.426308

Balaman, F. (2016). The effect of digital storytelling technique on the attitudes of students toward teaching technologies. *Egitim ve Ögretim*, *6*(2), 147–168. doi:10.14527/pegegog.2016.009

Bell, S. (2010). Project-based learning for the 21st century: Skills for the future. *The Clearing House: A Journal of Educational Strategies, Issues and Ideas*, *83*(2), 39–43. https://www.jstor.org/stable/20697896. doi:10.1080/00098650903505415

Blumenfeld, P. C., Soloway, E., Marx, R. W., Krajcik, J. S., Guzdial, M., & Palincsar, A. (1991). Motivating project-based learning: Sustaining the doing, supporting the learning. *Educational Psychologist*, *26*(3-4), 369–398. doi:10.1080/00461520.1991.9653139

Bran, R. (2010). Message in a bottle Telling stories in a digital world. *Procedia: Social and Behavioral Sciences*, *2*(2), 1790–1793. doi:10.1016/j.sbspro.2010.03.986

Chadwick, C., & Muilenburg, L. (2011). Digital Storytelling in the Science Classroom: Using Analogies to Improve Understanding. In M. Koehler & P. Mishra (Eds.), *Proceedings of SITE 2011--Society for Information Technology & Teacher Education International Conference* (pp. 1087-1092). Nashville, Tennessee, USA: Association for the Advancement of Computing in Education (AACE).

Chan, B. S., Churchill, D., & Chiu, T. K. (2017). Digital literacy learning in higher education through digital storytelling approach. [JIER]. *Journal of International Education Research, 13*(1), 1–16. doi:10.19030/jier.v13i1.9907

Cohen, J. (1988). *Statistical power analysis for the behavioral sciences* (2nd ed.). Lawrence Earlbaum Associates.

Collins, S. N. (2021). The importance of storytelling in chemical education. *Nature Chemistry, 13*(1), 1–2. doi:10.103841557-020-00617-7 PMID:33353969

Condy, J., Chigona, A., Gachago, D., & Ivala, E. (2012). Pre-service students' perceptions and experiences of digital storytelling in diverse classrooms. *The Turkish Online Journal of Educational Technology, 11*(3), 278–285.

Çubukçu, Z. (2012). Proje Tabanlı Öğrenme [Project based learning]. B. Oral (Ed.), Öğrenme Öğretme Kuram ve Yaklaşımları [Learning Teaching Theory and Approaches] (527-539). Pegem Akademi.

Dağ, F., & Durdu, L. (2012). Opinions of prospective teachers about project-based learning process. *e-Journal of New World Sciences Academy, 7*(1), 200-211. https://doi.org/ doi:10.12739/10.12739

Demir, S., & Bozkurt, A. (2011). Primary mathematics teachers' views about their competencies concerning the integration of technology. *Elementary Education Online, 10*(3), 850–860.

Demircioğlu, H., Demircioğlu, G., & Ayas, A. (2006). Stories and chemistry education. *Hacettepe University Journal of Education, 30*, 110–119.

Diffily, D. (2002). Project-based learning: Meeting social studies standards and the needs of gifted learners. *Gifted Child Today, 25*(3), 40–59. doi:10.4219/gct-2002-69

Dinçol Özgür, S., & Yılmaz, A. (2020). The effect of project-based learning approach on prospective teachers' adopted learning approach, self-efficacy and level of knowledge. *Necatibey Faculty of Education Electronic Journal of Science and Mathematics Education, 14*(1), 761–786. doi:10.17522/balikesirnef.673060

Duncan, T. G., & McKeachie, W. J. (2005). The making of the motivated strategies for learning questionnaire. *Educational Psychologist, 40*(2), 117–128. doi:10.120715326985ep4002_6

Eilam, B., & Aharon, I. (2003). Students' planning in the process of self-regulated learning. *Contemporary Educational Psychology, 28*(3), 304–334. doi:10.1016/S0361-476X(02)00042-5

Ekawati, E., & Prastyo, A. (2022). Optimization of tpack-based project learning in micro-teaching courses in physics education study programs during the pandemic. *Journal of Physics: Conference Series, 2392*(1), 012035. doi:10.1088/1742-6596/2392/1/012035

Ertmer, P. A. (2005). Teacher pedagogical beliefs: The final frontier in our quest for technology integration? *Educational Technology Research and Development, 4*(53), 25–39. doi:10.1007/BF02504683

Ertmer, P. A., Conklin, D., Lewandowski, J., Osika, E., Selo, M., & Wignall, E. (2003). Increasing preservice teachers' capacity for technology integration through the use of electronic models. *Teacher Education Quarterly, 30*(1), 95–112. https://www.jstor.org/stable/23478427

Fraenkel, J. R., Wallen, N. E., & Hyun, H. H. (2015). *How to design and evaluate research in education* (9th ed.). McGraw-Hill Education.

Garnett, P., & Tobin, K. (1989). Teaching for understanding: Exemplary practice in high school chemistry. *Journal of Research in Science Teaching*, *26*(1), 1–14. doi:10.1002/tea.3660260102

Geisinger, K. F. (2016). 21st century skills: What are they and how do we assess them? *Applied Measurement in Education*, *29*(4), 245–249. doi:10.1080/08957347.2016.1209207

Gómez-Pablos, V. B., del Pozo, M. M., & Muñoz-Repiso, A. G. V. (2017). Project-based learning (PBL) through the incorporation of digital technologies: An evaluation based on the experience of serving teachers. *Computers in Human Behavior*, *68*, 501–512. doi:10.1016/j.chb.2016.11.056

Gorder, L. M. (2008). A study of teacher perceptions of instructional technology integration in the classroom. *Delta Pi Epsilon Journal*, *L*(2), 63–76.

Hare, S., Howard, E., & Pope, M. (2002). Technology integration: Closing the gap between what preservice teachers are taught to do and what they can do. *Journal of Technology and Teacher Education*, *10*(2), 191–203.

Haşlaman, T. (2017). Supporting self-regulated learning: A digital storytelling implementation. *Elementary Education Online*, *16*(4), 1407–1424. doi:10.17051/ilkonline.2017.342964

Hava, K. (2021). Exploring the role of digital storytelling in student motivation and satisfaction in EFL education. *Computer Assisted Language Learning*, *34*(7), 958–978. doi:10.1080/09588221.2019.1650071

Hennessy, S., Ruthven, K., & Brindley, S. (2005). Teacher perspectives on integrating ICT into subject teaching: Commitment, constraints, caution, and change. *Journal of Curriculum Studies*, *37*(2), 155–192. doi:10.1080/0022027032000276961

Heo, M. (2009). Digital storytelling: An empirical study of the impact of digital storytelling on preservice teachers' self-efficacy and dispositions towards educational technology. *Journal of Educational Multimedia and Hypermedia*, *18*(4), 405–428.

Hung, C.-M., Hwang, G.-J., & Huang, I. (2012). A project-based digital storytelling approach for improving students' learning motivation, problem-solving competence and learning achievement. *Journal of Educational Technology & Society*, *15*(4), 368–379.

Istenic Starčič, A., Cotic, M., Solomonides, I., & Volk, M. (2016). Engaging preservice primary and preprimary school teachers in digital storytelling for the teaching and learning of mathematics. *British Journal of Educational Technology*, *47*(1), 29–50. doi:10.1111/bjet.12253

Jacobsen, M. (2001). *Building different bridges: Technology integration, engaged student learning, and new approaches to professional development.* Paper presented at AERA 2001: What We Know and How We Know It, the 82nd Annual Meeting of the American Educational Research Association, Seattle, WA.

Jakes, D. (2006). *Standards-Proof your digital storytelling Efforts.* TechLearning. https://www.techlearning.com/news/standardsproof-your-digital-storytelling-efforts

Jakes, D. S., & Brennan, J. (2005). *Capturing stories, capturing lives: An Introduction to digital storytelling.* Jake's Online. http://www.jakesonline.org/dst_techforum.pdf

Karakoyun, F., & Kuzu, A. (2016). The investigation of preservice teachers' and primary school students' views about online digital storytelling. *European Journal of Contemporary Education, 15*(1), 51–64.

Karaoğlan Yılmaz, F. G., Özdemir, B. G., & Yaşar, Z. (2018). Using digital stories to reduce misconceptions and mistakes about fractions: An action study. *International Journal of Mathematical Education in Science and Technology, 49*(8), 867–898. doi:10.1080/0020739X.2017.1418919

Kim, D., & Li, M. (2020). Digital storytelling: Facilitating learning and identity development. *Journal of Computers in Education, 8*(1), 33–61. doi:10.100740692-020-00170-9

Kotluk, N., & Kocakaya, S. (2016). Researching and evaluating digital storytelling as a distance education tool in physics instruction: An application with pre-service physics teachers. *Turkish Online Journal of Distance Education, 17*(1), 87–99. doi:10.17718/tojde.59900

Lambert, J. (2013). *Digital storytelling: Capturing lives, creating community* (4th ed.). Routledge. doi:10.4324/9780203102329

Lin, C., & Lu, M. (2010). The study of teachers' task values and self-efficacy on their commitment and effectiveness for technology-instruction integration. *US-China Education Review, 7*(5), 1–11.

Mandell, S., Sorge, D. H., & Russell, J. D. (2002). TIPS for technology integration. *TechTrends for Leaders in Education and Training, 46*(5), 39–43.

Meadows, D. (2003). Digital storytelling-research-based practice in new media. *Visual Communication, 2*(2), 189–193. doi:10.1177/1470357203002002004

Meyer, H. (2004). Novice and expert teachers' conceptions of learners' prior knowledge. *Science Education, 88*(6), 970–983. doi:10.1002ce.20006

Morgil, İ., Temel, S., Seyhan, H. G., & Alşan, E. U. (2009). The effect of project based laboratory application on pre-service teachers' understanding of nature of science. *Journal of Turkish Science Education, 6*(2), 92–109.

Moursund, D. G. (2003). *Project-based learning using information technology* (2nd ed.). International Society for Technology in Education.

Nam, C. W. (2017). The effects of digital storytelling on student achievement, social presence, and attitude in online collaborative learning environments. *Interactive Learning Environments, 25*(3), 412–427. doi:10.1080/10494820.2015.1135173

Nuroh, E. Z., Kusumawardana, M. D., & Destiana, E. (2022). Developing digital literacy skill for initial teacher education through digital storytelling. *KnE Social Sciences, 7*(10), 475–496. doi:10.18502/kss.v7i10.11250

Öztuna Kaplan, A., & Diker Coşkun, Y. (2012). Proje tabanlı öğretim uygulamalarında karşılaşılan güçlükler ve çözüm önerilerine yönelik bir eylem araştırması [An action research on the difficulties encountered in project-based teaching practices and solution suggestions]. *Mersin University Journal of the Faculty of Education, 8*(1), 137–159.

Pallant, J. (2007). *SPSS Survival Manual* (3rd ed.). Mcgrath Hill.

Pintrich, P. R., & De Groot, E. V. (1990). Motivational and self-regulated learning components of classroom academic performance. *Journal of Educational Psychology, 82*(1), 33–40. doi:10.1037/0022-0663.82.1.33

Pintrich, P. R., Smith, D., Garcia, T., & McKeachie, W. (1991). *A Manual for the Use of the Motivated Strategies for Learning Questionnaire (MSLQ).* The University of Michigan.

Robin, B. R. (2008). Digital storytelling: A powerful technology tool for the 21st century classroom. *Theory into Practice, 47*(3), 220–228. doi:10.1080/00405840802153916

Sabari, N. A. S., & Hashim, H. (2023). Sustaining education with digital storytelling in the English language teaching and learning: A systematic review. *International Journal of Academic Research in Business & Social Sciences, 13*(4), 214–231. doi:10.6007/IJARBSS/v13-i4/16860

Sadik, A. (2008). Digital storytelling: A meaningful technology-integrated approach for engaged student learning. *Educational Technology Research and Development, 56*(4), 487–506. doi:10.100711423-008-9091-8

Sakka, Z. I., & Zualkernan, I. A. (2005). Digital storytelling in higher education: a case study in a civil engineering laboratory. *Fifth IEEE International Conference on Advanced Learning Technologies (ICALT'05),* (pp. 365-367). IEEE. 10.1109/ICALT.2005.124

Sancar-Tokmak, H., Surmeli, H., & Ozgelen, S. (2014). Preservice science teachers' perceptions of their tpack development after creating digital stories. *International Journal of Environmental and Science Education, 9*(3), 247–264. doi:10.12973/ijese.2014.214a

Şen, Ş. (2011). *Effect of conceptual change texts and dual situated learning model on students' achievement and motivation in the concepts of melting and dissolving* [Master's thesis, Hacettepe University]. Council of Higher Education Thesis Center. https://tez.yok.gov.tr/UlusalTezMerkezi/giris.jsp

Shelton, C. C., Archambault, L. M., & Hale, A. E. (2017). Bringing digital storytelling to the elementary classroom: Video production for preservice teachers. *Journal of Digital Learning in Teacher Education, 33*(2), 58–68. doi:10.1080/21532974.2016.1276871

Shin, W. S., Han, I., & Kim, I. (2014). Teachers' technology use and the change of their pedagogical beliefs in Korean educational context. *International Education Studies, 7*(8), 11–22. doi:10.5539/ies.v7n8p11

Sintawati, M., Yuli Erviana, V., Bhattacharyya, E., Habil, H., & Fatmawati, L. (2022). The effect of project-based learning on technological pedagogical content knowledge among elementary school pre-service teacher. *Pegem Journal of Education and Instruction, 12*(2), 151–156. doi:10.47750/pegegog.12.02.15

Smeda, N., Dakich, E., & Sharda, N. (2014). The effectiveness of digital storytelling in the classrooms: A comprehensive study. *Smart Learning Environments, 1*(6), 1–21. doi:10.118640561-014-0006-3

Song, Y. (2018). Improving primary students' collaborative problem solving competency in project-based science learning with productive failure instructional design in a seamless learning environment. *Educational Technology Research and Development, 66*(4), 979–1008. doi:10.100711423-018-9600-3

Sunzuma, G., & Maharaj, A. (2019). In-service teachers' geometry content knowledge: Implications for how geometry is taught in teacher training institutions. *International Electronic Journal of Mathematics Education*, *14*(3), 633–646. doi:10.29333/iejme/5776

Trilling, B., & Fadel, C. (2009). *21st century skills: Learning for life in our times*. John Wiley & Sons.

Tsybulsky, D., Gatenio-Kalush, M., Abu Ganem, M., & Grobgeld, E. (2020). Experiences of preservice teachers exposed to project-based learning. *European Journal of Teacher Education*, *43*(3), 368–383. doi:10.1080/02619768.2019.1711052

Tsybulsky, D., & Muchnik-Rozanov, Y. (2023). The contribution of a project-based learning course, designed as a pedagogy of practice, to the development of preservice teachers' professional identity. *Teaching and Teacher Education*, *124*, 104020. doi:10.1016/j.tate.2023.104020

Weinstein, C. E., & Mayer, R. E. (1986). The teaching of learning strategies. In M. C. Wittrock (Ed.), *Handbook of Research on Teaching* (pp. 315–327). Macmilian Publishing Company.

Wittrock, M. C. (1986). Studens thought processes. In M. C. Wittrock (Ed.), *Handbook of Research on Teaching* (pp. 255–296). Macmilian Publishing Company.

Yılmaz, Y., Üstündağ, M. T., & Güneş, E. (2017b). Investigation of digital story development stages and tools as teaching materials. *Abant İzzet Baysal Üniversitesi Eğitim Fakültesi Dergisi*, *17*(3), 1621–1640. doi:10.17240/aibuefd.2017.17.31178-338851

Yılmaz, Y., Üstündağ, M. T., Güneş, E., & Çalişkan, G. (2017a). Utilizing digital storytelling method for effective Turkish language teaching. *Educational Technology Theory and Practice*, *7*(2), 254–275.

Yüzer, T. V., & Kılınç, A. G. H. (2015). Benefit from the digital storytelling in the open learning system. *Journal of Research in Education and Teaching*, *4*(1), 243–250.

Zimmerman, B. J., & Martinez-Pons, M. (1990). Student differences in self-regulated learning: Relating grade, sex, and giftedness to self-efficacy and strategy use. *Journal of Educational Psychology*, *82*(1), 51–59. doi:10.1037/0022-0663.82.1.51

KEY TERMS AND DEFINITIONS

21st-Century Skills: The skills that society expects students to acquire in the 21st century.

Chemistry Education: A branch of science that deals with how students are taught chemistry topics and concepts.

Information and Communication Technologies (ICT): All the technologies that make our lives easier today, such as computers, mobile phones and television.

Metacognitive Learning Strategies: Learning strategies that enable learners to be aware of how they learn.

Storytelling: The act of expressing one's emotions, thoughts and ideas through the art of storytelling.

Technology Integration: The use of technology to support the learning and teaching process.

Web 2.0 Tools: Tools that facilitate the use of web sites.

Chapter 13
Pitfalls in Online Digital Content Creation for Undergraduate Dental Education

Gururajaprasad Kaggal Lakshmana Rao
https://orcid.org/0000-0002-5697-2402
Penang International Dental College, Malaysia

ABSTRACT

Undergraduate dental education, which is at the forefront of utilizing innovative pedagogies and instructional methods to deliver learning content, saw an unprecedented disruption globally due to the pandemic. This disruption in dental education resulted in limited access to traditional forms of learning content, which relies heavily on face-to-face teaching. An asynchronous mode of delivery was used to support and maintain the continuity of lectures and knowledge exchange. The mainstream method used was through pre-recorded video lectures, using PowerPoint lecture slides hosted on YouTube. This approach worked for maintaining the knowledge transfer continuum; though the creation and distribution of online content was in itself a challenge to dental educators. Thus, the chapter aimed to identify the pitfalls in digital content creation in undergraduate dental education. Furthermore, the chapter highlights the pathways needed to overcome the hindrances of digital content creation both from a pedagogical and technological perspective.

INTRODUCTION

Dental education with its wide arsenal of pedagogies and instructional methods is considered to be at the forefront in utilizing innovative approaches to deliver learning content at various levels of curriculum. The curriculum is rich in both theoretical and clinical knowledge to equip the student to deal with wide-ranging problems affecting dental health and well-being. The impetus to deliver content online through various approaches has been studied by numerous authors (Kumar et al., 2020). The use of technology and innovative teaching methods was available to students even before the onset of the pandemic (Nicoll

DOI: 10.4018/979-8-3693-3128-6.ch013

Copyright © 2024, IGI Global. Copying or distributing in print or electronic forms without written permission of IGI Global is prohibited.

et al., 2018). Nevertheless, what the pandemic taught us was the need to have a foolproof method to create, and deliver content along with assessing student performance.

Undergraduate dental education which is at the forefront of utilizing innovative pedagogies and instructional methods to deliver learning content saw an unprecedented disruption globally due to the pandemic (Kerkstra et al., 2022). This disruption in dental education resulted in limited access to traditional forms of learning content and a total disruption of clinical training (Hattar et al., 2021). Not only did this disruption affect the student learning progression but also crippled the overall skill set of the affected learners.

The non-clinical learning content, which relied heavily on face-to-face teaching and tutoring saw a complete shutdown. The hands-on training and apprenticeship were unavailable to the students. The task-based learning, an approach extensively employed to teach procedural tasks halted.

Patient care which is an inseparable training requirement saw the most disruption as the dental training centres were ill-prepared to assist student clinical training needs in a controlled environment (Elangovan et al., 2020). The training centers were not only grappling with learning disruptions but also with fear of transmission amongst the faculty and students.

However, the dental fraternity was quick to adapt and resorted to the use of technology to strengthen the knowledge continuum. Due to the need for physical separation, an asynchronous mode of delivery was used to support and maintain the continuity of lectures and knowledge exchange (Nasseripour et al., 2021). The mainstream method used was through pre-recorded video lectures, PowerPoint lecture slides, and external video hosting platforms such as YouTube videos or through internal or external educational websites, offline tests, and assignments (Azlan et al., 2020). This transition was rather slow and painstaking as the faculty unlike students are not technology savvy (Li et al., 2022). The creation and distribution of online content was in itself a challenge to dental educators. What started as bits of information posted online, spread to bytes of data for the learner to access. This opened the floodgates for content creation from all faculties in real time. The online content generation surpassed the total content generated in traditional formats.

The previously guarded training centers became a powerhouse of content generation and dissemination. This approach although worked for maintaining the knowledge transfer continuum, was limited in maintaining student engagement and retention. This is a very important aspect of digital content in the context of dental education. The extremely limited understanding of student digital learning analytics creates multiple challenges to the current training needs and competencies of the learners. The type, quality, mode, and amount of digital learning content consumed by the learner remain hugely unexplored.

The training centers' educational portals saw an uprising and served as a go-to platform for the affected learners. However, these portals have minimum features to keep the learner interested, as the level of interaction is limited to likes and shares.

Although these have served the dental faculties and students for decades, the above modes of content creation and knowledge transfer have been limited to the creation and dissemination of learning content in read/ write/ watch modes. With an unprecedented disruption secondary to a pandemic, the dental faculty realized the need to digitize learning content to cope with the ever-demanding needs of the student community, dental schools, and dental councils to maintain the continuity of knowledge transfer.

BACKGROUND

Dental education is a faculty dealing with oral health and comprises various aspects of theoretical, pre-clinical, and clinical learning. The students start their understanding of the basic sciences followed by diagnosis and treatment planning and extend to carrying out specialized clinical procedures. As the learning centers around, repetitive practice and competency, the learning content is highly regulated with every learning outcome weighed against the curricular needs of the course. The learning cycles can range from one-time lectures to extensive diagnosis and treatment planning sessions.

Dental education, which follows a didactic approach, still places a strong emphasis on traditional learning methods such as apprenticeship (Rao, Iskandar & Mokhtar, 2019) problem-based and case-based learning (Wang et al., 2021). The clinical procedures follow a task-based simulation to improve the competency of the learners who then progress on to perform these tasks on live patients (Higgins et al., 2020). The learner is exposed to theoretical, pre-clinical, and clinical tasks and procedures in a staggered manner. The learner is thus expected to make connections with new knowledge based on existing and prior learning experiences (Rao & Mokhtar, 2023).). This requires a constant flow of new information and reinforcement of existing understanding. Blended learning approaches (Alhaija et al., 2023) have been utilized to combine both traditional and digital modes catering to learners of all ages, a vast majority of whom are digital natives.

The same principle is employed in the transfer of clinical skills. The learner is exposed to a clinical task in a simulated and safe environment in which the learner is allowed to make errors. Following the development of basic skills in hand-eye coordination, usage of instruments, and correlation of prior theoretical knowledge, the learner is then allowed to engage in handling live patients under the close supervision of tutors. The learner progresses through different levels of competencies with the final aim of performing a clinical procedure independently.

To cater to these learning cycles, content creation becomes a herculean task. In a traditional setup, learning content creation has always been a forte of educators. The content requires the educator to create, refine, and recreate content based on the evolving needs of the learners. As educators are clinicians by training, the content creation, assimilation, and distribution utilize a substantial amount of time and resources. Therefore, the educators unless required by the educational institution to innovate and apply educational technology often resort to age-old methods of lectures and presentations. However, with the unprecedented disruption seen in recent times (Elangovan et al., 2020) educators had to quickly adapt and modify existing learning resources. This involved the creation of digital content covering areas of both theoretical and clinical training. With this challenge, the educators grappled not only with the ability to adapt but also with the use of educational technology to create meaningful learning outcomes.

The time and location-bound primary mode of knowledge transfer evolved into a digital and ubiquitous training mode for both the educators and the learners. However, this did not involve large-scale educational technology and innovation but used existing tools and online platforms for content creation and dissemination. The use of YOUTUBE as a go-to source for lectures became extremely relevant and institutions started creating dedicated channels and uploading content (Gross et al., 2023).

THE MAIN FOCUS OF THE CHAPTER

The chapter aims primarily to understand the large-scale shift of knowledge transfer and the methods of dissemination, the phenomenon of digital content creation, and their need and pitfalls in an undergraduate dental education setup. The advantages and disadvantages of adopting YouTube lecture videos and a brief discussion on the benefits of YouTube lecture video lectures are explained to gain insight into their pedagogical implications. Furthermore, the chapter highlights the pathways needed to overcome the hindrances of digital content creation both from a pedagogical and technological perspective.

DENTAL EDUCATION CONTENT CREATION

With dental education relying heavily on traditional learning formats such as lectures, seminars, case discussions, and clinical reasoning, the modes of content delivery have been extensively didactic (Parikh, et al., 2022). The curriculum mandates the use of lectures as an essential tool (Parolia, et al., 2012; Kunin, et al., 2014). The dental curriculum closely follows the pre-determined learning outcomes, which are reflected in the created content of a topic. However, the curriculum does not mandate the use of any format for creating this but outlines a brief pathway for achieving this.

Dental education can be broadly divided into traditional, semi-digital, and digital modes. These divisions are not an actual classification but a wider representation of how the content is created and the means used to create it.

The traditional mode follows the principles of didactic learning as the entire curriculum places a strong emphasis on lectures, lecture slides, and lecture notes. The educators are expected to create standardized lectures to reflect the learning outcomes outlined in the curriculum. The technology used mainly focuses on the dental faculty utilizing computer-assisted learning (CAL) methods such as PowerPoint presentations and simple illustrations. The concepts and principles behind clinical techniques and procedures are shown as either 2D illustrated images or clinical photographs.

Textual data still holds a large chunk of knowledge transfer as factual information and recall are part of the learning principles. Educators rely on content creation to cater to this need. The principles and techniques are broken down into smaller pieces of information under different headings to create a structured outlook. The content thus becomes extensive as every topic created follows this pattern. The learners receive handouts of lecture slides to enable a comprehensive understanding of the topic in question. Thus, the traditional modes take precedence over other formats, as it is easy to conceive and put forth lectures promptly.

The semi-digital mode utilizes technology to assist in content creation and delivery. With the CAL applications available to most educators, the use of these methods has seen a larger uptake among the faculty resulting in the creation of digital content. As technology evolves, educators have utilized simpler tools to create more learning formats to support a wider audience. With the feature-rich resources now available with ease, content creation has adopted tools such as Google Classroom, Google Forms, and online quizzes and assessments. These channels have made content accessible to learners outside the physical buildings and libraries. As the theoretical training still mandates attendance on campus, the content is passed on to learners through a mix of traditional modes using technology.

The digital mode is where learning content is accessible only in a digital format. The existing teaching cycles have used fully online modes to teach certain modules as refresher courses and have not incorporated these into the regular curriculum. The modules are parts of the topic but not a standalone module covering the entire course content.

NEED FOR DIGITAL CONTENT CREATION

The pedagogical applications of asynchronous learning methods provide a valuable tool for a curriculum-focused discipline such as dental education. The commonly utilized modes are pre-recorded lecture videos hosted on either YouTube, institutional portals, or external educational portals, voice-over PowerPoint presentations, and YouTube videos. These modes of interaction require specialized training modules for both content creation and delivery. The ability to self-pace and engage with the learning content at the learner's discretion is what makes pre-recorded lecture videos popular (Botelho, Gao & Jagannathan 2019). These videos provide a powerful channel and resource for dental educators and learners respectively.

Studies have identified that videos were perceived as positive on several fronts such as maximizing attention (Choi and Johnson, 2005) and improving learning outcomes and procedural skills (Mehrpour et al., 2013). The pre-recorded lecture videos were found to be as effective as traditional formats or synchronous face-to-face lectures (Brockfeld, Müller & Laffolie, 2018). Studies further claim the benefits of using lecture videos that support individualized and self-directed learning (Al-Azzam, Elsalem & Gombedza, 2020). Qualitative research in this area supports the advantages of learning from videos for their ease of access in addition to showing better cognitive engagement (Botelho, Gao & Jagannathan 2019).

Furthermore, the pre-recorded PowerPoint lecture videos showed better results in comparison to other asynchronous methods due to several factors such as being simple to use, easily downloadable, and accessible across different devices ubiquitously (Kunin, Julliard, & Rodriguez, 2014).

CHALLENGES OF DIGITAL CONTENT CREATION IN DENTAL EDUCATION

The digital mode is when the content creation, distribution, and absorption of learning resources happens fully in an online format without the presence of learners at physical locations. Albeit the dental training requires mandatory attendance for pre-clinical and clinical procedures, the faculty has adopted interactive technology and simulation-based training in pre-clinical and clinical domains.

However, the theoretical and basic sciences courses, which have a huge didactic component, have remained traditional. There remains a void in digital content creation, as the adoption of these tools requires specialized training in instructional design and educational technology. The excitement to create new and interactive content although remains an exciting area has stagnated. The factors responsible for such stagnation are discussed in the following sections as perspectives. Due to the teaching methods, working well across the student learning cycles, further innovation and progression to newer methods had become limited.

For digital content creation to be effective, it needs to reflect on the ability of the tutors/academicians to create meaningful educational learning experiences. These experiences have to follow the wider framework of instructional design and the use of technology to create educational content. In the face of a pandemic, the faculty resorted to digital means of content creation. However, one faced several issues from a sudden migration from traditional to online modes in a split second.

The disruption affected the preclinical and clinical learning cycles the most. Hence, in the context of psychomotor skill development and transfer of pre-clinical and clinical knowledge, the following sections will discuss the use of YOUTUBE as a standalone tool used by the faculty to deliver both lectures, and procedural demonstrations. Tools such as EXAM.NET, Google Classroom, Google Meet, and Google Forms were some of the other tools used for assessment and evaluation.

Digital content creation is a grey area for which educators have not received any formal training. However, with the unprecedented disruption, educators had to innovate and create teaching content. Although YOUTUBE has become an established platform for educational content, it was only during the pandemic that the platform was overwhelmingly used to create and deliver content. However, this content creation had many pitfalls, and will be discussed in the following sections.

As the process of content creation involves the use of pre-recorded videos, these videos can present a challenge for both content creation and delivery. The ability to cover not only the topic in full but to summarize, use appropriate jargon, and maintain continuity in the flow of content is what makes the videos stand out. The effective use of illustrations and other tools to enhance the content forms the essential features for benefitting the audience.

The pre-recorded videos can have inadequacies on several fronts and are listed below. These inadequacies are generic to any pre-recorded video, however, a brief correlation with dental lectures will be established to provide clarity from a dental education perspective.

The factors responsible for poor pre-recorded lecture video recordings are categorized as general and learner-related.

The general factors contributing to poor pre-recorded lecture video recordings are:

1. Lack of Audibility/ comprehensibility: If the pre-recorded lecture videos lack clear recordings in the voice-over presentation, the content communicated becomes confusing and uninteresting. The audibility might pose a challenge to the presenter, as the presenter has no control over the content heard by the learner (Shrivastava et al., 2022). This can lead to unwatched content or the video might not be watched in full length thereby preventing the learner from having an overall understanding of the topic being taught.

2. Lack of Thoroughness: If the presented topics and the content of the pre-recorded lecture video are not thorough in the content delivered, the learners will find it hard to piece together any missing information by themselves. This creates a knowledge gap (Morgado, Mendes & Proença, 2021), as the learner is left wanting for more information. This might further create difficulty in understanding the topic, as the learner is unable to raise questions and receive feedback immediately (Meguid & Collins, 2017). The unpreparedness of an instructor/ tutor affects the overall quality of the lecture by making the audience disinterested (Moulton, Türkay & Kosslyn, 2017) both about the topic in question and any future lecture videos of that instructor.

3. Subjective reasoning: The learner who is at the receiving end of the video will find it hard to decipher implied meanings and explanations. The learner might feel overwhelmed with new information and might have difficulties establishing a reasonable connection with prior learning. The tutor's subjective reasoning and line of thought if not conveyed or broken down into small packets of information, the learner will find it hard to tie everything together and may leave out important information without giving it a thought (Rao & Mokhtar, 2023).

4. Lack of visualization: The learning content utilized by the tutors might include illustrations or complex diagrams, which vary in type and extent depending on the topic in question. The lack of

visualization decreases effective understanding (Rao, Iskandar & Mokhtar, 2020) as the concepts or principles presented in the lecture might be confusing. When a limited range of visualization techniques is employed, the learner eventually might become disinterested in watching the pre-recorded lecture videos. Visualization of technical and or principles of treatment is difficult to achieve in the absence of hands-on or face-to-face teaching.

5. Lack of structure: The content structure is an important aspect of a didactic lecture and it takes more precedence when the topic is communicated as a pre-recorded lecture video (Khalil & Elkhider, 2016). If the lecture does not use appropriate illustrations, the means of displaying information becomes irrelevant. Ill-structured pre-recorded lecture videos can give rise to problems with the arrangement of the sub-topics, the continuity of the subject matter, and the overall flow.

6. Lack of coherence: A lecture both, face-to-face or virtual requires the tutor to be proficient in both the language of communication and the subject matter at hand. The dental curriculum with its complex pedagogical requirements creates challenges (Lyon, 2014) in both conveying information on the tutor's end to understanding information on the student's end without an appropriate and planned structure. The pre-recorded lecture video becomes uninteresting if the content presented is random. This further can complicate knowledge and skills acquired at a later stage (Smeby & Vågan, 2008).

7. Use of heavy-worded phrases or dental/ medical jargon: As the field of dental science is a highly technical field, a pre-recorded lecture video might use heavy-worded phrases and or dental/ medical jargon. Extensive use of these will lead to difficulty in understanding concepts unless the subject matter was dealt with earlier. The non-comprehension of new terminologies can further limit the scope of explanation of a topic (McGrath & Laksov, 2014). When several such occurrences happen in a single pre-recorded lecture video, the knowledge gained by the learner might be deficient thereby becoming detrimental to the broader understanding cycles of the learner. The use of dental jargon becomes problematic for the tutor as it prevents the general understanding of a new terminology due to different individual understandings by the learners. (Brown, Reinhardt & Korner, 2023).

8. Content selection: The content selection for a given topic needs careful consideration to both match the learning outcomes and prior knowledge of the learners. Poor selection of precise and succinct content can lead to difficulties in cognition (Choe et al., 2019). The content in the pre-recorded lecture video if vague and complex might result in uninterested learners. The learners might skip content leading to gaps in the overall understanding of a subject matter.

9. Quality of Content presentation: The subject matter and its presentation should correspond to the audience the lecture is aimed at. If the presentation slides, use flashy and neon coloring to highlight sub-topics may create difficulty in reading the explanation parts of the slide. The size, font, and style of writing can all have an impact on the readability and subsequent understanding of the topic. Lengthy and illegible writings when used in a pre-recorded lecture video might create difficulty in following the deeper meanings and thereby disinterest learners. Overall structure and arrangement of a presentation might create difficulties in grasping the subject matter (Grech, 2018).

10. Lack of language proficiency: As English Medium Instruction (EMI) is the core instructional language of instruction, The enthusiasm in any pre-recorded lecture video disappears as soon as the language used for communication uses improper sentences, grammar, pace, and pronunciation. A lack of these might make an interesting topic uninteresting. Lectures conducted by both native and non-native speakers can give rise to issues in comprehension of ideas or concepts, and problems

with listening comprehension based on students' English proficiency (Querol Julián & Camiciottoli, 2019).

The above points describe the different aspects of a pre-recorded video lecture, which can contribute to or give rise to student learning difficulties. These factors represent the various layers of information exchange from selection, compilation, communication, and delivery.

The learner-related factors contributing to poor pre-recorded lecture video recordings are:

1. Lack of interaction: As the pre-recorded video lectures are posted in an online accessible format, the learner might feel the videos to be monotonous lacking any interaction as compared to a live session or face-to-face lecture (Moazami et al., 2014). The pre-recorded video lectures do not provide any channels for two-way communication, peer communication, or elaboration of complex topics. Any gaps in the knowledge continuum cannot be removed as the learner is left with no means of getting feedback. Active engagement during a lecture or immediately post-lecture isn't available for learners leaving the feedback or clarifications to be reserved for another session or communicated through online queries or emails, which renders the process of knowledge delivery difficult and less fulfilling.

2. Lack of attention and or focus: When the mode of content delivery is fully through an online pre-recorded video lecture format, the learner's behavior is impossible to ascertain (Crook & Schofield, 2017). This leads to difficulties in understanding essential factors such as attention, focus, distractions, and non-commitment. It is impossible to assess the learners' online behavior as the means available for such a task aren't available.

3. Lack of tools to determine motivation: The inherent determination of learners to pay attention, be involved, and actively participate in a lecture is essential for the overall understanding and knowledge gain. The pre-recorded video lecture does not provide a gateway to determine these factors. When these factors are not given consideration, the motivation to undertake self-directed learning becomes a difficult task for the learner and a complex task for the tutor to solve problems arising due to this format of learning (Ozan & Ozarslan, 2016).

4. Lack of inclusivity: As the learning styles of individual learners have strong implications on the knowledge gain and acceptance of a particular mode of delivery, the pre-recorded video lecture provides a limited channel for learners' of varied learning styles of aural, read/write and kinaesthetic modes (Chang-Tik, 2018). Thus, the lack of inclusivity in this mode might create difficulties for learners and thereby prevent them from accessing or utilizing these educational resources to their full potential.

5. Lack of implementation: The usage and implementation of technological advances for teaching and learning depend on an institution's policies and commitment to student training. It also depends on the skill set and technological literacy of the faculty. The usage might further depend on the class size and age of the institution rather than the funding source and geographic location (Brownstein, Murad, & Hunt, 2015). The provision of limited educational resources deters the faculty from creating digital content leading to challenges in content delivery and instruction.

6. Internet connectivity: In the era of digitalization and the Internet of Things, internet connectivity is taken as a given. However, not all countries have adequate infrastructure to cater to the connectivity issues. The learner is thus reliant on the available infrastructure. The inability to access digital content in a timely manner will affect the progress and continuity of learning cycles (Shrivastava

Table 1. List of factors and affected stakeholders

Domains	Affected Stakeholders	
	Faculty	Student
Audibility/ Comprehensibility		✓
Thoroughness		✓
Subjective reasoning	✓	✓
Visualization	✓	✓
Structure		✓
Coherence		✓
Dental/Medical Jargon		✓
Content Selection	✓	✓
Content Presentation	✓	✓
Language Proficiency		✓
Interaction	✓	✓
Attention/ Focus	✓	✓
Motivation	✓	✓
Inclusivity		✓
Implementation	✓	✓
Internet connectivity	✓	✓

et al., 2022). This factor although has been listed under the factors affecting learners, on a wider scale can affect the tutor or an institution.

In summary, a face-to-face lecture and its merits are extremely relevant and receptive to learning. The factors contributing to a positive learning environment through a physical mode outperform a pre-recorded video lecture as has been described. These factors contribute to the poor pre-recorded lecture video recordings and might affect the acceptance and usage by a wider audience. Table 1 describes the factors and the stakeholders affected.

As seen in Table 1, there are several domains affected for both the tutor and the learner, but the vast majority of the factors affect the learners who are at the receiving end of the learning process. As the students are one of the stakeholders in dental education (Lin, Goh, & Halil, 2023) the pitfalls identified can affect their learning cycles.

YOUTUBE LECTURE VIDEOS

The current section of the chapter will discuss the use of YouTube as a platform for hosting pre-recorded lecture videos. The section will discuss the advantages and disadvantages of adopting YouTube lecture videos with a brief discussion on their learning analytics drawn from the lectures of orthodontics, a specialized faculty in dental sciences.

These lectures served as the core mode of delivery during the pandemic and continue to serve as an educational resource to learners of orthodontics worldwide. YouTube became the go-to source of information during the pandemic (Sophia et al., 2020). The trend, however, continues to enrich learners' experiences through a variety of content post-pandemic.

The pre-recorded lecture videos posted on YouTube have their share of advantages and disadvantages.

The advantages of this include ubiquitous access, uninterrupted access, self-paced learning, non-interference in daily activities, and multi-device access. They also support barrier-free and flexible learning without the constraints of geographical separation.

The disadvantages of the pre-recorded lecture videos posted on YouTube have been discussed at length in the section on "challenges of digital content creation in dental education."

With this information on the pitfalls of digital content creation and the pre-recorded lecture videos hosted on YouTube, the next section will discuss and provide useful suggestions for overcoming these challenges in a dental education set-up drawing from both the pedagogy of dental education and the advances in technology.

OVERCOMING THE CHALLENGES OF DIGITAL CONTENT CREATION IN DENTAL EDUCATION

The pitfalls identified in this chapter can serve as a reminder of the technical difficulties and pedagogical challenges faced by dental educators. To address these, suggestions are made for creating digital content, which is both pedagogically sound, relevant to current standards of delivery, and provides insights into advances in technology thereby enabling the creation of enriching digital content by dental educators.

The recommendations are classified into three categories.

Category 1: Institutional support for technology-based learning
1. Provision of educational technology (hardware and software) and high-speed internet access.
2. Allocation of finances for purchasing and maintaining good quality audio and video recording equipment.
3. Information technology support is available to all faculty responsible for digital content creation.
4. Optimization of educational technology resources to maximize the equipment's use to support teaching and learning.
5. Step-wise approach to handling a device/software/web application.
6. Encouraging faculty research in educational technology.
7. Faculty support for training needs in skill development for language proficiency, communication, and scholarship.

Category 2: Formal training in learning theories and the science of instruction for dental educators
1. Vetting process to identify lack of knowledge in instructional design and theories of learning.
2. Workshops on pedagogy and andragogy.
3. Short-term training or continued professional development programs on instructional design and theories of learning, learner engagement, and educational content management.

Category 3: Technology literacy of dental educators

1. Faculty training in handling and using the equipment to enable the appropriate use of equipment features, functions, and troubleshooting.
2. Faculty training in the implementation of technology usage for educational content delivery.
3. Hands-on training sessions for senior faculty or those who are unenthusiastic about technology use in education.
4. Educating clinicians/ dental educators on non-clinical uses of technology.
5. Faculty training on the use of educational content management systems.

Furthermore, the general and learner-related factors can be overcome by following basic recommendations on content creation, handling, and delivery.

The focus on subject matter and learning outcomes needs a strong emphasis. Any deviation can give rise to cognitive overload and or cognitive dissonance (Rao, 2020; Rao & Mokhtar, 2023). To avoid such a phenomenon, the content of the lecture should closely follow the learning outcomes of each lecture topic. Any new information or concept should be introduced in small bits. New content should always be added with an emphasis and correlation with prior knowledge to maintain continuity and relevance. The lectures should reflect these in the arrangement thereby preventing cognitive dissonance.

When a new concept is introduced, the educator should avoid using heavy-worded technical dental or medical jargon. Failure to avoid using these creates a gap in understanding, as the learners are unable to receive immediate clarifications. As the need for using technical words or jargon is necessary for effective clinical communication, introducing jargon by listing them as new terminologies at the beginning of the lecture will help the educator communicate concepts and principles more effectively.

In dental education, the need for reasoning takes precedence over factual information. When clinical reasoning is taught to dental students, the educator invariably draws from prior knowledge and their own experiences. As dental education still relies on the apprenticeship model, the subjective reasoning of an educator becomes part of the teaching process. To overcome this, the educator should provide reasoning based on evidence and correlate it to their own belief systems. This will enable the educator to follow the requirements of the curriculum along with sharing their own experiences in dealing with patients in real-life scenarios.

The subject matter must be broken down into bits of understandable and relatable information to maintain relevancy and interest. The structure should emphasize learning outcomes and provide a channel for constructive thinking and correlation to prior knowledge. Any new terminology, if introduced during the pre-recorded lecture should provide an explanation of the terminology with examples of usage. Dental jargon should be limited to the ones, which have been introduced earlier.

Every educator has to develop their own skill set and equip themselves with the current pedagogical principles in knowledge consumption and delivery. The ability to coherently convey learning content is a skill that has to be individually developed. The teaching skills of the tutor also play a role in the content selection, presentation, and structuring of the overall lecture and information delivery.

Proficiency in the language of instruction must be a requirement enforced by the institution. For effective communication to take place, the ability of one's command of both academic and non-academic language skills is essential. The skill should be enhanced using specific usage of vocabulary and sentence structures.

The educator's ability to engage the audience during a pre-recorded lecture video lies in soft- skills, language proficiency, content structuring, and subject matter expertise. The tone, pronunciation, and pace are some of the additional factors, which play a role in capturing the viewer's attention. These skills should be actively developed to aid learner engagement and interaction. The educator might also use additional tools such as sounds, animations, anecdotes, tips, clinical photographs, historical perspectives, futuristic PowerPoint themes, and polls during a lecture to increase viewership.

Online viewing and hosting platforms such as YouTube provide an excellent tool for uploading pre-recorded lecture videos for easy dissemination among students. The platform has easy-to-use features, which do not require any specialized skills for uploading and managing content. The educators are provided with resources and viewership analytics to track and monitor the impact of their videos both locally and globally. Monitoring the number of viewers and their geographical spread by itself can provide the needed impetus and motivation for creating more such content.

As the innovative teaching and learning practices evolved during the learners absence from the physical locations, the online activities saw a renewed interest among both the teachers and students (Quinn 2022). The online activities were not limited to pre-recorded lecture videos but included reframing interaction pathways through different formats, such as online discussions, quizzes, and assessment.

The Google Classroom is a tool used extensively for online teaching and instruction. It provided a rich source of educational content as the platform supports uploading links, educational resources and assignments. The platform supports evaluation of assignments with both grades and written feedback. The platform allowed setting up of deadlines, and resubmissions to track learner progress.

The Google Meet is an online platform used for teacher-student interaction. The Google Meet allowed multiple participant access without restrictions of duration. The camera feature with audio further enabled both parties to interact with learning content easily. As the platform allowed real-time interaction, technical knowledge and complex principles were easily conveyed with immediate feedback and clarifications.

For conducting formative assessment and post lecture assignments, Google Forms provided an excellent handy tool. The assignments can be turned into quizzes, essays, match the item or picture tests. Google Forms provided tools for auto-marking, deadlines, and self-reflection through provision of immediate answer keys at the time of submission. This helps learners reflect on their mistakes and helps them to re-analyse the line of questioning and or knowledge gaps. Furthermore, these post-lecture quizzes can reinforce learning and help learners develop deeper understanding of the topic at hand.

For continued evaluation of learners, both summative and formative assessments were conducted online and remotely. However, the critical assessments and exams, which needed greater supervision and invigilation, were conducted using an online platform. The platform named Exam.net enabled the teachers to administer exams online in a secured manner. The platform is highly secure with several features. The platform allows the teachers to upload question papers, allows control on entry and exit of examinees, allows monitoring of inactive cursor movements, blocks opening of webpages other than the exam.net page, talking to others and notifies the invigilator on long pauses in writing. The most important feature of real-time visualization of examinees' writing progress further elevates the transparency of the examination. The platform is secured using the latest encryption software. Additional features of marking answers, downloading answer sheets are available for use by the teachers.

This was a critical need during the pandemic as the examinees and examiners/ invigilators were at different physical locations but were able to conduct wide range of assessments. The exam process can be. The author's affiliate place of teaching further strengthened the exam process by adding video surveillance during the duration of exam to deter any malpractice. Google Meet was the platform utilised for video surveillance where the examinees were instructed to turn on their cameras for invigilators to monitor any suspicious behaviour or activity.

The advances in technology further enables both the learners and the teachers to imbibe from the features of mobile augmented reality (Lim et al., 2023; Rao, Iskandar, & Mokhtar 2020). The use of augmented reality opens up pathways for easier transition between different levels and formats of training such as from theoretical to pre-clinical to clinical training (Murbay et al., 2020; Dzyuba et al., 2022). The AR systems allow ubiquitous access to learning content and do not require the learner or the teacher to be present at the physical location. These systems can further allow demonstration of procedural tasks with feedback and multi format support for learners (Freina & Ott, 2015; Rao & Mokhtar, 2023).

In conclusion, although the success of a lecture depends on the educator's scientific competence, instructional skills, and personal capacity to engage and inspire students (Copeland, Longworth, Hewson, & Stoller, 2000), the high level of autonomy is what sets the pre-recorded lectures as a preferable mode of learning. The possibility of innumerable cycles of repetition: (Reissmann et al., 2015) is another important determinant in favour of this mode of learning. However, the lack of immediacy of feedback might be the one important factor detrimental to the success of a pre-recorded lecture from a pedagogical viewpoint.

FUTURE RESEARCH DIRECTIONS

With the advances in educational technology, content creation, and delivery can be streamlined in a multitude of ways. Dental educators should engage in educational research to identify and address pedagogical problems in digital content creation, delivery, and consumption. The next generation of smart technologies in education such as autonomous smart learning environments (Rao & Mokhtar, 2023) generative artificial intelligence (Bahroun et al., 2023), and smart hybrid learning environments (Rao, Iskandar, & Mokhtar, 2022) will require extensive validation by adopting these technologies for routine curricular usage. The impetus to think beyond traditional learning pathways to synergize their benefits should take the front seat if we are to reap the success of these technologies for the greater good of dental education.

CONCLUSION

The overwhelming need of society to develop a technology-rich skill set for the trainee pushes educators to become digitally active content designers and creators. With the commonly understated aspect of content creation in digital formats, the chapter has provided a fresh perspective on the challenges faced by the dental clinicians who shoulder the responsibilities of an educator. As hybrid-learning strategies continue to gain popularity post-pandemic, the skill set of the traditional dental educator has to change lanes and keep abreast with advances in educational technology.

The chapter has highlighted an area generally seen as a non-determinant of teaching and learning. However, the correlations brought out here are not specific to dental education but are broadly discussed for the reader to have an understanding of the potential implications and challenges of digital content creation in teaching and learning.

The availability of educational technology in itself will not enable enhanced training if the technology and its features are not fully understood. As the current generation of learners are technology ready, the impetus for change to avoid failure in optimally utilising the advances of educational technology by both the learners and the teachers becomes evident.

With evolving technology, comes challenges and the need for upskilling of the educational work force. By identifying the issues at hand and by incorporating necessary measures such as self-reflection at an individual, school, university level, policy changes can be mandated for effective training of the faculty to handle such disruptions in future. Thus, to avoid becoming redundant, the current fact-based knowledge exchange needs revival to become fast-paced.

REFERENCES

Abdel Meguid, E., & Collins, M. (2017). Students' perceptions of lecturing approaches: Traditional versus interactive teaching. *Advances in Medical Education and Practice*, 8, 229–241. doi:10.2147/AMEP.S131851 PMID:28360541

Adcock, A. (2012). Cognitive Dissonance in the Learning Processes. In N. M. Seel (Ed.), *Encyclopedia of the Sciences of Learning*. Springer. doi:10.1007/978-1-4419-1428-6_5

Aebersold, M. (2018). Simulation-Based Learning: No Longer a Novelty in Undergraduate Education OJIN. *Online Journal of Issues in Nursing*, 23(2), 1–1. doi:10.3912/OJIN.Vol23No02PPT39

Al-Azzam, N., Elsalem, L., & Gombedza, F. (2020). A cross-sectional study to determine factors affecting dental and medical students' preference for virtual learning during the COVID-19 outbreak. *Heliyon*, 6(12), e05704. doi:10.1016/j.heliyon.2020.e05704 PMID:33324768

Azlan, C. A., Wong, J. H. D., Tan, L. K., Huri, M. S. N. A., Ung, N. M., Pallath, V., & Ng, K. H. (2020). Teaching and learning of postgraduate medical physics using Internet-based e-learning during the COVID-19 pandemic–A case study from Malaysia. *Physica Medica*, 80, 10–16. doi:10.1016/j.ejmp.2020.10.002 PMID:33070007

Bahroun, Z., Anane, C., Ahmed, V., & Zacca, A. (2023). Transforming Education: A Comprehensive Review of Generative Artificial Intelligence in Educational Settings through Bibliometric and Content Analysis. *Sustainability (Basel)*, 15(17), 12983. doi:10.3390u151712983

Botelho, M. G., Gao, X., & Jagannathan, N. (2019). A qualitative analysis of students' perceptions of videos to support learning in a psychomotor skills course. *European Journal of Dental Education*, 23(1), 20–27. doi:10.1111/eje.12373 PMID:29920878

Brockfeld, T., Müller, B., & de Laffolie, J. (2018). Video versus live lecture courses: A comparative evaluation of lecture types and results. *Medical Education Online*, 23(1), 1. doi:10.1080/10872981.2018.1555434 PMID:30560721

Brown, K., Reinhardt, A., & Korner, T. (2023). Lecturer decision-making in the context of pandemic teaching: Rationales and evidence, International Journal for Academic Development Kerkstra, RL, Rustagi, KA, Grimshaw, AA, Minges, KE. Dental education practices during COVID-19: A scoping review. *Journal of Dental Education*, 2022(86), 546–573.

Brownstein, S. A., Murad, A., & Hunt, R. J. (2015). Implementation of new technologies in US dental school curricula. *Journal of Dental Education*, *79*(3), 259–264. doi:10.1002/j.0022-0337.2015.79.3.tb05880.x PMID:25729019

Chang-Tik, C. (2018). Impact of learning styles on the community of inquiry presences in multi-disciplinary blended learning environments. *Interactive Learning Environments*, *26*(6), 827–838. doi:10.10 80/10494820.2017.1419495

Copeland, H. L., Longworth, D. L., Hewson, M. G., & Stoller, J. K. (2000). Successful lecturing: A prospective study to validate attributes of the effective medical lecture. *Journal of General Internal Medicine*, *15*(6), 366–371. doi:10.1046/j.1525-1497.2000.06439.x PMID:10886470

Crook, C., & Schofield, L. (2017). The video lecture. *The Internet and Higher Education*, *34*, 56–64. doi:10.1016/j.iheduc.2017.05.003

Dzyuba, N., Jandu, J., Yates, J., & Kushnerev, E. (2022). Virtual and augmented reality in dental education: The good, the bad and the better. *European Journal of Dental Education*, *00*, 1–19. doi:10.1111/eje.12871 PMID:36336847

Elangovan, S., Mahrous, A., & Marchini, L. (2020). Disruptions during a pandemic: Gaps identified and lessons learned. *Journal of Dental Education*, *84*(11), 1270–1274. doi:10.1002/jdd.12236 PMID:32500586

Freina, L., & Ott, M. (2015, April). A literature review on immersive virtual reality in education: state of the art and perspectives. In The international scientific conference elearning and software for education (Vol. 1, No. 133, pp. 10-1007). doi:10.12753/2066-026X-15-020

Goob, J., Erdelt, K., Güth, J. F., & Liebermann, A. (2021). Dental education during the pandemic: Cross-sectional evaluation of four different teaching concepts. *Journal of Dental Education*, *85*(10), 1574–1587. doi:10.1002/jdd.12653 PMID:34046898

Grech, V. (2018). The application of the Mayer multimedia learning theory to medical PowerPoint slide show presentations. *Journal of Visual Communication in Medicine*, *41*(1), 36–41. doi:10.1080/174530 54.2017.1408400 PMID:29381105

Gross, R. T., Ghaltakhchyan, N., Nanney, E. M., Jackson, T. H., Wiesen, C. A., Mihas, P., Persky, A. M., Frazier-Bowers, S. A., & Jacox, L. A. (2023). Evaluating video-based lectures on YouTube for dental education. *Orthodontics & Craniofacial Research*, ocr.12669. doi:10.1111/ocr.12669 PMID:37184946

Gururajaprasad, R., & Lakshmana, K. (2020). *Smart Mobile Augmented Reality For Orthodontics Teaching And Learning Environment*. [PhD thesis, Universiti Sains Malaysia].

Hattar, S., AlHadidi, A., Sawair, F. A., Alraheam, I. A., El-Ma'aita, A., & Wahab, F. K. (2021). Impact of COVID-19 pandemic on dental education: Online experience and practice expectations among dental students at the University of Jordan. *BMC Medical Education*, *21*(1), 151. doi:10.118612909-021-02584-0 PMID:33685451

Higgins, D., Hayes, M., Taylor, J., & Wallace, J. (2020). A scoping review of simulation-based dental education. *MedEdPublish*, *9*(36), 36. doi:10.15694/mep.2020.000036.1 PMID:38058871

Kamran Ali, E. S. A. (2023). Blended learning in undergraduate dental education: A global pilot study. *Medical Education Online, 28*, 1. PMID:36751853

Kumar, P. M., Gottumukkala, S. N. V. S., Ramesh, K. S. V., Bharath, T. S., Penmetsa, G. S., & Kumar, C. N. (2020). Effect of e-learning methods on Dental education: An observational study. *Journal of Education and Health Promotion, 9*(1), 235. doi:10.4103/jehp.jehp_209_20 PMID:33209927

Kunin, M., Julliard, K. N., & Rodriguez, T. E. (2014). Comparing face-to-face, synchronous, and asynchronous learning: Postgraduate dental resident preferences. *Journal of Dental Education, 78*(6), 856–866. doi:10.1002/j.0022-0337.2014.78.6.tb05739.x PMID:24882771

Kunin, M., Julliard, K. N., & Rodriguez, T. E. (2014). Comparing face-to-face, synchronous, Li, B., Cheng, L., & Wang, H. (2022). Challenges and Opportunities for Dental Education from COVID-19. *Dentistry Journal, 10*(10), 188. doi:10.3390/dj10100188

Lim, E. J., Kim, Y. S., Im, J. E., & Lee, J. G. (2023). Mobile educational tool based on augmented reality technology for tooth carving: Results of a prospective cohort study. *BMC Medical Education, 23*(1), 1–10. doi:10.118612909-023-04443-6 PMID:37344879

Lin, G. S. S., Goh, S. M., & Halil, M. H. M. (2023). Unravelling the impact of dental workforce training and education programmes on policy evolution: A mixed-method study protocol. *Health Research Policy and Systems, 21*(1), 95. doi:10.118612961-023-01048-9 PMID:37700266

Lyon, L. J. (2014). Development of teaching expertise viewed through the Dreyfus Model of Skill Acquisition. *The Journal of Scholarship of Teaching and Learning, 15*(1), 88–105. doi:10.14434/josotl.v15i1.12866

McGrath, C., & Bolander Laksov, K. (2014). Laying bare educational crosstalk: A study of discursive repertoires in the wake of educational reform. *The International Journal for Academic Development, 19*(2), 139–149. doi:10.1080/1360144X.2012.716760

Moazami, F., Bahrampour, E., Azar, M. R., Jahedi, F., & Moattari, M. (2014). Comparing two methods of education (virtual versus traditional) on learning of Iranian dental students: A post-test only design study. *BMC Medical Education, 14*(1), 45. doi:10.1186/1472-6920-14-45 PMID:24597923

Mohammed, K. (2016). Khalil and Ihsan A. Elkhider. Applying learning theories and instructional design models for effective instruction. *Advances in Physiology Education, 40*(2), 147–156. doi:10.1152/advan.00138.2015 PMID:27068989

Morgado, M., Mendes, J. J., & Proença, L. (2021). Online Problem-Based Learning in Clinical Dental Education: Students' Self-Perception and Motivation. *Healthcare, 9*(4), 420. MDPI AG. doi:10.3390/healthcare9040420

Moulton, S. T., Türkay, S., & Kosslyn, S. M. (2017). Does a presentation's medium affect its message? PowerPoint, Prezi, and oral presentations. *PLoS One, 12*(7), e0178774. doi:10.1371/journal.pone.0178774 PMID:28678855

Murbay, S., Neelakantan, P., Chang, J. W. W., & Yeung, S. (2020). Evaluation of the introduction of a dental virtual simulator on the performance of undergraduate dental students in the pre-clinical operative dentistry course. *European Journal of Dental Education*, *24*(1), 5–16. doi:10.1111/eje.12453 PMID:31278815

Nasseripour, M., Turner, J., Rajadurai, S., San Diego, J., Quinn, B., Bartlett, A., & Volponi, A. A. (2021). COVID 19 and dental education: Transitioning from a well-established synchronous format and face to face teaching to an asynchronous format of dental clinical teaching and learning. *Journal of Medical Education and Curricular Development*, *8*, 2382120521999667. doi:10.1177/2382120521999667 PMID:33796791

Nicoll, P., MacRury, S., Van Woerden, H. C., & Smyth, K. (2018). Evaluation of technology-enhanced learning programs for health care professionals: Systematic review. *Journal of Medical Internet Research*, *20*(4), e9085. doi:10.2196/jmir.9085 PMID:29643049

Ozan, O., & Ozarslan, Y. (2016). Video lecture watching behaviors of learners in online courses. *Educational Media International*, *53*(1), 27–41. doi:10.1080/09523987.2016.1189255

Parikh, N., Risinger, D., Holland, J. N., Molony, D. A., & van der Hoeven, D. (2022). Evaluating dental students' perspectives on the concurrent teaching of didactic and case-based courses. *Journal of Dental Education*, *86*(12), 1643–1652. doi:10.1002/jdd.13081 PMID:35994207

Parolia, A., Mohan, M., Kundabala, M., & Shenoy, R. (2012). Indian dental students' preferences regarding lecture courses. *Journal of Dental Education*, *76*(3), 366–371. doi:10.1002/j.0022-0337.2012.76.3.tb05268.x PMID:22383607

Querol Julián, M., & Crawford Camiciottoli, B. (2019). The impact of online technologies and English medium instruction on university lectures in international learning contexts. *Systematic Reviews*.

Quinn, B. F. A. (2022). Challenges and opportunities of online education in dentistry post-COVID-19. *British Dental Journal*, *233*(6), 491. doi:10.103841415-022-4979-y PMID:36151177

Rao, G. K., Iskandar, Y. H., & Mokhtar, N. (2020). Enabling Training in Orthodontics Through Mobile Augmented Reality: A Novel Perspective. In Y. Qian (Ed.), *Teaching, Learning, and Leading With Computer Simulations* (pp. 68–103). IGI Global. doi:10.4018/978-1-7998-0004-0.ch003

Rao, G. K., Iskandar, Y. H., & Mokhtar, N. (2022). Bolstering the Pedagogies of Orthodontic Education Using Smart Technologies. In A. Lopes & F. Soares (Eds.), *Online Distance Learning Course Design and Multimedia in E-Learning* (pp. 225–253). IGI Global. doi:10.4018/978-1-7998-9706-4.ch010

Rao, G. K. L., Iskandar, Y. H. P., & Mokhtar, N. (2020). Understanding the nuances of E-learning in orthodontic education. *Education and Information Technologies*, *25*(1), 307–328. doi:10.100710639-019-09976-2

Rao, G. K. L., & Mokhtar, N. (2023). Dental Education in the Information Age: Teaching Dentistry to Generation Z Learners Using an Autonomous Smart Learning Environment. In Handbook of Research on Instructional Technologies in Health Education and Allied Disciplines (pp. 243-264). IGI Global.

Reissmann, D. R., Sierwald, I., Berger, F., & Heydecke, G. (2015). A model of blended learning in a pre-clinical course in prosthetic dentistry. *Journal of Dental Education, 79*(2), 157–165. doi:10.1002/j.0022-0337.2015.79.2.tb05870.x PMID:25640620

Ronny, C. (2019). Student Satisfaction and Learning Outcomes in Asynchronous Online Lecture Videos. *CBE Life Sciences Education, 18*, 4.

Schönwetter, D. J., Gareau-Wilson, N., Cunha, R. S., & Mello, I. (2016). Assessing the Impact of Voice-Over Screen-Captured Presentations Delivered Online on Dental Students' Learning. *Journal of Dental Education, 80*(2), 141–148. doi:10.1002/j.0022-0337.2016.80.2.tb06069.x PMID:26834131

Sharma, N., & Patnaik, S. (2018). Is jargon deterrent to effective communication in dental practice? the budding dentists' outlook. *The Journal of the Indian Association of Public Health Dentistry, 16*(1), 48–53. doi:10.4103/jiaphd.jiaphd_123_17

Smeby, J.-C., & Vågan, A. (2008). Recontextualising professional knowledge – newly qualified nurses and physicians. *Journal of Education and Work, 21*(2), 159–173. doi:10.1080/13639080802018014

Wang, H., Xuan, J., Liu, L., Shen, X., & Xiong, Y. (2021). Problem-based learning and case-based learning in dental education. *Annals of Translational Medicine, 9*(14), 1137. doi:10.21037/atm-21-165 PMID:34430578

ADDITIONAL READING

Crawford, C. M. (Ed.). (2021). *Shifting to Online Learning Through Faculty Collaborative Support*. IGI Global. doi:10.4018/978-1-7998-6944-3

Rao, G. K., Iskandar, Y. H., & Mokhtar, N. (2022). Bolstering the Pedagogies of Orthodontic Education Using Smart Technologies. In A. Lopes & F. Soares (Eds.), *Online Distance Learning Course Design and Multimedia in E-Learning* (pp. 225–253). IGI Global. doi:10.4018/978-1-7998-9706-4.ch010

Rao, G. K., & Mokhtar, N. (2023). Dental Education in the Information Age: Teaching Dentistry to Generation Z Learners Using an Autonomous Smart Learning Environment. In M. Garcia, M. Lopez Cabrera, & R. de Almeida (Eds.), *Handbook of Research on Instructional Technologies in Health Education and Allied Disciplines* (pp. 243–264). doi:10.4018/978-1-6684-7164-7.ch011

KEY TERMS AND DEFINITIONS

Asynchronous Learning: This is a general term used to describe forms of education, instruction, and learning that do not occur in the same place or at the same time. The term is most commonly applied to various forms of digital and online learning in which students learn from instruction—such as pre-recorded video lessons or game-based learning tasks that students complete on their own—that are not being delivered in person or in real-time.

Cognitive Dissonance: This is described as an uncomfortable internal state occurring when new information conflicts with commonly held beliefs. From the educational psychology perspective, cognitive dissonance is seen as a means to facilitate the cognitive processes of accommodation and assimilation, which are central to knowledge development. Accommodation and assimilation occur when learners are presented with new knowledge and must expend mental effort to integrate this information into their existing schema.

Dental Education: A field of science, that involves the teaching, and learning of the future generations of dentists to prevent, diagnose, and treat oral diseases and meet the dental needs and demands of the individual patients and the public.

Smart Learning Environment: A smart learning environment can be conceptualized as a learning environment that emphasizes learning flexibility, effectiveness, efficiency, engagement, adaptivity, and reflectiveness where both formal learning and informal learning are integrated.

Technology-Based Learning: This style of instructional engagement and cognitive understanding with conceptual enhancement in implicit and explicit cognitive engagement may occur through in-person, hybrid, or distance learning approaches. The differentiation within this type of environment is the primary support of technology as the way through which the learner engages with new information to be learned.

Chapter 14
Teaching the Scientific Discourse at the Secondary Level Schools:
Towards Critical and Digital Literacy

Georgios Alexandropoulos
University of Thessaly, Greece

ABSTRACT

After the pandemic with the coronavirus, many teachers and students were trained in the use of digital tools. Indeed, many of these tools are being used more and more frequently and facilitate learning in combination with other methods. In this study, the authors present the teaching approach of scientific discourse to high school students, aged 17-18 (secondary level education in Greece). Scientific discourse is characterized by specific conventions, standards, and practices that are recognized and accepted within the scientific community. It typically involves various forms of communication, including scientific papers, research articles, conference presentations, and scientific discussions. Through this didactic scenario, students will acquire the knowledge required for communication, discourse, persuasion techniques, and means.

INTRODUCTION

Scientific discourse within a classroom context has been described as encompassing knowledge, practical application, verbal communication, reading, and writing (Moje, Collazo, Carillo, & Marx 2001) or as a fusion of scientific modes of communication, understanding, practical application, and the utilization of relevant forms of evidence (Lemke, 1990). Newton, Driver, and Osborne (1999) contend that scientific discourse plays a role in fostering conceptual comprehension, infuses a classroom with a sense of scientific community, and enhances students' overall education. Given that scientific discourse is shaped and influenced by social interaction, students are required to acquire the conventions of discourse

DOI: 10.4018/979-8-3693-3128-6.ch014

Copyright © 2024, IGI Global. Copying or distributing in print or electronic forms without written permission of IGI Global is prohibited.

through active engagement in scientific discussions and receiving clear guidance from their teachers, as advocated by Kelly and Chen (1999).

Recent research has shed light on the significance of scientific discourse in education. Studies such as those by Hand, Prain, and Yore (2001) emphasize the importance of incorporating scientific discourse as it promotes students' deeper understanding of scientific concepts and encourages the development of critical thinking skills. Their findings highlight that students who engage in scientific discourse are better equipped to analyze and communicate scientific ideas effectively. Furthermore, research by Nystrand, Wu, Gamoran, Zeiser, and Long (2003) underscores the role of teacher-student interactions in fostering scientific discourse. These interactions provide a framework for students to engage in dialogue and argumentation, which can enhance their ability to construct scientific knowledge and communicate their findings. To incorporate these recent research findings, educators should consider strategies that encourage student engagement in scientific discourse. This may involve the use of structured argumentation frameworks (Toulmin, 1958), collaborative group work, and the integration of technology tools for real-time feedback and discussions.

In the Greek syllabus the aim is for students to recognize the author's personal stance in argumentative texts and understand the purpose and conclusion of the arguments. Students are encouraged to form their own opinions on the texts and acknowledge that there can be different viewpoints on the issues raised. The Greek Language Curriculum in high school acknowledges the diversity, needs, capabilities, and overall backgrounds of students. It is designed to allow each student to develop their own perspective within the framework, connecting their individuality with linguistic awareness and development. Through tailored teaching and learning, students become aware of how their language choices are linked to their communication goals and their identity. They gain insight into why they choose certain expressions, how these choices shape their identity, and the impact of these choices. The curriculum covers phonological, morphological, and syntactical structures of the Greek language and their subsystems. It also focuses on vocabulary development, oral and written communication skills, and textual literacy within a critical context, emphasizing different forms of the language and literature.

In the realm of education, it is essential to craft curricula and teaching materials that not only cover fundamental subjects but also address the evolving requirements of students in our modern digital era. In this context, a pivotal component of the secondary level curriculum involves the instruction of scientific discourse, persuasion techniques, and digital literacy. These proficiencies are indispensable for students to flourish in our information-rich, technology-driven society.

Teaching scientific discourse entails equipping students with the ability to effectively communicate within the realm of science. This encompasses developing proficiency in scientific language, understanding the conventions of scientific writing and communication, and engaging in meaningful discussions and debates on scientific topics. Expected learning outcomes in this domain encompass students' capacity to read, comprehend, and produce scientific texts, as well as their ability to participate in scientific inquiry and critical analysis.

Persuasion techniques represent another vital skill, particularly in a world saturated with information and diverse media forms. Educating students on how to comprehend, identify, and employ persuasive methods enables them to become discerning consumers of information. Anticipated learning outcomes in this area should encompass students' ability to critically evaluate persuasive content, distinguish between reliable and biased sources, and enhance their persuasive communication skills, ensuring they can effectively express their perspectives and engage in informed debates.

Digital literacy stands as a foundational skill in today's digital age. Students must possess proficiency in using digital tools and platforms for research, communication, and collaboration. Equally crucial is their ability to navigate the digital landscape responsibly and ethically. Expected learning outcomes for digital literacy should cover students' capacities to effectively employ digital resources, critically assess online information, safeguard their online privacy, and participate in responsible digital citizenship.

To bolster the inclusion of these subsections in the curriculum, it is essential to reference pertinent literature on each of these topics. Drawing upon academic research and established best practices in teaching scientific discourse, persuasion techniques, and digital literacy not only bolsters the credibility of the educational materials but also equips educators with valuable insights and resources to effectively impart these skills.

Integrating a dedicated subsection within the secondary level curriculum focused on scientific discourse, persuasion techniques, and digital literacy is pivotal in preparing students to excel in our intricate, information-driven world. This approach ensures that students acquire the knowledge and proficiencies necessary for academic success, critical evaluation of information, and responsible digital citizenship. The incorporation of relevant literature further enhances the quality of educational materials and provides educators with valuable guidance.

In the realm of digital literacy, the proliferation of online information and communication technologies has reshaped the educational landscape. Recent research and literature offer valuable insights into how educators can navigate this changing terrain. One study by Hobbs (2010) emphasizes the importance of media literacy as a component of digital literacy. It highlights the need for students to critically assess and analyze media content in an age of information overload. Hobbs suggests that educators should focus on teaching students to evaluate the credibility of digital sources and consider the potential biases in online information. Moreover, the work of Wachira and Keengwe (2011) explores the role of digital storytelling in enhancing digital literacy. Their findings suggest that digital storytelling can be a powerful tool for developing students' communication and technology skills, while also promoting creativity and critical thinking. To incorporate these recent findings into the teaching of digital literacy, educators should emphasize critical media literacy and provide students with the skills to critically evaluate digital content. They should also consider incorporating digital storytelling projects into the curriculum to foster creativity and enhance digital communication skills.

In the digital era, where online interactions have become an integral part of our daily lives, the importance of digital literacy extends beyond mere technical proficiency. It encompasses ethical considerations that play a pivotal role in shaping online behaviors and influencing broader societal outcomes. Fundamental to ethical digital conduct is online etiquette, which underscores the significance of polite and respectful interactions in digital realms. Fostering positive online communities' hinges on the impact of courteous behavior in shaping constructive digital discourse. Recognizing that words and actions online bear the same weight as those in the physical world marks the initial stride toward responsible digital citizenship. Ethical digital literacy encompasses responsible digital citizenship as a pivotal component. This entails adhering to ethical guidelines, respecting digital rights, and advocating for a secure online environment for all. Encouraging users to contemplate the consequences of their online actions on a broader scale is essential in fostering a more ethical online community. The digital landscape raises intricate privacy concerns as users navigate the balance between sharing information and safeguarding personal data. Addressing privacy within digital literacy necessitates comprehending the implications of data collection, surveillance, and the potential fallout of sharing personal information online. Equipping individuals with knowledge about privacy settings, data protection, and informed decision-making forms a crucial facet of ethical digital literacy. Signifying the repercussions of unethical online behavior holds pivotal importance in cultivating ethical digital literacy. This entails discussing potential legal and personal consequences tied to actions such as cyberbullying, online harassment, or the dissemination of false information. Grasping these consequences underscores the significance of ethical conduct in digital spaces. Digital literacy serves as a potent tool in combatting the dissemination of misinformation and disinformation. Proficiency in critically evaluating online information enables individuals to differentiate credible sources from false or biased information. Individuals equipped with robust digital literacy skills contribute to a more informed and discerning society, less susceptible to misinformation. Digital literacy plays a significant role in addressing issues like cyberbullying and online harassment, which exact detrimental effects on individuals and society at large. Empowering individuals with digital literacy skills equips them to combat these issues, paving the way for online spaces free from harassment and hostility. Digital literacy serves as an instrumental force in nurturing informed and responsible citizens. Proficiency in digital literacy enables individuals to engage in critical thinking, uphold ethical online behavior, and partake in civic activities. A populace well-versed in digital literacy contributes to a more engaged and responsible citizenry. The digital divide, characterized by disparities in access to digital resources, raises ethical and social quandaries. These disparities are intrinsically tied to societal inequalities. This segment delves into the ethical concerns surrounding the digital divide and investigates how unequal access to digital resources can exacerbate existing societal divisions. It also explores the endeavors undertaken to bridge this divide, ensuring that technology is harnessed ethically to empower underserved communities.

With constant advancements in technology and communication practices, educators must be flexible and adaptable to maintain their effectiveness. It will be useful to emphasize the significance of educators staying informed about emerging technologies, digital tools, and teaching methodologies that can enhance their instruction in scientific discourse and digital literacy. It is necessary to encourage them to participate in professional development opportunities, attend relevant conferences, and establish connections with colleagues in their field. This ongoing learning and collaborative spirit can aid educators in refining their teaching methods, ultimately providing students with the highest quality education. Furthermore, we must stress the importance of fostering in students the desire to become independent, lifelong learners in these domains.

CURRICULUM OF THE MODERN GREEK MODERN LANGUAGE

In the following lines, we shall present some information about the curriculum of the Modern Greek Language course for the 1st, 2nd, and 3rd grades of General High School (Ministerial Decision No. 33127/D2/2023, Government Gazette 1948/B/24-3-2023). The cognitive object of the Modern Greek Language is distinguished for its specificity compared to all other subjects in school. Its main content, the language system, is usually acquired naturally and spontaneously before the start of formal education. Students do not come to the Modern Greek Language class solely to learn the Greek language, but also to expand their linguistic repertoire with tropes such as written discourse and linguistic varieties, including standard language and other geographical, social, and functional variations, as well as textual genres they may not have been familiar with through their socialization in the linguistic communities they belong to. Language is cultivated in school as a necessary means of accessing all aspects of the complex objective and subjective reality and as an indicator of individual, social, and cultural identity.

The cultivation of language perception and oral and written expression is a necessary prerequisite for the cognitive, social, and linguistic development of students since developed linguistic structures are interconnected and interact with the maturation of cognitive processes. The Greek language, with its long oral and written tradition and a wide range of linguistic varieties, is closely associated with the existence and history of education in Greek-speaking communities and the Greek state. It represents a central reference point for cultural heritage and an indicator of national identity. That is why Modern Greek Language has a central position in the curriculum at all levels. The teaching of Modern Greek Language aims at the gradual transformation of language awareness into an understanding of the Greek language system and, specifically, lexical choices and textual patterns available to speakers for creating meanings in various communicative contexts. The main elements of linguistic education content consist of presenting and analyzing the interrelated phonological, morphological, and syntactic structures of Greek and their subsystems (e.g., nominal and verbal systems), developing basic and specialized vocabulary, practicing basic skills of comprehension and production of oral and written speech, and developing textual literacy within a critical framework, with an emphasis on linguistic (synchronic and diachronic) varieties and literature. Especially at the high school level, students are called upon to achieve a more comprehensive cognitive autonomy, combined with increased emotional maturity and independence. The cognitive object of Modern Greek Language significantly contributes to their preparation for active participation in social and political events, the formation of social consciousness, and the qualities of an academic citizen and/or future professional. Through the knowledge and skills related to language, students understand, analyze, and evaluate information, participate in the creation of meanings, present their ideas and opinions, have access to all academic subjects, interact with others, and participate in school activities as well as in their lives outside school. Therefore, Modern Greek Language contributes to the preparation of adolescents to participate as equal members in the adult society.

Program of Study Identity

The Program of Study for Modern Greek Language in high school is a multidimensional program, both in its theoretical foundation and in the principles of instructional framing and learning. It follows the tradition of text-centered and communicative language approaches that have been adopted in previous Study Programs and clearly contrasts with older teaching methods that focused exclusively on linguistic forms. At the same time, it attempts to combine elements of traditional teaching with contemporary approaches without adopting a single theoretical framework. It also emphasizes the critical dimension of language and the cultivation of multiple literacies as a pedagogical orientation. Thus, the new Program of Study incorporates three basic dimensions of language teaching, encompassing the structural framework of language instruction connected to language learning, the functional framework linked to language use, the genre framework, and the framework of activities associated with language acquisition. In doing so, it creates a flexible field for the application of theoretical principles and orientations that can be adapted to the specific educational conditions within the Greek educational system. Within this framework, the Program of Study for Modern Greek Language in high school, as in the Study Programs for primary and lower secondary education, aims for a holistic approach. The expected learning outcomes focus on both language proficiency and language use, as well as the strategies available to students. The general and specific objectives of language teaching determine the emphasis on different aspects of language, enabling the transition from words and sentences to texts, always within the context of communicative language teaching. Based on these principles, the Program of Study relies on the following:

- Organic continuity of language teaching and functional transition from lower secondary to high school and from one grade of high school to the next.
- Holistic approach to language: Language is treated as a unified whole (vocabulary-grammar-text), and its teaching aims to achieve both communicative fluency and linguistic accuracy.
- Explicit teaching of linguistic means used by speakers and writers to achieve their communicative goals in specific contexts, connecting their lexical and grammatical choices with textual patterns and providing focused instruction on vocabulary, grammar, and text depending on the grade level and students' needs.
- Focus on expected learning outcomes rather than the content of the language course as material.
- Authentic use of language through real, not contrived or invented, examples in all language comprehension and production activities.
- Explicit distinction between the linguistic varieties of Greek in their social and textual contexts and within the framework of multiple literacies.
- Differentiated teaching regarding content, process, learning products, and learning environment based on students' readiness, interests, and profiles (personal learning styles and pace, unique experiences, cultural background, etc.).
- Student-centered approach with an emphasis on discovery, collaboration, and active learning, encouraging critical thinking, creativity, and the development of metacognitive skills.

Overall, the Program of Study for Modern Greek Language in high school aims to foster language proficiency, language use, and metalinguistic awareness, enabling students to become competent and confident communicators in a range of linguistic and sociocultural contexts.

The Objectives of Language Teaching in Primary School, Gymnasium (Lower Secondary School), and Lyceum (Upper Secondary School) in Greece

The main objective is for all students to be able to express themselves orally and in writing with ease, accuracy, and appropriateness in order to convey their ideas and evaluations to others and actively communicate with them through speech production and comprehension. The program of study emphasizes the differentiated approach to teaching and learning, which recognizes the diversity, needs, abilities, individuality, and overall background of all students. It aims to cultivate students' language skills and knowledge by considering language as a system of structures and interconnected elements. Additionally, it focuses on functional language use, expanding pragmatic abilities, and understanding the role of linguistic choices as means of expressing social relationships, positions, attitudes, and identities. The general objectives of language teaching in lyceum combine various aspects of the Greek language, such as its structural dimension (grammar), functional dimension (language use), and the interrelation between linguistic choices and language functions in specific contexts. These objectives include the development of textual competence, which involves creating and comprehending oral and written texts, and linguistic awareness regarding the role of each linguistic choice as a mechanism for creating meaning and identity. Furthermore, the language, pragmatic, and textual competence of students are connected to the overall goal of developing social and functional literacy, enabling equal participation in society and the utilization of social and professional opportunities. In comparison to primary and gymnasium levels, the objectives of language teaching in lyceum emphasize specific aspects of the language while maintaining necessary coherence in teaching between different school levels. Overall, the objectives of teaching the

Greek language in lyceum involve raising students' awareness of linguistic structures, expanding their vocabulary, improving spelling skills, understanding the connection between lexical and grammatical choices, and developing textual competence.

Special Purposes

The above general objectives of teaching the Modern Greek Language in high school are specialized in specific purposes that concern the abilities of students, which correspond, without being exclusively identified, with the communicative skills, cognitive and textual processes, linguistic awareness, and social and functional literacy that students in high school are expected to develop. Specifically, the special purposes are organized into four dimensions and specialized in specific expected learning outcomes as follows: Understanding, Analysis, Interpretation, and Text Creation.

- Students are intended to be able to:
- Understand the communicative goal of the text, the intentions of its creator, the important general and specific information, the textual genre, and the different perspectives that can be adopted within it.
- Evaluate, using appropriate metalanguage, the linguistic mechanisms used in various texts in terms of their communicative effectiveness.
- Identify and evaluate the representations, attitudes, and values expressed in extensive texts, as well as the perspectives that are silenced or marginalized in those texts.
- Develop their personal stance toward the texts they read or listen to, recognizing the logic of different positions.
- Produce extensive oral and written texts with accuracy, fluency, and effectiveness that correspond to a wide range of communicative goals, utilizing various semiotic resources.

Reasoning and Argumentation

Students are intended to be able to:

- Identify and present the reasoning and arguments of a text, assessing their persuasiveness and effectiveness.
- Develop and substantiate their own opinion, in writing or orally, regarding significant issues concerning their immediate and broader social environment, as well as aspects of contemporary reality.
- Plan their contribution to an oral or written public dialogue, organizing their ideas and arguments effectively and persuasively.
- Use appropriate linguistic elements and textual structures to present their arguments in written and oral discourse.
- Use persuasive strategies to support or refute an argument or to develop a line of reasoning.

Linguistic Awareness

Students are intended to be able to:

- Possess a comprehensive understanding of the linguistic system of Greek, with an emphasis on the verbal and nominal systems.
- Recognize and use appropriate linguistic elements in relation to content, communicative purpose, textual genre, and context.
- Be able to evaluate the grammar, vocabulary, and spelling of the texts they create and refer to appropriate reference materials for checking their texts.
- Have basic knowledge of diachronic and synchronic variations of Greek and be able to assess their role and significance in the perception and creation of meaning.

Social and Functional Literacy

Students are intended to be able to:

- Utilize their knowledge of the world and various specialized topics to create their texts.
- Utilize their linguistic abilities and knowledge to develop their academic and professional interests in specialized fields.

Within the framework of the basic principles and aims of the Curriculum for the Modern Greek Language in high school, the treatment of extensive texts is introduced as a complement to the textual excerpts or limited-length complete texts used in the other two thematic fields and in combination with the extensive texts taught in Literature.

The use of "long" texts and their guided study in language teaching provides authentic writing models, engagement with the world of books, reading enjoyment, as well as increased opportunities for familiarity with authentic choices and strategies of language content and form, which promote comprehension, analysis, interpretation, and the creation of new texts by students. The extensively studied texts should belong to specific textual genres for each grade and be selected based on specific criteria:

- They should not be translations.
- They should be products of the 20th and 21st centuries.
- They should be written in understandable language, without being simplistic, and open to variations.
- They should have a moderate length manageable within the school curriculum.
- They should draw their thematic content from a wide range of contemporary and historical issues.
- They should align with the interests of the students, providing both knowledge and enjoyment.
- They should be accompanied by audiovisual material.

Specifically, for the first year of high school, extended non-fiction narrative texts are recommended (mainly biographies). For the second and third years of high school, extended non-narrative texts, particularly essays, are proposed: reflective essays for the second year (reflective essay: the established genre cultivated by thinkers and writers aiming for non-fictional expression on a specific subject) and academic essays for the third year (academic essay: the textual genre usually cultivated in an educational context with the goal of presenting information and argumentation on a specific subject).

Teaching Framework: Learning Design

The Curriculum for Modern Greek Language in high school promotes creativity and highlights the individuality of the protagonists of the educational process. It consciously allows for significant initiative and recognizes educators as important designers of teaching and as scientists who can draw on and process resources from various communicative, conventional, and digital environments with their students. Additionally, the Curriculum for Modern Greek Language in high school recognizes that participation in a democratic society requires voluntary mobilization and personal commitment from adolescent students. It supports and seeks to foster their freedom of expression, taking into account their interests, priorities, and the biography of their individual and collective identities. Students are co-creators of knowledge with educators in collective processes of reflection and introspection in the classroom, which educators coordinate with sensitivity and awareness of the individuality of the students. From this perspective and in accordance with the principles of humanistic teaching and learning approaches in language education, the selection and organization of content, the format of activities, and the utilization of educational materials are based on both presentation by the educator and processing by the students. This is achieved through collaborative activities of exploratory nature aimed at developing communicative skills, creating knowledge, and fostering aesthetic, emotional, and social aspects of their personalities. The role of educators extends beyond the reproduction of knowledge and encompasses the coordination and organization of activities, as well as the encouragement of students in dealing with the difficulties encountered during the completion of activities. Similarly, the role of students does not simply involve being passive recipients of instruction but rather entails participation in authentic, playful, and simulated actions, as well as engaging in research activities. Based on the above, the teaching of grammar, vocabulary, production, and comprehension of written and oral speech requires the combination of productive and inductive teaching approaches. In the former, educators present and analyze previous or new knowledge, while in the latter, students are called upon to utilize the content of language instruction in receptive and productive actions in which they are involved. However, despite the combined application of both methods in the educational practice, particular emphasis is placed on inductive teaching approaches, where students play a leading role, both in the presentation of grammatical and lexical phenomena and in the processing of text genres and textual structures that they are called upon to utilize in the activities in which they participate.

The Ministerial Decision No. 33127/D2/2023 and Government Gazette 1948/B/24-3-2023 present the curriculum of the Modern Greek Language course for the 1st, 2nd, and 3rd grades of General High School. The inclusion of a specific Ministerial Decision indicates a level of official endorsement and regulation for the curriculum. By detailing the curriculum, it is obvious that it offers transparency and clarity to both students and educators regarding the learning objectives, content, and skills to be covered in the Modern Greek Language course. This can help ensure consistency in teaching practices and facilitate effective learning outcomes. Overall, the Ministerial Decision and Government Gazette provide a foundation for curriculum planning and implementation, enabling students to acquire essential language skills and knowledge throughout their General High School education.

OBJECTIVES AND METHODOLOGICAL FRAMEWORK

Scientific discourse refers to the communication and exchange of ideas, information, and knowledge within the scientific community. It encompasses the various forms of communication used by scientists to share their research findings, theories, methodologies, and interpretations of data. Scientific discourse plays a crucial role in advancing scientific knowledge, fostering collaboration, and promoting critical evaluation and scrutiny of scientific claims. Key features of scientific discourse include:

- Objectivity: Scientific discourse aims to present information objectively, based on empirical evidence, data, and logical reasoning. It strives to minimize personal bias and subjective interpretation.
- Precision and Clarity: Scientific communication emphasizes clear and precise language to ensure that ideas and findings are accurately conveyed. Terminology and jargon specific to the field are used to enhance precision and facilitate effective communication among experts.
- Methodology and Reproducibility: Scientific discourse often includes detailed descriptions of research methodologies, experimental procedures, and data analysis techniques. This facilitates transparency and allows other researchers to replicate and validate the findings.
- Logical Structure: Scientific discourse typically follows a structured format, such as introduction, methods, results, and discussion, to provide a clear and logical flow of information. This allows readers to easily comprehend the research and its implications.
- Citation and Referencing: Scientific discourse requires proper citation and referencing of previous works and sources to acknowledge the existing body of knowledge and give credit to other researchers. This promotes intellectual integrity and helps build upon the work of others.

It is a fact that texts, according to researchers such as Tentolouris & Chatzisavvidis (2014) and Stamou et al. (2016), are no longer considered neutral semantic entities but ideological constructs that promote a particular worldview and maintain specific power relations. Fairclough (1992) connects language and discourse with the interpretation of capitalist society, as critical discourse analysis reveals many changes taking place through discourse or reflected in discourse. Janks (2000) argues that today it is crucial for education to prepare young people to read both words and the world with a critical perspective. Koutsogiannis (2017:38-42) proposes shifting the scientific community's focus to critically reading the Greek example and developing reflections on the type of learning identities that Greek schools will seek to cultivate in the 21st century.

Critical literacy through the theoretical framework of multiliteracies can contribute to this direction of approaching texts as carriers of ideological predispositions. Multiliteracies encompass various text types that emerge within a multilingual and multicultural society and are connected to new technologies and their integration into the learning process.

The multiliteracies model (Kallantzis & Cope 2000) is based on four pillars:

a. Situated practice: Students' engagement with elements derived from their daily lives and social reality.
b. Overt instruction: The way linguistic elements function.
c. Critical framing: At this stage, students engage in critical interpretation of the text.
d. Transformed practice: Transformed production of discourse.

Regarding the use of technology, the goal of instructional scenarios is for students to learn to utilize the Internet, the Google website, access their class blog, conduct searches and make posts, search for information, images, and photos on Google, find videos, explore pages of educational and social interest, use electronic dictionaries, the e-class online platform, and use collaborative documents and their email within the context of situated practice and open-ended pedagogies. Within the framework of transformed practice, students will be able to utilize digital storytelling tools (Moviemaker) and digital posters (Glogster). Besides this, students will acquire eloquence through drama strategies[1] in education.

All of the above are applied within the framework of collaborative teaching according to Bruner (1997), Vygotsky (1986), and McConnell (1994). In collaborative learning, tasks are transferred from the educator to the learning group, with students collaborating and influencing each other to achieve a common goal. According to Vygotsky (1986), Collaborative Learning is a form of teaching with a learner-centered approach, where small groups of students collaborate to solve a problem. Collaborative Learning is based on the theory of constructivism and the belief that knowledge is a social construction, while learning is a social process. McConnell (1994) describes how collaborative learning benefits individuals by utilizing the resources of the group. He claims that collaborative learning yields valuable outcomes that have not yet been fully recognized in academic and continuing education settings, such as increased ability in teamwork, self-confidence, etc. McConnell also appreciates how individuals gain a better understanding of a subject by publicizing their knowledge. Collaborative learning is based on the axis of cooperation, with the following structural elements:

- Group work: Students work together in small groups to achieve a common goal.
- Mutual support): Students support and assist each other in the learning process.
- Shared responsibility): Students share responsibility for the success of the group's outcomes.
- Communication: Effective communication is essential for collaboration and knowledge sharing.
- Critical thinking: Students engage in critical thinking to analyze and evaluate ideas and information.
- Collaborative assessment: Evaluation is conducted collectively, allowing students to provide feedback and assess their own and others' work.
- Personal autonomy: Students have a degree of autonomy and independence within the collaborative learning process.
- Active participation: All students actively participate in group activities and contribute their ideas and perspectives.

Through these elements, collaborative learning fosters a dynamic and interactive learning environment that promotes engagement, critical thinking, and social interaction among students.

The advantages of cooperative learning are numerous. Firstly, individuals interact with others, engage in socialization, establish trust bonds with fellow members, undertake tasks based on the division of labor, cultivate members' skills, and achieve cognitive and emotional development. Moreover, within the framework of cooperative learning, educators can dynamically create lessons to transfer knowledge, teach students how to learn the material, foster students' responsibility, promote active learning, encourage students, intellectually guide them towards new knowledge, cultivate social skills, and ultimately act as a mediator in student interactions.

Cooperative learning, within a social theory combined with the use of information and communication technologies, can significantly contribute to the achievement of educational goals. According to Haralambous (2000), cooperative learning follows the following stages:

i)   Preparatory Stage: Organizing the space, Group formation, Role distribution within the group, Determination of the cognitive objective, Specification of the learning and collaborative goals, Determination of the resources on which the groups will work, Evaluation sheet.

ii)   Implementation of Cooperative Learning: Introduction to the activity, Oral or written instructions, Group work based on the group worksheet, Guidance and intervention by the educator, when necessary, in an encouraging and motivating manner.

iii) Evaluation of Cooperative Learning: Presentation of the generated material by the groups, Evaluation of the work, quality of collaboration, and Discussion for potential improvements.

As a social learning theory, the social constructivism of Vygotsky is chosen. The main axes of this particular theory are as follows:

I.   The social environment.
II.   Tools for cognitive development, e.g., Language - Cultural tradition.
III. The zone of proximal development, which refers to the range of abilities that an individual can achieve with the help of an expert but cannot master independently without support.

TEACHING SCENARIO ON PERSUASION IN SCIENTIFIC DISCOURSE

Phases of Teaching

i) Overt instruction

In this stage, the concept of scientific discourse is defined, and students are asked:

- if they have read scientific texts
- if they are familiar with scientific terms by field

Then, students will watch scientists deliver speeches to the public. It follows a discussion about the context of these speeches. We can ask them the following questions: a. Who is the speaker? b. Who is the audience? c. What is the message of the speech?

ii)   Situated practice

In this stage of the educational process, students are instructed to gather scientific texts and record them in Word format on a computer. These texts will form a corpus, which is a collection of texts used for analysis and study. The corpus will be processed and analyzed using the computational tool Voyant Tools. Voyant Tools allows students to explore the corpus and generate valuable information. For example, it can generate a list of the most frequently occurring words in the corpus, excluding common words found in all languages (such as functional connectors). This analysis can provide insights into the vocabulary and terminology used in the scientific texts. Furthermore, Voyant Tools can help extract information about verb usage, such as identifying active or passive syntax. It can also identify intertextual sources, which refer to references or connections between different texts. Additionally, students can analyze persuasive methods employed in the scientific texts. After conducting their analysis, students are expected to present their findings and data in tables on their class blog. This allows them to share their discoveries and insights with their classmates and potentially engage in discussions and further analysis.

iii)   Critical Framing

Students are called upon to observe how many scientific studies have been conducted by women. They are also encouraged to reflect on what this means for society and the world we live in.

iv)   Interdisciplinary and intersectionality activities

At this stage, students are asked (through e-class/flipped classroom) to find information about the relationship between women and science and present female personalities who have excelled in the scientific field. Specifically, they are asked to study the case of Hypatia and Marie Curie. In addition, they are asked to study several texts uploaded in e-class about the pros and cons of science in our life.

v)   Transformed practice

At this point, students will be asked to apply what they have learned in the previous stage by engaging in practical applications working in groups. Specifically, students will be expected to:

- Interview with a scientist. Record a video interview and then present the text of the interview in the school magazine using transcriptor.com.
- Create a scientific poster using Glogster for a convention. They can also use DALL-E for creating pictures.
- Develop a one-minute digital storytelling commercial to present their data on scientific project using Movie Maker.

Write a scientific speech of 400 words individually or in groups on a selected topic using collaborative documents on Google. The correctness criteria for the speech will include deontic modality, parallelism, emotional words, epistemic verbs, repetition, and all modes of persuasion.

Participate in rhetorical contests or debates on a topic using the investigative method. Alternatively, students may engage in a hot chair of rhetoric by interrogating a scientist about his/her purpose when he/she conducts research.

After completing the above tasks, students will engage in peer and self-assessment activities using google forms.

Worksheet on Persuasion in Scientific Discourse

First Hour

Activities:

- What do you know about scientific discourse?
- Have you read scientific texts?

- Do you know scientific terms by field?
- Mention scientific terms by field: history, philosophy, justice, medicine, physics, chemistry, theology, technology, music, art. And then create a word cloud for each discipline with wordle.

Second Hour

Activities:

- What are the stylistic devices of these texts?
- What are the most frequently used nouns and verbs in the corpora?
- Present them on your blog.

Third Hour

Activities:

- How many scientific studies have been conducted by women?
- What this means for society and the world we live in?

Fourth Hour

Activities
   Discuss these topics:

- Which is the relation between women and science? Present female personalities who have excelled in the scientific field such as Hypatia and Marie Curie.
- Study the texts in e-class that discuss the pros and cons of science in our life.

From the Fifth to the Eighth Hour

Activities

Group A

Interview with a scientist. Record a video interview and then present the text of the interview in the school magazine using transcriptor.com.

Group B

Create a scientific poster for a convention using Glogster and DALL-E.

Group C

Develop a one-minute digital storytelling commercial to present their data on scientific project using Movie Maker.

Common Work for All Groups

- Write a scientific speech of 400 words in groups on a selected topic using collaborative documents on Google. The correctness criteria for the speech will include deontic modality, parallelism, emotional words, epistemic verbs, repetition, and all modes of persuasion.
- Participate in rhetorical contests or debates on a topic using the investigative method. Alternatively, students may engage in drama strategies such as a hot seating by interrogating a scientist about his/her purpose when he/she conducts research.

After completing the above tasks, students will engage in peer and self-assessment activities using Google Forms2.

CONCLUSION

In conclusion, the students were provided with an opportunity to gain knowledge about various methods of persuasion. They studied the stylistic devices of the scientific discourse. The existing theoretical model was expanded to include an additional stage, that of interdisciplinary study. The teaching intervention spanned eight instructional hours, conducted both in the classroom and computer lab. Collaborative documents and the e-class platform of the Panhellenic School Network were utilized for completing student assignments. Information and Communications Technology (ICT) was creatively and critically employed to foster collaborative work, encourage initiative, creativity, and independent action. Overall, the students worked in groups and employed various tools such as e-class, blog, Web 2.0, Voyant, DALL-E, Glogster, Wordle, Movie Maker, Google Forms and Google Docs. Additionally, the drama education technique known as "hot seating" was utilized. By combining critical and digital literacy skills, the students developed an understanding of the importance of critically analyzing texts. Recent research findings and literature offer valuable insights into teaching scientific discourse and digital literacy. By integrating these findings into educational practices, educators can better equip students with the skills necessary to thrive in a world where effective communication, critical thinking, and digital literacy are paramount. To stay at the forefront of education, it is essential to continually update teaching methods and materials based on the latest research and scholarly contributions in these areas. It is essential to underscore the ongoing opportunities for learning and development within the realms of scientific discourse and digital literacy. Education exists within a continuously evolving landscape, making it imperative to remain updated on progress and changes.

ACKNOWLEDGMENT

I would like to express my sincere gratitude to my supervisor, Assistant Professor Phillipos Tentolouris, for his helpful information and practical advice that have helped me tremendously at all times in my research and writing of this study.

REFERENCES

Bruner, J. (1997). *The acts of meaning*. Harvard University Press.

Cope, B., & Kalantzis, M. (2000). *Multiliteracies. Literacy learning and the design of social futures*. Routledge.

Fairclough, N. (1992). *Critical Language Awareness*. Longman.

Freedman, A. (2015). *Genre and the New Rhetoric*. Routledge.

Hand, B., Prain, V., & Yore, L. D. (2001). Contributing to a Project-Based Elementary Science Program: The Nature of Language. *Research in Science Education, 31*(3), 289–307.

Hobbs, R. (2010). *Digital and Media Literacy: A Plan of Action*. The Aspen Institute.

Hofmann, A. H., & Ristroph, K. A. (2019). *Scientific Writing and Communication: Papers, Proposals, and Presentations* (4th ed.). Oxford University Press.

Janks, H. (2005). Language and the design of texts. *English Teaching: Practice and Critique*. ERIC. (https://files.eric.ed.gov/fulltext/EJ847267.pdf)

Kelly, G., & Chen, C. (1999). The sound of music: Constructing science as sociocultural practices through oral and written discourse. *Journal of Research in Science Teaching, 36*(8), 883–915. doi:10.1002/(SICI)1098-2736(199910)36:8<883::AID-TEA1>3.0.CO;2-I

Koutsogiannis, D. (2017). *Language Teaching Yesterday, Today, Tomorrow. A Political Approach*. Institute of Modern Greek Studies.

Lemke, J. (1990). *Talking science*. Ablex.

McConnell, D. (1994). What is Cooperative Learning. In *Implementing Computer Supported Cooperative Learning?* Kogan Page Limited.

Ministerial Decision No. 33127/D2/2023, Government Gazette 1948/B/24-3-2023.

Moje, E. B., Collazo, T., Carrillo, R., & Marx, R. (2001). "Maestro, what is 'quality'?" Language, literacy and discourse in project-based science. *Journal of Research in Science Teaching, 38*(4), 469–498. doi:10.1002/tea.1014

Neelands, J. (2002). *Making sense of Drama: A guide to classroom practice*. Heinemann Educational Publishers.

Newton, P., Driver, R., & Osborne, J. (1999). The place of argumentation in the pedagogy of school science. *International Journal of Science Education, 21*(5), 553–576. doi:10.1080/095006999290570

Nystrand, M., Wu, L. L., Gamoran, A., Zeiser, S., & Long, D. A. (2003). Questions in Time: Investigating the Structure and Dynamics of Unfolding Classroom Discourse. *Discourse Processes, 35*(2), 135–198. doi:10.1207/S15326950DP3502_3

Stamou, G. A., Politis, P., & Archakis, A. (Eds.). (2016). *Linguistic Diversity and Critical Literacies in the Discourse of Mass Culture: Educational Proposals for Language Education. Kavala*. Saita Publications.

Sword, H. (2012). *Stylish Academic Writing*. Harvard University Press.

Tentolouris, F., & Chatzisavvidis, S. (2014). Discourses of Critical Literacies and Their 'Placement' in School Practice: Towards a Reflective Language Teaching. *Studies on the Greek Language, 34,* 411–421.

Toulmin, S. E. (1958). *The Uses of Argument*. Cambridge University Press.

Vygotsky, L. S. (1986). Thought and language (rev. ed.) A. Kozulin (ed.). Cambridge, M.A.: The MIT Press.

Wachira, P., & Keengwe, J. (2011). Technology Integration in K-12: Teachers' Perceptions and Use of Digital Media in the Classroom. *International Journal of Education and Development Using Information and Communication Technology, 7*(2), 136–149.

ENDNOTES

[1]   For more details about drama strategies in education see Neelands (2002).
[2]   Google Forms allows you to create customized surveys or quizzes for students to assess their own work or provide feedback to their peers. Students can submit their responses digitally, and you can easily analyze the results.

Chapter 15
The Contribution of ICTE to the Teaching of Literature Within the Action–Oriented Perspective

Mohammed Zine El Abidine
https://orcid.org/0000-0002-8767-4504
Abdelmalek Essaadi University, Morocco

Fatima Zahra Ouariach
https://orcid.org/0009-0000-1360-9286
Abdelmalek Essaadi University, Morocco

Amel Nejjari
https://orcid.org/0000-0002-7323-1286
Abdelmalek Essaadi University, Morocco

ABSTRACT

In recent years, increasing emphasis has been placed on the integration of ICTE. In particular, the teaching of literature has been at the center of this integration, with the aim of improving student engagement and learning outcomes. In this regard, the action-based approach emphasizes the active engagement of students and the concrete relevance of teaching literature. This chapter aims to explore the integration of ICT into the teaching of literature within the framework of the action-based approach. More specifically, the chapter will address the following questions: What is the action-based approach to teaching literature? How can ICT be used to improve the teaching of literature within the action-based approach? And what are the challenges of integrating ICT into the teaching of literature using the action-based approach? In addressing these questions, this chapter seeks to provide an overview of the potential benefits and challenges of integrating ICT into the teaching of literature, and to offer practical suggestions for educators seeking to do so.

DOI: 10.4018/979-8-3693-3128-6.ch015

Copyright © 2024, IGI Global. Copying or distributing in print or electronic forms without written permission of IGI Global is prohibited.

INTRODUCTION

Literature, as a medium of expression, has traversed the annals of human existence since time immemorial. Its essence transcends epochs, leaving an indelible imprint on the growth and evolution of civilizations. Through the creative genius of writers, who weave intricate tales within novels, poems, and plays, the profound potential to ignite profound transformations within individuals' minds and souls is realized. It is through the immersive experience of engaging with literary works that individuals attain the highest level of comprehension and assimilation. Therefore, it is incumbent upon educational institutions to foster an environment that encourages both teachers and students to harness the transformative power of literature, for the fundamental pedagogical approach to foreign language instruction rests upon its integration within the classroom. In light of this, it behooves us to reevaluate the untapped possibilities that lie in augmenting the multifaceted roles ascribed to literature within the language learning milieu.

Literature, revered as a ubiquitous tool of instruction worldwide, encompasses a myriad of pedagogical approaches, including the realms of aesthetics, culture, training, and language. Indeed, when a literary work is unveiled within a designated sphere, the very fabric of language and culture finds itself at the forefront of scrutiny. It is within this hallowed literary realm that educators of the present era unanimously concur lies the crucible wherein language(s) and culture(s) intertwine, facilitating the cultivation of an intercultural communicative competence that stands as an indispensable asset for individuals navigating the complexities of today's plurilingual and pluricultural societies.

Across the passage of time, the enduring and intricate relationship between French as a foreign language and the realm of literature has become increasingly apparent. Notably, these enduring bonds have weathered periods of turmoil, while simultaneously sparking contentious debates concerning the rightful place and role that literary texts should assume within the act of teaching and learning a living language. Consequently, the position of literature in education, both in a broader context and specifically in the field of foreign language instruction, elicits a multifaceted array of inquiries regarding the significance of literary language in fostering the learner's overall and communicative proficiencies. Does literature not epitomize the aesthetic culmination of language, an inherent entity germane to the realm of language instruction? Or does it not function as a linguistic crucible, a revered "language laboratory" that unveils the latent potentialities inherent within the written and spoken word, as solemnly proclaimed by Peytard and Moirand (1992)? Moreover, how can we harness the untapped potential of this literary medium in innovative and transformative ways?

THE PLACE OF LITERATURE IN FLE TEACHING

Within the realm of teaching French as a foreign language (FLE), literature assumes a paramount position of influence, boasting an undeniable and exhilarating pertinence. It stands as an esteemed conduit that grants learners privileged access, facilitating their profound immersion into the essence of the French language through a rich tapestry of literary creations. Thus, literature emerges as an instrumental force, wielding its potency to mold and refine students' linguistic acumen while concurrently fostering their intercultural competencies.

In this evocative milieu, literature unveils an inexhaustible reservoir of marvel and sentiment. Its literary opuses ensnare readers, bewitching them with their enthralling narratives, eloquent prose, and memorable protagonists. Through the integration of literature into the fabric of FLE instruction, learners are beckoned to cultivate the sheer joy of reading, embarking upon transformative journeys into realms of imagination, where the boundless wonders of the human spirit lay.

A Brief History

Throughout the course of pedagogical evolution and the advent of communicative approaches, the centrality of the literary text in the realm of teaching and learning French as a second or foreign language has remained a subject of fervent debate. However, it is worth noting that the didactic practices employed in teaching French as a mother tongue (FLM) have traditionally exhibited a conservative disposition, consistently emphasizing the significance of literary materials within language courses. From kindergarten to lycée, official guidelines unambiguously position the study of literary texts as a cornerstone of educational objectives. This stands in stark contrast to the domain of FLE, where the role of literature varies, ranging from a prominent position to a marginalized one. In certain instances, FLE methodologies develop independently from the realm of literature and occasionally even in opposition to it.

Let us delve into the annals of history, casting our gaze upon the direct method that emerged in the late 19th century. During this era, literature reigned supreme in language acquisition, with "literary texts serving as the foundation for the study of civilization" (Puren, 1988). This predominantly grammatical approach allowed foreign learners of French to forge a profound connection with one of the most illustrious civilizations of the modern world, cultivating and adorning their minds through the study of a resplendent literary language, thereby attaining true distinction (Blancpain, 1953). The primary aim was to offer a corpus of renowned authors, universally acknowledged by educational institutions and universities. In the subsequent years, commencing around 1920, the advent of active methodology brought about a subtle transformation in the treatment of literary texts. They assumed the role of foundational texts, accompanied by explanatory annotations, serving as vehicles for fundamental formative and cultural objectives.

The winds of change, propelled by shifts in public sentiment, psycho-pedagogical innovations, and philosophical theories, have exerted a decisive influence on the landscape of French language learning classes, shaping the very essence of FLE didactics. Within the framework of the structuro-global audiovisual methodology, the once-unchallenged dominion of literary texts undergoes reevaluation, as instructional materials diversify and the prominence of literary works diminishes (Puren, 1988). This method, which perceives language primarily as an oral practice, relegates literature to the periphery of FLE instruction, distancing itself from the confines of literary norms. It engenders an educational milieu wherein each student's expression is received in relation to their unique communicative objectives, liberated from the scrutiny of standardized achievements and the reductionist lens of deviance (Massacret, 1993). Consequently, we bear witness to a devaluation of the written text and literary compositions, as they are deemed inconducive to the acquisition of oral language skills.

However, with the advent of communicative approaches during the 1980s, the intrinsic value of written language as a whole experiences a renaissance. Experts advocate for the inclusion of authentic documents, recognizing the pressing need for diverse support texts. These documents proliferate indiscriminately within the language classroom, marking the resurgence of literary works, reintegrated as one among myriad authentic materials, all evaluated without prejudice (L. Collès, 1994; A. Séoud, 1997; M.C. Albert & M. Souchon, 2000; J.P. Cuq & I. Gruca, 2005). Similarly, the Common European Framework of Reference acknowledges the multifaceted educational, intellectual, linguistic, and cultural objectives of literary studies, extending beyond the realm of aesthetics alone (2001).

DIDACTIC APPROACHES TO LITERATURE

Literary Text?

According to Zine El Abidine et al (2023), "A literary text is any text that meets the criteria for literarity. These include syntax and punctuation, lexical and grammatical spelling, the relevance and richness of vocabulary, the presence of figures of speech, language register and intended function (narrative, descriptive, expressive, argumentative, injunctive, poetic). The aim of this arsenal is to create a sophisticated style woven from the aesthetic concerns of the authors to capture the reader's interest".

The Need to Integrate the Literary Text

In response to the evident challenges encountered in classroom communication, proponents of communicative approaches propose the utilization of authentic documents. However, it is crucial to recognize that these documents, as previously employed, possess a transitory nature, inherently tied to specific temporal and spatial contexts. In contrast, the authenticity intrinsic to literary works bestows upon them a distinct advantage, for they are versatile and possess a timeless quality. These texts, in their enduring relevance, not only provide a source of intellectual gratification but also serve as catalysts for dialogue, generators of tasks, and provocateurs of reactions.

Séoud astutely asserts that when an authentic document is transposed into the classroom, it inevitably relinquishes its authenticity. Conversely, the literary document stands as an entity unto itself, self-sufficient, and endowed with a polysemic nature and universal dimension, capable of resonating with individuals across time and space (Séoud, 1994). It is worth recalling that the distinguishing essence of the literary text, one that merits acknowledgement within didactics, lies in its ability to embody multiple meanings, enabling it to speak to and be spoken by all (ibid). Moreover, the symbiotic relationship between language and literature becomes apparent, as literature both emanates from and supports language (ibid). In light of these reflections, FLE didactics would greatly benefit from forsaking monolithic choices and embracing an array of text types, thereby fostering pluralistic readings.

Consequently, the notion of language divorced from literature has been called into question, prompting numerous didacticians to expound on the ways in which the integration of literature enriches educational practices. Firstly, the literary text emerges as a veritable "language laboratory," as eloquently articulated by J. Peytard (1988), wherein language not only operates but also undergoes profound transformation. This sentiment is echoed by H. Besse (1991), who emphasizes that within the literary text, language is scrutinized and manipulated to a greater extent than in any other textual form. In essence, as observed by Spitzer (1970), the truest reflection of a nation's soul lies in its literature, which serves as a testament to its language, as crafted by its most discerning wordsmiths.

In contemporary discourse, a unanimous consensus has emerged, acknowledging francophone literature as the quintessential realm wherein language and culture converge, transcending the labyrinthine corridors of history, politics, and economics—its facets both embraced and contested. It stands as the venerated domain of confluence, fostering the exchange of ideas and facilitating dialogue between language and culture. To perceive language as a vehicle for communication and cultural expression is to affirm the indispensable role of texts in the pedagogy of foreign languages, which serve multifarious educational, intellectual, moral, emotional, linguistic, and cultural objectives, extending far beyond the realms of aesthetics alone (Council of Europe, 2001). Such objectives encompass the cultivation of analytical acumen, linguistic proficiency, reading and writing prowess, literary knowledge, cultural literacy, critical thinking, the acquisition of heritage, the refinement of aesthetic sensibilities, the nurturing of pleasure, and the molding of personal identity (Reuter, 1999).

In light of their inherent richness and multivalent nature, literary texts assume a paramount role in fostering the development of learners' communicative language skills, encompassing linguistic competence, socio-linguistic acuity, and pragmatic proficiency, while also nurturing broader competencies in socio-cultural understanding, interpersonal aptitude, and intercultural consciousness. Consequently, the teaching of literary texts, as a medium of mediation, possesses the profound capacity to foster dialogue within a nation, as well as between nations, engendering authentic and fruitful intercultural exchanges amongst individuals of diverse social identities. It serves as a catalyst for acknowledging and embracing the intricate tapestry of reciprocal identities, ensuring that the intricacies and complexities of these multifaceted identities are duly recognized and celebrated (CECRL).

The Constraints of This Integration

The integration of literary texts into the realm of French as a foreign language (FLE) instruction necessitates a delicate balance, demanding a judicious and meticulous adaptation of pedagogical methodologies. While this practice bears numerous merits, it is not devoid of challenges and unique prerequisites.

In a renowned discourse, Doubrovsky (1971) boldly proclaims that "literature cannot be taught." Drawing an analogy from other disciplines, he posits that just as one emerges from a mathematics or art class with the ability to perform calculations or create drawings, attending a poetry class does not necessarily bestow the capacity to compose a single exquisite verse. Likewise, Naturel (1995) expounds upon the intricate and intricate relationship between literature and French as a foreign language, highlighting its inherent complexity.

The aspiration underlying the teaching of literary texts lies in engendering the creation of new texts, springing forth from those that have been read, offering fresh interpretations of existing works, or empowering learners to craft their own compositions in a distinctive mode. Active engagement with texts inevitably leads to writing, serving as an end in itself, and fostering the development of learners' innate creative and aesthetic talents (Sorin, 2005). Nonetheless, this disconnection arises from the profound influence of the prevailing tradition of text explanation—an imposing obstacle, according to didacticians, hindering the evolution of pedagogical thinking. It is crucial, however, to recognize that the conflation of teaching literature with its critique, or teaching literature with the mere elucidation of its texts, has led us astray. Textual explanations, while valuable in their interpretative endeavors, primarily center on the text itself, thereby bypassing and regrettably excluding all that exists beyond its confines. Consequently, the student, the learner-reader, has persistently been neglected and marginalized.

With the advent and evolution of reception theories, a transformative shift commenced, steering the course towards a more auspicious direction. At the heart of this paradigm lies the learner, occupying a paramount position within the pedagogical framework, while primacy is accorded to reading as a vehicle for the construction of meaning by the student reader. The crux of the matter resides in the demarcation between the venerable tradition of object-centered approaches and the subject-centered constructivist perspective, with an emphasis on leveraging reading as a means to attain foreign language learning objectives. However, the challenge lies in the endeavor to introduce French as a foreign language (FLE) learners to the realm of literary texts right from the inception of their linguistic journey, aiming to instill within them a profound appreciation for the literary domain and fostering a gradual enjoyment of it, thereby enabling them to unravel the conveyed message.

Literary texts, often perceived as formidable instruments to wield within the FLE classroom, particularly at elementary and intermediate levels, present a multitude of difficulties. These hurdles encompass linguistic intricacies, manifested through lexical density and syntactic complexity, as well as cultural intricacies, where the presence of culturally implicit elements within a text poses a formidable barrier for foreign learners to penetrate. Furthermore, conceptual challenges arise when confronted with texts that delve into intricate and profound ideas.

Notwithstanding these constraints, the integration of literary texts into FLE instruction persists as a valuable conduit, enriching the acquisition of the French language and its accompanying culture. By adeptly adapting literary works to suit the needs and proficiency levels of learners, offering a diverse range of pedagogical activities, and providing support in comprehending and interpreting texts, it becomes feasible to surmount these challenges and fully harvest the benefits that literature bestows upon the teaching of FLE.

NEW PERSPECTIVES

Use of ICTE in the Language Classroom

Within the realm of language pedagogy, specifically pertaining to the teaching of French, the advent of Information and Communication Technologies in Education (ICTE) ushers forth novel instructional tools, fostering an environment conducive to playful activities that facilitate practice, kindle learners' motivation, and stimulate interaction. In this era, as affirmed by Zine El Abidine et al (2022), the relentless march of technological progress renders it inconceivable for students to remain passive spectators before screens. Scholars such as Perrenoud (1998) and Karsenti et al. (2002) further endorse the notion that these emerging technologies contribute to the implementation of alternative methodologies, thereby paving the way for self-directed learning through multimedia applications, communication techniques, and information production and dissemination. Consequently, they play a pivotal role in fostering an enhanced rapport with knowledge.

Adopting a systemic perspective, and cognizant of the paramount significance of digital technology in the realm of teaching French as a foreign language (FLE), information and communication technologies assume a position of profound importance. Their integration is not a mere indulgence or passing trend ; rather, it stands as an imperative, a necessity that demands the embrace of both educators and learners alike, ultimately yielding substantial savings in time and effort. These technologies undeniably represent a momentous opportunity, as they not only provide innovative means for the transmission of knowledge but also facilitate the exploration of learning strategies that foster the evolution of teaching practices and the reinforcement, if not the construction, of essential skills. In this regard, H. Knoerr (2005) astutely observes that the utilization of ICTE engenders a more positive attitude towards learning and fosters greater collaboration among the various stakeholders: the educational institution, the family, and the wider community.

It is imperative to bear in mind that the action-oriented approach is grounded in a constructivist and socio-cognitive understanding of learning, positing that learners must enhance their cognitive capabilities to autonomously construct knowledge. Within this framework, it is crucial to underscore that ICTE aligns itself with these two perspectives, as it encourages learners to embrace a novel modality of knowledge and skill acquisition. Notably, ICTE kindles their curiosity and motivation, engendering a shift towards co-constructing knowledge through interactive exchanges with their peers, while fostering reflection and refining their own productions. Thus, in accordance with ICTE and the action-oriented viewpoint, the learner assumes an active role within their learning environment, engaging in the co-construction of knowledge alongside other members of their educational and social community, encompassing teachers, classmates, and friends. The vast array of online tools at their disposal serves as instrumental means or scaffolds for the realization of concrete tasks.

In Morocco, as stipulated in official documents, learners are expected, upon completion of the qualifying secondary cycle, to "generate appropriate utterances in communication situations and engage in creative and personal writing" (Orientations pédagogiques et programmes spécifiques de l'enseignement de la langue française au second cycle qualifiant, 2007, p. 4). This signifies that students are called upon to cultivate skills by mobilizing linguistic and social resources within the target language, in response to contextualized communication scenarios. Our objective lies in accentuating the added value of integrating ICTE into the pedagogical practices of French as a foreign language classes in Moroccan secondary schools. Indeed, for teachers to assist learners in mastering these skills, they are tasked with crafting a deliberate and well-structured progression that harmonizes objectives, teaching materials, and pedagogical methodologies. To accomplish this feat, it is preferable to embrace innovative modalities, notably the utilization of emerging information and communication technologies.

The "TriSociale" Approach, a New Lease of Life

Set your sights high to find your true mark. The trajectory that literary education must embrace, including within the realm of FLE, finds its foundation in reception theories and the resplendent marvel of reading extolled by Proust. It is through this wondrous phenomenon that the full spectrum of objectives in foreign language acquisition can be attained, encompassing not only linguistic proficiency but also the cultivation of one's character and beyond. The act of active-productive reading engenders a fertile ground for the blossoming of learner and reader alike, stimulating their imagination, interpretation, and creative output, while nurturing the development of critical thinking skills and fostering affective and emotional engagement. In light of this, we must relinquish the confines of a traditional, linguistically centered lens through which literary texts have been viewed, in favor of embracing "the task [...] that most closely resembles the social action for which we want to prepare students" (Puren, 2009). The ultimate aim is to equip students with the capacity to become active citizens in the future, by empowering them to assume the role of active citizens within the micro-society of the classroom itself and by encouraging them to engage in meaningful actions within the broader society beyond its walls (ibid).

From this perspective, the reader now assumes a central position within the realm of literary education, aligning harmoniously with the action-oriented approach that places the learner as the protagonist of their educational journey. Thus, the pedagogical approach to cultivating comprehension of literary works necessitates guiding students through pivotal junctures, enabling them to grasp how each narrative component contributes to the construction of meaning. This process demands patience and forbearance, eschewing the hasty imposition of a prescriptive questionnaire. Instead, a carefully calibrated interplay of questions and answers should be employed to foster focused attention on the guiding threads that weave the tapestry of meaning.

Figure 1. A new process for teaching literary texts
Source: Zine El Abidine et al. (2023)

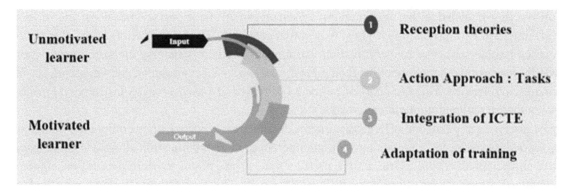

The meticulous and discerning selection of literary texts for inclusion in the FLE classroom stands as a pivotal matter that educational institutions must approach with utmost care. Several pertinent queries arise, demanding thoughtful contemplation: Does the chosen text possess themes likely to captivate and engross learners? Can learners decipher the implicit and concealed communicative intentions embedded within the literary artifact to be explored? If a text proves exceedingly arduous, prudence dictates its exclusion from the FLE classroom. Instead, an alternative text, one that is more accessible and accommodating to learners' interests and proficiency levels, can be judiciously chosen. The teacher wields the authority to elect the literary text to be employed, further adapting it to suit the learners' age, linguistic aptitude, personal inclinations, as well as considering the inherent motivational appeal of the text itself and the objectives to be attained. And in delving into the realm of the teacher, it is inevitable to expound upon the paramount importance of the quality of training that aspiring educators ought to receive, particularly in the realm of literature.

The artful adaptation of literary masterpieces for didactic purposes within the language classroom, achieved through the gradual cultivation of learner autonomy in the realm of reading, holds great validity in light of the modern approaches influenced by the integration of information and communication technologies in education (ICTE). This pedagogical undertaking finds resonance with the tenets of the action-oriented perspective, wherein autonomy and individualization emerge as focal points of convergence that we must exploit to enhance the caliber of FLE instruction and learning. "From this vantage point, we can perceive adaptive e-learning as an instrumentality for this endeavor, a veritable boon bestowed upon our field" (ibid). "The crux of the matter lies in comprehending the learner's behavior and proffering content tailored to their unique needs. To achieve this, the process of adaptation must duly account for the learner's evolving profile throughout the course of their educational journey" (Zine El Abidine et al., 2022). By incorporating adaptive e-learning within the FLE classroom, we gain the ability to flexibly modulate the difficulty of activities, tasks, and even the literary texts themselves, ensuring a dynamic and responsive learning experience.

By embracing the precepts of the action-oriented approach, which positions the learner as a "social actor" within the educational landscape, the utilization of information and communication technologies (ICT), with their inherent social function, paves the way for the establishment of social and interactive tasks aimed at comprehending the literary text in its multifaceted social dimension. Such tasks encompass a rich tapestry of endeavors, including online reading reviews, spirited debates, immersive role-playing,

Figure 2. TriSocial" approach
Source: Zine El Abidine et al. (2023)

the cultivation of creative writing, dynamic simulations, as well as individual or collaborative projects. It is within this realm of social interplay that the triumvirate of literature, the action-oriented approach, and ICTE find a harmonious convergence, entailing the quintessence of success in this novel perspective on the didactics of literature in the pedagogical realm of French as a foreign language. This heralds a novel "TriSocial" approach, hinging upon the amalgamation of social dynamics to achieve the desired objectives, thereby emancipating the literary text from its enduring predicaments, liberating it from its chronic malaise (ibid).

CONVERGENCE OF THE PILLARS OF THE "TRISOCIAL" APPROACH

Action-Oriented Approach and ICTE

Within the realm of educational endeavors, the Common European Framework of Reference for Languages assumes a paramount role in instructing the French language. At its core, this framework advocates for the Action Perspective, recognizing the learner as an active participant in their own educational journey, as well as a social agent who navigates and influences their surroundings. The learner undertakes tasks that extend beyond the confines of mere linguistic exercises, operating within specific circumstances and environments, encompassing distinct domains of action (CEFR, 2000, p. 15). Concurrently, educational institutions are increasingly inclined to integrate and harness the potential of Information and Communication Technologies (ICT) within the language teaching and learning process. In this regard, mediatization emerges as a favored and endorsed solution, fostering the development of novel pedagogical modalities. A study conducted by Catroux (2006) expounds on the profound interplay between the emergent action-oriented perspective and the authentic potential embedded within available ICTE, wherein the responsibility of social actors becomes fundamentally engaged.

According to Christian Puren (2009), the utilization of Information and Communication Technologies (ICT) facilitates a transition from mere communication to a state of co-action. More specifically, the advent of Web 2.0, with its inherent social and interactive nature, seamlessly integrates into educational activities, harnessing its "authentic" immediacy within the educational framework. These technologies serve as a pivotal element, enabling the accomplishment of pedagogically oriented tasks or activities, grounded in the genuine social and interactive dynamics that mirror the classroom environment. A compelling illustration of this phenomenon can be found in the captivating experience of Cultura, wherein French and American students are brought together through a dedicated platform. Through tasks centered around film excerpts, news items, proverbs, and surveys that embody each other's cultures, students engage in hypothesizing about the cultural values of both nations. In doing so, they cultivate the ability to modify linguistic and cultural representations associated with the two languages, while simultaneously refining their understanding of the other's culture and honing their reading and listening comprehension skills (Furstenberg et al., 2001). Consequently, learners are now equipped to develop their language proficiency utilizing technological tools such as Internet chats, blogs, and other technological devices beyond the confines of the classroom. The contemporary learner occupies a markedly distinct position from their predecessors, as the focus has shifted from rote memorization to the active construction of meaning through their own agency.

As functional devices continue to evolve, so too have the theories of learning experienced transformation. Initially, the application of Information and Communication Technologies in Education (ICTE) found its roots in behaviorism, wherein stimulus-response activities were proposed. However, constructivism emerged as a paradigm that seamlessly intertwined with ICTs, as learners were no longer expected to passively memorize knowledge but rather to autonomously construct it. Linard (1996) aptly characterizes constructivism as "the humanist version of the computer," while Legros and Crinon (2002) emphasize the resurgence of constructivist theories as the cornerstone for developing ICT-enabled environments and propelling their integration within the classroom. In light of this, current trends lean towards a more independent approach to technology utilization, encompassing its application across diverse contexts, situations, and complex tasks.

Within the realm of teaching and learning French as a foreign language (FLE), these developments can also be attributed to the advent of the action-oriented perspective, rooted in the notion of tasks. In parallel, Puren asserts that in the present era, characterized by the proliferation of Web 2.0, learner-users are not only able to interact with webpage content but also engage in co-action with one another. The availability of collaborative tools and environments empowers educators to design tasks that transcend occasional exchanges, fostering sustained and collaborative endeavors. Thus, the landscape of learning has been reshaped, offering fertile ground for long-term joint work and collective engagement.

In brief, when juxtaposed with preceding educational systems, the contemporary pedagogical triad assumes a markedly distinct form, primarily attributable to the ascendancy of constructivism and cognitivism. These influential theories have engendered a profound transformation in the perception of learners. No longer relegated to the role of passive observers of information, learners now embrace their agency as active protagonists in their own educational odyssey.

Literature and the Action Approach

The pedagogical incorporation of literature within the action-oriented approach epitomizes a profound educational methodology that accentuates the practical and utilitarian utilization of language, placing learners at the epicenter of their own educational expedition. This approach endeavors to cultivate students' communicative aptitude while simultaneously enabling them to actively explore and foster an appreciation for the realm of literature.

The action-oriented approach impels learners to employ the target language in the execution of tangible and meaningful tasks, directing their focus towards genuine communicative objectives. In the context of teaching literature, this signifies that students transcend the role of mere passive recipients of literary texts, assuming the mantle of engaged actors who dynamically interact with the artistic tapestry of literary works.

Outlined below are key tenets underpinning the teaching of literature within the action-oriented approach:

- Authentic literary tasks: Educators can meticulously devise authentic tasks grounded in literary texts, spanning the gamut from group discussions, debates, presentations, re-enactments, artistic creations, to theatrical adaptations. These tasks offer students a platform to hone their language skills while actively engaging with the manifold dimensions of literary masterpieces.
- Interaction and collaboration: The action-oriented approach fosters an ethos of exchange and collaboration among learners. Students can collaboratively analyze, discuss, and interpret literary texts within group settings. Moreover, they can partake in co-creative endeavors, where they are encouraged to produce their own written compositions inspired by the literary works under study.
- Integration of skills: The teaching of literature within the action-oriented approach seamlessly amalgamates the diverse strands of language skills—namely, oral and written comprehension, as well as oral and written expression—within a holistic framework. Students are invited to read, listen, speak, and write, employing the target language in real-life contexts intricately linked to the realm of literature.
- Cultural contextualization: The action-oriented approach accords paramount importance to the cultural tapestry interwoven within literary works. Educators can prompt students to delve into the cultural facets ingrained within such texts, encompassing values, norms, traditions, customs, and social perspectives. This enables students to forge a profound understanding of the cultural milieu associated with the target language.
- Critical thinking: Teaching literature within the action-oriented approach nurtures and stimulates critical thinking, inviting students to delve into the depths of literary texts, interpret their meanings, articulate their opinions, substantiate their arguments, and refine their capacity for discerning analysis.

Puren (2012) expounds upon two distinct actional perspectives: the weak perspective and the strong perspective. The former revolves around literature as a conduit for ancillary activities within the scholastic milieu, mobilizing students around literary texts. Puren provides illustrative examples, including inquiries posed by pupils regarding a text, the comprehensive reading of a literary work, the division of text segments among groups, students' freedom to select works and organize their own reading programs, the study of a work accompanied by direct contact with the author, writing workshops, imaginative re-writes encompassing alterations of genre, point of view, and scenario, collaborative writing endeavors, creative writing ventures, theatrical performances, and an array of pedagogical projects. These actions are driven by purpose, although they lack the authentic essence embodied by the strong perspective.

The more recent action-oriented perspective, the strong perspective, entails the creation of social actions through texts—actions that transcend the confines of the classroom and resonate with society at large. Under this paradigm, students transcend the role of mere readers, assuming the mantle of agents within the social realm of literature. The projects that emerge from this perspective are inherently editorial, journalistic, or socio-cultural in nature. They encompass activities such as penning reviews for newspapers, magazines, radio, television, publishers' websites, or blogs; crafting press reviews; organizing launch campaigns; conducting interviews with authors and literary critics; orchestrating public debates; arranging literary prizes; curating "literature/poetry/novel/theater festivals"; and engaging in professional and editorial translation endeavors. In essence, Puren delineates two distinct categories of action tasks: those that mobilize students around literary works, constituting pedagogical projects, and those that empower students to act through literary texts, manifesting as social projects.

By seamlessly integrating the teaching of literature within the action-oriented approach, educators can elicit students' interest, foster their commitment, and concurrently cultivate their language proficiency and appreciation for the realm of literature. This approach empowers students to assume an active and reflective role in the learning process, while expanding their comprehension of language and enriching their literary-cultural acumen.

Literature and ICTE

The essence of text has become inextricably intertwined with its technical milieu, as it inevitably becomes entangled with the media that occupies its realm. Consequently, literature transcends its traditional confinement within the pages of books, as a new form of "literature" emerges, accessible only through the electronic realm and reliant upon the medium of information technology for its very existence.

Multiple scholarly investigations, including the works of Détrez (2011) and Donnat (2012), shed light on the diminishing engagement of young individuals with literary works, a practice that now struggles to compete against the allure of digital leisure pursuits (Donnat, 2009). In the face of this evolving landscape and the transformative dynamics governing knowledge acquisition and transmission, it becomes imperative to foster innovative pedagogical approaches that effectively address the educational challenges posed by the digital society.

Digital literature, referred to by various appellations such as "computer literature," "electronic literature," "e-literature," or "cyberliterature," as outlined by Bouchardon et al. (2007), encompasses literary practices that find their genesis within the realm of digital devices. It is a form of literature that resists being confined to the printed page, as doing so would result in the forfeiture of its defining characteristics, its raison d'être, as elucidated by Bouchardon et al. (2007). Thus, the digital literary artifact is conceived and crafted in tandem with the digital domain, where the digitality permeates not only the object itself but also the medium through which it is consumed.

Digital literature, or as Saemmer (2015) terms it, "digital text," can manifest in narrative or poetic forms, leveraging the distinctive properties inherent to the digital medium, as expounded upon by Bootz et al. (2003). It diverges notably from digitized text, which merely transposes a preexisting paper-based text into digital format, as emphasized by Bouchardon et al. (2007) and Souchier et al. (2003). Moreover, it stands apart from augmented text, which originates from a paper-based source but incorporates enrichments made possible by the digital realm, as explicated by Saemmer (2015).

The experimental essence permeating this form of literature, intricately entwined with the realm of technology rather than the erudite domain traditionally associated with print literature, engenders a certain resistance among literary critics. Consequently, there is a tendency, for instance, to disavow its classification as "literature" (Saemmer, 2017). Furthermore, conventional analytical tools often prove inadequate for comprehending this literary form, given that its constituent characteristics diverge fundamentally from those of print literature.

Indeed, while digital literature frequently encompasses a significant textual dimension, the presence of other semiotic modes such as images, sounds, animations, and more, necessitates the adoption of a more encompassing term that encompasses the artistic and multimodal aspects of these works (Lacelle et al., 2017), in conjunction with their digital essence. As digital literary works inherently embody a multi-semiotic nature, they are grounded in the concept of hybridity. Within a single work, texts, illustrations, photographs, music, videos, and animations coexist, either simultaneously or in a linear progression, fostering interaction with the reader as the narrative unfolds. This interactive dimension, in turn, entices the reader to manipulate the work on the screen, forging a personalized reading path.

Given these distinctive attributes, engaging with digital literature demands a profound commitment on the part of the reader. The reader is called upon to navigate a text that is simultaneously legible, visible, and manipulable, while crafting interpretive hypotheses in the face of reading experiences that remain perpetually suspended, oscillating between coherence and decoherence, affirming and challenging one's expectations (Saemmer, 2015).

Impact of ICTE on the Teaching of Literature

The proliferation of diverse technological mediums and the perpetual advancement of novel social communication tools have engendered unforeseen repercussions on the pedagogy of language-cultures. Within this milieu, C. Puren (2004) posits, "It becomes evident to me that the present juncture, marked by the convergence of language-culture pedagogy and emerging educational technologies, corresponds to one of those tumultuous epochs where new harmonies shall inevitably arise, eluding our current endeavors and prognostications."

On one hand, the integration of information and communication technologies (ICT) in the realm of literary instruction not only facilitates the modernization of literary approaches but, more importantly, emancipates literature from the confines of institutional rigidity. Indeed, the utilization of tools that foster discussion and collaborative work, such as blogs, situates students at the epicenter of their literary education, mirroring the emphasis placed on language acquisition. Students find themselves engaged in literary discourse, exchanging diverse perspectives, and endeavoring to forge connections among literary texts, information retrieval, and the construction of meaning.

Information and Communication Technologies (ICT) serve as invaluable aids for both language-culture learners and educators, granting them access to a wide array of literary resources. Online libraries, multimedia documents encompassing textual, video, and audio formats, and an assortment of literary texts are readily available through these digital means. Moreover, ICT enables the creation of exercises employing literary texts as supportive material, all while enhancing the allure of learning through diversified tools and mediums. Software designed to rectify language errors, visually captivating images, and engaging videos contribute to the enrichment of learners' memory, thereby affording individuals with learning disabilities an enhanced opportunity for autonomy, triumph, and a bolstered sense of self-assurance.

To foster these profound benefits, teachers must meticulously devise their instructional sequences, taking full cognizance of the potential offered by these novel tools. They must not only integrate their usage within the framework of learning objectives but also cultivate novel proficiencies in their students.

By prompting learners to reflect upon the impact of employing new media, teachers empower them to contemplate the implications for their relationship with information and knowledge. Furthermore, they facilitate constructive exchanges among peers via social networks, encouraging a collaborative approach to writing and reading. Through this exploration, students gain insight into the evolving roles of readers and authors, as well as the transformative influence of digitized media on cognition, self-expression, and behavior.

These exemplifications poignantly underscore the tangible value added by digital tools, fostering access to culture, forging connections between the educational institution and its broader environment, bridging in-school and out-of-school experiences, enabling the diversification of pedagogical scenarios, nurturing writing and linguistic proficiency, and reigniting students' enthusiasm for engaging with literary endeavors.

CONCLUSION

We maintain that Information and Communication Technologies in Education (ICTE) present highly valuable tools for language instruction and acquisition, but their efficacy can only be realized when we possess the requisite competencies to seamlessly integrate them into our didactic framework. It is imperative to seize upon their existence and multifaceted nature, harnessing their potential through astute pedagogical and technological choices, and subsequently acquiring the proficiency to craft interactive online content. Our objective resides in effectuating a genuine integration of ICTE within the domain of literature instruction, specifically in the realm of French language pedagogy, a feat that can only be accomplished when these technologies are effectively harnessed to serve the purpose of learning.

In undertaking this undertaking, it becomes evident that success in teaching and learning literature necessitates concerted efforts on the part of both learners and educators, irrespective of the prevailing social milieu. Literature has the capacity to transcend boundaries and become a meeting ground for inquisitive minds yearning for enrichment, personal growth, and the discovery of the profound harmony that literature so magnanimously bestows.

REFERENCES

Albert, M.C. & Souchon, M. (2000). *Les textes littéraires en classe de langue.* Hachette.

Besse, H. (1991). Comment utiliser la littérature dans l'enseignement du français langue étrangère. *Ici et là,, 20,* 51-55.

Blancpain M. (1953). Préface. In Mauger G., (ed.), *Cours de langue et de civilisation françaises I* (pp. V–VI). Hachette.

Bootz, P., Gherban, A., & Papp, T. (2003). *Transitoire observable: texte fondateur.* Transitoire Observable.

Bouchardon, S. (dir.), Broudoux, E., Deseilligny, O. & Ghitalla, F. (2007). *Un laboratoire de littératures: littérature numérique et Internet.* Bibliothèque publique d'information.

Catroux, M. (2006). *Perspective co-actionnelle et tice: quelles convergences pour l'enseignement de la langue de spécialité?* Langues Vivantes. http://www.langues-vivantes.u-bordeaux2.fr/frsa/pdf/CA-TROUX.pdf

Puren, C. (1999). De l'approche communicative à la perspective actionnelle. *Contact+, 44*, 50-54.

Colles, L. (1994). *Littérature comparée et reconnaissance interculturelle.* De Boeck-Duculot.

Conseil De L'europe. (2001). *Cadre européen commun de référence pour les langues: apprendre, enseigner, évaluer.* Didier.

Conseil De L'europe. (2001). *Un cadre européen commun de référence pour les langues: apprendre, enseigner, évaluer.* Didier.

Cuq J.-P. & Gruca I. (2005). Cours de didactique du français langue étrangère et seconde, (2e éd). Grenoble, PUG.

Détrez, C. (2011). Les adolescents et la lecture, quinze ans après. *Bulletin des bibliothèques de France, 5*, 32-35. https://bbf.enssib.fr/consulter/bbf-2011-05-0032-005.pdf

Donnat, O. (2009). Les pratiques culturelles des Français à l'ère numérique: éléments de synthèse 1997-2008. *Culture études, 5*(5), 1-12. doi:10.3917/cule.095.0001

Donnat, O. (2012). La lecture régulière de livres: un recul ancien et général. *Le Débat, 170*(3), 42 51. doi:10.3917/deba.170.0042

Doubrovsky S. & Todorov T. (dir.). (1971). *L'Enseignement de la littérature.* Centre culturel de Cerisy-la-salle, Paris, Plon.

Furstenberg. G., Levet, S. & Maillet, K. (2001). Giving a virtual voice to the silent language of culture: the Cultura project. Language Learning and Technology Journal, 5(1), 55-102.

Karsenti, T., Peraya, D., & Viens, J. (2004). Conclusion: Bilan et prospectives de la recherche sur la formation des maîtres à l'intégration pédagogique des TIC. *Revue des Sciences de l'Education, 28*(2), 459–470. doi:10.7202/007363ar

Knoerr, H. (2005). TIC et motivation en apprentissage/enseignement des langues. Une perspective canadienne. *Cahiers de l'APLIUT, XXIV*(3), 53–73. doi:10.4000/apliut.2889

Lacelle, N., Boutin, J.-F., & Lebrun, M. (2017). *La littératie médiatique multimodale appliquée en contexte numérique - LMM@: outils conceptuels et didactiques.* Presses de l'Université du Québec.

Legros. D. & Crinon, J. (dir.). (2002). Psychologie des apprentissages et multimédia. Paris: Armand Colin.

Linard, M. (1996). Des machines et des hommes. Paris: L'Harmattan.

Massacret, M. (1993). Français, langue maternelle, langue étrangère: une double culture? *L'Ecole des lettres, 9* (mars), 17-24.

Mohammed, Z. E. A., Amel, N., & Mohamed, K. (2022). Reflection on E-Learning and Adaptability in the Teaching and Learning of French as Foreign Language. *RA Journal Of Applied Research, 8*(5), 408–411. doi:10.47191/rajar/v8i5.17

Mohammed, Z. E. A., Amel, N., & Mohamed, K. (2023). *Literature and the Teaching of French as a Foreign Language in Morocco: Rethinking the importance of the literary text using new approaches.*

Naturel, M. (1995). *Pour la littérature: de l'extrait à l'oeuvre.* FeniXX.

Peytard J. (1988). Des usages de la littérature en classe de langue. *Le Français dans le monde, Littérature et enseignement, la Perspective du lecteur,* 8-17.

Peytard, J. & Moirand, S. (1992). Discours et enseignement du français. Les lieux d'une rencontre, Paris, Hachette.

Puren, C. (2012). *Perspectives actionnelles sur la littérature dans l'enseignement scolaire et universitaire des langues-cultures: des tâches scolaires sur les textes aux actions sociales par les textes.* Christian Puren. https://www.christianpuren.com/mestravaux/2012d/

Puren, C. (2009). Nouvelle perspective actionnelle et (nouvelles) technologies éducatives: Quelles convergences... et quelles divergences? *Cyber-Langues.* http://www.aplvlanguesmodernes.org/spip.php?article2673

Puren, C. (1988). *Histoire des méthodologies de l'enseignement des langues.* Nathan - Clé International.

Puren, C. (2004). Quels modèles didactiques pour la conception de dispositifs d'enseignement/apprentissage en environnement numérique? In Études de linguistique appliquée, 134.

Reuter Y. (1999). L'Enseignement de la littérature en question. *Enjeux,* (43), 191–203.

Saemmer, A. (2015). *Rhétorique du texte numérique: figures de la lecture, anticipations de pratiques.* Presses de l'Enssib. doi:10.4000/books.pressesenssib.3870

Saemmer, A. (2017). Interpréter l'hyperlien en contexte pédagogique: éléments d'une sémiotique sociale. *Le français aujourd'hui, 196*(1), 25-34.

Séoud, A. (1994, January-March). « Document authentique ou texte littéraire », Littérature et cultures en situation didactique. *ELA,* (93), 8–24.

Seoud, A. (1997). *Pour une didactique de la littérature, Paris.* Hatier-Didier, (LAL).

Sorin, N. (2005). Vers une didactique de l'écriture littéraire du récit de fiction au primaire. Nouveaux cahiers de la recherche en éducation, 65-78.

Souchier, E., Jeanneret, Y. et Le Marec, J. (dir.). (2003). *Lire, écrire, récrire.* Bibliothèque publique d'information.

Spitzer, L. (1970). *Etudes de style.* Gallimard.

Chapter 16

The Axiological Dimension in the Study of Literary Works in the Qualifying Cycle Between Possibility and Difficulties of Implementation

Chafik Azirar

https://orcid.org/0009-0001-3966-9903

ENS, Abdelmalek Essaadi University, Morocco

ABSTRACT

According to the Pedagogical Guidelines (July 2007) for qualifying secondary education, the teaching of the French language is done through three inputs: entry through skills, actional entry, and entry through values. While the first and second entries are of particular interest, the third remains vague insofar as its field of investigation is thorny and impossible to define in terms of didactic implementation. The aim of this chapter is to highlight the various reasons justifying the didactic and docimological ambiguities regarding the implementation of the axiological dimension in the study of literary works programmed in the qualifying cycle, in particular, on a theoretical basis and according to a sample collected and analysed from 50 French-language teachers.

INTRODUCTION

Learning to coexist in an increasingly globalized environment such as ours requires the acquisition of skills and values that enable all human beings to live in a context strongly marked by linguistic and cultural diversity. This diversity is no longer just a feature of societies that we once considered distant, it is now part of our daily lives as our own lives are permeated by what is other and different. This phenomenon is due, on the one hand, to the growing predominance of new information technologies, which allow us to come into contact with worlds of different cultures and languages, and, on the other hand, to

DOI: 10.4018/979-8-3693-3128-6.ch016

Copyright © 2024, IGI Global. Copying or distributing in print or electronic forms without written permission of IGI Global is prohibited.

the increasing population displacement of individuals from regions and countries other than our own. Schools, in the generic sense, must therefore take up a real challenge in this new context. To prepare us to coexist with what is different, the Moroccan curriculum, which is part of the reform initiated in 1999, should allow, in the first place, the acquisition of different social skills that will lead everyone to recognize, respect and appreciate this diversity that is necessary today more than ever. Our students should learn to accept the fact that linguistic and cultural heterogeneity is not only a reality, but also, and above all, an inherent characteristic of the human race. Indeed, human beings are by nature different, we are bearers of specific and different cultures, we read the world in a particular way and in accordance with the vision that we have assimilated from the moment we have learned to be part of our family and community. We learn in a particular way and communicate in an equally particular language or dialect that denotes our filiation and our belonging to a historical and social group with particular values. As a result, the question of values remains a vast and fertile field for both social and pedagogical exploitation.

It is in this perspective that the present chapter is inscribed, in which we intend first to highlight the importance and difficulties of teaching through values from a general point of view and then from the official texts that govern the teaching-learning process in Morocco. This first phase of our approach will lead us to a much more empirical analysis in which we intend to experiment the axiological approach with practicing teachers and which will allow us to demonstrate how problematic the axiological approach is in teaching and how urgent it is to make devices, both didactic and pedagogical, available to them in order toto improve the notion of values-based learning in the teaching of languages, in particular French and, in particular, in the complete works studied in the qualifying cycle.

THE CONCEPT OF VALUES AND THE PRINCIPLE OF EDUCABILITY

This work, in its theoretical framework, addresses the notion of value as an undeniably founding element in the official texts that justify the teaching-learning process declined in terms of knowledge, know-how and interpersonal skills, particularly at the level of the integration of integral works at the level of the qualifying cycle.

The Concept and Definition of Values

Living in society requires an agreement that makes it necessary to have values, which are standardized elements that can be identified by the individual. Individual behaviour that does not take into account the values of a society would be considered individualism or deviance from the point of view of its society. As a result, "values-based entry" corresponds to the school's action of moving from the values that characterize society to their operationalization through the proposed teaching content. However, the concept of values requires meanings that are both diverse and complex depending on the fields of knowledge it invokes. What makes a value a value? The fact that it appears as a foundation for thought (the true), a reference point for taste (the beautiful), an ethical principle (the good). It is therefore a criterion for intellectual, ethical, and aesthetic judgment. For some, values are anchored in a transcendent, rational, universal, intangible absolute. For others, they are evolutionary, sociologically and psychologically relative and subjective. It's not that simple to name the values. They are often implicit and constantly finalize our actions. Obvious to everyone, so rarely explained. As soon as you think about it, everything becomes blurred: politeness, or hypocrisy? Is health a value (e.g. the right to health) or a de facto biological state?

Is trust a value or a psychological process? Is listening a value or a behavioral indicator of respect? In short, values are not easy to define, especially since they involve several fields of knowledge. According to him, "every society necessarily needs a certain number of values that shape and justify its ways of thinking, acting and feeling". To the question of why values exist in any society, Kluckhohn replies: "Because social life would be impossible without them. The functioning of the social system as a whole would be thwarted in the attainment of collective goals." As a result, we see that values (Kluckhohn, 1961)and social actions are linked. Values are then an essential element of social functioning, as they drive action and channel motivational forces in the individual to direct them towards the achievement of goals. In the context of a psychosociological approach to values, Rokesch (1973) proposes a definition of values that has been taken up and translated by several researchers. According to him, "a value is an enduring belief, a specific mode of behavior or purpose of existence that is personally or socially preferable to another opposite or converging mode or purpose of existence." Values are organized into hierarchical systems, after having been integrated by individuals. They are then "prioritized" in relation to each other. Ultimately, value systems have the property of being relatively stable over time, even if rearrangements are always possible due to cultural and societal changes. To the previous definitions of the notion of value, by Kluckhohn and Rockeach. Shalom Schwartz adds another: "Values [he says] correspond to beliefs related to affects that, across a diversity of contexts, motivate action and guide the evaluation of the actions of others, policies, people, and events." regardless of the crops studied. (SCHWARTZ, 2006)

Values and the Principle of Educability

Human beings in general, and pupils in particular, are essentially educable, since they live within a specific social group which operates, through education, a particularizing modelling. From this perspective,, defines education as "a methodical socialization of the younger generation." The object of this action exercised by adults on the younger ones is to bring about and develop a certain number of physical, intellectual and moral states which are demanded in a general way by political society and, more specifically, by the special environment to which each is particularly destined. (Émile, 1977)

Values and Ideology

Values run through all education systems and disciplines. However, each system makes specific axiological choices emanating from the ideological system on which it is founded. As a result, the approach to the question of values necessarily invokes the concept of ideology, which is generally considered as a predefined system of ideas, which are also called categories and on the basis of which reality is analyzed, as opposed to an intuitive knowledge of perceived sensible reality. Systems considered ideological exist in the political, social, economic, cultural and religious spheres. An ideology often appeals to the cultural dimension of a social institution or a system of power. It is thus typically imposed by authority, by indoctrination (in the case of teaching, for example) or imperceptibly in everyday life (in the family, in the media, etc.). An ideology may be dominant and pervasive, but it is usually invisible to the person who shares it, by the very fact that this ideology founds and shapes the perception of the world. First of all, it has a cognitive dimension corresponding to the set of dogmas and beliefs that determine what is true in a given society. Moreover, its normative dimension is equivalent to the set of prescriptions to be respected in life in society. Finally, the values that define what is good and what is not within a social group correspond to the moral dimension of ideology.

Sociological Values and Requirements

If Emile Durkheim attaches great importance to the social being, with a tendency to reduce education to its strictly social dimension, it will certainly be futile not to look at the legitimacy of values in relation to social demands. Each individual is part of a specific set of groups within a given society, and each type of people therefore has its own education. The result, first of all, according to the sociologist of education, is "the impossibility of giving a relativistic education, since it is not really possible to produce a cultured man who would be the native of all cultures." Education is, in fact, necessarily particularizing. We could then say that each person, as a social being, is only the child of his time and his environment. Secondly, it follows that the entry into education by values is necessarily arbitrary. All pedagogical action is the imposition and inculcation of an axiological arbitrariness, since in addition to the arbitrariness of the imposed content (set of meanings, dispositions and values inculcated) there is the arbitrariness of the modalities of inculcation (forms taken by pedagogical work, behaviour and procedures). The arbitrariness of the axiological content follows immediately from the plurality of social groups and cultures peculiar to them. It does not seem possible, it seems, simply because of this plurality, to link one or other of the cultures more particularly to a universal principle from which it could be deduced. None has an absolute value, and each axiological system is only a particular variation within the set of possible cultures. Educational action is "normosing" because it provides the norms, the rules, the guiding ideas, the models of functioning, without which the individual - the pupil - uneducated could not live the life of a human being. But it is also "normalizing" because educational action contains norms whose arbitrary nature makes them fundamentally questionable. (Bourdieu, 1970)

As a result, the problem of social demands in values education across the different teaching disciplines is far from being a false problem, but it is difficult to solve. If everything is legitimate, nothing is truly legitimate, and there is no longer a boundary between the "normosing" and the "normalizing". Attempting to reintroduce it cannot be done without incurring the reproach of falling into ideology. It is now necessary to ensure that education is plural, not according to individuals, in order to adapt to their characteristics, but according to the requirements of social groups. Only mediation, that of the educational environment, can make the action of the former effective on the latter. It should also be emphasized that the domain of values in education and teaching varies its meanings indefinitely, according to social and axiological perspectives. There is an infinite field of means or obstacles that regulate and regulate conduct. In him, the freedom of the individual constantly chooses the universe it postulates or the one it rejects. Every course of action leads to values, every value has a choice, and every choice is a world project or a world in the making. At this point in the analysis, the philosopher Joseph Combès indicates (1967) that the reality of value depends neither on the subject nor on the object; it belongs to the indissoluble system of activity aiming at an ideal through a form: "Man, unlike the animal, objectifies his environment and establishes a multitude of relationships which are judgments of all kinds. These allow him to use everything in a rational way. In doing so, man organizes his axiological universe. He invests it in the infinitely supple play of his freedom." Thus, in order to give more importance to the notion of values in the field of education, several education systems have undergone in-depth reforms in recent years. These reforms, as noted by a Quebecois researcher in education sciences in relation to curriculum training, "have as their main raison d'être to substantially modify both the modes of training with a view to professionalization and the teaching curriculum, with the hope that they will give rise to profoundly renewed practices on the part of teachers, [...] to foster learning that is more in line with social needs and expectations." In other words, the question of the choice of values is eminently cardinal. What, then, are the values that educators claim to impose worth? Isn't there a great risk of normalizing cheaply, and destroying with a clear conscience? What are the sociological requirements of such a conception in the Moroccan education system? (LENOIR, 2016)

VALUES IN THE MOROCCAN EDUCATION SYSTEM

It goes without saying that values are everywhere. They are first and foremost found in the ideologies that underpin educational policies. The school's function, and not the only one, is to enable its users who have become captives to acquire content. This content is presented in the form of disciplines. Such an idea is confirmed by, "The educational institution [he says] is not only a place for the acquisition of content, but it also presents itself as a place for the integration of attitudes." Thus, values education in schools operates according to orientations and axiological choices stipulated by official texts. Like other countries, Morocco's education system is dependent on choices based on local and universal values. (HOUSSAYE Jean, 1991)

What Our Official Texts Say

The reform of the Moroccan education system is part of a global context that is characterized by major changes to which schools must respond. Thus, one of the constant aims of any educational system is the transmission of a certain number of national and universal values often set out in official texts and which aim to lead the pupil to build his or her personality. Indeed, it is impossible to approach the question of education without taking into consideration the normative reference that underlies it and which should be related to an expected social project. In his speech at the opening of the autumn session of the third legislative year, His Majesty King Mohamed 6 stated in explicit terms: *"Our objective is to form a good citizen capable of acquiring knowledge and skills while being deeply attached to his identity and proud of his belonging, aware of his rights and duties, Fully apprehensive of the local situation, his civic obligations and his commitments to himself, his family and his community, willing to serve his homeland with loyalty, dedication, self-sacrifice and sacrifice, to rely on himself and to show a spirit of initiative with confidence, courage, faith and optimism (Excerpt from the Royal Speech, Rabat, October 8, 1999).»*. In this sense, the report of the Higher Council for Education, Training and Scientific Research (COSEFRS) published in 2017 bases its approach on the conviction that values education is an integral part of the functions of the school and constitutes one of the main vectors of the social and cultural inclusion of generations of learners and the guarantee of social cohesion. At the same time, it is one of the levers for building and upgrading human capital. Development and imbuing with values are ultimately a lever for the promotion of the education system and for the improvement of its quality at all levels.

The National Charter for Education and Training (1999)

According to this founding text, Morocco's education system is based on the principles and values of the Islamic faith. It aims to form a virtuous citizen, a model of rectitude, moderation and tolerance, open to science and knowledge and endowed with a spirit of initiative, creativity and enterprise. On the other hand, the Kingdom's education system respects and reveals the ancestral identity of the Nation. It manifests its sacred and intangible values: *faith in God, love of the Fatherland and attachment to the Constitutional Monarchy*. On these foundations, education cultivates the values of citizenship that enable all to participate fully in public and private affairs with full knowledge of the rights and duties of each individual. The education system ensures oral and written proficiency in Arabic, the official language of the country, for all and, in addition, is open to the use of the most widely used foreign languages in the world. Education also seeks to develop a spirit of dialogue, of acceptance of difference through its openness to universal values. As a result, Moroccan schools according to the National Charter of Education and Training do not only aim at the acquisition of knowledge by students but also aspire to transmit values to them. According to the orientations of this framework text, "entry through values" corresponds to a crucial choice including major axiological orientations.

Teaching and Gender of Values in Morocco

Four constant and fundamental principles form the framework of the various official texts (royal speeches, the CNEF, the New Constitution of 2011, the White Paper, pedagogical guidelines organizing each discipline):

1- The values of the Islamic religion and faith (values of tolerance, peace, solidarity, etc.);
2- The values of national identity that are based on the principles of our civilization and its ethical principles and cultural specificities;
3- The fundamental values of citizenship;
4- The values of human rights and their universal foundations (women's rights, children's rights, etc.).

The White Paper, for its part, is in line with the four fundamental areas set out in the Charter and sets out, among other things, the following major objectives:

- Consolidation of national civilizational identity;
- Strengthening the love of one's homeland and the willingness to serve it;
- The development of awareness of rights and duties;
- Imbuing the spirit of dialogue, tolerance and acceptance of difference;
- Strengthening the values of modernity and communication in all its forms;

According to the White Paper, the Moroccan education and training system is working to meet the needs of learners through various means, including:

- Self-confidence and openness to the Other;
- Autonomy in thought and practice;
- Positive interaction with the social environment at all levels;
- The spirit of responsibility and the sense of discipline;
- The practice of citizenship and democracy;

This axiological framework governing the Moroccan education system covers all cycles and all teaching disciplines. The various programs and curricula must implement it. A simple examination of this frame of reference shows that Morocco opts for a happy combination of universal values drawn from the various international treaties and documents and values referring to its history and cultural heritage. As a result, this aspiration is part of a logic of positive, dynamic and constructive interaction between the local axiological referent and the universal axiological referent. In the light of these fundamental constants, it is clear that the reference framework of values in the Moroccan education system can be broken down into two axiological poles: the one relating to the preservation of the local national cultural identity and the one relating to openness to human values drawn from the universal reference system.

PEDAGOGY AND KINDS OF VALUE

The pedagogy of its Greek origin corresponds to the action of leading, of educating the child and thus designates the art of education. This term generally refers to the teaching methods and practices required to transmit not only knowledge or know-how but also interpersonal skills, i.e. attitudes.

The Pedagogy of Values in the E/A of French at the Qualifying Secondary School

The Pedagogical Guidelines for the Teaching and Learning of French to the Qualifying Student are no exception to the rule and emphasize that French should, like all other subjects, *"contribute to the development of national and universal values"*. (Pedagogical Guidelines for the Teaching of French in the Qualifying Secondary Cycle, 2007, p.2.) They also insist on *"the formation of an autonomous citizen through the appropriation of universal civic and human values"*. (Ibid.p.2). Implicitly, there should therefore be a relationship between the autonomy of the learner and the values to be transmitted in a classroom. In addition to the entry through skills, the same text prescribes an entry through values which refers to the content to be used wisely by the teacher in the language class, *"Like other subjects, French contributes to the development of national and universal values, as set out in the official reference texts. The selected pedagogical proposals take this requirement into account. It is up to the teacher to highlight the values conveyed in the works studied"* (ibid.p3). Teaching then consists of knowing how to manage what is related to official values and what is related to the personal values of Moroccan learners.

National and Universal Values

The most recent report (2017) of the Conseil supérieur on values education in the teaching of school subjects, including the French language, comes in a rapidly changing national and international context. As a result, Morocco embarked on a number of institutional and legislative reforms, culminating in the adoption of the 2011 Constitution. It has put in place the foundation of the values common to the nation, in particular:

- the organisation of social life around the values of democracy, human rights, the rule of law, justice, freedom, dignity, equality between men and women, responsible citizenship and solidarity;
- the preponderant place of the Islamic religion in Moroccan identity;

- national and territorial unity;
- the plural identity resulting from the interbreeding of its multiple tributaries;
- openness, moderation, tolerance and creativity;
- Dialogue and understanding among the cultures and civilizations of the world.

A simple examination of such axiological choices leads us to say that the teaching content of the various school subjects, including French in high school, must be grasped and transmitted in the perspective of a coherent coalition between the reinforcement of the different values of the Moroccan national identity and the promotion of the learner's openness to values.

In this regard, would the return of the literary text in the current curricula in French classes in high school be a real opportunity for the promotion of values?

DIDACTICS, LITERATURE, AND VALUES

The literary text in the E/A of French in high school, in other words the introduction of literature in school, has often been equated with the transmission of values. In this sense, they affirm that (CAN-VAT, 2004): *"Schools have made literature a subject of compulsory education for the sake of education rather than instruction, and of morality rather than aesthetics, since one of the objectives most regularly proclaimed by teachers is the discovery of the values that give meaning to life."* Indeed, questions about the formation of individuals and the transmission of values form the basis of a reflection on society that the literature reveals. In a way, the Pedagogical Orientations of the French Language in High School are part of this perspective and propose a certain approach to the values represented first and foremost by prescribed literary works. Thus, in order to appropriate a certain number of values in the language classroom, this official text recommends a very specific corpus.: Maupassant, Molière, Victor Hugo, Balzac, Voltaire, and Khair-Eddine among others. The choice of the literary corpus indicated below is in line with the institutional desire to contribute to the development of attitudes and interpretive reflections among Moroccan learners around values related to their identity and otherness.

Literary Text and Identity

The proposal of literary works by Moroccan writers in the curricula of qualifying secondary school meets a twofold objective. The first is to enable learners to become aware of their Moroccanness, since literature is a cultural fact that allows them to develop a sense of identity. In this regard, literature is considered by Amor Séoud as the royal road that leads to the construction of identity: *"It (literature) is a unique opportunity to access an imaginary universe that will serve as the foundation for the constitution of their own identity"*.(CUQ Jean-Pierre & GRUCA, Cours de didactique du français langue étrangère et seconde, 2002) Literature is therefore necessary for the constitution of both the personal and collective identity of learners. On the other hand, it must be admitted that the cultural dimension of French-language literary texts is the manifestation of a cultural commitment to oneself and to the social group to which the learner belongs, because, in fact, *"the fact of participating in a linguistic community implies more or less consciously a cultural positioning"* (BESSE, Educating Intercultural Perception, 1984) As for the second objective, which follows on from the first, the affirmation of the learner's identity and origins implies a way of marking his or her difference with the otherness contained in literary fiction.

But this does not mean denial and denigration of the Other. It is, in reality, only a way of expressing and perceiving one's axiological differences vis-à-vis this Franco-Western otherness. Such a dialectic covering the inside and the outside takes place on the basis of a constructive comparative activity that eliminates false or distorted representations that the teacher and the learner might have of the Other and that would prevent true self-knowledge: It is not possible for students to perceive what constitutes their own cultural environment without a term of comparison: *"It is only after I have discovered the culture of the Other that I can see what is the basis of my cultural particularities."* said by the way(CUQ Jean-Pierre & GRUCA, Didactics of French as a Foreign and Second Language, 1997).

Literary Text and Otherness According to its Latin Origin (alterĭtas)

Otherness is the condition of being another. The term alter refers to the "other" from the point of view of the "me". The concept of otherness is thus used in the philosophical sense to designate the discovery of the conception of the world and the interests of an "other". Otherness must be understood on the basis of a division between "self" and "the other" or between "us" and "them". The "other" has different customs, traditions and representations than the "self". Otherness then implies putting oneself in the place of the "other", alternating with one's own point of view and that of others. This means that otherness is a desire for understanding that encourages dialogue and fosters peaceful relationships. At a time when the challenges of opening up to the world are essential, literature is the privileged place for a communicative approach between different cultures. The literary text, because of its plurality of points of view, is the place par excellence for the manifestation of otherness. , considers it (PRETCEILLE, 2010) *as "the pledge of a testimony of individual experience and of the learning of otherness and diversity".* No one doubts that literature is addressed first and foremost to the mind, to the emotion and at the same time to an infinite number of people who share the same ideas, the same ideological conceptions, but from a different angle from ours. This common and singular character is omnipresent in literature where the individual is totally incomparable and irreducible and at the same time as a human being. In this context, states: (Sartre, 1970)*"There is always a way to understand the idiot, the child, the primitive or the foreigner, provided one has sufficient information. In this sense, we can say that there is universality of man; But it is not given, it is perpetually constructed. I build the universal by choosing myself."* In the same vein, Luc Collès emphasizes the importance of the literary text in the process of discovering otherness. In this regard, he explicitly states that: *"The literary text (is) like a look that sheds light on a cultural model, fragmentarily. The multiplicity of perspectives will allow us to identify little by little the values around which it is organized."* (COLLES, 1994)Generally speaking, it goes without saying that learning the literary text apprehends the Other through its various manifestations in fiction. Such learning is therefore not a phenomenon that can be confined to sacralization, on the contrary, it bases its reality on the specificity of the Other as a whole, not detached from its humanistic nature and conveying a culture of otherness. The singularity of otherness also makes it possible to describe and present all kinds of differences and diversity of attitudes and behaviors, as the organizing principle of the open society. In this sense, emphasizes the following idea: (BESSE, Some Reflections on the Literary Text and Its Practices in the Teaching of French as a Second Language or Foreign Language, 1989)*"The teaching-learning of the literary text takes on an intercultural dimension that promotes the reciprocal discovery of cultures. It is a means that stimulates the encounter and confrontation between profoundly divergent cultural universes. The intercultural approach is a decentration in relation to one's own culture, it aims at an understanding of the Other through one's culture."*

PRACTICAL INVESTIGATION OF VALUES AND ANALYSIS OF RESULTS

The theoretical aspect mentioned above leads us to experiment with this axiological aspect of the teaching/learning process as follows:

Research Hypotheses

The practical investigation carried out in the field aims to verify the extent to which the reality of the teaching of qualifying French at the secondary level through the literary text confirms or invalidates the following hypotheses regarding entry through values. First of all, interpretative interaction, when it begins with literary fiction, would develop in learners, through the establishment of an adequate didactic and docimological device, ethical requirements and a capacity for autonomous and in-depth reflection on values. Secondly, the role of cultural mediation for the teacher in the French classroom is one of the keys to the development and integration of the learner into a global and healthy axiological dynamic of the world. Finally, in the absence of a clear didactic framework to do this, the values component in the teaching/learning of French in high school would be subject to the vagaries of improvisation on the part of teachers.

Samples and Research Tools

The investigation that we propose to carry out concerns a global sample of 50 high school French teachers working in the territory of the Taza-Hoceima-Taounate academy in four schools. (Table 1). This work is based on a questionnaire as a research tool, intended for these 50 professors, aimed at collecting, through the different answers obtained, the representations that the teaching staff has of the entry through values in the teaching/learning of the French language to the qualifier in relation to the official texts. This investigative tool will make it possible to examine the place given by these teachers to the axiological component in their planning and management of the content conveyed by the integral works in the program for the three levels: common core, first and second year of the baccalaureate.

Table 1. Representative table of teachers and schools

Head to Taza	Number of professors	Frequency	Percentage
Establishment1	14	0,3	30%
Establishment2	14	0,3	30%
Establishment3	11	0,2	20%
Establishment4	11	0,2	20%
Total	50	1	100

Figure 1. Graphical representation of Table 1

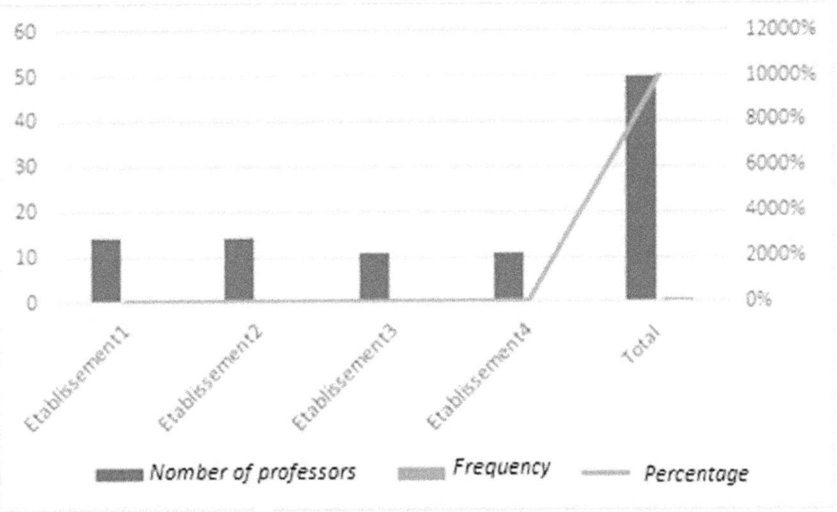

Analysis of the Results Obtained by the Questionnaire

Table 2. Representative table of the three entries

1- Is the teaching of the French language in high school done through	
Proposed Responses	**Percentages**
Entry-in-skills?	90%
Entry through values?	2%
Entry through gender?	0%
All three entries at once?	**8%**

Figure 2. Representative of the three inputs

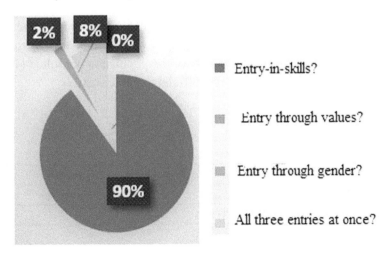

Table 3. Representative table of the values of the national charter

2- Do you already have an idea about the value system established by the National Charter for Education and Training (CNEF)?	
Suggested Responses	**Percentages**
Yes	12%
No	88%

Figure 3. Representative table of the values of the national charter

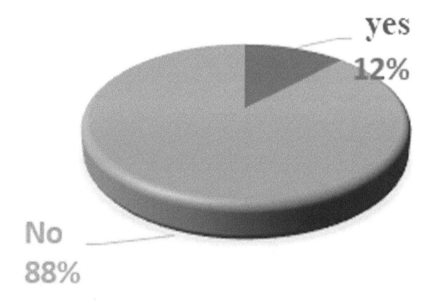

In view of the answers obtained, most of the teachers surveyed believe that the teaching of the French language is done through the one and only entry by skills (90%). Few associate it with entry through values (2%). Subsequently, only a minority of them have sufficiently familiarized themselves with the normative texts, in particular the Pedagogical Guidelines for the Teaching of French in the Qualifying Secondary Cycle.

This state of non-knowledge about the existence and place of "entry through values" in the Pedagogical Guidelines is similar to that of ignorance of the system of values established by the National Charter for Education and Training (CNEF). Only a minority of the population consulted (12%) claim to have an idea of the axiological system advocated by this official reference text.

Table 4. Values of the new constitution

3- Do you have any idea of the values established by the New Constitution?	
Suggested Responses	**Percentages**
Yes	31%
No	69%

Figure 4. S-values of the new constitution

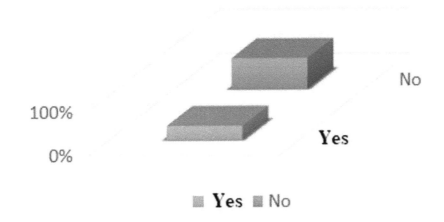

Table 5. Pedagogical orientations

4- Have you ever read the Pedagogical Guidelines for the Teaching of French in High School?	
Suggested Responses	**Percentages**
Yes	94%
No	6%

With regard to the state of knowledge of the values contained in the New Constitution (2011), the situation is almost the same. More than two-thirds of professors have no idea of the value system stipulated by this founding official text (69%)

With regard to the pedagogical guidelines governing the teaching/learning of the French language in high school, an overwhelming majority of teachers say they have read the normative text in question (94%). However, it should be noted in passing that such a rate is far from reliable for one of two reasons: either because the answers collected are not truthful or because the reading of the Guidelines in question is not sufficiently thoughtful to the point of omitting the part relating to "entry by values".

Regarding the question of whether French teachers are aware of the values stipulated by the Pedagogical Guidelines, the majority of them say that it is fundamentally vague and vague (83%). On the other hand, a minority of them (7%) admit that this idea is more or less accurate and only (10%) say that it is

Figure 5. Pedagogical guidelines

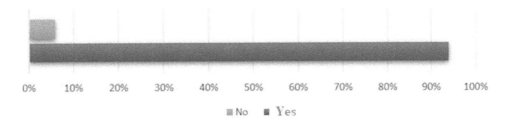

Table 6. Values of pedagogical orientations

5- What is your idea of the values expected by POs?	
Suggested Responses	**Percentages**
Precise	10%
Blurred	83%
+ or – precise	7

Figure 6. The values of the pedagogical orientations

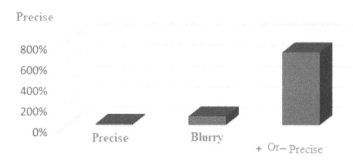

clear. In short, the idea of axiological expectations stipulated in the Pedagogical Guidelines is mostly absent among teachers.

Training a pupil who speaks and writes French well seems to be the only aim expected by the teaching of French in high school for almost half of the teachers surveyed (44%). 27% of the sample concerned believe that the purpose of teaching French at the qualifying secondary level is to train a pupil who masters the language in its functional dimension. However, the axiological component is taken into

Table 7. The purpose of the French language curriculum

6- Does the curriculum relating to the teaching of French in high school aim to:	
Suggested Responses	**Percentages**
To train a student who speaks and writes well in French?	44%
To train a student who has mastered functional French?	27%
To form a future citizen open to other cultures?	29%

Figure 7. The purpose of the French language curriculum

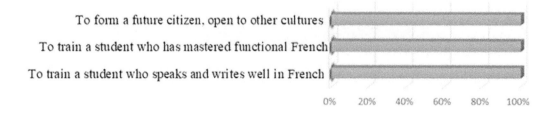

Table 8. Types of knowledge provided by the works in the programme

7- Is the knowledge provided by the works in the program purely	
Responses collected	**Percentages**
Literary?	81%
Language?	4%
Functional?	1%
Cultural?	14%

Figure 8. Types of knowledge provided by works in the program

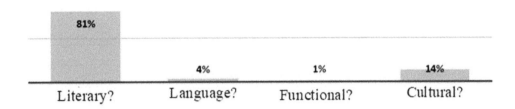

account by only a minority (29%). As a result, the current conception of language teaching is reduced in most cases to language learning alone and, as a result, the French teacher often overlooks one of the major aims governing school in general and its pedagogical action in particular, namely the formation of a future citizen attached to national values and open to the values of other cultures.

Professors' opinions on the teaching object of the complete work are fundamentally divergent. However, in the light of the statistical data obtained, it appears that the most common conception that these professors have of the complete work is that it is a medium for teaching literature exclusively. Some believe that the latter is a support for learning linguistic and functional tools. But all these three conceptions have in common the fact that they do not take into account the values that the literary text conveys.

According to almost half of the professors surveyed, the teaching of the French language through the complete works allows more or less respect for the national axiological system and promotes openness to universal values (49%). In addition, a significant proportion of them feel that their teaching through the integral work actually allows this. Nevertheless, it should be noted that while teachers are generally aware of the dual objective of teaching French through literary works, namely the appropriation by

Table 9. Literary works as national and universal values

8- Does the teaching of French through literary works allow respect for national values and openness to universal values?	
Suggested Responses	**Percentages**
Yes	33%
No	18%
+or-	49%

Figure 9. Literary works as national and universal values

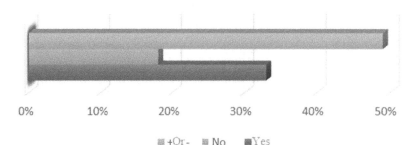

Table 10. The exit profile of the Moroccan high school student

9- Is the exit profile of the Moroccan high school student based on:	
Suggested Responses	**Percentages**
- The acquisition of skills and content?	93%
- The degree of integration into the system of national and universal values?	5%
- The degree of personal involvement in the dynamics of the world?	2%

Figure 10. The exit profile of the Moroccan high school student

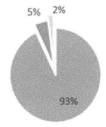

= The acquisition of skills and content?

= The degree of integration into the system of national and universal values?

= The degree of personal involvement in the dynamics of the world?

learners of national values and their openness to the values of other cultures, the fact remains that its implementation in the classroom is delicate.

The survey in question shows that the teachers questioned think that the expected exit profile of Moroccan high school students corresponds solely and solely to the acquisition of skills and content (93%). The dimensions corresponding to the degree of integration into the system of national and universal values as well as that of personal involvement in the dynamics of the world are mostly obscured and/or ignored by the target audience. As a result, most teachers continue to have an incomplete and exclusively transmissive vision of its pedagogical action. The knowledge paradigm is privileged to the detriment of the paradigms relating to know-how and interpersonal skills.

When asked what central value the axiological system advocated by the curriculum should be reduced to, the majority places responsibility and fidelity at the top The value of respect for difference, although cardinal and recurrent in official texts, enjoys little interest among teachers (12%).

In view of the responses received concerning the integration of values into teaching, a minority of the teachers surveyed say that they use this dimension when the content lends itself to it (18%). Con-

Table 11. The axiological scope of the curriculum

10- If you are asked to summarize the axiological system established by the curriculum into a central value, which one would you choose?	
Suggested Responses	**Percentages**
Respect for difference	12%
Loyalty	43%
Accountability	45%

Figure 11. The axiological scope of the curriculum

Table 12. Degree of involvement of the axiological system

11- When you teach French, you use the axiological system:	
Suggested Responses	**Percentages**
Always	0%
Sometimes	17%
Never	65%
When the nature of the content allows it	18%

Figure 12. Degree of involvement of the axiological system

Table 13. Teacher's knowledge of French culture and civilisation

12- Do you think that a teacher's knowledge of French culture and civilization is:	
Suggested Responses	**Percentages**
Necessary?	12%
Not always necessary?	81%
Not necessary at all?	7%

Figure 13. The teacher's knowledge of French culture and civilization

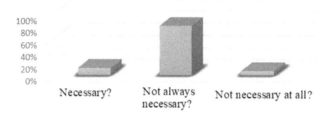

versely, some say they use it (65%). Entering the French class in high school by starting from texts with an axiological dimension is an idea that is almost absent among teachers. As a result, the works on the programme are rarely the subject of an adequate axiological exploitation.

Teaching a language presupposes a knowledge of the culture and civilization of which it is the vector and manifestation. However, most French teachers believe that this knowledge is not always necessary. Such a departure from the initial premise confirms the idea that the majority of teachers of the French language are almost totally unaware of the need to integrate the paradigm of values conveyed by works into their educational practices.

The answers collected concerning the source of the transmission of values justify the above deductions in the sense that more than half of the teachers say that this transmission must be based on their own convictions (65%). Such a drift is therefore not without transforming the French course into a moment of indoctrination punctuated by moralizing and moralizing speeches on the part of the teacher. This also attests to the lack of initial and continuing training in the teaching of interculturalism.

If the values component is almost ignored from a didactic point of view, the same is true for the evaluation component. When asked whether the values expressed are evaluable, 77% of teachers say that this is impossible. We therefore deduce that it is quite normal to think this way since the teaching staff

Table 14. Teaching between personal conviction and literary content

13- In your opinion, should the transmission of values be based on:	
Suggested Responses	**Percentages**
Of the content of the literary text alone?	28%
The teacher's own convictions?	65%
Students' own convictions?	7%

Figure 14. Teaching between personal conviction and literary content

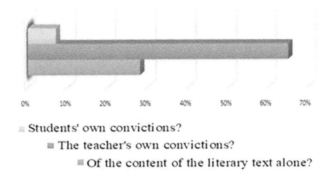

■ Students' own convictions?
■ The teacher's own convictions?
■ Of the content of the literary text alone?

Table 15. Possibility of assessing values-based entry in French language teaching

14- Is it possible to evaluate values-based entry into the teaching of French?	
Suggested Responses	**Percentages**
Possible	**9%**
Impossible	**77%**
When the content allows it	**14%**

Figure 15. Possibility of assessing values-based entry into the teaching of French

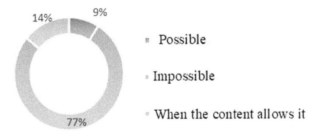

■ Possible

■ Impossible

■ When the content allows it

of French in high school continues to believe that, unlike "entry through skills", "entry through values", if it is taken into account, is neither didactic nor evaluable.

DISCUSSION AND INTERPRETATION OF RESULTS

In view of the data collected during this investigative work, the objective of which is to examine the representations that French teachers in high school have of entry through values, a certain number of points emerge and deserve analysis and interpretation. The answers given by the professors questioned on the degree of their knowledge of the values conveyed by the various official reference texts (the CNEF, the New Constitution, the White Paper, the Pedagogical Guidelines), attest to an alarming lack of knowledge in this area. There is no need to recall that a teacher is first and foremost a civil servant who is required to carry out his or her mission in accordance with a certain number of guidelines contained in official texts. However, this normative culture is almost absent among our teachers of the French language at the secondary level, in this case the one relating to the axiological dimension. That being said, this state of intellectual scarcity in terms of the values governing society certainly has a most unfortunate impact on the quality and efficiency of our education system. Indeed, this quality and efficiency at the level of teaching/learning French in high school can be measured first of all by the degree of mastery and application on the part of the teacher of the official founding texts as well as by a deep and thoughtful awareness of the axiological system guiding society in general and the pedagogical action of the school in particular. Without this, the school would be reduced to the sole function of transmitting knowledge and the French class in high school would be transformed into a space for inculcating content, as we have often observed. The glaring lack of knowledge of the axiological aspect at the level of official texts also corresponds to the failure of most of the public concerned to take into account the integration of values as didactic and docimological objects into classroom practices. If there is consciousness, it is reduced to the belief of some that values pass only through disciplinary knowledge or even through the teacher's own axiological system. These two major observations, linked to the majority absence of the values component, both at the level of theoretical knowledge and at the level of professional and pedagogical practices of French teachers in high school, imply the responsibility of researchers. Indeed, the pedagogical supervision/training of teaching staff should henceforth integrate the axiological aspect into the training through the common analysis of the expectations of curricular texts and the implementation of didactic and evaluative devices of the values expected by the teaching of the French language in high school. With regard to the third and final axis, the questions of which concern teachers' representations of values at the level of their practices, the results collected largely show the pervasiveness of two major conceptions: a strictly cognitive conception centred on knowledge, emanating from a conviction according to which values are transmissible by the source of content alone, and another subjective conception centred on the teacher postulating that the The transmission of values in the French classroom in high school should only operate through the teacher's own axiological system.

Challenges and Considerations

The objective of this work was to examine the state of play relating to values-based entry into the teaching/learning of the French language at the qualifying secondary level, based on theoretical considerations on the subject and then on the basis of a sample developed and subjected to a qualitative and quantitative analysis of 50 French-language teachers. In spite of the official recommendations, the introduction of values and its use in the French class in high school is not without its didactic problems that our contact with the pedagogical reality has brought to light. In this context,, rightly states the following, "From the experience of tested values to a (MASSERON, 2003)*work on values, from the theorization to the practical implementation of a didactic device likely to promote the entry through values, there is a state of affairs"* (Revue *Pratiques*, pages 117/118).

CONCLUSION

The question of values and the possibility or necessity of introducing them into the ranks of didactic objects arouses a mixed feeling of circumspection and questioning among the French teachers consulted. If a reflection were to be carried out with their students, they would ask themselves how to do it and how to determine the ethical limits of the situations to be established. They are also helpless, both in terms of the knowledge to be used to define the notion of value and in terms of the professional know-how to be used to teach the literary texts of French and Maghreb authors. Moreover, the component of values and its axiological scope, as indicated in our work, is difficult to apply since the official reference texts remain too general and give rise, in most cases, to vague and/or impressionistic interpretations.

In view of the paucity of research on the value component in the teaching of French in Moroccan schools, and despite some attempts at research on the didacticization of values in the qualifying secondary cycle, the didactic implementation of such a project is almost non-existent. Hence the need to renew, or even refound, the didactics of the integral work in high school, especially since the results of our research show a case that could not be more alarming. Indeed, since the introduction of literary works by the curriculum as a pretext for learning the French language in all its forms, axiological tendencies/objectives are most often hidden or not properly exploited by teachers of French in the qualifying cycle. The status of the literary text and its presence in the curriculum, the ambiguity of didactic approaches do not offer plausible anchor points for the development of the cultural competences and reflective capacities of the Moroccan student, knowing that it is necessary to go beyond the simple language laboratory to form the skills of the authentic reader by arousing in him the capacity to live with the Other and his culture and by endowing him with a certain number of resonances linguistic and cultural issues that are likely to make differences interact in contact with the literary text, considered as an entity carrying both universal and local values. This being the case, and with the aim of curbing this haemorrhage in terms of entry through values, it is necessary to think about the development of a remedial system aimed at making the French classroom not only a moment of transmission of knowledge on values but also and above all a space where the procedural approaches and postures of the teacher must work in the direction of the development of both individual values both local and universal.

Perspective and Recommendations

In this perspective, the proposed recommendations can by no means be exhaustive since our project intends to be part of a broader and more ambitious dynamic that considers the values-based entry into the teaching of the French language through integral works as a fertile ground for the development of emotional intelligence in Moroccan students. Such a project leads us to ask: To what extent can the student-subject-reader, based on his or her cultural convictions, transform the text? What limits and legitimacy should be given to this reconfiguration? How to construct the posture of a fulfilled and expert student/reader based on subjective readings since, as the reader states,(LACELLE, 2007) *"the subjective investment of the reader is first and foremost valid as a means of access to the works"*.

REFERENCES

Besse, H. (1984). Educating intercultural perception. France: Hachette Edicef.

Besse, H. (1989). *Some reflections on the literary text and its practices in the teaching of French as a second language or as a foreign language.* Lyon: Trefoil, n°9.

Bourdieu, P. (1970). *Reproduction.* Taylor & Francis.

Canvat, K. (2004). *Values in/from literature.* P.U of Namur.

Colles, L. (1994). Comparative Literature and Intercultural Recognition. Brussels: De Boeck.

Combes, J. (1967). Value and Freedom. Paris: PUF.

Émile, D. (1977). *Education and Sociology.* Humensis.

Gruca, I. (1997). *Didactics of French as a foreign and second language.* Deir Publishing.

Gruca, I. (2002). *Didactic courses in French as a foreign and second language.* Paris: Horizon Groupe.

Hadiji, C. (1995). *Thinking and acting on education.* Paris: ESF éditeur.

Jean, H. (1991). Values: School Choices. *Revue Française de Pédagogie.*

Kluckhohn, C. (1961). *Anthropology And The Classics.*

Lenoir, Y. (2016). *School disciplines and life outside of school. The case of "education to" in Quebec. Health education, environmental education and citizenship education.* Saint-Lambert: Group- éditions Editeurs.

Masseron, C. (2003). *Reading practices: what ways to promote the expression of the reading subject?* Review number 117/118.

Piaget, J. (1967). *The Psychology of Intelligence.* Armand Colin.

Pretceille, M.-A. (2010). Literature as a Learning Space for Otherness and Diversity. *Synergies Brazil, 2.*

Rokeach, P. (1973). *The Nature of Human Values.* UK: Free Press. A division of Macmillan.

Sartre. J.-P. (1970). Existentialism is a Humanism (1947). Paris: Éditions Nagel.

Schwartz. S. (2006). *The basic values of the person: theory, measures and applications.* Cairn. www.cairn.info/revue-francaise-de-sociologie-2006-4-page-929.htm

Chapter 17
The Place of E-Learning in Language Learning:
Its Contribution to the Enhancement of Language Proficiency

Aicha Ait-Hroch

ENS, Abdelmalek Essaadi University, Morocco

Ahmed Ibrahimi

https://orcid.org/0009-0004-8879-5561

ENS, Abdelmalek Essaadi University, Morocco

ABSTRACT

The way languages are learned in today's educational environment has changed dramatically due to the incorporation of technology and the introduction of new methods and approaches, such as e-learning. This chapter breaks down aspects that relate e-learning to language acquisition. It explains e-learning, its emergence, its history throughout the years, and its most efficient platforms and systems. Then, it discusses language learning, its importance, and the basic language skills that provide an effective basis for language learning. Next, it discusses the relationship between e-learning and the development of language skills, how to learn languages through e-learning, and its contribution to language acquisition. Further on, it focuses on instructional design, which plays a major role in the success of training programs; discovers some of the most used instructional design models; and digs into the ADDIE model and how to design educational devices through it. Afterwards, it illustrates all of that with an example of an e-learning educational scenario designed using the ADDIE model.

INTRODUCTION

The unprecedented technological advancement over the last few decades has changed almost every area of our existence. Communication, healthcare, education, and other advances have completely changed the

DOI: 10.4018/979-8-3693-3128-6.ch017

Copyright © 2024, IGI Global. Copying or distributing in print or electronic forms without written permission of IGI Global is prohibited.

way we think, work, live, and communicate. Particularly in the field of education, tremendous technology advancements over the last several decades have drastically changed conventional teaching and learning approaches. New methods and resources that improve the learning process have emerged as a result of the use of technology in education. The way languages are learned and mastered in today's educational environment has changed dramatically due to the incorporation of technology and the introduction of new methods and approaches. E-learning, which comprises a diverse range of digital platforms and resources, has become a crucial component of language acquisition, substantially augmenting language acquisition. Language learning which also gained more importance and value among individuals as technological advancement has made it easier for people from different cultures, different linguistic backgrounds, and from all over the world to reach and communicate, and as interacting with communities on other sides of the world on a daily basis has become a necessity, people has become more interested, and in some cases bound, to learn new foreign languages. This dynamic and expanding method that is of e-learning not only helps traditional language instruction but also creates new opportunities for learners to connect with language information and the rich cultures behind them in a variety of ways, which makes it an ideal instrument for developing language skills and enhancing proficiency.

The purpose of this chapter, is to show the importance and contribution of online learning to language learning and its role in the enhancement of language proficiency and the development of language skills, as well as to show the importance of instructional design in ensuring a successful and efficient e-learning language course. Thus, throughout this chapter, we will get to break down some of the most relevant aspects that relate e-learning as a learning method, and language acquisition. We will start by understanding what e-learning is, its emergence, its history throughout the years, and some of its most used and most efficient platforms and systems. Then we will move on to language acquisition to get a better understanding of what language learning is; its importance in an educational context, work field, personal aspect, or even the day-to-day life; and the basic language skills that build and give an effective basis to the language learning and proficiency. Next, we will be discussing the relationship between E-learning and the development of language skills, how to learn languages through e-learning, its contribution to language acquisition, and even the role of an instructor in an e-learning language class. Further on, we will focus on instructional design that plays a major role in the success of a training program, we will discover some of the most accepted and used instructional design models, and then, we will dig deep into the ADDIE model, how it works, and how to design an educational device through it. Later on, we will illustrate all of that with an example of an e-learning educational scenario designed using the ADDIE model.

E-LEARNING

E-Learning Definitions

The technological development that the world has known in recent years has had a significant impact on the evolution and growth of educational methods and approaches. It has completely altered the way we learn and teach, and has transformed the way education is delivered and accessed. One of the various learning systems that have occurred with the immense technological advancement is what we call the E-learning system. E-learning, which stands for "electronic learning," is a type of education that makes use of electronic technologies and digital resources to provide instructional content and educational material and support learning over the internet or other digital means. This method of learning which is also commonly referred to as online learning, is the process of acquiring information and knowledge or developing skills using digital tools as well as the internet. It requires using electronic devices such as computers and mobile devices; online platforms, websites, and apps to access educational resources. It is a formalized teaching-based learning system that makes use of electronic resources. E-learning is primarily based on using computers and the Internet, while teaching and learning can also take place in or outside of formal classroom settings. According to George Siemens, E-learning is a technology-enhanced approach to facilitating and delivering learning that is distinguished by making use of networked connections and resources. Jabeen & Thomas (2015) define E-learning as a modern teaching-learning viewpoint for both instructors and students to give an efficient educational process by incorporating computers and the Internet. This definition emphasizes e-learning's modern and efficient nature as a teaching and learning strategy. It emphasizes the importance of computers and the internet in making the educational process easier for both educators and students. it also aligns with the fundamental basics of e-learning as a digital web-based instructional system aimed to improve the teaching and learning experience.

In a similar vein, D. R. Garrison and Terry Anderson state that E-learning is the convergence of the Internet and learning, including the usage of multimedia applications, computer-based training, and distance learning. According to them, it covers the Internet, intranet/extranet (LAN/WAN), audio and videotape, satellite broadcast, interactive TV, and CD-ROM content delivery. They emphasize the inclusive and holistic nature of e-learning as a result of the Internet's integration into the learning process, and include a diverse range of digital and online learning technologies. They also encompass multiple content delivery technology means which highlights the various technologies and platforms that come under the e-learning umbrella, illustrating the multidimensional character of modern digital learning.

According to Mark J. W. Lee and Catherine McLoughlin, E-learning is the acquisition and application of information that is largely provided and facilitated by electronic methods. It includes all levels of learning, both official and informal, and it may occur in an array of settings, including lifetime learning, workplace learning, and education. They, like D. R. Garrison and Terry Anderson, emphasize the holistic aspect of e-learning, emphasizing its role in the acquisition and use of information via electronic methods at various levels and situations. They also highlight the flexible and adaptable nature of e-learning as an educational medium.

The Emergence and History of E-Learning

E-learning did not magically emerge out of the blue, out of nowhere. It is the result of years of human intellect, years of researchers' hard work, and it has a rich history that has resulted from years of invention. Compared to other educational fields, e-learning, especially online language instruction, has a lengthy history (Wang & Sun, 2001). There were a series of historical events that led to the creation of this method of instruction.

E-learning has a long history that has grown substantially with technological improvements. It first appeared in the 1960s and 1970s, when the notion of computer-based training (CBT), in which computers are used to provide instructional material, began to form.

The introduction of personal computers and the growing popularity of the internet in the 1980s paved the way for more participatory and accessible types of e-learning despite the primitive nature of personal computers and systems used back then that were often text-based read-only technologies. In 1840, Sir Isaac Pitman established a shorthand correspondence class. This was one of the first examples of online learning, with written materials sent over mail. With its free HyperCard program, the Macintosh also aided a generation of tech-savvy teachers in creating their own software and lessons for pupils. Commercial software businesses jumped at the chance to create computer-based instructional resources and learning games.

With the introduction of multimedia and the World Wide Web in the 1990s, e-learning underwent a substantial transformation. This era saw the creation of increasingly interactive e-learning materials, which included the incorporation of graphics, audio, and video. The Multimedia PC started to come with a CD-ROM drive, which implies it can allow students to display videos that are synchronized with audio. Along with that, the presentation program Microsoft PowerPoint emerged and swiftly started being adopted by lecturers, instructors, and students. A considerable amount of schools that offer only online courses were also formed in the early 1990s. In the late 1990s, Learning Management Systems (LMS) and virtual learning environments emerged, making it simpler to develop, deliver, and administer online courses. Throughout this time, educational platforms such as Blackboard, and Moodle gained prominence. Despite the fact that E-learning existed since the 1960s, it was until November 1999 when Elliott Masie, according to Shiftelearning, coined the term "E-Learning" at his TechLearn Conference at Disneyworld making it the first time the phrase had been used in a professional setting. beforehand, the industry has been using the phrase "online learning," essentially referring to the same notion.

In the 2000s, the growth of open educational resources (OER) and the creation of MOOCs which stands for Massive Open Online Courses, occurred. These projects, such as MIT's OpenCourseWare project, helped making educational content available to a worldwide audience for free or at a cheap cost. It was also during this decade that the Web 2.0, as we know it now, was introduced for the first time in 2004 Making the world shift away from the read-only environment of Web 1.0 and toward a two-way discourse in which users can participate, cooperate, and create using various platforms such as social media, blogs, wikis, and forums. The rise of Flash Video and the release of YouTube made embedding and playing back videos easier and faster. By 2008, the mobile web had begun with the introduction of Smartphones, followed by Internet-enabled tablets, which helped revolutionize the way developers develop educational software, educators teach, and pupils study.

The widespread adoption of smartphones and tablets in the 2010s fueled the expansion of mobile learning within the field of E-learning. Mobile devices have made E-learning courses and material readily available, making learning more versatile and on-the-go.

The coronavirus pandemic that hit the world in 2020 boosted e-learning adoption as educational institutions throughout the world were forced to switch to distance learning. During this time, new technologies such as virtual reality (VR) and augmented reality (AR) were also integrated into the e-learning method.

And as we look ahead, E-Learning will keep on growing and improving. Adaptive learning, individualized learning paths, and AI-driven education are among the innovations that are expected to impact the future of E-Learning, making teaching and learning more personalized and easily accessible.

E-Learning Platforms, Apps, Tools, and Software

Learning is a dynamic and lifelong process, and the internet has revolutionized the way we access and acquire knowledge. Not only has education progressed into the digital sphere, but it has also made a wide range of resources available. E-learning platforms, applications, tools, and software are an extensive variety of technological resources for developing, delivering, and administering online education.

Here are some examples from each of these categories:

E-Learning Platforms (LMS - Learning Management Systems): that enable instructors to develop digital courses and keep educational content online:

- Moodle: An open-source learning management system (LMS) that is extremely adaptable and frequently utilized in education.
- Blackboard Learn: it's a prominent learning management system (LMS) in higher education, with features for course development and student participation.
- Canvas (Instructure): Famous for its easy-to-use interface and contemporary design, Canvas provides an array of course administration capabilities.
- Google Classroom: which is a component of Google Workspace for education purposes that provides instructors and students with an easy and interactive platform.
- Pocket Study: is a learning platform that enables teachers to stay engaged with their students and effectively exchange learning resources. Students get to learn using flashcards, and they can have access to high-quality information at any time and in the comfort of their homes.
- Edmodo: is a social learning platform that focuses on communication, interaction, and collaboration.

Online learning apps: are mobile apps that provide users with educational content and courses that can be accessed through the Internet:

- Duolingo: An app for language learning that provides interactive and game-like courses.
- Khan Academy: Offers free instructional information and exercises on a wide range of topics.
- Quizlet: is a learning tool that lets users make and share flashcards and other study materials.
- Buusuu: Learn Languages: a collaborative mobile app that teaches languages by connecting users with a supportive community of native speakers for authentic feedback and cultural insights.
- Coursera: is an app that allows students to access online classes from universities and organizations.
- LinkedIn Learning: provides professional development classes on the move.

E-Learning Authoring Tools: are software programs that enable the creation, development, and production of digital learning content such as online courses, interactive modules, and instructional materials:

- Adobe Captivate: Allows users to create interactive e-learning programs.
- Articulate Storyline: Makes it easier to create interactive e-learning content.
- uQualio: is a cloud-based online video learning platform, that allows teachers to film and share instructional videos with students, create courses that they can re-visit at any time, and monitor their activity and test scores. It also allows instructors to turn any video into micro-learning videos with our bite-sizing tool.
- Camtasia: A software application for generating screen recordings and video lessons.
- ProProfs Training Maker: an e-learning authoring software that is a web-based tool for generating online learning and educational content such as courses, lessons, and even tests.
- iSpring Suite: Provides tools for producing PowerPoint-based e-learning courses.
- Lectora: is an authoring tool that allows for the creation of responsive e-learning courses.

Collaboration and Communication E-learning Tools: In the context of online education, collaboration, and communication e-learning tools are software and platforms that promote interactions, conversations, and information exchange among students, teachers, and peers. These technologies are critical for fostering community and participation in online learning settings:

- Zoom: A popular tool for virtual meetings and webinars, in the context of online education, is also used for virtual classrooms and live lessons and discussions.
- Microsoft Teams: is a part of Microsoft 365 that provides teachers and pupils with chat, video conferencing, as well as collaboration tools.
- Webex Meetings: It is a web and video conferencing software that allows people and organizations to hold online meetings, webinars, and virtual interactions. It is a component of the Cisco Webex range of communication and collaboration tools.
- Slack: is a communication and team collaboration tool that is used in educational institutions.
- AnyMeeting Webinars: is a free intermedia platform that enables users to attend and actively engage in webinars on-the-go. It is only available to webinar attendees.
- Google Workspace: Provides an array of tools for online collaboration and document sharing, including both Google Meet and Google Drive.

Learning Management Systems for Organizations: are specialized software systems for managing and administering online learning and educational programs. These platforms are designed to fulfill the specific requirements and needs of educational institutions, companies, corporations, and organizations aiming to deliver e-learning material.

- TalentLMS: A cloud-based LMS built for organizations, with an easy-to-use interface and content authoring tools.
- Cornerstone OnDemand: it provides enterprises with a variety of instructional content and talent management tools, including an LMS.
- Adobe Captivate Prime: A business LMS with e-learning material distribution and tracking capabilities.
- SAP Litmos: is a corporate learning management system noted for its flexibility and monitoring features.

These platforms address a wide range of the requirements of the e-learning system, from developing and delivering lessons to facilitating communication, interaction, and collaboration in the educational and business sectors. The tools adopted are dictated by the specific needs and goals of pupils, teachers, and organizations.

LANGUAGE LEARNING

What is Language Learning

Language learning is a dynamic process that starts from one's birth and lasts throughout one's entire life. It is the process through which one learns to understand, speak, read, and write in a language. It entails acquiring the essential skills and knowledge to successfully communicate and engage using a language whether it is one's native language or mother tongue or not. People learn a language by using it to convey their ideas, thoughts, feelings, and experiences, to build relationships with others and form connections with family and friends, and to seek to make sense of and create order and consciousness of their surroundings. Vocabulary, grammar, pronunciation, and cultural knowledge are all facets of language acquisition.

According to the Manitoba Education and Early Childhood Learning Structure, children learn language informally during their earliest years of life. Long before infants learn formal language norms, rules, and conventions, they imitate and make use of language to generate and express new meanings. As soon as they are born, children begin to interact with and learn language. They learn to communicate and comprehend language long before they understand explicit language norms and conventions throughout their early years.

Beyond the early stages of development, language acquisition becomes purpose-driven and context-specific. Individuals go on language learning journeys to achieve different goals, such as expanding their knowledge, actively participating in their communities, progressing in their profession, or just improving their leisure activities such as hobbies and interests. Within these specified circumstances, language acquisition becomes a tool for interaction and comprehension, requiring learners to gain specialized vocabulary, adjust to specific communication standards, and develop insights into the cultural subtleties connected with the language they are in the process of acquiring. This type of language acquisition indicates the constantly evolving interaction between language and the various aspects of human existence, in which language serves as a bridge linking people to the multifarious aspects of life. According to Stephen D. Krashen (1982), a renowned linguist and language acquisition theorist, language development does not need significant application of conscious grammatical rules or tiresome practice. Language learning does not require a heavy dependence on grammatical rules or tiresome exercises. Krashen's hypothesis, known as the Input Hypothesis, states that language acquisition is most successful when learners are exposed to intelligible input, meaning language that is somewhat above their present level of ability and language proficiency, yet nonetheless understandable within the related context. The emphasis, in this idea, is on meaningful communication and comprehension rather than formal rule memorization, on the value of engaging usage of language throughout the learning process. Language is not taught through the application of formal rules or conscious learning that play only a minor part in language performance, but rather through a subconscious process that happens when pupils are exposed to the language in a way in which they can grasp it (Stephen D. Krashen, 1982). According to Vivian Cook (2008), Second language learning is a subconscious process that results from actual conversation and communication. As defined by Noam Chomsky (2012), language acquisition is a mental process that occurs when an individual gains linguistic competence. Language speakers have a subconscious awareness of norms, an intuitive comprehension of meanings, the capacity to interact in social circumstances, a variety of language abilities, and language inventiveness (Stern, 1983). Similarly, Ellis and Larsen-Freeman (2006) assert that language learning is simultaneously incidental and subconscious. Language learning frequently occurs in an unplanned and unintentional way. This viewpoint lines up with language acquisition theories that highlight the importance of exposure and engagement in a language-rich environment. Therefore, language acquisition is a multidimensional process that is frequently subconscious, consists of connection, and is impacted by motivation and meaningful interaction and communication which illustrates the crucial role of exposure to the language and genuine conversation in the language learning process.

The Importance of Language Learning

Language is an extraordinary and distinctively human phenomenon that serves as a basic tool for representing, and transmitting meaning in our complicated environment. It is a distinctively social and human way of representing, investigating, and sharing meaning (Manitoba Education and Early Childhood Learning Structure). It is intrinsically social, with the goal of bridging barriers between people, cultures, and communities. Humans use language to not only transmit ideas and notions, but also to connect on a deeper level by expressing thoughts, feelings, experiences, and stories. Language enables individuals to scout the complexities of our existence, exhibit our creativity, and preserve the immense tapestry that constitutes human culture and knowledge. Language, whether spoken or written, is a monument to our potential for common understanding, allowing us to connect, learn, and progress as individuals, as communities, and as a society.

Language learning is critical because it is an essential component to effective communication and comprehension in our varied and interconnected world. Language provides a link between individuals, groups, and cultures, enabling people to communicate ideas, feelings, and knowledge. Language is an undeniable signature of human identity, as well as a distinguishing aspect of culture. It is necessary for developing interpersonal connections, comprehending social circumstances, enriching experiences, reflecting on ideas and behavior, and taking part in human society (Manitoba Education and Early Childhood Learning Structure). It is the cornerstone of learning, allowing access to education, literature, science, and humankind's collective knowledge. Language learning is critical for social interplay, whether it is within interpersonal relationships or professional contexts, and it plays a key role in cognitive development.

Specially in our increasingly globalized, and super connected world, foreign language learning is of paramount importance. Learning a second language not only exposes one to other cultures and ideas, but it also improves one's ability to interact and connect with people from all walks of life and different backgrounds. It fosters cross-cultural understanding and empathy. It aids in the development of a broader knowledge and regard for other people's traditions and customs that differ from theirs (The Government of Western Australia). Foreign language proficiency broadens travel opportunities by increasing opportunities to enjoy local culture, interact with locals, and travel with ease; work and business in worldwide markets, making individuals stronger competitors in an economically globalized world, and creating more career opportunities as companies seek employees who can speak multiple languages due to their ability to cross cultural and language barriers. Furthermore, learning a foreign language improves cognitive abilities such as problem-solving and multitasking, and can have a favorable influence on academic and professional growth by allowing learners to better analyze material and solve problems. It can also improve memory and brain function by strengthening the brain region responsible for memory, speech, and sensory perception. According to The Government of Western Australia, bilingual people remember lists, sequences, names, and instructions better. They are also more creative, intuitive, and can focus for longer periods of time. Finally, acquiring a foreign language enhances one's life both on the personal and professional level by providing a more expanded perspective and better understanding of the rich tapestry of the world's culture.

Language Skills

As we discussed language learning and the importance it holds, now we move to language skills which are the cornerstone of learning and mastering a foreign language. In the educational context, a skill is a specialized ability or aptitude that is acquired and enhanced via learning, practice, and experience. Academic skills cover a wide variety of competencies that pupils and researchers employ to effectively connect with and achieve in schools and universities. According to the European Center for the Development of Vocational Training, it is the capacity to apply information learned and the ability to know how to effectively use it in order to fulfill tasks and solve problems. Knowledge acquisition, coursework completion, and the pursuit of cognitive growth and performance in an academic setting all depend on having strong educational skills. They are an essential component of the pupil's toolset for lifetime development and academic achievement.

The range of skills needed to communicate well in a given language is called language skills. These are the skills and capacities required to effectively communicate in a particular language. They require proficiency in a variety of areas, including understanding, articulation, and interaction, which enable people to take part in meaningful and cogent conversations. Language skills include listening, speaking, reading, and writing:

- **Listening skills:** The capacity to actively and successfully understand spoken language. They entail having the ability to grasp spoken language and comprehend the nuances of pronunciation, intonation, and tone that give context and meaning. Effective communication requires good listening skills, whether in regular interactions, academic settings, or professional discussions, since they allow people to understand the intended message and enable them to respond properly.

- **Speaking skills:** They include the ability to use spoken language to communicate ideas, thoughts, and knowledge in an understandable and cohesive manner. Speaking with proficiency is knowing how to communicate effectively by utilizing the right words, grammar, and pronunciation. For daily interactions, public speaking, corporate speeches, and classroom debates, these abilities are essential. Good speakers are useful in personal as well as professional settings because they can communicate clearly, participate in insightful conversations, and deliver their points succinctly.

- **Reading skills:** refers to the capacity to decipher written language, comprehend its meaning, and interact with a variety of materials, from common texts such as emails, newspapers, and subtitles to more sophisticated literary and academic content. Reading effectively requires not solely being able to recognize and understand words but also understanding the ideas, notions, and context that are presented in the written text. These abilities are critical for learning, acquiring information, and expanding knowledge in different interests and fields, which makes them a necessary part of professional, academic, and even personal growth.

- **Writing skills:** include the capacity to effectively communicate concepts, ideas, and information using written text. Effective writing entails arranging sentences and content in a clear, coherent, and proper style while following grammar and syntax rules. These abilities are critical for a variety of situations, such as typical written encounters such as texting, professional communication such as emailing, academic writing such as dissertations, and creative or artistic expression. Effective communication can be achievable through having excellent writing skills, regardless of the type of written communication: essays, reports, business papers, artistic works, etc.

E-LEARNING AND LANGUAGE LEARNING

How to Learn Languages Through E-Learning

The emergence and growth of E-learning over the years has made learning everything about anything possible and extremely easy. Individuals can literally learn about their areas of interest, no matter the complexity and difficulty of the subject, in the comfort of their homes as the wide availability of the internet, electronic devices, and educational platforms have facilitated access to knowledge and provided several learning approaches suited to different learning styles. Language learning is one of the several areas of interest that e-learning has facilitated as it provides a convenient and efficient means of acquiring new language skills. Yumnam's (2021) study found that the usage of e-learning technologies helped facilitate the teaching and learning process (Yumnam, 2021). However, it is worth mentioning that in order to efficiently implement this learning method, one has to not only implement it for the sole sake of implementing it as this will have no benefits for the learner. A well-designed learning plan is the first step toward effective e-learning implementation in language acquisition. According to Yumnam (2021), e-learning, with adequate planning, may help learners establish their own learning styles while also successfully improving language skills, grammar, and vocabulary. Teachers should develop and design learning plans that seek the gradual development of students' language skills, plans that challenge their current level of language proficiency, but not too far to make it too complicated to understand or seem "unattainable". Instructors, or even students themselves, must then select an accurate language learning platform or software that meets their objectives. Choose a reliable e-learning site or language learning software that provides courses in the desired language, and meets their requirements and needs. Next is to define the language learning objectives, whether it is to improve fundamental conversational skills, fluency, or reading and writing ability. Defining specific goals is going to help the teachers/learners in selecting the appropriate courses and materials. Making use of multimedia resources such as interactive activities, audio snippets, video lectures, and other multimedia content that are often available on e-learning platforms can also help students to enhance their language proficiency, and teachers to make their courses more efficient. According to Arkorful & Abaidoo (2015) and Mohammadi et al. (2011), the interactive, repetitious, adjustable, and customizable aspect of online learning is one of the aspects that contribute to its uniqueness. An effective integration of online learning also requires the development of autonomous learning habits, it requires responsibility, independence, and autonomy from the students. According to a study conducted by Erarslan and Arslan (2020), e-autonomous learning behaviors among pupils must be developed, and students need assistance and guidance in making deliberate work, in order for online learning to be successfully implemented. They also suggest that after gaining e-autonomy in their online learning, learners might discover their efficient learning styles and outputs (Erarslan and Arslan, 2020; Al Hadef, 2021; Yumnam, 2021). Utilizing online learning tools to the fullest can improve speaking and listening abilities. According to Zakarneh's (2018) investigation on the efficacy of e-learning as a learning method at Arab educational institutions, e-learning helps with vocabulary acquisition and development, language skill improvement, as well as the mastery of English grammar. Learners can also join one of the many online forums or communities offered by e-learning platforms where they may communicate with other students and native speakers. Participating in these groups might offer more support and practice, which helps students acquire better communication skills in the desired language. Various studies show that students benefit from e-learning when it comes to the process of language acquisition because it gives students independence in their learning journey, and the ability to take full advantage of learning opportunities across a variety of online resources, software programs, or, in a more modern way, social media platforms and websites (Abney et al., 2019; Aydin, 2012; Brick, 2012; Chawinga, 2017; Faizi et al., 2013; Wong et al., 2017; Erarslan & Arslan, 2020). E-learning also allows not only instructors, but also students to monitor their own progress in the language learning process as progress monitoring options are now available on a lot of e-learning platforms. Tracking one's development to determine how far they have gone and to pinpoint any areas that could require additional attention is so beneficial as it assists and helps mediating to any gaps or difficulties the learners are facing, and thus allowing the learning process to proceed faster and smoother. Using e-learning and the numerous benefits it provides, educators and pupils can customize the language acquisition experience to fit their requirements and preferences. E-learning materials can be used to significantly further the language learning experience.

The Contribution of E-Learning in Language Learning

In addition to the numerous contributions of E-learning and the diverse range of platforms and software it offers that were mentioned above, and which offer plenty of features to boost the learning experience of language students, e-learning can significantly enhance the teaching and learning process of foreign languages and improve pupils' language proficiency. In the modern educational era, e-learning has emerged as an important tool for language training. it can be exceedingly advantageous to language instruction when employed in a language course due to several reasons including the accessibility it offers as it has made language acquisition available to people all over the world, removing geographical and financial restrictions. Language courses and materials may be accessed from practically any location with an internet connection, allowing individuals in distant places or with restricted access to traditional language programs to engage in language learning. According to Mohammadi, Neda, V. Ghorbani, and F. Hamidi (2011), e-learning material is convenient for students to access at any time, and in any place. It also enables professors and students to connect more effectively with one another and create meaningful relationships using educational apps and social media platforms such as Zoom, or Google Meet, or even Facebook and WhatsApp. Furthermore, e-learning systems provide unrivaled flexibility allowing learners to decide their own study plans, choosing when and where to interact with language learning resources. According to Sun and Chen (2016), e-learning is being used in universities and higher education institutions all over the world, but especially in the United States, either fully online (distant) or in a hybrid format, in order to give students more flexibility with their schedules, give them access to universities, increase the number of courses that are offered, and ultimately boost university enrollment (Erarslan & Arslan, 2020). This adaptability of e-learning in a language-learning context allows students to develop at their own speed and at their own rate. Costley and Lange (2018) state that e-learning programs catered to the requirements of individual students and gave them flexibility with regard to time, place, as well as resources. Students are able to return to topics and revise them as many times as needed and devote more time to difficult elements, guaranteeing thorough understanding and skill improvement. Teachers can use e-learning to get around some of the challenges they encounter in the classroom, such as the restricted lecture time, the high number of pupils, and the passive educational settings (Limniou & Whitehead, 2010; Tuncay & Uzunboylu, 2012). It also enables teachers to use a variety of multimedia materials in language courses such as video lessons, audio clips, interactive exercises, and quizzes that can help in enhancing listening and speaking skills; use tailored evaluation tools according to the requirements of the students, and make use of technology to enhance content delivery techniques over the traditional blackboard and textbooks techniques which develops students' language skills, proficiency, and pronunciation. According to Gilakjani, and Abbas Pourhosein (2017), more depth in the content-area curriculum would be attainable by incorporating technology. Moreover, e-learning offers learners immediate feedback through interactive exercises and online quizzes which enables them to evaluate their language abilities in real-time. This immediate feedback assists students in identifying areas for progress, allowing them to concentrate on specific language components for mediation, and therefore encourages active involvement with language material and speeds up the language acquisition process. Additionally, it makes students more interested in learning about new topics that are addressed in lectures or reading assignments and so they can even take it further and look up more depth to subjects and seek more knowledge using the internet and technological tools, it also creates scenarios and real-world situations that foster creativity and problem-solving skills, pushing pupils to think critically instead of automatically receiving and memorizing facts. The study conducted by Yumnam (2021) proves that e-learning tools boost students' creativity, critical thinking, and motivation, resulting in better academic writing skills (Yumnam, 2021). E-learning can also help students improve their writing skills since it offers numerous online writing platforms and tools that provide real-time feedback, allowing learners to improve their grammar and style. in a study conducted by Ramos and Gatcho (2020), they evaluated the frequent writing challenges encountered by Filipino first-year college students in the e-learning setting and discovered that the majority of the students' writing skills are either improving or reasonably developing. Moreover, e-learning makes learning more personalized as certain systems employ adaptive algorithms to evaluate every pupil's requirements and progress, and thus, customizing material to meet the unique needs of the students based on the results of their evaluation, and guaranteeing a productive and successful learning environment. In his study on e-learning English as a Foreign Language (EFL) in Saudi Arabia, Mutambik (2018) underlines the significance of utilizing e-learning technologies to successfully satisfy the needs of both educators and learners (Yumnam, 2021). by maximizing their language learning process through practice and instruction that is specifically tailored to them. Furthermore, the idea that teachers are the primary and exclusive source of knowledge will also disappear with e-learning since students now have access to a variety of educational platforms and technologies that provide them with a limitless supply of knowledge that they can subsequently share and debate with their peers. Additionally, cultural insights are frequently incorporated into e-learning to guarantee that students get a better comprehension of the language's background and culture. The awareness of cultures and not only of languages improves communication across cultural boundaries and adds value to language acquisition. One of the most important and note-worthy aspects of e-learning is its cost-free nature, e-learning lowers the total cost of language instruction by doing away with the requirement for physical textbooks, travel costs, and classroom equipment. A larger audience is able to afford language instruction thanks to its affordability and cost-effectiveness. Several studies have found the same results according to Erarslan and Arslan (2020), stating that online learning grants students comfort, practicality, and time and financial freedom (Kemp & Grieve, 2014; Salamat et al.,2018; Sun & Chen, 2016; Young, 2006).

However, despite being highly beneficial and despite its significant contributions to language learning, e-learning in language learning and teaching is fraught with challenges and obstacles. One key barrier is the absence of face-to-face connection, which might impede the development of social and oral communication skills and real-life language practice. The lack of face-to-face feedback can also make resolving pronunciation issues, delicate language nuances, and learning idioms and expressions difficult. This was demonstrated in research done by Erarslan and Arslan (2020) that found several drawbacks to e-learning, including little to no contact, a lack of fast or delayed feedback, and online distractions. In addition to this study, other studies done on the subject also demonstrate that these aspects are some of the limiting drawbacks of e-learning (Yuce, 2019; Berge, 2013; Muilenburg & Berge, 2005; Gillett-Swan, 2017). Poor internet connectivity or restricted access to electronic devices, as well, might create disparities among learners, and reduce, or even prevent, their involvement and participation. Furthermore, consistent language practice may be hampered by a lack of ambition, motivation, and discipline, as well as a high level of distraction brought on by the self-paced and autonomous aspect of online learning which makes it require a lot of responsibility and self-control. Another problem that teachers especially face, is in creating successful language exams for virtual environments since it could be more challenging to evaluate spoken language skills and offer helpful feedback than in typical educational environments. The shortcomings and difficulties of e-learning in language education, in spite of all of its benefits, highlight the necessity of careful planning, innovative teaching strategies, and continuous work to resolve accessibility concerns, which draws more importance to the role a teacher plays in an online learning setting.

The Role of the Teacher in an Online Language Course

In a traditional classroom setting, professors had complete control over the classroom and were endowed with authority, power, and absolute responsibility. In the classroom, teachers were seen as the primary and exclusive information source. learning was therefore teacher-centered. Even if the dynamics of the traditional classroom might shift in the online and e-learning training, the teacher is still crucial in guiding and assisting in language learning. In an online language course, the role that the instructor plays is complex and vital to the learning process. In the traditional classroom setting, the instructor is physically present to give courses and provide real-time training. In contrast, e-learning changes this dynamic by making learning resources available to learners outside of the boundaries of a physical classroom. According to Bates, Almekdash, and Gilchrest-Dunnam, (2017), This shift in learning positions the teacher as a facilitator and guide in the classroom rather than as the primary source of knowledge. In online learning settings, instructors frequently play the role of facilitators and guides instead of being the main or only source of knowledge, which encourages pupils to evolve into active, self-motivated learners, develop their critical thinking skills, and become self-directed learners, which are beneficial components for language acquisition. In addition to facilitating and guiding, teachers take on a variety of duties and responsibilities that are critical to the success of the e-learning language training including designing online curriculum and adapting course material for online delivery; providing remote support and communication through email, interaction platforms, discussion forums, and video conferencing software; offering feedback and assessment; Keeping pupils engaged and self-directed in their study, and promoting self-discipline and time management; monitoring students' progress, engagement and accomplishment; providing explanations of content through video lectures, written explanations, webinars; adapting teaching techniques to meet the requirements and learning styles of individual pupils, as well as offering individualized assistance; engaging pupils in their learning and in interactions with their peers through discussion forums and live chat sessions; and providing technical support to assist students in solving technical issues they might face.

INSTRUCTIONAL DESIGN MODELS: ADDIE

Importance of Instructional Design

With the aim of promoting efficient and effective learning, instructional design is a methodical, inter-disciplinary process that includes the planning, conception, development, and evaluation of educational resources, experiences, and activities. Instructional Design, according to Instructional Design Australia, is the process of applying our understanding of the way individuals learn to drive our choices of instructional sequences and approaches to suit the goals and needs of students, as well as their intended learning outcomes. It is a systematic strategy to creating learning experiences that are personalized to the requirements of students and strive to achieve specified learning goals. In order to develop educational material that engages pupils, promotes comprehension, and fosters the acquisition of knowledge and abilities, instructional designers make use of concepts derived from learning theory, pedagogy, and technology. The importance of instructional design stems from its effectiveness in making the instructions efficient, engaging, appealing, useful, and affordable. It improves learning outcomes as Learning experiences are

Figure 1. What do instructional designers do job description

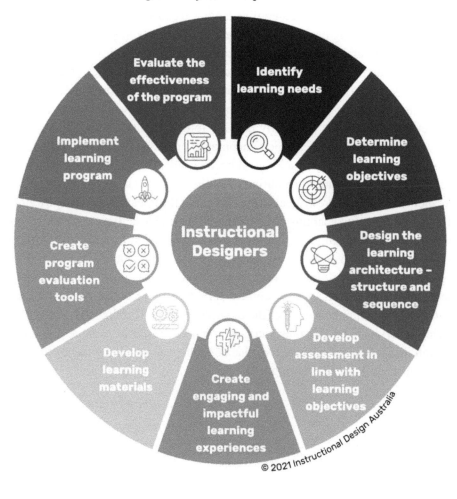

made as effective as possible when training is well planned. It guarantees that the information is coherently organized, in line with learning goals, and efficiently engages students; simplifies the teaching and learning process, maximizing time and resources which improves the efficiency of training and learning; motivates and engages students in their learning by integrating a range of interesting and interactive components such as games, multimedia, simulations, and AI which improves the enjoyment of the learning experience; guarantees that the targeted learning objectives and needs and the instructional materials are correlated; It enables continuous evaluation and enhancement of educational trainings and programs through feedback, and evolving educational trends; helps saving costs related to time, money, and materials since a larger audience may be reached and return on investment can be maximized with well-designed courses; enables personalized learning experiences, and employs a learner-centered approach instead of a teacher-centered one.

Instructional Design Models

Models of instructional design were created to offer a systematic, methodical, and structured approach to training and teaching. Though there are many models and processes for instructional design, only a select few have become widely accepted and are frequently employed by experts, professionals, instructors, and instructional designers. Several of the most often used and most effective models for instructional design include:

- **ADDIE Model:** The ADDIE model, which stands for Analysis, Design, Development, Implementation, and Evaluation, is a well-known and adaptable model used in instructional design. Because it offers a methodical approach to creating and enhancing learning experiences, it is extensively used in a variety of business and educational contexts. It is a dynamic, adaptable, and iterative guideline that instructional designers may use to create successful e-learning courses. it also offers an efficient, targeted method with feedback for ongoing development (Disha Gupta, 2023).
- **Bloom's Taxonomy:** Bloom's Taxonomy is frequently utilized in the creation of learning objectives and evaluations. It offers assessments that focus on certain cognitive skills and divides learning objectives into many cognitive domains, assisting designers in creating precise and quantifiable goals.
- **Merrill's Principles of Instruction (MPI):** According to Disha Gupta (2023), the task-centered Merrill's Principles of Instruction (MPI) method concentrates on strategies that promote and facilitate learning. This instructional design model incorporates five MPI principles, which are as follows: Task-centered, Activation, Demonstration, Application, and Integration.
- **Dick and Carey Model:** The Dick and Carey Model provides a thorough framework for assessing learning requirements, creating lessons, and carrying out formative and summative assessments. It is based on a systemic approach to instructional design.
- **SAM Model:** SAM, which stands for Successful Approximation Model, is an approach to instructional design that puts an emphasis on efficiency, teamwork, quick iterations and prototyping, and subject matter expert participation. Its approach to instructional design is marked by agility and iteration.
- **Gagne's Nine Events of Instructions:** The behaviorist approach to learning is the foundation of Gagne's Nine Events of Instruction model (Disha Gupta, 2023). As its name suggests, nine es-

sential instructional events are identified by the framework and should be addressed in order to optimize learning: Gain attention, inform learners of the objectives, recall prior learning, Present the material, provide guidance, elicit performance, provide feedback, assess performance, and Enhance retention (Disha Gupta, 2023).

ADDIE Model, and How to Design an Educational Device Through It

One of the most popular approaches for instructional design is the ADDIE Model. It was developed by Florida State University's Center for Educational Technology in 1975 (Branson, Rayner, Cox, Furman, King, Hannum, 1975), but it was first conceived by Gagné in 1967 (Moulton, Shane, Jane Strickland, Al Strickland, Jerry White, and Lauralee Zimmerly, 2010). This instructional design model is renowned for using systematic methods to provide engaging educational opportunities. When developing educational materials, it provides educators, instructors, trainers, and instructional designers with a framework to operate within.

As it was stated before, ADDIE stands for Analysis, Design, Development, Implementation, and Evaluation. Each one of these five phases is essential for planning and delivering effective educational courses.

- **Analysis:** It constitutes the foundation of the following phases. Every other phase is built upon the analysis phase. Instructional designers determine the goals and requirements for learning during this phase. This entails a careful analysis of the intended audience, their background knowledge, skill gap analysis, and the particular objectives of the educational initiative. Information on the learning environment, the resources that are available, and any restrictions or limits are also gathered by designers in this phase.
- **Design:** The goal of the design phase is to create a comprehensive plan for the educational program by utilizing the analysis phase's results to determine an approach to creating the instructional program. This entails creating the general framework and arrangement of the material as well as specifying learning objectives and evaluation techniques. In this phase, designers create a course plan that outlines the instructional methods, activities, time frames, and resources to be used by teachers.
- **Development:** This phase brings the previous one (design) to life, the training resources and educational content are created during the development process. During this phase, educators create lesson plans, multimedia assets, tests, determine the delivery method, and any additional teaching tools or technologies required for the program of study.
- **Implementation:** The launch, presentation, and delivery of the educational program and course materials to the students occur during the Implementation phase. This includes guiding the course, configuring the learning management system, and offering assistance to students as required. Whether the instruction is done in a classroom, online, or in another learning setting, the implementation phase requires real teaching and learning activities and course delivery.
- **Evaluation:** The evaluation phase evaluates and assesses the educational program's efficiency. To assess if the learning objectives were met, and the goals set were achieved, instructors compile information on student performance as well as their feedback. in light of the outcomes, they get to decide whether to make adjustments and enhancements, or start the ADDIE process all over again.

Using the ADDIE model for educational device design entails a methodical, iterative approach that aims to produce a useful and efficient learning course. In order to design an educational device through the instructional design model ADDIE, educators, or designers should follow the five phases of this model. Each and every one of these phases is crucial to the instructional design process and assures the effectiveness and efficiency of the training program and instructional course, it ensures the students' educational success, helps achieve learning objectives and goals, and facilitates customization to fit different individual learning needs.

EXAMPLE OF AN E-LEARNING EDUCATIONAL SCENARIO DESIGNED USING THE ADDIE MODEL

Below is an example of an e-learning educational scenario that was designed through the ADDIE model for a freshman French language course. It was designed following the first three phases of the ADDIE model starting from the analysis determining the goals and requirements for learning; design, creating the general framework and structure of the material and content and specifying learning objectives; development, creating the plan of the lesson, multimedia resources, exercises, and defining the delivery method. The implementation and evaluation phases are phases that occur during, or after the application and execution of the lesson. This bellow is a vocabulary lesson that aims to teach students sports vocabulary in French:

- Nature de l'activité: Activité de langue.
- Objectif intermédiaire: Reconnaître et identifier le lexique sportif.
- Tâche: Organiser une activité sportive lors d'un voyage.
- Intitulé du cours: Parler de son sport préféré.
- Support: Image.
- Consigne de la tâche:
  ○ Reconnaît le lexique sportif.
  ○ Emploie le lexique sportif pour parler de ses activités sportives.
- Mode d'enseignement: A distance.
- Domaine de la discipline: lexique
- Durée: 1h

Table 1. Course of the lesson, activities, the teacher's role and instructions, students tasks, and the duration of every step

Etapes de l'activité	Consignes du professeur	Rôle du professeur	Tâches de l'apprenant	Durée
Mise en situation **- Tâche à accomplir:** Reconnaître les types de sports		- Présente le cours. - Affiche le support de départ. (Voir document 1)		10min

Document 1:

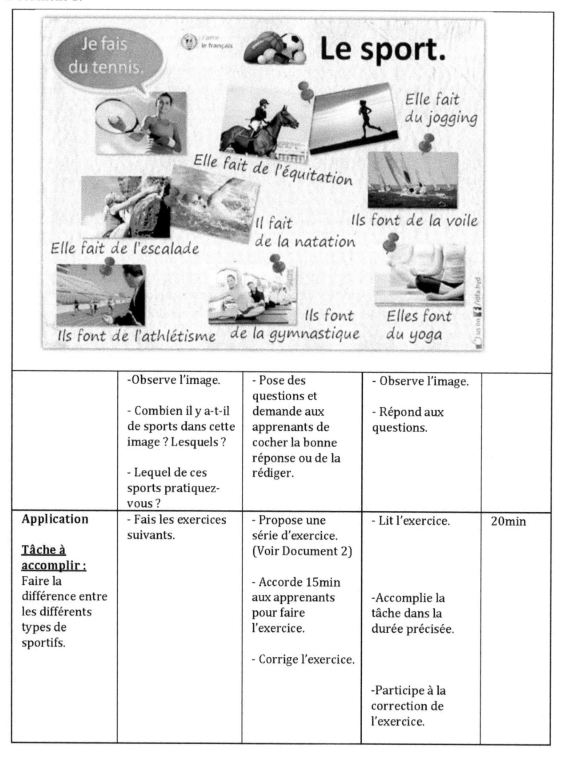

	-Observe l'image. - Combien il y a-t-il de sports dans cette image ? Lesquels ? - Lequel de ces sports pratiquez-vous ?	- Pose des questions et demande aux apprenants de cocher la bonne réponse ou de la rédiger.	- Observe l'image. - Répond aux questions.	
Application <u>**Tâche à accomplir :**</u> Faire la différence entre les différents types de sportifs.	- Fais les exercices suivants.	- Propose une série d'exercice. (Voir Document 2) - Accorde 15min aux apprenants pour faire l'exercice. - Corrige l'exercice.	- Lit l'exercice. -Accomplie la tâche dans la durée précisée. -Participe à la correction de l'exercice.	20min

Document 2:

1) Classe les mots dans le tableau :

Le tennis – le ski – le football – le tir à l'arc – la natation – l'escalade – le judo – le saut en hauteur – le volleyball – le hockey sur glace – l'escrime – le baseball.

Sports individuels	Sports à deux	Sports collectifs

2) a- Entoure les verbes qui indiquent des actions en natation :

nager – dribbler – couler - pédaler – plonger – flotter

b- À quelles autres activités renvoient les autres verbes ?

3) Associe chaque sport à sa surface ou au lieu correspondant.

La natation	La patinoire
La gymnastique	Le gymnase
Le ski	La piscine
Le football	Le ring
Le hockey sur glace	Le tatami
L'équitation	La piste
Le judo	Le manège
La boxe	Le terrain

Transfert - __Tâche à accomplir__ : Rédiger la liste des activités sportives à faire lors d'un voyage.	- Rédige une liste dans laquelle tu cites le programme d'activités sportives lors d'un voyage organisé par l'université.	- Affiche la consigne de l'exercice de transfert. - Met les mots clé en gras. - Accorde 20min aux apprenants pour envoyer la tâche. - Publie sur la plateforme un exemplaire de production.	- Lit la consigne. - Schématise à l'aide d'un mind-map la consigne. - Accomplit la tâche dans la durée précisée. - Envoie son travail.	30min

CONCLUSION

As we just proved, the importance of language in our current era is undeniable due to various reasons, and in the future, it might get even more valuable as the world barriers and distances disappear more and more with the technological improvement. The same goes for e-learning, which with time, will see a massive improvement driven by ongoing technological innovations, educational research, innovative instructional design models, and increasing learning demands. With the emergence of AI technologies and all these trends coming together, e-learning has the potential to completely transform education in the future. In the years to come, e-learning will continue to progress and get better due to the constant cooperation between educators, software developers, designers, and students which is going to help it overcome the challenges and difficulties faced while using it. These future e-learning advancements are expected to have a major positive impact on language acquisition. There are a number of significant trends and developments that indicate that language students will benefit from improved and more successful educational experiences especially if e-learning is successfully implemented and the courses are well designed following the most efficient instructional design models, teachers are following their roles effectively, and students are responsibly interacting with content and lessons. However, will e-learning ever be able to completely replace the traditional face-to-face learning experiences and the important real-life interactions it offers?

REFERENCES

Abney, A. K., Cook, L. A., Fox, A. K., & Stevens, J. (2019). Intercollegiate social media education ecosystem. *Journal of Marketing Education*, *41*(3), 254–269. doi:10.1177/0273475318786026

- Arkorful, V., & Abaidoo, N. (2015). The role of e-learning, advantages, and disadvantages of its adoption in higher education. *International journal of instructional technology and distance learning*, *12*(1), 29-42.

Aydin, S. (2012). A review of research on Facebook as an educational environment. *Educational Technology Research and Development*, *60*(6), 1093–1106. doi:10.100711423-012-9260-7

- Branson, R. K., Rayner, G. T., Cox, J. L., Furman, J. P., King, F. J., & Hannum, W. H. (1975). Interservice procedures for instructional systems development. (5 vols.)(TRADOC Pam 350-30 NAVEDTRA 106A). Ft. Monroe, VA: US Army Training and Doctrine Command.

Berge, Z. L. (2013). Barriers to communication in distance education. *Turkish Online Journal of Distance Education*, *14*(1), 374–388.

Bates, J. E., Almekdash, H., & Gilchrest-Dunnam, M. J. (2017). The flipped classroom: A brief, brief history. *The flipped college classroom: Conceptualized and re-conceptualized*, 3-10.

Brick, B. (2012). The Role of Social Networking Sites for Language Learning in UK Higher Education: The Views of Learners and Practitioners. [IJCALLT]. *International Journal of Computer-Assisted Language Learning and Teaching*, *2*(3), 35–53. doi:10.4018/ijcallt.2012070103

Chomsky, N. (2012). On the nature, use and acquisition of language. In *Language and meaning in cognitive science* (pp. 1–20). Routledge.

Chawinga, W. D. (2017). Taking social media to a university classroom: Teaching and learning using Twitter and blogs. *International Journal of Educational Technology in Higher Education, 14*(1), 1–19.

Costley, J., & Lange, C. (2018). The moderating effects of group work on the relationship between motivation and cognitive load. *The International Review of Research in Open and Distributed Learning, 19*(1).

Cook, V. (2008). Second Language Learning and Language Learning—Vivian Cook-2008. *Structure (London, England), 18*, 2–2.

Disha Gupta. (2023). *8 Effective Instructional Design Models in 2023.* Whatfix. https://whatfix.com/blog/instructional-design-models/

El Hadef, S. (2021). The Implication of Online Learning on the Motivation of Students:(Students of University Mohammed First as a Case Study). *International Journal of Linguistics and Translation Studies, 2*(3), 12–22. doi:10.36892/ijlts.v2i3.164

Ellis, N. C., & Larsen-Freeman, D. (2006). Language emergence: Implications for applied linguistics—Introduction to the special issue. *Applied Linguistics, 27*(4), 558–589. doi:10.1093/applin/aml028

Erarslan, A., & Arslan, A. (2020). Online learning experiences of university students in ELT and the effects of online learning on their learning practices. *Language and Technology, 2*(1), 44–58.

Erarslan, A., & Arslan, A. (2020). Online learning experiences of university students and the effects of online learning on their learning practices. *Language and Technology, 2*(1), 44–58.

Faizi, R., El Afia, A., & Chiheb, R. (2013). Exploring the potential benefits of using social media in education. [iJEP]. *International Journal of Engineering Pedagogy, 3*(4), 50–53. doi:10.3991/ijep.v3i4.2836

- Garrison, D. R., & Anderson, T. (2005). El e-learning en el siglo XXI: Investigación y práctica. *El e-learning en el siglo XXI: investigación y práctica*, 0-0.

Gatcho, A. R., & Ramos, E. T. (2020). Common Writing Problems and Writing Attitudes among Freshman University Students in Online Learning Environments: An Exploratory Study. *Journal of Translation and Language Studies, 1*(1), 49–66. doi:10.48185/jtls.v1i1.6

Gilakjani, A. P. (2017). A review of the literature on the integration of technology into the learning and teaching of English language skills. *International Journal of English Linguistics, 7*(5), 95–106. doi:10.5539/ijel.v7n5p95

Gillett-Swan, J. (2017). The challenges of online learning: Supporting and engaging the isolated learner. *Journal of Learning Design, 10*(1), 20–30. doi:10.5204/jld.v9i3.293

Krashen, S. (1982). *Principles and practice in second language acquisition.*

Lee, M. J., & McLoughlin, C. (Eds.). (2010). *Web 2.0-based e-learning: Applying social informatics for tertiary teaching: Applying social informatics for tertiary teaching.* IGI Global.

Kemp, N., & Grieve, R. (2014). Face-to-face or face-to-screen? Undergraduates' opinions and test performance in classroom vs. online learning. *Frontiers in Psychology, 5*, 1278. PMID:25429276

Jabeen, S. S., & Thomas, A. J. (2015, October). Effectiveness of online language learning. In *Proceedings of the World Congress on Engineering and Computer Science* (Vol. 1, pp. 15).

Mohammadi, N., Ghorbani, V., & Hamidi, F. (2011). Effects of elearning on language learning. *Procedia Computer Science*, *3*, 464–468. doi:10.1016/j.procs.2010.12.078

Moulton, S., Strickland, J., Strickland, A., White, J., & Zimmerly, L. (2010, October). Online course development using the ADDIE model of instruction design: The need to establish validity in the analysis phase. In *ELearn: World Conference on ELearning in Corporate, Government, Healthcare, and Higher Education* (pp. 20462054). Association for the Advancement of Computing in Education (AACE).

Muilenburg, L. Y., & Berge, Z. L. (2005). Student barriers to online learning: A factor analytic study. *Distance Education*, *26*(1), 29–48. doi:10.1080/01587910500081269

Mutambik, I. (2018). The Role of eLearning in Studying English as a Foreign Language in Saudi Arabia: Students' and Teachers' Perspectives. *English Language Teaching*, *11*(5), 74–83. doi:10.5539/elt.v11n5p74

Stern, H. H. (1983). *Fundamental concepts of language teaching: Historical and interdisciplinary perspectives on applied linguistic research*. Oxford university press.

Siemens, G., & Yurkiw, S. (2003). The roles of the learner and the instructor in elearning. *Preparing learners for elearning*, 123138.

Sun, A., & Chen, X. (2016). Online education and its effective practice: A research review. *Journal of Information Technology Education*, 15.

Salamat, L., Ahmad, G., Bakht, M. I., & Saifi, I. L. (2018). Effects of elearning on students' academic learning at university level. *Asian Innovative Journal of Social Sciences and Humanities*, *2*(2), 1–12.

Tuncay, N., & Uzunboylu, H. (2012). English language teachers' success in blended and online elearning. *Procedia: Social and Behavioral Sciences*, *47*, 131–137. doi:10.1016/j.sbspro.2012.06.626

Wang, Y., & Sun, C. (2001). Internetbased real time language education: Towards a fourth generation distance education. *CALICO Journal*, 539–561.

Whitehead, J. C., & Limniou, M. (2010). Online general prelaboratory training course for facilitating first year chemical laboratory. *Cypriot Journal of Educational Sciences*, *5*, 39–55.

Wong, L.H., SingChai, C., & PohAw, G. (2017). Seamless language learning: Second language learning with social media. *Comunicar: Revista Científica de Comunicacíon y Educacíon*, *25*(50), 9–21. doi:10.3916/C50-2017-01

Young, S. (2006). Student views of effective online teaching in higher education. *American Journal of Distance Education*, *20*(2), 65–77. doi:10.120715389286ajde2002_2

Yüce, E. (2019). Possible problems in online foreign language teaching at a university context. *International Journal of Curriculum and Instruction*, *11*(2), 75–86.

Yumnam, R. (2021). Elearning: An effective mode of teaching English as a Second Language. *Journal of Translation and Language Studies*, *2*(2), 1–9. doi:10.48185/jtls.v2i2.275

Zakarneh, B. M. (2018). Effectiveness of Elearning mode for teaching English language in Arab Universities. *International Journal of Applied Linguistics and English Literature*, *7*(7), 171–181. doi:10.7575/aiac.ijalel.v.7n.7p.171

Chapter 18
The Potential of Content and Language Integrated Learning in Curriculum–Based Ideological and Political Education

Hengzhi Hu

https://orcid.org/0000-0001-5232-913X
Universiti Kebangsaan Malaysia, Malaysia

Harwati Hashim

https://orcid.org/0000-0002-8817-427X
Universiti Kebangsaan Malaysia, Malaysia

Nur Ehsan Mohd Said

Universiti Kebangsaan Malaysia, Malaysia

ABSTRACT

The innovative curriculum-based ideological and political education (CIPE) trend in China's higher education integrates ideological and political education (IPE) into curricula to develop students' citizenship skills. Foreign language teaching (FLT) has leveraged CIPE's advancement due to its rich cultural nuances. Yet, effectively implementing IPE within FLT remains complex and demands academic attention. The authors suggest content and language integrated learning (CLIL) holds significant potential for IPE-based FLT. This potential arises from the shared attributes between CLIL and IPE-based FLT, which encompass diverse language learning facets, the acquisition of content knowledge and the cultivation of cross-cultural understanding. This chapter compares CLIL and IPE-based FLT, based on which a coherent conceptual framework is introduced and justified for implementing IPE-based FLT. However, a comprehensive agenda is needed to address a multitude of issues beyond the scope of this chapter, which is pivotal in unlocking the full potential of CIPE and ensuring its enduring viability.

DOI: 10.4018/979-8-3693-3128-6.ch018

Copyright © 2024, IGI Global. Copying or distributing in print or electronic forms without written permission of IGI Global is prohibited.

INTRODUCTION: SETTING THE CONTEXT

The evolution of foreign language teaching (FLT) theories in China has undergone three significant phases: the importation and adaptation of foreign theories, the creation of context-specific theories rooted in local circumstances and the amalgamation of theories stemming from both domestic and foreign practices (Wen, 2019). A series of theoretical achievements have been constituted against this backdrop, whereas they still cannot satisfy the practical needs of FLT in China, with domestic scholars appealing for an innovative and localised endeavour to refine FLT theories and explore educational possibilities to attain the national goal of improving FLT quality and developing learners' competency to use a foreign language (FL) and engage in international and cross-cultural communication (An & Pan, 2023; Ma & Liu, 2021).

Amidst the surge of FLT theories, the concept of Curriculum-based Ideological and Political Education (CIPE), also referred to as *ke-cheng si-zheng*[1], has gained renewed prominence through the recent introduction of *The Guiding Outline for Ideological and Political Construction of Courses in Colleges and Universities*, a government-issued directive underscoring the imperative for nurturing talent within higher education providers (HEPs) and the importance of constructing and reforming CIPE (Lou, 2021). CIPE is a pedagogical initiative put forth by Chinese authorities to realise the objective of developing well-rounded citizens with positive perspectives on the nation, ethnicity, history, culture, world, life and values, by "running ideological and political work through the whole process of education and teaching" in a holistic manner (Gao, 2021, p. 308). Embracing the philosophy that courses within HEPs serve a dual purpose of imparting professional expertise alongside fostering students' political and ideological development, the potential of CIPE to harmonise Ideological and Political Education (IPE) with FLT has been extensively deliberated upon (Gao, 2021; Huang, 2021; Li & Zhang, 2023; Ren, 2022). However, the effective utilisation of this potential remains an intricate matter, warranting immediate attention due to its pivotal role in shaping the future organisation of CIPE (Huang & Xiao, 2021).

Given that FLT sets itself apart from the education of other subjects by highlighting the interconnection of languages, cultures and cognition, and that language discourse serves as a conduit for unveiling the underlying beliefs, values and expressions inherent in social and cultural institutions (Gao, 2021; Hu, 2021), we aim to propel and rationalise the potential of Content and Language Integrated Learning (CLIL) within the context of China's higher education agenda, which is undergoing an influence from CIPE considerations within FLT. It is suggested that, in the current stage where both domestic and foreign theories and practices of FLT are integral to the Chinese FLT landscape (Wen, 2019), CLIL, a pedagogical approach that originated from the Western hemisphere, holds significant theoretical implications for IPE-based FLT due to its distinct characteristic of simultaneous emphasis on both language acquisition and content comprehension. Following a brief literature review on CLIL and IPE-based FLT, a comparative analysis of these pedagogical concepts is conducted in this chapter, culminating in the introduction of a framework for conceptualising the integration of CLIL into IPE-based FLT, with a primary focus on guiding FL teachers in implementing the CIPE initiative.

CIPE: AN INNOVATIVE EDUCATIONAL TREND IN CHINA

IPE "refers to the activities of cultivating people's ideological and moral qualities that are common to all class societies of mankind" (Li, 2018, p. 1379), encompassing a purposeful, well-planned and organised endeavour that influences members of society through the dissemination of specific ideas, political stances and moral principles (Cheng et al., 2016). This definition positions IPE in close alignment with citizenship education, an academic discipline geared towards disseminating the essential knowledge necessary for fostering a continuous supply of new citizens who are willing to actively participate in and contribute to the progress of a civilised society (Zhang & Fagan, 2016). Given that the Chinese government and educational bodies have yet to establish a systematic curriculum for citizenship education (Zhou, 2021), IPE takes on a pivotal role in ensuring that students possess the requisite knowledge, skills and attitudes essential for effective engagement in civic life.

In China's higher education agenda, the concept of CIPE, a more specialised form of IPE, emphasises the utilisation of classroom teaching to create a synergistic effect (Ren, 2022). This is achieved by "running ideological and political work through the whole process of education and teaching" and improving the affinity and pertinence of IPE in university courses, ultimately working towards the IPE objectives of nurturing well-rounded citizens with positive ideological and moral attributes (Gao, 2021, p. 308). This aligns with the perspective that curriculums in HEPs serve as the foundational cornerstone and conduit for effective IPE (Yu, 2021).

Although CIPE is indeed a novel concept, Chinese scholars believe that its roots can be traced back to a much earlier period. In the late twentieth century, moral education, especially for teenagers, began to gain prominence in China, as an integral part of the government's broader effort to achieve the nation's modernisation, and against the backdrop of significant socio-economic shifts initiated by the *Reform and Opening-Up* policies (i.e. a series of economic and political reforms initiated by the Chinese government to change China's previously closed and centrally planned economy) (Chu, 1998; Song & Xiao, 1992). While this initiative initially operated as a distinct educational endeavour, it is now regarded as a precursor to China's ongoing efforts to integrate IPE into the curricula of various subjects (Li & Zhang, 2023).

The effort continued in the earlier part of this century, and it was not until 2010 that CIPE-wise education began to emerge, coincided with the implementation of a trial project of strengthening and improving moral education work in several developed Chinese cities (e.g. Shanghai), aimed at integrating China's core socialist ideology into the curricula at all levels of education (Cheng et al., 2016; Ren, 2022). An academic example widely recognised as the pioneering and relatively systematic CIPE-wise education is the introduction of liberal arts courses at Shanghai University in 2016. This initiative aimed to transition from the traditional, teacher-centred, didactic approach to IPE and instead adopt a multidisciplinary paradigm that integrated IPE into curricula, particularly within hidden curricula (Xin & Yin, 2016).

First introduced in 2017, the notion of CIPE was officially mentioned and elaborated upon in the *Implementation Outline of the Quality Improvement Project of Ideological and Political Work in Colleges and Universities*, a report issued by the Ministry of Education of The People's Republic of China (2017, December 6), aimed to further enhance IPE. Since its inception, it has gained widespread recognition and adoption, with a national effort to reinforce its presence. This reflects the development of a collaborative educational framework that emphasises "knowledge transfer, ability cultivation and value guidance" are achieved in a whole-curriculum approach (Yu, 2021, p. 2). Consequently, this enriches the organisational structure of higher education programmes by preserving the inherent academic attributes of specialised subjects while simultaneously addressing the intricate relationship between a political orientation and an academic orientation in teaching (Li & Li, 2023; Ren, 2022).

In other words, the purpose of implementing CIPE is not to establish an entirely new course but rather to supplement the existing educational agenda with IPE in a subtle and implicit manner. This educational move is justified by the penetration theory, which spotlights the integration of the IPE content (i.e. the knowledge of politics, traditional moralities and socialist core values) "into the mind of the instructional objects through various ways under certain circumstances", as well as by the conception of holistic education embedded in humanism and the development of students' civic values (Li & Fu, 2020, p. 999).

FLT has provided a significant opportunity for the incorporation of CIPE. Language, in this context, is far more than a mere communication tool; it serves as a mirror reflecting culture, thought and society. This inherent connection of language, culture and social values implies that language can effectively convey the essence of IPE. Therefore, many scholars and researchers have actively explored to unlock the potential synergy between FLT and IPE, both in theory and practice (Gao, 2021; Hu, 2021; Huang, 2021; Lai et al., 2020; Li & Zeng, 2019; Wang et al., 2022). According to Huang and Xiao (2021), given that CIPE in FLT is an emergent issue, the exploration of it should be grounded in the consideration of six fundamental questions: (1) *Why should CIPE be implemented in FLT?* (2) *What is CIPE in FLT?* (3) *Who will provide CIPE in FLT?* (4) *When should CIPE be organised in FLT?* (5) *Where should CIPE be organised?* (6) *How should CIPE be organised in FLT?*.

The answers to the first five inquiries are readily apparent, as it is widely recognised that CIPE in FLT involves the harmonious fusion of IPE and FLT, engaging a diverse array of participants (e.g. researchers, FL teachers and students) in daily classroom interactions (Sun, 2021; Xiao & Huang, 2020). This integration aims to fulfil the imperative that FL "courses [should] strengthen the national cultural confidence, expand the international influence and attraction of Chinese culture … promote students' understanding, respect and tolerance for exotic cultures, help students to establish correct cultural viewpoint and advance Sino-foreign cultural exchange and cooperation" (Li & Fu, 2020, p. 999). Nevertheless, the effective implementation of CIPE remains a complex challenge. Teachers, who constitute the most direct stakeholders in FLT, often grapple with misconceptions stemming from inadequate professional training and guidance (Li et al., 2020). Some perceive CIPE in FLT as a mere additive process, while others adhere rigidly to traditional didactic teaching methodologies or struggle to incorporate IPE due to uncertainty about effectively merging ideological and political content with language learning (Li & Li, 2023; Lou, 2021).

Undoubtedly, the implementation of CIPE is a multifaceted process encompassing intricate elements, such as lesson planning, class delivery and assessment (Hu, 2021). Equally important is the challenge of engaging learners on both intellectual and emotional levels (Duan, 2019). Li et al. (2020) posit that the myriad challenges encountered in CIPE signify a shift from the initial stage, where a foundational comprehension of CIPE is acquired, to a more advanced developmental phase centred around practical classroom application. Contrarily, an alternative perspective suggests that FLT should revert to the primary phase of theoretical exploration to deepen educators' grasp of CIPE within their respective fields, the feasibility of which lies in the crucial role that theoretical development plays in guiding teachers towards embracing favourable theoretical perspectives and implications aligned with the specific learning contexts they address (Sun, 2021). From this standpoint, which appears to be more feasible given the challenges mentioned earlier for educators, it becomes imperative to systematically organise elements beneficial to IPE-based FLT, thereby aiding educators in introspectively assessing their practices and enhancing their pedagogical approaches within CIPE.

Numerous Chinese researchers have embarked on theoretical explorations within the context of IPE-based FLT. However, their inclination has been to formalise the processes and rationales of learning through a general educational lens, rather than anchoring them within the realm of well-defined FLT theories. For instance, Li and Fu (2020) endeavour to establish the viability of CIPE within the domain of College English, a mandatory English course for Chinese undergraduates. They base their argument on the aforementioned penetration theory and holistic education theory yet allocate comparatively less attention to the actual mechanics of language acquisition, without drawing upon established FLT theories. Moreover, in light of the ideological and political dimensions inherent to CIPE (Gao, 2021), certain scholars confine their interpretation to national education requirements and policies. For example, Lai et al. (2020), and Li and Li (2023) propose that FL teachers should champion and comprehend the ethical precepts outlined by national congress and societal leaders to promote CIPE. However, their proposition is characterised by a dearth of practical insights, often lapsing into repetitive interpretations of policies.

Furthermore, the discourse surrounding the methodologies and strategies employed in IPE-based FLT occasionally leans towards abstraction, lacking comprehensive elucidation. For example, Wen (2021), echoing Hu (2021), contends that the crux of designing IPE-based FLT content lies in *qian-yi mo-hua* and *run-wu wu-sheng*, which roughly translates to *subtly and imperceptibly influencing temperament* and conveys the underlying implicit impact of CIPE. Nonetheless, educators may grapple with effectively achieving this unobtrusive, positive influence without the benefit of a coherent and substantiated explanation. Hu's (2019) IPE-based FLT framework tends to be more detailed, emphasising the fusion of China's socialist core values with Western principles drawn from both prescribed and supplementary learning materials in the development of context-specific learning tasks. While classroom research has validated its effectiveness in enhancing educational quality, the framework itself lacks specific guidance on the practical implementation of task design and execution, potentially leading to confusion for educators. These challenges collectively warrant a reconsideration of the CIPE agenda and the fundamental tenets of IPE-based FLT. Such re-evaluation calls for a broader and more accessible perspective, extending beyond established educational theories and policies, to address the complexities and intricacies associated with this evolving pedagogical approach.

CLIL: A CONTENT-BASED INSTRUCTIONAL APPROACH TO FL PEDAGOGY

CLIL, a pedagogical term coined in the 1990s, may not be an entirely novel concept, as similar practice that emphasises both language and content learning within a single classroom can be traced back around 5,000 years to the Akkadian Empire in what is now central Iraq (Hanesová, 2015). Nonetheless, it is important to recognise that the essence of CLIL sets it apart from other FLT approaches, since it is "a generic umbrella term that represents a dual-focussed flexible educational approach with multiple dimensions and applications, in which an additional language is used for learning both content and language" (Gabillon, 2020, para. 10). While variations of CLIL exist across different contexts, such as strong CLIL that prioritises the teaching and learning of content subjects and weak CLIL that underscores language learning (Ikeda et al., 2021), what distinguishes CLIL is its unique emphasis on using the target language (TL) as a means to acquire content knowledge, which in turn contextualises and facilitates language learning. This reciprocal process aids in the enhancement of language proficiency and its practical application.

Influenced by sociocultural theory, which perceives the construction of knowledge and language as a collaborative social process, and drawing from the cognitivist orientation, which considers language acquisition as a complex adaptive system involving conscious and reasoned thinking (Klewitz, 2021), CLIL is underpinned by various frameworks. One of the most enduring is The 4Cs Framework, which harmonises content, communication, cognition and culture (Coyle, 2008; Coyle et al., 2010). While this framework exhibits multiple variations, the original interpretation commonly posits that culture (encompassing intercultural awareness and understanding) interweaves and links content (representing

Figure 1. The 4Cs framework

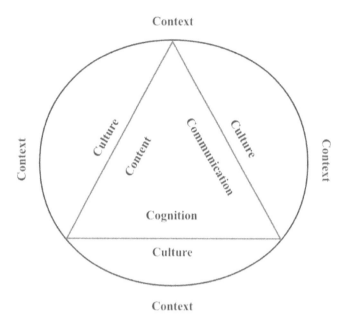

the foundational subject knowledge for the programme), communication (comprising the TL necessary for conveying subject-related meaning) and cognition (comprising the learning and thinking abilities essential for engaging in instructional processes), all in a mutually reinforcing manner (Chaya & Inpin, 2020; Kamis et al., 2021; Nawrot-Lis, 2019). In this sense, scholars emphasise that "culture and intercultural understanding constitute an important part of the CLIL conceptual framework" (Vourdanou, 2019, p. 90), as they enrich language learning, promote meaningful learning and facilitate social connection (Bernaus & Furlong, 2017). These four fundamental components serve as the bedrock for CLIL curriculum design and development, each finding placement within an authentic context (see Figure 1), an additional dimension incorporated into the framework, which underscores the intricate interconnectedness among the other elements (Gabillon, 2020).

Despite the dual-focused nature of CLIL, there has been a significant shift from content-led, strong CLIL programmes to weaker ones, placing primary emphasis on the development of language proficiency because of its increasingly important role in international communication (Kováčiková, 2020). This educational shift has underscored the critical role of teachers' language awareness in ensuring successful CLIL implementation and has further highlighted the importance of The Language Triptych, a conceptual framework that bridges content and language objectives in the teaching process and identifies three types of language essential to CLIL: language of learning (i.e. the language needed to access concepts and skills of a discipline of knowledge), language for learning (i.e. the classroom language and academic language that enable learners to function well in the TL environment) and language through learning (i.e. the new language produced in the learning process) (Coyle et al., 2010; Nawrot-Lis, 2019). It is a useful tool to analyse and differentiate linguistic needs and demands across different contexts so that language use can be conceptualised as the process of knowledge construction, and this tripartite division "stresses, inter alia, that the focus of CLIL ought not to be only on form but also on function and meaning with the objective of developing effective linguistic communicative skills" (Nikolić, 2017, p. 123).

CLIL has gained significant popularity in recent decades and has been likened to "an unstoppable train which has already left the station" with irresistible momentum (Macaro et al., 2019, p. 232). Consequently, there have been successful instances of integrating CLIL with IPE, though the latter is frequently approached with different terminology. For example, in the CLIL for Young European Citizens project, Lazăr et al. (2023) endeavoured to implement CLIL in citizenship, environmental and financial education in Romania, with the goal of enhancing students' competencies in European citizenship. This initiative demonstrated that the content and cultural components of CLIL could be well-suited for accommodating civic education, effectively harmonising it with language communication. This concept is also evident in other instances, such as Griva and Chostelidou's (2017) CLIL project aiming to foster multicultural citizenship awareness in primary education in Greece, Keogh's (2021) case in Colombia where CLIL materials facilitated university students' critical thinking and active citizenship and Porto's (2021) proposal to align intercultural citizenship theory with The 4Cs Framework to enhance the quality of education in Europe.

While CLIL has been embraced in the Western world, it remains a nascent topic in China, awaiting thorough exploration by researchers and educators within empirical contexts (Hu, 2023; Hu et al., 2023). Nonetheless, Chinese scholars and researchers have embarked on CLIL-related work, contributing to its theoretical comprehension. Drawing upon an analysis of CLIL-related literature, for instance, scholars propose that the implementation of CLIL within the Chinese educational context should not only adhere to the original tenets of this approach, such as dual-focused learning objectives, flexible integration of content and language learning and student-centred pedagogy, but also undergo localisation (C. H. Hu, 2022; Wang & Xing, 2021). This entails infusing teaching practices with culturally rich and humanistic content specific to China (Chang & Zhao, 2020) and rekindles an idea, articulated more than a decade ago but regrettably overlooked by academia, that the vitality of CLIL necessitates ongoing renewal through continuous localisation (Zhou, 2004). Consequently, this underscores the imperative of reforming CLIL and imbuing it with distinctive Chinese characteristics.

The Comparison of CLIL and IPE-Based FLT

The implementation of IPE-based FL classes within a comprehensive curriculum framework mirrors the concept of transdisciplinary or cross-curricular instruction (Yu, 2021), recognising that no curriculum exists in isolation when IPE principles are integrated into another curriculum or subject that could independently stand on its own (Shen, 2023). From this standpoint, CLIL coincides with IPE-based FLT, as the nature of the former is also interdisciplinary and features a "dual-focused approach that includes teaching-learning processes that emphasise equally on content and language" (Dack et al., 2020, p. 42).

However, it is important to note that this dual focus does not imply an equal distribution of emphasis between content and language teaching. As previously mentioned, varying degrees of emphasis exist in strong CLIL lessons compared to weaker ones (Coyle et al., 2010). This distribution of emphasis falls along a continuum, with subject-driven lessons and language-driven lessons situated at opposite ends (see Figure 2). The shift between these two ends is adaptable and contingent upon specific contextual needs and requirements (Ikeda et al., 2021). Huang and Xiao (2021) also propose a similar continuum within IPE-based FLT (see Figure 3), encompassing IPE at one end and regular or traditional language teaching at the other. Although a simultaneous focus on language acquisition and IPE occurs, certain researchers advocate for a flexible allocation of emphasis based on contextual factors, generally leaning towards the stronger ideological and political curriculum side (Li & Zeng, 2019; Sun, 2021).

Figure 2. The strong and weak CLIL continuum

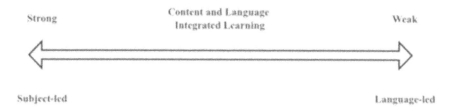

Figure 3. The strong and weak IPE-based FLT continuum

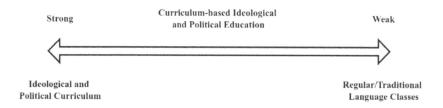

While this perspective highlights the rich humanistic and cultural connotations that language holds for IPE (Chang & Li, 2020; Huang & Xiao, 2021; Shen, 2023), it does raise concerns as it contradicts the core, accepted objective of FLT, which is to enhance students' language proficiency (Wen, 2019). Consequently, the inherent academic attributes of FL curricula must predominantly remain intact within IPE-based FLT (Gao, 2021; Yu, 2021). This approach contrasts somewhat with the flexible allocation of content learning and language learning in CLIL, since IPE-based FLT should prioritise language development, employing ideological and political content as thematic tools for instruction. While these thematic elements also constitute learning objectives, their primary role is to enhance learners' proficiency in the TL.

To iterate and simply put, the aim of integrating IPE with other disciplines is to enhance national cultural confidence by deepening students' comprehension of cultures, societal values and political perspectives (Li & Fu, 2020). These educational objectives within IPE-based FLT fulfil a role akin to that of content and culture in CLIL. Generally, content pertains to subject matters and goals that form the foundation of FL classes, reflecting the imperative of acquiring professional knowledge, skills and insights (Ji, 2019; Wang, 2019). Similarly, the ideological and political content serves not only as a subject of FLT but also as a target of learning.

Some scholars argue that culture within CLIL is largely confined to the TL and its relevant community and should be internalised by learners to enhance language proficiency (Diab et al., 2018), and this perspective is indeed applicable to numerous CLIL programmes in China (Duan, 2019; Ji, 2019; Ren, 2020). However, we prefer a much more inclusive viewpoint, considering culture as the 'self' and 'other' awareness, identity, citizenship and progression towards pluricultural understanding. This is in line with the idea that the CLIL culture "holds all of our experiences acquired in particular contexts and over time" and that "in itself, language holds a way of life with the values that define, for example, people's perceptions of what is right or wrong, acceptable or not acceptable" and constitute the foundational components of individuals' identities within specific communities (Bernaus & Furlong, 2017, p. 35). IPE-based FLT, therefore, also overlaps with the cultural facet of CLIL, and it has been gradually acknowledged that Chinese CLIL programmes should embrace the diversity of not only the cultures of the TL but also those indigenous to China (Chang & Zhao, 2020; Zhang, 2021).

There have been notable instances of experimentation with the fusion of domestic and exotic cultures within CLIL programmes, aimed at improving cross-cultural comprehension and enriching learners' appreciation of Chinese cultures and societal values. A case in point is the curriculum offered at Shanghai Jiao Tong University for students majoring in German, which necessitates an exploration of the humanities and social sciences pertaining to Germany, alongside a comparative analysis of TL cultures and Chinese counterparts, to delve into the core socialist values (Fan, 2021). Similarly, the programme at Jiangsu Food and Pharmaceutical Science College seamlessly integrates College English with specialised subjects, such as Chinese food cultural profiles and traditional Chinese medicine, which aligns with the national mandate that English instruction should not only enhance English proficiency but also cultivate content knowledge and humanistic qualities (Wang, 2019). Additionally, in pursuit of The Belt and Road Initiative—a global infrastructure development strategy formulated by the Chinese government—a preliminary blueprint for an expansive CLIL initiative has emerged, entailing a comparative exploration of Chinese cultures, social norms and political values vis-à-vis those of the TL communities (e.g. Russia, Kazakhstan, Kyrgyzstan and Cuba) involved in this geopolitical scheme (Yang, 2019). It is noteworthy that while these initiatives or concepts may not explicitly be classified as IPE-based FLT, they effectively showcase how CLIL implementation in China is aligning with the burgeoning trend of CIPE, and these efforts are deliberately designed to encompass language acquisition, content assimilation and the cultivation of cross-cultural awareness as integral learning objectives.

Applying CLIL to CIPE

To facilitate the organisation of IPE-based FLT, Chinese scholars have introduced various frameworks aimed at guiding teachers in curriculum design and development (Hu, 2019; Li & Fu, 2020; Wen, 2021). However, a notable gap in this body of literature pertains to the implementation of CIPE, which remains ambiguous. Scholars, too, have often placed excessive emphasis on IPE objectives and content for inclusion in FLT, neglecting to provide a comprehensive explanation of how IPE and languages can be effectively integrated based on established theories.

To address this deficiency and based on the discussions and theories related to CLIL and FLT, a proposed framework (see Figure 4) is presented for educators, particularly language instructors, seeking to enhance existing FLT with ideological and political content. It is imperative that teachers' comprehension of the learning objectives plays a pivotal role in ensuring the successful organisation of IPE-based FLT (Wen, 2021). This perspective extends to the notion that the identification of learning objectives, encompassing both TL learning objectives and IPE objectives, serves as the foundation for lesson planning, delivery and assessment (Li & Fu, 2020). In alignment with this concept, three key components are delineated and incorporated within the framework: the identification of learning objectives and lesson planning, lesson delivery and evaluation. While CIPE scholars typically view the *identification of learning objectives and lesson planning* as discrete activities (Hu, 2019; Li et al., 2020), they are consolidated within the initial stage of the framework due to their inseparability in practical application.

Figure 4. The CIPE-oriented FLT framework

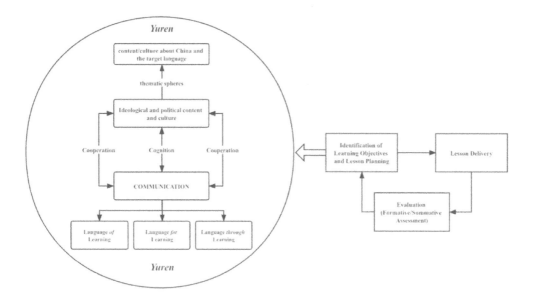

Certainly, the primary step is underscored throughout the entire framework, extending in alignment with CLIL theories. Given the parallels between CLIL and IPE-based FLT, the framework's left segment has been partially fashioned based on The 4Cs Framework as aforementioned. However, a departure from the original framework lies in the foregrounding of *communication* (in capital letters), which pertains to the TL employed for content analysis, comprehension and interactions. Its prominence is attributed to the obligatory mandate that the academic attributes of FLT must largely be retained within the CIPE context, which is aimed at cultivating learners' language proficiency (Gao, 2021; Yu, 2021). Consequently, *communication*, serving as the cohesive element among the other mechanisms, occupies a central role in the framework. In order to establish language learning objectives, The Language Triptych is also integrated into the framework, prompting educators to contemplate this matter from the vantage points of the *language of learning*, *language for learning* and *language through learning*.

In addition to language learning, content learning holds significant importance within the framework. *Content* and *culture* are intertwined elements within this framework, representing the objectives of IPE to equip FL learners with essential knowledge, skills and cross-cultural understanding necessary for active civic participation (Li & Fu, 2020). While they constitute an integral component of IPE-based FLT, it is imperative to underscore the prominence of language learning.

In terms of selecting subject matters and cultural themes for FLT, the framework allows for considerable flexibility. IPE content and culture are organised into *thematic spheres*, which is justified by the content-based learning theory that "any topic, theme or non-language issue of interest or importance to the learners" can be used for FLT, as long as they are "cognitively engaging and demanding for the learners, as well as appropriate to their linguistic level" (Dueñas, 2004, p. 75). Consequently, educators possess the agency to choose subject matters or themes that are deemed suitable for IPE-based learning, such as identity politics, traditional Chinese cultures, socialist values, rules of law, professional ethics, among others (Li et al., 2021). However, the framework adopts a broader stance towards *content* and *culture*, encouraging instructors to approach IPE from the vantage points of issues pertinent to China and the TL. This perspective aligns with the proposition presented by Hu (2019), emphasising that the content in IPE-based FLT should be grounded in the core tenets of socialism (i.e. a set of values endorsed by the central government to underscore national identity), Western values (i.e. universal values) and their comparative analysis.

Both language education and IPE are enmeshed within the Chinese concept of *yuren*, signifying students' comprehensive development encompassing knowledge, skills and attributes. This corresponds with the notion that IPE-based FLT should be approached through the lens of "cultivation of socialist core values, college talents training objectives and curriculum objectives" (Li & Fu, 2020, p. 1003), as well as the recommendation that instructors should consider the anticipated achievements of students within each learning unit, the overarching curriculum, the entirety of their degree programme and even in congruence with national educational goals (Li & Fu, 2020; Wen, 2021).

To effectively integrate language learning with IPE-related content and culture, while achieving multiple learning objectives, it is essential for teachers to consider *cognitive* aspects, specifically thinking mechanisms. They should sequence learning activities appropriately, engage students in higher-order thinking and foster personal avenues of comprehension. Language teachers may find the cognitive component of this framework challenging to address, as their training often focuses on others, such as macro language skills (H. Hu, 2022). However, cognition is a pivotal dimension of CLIL that, when improved, can significantly enhance learning outcomes (Coyle et al., 2010). This also holds true for both CIPE (Li & Li, 2023) and IPE-based FLT (Zhang, 2021). That means, when teachers apply CLIL theories to IPE-based FLT, they must acknowledge the inherent heavy intrinsic cognitive load due to the intricate ideological and political content integrated into language learning; moreover, the cognitive demand can escalate when conveying content knowledge in an FL. This preliminary awareness of learning demands is paramount, as it forms the basis for subsequent instructional decisions made by teachers to progress teaching and learning from lower-order skills (e.g. remembering, understanding and applying) to higher-order skills (e.g. analysing, evaluating and creating).

An additional element, referred to as *cooperation*, has been integrated into this framework, highlighting the crucial role of professional collaboration in the organisation of IPE-based FLT. Within the context of CIPE, this entails close collaboration among FL teachers, IPE teachers and at times other stakeholders, such as programme organisers, administrators and students. This collaborative effort aims to collectively determine the learning objectives for the TL, as well as the incorporation of ideological and political content, cultural elements and effective teaching methodologies (Chang & Li, 2020). While cooperation occurs on *micro* levels involving FL and IPE teachers, as well as on *meso* levels involving diverse stakeholders within educational institutions, it is also imperative to achieve cooperation on a *macro* dimension. This involves establishing a network among HEPs to facilitate knowledge sharing and programme evaluation for IPE-based FLT programmes (Li et al., 2021).

Recent studies focusing on FL teachers have highlighted the challenges they may encounter in integrating FLT with content teaching in CLIL or in enhancing intercultural learning, underscoring the necessity for ongoing professional development (H. Hu, 2022). Furthermore, recent research suggests that professional collaboration can also contribute to raising the cognitive learning awareness of CLIL teachers, ensuring a robust pool of educators to assist students in enhancing their thinking and cognitive skills (Campillo-Ferrer et al., 2020). Thus, we believe the *cooperation* component serves as a unifying force in our framework and brings together *communication*, *content*, *culture* and *cognition* in IPE-based FLT.

The initial step in identifying learning objectives and lesson planning is rooted in constructive theories specific to CLIL and CIPE. What sets the framework presented above apart is its emphasis on language proficiency development over content learning. It allows for significant flexibility in defining IPE objectives and places critical importance on professional cooperation. Given the intricate nature of teaching activities and diverse classroom contexts (Ikeda et al., 2021), teachers are granted substantial flexibility in determining how to *deliver* IPE-based language classes, the second step of the framework. This adaptability arises from CLIL, the foundational methodology underlying the framework, which leverages a range of teaching strategies in the post-method era (Coyle et al., 2010). For instance, a task-based approach can be used in CLIL, which involves teaching structured around pre-task (introduction of topic and task), task cycle (task completion, planning, and reporting) and language focus (language form analysis and practice); project-based learning empowers students to acquire knowledge and skills by investigating authentic and engaging problems or questions; technology-enhanced active learning integrates technology to aid student exploration and discussion of topics (Klewitz, 2021).

Indeed, scholars have proposed and justified a comprehensive array of teaching methods (Fan, 2021; Hu, 2021; Li et al., 2020). While a detailed review of these methods is beyond the scope due to page limitations, several key points must be noted in this teaching stage, as indicated by relevant literature (Chang & Zhao, 2020; Hu et al., 2023). First, teachers and students must adhere to the dual-focused rule of learning the TL and IPE-related matters while fostering cross-cultural understanding. Second, teachers should create opportunities and provide support for learning within a student-centred classroom. Third, an engaging and motivating environment should be established for learners through the utilisation of diverse learning materials, the organisation of various learning activities, facilitation of teacher-student and student-student interaction, and encouragement of mixed usage of Chinese and the TL as mediums of instruction, among other strategies.

The *evaluation* of teaching is positioned at the culmination of the framework and encompasses formative assessment, a deliberate and ongoing process of collecting evidence about students' learning to adapt teaching activities, and summative assessment, focused on the outcome of a programme. However, evaluation serves a more profound purpose than merely concluding the teaching process (C. H. Hu, 2022). Instead, it assumes an indispensable role in shaping implications for lesson planning and teaching, becoming interwoven with the entire teaching trajectory.

Again, the integration of IPE-based FLT intersects with CLIL. Consequently, the assessment considerations specific to CLIL gain relevance in informing IPE-based FLT. In CLIL, the assessment landscape is subject to ongoing debate regarding the evaluators of learning, the scope of evaluation and the methods employed to appraise learning (C. H. Hu, 2022). Notably, standardised formal tests are frequently employed by educators to assess CLIL outcomes, particularly those related to language acquisition, a trend attributed to the innovative nature of this methodology (Babocká, 2015). Therefore, the credibility of assessment validity and reliability is often questioned, stemming from concerns that content acquisition is inadequately evaluated within this dual-focused pedagogical paradigm or that instructional content remains unassessed.

Furthermore, as CLIL learners often encounter challenges when acquiring a non-native language, the risk of imprecise assessment outcomes arises in instances where students possess subject knowledge but struggle to articulate it in the TL (Zhetpisbayeva et al., 2018). To address these intricacies, both formative and summative assessment strategies, often discussed as assessment for, as, and of learning, emerge as vital tools, which serve as robust mechanisms to engage students and educators in the learning process and consequently contribute "to more soundly based assessment procedures" (Otto & Estrada, 2019,

p. 32). Given China's context of examination-focused education, educators are frequently compelled to employ pre-designed tests, particularly in the realm of language testing, within IPE-based FL programmes or modules for summative assessment purposes or due to institutional requirements, as observed in our ongoing research. In this context, formative assessment assumes heightened importance. These adaptive and informal assessment practices, intrinsic to the learning experience, facilitate the extraction of evidence regarding student learning. Subsequently, educators can tailor their instructional design and provide learners with feedback that enhances the learning process. Simultaneously, such practices empower learners to comprehend their expected achievements in both FLT and IPE, fostering self-reflection and encouraging them to assume responsibility for their educational journey.

CONCLUSION

In the realm of China's higher education, this paper delves into the integration of IPE with FLT under the umbrella of the CIPE. This paper highlights the synergistic relationship between IPE-based FLT and CLIL. These approaches share a cross-disciplinary and cross-cultural nature, emphasising concurrent content and language acquisition and fostering comprehension of, for example, cultures, societal values and political perspectives.

Nevertheless, this proposed framework in this paper is preliminary, primarily foregrounding the identification of IPE-based FLT objectives within China's unique context and serves as an initial endeavour to address the challenges faced by teachers in integrating IPE with FLT. CLIL and IPE-based FLT are both relatively nascent in China, with limited empirical research and classroom application. Therefore, there is ample room for further exploration in these areas, necessitating a more comprehensive research agenda.

For us, it is important to acknowledge the challenges encountered during the construction of this paper and the subsequent agenda. One significant challenge was deciphering the historical evolution of logic and its connection to CIPE, namely how the sciences and theories of valid inference regarding CIPE had developed beforehand. This historical perspective is vital, given the continuous reorganisation, reconstruction and integration inherent in education, including CIPE, FLT and IPE-based FLT. Understanding the development of various disciplines within the CIPE framework is fundamental to assessing theoretical feasibility and constructing a coherent educational system.

Balancing existing academic knowledge and personal experience was also a hurdle for us. The proposals and assumptions put forth in this paper are largely influenced by FLT wisdom, rather than an exhaustive grasp of CIPE theories. To overcome this limitation, a departure from path dependency—a hindrance to innovation and initiative—is necessary for the transformation of FLT in China. Adopting a multidisciplinary approach to innovative educational practice and fostering professional collaboration is critical, requiring stakeholders from diverse fields to unite to refine and invigorate CIPE.

We firmly believe that CIPE, despite its localisation in China, holds global academic significance in the evolution of education in the modern era. Sharing knowledge is crucial to amplify the voices of China within the international academic community, especially considering the limited access for foreign researchers and scholars to abundant academic resources related to CIPE or similar context-specific educational practices[2]. To promote mutual understanding in global academia, knowledge dissemination is a prerequisite for knowledge creation and subsequent innovation to thrive.

REFERENCES

An, X., & Pan, S. (2023). 核心素养融入外语教学研究的现状与展望——基于CiteSpace的可视化分析 [Research status and future trends on the integration of core literacy into foreign language teaching—based on the visualized analysis of CiteSpace]. 创新教育研究 *[Creative Education Studies], 11*(7), 1944–1952. doi:10.12677/CES.2023.117289

Babocká, M. (2015). Assessment in CLIL classes. In S. Pokrivčáková (Ed.), *CLIL in foreign language education: e-textbook for foreign language teachers* (pp. 176–199). Constantine the Philosopher University. doi:10.17846/CLIL.2015.176-188

Bernaus, M., & Furlong, Á. (2017). CLIL as a plurilingual approach or language of real life and language as carrier of culture. *Research Papers in Language Teaching and Learning, 8*(1), 34–43. https://rpltl.eap.gr/images/2017/08-01-034-Furlong-Bernaus.pdf

Campillo-Ferrer, J.-M., Miralles-Martínez, P., & Sánchez-Ibáñez, R. (2020). CLIL teachers' views on cognitive development in primary education. *Palgrave Communications, 6*(1), 97. doi:10.105741599-020-0480-x

Chang, Y., & Li, C. (2020). 发挥外语专业自身特殊优势,促进思政与专业教育深度融合 [On deeper integration of IP and FL education by fully utilizing the strengths of FL majors]. 外语电化教学 *[Technology Enhanced Foreign Language Education],* (6), 17–22. http://www.cnki.com.cn/Article/CJFDTotal-WYDH202006002.htm

Chang, Y., & Zhao, Y. (2020). 内容语言融合教育理念(CLI)的提出、内涵及意义——从内容依托教学到内容语言融合教育 [The proposal, connotation and significance of the concept of content-language integration (CLI) — From content-based instruction to content-language integration education]. 外语教学 *[Foreign Language Education], 41*(5), 49–54. http://www.cnki.com.cn/Article/CJFDTotal-TEAC202005010.htm

Chaya, P., & Inpin, B. (2020). Effects of integrating movie-based mobile learning instruction for enhancing Thai university students' speaking skills and intercultural communicative competence. *English Language Teaching, 13*(7), 27–45. doi:10.5539/elt.v13n7p27

Cheng, H., Cui, F., & Sun, N. (2016). 中国高校思想政治教育史论 [A critical history of ideological and political education in universities of China]. Social Sciences Academic Press.

Chu, P. (1998). 德育论 [Theory of moral education]. Fujian Education Publishing House.

Coyle, D. (2008). CLIL — a pedagogical approach from the European perspective. In N. V. Deusen-Scholl & N. H. Hornberger (Eds.), *Encyclopedia of language and education* (2nd ed., Vol. 4, pp. 97–111). Springer. doi:10.1007/978-0-387-30424-3_92

Coyle, D., Hood, P., & Marsh, D. (2010). *CLIL: content and language integrated learning.* Cambridge University Press. doi:10.1017/9781009024549

Dack, T. M. F., Argudo, J., & Abad, M. (2020). Language and teaching methodology features of CLIL in university classrooms: A research synthesis. *Colombian Applied Linguistics Journal, 22*(1), 40–54. doi:10.14483/22487085.13878

Diab, A. A. M., Abdel-Haq, E. M., & Aly, M. A.-S. (2018). The effectiveness of using content and language integrated learning (CLIL) approach to enhance EFL student teachers' cultural awareness. *Journal of Faculty of Education, 31*(122), 37–56. doi:10.21608/jfeb.2020.147494

Duan, S. (2019). Cultivation of students' critical thinking ability through CLIL mixed teaching model — a case study of "An Introduction to English Literature". In J. Guo, X. Xiao, & J. Liu (Eds.), *Proceedings of the 2019 3rd International Conference on Education, Economics and Management Rese*arch (pp. 665–669). Atlantis Presss. 10.2991/assehr.k.191221.159

Dueñas, M. (2004). The whats, whys, hows and whos of content-based instruction in second/foreign language education. *International Journal of English Studies, 4*(1), 73–96. doi:10.6018/ijes.4.1.48061

Fan, L. (2021). 高校外语课程思政实践探索——以"基础德语"为例 [On ideological and political practice of foreign language courses in colleges and universities — taking "basic German" as an example]. 外语与翻译 *[Foreign Languages and Translation],* (3), 71–76. doi:10.19502/j.cnki.2095-9648.2021.03.012

Gabillon, Z. (2020). Revisiting CLIL: background, pedagogy, and theoretical underpinnings. *Contextes et didactiques, 15.* doi:10.4000/ced.1836

Gao, H. (2021). On the construction of "Curriculum Ideological and Political Education" in college English. In Z. Zhu, & S. Zhao (Eds.), *Proceedings of the 6th Annual International Conference on Social Science and Contemporary Humanity Development* (pp. 308–312). Atlantis Press. 10.2991/assehr.k.210121.065

Griva, E., & Chostelidou, D. (2017). CLIL in primary education: promoting multicultural citizenship awareness in the foreign language classroom. *Research Papers in Language Teaching and Learning, 8*(2), 9–23. https://rpltl.eap.gr/images/2017/08-02-009-Griva-Chostelidou.pdf

Hanesová, D. (2015). History of CLIL. In S. Pokrivčáková (Ed.), *CLIL in foreign language education: e-textbook for foreign language teachers* (pp. 7–16). Constantine the Philosopher University. doi:10.17846/CLIL.2015.7-16

Hu, C. H. (2022). Assessment and learning in content and language integrated learning (CLIL) classrooms: Approaches and conceptualisations. *Language Value, 15*(2), 112–117. doi:10.6035/languagev.6618

Hu, H. (2022). Examining teacher competencies in content and language integrated learning: Professional profiles and ways forward. *Rupkatha Journal on Interdisciplinary Studies in Humanities, 14*(2). doi:10.21659/rupkatha.v14n2.26

Hu, H. (2023). Emerging from content and language integrated learning and English-medium instruction, is CLIL-ised EMI the next trend of education? *Higher Learning Research Communications, 13*(2), 1–8. doi:10.18870/hlrc.v13i2.1422

Hu, H., Said, N. E. M., & Hashim, H. (2023). Sustaining content and language integrated learning in China: A systematic review. *Sustainability (Basel), 15*(5), 3894. doi:10.3390u15053894

Hu, J. (2019). "课程思政"理念融入高职外语课程的生成路径研究 [A study on the path of integrating the idea of "ideological and political education through curriculum" into college foreign language courses]. 职教通讯 *[Communication of Vocational Education],* (2), 30–34. doi:10.3969/j.issn.1674-7747.2019.02.009

Hu, J. (2021). 外语课程思政视角下的教学设计研究 [Foreign language instructional design from the ideological-political perspective]. 中国外语 *[Journal of the Foreign Languages in China], 18*(2), 53–59. doi:10.13564/j.cnki.issn.1672-9382.2021.02.010

Huang, G., & Xiao, Q. (2021). 外语课程思政建设六要素 [Six elements in the ideological-political construction]. 中国外语 *[Journal of the Foreign Languages in China], 18*(2), 10–16. doi:10.13564/j.cnki.issn.1672-9382.2021.02.001

Huang, Y. (2021). Research on innovative practice of ideological and political in college English courses. *OAlib, 8*(8, e7600), 1–6. doi:10.4236/oalib.1107600

Ikeda, M., Izumi, S., Watanabe, Y., Pinner, R., & Davis, M. (2021). *Soft CLIL and English language teaching: understanding Japanese policy, practice, and implications.* Routledge., doi:10.4324/9780429032332

Ji, X. (2019). Teaching "Greek and Roman mythology" in a CLIL classroom: towards a new approach. In L. P. Mun (Ed.), *Proceedings of the 2019 4th International Conference on Social Sciences and Economic Development* (pp. 410–413). Atlantis Press. 10.2991/icssed-19.2019.77

Kamis, M. S., Ismail, M. J., Alias, M. N., Mikeng, D., Abidin, S. G. Z., & Yusof, R. (2021). CLIL approach in encouraging self-efficacy amongst Malaysian gifted students for Arabic tasks accomplishment. *Journal of Language and Linguistic Studies, 17*(2), 1001–1012. doi:10.52462/jlls.69

Keogh, C. (2022). Student and teacher perspectives on co-created CLIL-appropriate materials focused on critical thinking and active citizenship. *Latin American Journal of Content & Language Integrated Learning, 15*(1), e1512. doi:10.5294/laclil.2022.15.1.2

Klewitz, B. (2021). *Content and language integrated learning (CLIL): a methodology of bilingual teaching.* ibidem Press.

Kováčiková, E. (2020). *English for specific purposes in higher education through content and language integrated learning.* Cambridge Scholars Publishing.

Lai, Y., Xie, M., & Chen, Y. (2020). The application of the teaching mode for "ideological and political education" in college English teaching. *International Journal of New Developments in Education, 2*(7), 48–51. doi:10.25236/IJNDE.2020.020710

Lazăr, A., Langa, C., Loredana, T. S., Magdalena, S. M., & Luiza, V. S. (2023). Using CLIL in cross-curricular education to develop European citizenship. In E. Soare, & C. Langa (Eds.), Education Facing Contemporary World Issues - EDU WORLD 2022, (pp. 25–35). European Publisher. doi:10.15405/epes.23045.4

Li, F., & Fu, H. (2020). Study on college English teaching based on the concept of ideological and political education in all courses. *Creative Education, 11*(7), 997–1007. doi:10.4236/ce.2020.117072

Li, L., Pan, Q., Chen, T., & Huang, X. (2021). Curriculum ideological and political construction: Essence, connotation and realization path. *Advances in Soil Science, 10*(2), 378–383. doi:10.12677/ASS.2021.102055

Li, L., Xiang, Y., & Ding, Q. (2020). 思政反哺课程:我国高校课程思政深入发展的实现路径 [Ideological and political back-feeding curriculum: the path of in-depth development of curriculum ideology and politics in college and universities in China]. 大理大学学报 [*Journal of Dali University*], 5(11), 75–80. doi:10.3969/j.issn.2096-2266.2020.11.012

Li, L., & Zhang, G. (2023). 中国式现代化视域下的思想政治教育新形态研究 [Research on the new form of ideological and political education from the perspective of Chinese modernization]. 西南政法大学学报 [*Journal of Southwest University of Political Science & Law*], 25(1), 3–15. doi:10.3969/j.issn.1008-4355.2023.01.01

Li, Q., & Zeng, R. (2019). Implementation of ideological and political education in China's foreign language teaching. In J. Guo, X. Xiao, & J. Liu (Eds.), *Proceedings of the 2019 3rd International Conference on Education, Economics and Management Research* (pp. 549–552). Atlantis Press. 10.2991/assehr.k.191221.133

Li, R. (2018). The current situation and thinking of ideological and political education in college students. *KnE Social Sciences*, 3(10), 1378–1387. doi:10.18502/kss.v3i10.3477

Li, Y., & Li, A. (2023). Research on teaching quality improvement path of ideological and political course in universities. *Teacher Education and Curriculum Studies*, 8(3), 117–120. doi:10.11648/j.tecs.20230803.11

Li, Y., & Wang, C. (2020). 科研生产力与中文首发制度 [Scientific research productivity and 'Chinese First' publishing system]. 语言战略研究 [*Chinese Journal of Language Policy and Planning*], 26(2), 10–11. https://doi.org/CNKI:SUN:YZLY.0.2020-02-006

Lou, L. (2021). Practice of curriculum ideological and political education in specialized courses of English school under the guidance of optimization theory. *Journal of Critical Studies in Language and Literature*, 2(4), 14–19. doi:10.46809/jcsll.v2i4.71

Ma, R., & Liu, Y. (2021). 我国外语教学研究的热点、前沿及演进——基于中国知网学术期刊文献的共词可视化分析 [Hotspots, frontiers and evolution of foreign language teaching research in China — co-word visualization analysis based on CNKI academic journal articles]. 北京第二外国语学院学报 [*Journal of Beijing International Studies University*], (4), 19–32. http://www.cnki.com.cn/Article/CJFDTOTAL-JDEW202104002.htm

Macaro, E., Hultgren, A. K., Kirkpatrick, A., & Lasagabaster, D. (2019). English medium instruction: Global views and countries in focus. *Language Teaching*, 52(3), 231–232. doi:10.1017/S0261444816000380

Ministry of Education of The People's Republic of China. (2017, December 6). 中共教育部党组关于印发《高校思想政治工作质量提升工程实施纲要》的通知 [*Notice of the Ministry of Education of the Communist Party of China on issuing the "Implementation Outline of the Project to Improve the Quality of Ideological and Political Work in Colleges and Universities"*]. MoE. http://www.moe.gov.cn/srcsite/A12/s7060/201712/t20171206_320698.html

Nawrot-Lis, B. (2019). *The challenges of content acquisition in a CLIL course: a CLIL-based chemistry course at the lower secondary school level.* Springer. doi:10.1007/978-3-476-05139-4

Nikolić, D. (2017). Intelligibility within a modified CLIL framework. Glottodidactica. *International Journal of Applied Linguistics, 44*(1), 119–130. doi:10.14746/gl.2017.44.1.07

Otto, A., & Estrada, J. L. (2019). Towards an understanding of CLIL in a European context: Main assessment tools and the role of language in content subjects. *CLIL Journal of Innovation and Research in Plurilingual and Pluricultural Education, 2*(1), 31–42. doi:10.5565/rev/clil.11

Porto, M. (2021). Intercultural citizenship in foreign language education: An opportunity to broaden CLIL's theoretical outlook and pedagogy. *International Journal of Bilingual Education and Bilingualism, 24*(7), 927–947. doi:10.1080/13670050.2018.1526886

Ren, J. (2022). "课程思政"内涵的演进及其体用的发展 [The evolution of the connotation of "ideological and political education of curriculum" and the development of its application]. 创新教育研究 *[Creative Educaton Studies], 10*(1), 78–85. doi:10.12677/CES.2022.101015

Ren, N. (2020). A proposal for teaching MTI courses in China through a CLIL approach: Using the lesson on "Intellectual Property Law" as an example. *Journal of Education and Teaching Management Research, 1*(1), 24–26. doi:10.33969/twjournals.jetmr.2020.010107

Shen, Y. (2023). 一流课程建设背景下大学英语课程思政的内涵和实施路径 [The connotation and implementation path of values education in college English courses under the background of first-class course construction]. 教育进展 *[Advances in Education], 13*(3), 1047–1055. doi:10.12677/AE.2023.133166

Song, Q., & Xiao, W. (1992). 当代思想政治教育热点问题思考 [Reflections on hot issues in contemporary ideological and political education]. China Procurational Press.

Sun, B. (2021). Reflection on ideological and political education in foreign language teaching. In Y. Zhang (Ed.), *Proceedings of the 2nd International Conference on Education Studies: Experience and Innovation* (pp. 307–311). Atlantis Press. 10.2991/assehr.k.211217.049

Vourdanou, K. (2019). Challenging curricular boundaries and identities through CLIL: an e-learning professional development program for CLIL teachers. In A. Kostoulas (Ed.), *Challenging boundaries in language education: second language learning and teaching* (pp. 89–106). Springer. doi:10.1007/978-3-030-17057-8_6

Wang, S., & Xing, J. (2021). 国内 CLIL 教学研究回顾与展望 [Retrospect and prospect of CLIL teaching research in China]. 考试与评价·大学英语教研版 *[Testing and Evaluation (College English Teaching & Research)], (2)*, 90–95. doi:10.16830/j.cnki.22-1387/g4.2021.02.018

Wang, X. (2019). 中国优秀传统文化融入大学英语教学路径研究——以江苏食品药品职业技术学院为例 [Research on the paths of integrating Chinese excellent traditional culture into college English teaching — take the Jiangsu Food and Pharmaceutical Science College as an example*]. 湖州职业技术学院学报 *[Journal of Huzhou Vocational and Technological College], (4)*, 53–56. doi:10.13690/j.cnki.hzyxb.issn.1672-2388.2019.04.15

Wang, Z., Lu, Y., Guang, Y., & Zhou, E. (2022). 医学人文教育视角下的医学英语课程思政教学探索 [Teaching medical English combined with ideological and political education from the perspective of medical humanities education]. 中华医学教育杂志 *[Chinese Journal of Medical Education]*, 42(1), 11–15. doi:10.3760/cma.j.cn115259-20210513-00629

Wen, Q. (2019). 新中国外语教学理论70年发展历程 [Foreign language teaching theories in China in the past 70 years]. 中国外语 *[Journal of the Foreign Languages in China]*, 16(5), 14–22. doi:10.13564/j.cnki.issn.1672-9382.2019.05.003

Wen, Q. (2021). 大学外语课程思政的内涵和实施框架 [A framework of integrating moral education into college foreign language teaching]. 中国外语 *[Journal of the Foreign Languages in China]*, 18(2), 47–52. doi:10.13564/j.cnki.issn.1672-9382.2021.02.008

Xiao, Q., & Huang, G. (2020). 关于外语课程思政建设的思考 [On the ideological-political construction of foreign language courses]. 中国外语 *[Journal of the Foreign Languages in China]*, 17(5), 10–14. doi:10.13564/j.cnki.issn.1672-9382.2020.05.001

Xin, P., & Yin, X. (2016). 打造精彩优秀的思政课程——以"大国方略"系列课程为例 [To forge high-quality curriculum of ideological and political education—a case study of "What Matters to Rising China" series]. 青年学报 *[Youth Research]*, (4), 19–24. doi:10.3969/j.issn.2095-7947.2016.04.004

Yang, Y. (2019). "一带一路"建设与高校语言人才培养 [A research on the development of "Belt and Road Initiatives" and language human resources]. 兴义民族师范学院学报 *[Journal of Xingyi Normal University for Nationalities]*, (2), 106–110. doi:10.3969/j.issn.1009-0673.2019.02.023

Yu, X. (2021). Exploration on the university curriculum ideological and political innovation system. *E3S Web of Conferences, 295*(2021), Article 05028. doi:10.1051/e3sconf/202129505028

Zhang, C., & Fagan, C. (2016). Examining the role of ideological and political education on university students' civic perceptions and civic participation in Mainland China: Some hints from contemporary citizenship theory. Citizenship. *Social and Economics Education*, 15(2), 117–142. doi:10.1177/2047173416681170

Zhang, X. (2021). 我国高校德语专业本土化的内容—语言融合教学策略探究——以跨文化交际课程为例 [The localisation of CLIL teaching strategies in the German language major programmes at Chinese universities: a study of intercultural communication course]. 外语教育研究前沿 *[Foreign Language Education in China]*, 4(3), 57–64. http://www.cnki.com.cn/Article/CJFDTotal-WYQY202103008.htm

Zhetpisbayeva, B. A., Kitibayeva, A. K., Kazimova, D. A., Akbayeva, G. N., & Zatyneiko, M. A. (2018). Assessment issues in content and language integrated learning (CLIL). *Journal of Advanced Pharmacy Education and Research*, 8(4), 32–38. https://japer.in/article/assessment-issues-in-content-and-language-integrated-learning-clil

Zhou, D. (2004). 双语教学与语言-内容融合学习教学法 [Bilingual teaching and content language integrated learning approach]. 比较教育研究. *Comparative Education Review*, (6), 28–32. doi:10.3969/j.issn.1003-7667.2004.06.006

Zhou, X. (2021). Global citizenship education in school curricula: A Chinese perspective. *Journal of Liberal Arts and Social Science*, 9(4), 40–60. https://ijlass.org/articles/9.4.6.40-60.pdf

ENDNOTES

1. Some other translations of *ke-cheng si-zheng* are, for instance, integrating moral education into curricula, value education through courses, ideological and political theories teaching in all courses, and the ideological and virtue awareness of the curriculum.

2. Most CIPE-related resources (e.g. academic publications) have been presented in Chinese and are available in local databases (e.g. China National Knowledge Infrastructure), rendering it difficult for researchers from other regions or countries to access the knowledge they are interested in. We presume this situation is probably associated with the *zhong-wen shou-fa* concept proposed in China, encouraging researchers and scholars to first share and publish their understandings and research findings in Chinese (Li & Wang, 2020).

Compilation of References

360Learning. (n. d.). *What Is Connectivism Learning Theory and How Can You Apply It in Learning and Development?* 360Learning. https://360learning.com/guide/learning-theories/connectivism-learning-theory/

Abbad, M. M., Morris, D., & de Nahlik, C. (2009). Looking under the Bonnet: Factors Affecting Student Adoption of E-Learning Systems in Jordan. *The International Review of Research in Open and Distance Learning.*

Abdel Meguid, E., & Collins, M. (2017). Students' perceptions of lecturing approaches: Traditional versus interactive teaching. *Advances in Medical Education and Practice, 8,* 229–241. doi:10.2147/AMEP.S131851 PMID:28360541

Abney, A. K., Cook, L. A., Fox, A. K., & Stevens, J. (2019). Intercollegiate social media education ecosystem. *Journal of Marketing Education, 41*(3), 254–269. doi:10.1177/0273475318786026

Above, P. (2008). What is teaching? Some necessary and sufficient conditions for this activity. *Revue Française de Pédagogie, 164,* 139–158.

Abrami, P., Chambers, B., Poulsen, C., De Simone, C., d'Appollonia, S., & Howden, J. (1995). *Apprentissage Coopératif: Théories, Méthodes, Activités.* Éditions la Chenelière.

Acar, G. (2013). The effect of project-based learning on students' motivation. *International Journal of Academic Research, 5*(2), 82–86. doi:10.7813/2075-4124.2013/5-2/B.11

Adamson, S., Banks, D., Burtch, M., Cox, F. III, Judson, E., Turley, J., Benford, R., & Lawson, A. (2003). Reformed undergraduate instruction and its subsequent impact on secondary school teaching practice and student achievement. *Journal of Research in Science Teaching, 40*(10), 939–957. doi:10.1002/tea.10117

Adcock, A. (2012). Cognitive Dissonance in the Learning Processes. In N. M. Seel (Ed.), *Encyclopedia of the Sciences of Learning.* Springer. doi:10.1007/978-1-4419-1428-6_5

Aebersold, M. (2018). Simulation-Based Learning: No Longer a Novelty in Undergraduate Education OJIN. *Online Journal of Issues in Nursing, 23*(2), 1–1. doi:10.3912/OJIN.Vol23No02PPT39

Ahshan, R. (2021). A framework of implementing strategies for active student engagement in remote/online teaching and learning during the COVID-19 pandemic. *Education Sciences, 11*(9), 483. doi:10.3390/educsci11090483

Akyol, G. (2009). *The contribution of cognitive and metacognitive strategy use to seventh grade students' science achievement* [Master's thesis, Middle East Technical University]. Council of Higher Education Thesis Center. https://tez.yok.gov.tr/UlusalTezMerkezi/giris.jsp

Akyol, G., Sungur, S., & Tekkaya, C. (2010). The contribution of cognitive and metacognitive strategy use to students' science achievement. *Educational Research and Evaluation, 16*(1), 1–21. doi:10.1080/13803611003672348

Alarifi, Y. (2003). E-learning Technology: Promising Method. *E-learning International Conference*. Riyadh: King Faisal School.

Al-Azzam, N., Elsalem, L., & Gombedza, F. (2020). A cross-sectional study to determine factors affecting dental and medical students' preference for virtual learning during the COVID-19 outbreak. *Heliyon*, 6(12), e05704. doi:10.1016/j.heliyon.2020.e05704 PMID:33324768

Albert, M.C. & Souchon, M. (2000). *Les textes littéraires en classe de langue*. Hachette.

Alexander, PA, & *Winne*, PH (Eds.). (*2006*). Handbook of educational psychology. Lawrence Erlbaum Associates Publishers.

Algahtani, A. F. (2011). *Evaluating the Effectiveness of the E-learning Experience in Some Universities in Saudi Arabia from Male Students' Perceptions, Durham theses*. Durham University.

Alismaiel, O. A., Cifuentes-Faura, J., & Al-Rahmi, W. M. (2022). Online learning, mobile learning, and social media technologies: An empirical study on constructivism theory during the COVID-19 pandemic. *Sustainability (Basel)*, 14(18), 11134. doi:10.3390u141811134

Aljafen, B. S. (2021). EdTech and the Saudi EFL learners: Bane or boon? *Linguistics and Culture Review*, 5(S2), 1630–1642. doi:10.21744/lingcure.v5nS2.2251

Alkin, M. C., & Christie, C. A. (2004). *Evaluation roots: Tracing theorists' views and influences*. Sage Publications. doi:10.4135/9781412984157

Alladatin, J., Gnanguenon, A., Borori, A., & Fonton, A. (2020). Distance Education Practices for Pedagogical Continuity in Beninese Universities in the Context of the COVID-19 Pandemic: The Views of Students at the University of Parakou. *International Journal of Technologies in Higher Education*, 17(3), 163–177.

Allal, L., & Lafortune, L. (2008). In search of professional judgment. In L. Allal & L. Lafortune (Eds.), Professional Judgement in Education: Teaching Practices in Quebec in Geneva (pp. 1-10). Québec: Presses de l'université du Québec.

Allal, L., & Mottier, L. (2008). A Better Understanding of Professional Judgment in Evaluation: Contributions and Implications of the Geneva Study. In L. Allal & L. Lafortune (Eds.), *Professional Judgement in Education: Teaching Practices in Quebec in Geneva* (pp.223-239). Québec: Presses de l'université du Québéc.

Allen, I. E., & Seaman, J. (2017). *Digital Compass Learning: Distance Education Enrollment Report 2017*. Babson survey research group.

Ally, M. (2004). Foundations of Educational Theory for Online Learning. In T. Anderson & F. Elloumi (Eds.), Theory and Practice of Online Learning (pp. 3-31). Athabasca University & Creative Commons.

Ally, M. (2004). Foundations of educational theory for online learning. *Theory and practice of online learning, 2*, 15-44.

Almahasees, Z., Mohsen, K., & Amin, M. O. (2021, May). Faculty's and students' perceptions of online learning during COVID-19. []. Frontiers Media SA.]. *Frontiers in Education, 6*, 638470. doi:10.3389/feduc.2021.638470

Almosa, A., & Almubarak, A. (2005). E-learning Foundations and Applications. Saudi Arabia: Riyadh.

Almosa, A. (2002). *Use of Computer in Education* (2nd ed.). Future Education Library.

Almufarreh, A., & Arshad, M. (2023). Promising Emerging Technologies for Teaching and Learning: Recent Developments and Future Challenges. *Sustainability (Basel)*, 15(8), 6917. doi:10.3390u15086917

Alonso, F., López, G., Manrique, D., & Viñes, J. M. (2005). An instructional model for web-based e-learning education with a blended learning process approach. *British Journal of Educational Technology, 36*(2), 217–235. doi:10.1111/j.1467-8535.2005.00454.x

Al-Samarraie, H., Selim, H., Teo, T., & Zaqout, F. (2017). Isolation and distinctiveness in the design of e-learning systems influence user preferences. *Interactive Learning Environments, 25*(4), 452–466. doi:10.1080/10494820.2016.1138313

Alter, N. (2000). *Ordinary innovation*. Presses Universitaires de France.

Altet, M. (1997/2006). *Pedagogies of learning*. PUF.

Alvarez, J., Djaouti, D., & Rampnoux, O. (2016). *Learning with Serious Games*. Canopé Network.

Amara, S., Macedo, J., Bendella, F., & Santos, A. (2016). Group formation in mobile computer supported collaborative learning contexts: A systematic literature review. *Journal of Educational Technology & Society, 19*(2), 258–273.

An, X., & Pan, S. (2023). 核心素养融入外语教学研究的现状与展望——基于CiteSpace的可视化分析 [Research status and future trends on the integration of core literacy into foreign language teaching —based on the visualized analysis of CiteSpace]. 创新教育研究 [*Creative Education Studies*], *11*(7), 1944–1952. doi:10.12677/CES.2023.117289

Anderson, T. (2003). Modes of interaction in distance education: Recent developments and research questions. Handbook of distance education, 129-144.

Anderson, J. R., Corbett, A. T., Koedinger, K. R., & Pelletier, R. (1995). Cognitive tutors: Lessons learned. *Journal of the Learning Sciences, 4*(2), 167–207. doi:10.120715327809jls0402_2

Anderson, L. W., & Krathwohl, D. R. (2001). *A Taxonomy for Learning, Teaching, and Assessing: A Revision of Bloom's Taxonomy of Educational Objectives*. Longman.

Anderson, L. W., Krathwohl, D. R., Airasian, P. W., Cruikshank, K. A., Mayer, R. E., Pintrich, P. R., Raths, J., & Wittrock, M. C. (2001). *A Taxonomy for learning, teaching, and assessing: A Revision of Bloom's taxonomy of educational objectives*. Longman.

Anderson, M., & Jackson, D. (2001). Computer systems for distributed and distance learning. *Journal of Computer Assisted Learning, 16*(3), 213–228. doi:10.1046/j.1365-2729.2000.00134.x

Anderson, T., & Rivera Vargas, P. (2020). A critical look at educational technology from a distance education perspective. *Digital Education Review, 2020*(37), 208–229. doi:10.1344/der.2020.37.208-229

Angeli, C. (2005). Transforming a teacher education method course through technology: Effects on preservice teachers' technology competency. *Computers & Education, 45*(4), 383–398. doi:10.1016/j.compedu.2004.06.002

Angelo State University. (n.d.). 1.3 Theories of Learning and the Online Environment. Angelo State University. https://www.angelo.edu/faculty-and-staff/instructional-design/online-teaching/section_13.php

Anılan, B., Berber, A., & Anılan, H. (2018). The digital storytelling adventures of the teacher candidates. *Turkish Online Journal of Qualitative Inquiry, 9*(3), 262–287. doi:10.17569/tojqi.426308

Anna. (2020, July 31). *Top 5 des avantages et inconvénients de l'apprentissage en ligne*. Easy LMS. https://www.easy-lms.com/fr/base-connaissances/apprentissage-en-ligne/avantages-inconvenients-apprentissage-en-ligne/item12529

Anne, J., , & Nathalie, D. (2019). *Evaluation, a lever for education and training*. De Boeck.

Anoir, L., Khaldi, M., Erradi, M., & Khaldi, M. (2023). From the Conceptualization of an Architecture of a Pedagogical Scenario to the Design of a Model of Pedagogical Scenarios in Online Education. In Handbook of Research on Scripting, Media Coverage, and Implementation of E-Learning Training in LMS Platforms (pp. 133-166). IGI Global. doi:10.4018/978-1-6684-7634-5.ch006

Anoir, L., Khaldi, M., & Erradi, M. (2022). Personalization in Adaptive E-Learning. In *Designing User Interfaces With a Data Science Approach* (pp. 40–67). IGI Global. doi:10.4018/978-1-7998-9121-5.ch003

Apriyanti, N., Razak, R. A., Rahim, S. S. A., Shaharom, M. S. N., & Baharuldin, Z. (2020). Infographic instructional media as a solution and innovation in physics learning for senior high school students in Indonesia. *International Journal of Information and Education Technology (IJIET)*, *10*(10), 773–780. doi:10.18178/ijiet.2020.10.10.1457

Arcueno, G., Arga, H., Manalili, T. A., Garcia, J. A., Arcueno, G. G., Arga, H. A., & Garcia, S. (2021, March). *TPACK and ERT: Understanding teacher decisions and challenges with integrating technology in planning lessons and instructions. DLSU Research Congress.*

Arkorful, V., & Abaidoo, N. (2015). The role of e-learning, advantages, and disadvantages of its adoption in higher education. *International journal of instructional technology and distance learning, 12*(1), 29-42.

Atkinson, S. (2011). Embodied and embedded theory in practice: The student-owned learning-engagement (SOLE) model. *International Review of Research in Open and Distance Learning*, *12*(2), 1–18. doi:10.19173/irrodl.v12i2.929

Audet, L. (2010). *Wikis, Blogs, and Web 2.0. Opportunities and impacts for distance learning.* Réseau d'enseignement francophone à distance du Canada (REFAD). https://www.refad.ca/nouveau/Wikis_blogues_et_Web_2_0.pdf

Aydin, S. (2012). A review of research on Facebook as an educational environment. *Educational Technology Research and Development*, *60*(6), 1093–1106. doi:10.100711423-012-9260-7

Azlan, C. A., Wong, J. H. D., Tan, L. K., Huri, M. S. N. A., Ung, N. M., Pallath, V., & Ng, K. H. (2020). Teaching and learning of postgraduate medical physics using Internet-based e-learning during the COVID-19 pandemic–A case study from Malaysia. *Physica Medica*, *80*, 10–16. doi:10.1016/j.ejmp.2020.10.002 PMID:33070007

B Online Learning. (2022, January 20). *Cognitive Theory of eLearning.* B Online Learning. https://bonlinelearning.com/cognitive-theory-of-elearning/. Récupéré le 10 Mai 2022

Babocká, M. (2015). Assessment in CLIL classes. In S. Pokrivčáková (Ed.), *CLIL in foreign language education: e-textbook for foreign language teachers* (pp. 176–199). Constantine the Philosopher University. doi:10.17846/CLIL.2015.176-188

Bada, S. O., & Olusegun, S. (2015). Constructivism learning theory: A paradigm for teaching and learning. *Journal of Research & Method in Education*, *5*(6), 66–70.

Bahroun, Z., Anane, C., Ahmed, V., & Zacca, A. (2023). Transforming Education: A Comprehensive Review of Generative Artificial Intelligence in Educational Settings through Bibliometric and Content Analysis. *Sustainability (Basel)*, *15*(17), 12983. doi:10.3390u151712983

Baker, M. (2003). Computer-mediated argumentative interactions for the co-elaboration of scientific notions. In J. Andriessen, M. Baker, & D. Suthers (Eds.), *Arguing to Learn: Confronting Cognitions in Computer-Supported Collaborative Learning environments* (pp. 47–78). Kluwer Academic Publishers. doi:10.1007/978-94-017-0781-7_3

Baker, R. S., Corbett, A. T., & Aleven, V. (2008). More accurate student modeling through contextual estimation of slip and guess probabilities in Bayesian knowledge tracing. In *Proceedings of the 9th International Conference on Intelligent Tutoring Systems* (pp. 406-415). Springer. 10.1007/978-3-540-69132-7_44

Balaman, F. (2016). The effect of digital storytelling technique on the attitudes of students toward teaching technologies. *Egitim ve Ögretim, 6*(2), 147–168. doi:10.14527/pegegog.2016.009

Balanyk, J. (2017). Developing English for academic purposes MOOCS using the ADDIE Model. In *Inted2017 Proceedings* (pp. 6514–6522). IATED. doi:10.21125/inted.2017.1506

Balslev, K., & Saada-Robert, M. (2002). Expliquer l'apprentissage situé de la littéracie: une démarche inductive/déductive. *Raisons éducatives*, (5), 89-110.

Bandura, A. (1997). *Self-efficacy: The exercise of control.* W H Freeman.

Banna, J., Lin, M. F. G., Stewart, M., & Fialkowski, M. K. (2015). Interaction matters: Strategies to promote engaged learning in an online introductory nutrition course. *Journal of online learning and teaching/MERLOT, 11*(2), 249.

Barker, S., Ansorge, J., & Mwangi, W. (2018). Personalised Learning in Special Education. In Handbook of Personalization in Education (pp. 187-207). Springer.

Barraket, J., Payne, A., Scott, G., & Cameron, L. (2000). *Equity and the Use of Communications Technology in Higher Education: A UTS Case Study.* Department of Education, Science and Training.

Basque, J., & Doré, S. (1998). The concept of computer-based learning environment [electronic version]. *Journal of Distance Education / Revue de l'enseignement à distance, 13*(1). http://cade.athabascau.ca/vol13.1/dore.html

Basque, J., Contamines, J., & Maina, M. (2010). Design approaches to learning environments. In B. Charlier & F. Henri (Eds.), *Learning with technologies* (pp. 109–119).

Bates, A. W. (2005). *Distance Education in a Dual Mode Higher Education Institution: A Canadian Case Study [Electronic Version].* Centre for Distance Education, Korean National Open University. https://www.tonybates.ca/papers/KNOUpaper.htm

Bates, J. E., Almekdash, H., & Gilchrest-Dunnam, M. J. (2017). The flipped classroom: A brief, brief history. *The flipped college classroom: Conceptualized and re-conceptualized*, 3-10.

Bates, T. (2014, July 29). *Learning theories and online learning.* Tony Bates. https://www.tonybates.ca/2014/07/29/learning-theories-and-online-learning/

Batier, C. (2012, July 25). *Should we be afraid of evaluation?* [Video]. Charles Hadji. https://youtu.be/sH2QDWxDr1c?si=YVmSvDYVvDf7xeEw

Baudrit, A. (2007). Apprentissage coopératif/Apprentissage collaboratif: D'un comparatisme conventionnel à un comparatisme critique. *Les Sciences de l'Education pour l'Ere Nouvelle, 40*(1), 115–136. doi:10.3917/lsdle.401.0115

Baumeister, R. F., & Leary, M. R. (1995). The need to belong: Desire for interpersonal attachments as a fundamental human motivation. *Psychological Bulletin, 117*(3), 497–529. https://pubmed.ncbi.nlm.nih.gov/7777651/. doi:10.1037/0033-2909.117.3.497 PMID:7777651

Bautier, E., Crinon, J., & Rochex, J.-Y. (2011). Introduction. In J.-Y. Rochex & J. Crinon (Eds.), *The Construction of Educational Inequalities: At the Heart of Teaching Practices and Practices* (pp. 9–16). De Boeck Supérieur.

Beacco, J. (2007). The Competency-Based Approach to Language Teaching. Paris: Didier.

Béchard, J. P. & Pelletier, P. (2001), Development of the innovations educational in academia: a case of organizational learning. In D. Raymond (dir.), New spaces of development professional And organizational (pp.131-149). Sherbrooke: Editions of CRP

Béchard, J.-P. (2001). Higher education and educational innovations: A review of the literature. *Journal of Educational Sciences, 272*, 257–281.

Beckers, J. (2002). *Developing and Evaluating Skills at School: Towards More Efficiency and Equity.* Éditions Labor.

Bedard, D. & Béchard, J. (2009). Innovation pedagogic. In *THE superior: A vast construction site ". In D. Bedard And J.-P. Béchard (dir.), Innovate In higher education* (pp. 29–43). Presses Academics of France.

Bédard, L., Déziel, J., & Lamarche, L. (1999). *Introduction à la psychologie sociale.* ERPI.

Belhaoues, T., Bensebaa, T., Abdessemed, M., & Bey, A. (2016). AlgoSkills: an ontology of Algorithmic Skills for exercises description and organization. *Journal of e-Learning and Knowledge Society, 12*(1).

Bell, S. (2010). Project-based learning for the 21st century: Skills for the future. *The Clearing House: A Journal of Educational Strategies, Issues and Ideas, 83*(2), 39–43. https://www.jstor.org/stable/20697896. doi:10.1080/00098650903505415

Belt, E. S., & Lowenthal, P. R. (2023). Synchronous video-based communication and online learning: An exploration of instructors' perceptions and experiences. *Education and Information Technologies, 28*(5), 4941-4964.

Bennani, Y. (2006). *Apprentissage connexionniste.* Hermes Science.

Berelson, B., & Steiner, G. (1964). *Human Behavior.* Harcourt, Brace, & World.

Berger, C. R., & Calabrese, R. J. (1974). Some explorations in initial interaction and beyond: Toward a developmental theory of interpersonal communication. *Human Communication Research, 1*(2), 99–112. doi:10.1111/j.1468-2958.1975.tb00258.x

Berge, Z. L. (2013). Barriers to communication in distance education. *Turkish Online Journal of Distance Education, 14*(1), 374–388.

Berge, Z. L., & Muilenburg, L. Y. (2013). *Handbook of Mobile Learning.* Routledge. doi:10.4324/9780203118764

Bernaus, M., & Furlong, Á. (2017). CLIL as a plurilingual approach or language of real life and language as carrier of culture. *Research Papers in Language Teaching and Learning, 8*(1), 34–43. https://rpltl.eap.gr/images/2017/08-01-034-Furlong-Bernaus.pdf

Besse, H. (1984). Educating intercultural perception. France: Hachette Edicef.

Besse, H. (1989). *Some reflections on the literary text and its practices in the teaching of French as a second language or as a foreign language.* Lyon: Trefoil, n°9.

Besse, H. (1991). Comment utiliser la littérature dans l'enseignement du français langue étrangère. *Ici et là,, 20*, 51-55.

Beuscart, J. S., Dagiral, É., & Parasie, S. (2009). A Sociology of Online Activities (Introduction). *Terrains & Travaux, 15*(1), 3–28. doi:10.3917/tt.015.0003

Bijeesh, N. A. (2017). Advantages and disadvantages of distance learning. *India Education.* http://www.indiaeducation.net/online-education/articles/advantages-and-disadvantages-of-distance learning.html

Blancpain M. (1953). Préface. In Mauger G., (ed.)*, Cours de langue et de civilisation françaises I* (pp. V–VI). Hachette.

Blum, K. (1999). Providing Equitable Adult Education. *Feminista!, 2*(8)

Blumenfeld, P. C., Soloway, E., Marx, R. W., Krajcik, J. S., Guzdial, M., & Palincsar, A. (1991). Motivating project-based learning: Sustaining the doing, supporting the learning. *Educational Psychologist, 26*(3-4), 369–398. doi:10.1080/00461520.1991.9653139

Bonal, X., & González, S. (2020). The impact of lockdown on the learning gap: Family and school divisions in times of crisis. *International Review of Education, 66*(5-6), 635–655. doi:10.100711159-020-09860-z PMID:32952208

Bootz, P., Gherban, A., & Papp, T. (2003). *Transitoire observable: texte fondateur.* Transitoire Observable.

Botelho, M. G., Gao, X., & Jagannathan, N. (2019). A qualitative analysis of students' perceptions of videos to support learning in a psychomotor skills course. *European Journal of Dental Education, 23*(1), 20–27. doi:10.1111/eje.12373 PMID:29920878

Bouchardon, S. (dir.), Broudoux, E., Deseilligny, O. & Ghitalla, F. (2007). *Un laboratoire de littératures: littérature numérique et Internet.* Bibliothèque publique d'information.

Boullier, D. (2013, 01 mars). Cours en ligne massifs et ouverts: la standardisation ou l'innovation? *Le Monde.*

Bourdieu, P. (1970). *Reproduction.* Taylor & Francis.

Bourgeois, E., & Nizet, J. (1997). *Apprentissage et formation des adultes.* Presses Universitaires de France.

Bouthry, A., Jourdain, C., Bodet, G., & Amalric, P.-H. (2007). *Build your online training project, Eyrolles-Editions d'organization.* Collection Books Tools Training.

Bowen, J. A., & Watson, C. E. (2017). *Teaching naked techniques: A practical guide to designing better classes.* John Wiley & Sons.

Boyinbode, O., Olotu, P., & Akintola, K. (2020). Development of an ontology-based adaptive personalized e-learning system. *Applied Computer Science, 16*(4), 64–84. doi:10.35784/acs-2020-30

Bran, R. (2010). Message in a bottle Telling stories in a digital world. *Procedia: Social and Behavioral Sciences, 2*(2), 1790–1793. doi:10.1016/j.sbspro.2010.03.986

Bransford, J. D., Barron, B., Pea, R. D., Meltzoff, A., Kuhl, P., Bell, P., & Sabelli, N. H. (2009). Foundations and Opportunities for an Interdisciplinary Science of Learning. In K. Sawyer (Ed.), *The Cambridge Handbook of Learning Sciences* (pp. 19–34). Cambridge University Press.

Branson, R. K., Rayner, G. T., Cox, J. L., Furman, J. P., King, F. J., & Hannum, W. H. (1975). Interservice procedures for instructional systems development. (5 vols.)(TRADOC Pam 350-30 NAVEDTRA 106A). Ft. Monroe, VA: US Army Training and Doctrine Command.

Brassard, C., & Daele, A. (2003). A reflective tool for designing an educational scenario integrating ICT. Computer Environments for Human Learning, Strasbourg, France.

Brennan, R. L. (2001). *Generalizability Theory.* Springer. doi:10.1007/978-1-4757-3456-0

Brick, B. (2012). The Role of Social Networking Sites for Language Learning in UK Higher Education: The Views of Learners and Practitioners. [IJCALLT]. *International Journal of Computer-Assisted Language Learning and Teaching, 2*(3), 35–53. doi:10.4018/ijcallt.2012070103

Brien, R. (1981). *Design pédagogique. Introduction à l'approche de Gagné et Briggs.* Editions Saint-Yves.

Briggs, L. J. (1981). Instructional design: principles and applications. Englewood Cliffs, NJ: educational Technology publications (3è édition).

Brindley, J. E., Blaschke, L. M., & Walti, C. (2009). Creating effective collaborative learning groups in an online environment. *International Review of Research in Open and Distance Learning, 10*(3). doi:10.19173/irrodl.v10i3.675

Brockfeld, T., Müller, B., & de Laffolie, J. (2018). Video versus live lecture courses: A comparative evaluation of lecture types and results. *Medical Education Online, 23*(1), 1. doi:10.1080/10872981.2018.1555434 PMID:30560721

Brodin, É. (n.d.). Innovation en éducation et innovation dans l'enseignement des langues: quels invariants? Document inédit. Université Paris 3. France.

Bronckart, J. P. (1985). *Le fonctionnement des discours.* Delachaux et Niestlé.

Brown, C. (2017). *Advantages and disadvantages of distance learning.* EZ Talks. https://www.eztalks.com/elearning/advantages-and-disadvantages-of-distance-learning.html

Brown, K., Reinhardt, A., & Korner, T. (2023). Lecturer decision-making in the context of pandemic teaching: Rationales and evidence, International Journal for Academic Development Kerkstra, RL, Rustagi, KA, Grimshaw, AA, Minges, KE. Dental education practices during COVID-19: A scoping review. *Journal of Dental Education, 2022*(86), 546–573.

Brownstein, S. A., Murad, A., & Hunt, R. J. (2015). Implementation of new technologies in US dental school curricula. *Journal of Dental Education, 79*(3), 259–264. doi:10.1002/j.0022-0337.2015.79.3.tb05880.x PMID:25729019

Bruce, L. R., & Sleeman, P. J. (2000). *Instructional Design: a primer.* Information Age Publishing.

Bruffee, K. A. (1999). *Collaborative Learning: Higher Education, Interdependence, and the Authority of Knowledge.* The Johns Hopkins University Press. doi:10.56021/9780801859731

Bruner, J. (1997). *The acts of meaning.* Harvard University Press.

Brusilovskiy, P. L. (1994). The construction and application of student models in intelligent tutoring systems. *Journal of Computer and Systems Sciences International, 32*(1), 70–89.

Brusilovsky, P. (2001). Adaptive Hypermedia. *User Modeling and User-Adapted Interaction, 11*(1-2), 87–110. doi:10.1023/A:1011143116306

Brusilovsky, P. (2015). Adaptive hypermedia. In *Handbook of Research on Educational Communications and Technology* (pp. 359–368). Springer.

Bureau, S., & Marchal, E. (2005). The quest for objectivity in workplace evaluation. *Practical Sociologies,* (1), 61–72.

Burgos, D. (2008). *Extension of the IMS Learning Design Specification based on Adaptation and Integration of Units of Learning.* [Doctoral Thesis, Carlos III University of Madrid, Leganes, Spain].

Caduceus International Publishing. (2023, April 20). *Pedagogical approaches to teaching in higher education.* Caduceus International Publishing. https://www.cipcourses.com/blog/pedagogical-approaches-to-teaching-in-higher-education/

Cailliez, J. (2017). *The flipped classroom. Educational innovation through changing posture.* Ellipses.

Calvert, J. (2006). Achieving Development Goals-Foundations: Open and Distance Learning, Lessons and Issues. *Retrieved,* (June), 6.

Camara, W. J., & Kimmel, E. W. (2005). *A Review of the Impact of Test Preparation on Test Performance: What We Know and What We Need to Know.* The College Board.

Campbell, J. D., & Mahling, D. E. (1998). A Visual Language System for Developing and Presenting Internet-Based Education. In *Proceedings of IEEE Symposium on Visual Languages.* IEEE. 10.1109/VL.1998.706135

Campillo-Ferrer, J.-M., Miralles-Martínez, P., & Sánchez-Ibáñez, R. (2020). CLIL teachers' views on cognitive development in primary education. *Palgrave Communications, 6*(1), 97. doi:10.105741599-020-0480-x

Canvat, K. (2004). *Values in/from literature.* P.U of Namur.

Capozzi, M. M. (2007). Knowledge Management Architectures Beyond Technology. *First Monday, 12*(6). http://first-monday.org/htbin/cgiwrap/bin/ojs/index.php/fm/article/view/1 871/1754

Cartier, F. A. (1959). The President's Letter. *Journal of Communication, 9*(1), 5. doi:10.1111/j.1460-2466.1959.tb00285.x

Casalfiore, S. (2000). *Teacher activity in class. Contribution to understanding the professional reality of teachers.* HALSHS.

Catroux, M. (2006). *Perspective co-actionnelle et tice: quelles convergences pour l'enseignement de la langue de spécialité?* Langues Vivantes. http://www.langues-vivantes.u-bordeaux2.fr/frsa/pdf/CATROUX.pdf

Cavanagh, S. R. (2019). How to make your teaching more engaging. *The Chronicle of Higher Education.* https://tacc.org/sites/default/files/documents/2019-08/how_to_make_your_teaching_more_engaging-che.pdf

Cavanagh, S. R. (2016). *The spark of learning: Energizing the college classroom with the science of emotion.* West Virginia University Press.

Chadwick, C., & Muilenburg, L. (2011). Digital Storytelling in the Science Classroom: Using Analogies to Improve Understanding. In M. Koehler & P. Mishra (Eds.), *Proceedings of SITE 2011--Society for Information Technology & Teacher Education International Conference* (pp. 1087-1092). Nashville, Tennessee, USA: Association for the Advancement of Computing in Education (AACE).

Chan, B. S., Churchill, D., & Chiu, T. K. (2017). Digital literacy learning in higher education through digital storytelling approach. [JIER]. *Journal of International Education Research, 13*(1), 1–16. doi:10.19030/jier.v13i1.9907

Chang, Y., & Li, C. (2020). 发挥外语专业自身特殊优势,促进思政与专业教育深度融合 [On deeper integration of IP and FL education by fully utilizing the strengths of FL majors]. 外语电化教学 *[Technology Enhanced Foreign Language Education], (6), 17–22.* http://www.cnki.com.cn/Article/CJFDTotal-WYDH202006002.htm

Chang, Y., & Zhao, Y. (2020). 内容语言融合教育理念(CLI)的提出、内涵及意义——从内容依托教学到内容语言融合教育 [The proposal, connotation and significance of the concept of content-language integration (CLI) — From content-based instruction to content-language integration education]. 外语教学 *[Foreign Language Education], 41*(5), 49–54. http://www.cnki.com.cn/Article/CJFDTotal-TEAC202005010.htm

Chang-Tik, C. (2018). Impact of learning styles on the community of inquiry presences in multi-disciplinary blended learning environments. *Interactive Learning Environments, 26*(6), 827–838. doi:10.1080/10494820.2017.1419495

Chartier, D. (2003). Les styles d'apprentissage: Entre flou conceptuel et intérêt pratique. *Savoirs,* (2), 7–28. doi:10.3917avo.002.0007

Chatti, M. A., Muslim, A., & Schroeder, U. (2012). Toward a Personal Learning Environment Framework. *Journal of Educational Technology & Society, 15*(4), 3–13.

Chawinga, W. D. (2017). Taking social media to a university classroom: Teaching and learning using Twitter and blogs. *International Journal of Educational Technology in Higher Education, 14*(1), 1–19.

Chaya, P., & Inpin, B. (2020). Effects of integrating movie-based mobile learning instruction for enhancing Thai university students' speaking skills and intercultural communicative competence. *English Language Teaching, 13*(7), 27–45. doi:10.5539/elt.v13n7p27

Chen, F. H. (2021). Sustainable education through e-learning: The case study of ilearn2. 0. *Sustainability (Basel), 13*(18), 10186. doi:10.3390u131810186

Chen, F., Ruiz, N., Choi, E., Epps, J., Khawaja, M. A., Taib, R., Yin, B., & Wang, Y. (2013). Multimodal behavior and interaction as indicators of cognitive load. [TiiS]. *ACM Transactions on Interactive Intelligent Systems*, *2*(4), 1–36. doi:10.1145/2395123.2395127

Cheng, H., Cui, F., & Sun, N. (2016). 中国高校思想政治教育史论 [A critical history of ideological and political education in universities of China]. Social Sciences Academic Press.

Chen, H. T. (2015). *Practical program evaluation: Assessing and improving planning, implementation, and effectiveness*. Sage Publications.

Chen, L., Liu, R., & Xu, X. (2018). Artificial intelligence in education: What is essential? *Journal of Educational Technology Development and Exchange*, *11*(1), 64–74.

Chergui, M., Tahiri, A., Chakir, A., & Mansouri, H. (2020). Towards a New Educational Engineering Model for Moroccan University Based on ICT. *Int. J. Eng. Pedagog.*, *10*(3), 49–63. doi:10.3991/ijep.v10i3.12421

Chevallard, Y. (2007). *Evaluation, verification, objectification. IREM of Aix-Marseille Faculty of Sciences of Luminy European Commission. (2017)*. Handbook on Results-Based Management and Evaluation for Development Cooperation.

Chomsky, N. (2012). On the nature, use and acquisition of language. In *Language and meaning in cognitive science* (pp. 1–20). Routledge.

Chu, P. (1998). 德育论 [Theory of moral education]. Fujian Education Publishing House.

Chu, R. J. C. (2010). How family support and Internet self-efficacy influence the effects of e-learning among higher aged adults–Analyses of gender and age differences. *Computers & Education*, *55*(1), 255–264. doi:10.1016/j.compedu.2010.01.011

Cialdini, R. B., & Cialdini, R. B. (2007). *Influence: The psychology of persuasion* (Vol. 55). Collins.

Cilla, G., Montes, M., Gomariz, M., Alkorta, M., Iturzaeta, A., Perez-Yarza, E. G., & Perez-Trallero, E. (2013). Rotavirus genotypes in children in the Basque Country (North of Spain): Rapid and intense emergence of the G12 [P8] genotype. *Epidemiology and Infection*, *141*(4), 868–874. doi:10.1017/S0950268812001306 PMID:22873952

Clark, R. C., & Mayer, R. E. (2016). *E-learning and the science of instruction: Proven guidelines for consumers and designers of multimedia learning*. john Wiley & sons.

Clark, R., & Mayer, R. (2008). e-Learning and the Science of Instruction: Proven Guidelines for Consumers and Designers of Multimedia Learning. Pfeiffer.

Clark, R. C. (2008). *Building expertise. Cognitive methods for training and performance improvement* (3rd ed.). Pfeiffer & International Society for Performance Improvement.

Clergue, M. (2015). *Réseaux de Neurones Artificiels*.

Clevenger, T. Jr. (1991). Can one not communicate? A conflict of models. *Communication Studies*, *42*(4), 340–353. doi:10.1080/10510979109368348

Cohen, J. (1988). *Statistical power analysis for the behavioral sciences* (2nd ed.). Lawrence Earlbaum Associates.

Colles, L. (1994). Comparative Literature and Intercultural Recognition. Brussels: De Boeck.

Colles, L. (1994). *Littérature comparée et reconnaissance interculturelle*. De Boeck-Duculot.

Collins, S. N. (2021). The importance of storytelling in chemical education. *Nature Chemistry*, *13*(1), 1–2. doi:10.103841557-020-00617-7 PMID:33353969

Combes, J. (1967). Value and Freedom. Paris: PUF.

Condy, J., Chigona, A., Gachago, D., & Ivala, E. (2012). Pre-service students' perceptions and experiences of digital storytelling in diverse classrooms. *The Turkish Online Journal of Educational Technology*, *11*(3), 278–285.

Connac, S. (2021). Pour différencier: individualiser ou personnaliser?. Éducation et socialisation. *Les Cahiers du CER-FEE*, (59).

Connac, S. (2018). *La personnalisation des apprentissages: agir face à l'hétérogénéité, à l'école et au collège.* ESF Sciences Humaines.

Conseil De L'europe. (2001). *Cadre européen commun de référence pour les langues: apprendre, enseigner, évaluer.* Didier.

Conseil De L'europe. (2001). *Un cadre européen commun de référence pour les langues: apprendre, enseigner, évaluer.* Didier.

Cook, V. (2008). Second Language Learning and Language Learning—Vivian Cook-2008. *Structure (London, England)*, *18*, 2–2.

Coomey, M., & Stephenson, J. (2018). Online learning: It is all about dialogue, involvement, support and control—according to the research. In *Teaching & learning online* (pp. 37–52). Routledge. doi:10.4324/9781315042527-6

Cope, B., & Kalantzis, M. (2000). *Multiliteracies. Literacy learning and the design of social futures.* Routledge.

Copeland, H. L., Longworth, D. L., Hewson, M. G., & Stoller, J. K. (2000). Successful lecturing: A prospective study to validate attributes of the effective medical lecture. *Journal of General Internal Medicine*, *15*(6), 366–371. doi:10.1046/j.1525-1497.2000.06439.x PMID:10886470

Corbett, A. T., & Anderson, J. R. (1995). Knowledge Tracing: Modeling the Acquisition of Procedural Knowledge. *User Modeling and User-Adapted Interaction*, *4*(4), 253–278. doi:10.1007/BF01099821

Corbett, F., & Spinello, E. (2020). Connectivism and leadership: Harnessing a learning theory for the digital age to redefine leadership in the twenty-first century. *Heliyon*, *6*(1), e03250. doi:10.1016/j.heliyon.2020.e03250 PMID:31993523

Costley, J., & Lange, C. (2018). The moderating effects of group work on the relationship between motivation and cognitive load. *The International Review of Research in Open and Distributed Learning*, *19*(1).

Cottier, P., Choquet, C., & Tchounikine, P. (2008). Rethinking EIAH engineering for teacher designers. In J. Dinet (Ed.), *Uses, users and information skills in the 21st century* (pp. 159–193). Edited by Hermes Lavoisier.

Coyle, D. (2008). CLIL — a pedagogical approach from the European perspective. In N. V. Deusen-Scholl & N. H. Hornberger (Eds.), *Encyclopedia of language and education* (2nd ed., Vol. 4, pp. 97–111). Springer. doi:10.1007/978-0-387-30424-3_92

Coyle, D., Hood, P., & Marsh, D. (2010). *CLIL: content and language integrated learning.* Cambridge University Press. doi:10.1017/9781009024549

Creasman, P. A. (2012). *Considerations in online course design* (IDEA paper# 52). IDEA.

Crocker, L., & Algina, J. (2008). *Introduction to Classical and Modern Test Theory.* Wadsworth Cengage Learning.

Cronbach, L. J. (1989). Six thoughts for evaluators. *Evaluation Practice*, *10*(2), 139–146.

Crook, C., & Schofield, L. (2017). The video lecture. *The Internet and Higher Education*, *34*, 56–64. doi:10.1016/j.iheduc.2017.05.003

Cros, F. (2002). National Innovation Council for Academic Success. Progress report to the Minister of National Education, France.

Cros, F. (n.d.). *Innovation in education and training. Meaning and use of the word: Final report*. INNOVA. European Observatory of Innovations in Education.

Cros, F. (1997). Innovation in education And in training. *Revue Française de Pédagogie, 118*.

Cros, F. (2001). *School innovation. Teachers and Researchers – Summary and debate – Paris*. INRP.

Cros, F. (2007). *Innovative action. Between creativity and training*. De Boeck.

Cross, J. (2004). *An informal history of eLearning*. Emerald.

Croxton, R. A. (2014). The role of interactivity in student satisfaction and persistence in online learning. *Journal of Online Learning and Teaching, 10*(2), 314.

Crozat, S., & Trigano, P. (2002). Structuring and scripting of digital educational documents in a massification logic. STE (Educational Sciences and Techniques), 9(3).

Çubukçu, Z. (2012). Proje Tabanlı Öğrenme [Project based learning]. B. Oral (Ed.), Öğrenme Öğretme Kuram ve Yaklaşımları [Learning Teaching Theory and Approaches] (527-539). Pegem Akademi.

Cullen, R., & Harris, M. (2009). Assessing learner-centeredness through course syllabi. *Assessment & Evaluation in Higher Education, 34*(1), 115–125. doi:10.1080/02602930801956018

Cuq J.-P. & Gruca I. (2005). Cours de didactique du français langue étrangère et seconde, (2e éd). Grenoble, PUG.

D'Halluin, C., Boudry, T., Charlet, D., Clavel, D., Desprez, C., Dewulf, B., Le Ven, O., Merveille, S., & Warocquier, A. (2003). Les formations en ligne: Points de vue de responsables de grandes entreprises de la distribution et des services. *Distances et Savoirs, 4*(4), 517–531. doi:10.3166/ds.1.517-531

D'Mello, S., Lehman, B., Pekrun, R., & Graesser, A. (2015). Confusion Can Be Beneficial for Learning. *Learning and Instruction, 36*, 11–21.

Dack, T. M. F., Argudo, J., & Abad, M. (2020). Language and teaching methodology features of CLIL in university classrooms: A research synthesis. *Colombian Applied Linguistics Journal, 22*(1), 40–54. doi:10.14483/22487085.13878

Daele, A., Brassard, C., Esnault, L., Donoghue, M., Uytterbrouk, E., Zeiliger, R. (2002). Design, implementation, analysis and evaluation of educational scenarios using ICT. *Recre@sup-WP2 FUNDP project report*.

Dağ, F., & Durdu, L. (2012). Opinions of prospective teachers about project-based learning process. *e-Journal of New World Sciences Academy, 7*(1), 200-211. https://doi.org/ doi:10.12739/10.12739

Dance, F. E. (1970). The "concept" of communication. *Journal of Communication, 20*(2), 201–210. doi:10.1111/j.1460-2466.1970.tb00877.x

Dance, F. E. X., & Larson, C. E. (1976). *The Functions of Human Communication: A Theoretical Approach*. Holt, Rinehart & Winston.

Daniel, J. (2016). *Making sense of flexibility as a defining element of online learning*. Athabasca University.

Davidson-Shiver, G., & Rasmussen, K. (2006). *Behaviorism Applied to Distance Education*. EDUC633 - Module 2. http://www.amandaszapkiw.com/artifacts/EDUC633_eXe_Module_2/behaviorism_applied_to_distance_education.html. Récupéré le 24 Juillet 2023.

Davis, A. L. (2013). Using instructional design principles to develop effective information literacy instruction: The ADDIE model. *College & Research Libraries News, 74*(4), 205–207. doi:10.5860/crln.74.4.8934

De Ketele, J. M. (1996). *Formative Assessment: Foundations and Practices*. De Boeck University.

De Ketele, J., & Hugonnier, B. (2020). Chapitre 1. Qu'est-ce que l'internationalisation? Un réseau conceptuel à clarifier. In L. Cosnefroy (Ed.), *L'internationalisation de l'enseignement supérieur: Le meilleur des mondes?* (pp. 17–32). De Boeck Supérieur., doi:10.3917/dbu.cosne.2020.01.0017

De Lièvre, B., Temperman, G., Cambier, J.-B., Decamps, S., & Depover, C. (2009). Analyse de l'influence des styles d'apprentissage sur les interactions dans les forums collaboratifs. In C. Develotte, F. Mangenot, E. Nissen (Eds.), *Actes du colloque Epal 2009 - Échanger pour apprendre en ligne: conception, instrumentation, interactions, multimodalité*. Grenoble, France: Université Stendhal – Grenoble 3. Retrieved from: https://shs.hal.science/halshs-01078945/document

De Lièvre, B., & Depover, C. (2007). Analyse des communications médiatisées au sein de paires de niveau différencié. In T. Nodenot, J. Wallet, & E. Fernandes (Eds.), *Environnements informatiques pour l'apprentissage humain 2007* (pp. 461–472).

Dean, C., & Whitlock, Q. (1992). *A handbook of computer-based training. Based Training*. Nichols Publishing Company.

Deans, T. (2019). Yes, your syllabus is way too long. *The Chronicle of Higher Education*. https://www.chronicle.com/article/yes-your-syllabus-is-way-too-long/

Decamps, S. (2014). *Educational scripting of online collaborative activities*. [Doctoral thesis in Psychological Sciences and Education. University of Mons, Faculty of Psychology and Educational Sciences].

Dejean-Thircuir, C., & Mangenot, F. (2014). Benefits and limitations of web 2.0 tasks in an asymmetrical tele-collaboration project. *Canadian Journal of Learning and Technology, 40*(1). doi:10.21432/T23019

Dejours, C. (1995). *The human factor*. PUF.

Delaby, A. (2008). *How to design and produce an online course: Create an online course, Eyrolles-Editions d'organization* (2nd ed.). Collection Books Tools Training.

Demircioğlu, H., Demircioğlu, G., & Ayas, A. (2006). Stories and chemistry education. *Hacettepe University Journal of Education, 30*, 110–119.

Demir, S., & Bozkurt, A. (2011). Primary mathematics teachers' views about their competencies concerning the integration of technology. *Elementary Education Online, 10*(3), 850–860.

Depover, C., De Lièvre, B., Decamps, S., & Porco, F. (2014). *Analysis and design of learning scenarios*. The Department of Educational Sciences and Technology University of Mons. (http:// deste.umons.ac.be/cours/scnr/)

Depover, C., Karsenti, T., & Komis, V. (2007). *Enseigner avec les technologies*. Presses de l'Université du Québec.

Depover, C., & Marchand, L. (2002). *E-learning et formation des adultes en contexte professionnel*. De Boeck-Université. doi:10.3917/dbu.depov.2002.01

Depover, C., Quintin, J.-J., & De Lièvre, B. (2003). Un outil de scénarisation de formations à distance basées sur la collaboration. In C. Desmoulins, P. Marquet, & D. Bouhineau (Eds.), *Environnements informatiques pour l'apprentissage humain 2003* (pp. 115–126).

Depover, C., & Strebelle, A. (1997). *A model and intervention strategy for the introduction of ICT into the educational process*. Educational Technology Unit, University of Mons-Hainaut.

Depover, C., Strebelle, A., & De Lièvre, B. (2007). A modeling of the innovation process based on the dynamics of networks of actors. In M. Baron, D. Guin, & L. Trouche (Eds.), *Computerized environments and digital resources for learning. Design and uses, combined perspectives* (pp. 140–169). Hermès and Lavoisier.

Desai, D. (2020). *Modeling Personalized E-Learning for Effective Distance Education.*

Détrez, C. (2011). Les adolescents et la lecture, quinze ans après. *Bulletin des bibliothèques de France, 5,* 32-35. https://bbf.enssib.fr/consulter/bbf-2011-05-0032-005.pdf

Develay, M. (1992). *From learning to teaching.* ESF.

Dewey, J. (2008). The Later Works of John Dewey: Vol. 12. *1925 - 1953: 1938, Logic: The Theory of Inquiry (Collected Works of John Dewey 1882-1953)* (1st ed.). Southern Illinois University Press.

DeWitz, S. J., Woolsey, M. L., & Walsh, W. B. (2009). College student retention: An exploration of the relationship between self-efficacy beliefs and purpose in life among college students. *Journal of College Student Development, 50*(1), 19–34. doi:10.1353/csd.0.0049

Diab, A. A. M., Abdel-Haq, E. M., & Aly, M. A.-S. (2018). The effectiveness of using content and language integrated learning (CLIL) approach to enhance EFL student teachers' cultural awareness. *Journal of Faculty of Education, 31*(122), 37–56. doi:10.21608/jfeb.2020.147494

Diffily, D. (2002). Project-based learning: Meeting social studies standards and the needs of gifted learners. *Gifted Child Today, 25*(3), 40–59. doi:10.4219/gct-2002-69

Dillenbourg, P., & Traum, D. (1999*). The long road from a shared screen to a shared understanding.* C., I., Hoadley, & J.R. (Eds.), Proceedings of the 3rd Conference on Computer Supported Collaborative Learning, Stanford.

Dillenbourg, P. (1996). What do you mean by collaborative learning? In P. Dillenbourg (Ed.), *Collaborative – learning: Cognitive and Computational Approaches* (pp. 1–19). Elsevier.

Dillenbourg, P. (1999). What do you mean by "collaborative learning"? In P. Dillenbourg (Ed.), *Collaborative Learning: Cognitive and Computational Approaches* (pp. 1–19). Pergamon.

Dillenbourg, P. (2002). Over-scripting CSCL: The risks of blending collaborative learning with instructional design. In P. Kirschner (Ed.), *Three worlds of CSCL: Can we support CSCL?* (pp. 61–69). Open Universiteit.

Dillenbourg, P., Järvelä, S., & Fischer, F. (2009). The Evolution of Research on Computer-Supported Collaborative Learning. In *Technology-Enhanced Learning* (pp. 3–19). Springer. doi:10.1007/978-1-4020-9827-7_1

Dillenbourg, P., & Jermann, P. (2006). Designing Integrative Scripts. In F. Fischer, I. Kollar, H. Mandl, & J. Haake (Eds.), *Scripting Computer-Supported Collaborative Learning* (pp. 277–302). Springer.

Dillenbourg, P., & Tchounikine, P. (2007). Flexibility in macro-scripts for computer supported collaborative learning. *Journal of Computer Assisted Learning, 23*(1), 1–13. doi:10.1111/j.1365-2729.2007.00191.x

Dimitrova, V., Valkanova, N., & Rensing, C. (2015). Enhancing Learning Analytics through Semantic Integration and Analysis of Multimodal Data. *Journal of Learning Analytics, 2*(2), 103–129.

Dinçol Özgür, S., & Yılmaz, A. (2020). The effect of project-based learning approach on prospective teachers' adopted learning approach, self-efficacy and level of knowledge. *Necatibey Faculty of Education Electronic Journal of Science and Mathematics Education, 14*(1), 761–786. doi:10.17522/balikesirnef.673060

Ding, L., Zhao, Z., & Wang, L. (2023). Does online teaching strategy matter: Exploring the effect of online teaching strategies on students' ambidextrous innovation capacities based on the online teaching situation in China. *Journal of Research on Technology in Education, 55*(5), 817–840. doi:10.1080/15391523.2022.2038315

Disha Gupta. (2023). *8 Effective Instructional Design Models in 2023*. Whatfix. https://whatfix.com/blog/instructional-design-models/

Doise, W., & Mugny, G. (1984). *Psychologie sociale et développement cognitif.* Armand Colin.

Donald, A. (1967). The Indirect but Constant Process of Innovation: Technology and Change. The New Heraclitus. Delacorte Press.

Donnat, O. (2009). Les pratiques culturelles des Français à l'ère numérique: éléments de synthèse 1997-2008. *Culture études, 5*(5), 1-12. doi:10.3917/cule.095.0001

Donnat, O. (2012). La lecture régulière de livres: un recul ancien et général. *Le Débat, 170*(3), 42 51. doi:10.3917/deba.170.0042

Doubrovsky S. & Todorov T. (dir.). (1971). *L'Enseignement de la littérature.* Centre culturel de Cerisy-la-salle, Paris, Plon.

Douglas, I. (2001). Instructional Design Based on Reusable Learning Object: Applying Lessons of Object-Oriented Software Engineering to Learning System Design. In *Proceeding ASEE/IEEE Frontiers in Education Conference.* IEEE. 10.1109/FIE.2001.963968

Downes, S. (2005). E-learning 2.0. *eLearn Magazine, 2005*(10).

Doyle, W. (1986). Classroom organization and management. In M. C. Wittrock (Ed.), *Handbook of research on teaching* (pp. 392–431). Macmillan.

Drew, P. J., & Monson, J. R. T. (2000). Artificial neural networks. *The Journal of Pathology, 127*(1), 3–11. PMID:10660751

Dreyfus, G., Martinez, J., Samuelides, M., Gordon, M. B., Badran, F., Thiria, S., & Hérault, L. (2008). *Réseaux de neurones: Méthodologie et applications (2e édition).* Eyrolles.

Duan, S. (2019). Cultivation of students' critical thinking ability through CLIL mixed teaching model — a case study of "An Introduction to English Literature". In J. Guo, X. Xiao, & J. Liu (Eds.), *Proceedings of the 2019 3rd International Conference on Education, Economics and Management Rese*arch (pp. 665–669). Atlantis Presss. 10.2991/assehr.k.191221.159

Dubet, F. (2002). *The decline of the institution.* Threshold.

Dubet, F., & Martuccelli, D. (1996). *At school. Sociology of the school experience.* Threshold.

Dueñas, M. (2004). The whats, whys, hows and whos of content-based instruction in second/foreign language education. *International Journal of English Studies, 4*(1), 73–96. doi:10.6018/ijes.4.1.48061

Dumulescu, D., Pop-Păcurar, I., & Necula, C. V. (2021). Learning Design for Future Higher Education – Insights From the Time of COVID-19. *Frontiers in Psychology, 12*, 647948. doi:10.3389/fpsyg.2021.647948 PMID:34539481

Duncan, T. G., & McKeachie, W. J. (2005). The making of the motivated strategies for learning questionnaire. *Educational Psychologist, 40*(2), 117–128. doi:10.120715326985ep4002_6

Dunlosky, J., Rawson, K. A., Marsh, E. J., Nathan, M. J., & Willingham, D. T. (2013). Improving Students' Learning With Effective Learning Techniques: Promising Directions From Cognitive and Educational Psychology. *Psychological Science in the Public Interest, 14*(1), 4–58. doi:10.1177/1529100612453266 PMID:26173288

Dunn, R., & Honigsfeld, A. (2013, April). Learning styles: What we know and what we need. [). Taylor & Francis Group.]. *The Educational Forum, 77*(2), 225–232. doi:10.1080/00131725.2013.765328

Dunn, R., Honigsfeld, A., Doolan, L. S., Bostrom, L., Russo, K., Schiering, M. S., & Tenedero, H. (2008). Impact of LearningStyle Instructional Strategies on Students' Achievement and Attitudes: Perceptions of Educators in DiverseInstitutions. *The Clearing House: A Journal of Educational Strategies, Issues and Ideas, 82*(3), 135–140. doi:10.3200/TCHS.82.3.135-140

Durand, M. (1996). *Teaching in schools.* PUF.

Dyrud, M. A. (2000). The third wave: A position paper. *Business Communication Quarterly, 63*(3), 81–93. doi:10.1177/108056990006300310

Dziubaniuk, O., Ivanova-Gongne, M., & Nyholm, M. (2023). Learning and teaching sustainable business in the digital era: A connectivism theory approach. *International Journal of Educational Technology in Higher Education, 20*(1), 1–23. doi:10.118641239-023-00390-w PMID:37096023

Dzyuba, N., Jandu, J., Yates, J., & Kushnerev, E. (2022). Virtual and augmented reality in dental education: The good, the bad and the better. *European Journal of Dental Education, 00*, 1–19. doi:10.1111/eje.12871 PMID:36336847

EduTech Wiki. (n.d.). *Piaget et le constructivisme.* EduTech Wiki. https://edutechwiki.unige.ch/fr/Piaget_et_le_constructivisme

EHL. (2021). Les avantages de l'apprentissage en ligne pour votre carrière hôtelière. *Hospitality Insights.* https://hospitalityinsights.ehl.edu/fr/avantages-apprentissage-en-ligne

Eilam, B., & Aharon, I. (2003). Students' planning in the process of self-regulated learning. *Contemporary Educational Psychology, 28*(3), 304–334. doi:10.1016/S0361-476X(02)00042-5

Ekawati, E., & Prastyo, A. (2022). Optimization of tpack-based project learning in micro-teaching courses in physics education study programs during the pandemic. *Journal of Physics: Conference Series, 2392*(1), 012035. doi:10.1088/1742-6596/2392/1/012035

El Asame, M., & Wakrim, M. (2018). Towards a competency model: A review of the literature and the competency standards. *Education and Information Technologies, 23*(1), 225–236. doi:10.100710639-017-9596-z

El Hadef, S. (2021). The Implication of Online Learning on the Motivation of Students:(Students of University Mohammed First as a Case Study). *International Journal of Linguistics and Translation Studies, 2*(3), 12–22. doi:10.36892/ijlts.v2i3.164

Elangovan, S., Mahrous, A., & Marchini, L. (2020). Disruptions during a pandemic: Gaps identified and lessons learned. *Journal of Dental Education, 84*(11), 1270–1274. doi:10.1002/jdd.12236 PMID:32500586

eLearning Industry. (2018, February 18*). The Learning Theory Of Cognitive Development In eLearning.* eLearning Industry. https://elearningindustry.com/learning-theory-of-cognitive-development-elearning. Récupéré le 14 Juillet 2023.

eLearning Industry. (2023, June 20). *From Behaviorism To Connectivism: A Comprehensive Guide To Instructional Design Theories For Online Learning.* eLearning Industry. https://elearningindustry.com/from-behaviorism-to-connectivism-comprehensive-guide-instructional-design-theories-online-learning

Elharbaoui, E., Matoussi, F., Ntebutse, J.G. & Ben-Attia, M. (2018). *The evolution of the representations of Tunisian students through the iterative design of an online learning system.*

Ellis, N. C., & Larsen-Freeman, D. (2006). Language emergence: Implications for applied linguistics—Introduction to the special issue. *Applied Linguistics*, *27*(4), 558–589. doi:10.1093/applin/aml028

Émile, D. (1977). *Education and Sociology*. Humensis.

Erarslan, A., & Arslan, A. (2020). Online learning experiences of university students in ELT and the effects of online learning on their learning practices. *Language and Technology*, *2*(1), 44–58.

Ertmer, P. A. (2005). Teacher pedagogical beliefs: The final frontier in our quest for technology integration? *Educational Technology Research and Development*, *4*(53), 25–39. doi:10.1007/BF02504683

Ertmer, P. A., Conklin, D., Lewandowski, J., Osika, E., Selo, M., & Wignall, E. (2003). Increasing preservice teachers' capacity for technology integration through the use of electronic models. *Teacher Education Quarterly*, *30*(1), 95–112. https://www.jstor.org/stable/23478427

Ertmer, P. A., & Newby, T. J. (2013). Behaviorism, cognitivism, constructivism: Comparing critical features from an instructional design perspective. *Performance Improvement Quarterly*, *26*(2), 43–71. doi:10.1002/piq.21143

Espino, D., Lee, S., Van Tress, L., & Hamilton, E. (2019). Application of the IBE-UNESCO Global Competences Framework in Assessing STEM-focused. *Global Collaborative Learning within a Digital Makerspace Environment*. UNESCO.

Evanick, J. (2023, June 20). *From Behaviorism To Connectivism: A Comprehensive Guide To Instructional Design Theories For Online Learning*. eLearning Industry. https://elearningindustry.com/from-behaviorism-to-connectivism-comprehensive-guide-instructional-design-theories-online-learning

Ezenwa-Ohaeto, N., & Ugochukwu, E. N. (2021). Language Learning Theories: Behaviourism, Mentalism and Affectivism. *Awka Journal of English Language and Literary Studies, 8*(1).

Faerber, R. (2003). Groupements, processus pédagogiques et quelques contraintes liés à un environnement virtuel d'apprentissage. In C. Desmoulins, P. Marquet & D. Bouhineau (Eds.), *Environnements informatiques pour l'apprentissage humain 2003* (p. 321-331). Strasbourg, France. https://edutice.hal.science/edutice-00000137

Fairclough, N. (1992). *Critical Language Awareness*. Longman.

Faizi, R., El Afia, A., & Chiheb, R. (2013). Exploring the potential benefits of using social media in education. [iJEP]. *International Journal of Engineering Pedagogy*, *3*(4), 50–53. doi:10.3991/ijep.v3i4.2836

Fan, L. (2021). 高校外语课程思政实践探索——以"基础德语"为例 [On ideological and political practice of foreign language courses in colleges and universities — taking "basic German" as an example]. 外语与翻译 *[Foreign Languages and Translation]*, (3), 71–76. doi:10.19502/j.cnki.2095-9648.2021.03.012

Farhan, W., Razmak, J., Demers, S., & Laflamme, S. (2019). E-learning systems versus instructional communication tools: Developing and testing a new e-learning user interface from the perspectives of teachers and students. *Technology in Society*, *59*, 101192. doi:10.1016/j.techsoc.2019.101192

Fayolle, A., Verzat, C., & Wapshott, R. (2016). In quest of legitimacy: The theoretical and methodological foundations of entrepreneurship education research. *International Small Business Journal*, *34*(7), 895–904. doi:10.1177/0266242616649250

Ferraris, C., Lejeune, A., Vignollet, L., & David, J. P. (2005). Modélisation de scénarios d'apprentissage collaboratif pour la classe: vers une opérationnalisation au sein d'un ENT. Actes de la conférence EIAH 2005, Ed. Pierre Tchounikine, Michelle Joab et Luc Trouche. INRP. Institut Montpellier II.

Figlio, D. N., Rouse, C. E., & Bhatt, R. (2018). Uniformity and adaptability in educational systems: Both are possible, but different. In R. Chakrabarti (Ed.), *Creating a New Teaching and Learning Ecosystem: A Report on the 3E Initiative* (pp. 31–58). Brookings Institution.

Fletcher, J. D., & Rockaway, M. R. (1986). *Military Contributions to Instructional Technology*. Praeger.

Fornaciari, C. J., & Dean, K. L. (2014). The 21st-century syllabus: From pedagogy to andragogy. *Journal of Management Education*, *38*(5), 701–723. doi:10.1177/1052562913504763

Fortun, V. (2016). *Les enjeux du e-learning «communautique» en formation continue d'enseignants* (Doctoral dissertation, Paris Est).

Fournier, M. A., & Grey, K. C. (2000). Assessing program outcomes: Comparison of four evaluation frameworks. *Journal of Personnel Evaluation in Education*, *14*(2), 143–170.

Fraenkel, J. R., Wallen, N. E., & Hyun, H. H. (2015). *How to design and evaluate research in education* (9th ed.). McGraw-Hill Education.

Françoise, C. (2002). Innovation in education And in training: topicals And challenges. In *NOT. Alter, THE logical of innovation* (pp. 211–240). There Discovery.

Freedman, A. (2015). *Genre and the New Rhetoric*. Routledge.

Freina, L., & Ott, M. (2015, April). A literature review on immersive virtual reality in education: state of the art and perspectives. In The international scientific conference elearning and software for education (Vol. 1, No. 133, pp. 10-1007). doi:10.12753/2066-026X-15-020

Fu, Q. K., & Hwang, G. J. (2018). Trends in mobile technology-supported collaborative learning: A systematic review of journal publications from 2007 to 2016. *Computers & Education*, *119*, 129–143. doi:10.1016/j.compedu.2018.01.004

Furstenberg. G., Levet, S. & Maillet, K. (2001). Giving a virtual voice to the silent language of culture: the Cultura project. Language Learning and Technology Journal, 5(1), 55-102.

Gabillon, Z. (2020). Revisiting CLIL: background, pedagogy, and theoretical underpinnings. *Contextes et didactiques, 15*. doi:10.4000/ced.1836

Gage, N. L. (2009). *A conception of teaching*. Springer. doi:10.1007/978-0-387-09446-5

Gagné, R., Briggs, L., & Wager, W. (1992). *Principles of Instructional design*. Hartcourt Brace Jovanovitch.

Gao, H. (2021). On the construction of "Curriculum Ideological and Political Education" in college English. In Z. Zhu, & S. Zhao (Eds.), *Proceedings of the 6th Annual International Conference on Social Science and Contemporary Humanity Development* (pp. 308–312). Atlantis Press. 10.2991/assehr.k.210121.065

Garnett, P., & Tobin, K. (1989). Teaching for understanding: Exemplary practice in high school chemistry. *Journal of Research in Science Teaching*, *26*(1), 1–14. doi:10.1002/tea.3660260102

Garrison, D. R. (2011). *E-learning in the 21st century: A framework for research and practice*. Routledge.

Garrison, D. R. (2011). *E-Learning in the 21st Century: A Framework for Research and Practice*. Routledge.

Garrison, D. R., & Anderson, T. (2005). El e-learning en el siglo XXI: Investigación y práctica. *El e-learning en el siglo XXI: investigación y práctica*, 0-0.

Garrison, D. R., & Kanuka, H. (2004). Blended learning: Uncovering its transformative potential in higher education. *The Internet and Higher Education*, *7*(2), 95–105. doi:10.1016/j.iheduc.2004.02.001

Garrison, D. R., & Vaughan, N. D. (2008). *Blended learning in higher education: Framework, principles, and guidelines.* John Wiley & Sons.

Gatcho, A. R., & Ramos, E. T. (2020). Common Writing Problems and Writing Attitudes among Freshman University Students in Online Learning Environments: An Exploratory Study. *Journal of Translation and Language Studies, 1*(1), 49–66. doi:10.48185/jtls.v1i1.6

Gauvreau, C. (1994). Armand Mattelart, L'invention de la communication, Éditions La Découverte, Paris, 1994, 376 p. *Cahiers de Recherche Sociologique*, (23), 202–204. doi:10.7202/1002258ar

Geisinger, K. F. (2016). 21st century skills: What are they and how do we assess them? *Applied Measurement in Education, 29*(4), 245–249. doi:10.1080/08957347.2016.1209207

Giardina, M. & Oubenaïssa, L. (2003). Projet d'apprentissage/enseignement en ligne. *Sciences et technologies de l'information et de la communication pour l'éducation et la formation, 10,* 20.

Gilakjani, A. P. (2017). A review of the literature on the integration of technology into the learning and teaching of English language skills. *International Journal of English Linguistics, 7*(5), 95–106. doi:10.5539/ijel.v7n5p95

Gillett-Swan, J. (2017). The challenges of online learning: Supporting and engaging the isolated learner. *Journal of Learning Design, 10*(1), 20–30. doi:10.5204/jld.v9i3.293

Glikman, V. (2002). From correspondence courses to e-learning: overview of open and distance learning. Presses universitaire de France.

Godin, B. (2012). Innovation Studies: The Invention of a Specialty, Minerva, volume 50. *Nummer, 4,* 397–421.

Goigoux, R. (2007). A model for analyzing teacher activity. *Education and didactics, 1*(3). http://journals.openedition.org/educationdidactic/232

Gómez-Pablos, V. B., del Pozo, M. M., & Muñoz-Repiso, A. G. V. (2017). Project-based learning (PBL) through the incorporation of digital technologies: An evaluation based on the experience of serving teachers. *Computers in Human Behavior, 68,* 501–512. doi:10.1016/j.chb.2016.11.056

Goob, J., Erdelt, K., Güth, J. F., & Liebermann, A. (2021). Dental education during the pandemic: Cross-sectional evaluation of four different teaching concepts. *Journal of Dental Education, 85*(10), 1574–1587. doi:10.1002/jdd.12653 PMID:34046898

Goralski, M. A. (2008). The concept of implementing effective criteria for learning assessments in a virtual environment. *Journal of International Business Disciplines, 2*(3), 127–141.

Gorder, L. M. (2008). A study of teacher perceptions of instructional technology integration in the classroom. *Delta Pi Epsilon Journal, L*(2), 63–76.

Gove, P. B. (1986). *New International Dictionary.* Merriam-Webster Inc.

GradePower Learning. (n.d.). *The Cognitive Learning Approach.* GradePower Learning. https://gradepowerlearning.com/cognitive-learning-theory/.

Graesser, A. C. (2009). Inaugural editorial for Journal of Educational Psychology. *Journal of Educational Psychology, 101*(2), 259–261. doi:10.1037/a0014883

Graf, S., Viola, S. R., Leo, T., & Kinshuk. (2007). In-depth analysis of the Felder-Silverman learning style dimensions. *Journal of Research on Technology in Education, 40*(1), 79–93. doi:10.1080/15391523.2007.10782498

Graham, S., & Harris, K. R. (2000). The Effects of Whole-Language Instruction: An Update and a Reappraisal. *Educational Psychology, 35*(6), 323–368.

Grandière, M., & Lahalle, A. (dir.) (2004). L'Innovation dans l'enseignement français (XVIe-XXe siècle). Nantes-Lyon: SCEREN CRDP Pays de la Loire/INRP, 172 p.

Grech, V. (2018). The application of the Mayer multimedia learning theory to medical PowerPoint slide show presentations. *Journal of Visual Communication in Medicine, 41*(1), 36–41. doi:10.1080/17453054.2017.1408400 PMID:29381105

Greitzer, F. L. (2002, September). A cognitive approach to student-centered e-learning. In *proceedings of the human factors and ergonomics society annual meeting* (*Vol. 46*, No. 25, pp. 2064-2068). Sage CA: Los Angeles, CA: SAGE Publications. 10.1177/154193120204602515

Griva, E., & Chostelidou, D. (2017). CLIL in primary education: promoting multicultural citizenship awareness in the foreign language classroom. *Research Papers in Language Teaching and Learning, 8*(2), 9–23. https://rpltl.eap.gr/images/2017/08-02-009-Griva-Chostelidou.pdf

Gronlund, N. E., & Brookhart, S. M. (2009). *How to Write and Use Instructional Objectives* (7th ed.). Pearson.

Gross, R. T., Ghaltakhchyan, N., Nanney, E. M., Jackson, T. H., Wiesen, C. A., Mihas, P., Persky, A. M., Frazier-Bowers, S. A., & Jacox, L. A. (2023). Evaluating video-based lectures on YouTube for dental education. *Orthodontics & Craniofacial Research*, ocr.12669. doi:10.1111/ocr.12669 PMID:37184946

Gruca, I. (1997). *Didactics of French as a foreign and second language.* Deir Publishing.

Gruca, I. (2002). *Didactic courses in French as a foreign and second language.* Paris: Horizon Groupe.

Guba, E. G., & Lincoln, Y. S. (1989). *Fourth Generation Evaluation.* Sage Publications.

Guéraud, V. (2006). *Author approach for Active Learning Situations: Scenarios, Monitoring and Engineering. HDR.* Joseph Fourier University. http://discas.qc.ca

Gupta, S. (2017, November 11). *9 Benefits of eLearning for Students.* eLearning Industry. https://elearningindustry.com/9-benefits-of-elearning-for-students ↗

Gupta, L. A. (2016). *Wreading, Performing, and Reflecting: The Application of Narrative Hypertext and Virtual World Experiences to Social Work Education.* Virginia Commonwealth University.

Gurung, R. A. R., & Galardi, N. R. (2022). Syllabus Tone, More Than Mental Health Statements, Influence Intentions to Seek Help. *Teaching of Psychology, 49*(3), 218–223. doi:10.1177/0098628321994632

Gururajaprasad, R., & Lakshmana, K. (2020). *Smart Mobile Augmented Reality For Orthodontics Teaching And Learning Environment.* [PhD thesis, Universiti Sains Malaysia].

Hadiji, C. (1995). *Thinking and acting on education.* Paris: ESF éditeur.

Hakkarainen, K., Palonen, T., Paavola, S., & Lehtinen, E. (2014). The Knowledge Creation Metaphor—An Emergent Epistemological Approach to Learning. *Science & Education, 23*(1), 63–84.

Haladyna, T. (2000). An Evaluation of Conjunctive and Compensatory Standard-setting Strategies for Test Decisions. *Educational Assessment, 6*(2), 129–153.

Hall, R. N. (1959). Recombination processes in semiconductors. *Proceedings of the IEE-Part B: Electronic and Communication Engineering, 106*(17S), 923-931. 10.1049/pi-b-2.1959.0171

Hambleton, R. K., Merenda, P. F., & Spielberger, C. D. (2000). *Adapting Educational and Psychological Tests for Cross-Cultural Assessment*. Lawrence Erlbaum Associates.

Hand, B., Prain, V., & Yore, L. D. (2001). Contributing to a Project-Based Elementary Science Program: The Nature of Language. *Research in Science Education, 31*(3), 289–307.

Hanesová, D. (2015). History of CLIL. In S. Pokrivčáková (Ed.), *CLIL in foreign language education: e-textbook for foreign language teachers* (pp. 7–16). Constantine the Philosopher University. doi:10.17846/CLIL.2015.7-16

Hannan, A., English, S., & Silver, H. (1999). Why innovate? Some preliminary findings from a research project on «Innovations in teaching and learning in higher education». *Studies in Higher Education, 24*(3), 279–289. doi:10.1080/03075079912331379895

Hansen, C. D., Graf, S., & Vienne, J. (2014). The Evolution of IMS Learning Tools Interoperability: LTI Version 2 and Beyond. *eLearning Papers, 37*, 1-11.

Hara, N., & Kling, R. (2000). Student distress in a web-based distance education course. *Information Communication and Society, 3*(4), 557–579. doi:10.1080/13691180010002297

Harden, R. M. (2002). Assessment within competency-based education. *Medical Teacher, 24*(5), 267–272. PMID:12450465

Hare, S., Howard, E., & Pope, M. (2002). Technology integration: Closing the gap between what preservice teachers are taught to do and what they can do. *Journal of Technology and Teacher Education, 10*(2), 191–203.

Harrington, C., & Thomas, M. (2023). *Designing a motivational syllabus: Creating a learning path for student engagement*. Taylor & Francis.

Haşlaman, T. (2017). Supporting self-regulated learning: A digital storytelling implementation. *Elementary Education Online, 16*(4), 1407–1424. doi:10.17051/ilkonline.2017.342964

Hastie, T., Tibshirani, R., & Friedman, J. (2009). *The Elements of Statistical Learning: Data Mining, Inference, and Prediction* (2nd ed.). Springer. doi:10.1007/978-0-387-84858-7

Hattar, S., AlHadidi, A., Sawair, F. A., Alraheam, I. A., El-Ma'aita, A., & Wahab, F. K. (2021). Impact of COVID-19 pandemic on dental education: Online experience and practice expectations among dental students at the University of Jordan. *BMC Medical Education, 21*(1), 151. doi:10.118612909-021-02584-0 PMID:33685451

Hattie, J. (2009). *Visible learning: A synthesis of over 800 meta-analyses relating to achievement*. Routledge.

Hattie, J. (2009). *Visible Learning: A synthesis of over 800 meta-analyses relating to achievement*. Routledge.

Hava, K. (2021). Exploring the role of digital storytelling in student motivation and satisfaction in EFL education. *Computer Assisted Language Learning, 34*(7), 958–978. doi:10.1080/09588221.2019.1650071

Heard, J., Harriott, C. E., & Adams, J. A. (2018). A survey of workload assessment algorithms. *IEEE Transactions on Human-Machine Systems, 48*(5), 434–451. doi:10.1109/THMS.2017.2782483

Hennessy, S., Ruthven, K., & Brindley, S. (2005). Teacher perspectives on integrating ICT into subject teaching: Commitment, constraints, caution, and change. *Journal of Curriculum Studies, 37*(2), 155–192. doi:10.1080/0022027032000276961

Henri, F., & Lundgren-Cayrol, K. (1997). *Apprentissage collaboratif à distance, téléconférence et télédiscussion. Rapport interne no 3 (version 1.7)*. Montréal: LICEF. http://www.licef.teluq.uquebec.ca/Bac/fiches/f48.htm

Henri, F., & Lundgren-Cayrol, K. (2000). *Apprentissage collaboratif à distance: pour comprendre et concevoir les environnements d'apprentissage virtuels.* Québec,Canada: Presses de l'Université du Québec. http://ebookcentral.proquest.com.tlqprox.teluq.uquebec.ca

Henri, F., & Lundgren-Cayrol, K. (2001). *Apprentissage collaboratif à distance: Pour comprendre et concevoir des environnements d'apprentissage virtuels.* Presses de l'Université du Québec.

Heo, M. (2009). Digital storytelling: An empirical study of the impact of digital storytelling on pre-service teachers' self-efficacy and dispositions towards educational technology. *Journal of Educational Multimedia and Hypermedia*, *18*(4), 405–428.

Hernández-Leo, D., Villasclaras-Fernández, E. D., Asensio-Pérez, J. I., Dimitriadis, Y., & Ruiz-Requies, I. (2006). COLLAGE: A Collaborative Learning Design Editor Based on Patterns. *Journal of Educational Technology & Society*, *9*(1), 58–71.

Herring, S. (1999). The rhetorical dynamics of gender harassment on-line. *The Information Society*, *15*(3), 151–167. doi:10.1080/019722499128466

Higgins, D., Hayes, M., Taylor, J., & Wallace, J. (2020). A scoping review of simulation-based dental education. *MedEdPublish*, *9*(36), 36. doi:10.15694/mep.2020.000036.1 PMID:38058871

Higher Education Council (CSÉ). (1995). Annual report on the state and needs of education (1994-1995). Managing change in education. Quebec. CSE.

Higher Education Council (CSÉ). (2000). Report on the state and needs of education (1999-2000). Education and new technologies: For successful integration in teaching and learning. Quebec. CSE.

Higher Education Council (CSÉ). (2006). Annual report on the state and needs of education (2004-2005). The dialogue between research and practice in education: a key to success. Quebec. CSE.

Hiltz, S.R. & Turoff, M. (2002). What makes learning networks effective? *Communications of the ACM.* ACM.

Hirst, P. H. (1971/2012). What is teaching? In S. M. Cahn (Ed.), *Classic and Contemporary Readings in the Philosophy of Education* (2nd ed., pp. 353–361). Oxford University Press.

Hoang, A. D., Pham, H. H., Nguyen, Y. C., Nguyen, L. K. N., Vuong, Q. H., Dam, M. Q., Tran, T., & Nguyen, T. T. (2020). Introducing a tool to gauge curriculum quality under Sustainable Development Goal 4: The case of primary schools in Vietnam. *International Review of Education*, *66*(4), 457–485. doi:10.100711159-020-09850-1

Hobbs, R. (2010). *Digital and Media Literacy: A Plan of Action.* The Aspen Institute.

Hoben, J. B. (1954). English Communication at Colgate Re-examined. *Journal of Communication*, *4*(3), 77. doi:10.1111/j.1460-2466.1954.tb00232.x

Hodges, C., Moore, S., Lockee, B., Trust, T., & Bond, A. (2020). The difference between emergency remote teaching and online learning. *EDUCAUSE Review*, 27.

Hofmann, A. H., & Ristroph, K. A. (2019). *Scientific Writing and Communication: Papers, Proposals, and Presentations* (4th ed.). Oxford University Press.

Holmes, B., & Gardner, J. (2006). *E-Learning: Concepts and Practice.* SAGE Publications. doi:10.4135/9781446212585

Hooper, S. (1992). Cooperative learning and computer-based instruction. *Educational Technology Research and Development*, *40*(3), 21–38. doi:10.1007/BF02296840

Hopfield, J. J. (1982). Neural networks and physical systems with emergent collective computational abilities (Réseaux neuronaux et systèmes physiques dotés de capacités de calcul collectives émergentes). *Proceedings of the National Academy of Sciences of the United States of America*, *79*(8), 2554–2558. doi:10.1073/pnas.79.8.2554 PMID:6953413

Horton, W. K. (2001). *Leading E-Learning*. ASTD.

Hrich, N., Lazaar, M., & Khaldi, M. (2017). A model for pedagogical supporting based on competencies evaluation and ontologies. *International Research Journal of Computer Science (IRJCS)*, 43-49.

Hrich, N., Lazaar, M., & Khaldi, M. (2019). Improving Cognitive Decision-Making into Adaptive Educational Systems through a Diagnosis Tool based on the Competency Approach. International Journal Emerging Technologies in Learning, 14(7). doi:10.3991/ijet.v14i07.9870

Hrich, N., Lazaar, M., & Khaldi, M. (2019). Problematic of the assessment activity within adaptive E-learning systems. [iJET]. *International Journal of Emerging Technologies in Learning*, *14*(17), 133–142. doi:10.3991/ijet.v14i17.10675

Hu, J. (2019). "课程思政"理念融入高职外语课程的生成路径研究 [A study on the path of integrating the idea of "ideological and political education through curriculum" into college foreign language courses]. 职教通讯 *[Communication of Vocational Education]*, (2), 30–34. doi:10.3969/j.issn.1674-7747.2019.02.009

Hu, J. (2021). 外语课程思政视角下的教学设计研究 [Foreign language instructional design from the ideological-political perspective]. 中国外语 *[Journal of the Foreign Languages in China]*, *18*(2), 53–59. doi:10.13564/j.cnki.issn.1672-9382.2021.02.010

Huang, G., & Xiao, Q. (2021). 外语课程思政建设六要素 [Six elements in the ideological-political construction]. 中国外语 *[Journal of the Foreign Languages in China]*, *18*(2), 10–16. doi:10.13564/j.cnki.issn.1672-9382.2021.02.001

Huang, Y. (2021). Research on innovative practice of ideological and political in college English courses. *OAlib*, *8*(8, e7600), 1–6. doi:10.4236/oalib.1107600

Huberman, A.M. (1973). How changes in education take place: contribution to the study of innovation. *Experience and innovation in education no. 4*. Unesco: IBE.

Hu, C. H. (2022). Assessment and learning in content and language integrated learning (CLIL) classrooms: Approaches and conceptualisations. *Language Value*, *15*(2), 112–117. doi:10.6035/languagev.6618

Huezo, E. (2017, July 7). Connectivism: The Future of Learning? *FIU Online Insider*. https://insider.fiu.edu/connectivism-future-learning/.

Hu, H. (2022). Examining teacher competencies in content and language integrated learning: Professional profiles and ways forward. *Rupkatha Journal on Interdisciplinary Studies in Humanities*, *14*(2). doi:10.21659/rupkatha.v14n2.26

Hu, H. (2023). Emerging from content and language integrated learning and English-medium instruction, is CLIL-ised EMI the next trend of education? *Higher Learning Research Communications*, *13*(2), 1–8. doi:10.18870/hlrc.v13i2.1422

Hu, H., Said, N. E. M., & Hashim, H. (2023). Sustaining content and language integrated learning in China: A systematic review. *Sustainability (Basel)*, *15*(5), 3894. doi:10.3390u15053894

Hung, C.-M., Hwang, G.-J., & Huang, I. (2012). A project-based digital storytelling approach for improving students' learning motivation, problem-solving competence and learning achievement. *Journal of Educational Technology & Society*, *15*(4), 368–379.

Hutabarat, Z. S., & Ekawarna, E. (2023). Development of Teaching Materials on Learning Economic Models to Improve Students' Cognitive Achievement. AL-ISHLAH. *Jurnal Pendidikan*, *15*(2), 1204–1212.

Hutt, M. (2017). Top 10 disadvantages of distance learning. *EZ Talks*. https://www.eztalks.com/elearning/top-10-disadvantages-of-distance-learning.html

Ibrahimi, A., Rais, O., & Khaldi, M. (2014). *Dispositif hybride en cours de langue à l'université marocaine*. Adjectif. net. http://www.adjectif.net/spip/spip.php

Ibrahimi, A., Khaldi, M., & Kaddouri, E. (2019). Processes of Knowledge Appropriation in an Online Collaboration Device. *RA JOURNAL OF APPLIED RESEARCH, Volume, 05*(07), 2495–2509.

Ikeda, M., Izumi, S., Watanabe, Y., Pinner, R., & Davis, M. (2021). *Soft CLIL and English language teaching: understanding Japanese policy, practice, and implications*. Routledge., doi:10.4324/9780429032332

Ikram, C., Mohamed, E., Souhaib, A., & Mohamed, K. (2021). Integration of pedagogical videos as learning object in an adaptive educational hypermedia systems according to the learner profile. *International Journal of Computer Trends and Technology*, *69*(6), 1–6. doi:10.14445/22312803/IJCTT-V69I6P101

Inês, P. (n.d.). *Instructional design for e-learning: Everything you need to know*. Easy Generator. https://www.easygenerator.com/en/guides/instructional-design-for-elearning/

Istenic Starčič, A., Cotic, M., Solomonides, I., & Volk, M. (2016). Engaging preservice primary and preprimary school teachers in digital storytelling for the teaching and learning of mathematics. *British Journal of Educational Technology*, *47*(1), 29–50. doi:10.1111/bjet.12253

Itçaina, X. (2010). Territorial Regimes of Social and Solidarity-Based Economy: The Case of the French Basque Country. *Geographie, economie, societe, 12*(1), 71-87.

Jabeen, S. S., & Thomas, A. J. (2015, October). Effectiveness of online language learning. In *Proceedings of the World Congress on Engineering and Computer Science* (Vol. 1, pp. 15).

Jackson, M., & Moreland, R. (2009). Transactive memory in the classroom. *Small Group Research*, *40*(5), 508–534. doi:10.1177/1046496409340703

Jacobsen, M. (2001). *Building different bridges: Technology integration, engaged student learning, and new approaches to professional development*. Paper presented at AERA 2001: What We Know and How We Know It, the 82nd Annual Meeting of the American Educational Research Association, Seattle, WA.

Jakes, D. (2006). *Standards-Proof your digital storytelling Efforts*. TechLearning. https://www.techlearning.com/news/standardsproof-your-digital-storytelling-efforts

Jakes, D. S., & Brennan, J. (2005). *Capturing stories, capturing lives: An Introduction to digital storytelling*. Jake's Online. http://www.jakesonline.org/dst_techforum.pdf

Janks, H. (2005). Language and the design of texts. *English Teaching: Practice and Critique*. ERIC. (https://files.eric.ed.gov/fulltext/EJ847267.pdf)

Jatmika, S., Kusmawati, V., Suranto, S., Rahmawati, D., & Setyawati, L. (2022). The Use of Mind Mapping as a Learning Delivery Medium for Business Entity Materials in a Vocational High School. *The International Journal of Technologies in Learning*, *29*(2), 1–13. doi:10.18848/2327-0144/CGP/v29i02/1-13

Jean, H. (1991). Values: School Choices. *Revue Française de Pédagogie*.

Jeffery, K. A., & Bauer, C. F. (2020). Students' responses to emergency remote online teaching reveal critical factors for all teaching. *Journal of Chemical Education*, *97*(9), 2472–2485. doi:10.1021/acs.jchemed.0c00736

Jeonghyun, K., & Jisu, L. (2014). Knowledge Construction and Information Seeking in Collaborative Learning. *Canadian Journal of Information and Library Science, 38*(1), 1–21. doi:10.1353/ils.2014.0005

Jermann, P. (2004). *Computer Support for Interaction Regulation in Collaborative Problem-Solving* [thèse de doctorat, Université de Genève, Suisse]. https://tecfa.unige.ch/tecfa/research/theses/jermann2004.pdf

Jézégou, A. (2012). La présence en e-learning: modèle théorique et perspective pour la recherche. *The Journal of Distance Education / Revue de l'Éducation à Distance, 26*(1). https://edutice.hal.science/edutice-00733742v2

Jézégou, A. (1998). *La formation à distance: enjeux, perspectives et limites de l'individualisation.* L'Harmattan.

Ji, X. (2019). Teaching "Greek and Roman mythology" in a CLIL classroom: towards a new approach. In L. P. Mun (Ed.), *Proceedings of the 2019 4th International Conference on Social Sciences and Economic Development* (pp. 410–413). Atlantis Press. 10.2991/icssed-19.2019.77

Johnson, D. W., & Johnson, R. T. (2017). Cooperative Learning in 21st Century. *Annual Review of Education, 3,* 225–251.

Johnson, W. L. (2018). Intelligent tutoring systems: Past, present, and future. In *Handbook of Research on Emerging Priorities and Trends in Distance Education* (pp. 222–241). IGI Global.

Jonassen, D., Davidson, M., Collins, M., Campbell, J., & Haag, B. (1995). Constructivism and computer-mediated communication in distance education. *American Journal of Distance Education, 9*(2), 7–26. doi:10.1080/08923649509526885

Jones, J. B. (2011). Creative approaches to the syllabus. *The Chronicle of Higher Education.* https://www.chronicle.com/blogs/profhacker/creative-approaches-to-the-syllabus

Jonnaert, P., & Vander Borght, C. (1999). *Créer des conditions d'apprentissage: un cadre de référence socio-constructiviste pour une formation didactique des enseignants.* De Boeck.

Julia, K., & Marco, K. (2021). Évolutivité pédagogique dans les MOOC: Analysing instructional designs to find best practices. *Computers & Education, 161,* 104054. doi:10.1016/j.compedu.2020.104054

Kahu, E. R., & Nelson, K. (2018). Student engagement in the educational interface: Understanding the mechanisms of student success. *Higher Education Research & Development, 37*(1), 58–71. doi:10.1080/07294360.2017.1344197

Kamis, M. S., Ismail, M. J., Alias, M. N., Mikeng, D., Abidin, S. G. Z., & Yusof, R. (2021). CLIL approach in encouraging self-efficacy amongst Malaysian gifted students for Arabic tasks accomplishment. *Journal of Language and Linguistic Studies, 17*(2), 1001–1012. doi:10.52462/jlls.69

Kamran Ali, E. S. A. (2023). Blended learning in undergraduate dental education: A global pilot study. *Medical Education Online, 28,* 1. PMID:36751853

Kane, M. T. (2006). Validation. In R. L. Brennan (Ed.), *Educational Measurement* (4th ed.). American Council on Education/Praeger.

Kaouni, M., Lakrami, F., & Labouidya, O. (2023). The Design of An Adaptive E-learning Model Based on Artificial Intelligence for Enhancing Online Teaching. *International Journal of Emerging Technologies in Learning, 18*(6), 202–219. doi:10.3991/ijet.v18i06.35839

Kaplan-Rakowski, R., Shih, B., & Thompson, C. (2014). Personalized E-Learning in the Workplace: A Multidimensional Model and Case Study. *Computers in Human Behavior, 30,* 35–47.

Karakoyun, F., & Kuzu, A. (2016). The investigation of preservice teachers' and primary school students' views about online digital storytelling. *European Journal of Contemporary Education, 15*(1), 51–64.

Karaoğlan Yılmaz, F. G., Özdemir, B. G., & Yaşar, Z. (2018). Using digital stories to reduce misconceptions and mistakes about fractions: An action study. *International Journal of Mathematical Education in Science and Technology, 49*(8), 867–898. doi:10.1080/0020739X.2017.1418919

Karima, A. D. (2009). Multilingualism And education intercultural has university, place of training And interaction. *Synergies Algeria,* (5), 151–158.

Karima, A. D. (2011). The impact of the ICT on teaching/learning of there language French in higher education: What training needs for what pedagogy? *Review of the School Doctoral of French, Synergies Algeria,* (12), 227–231.

Karsenti, T., Peraya, D., & Viens, J. (2004). Conclusion: Bilan et prospectives de la recherche sur la formation des maîtres à l'intégration pédagogique des TIC. *Revue des Sciences de l'Education, 28*(2), 459–470. doi:10.7202/007363ar

Kasowitz, A. (1998). *Tool for Automating Instructional Design*. ERIC elearning house in Information Technology in Education. http://ericit.org/digests/EDO-IR- 1998-01.shtml

Kawtar, Z., Mohamed, K., & Mohamed, E. (2021, March). Collaboration in Adaptive E Learning. In *International Conference On Big Data and Internet of Things* (pp. 235-244). Cham: Springer International Publishing.

Kazadi, C. (2006). Innovative approaches in mathematics textbooks. In Loiselle, J., Lafortune, L. and Rousseau, N. (eds.) Innovation in teacher training. Press of the University of Quebec.

Keegan, D. (1995). *Distance education technology for the new millennium: Compressed videoteaching.* ZIFF Papiere. Hagen, Germany: Institute for research into Distance education.

Keegan, D. (1986). *The foundations of distance education.* Croom Helm.

Kehoe, C., Blackmon, S., & Zoccoli, A. (2018). Implementing Single Sign-On in a Higher Education Environment: A Systematic Review. *Journal of Computing in Higher Education, 30*(2), 363–390.

Keller, C., & Cernerud, L. (2002). Students' perception of e-learning in university education. *Learning, Media and Technology, 27*(1), 55–67.

Kelly, G., & Chen, C. (1999). The sound of music: Constructing science as sociocultural practices through oral and written discourse. *Journal of Research in Science Teaching, 36*(8), 883–915. doi:10.1002/(SICI)1098-2736(199910)36:8<883::AID-TEA1>3.0.CO;2-I

Kemp, N., & Grieve, R. (2014). Face-to-face or face-to-screen? Undergraduates' opinions and test performance in classroom vs. online learning. *Frontiers in Psychology, 5,* 1278. PMID:25429276

Keogh, C. (2022). Student and teacher perspectives on co-created CLIL-appropriate materials focused on critical thinking and active citizenship. *Latin American Journal of Content & Language Integrated Learning, 15*(1), e1512. doi:10.5294/laclil.2022.15.1.2

Kerdtip, C., & Thammachat, P. (2023). Enhancing Thai Secondary Teacher Lifelong Learning Competencies In A Digital Age. *Journal of Namibian Studies: History Politics Culture, 34,* 4224–4350.

Kerr, P. (2015). Adaptive learning. *ELT Journal, 70*(1), 88–93. doi:10.1093/elt/ccv055

Khaldi, M., Erradi, M., & Khaldi, M. (2019). Learning Situation: The teacher management and decisions according to the context and the situation. *IMPACT: International Journal of Research in Engineering & Technology, 7*(5), 25-40.

Khan, B. H. (2005). *Managing E-learning: Design, Delivery, Implementation and Evaluation.* Information Science Publishing. doi:10.4018/978-1-59140-634-1

Kim, D., & Li, M. (2020). Digital storytelling: Facilitating learning and identity development. *Journal of Computers in Education*, 8(1), 33–61. doi:10.100740692-020-00170-9

Kim, Y., & Ekachai, D. G. (2020). Exploring the effects of different online syllabus formats on student engagement and course-taking intentions. *College Teaching*, 68(4), 176–186. doi:10.1080/87567555.2020.1785381

Kirkpatrick, D. L. (1996). Great ideas revisited. *Training & Development*, 50(1), 54–59.

Kizilcec, R. F., Pérez-Sanagustín, M., & Maldonado, J. J. (2017). Self-regulated learning strategies predict learner behavior and goal attainment in massive open online courses. *The International Review of Research in Open and Distributed Learning*, 18(2).

Klamma, R., Rohde, M., & Stahl, G. (2004). Community-based learning: Explorations into theoretical groundings, empirical findings and computer support. *SigGroup Bulletin*, 24 (4), 1-100. https://www.researchgate.net/publication/28675083_Community-based_learning_workshop_Explorations_into_theoretical_groundings_empirical_findings_and_computer_support

Klewitz, B. (2021). *Content and language integrated learning (CLIL): a methodology of bilingual teaching.* ibidem Press.

Kluckhohn, C. (1961). *Anthropology And The Classics.*

Knoerr, H. (2005). TIC et motivation en apprentissage/enseignement des langues. Une perspective canadienne. Recherche et pratiques pédagogiques en langues de spécialité. *Cahiers de l'Apliut*, 24(2), 53–73. doi:10.4000/apliut.2889

Knowles, M. S. (1978). Andragogy: Adult learning theory in perspective. *Community College Review*, 5(3), 9–20. doi:10.1177/009155217800500302

Koch, N. (2000). *Software Engineering for Adaptive Hypermedia Systems.* [PhD thesis, Eindhoven University of Technology].

Kohonen, T. (1988). An introduction to neural computing. *Neural Networks*, 1(1), 3–16. doi:10.1016/0893-6080(88)90020-2

Kolb, A. Y., & Kolb, D. A. (2005). Learning styles and learning spaces: Enhancing experiential learning in higher education. *Academy of Management Learning & Education*, 4(2), 193–212. doi:10.5465/amle.2005.17268566

Kolb, D. A. (1984). *Experiential learning: Experience as the source of learning and development.* Prentice-Hall.

Konstantinidis, A., Tsiatsos, T., & Pomportsis, A. (2009). Collaborative virtual learning environments: Design and evaluation. *Multimedia Tools and Applications*, 44(2), 279–304. doi:10.100711042-009-0289-5

Kotluk, N., & Kocakaya, S. (2016). Researching and evaluating digital storytelling as a distance education tool in physics instruction: An application with pre-service physics teachers. *Turkish Online Journal of Distance Education*, 17(1), 87–99. doi:10.17718/tojde.59900

Kotsilieris, T., & Dimopoulou, N. (2013). The Evolution of e-Learning in the Context of 3D Virtual Worlds. *Electronic Journal of e-Learning*, 11(2), 147–167.

Koutsogiannis, D. (2017). *Language Teaching Yesterday, Today, Tomorrow. A Political Approach.* Institute of Modern Greek Studies.

Kováčiková, E. (2020). *English for specific purposes in higher education through content and language integrated learning.* Cambridge Scholars Publishing.

Krashen, S. (1982). *Principles and practice in second language acquisition.*

Krishnan, S. D., Norman, H., & Md Yunus, M. (2021). Online gamified learning to enhance teachers' competencies using classcraft. *Sustainability (Basel)*, *13*(19), 10817. doi:10.3390u131910817

Kukulska-Hulme, A. (2005). *Mobile Learning: A Handbook for Educators and Trainers*. Routledge.

Kumar, P. M., Gottumukkala, S. N. V. S., Ramesh, K. S. V., Bharath, T. S., Penmetsa, G. S., & Kumar, C. N. (2020). Effect of e-learning methods on Dental education: An observational study. *Journal of Education and Health Promotion*, *9*(1), 235. doi:10.4103/jehp.jehp_209_20 PMID:33209927

Kunin, M., Julliard, K. N., & Rodriguez, T. E. (2014). Comparing face-to-face, synchronous, and asynchronous learning: Postgraduate dental resident preferences. *Journal of Dental Education*, *78*(6), 856–866. doi:10.1002/j.0022-0337.2014.78.6.tb05739.x PMID:24882771

Kunin, M., Julliard, K. N., & Rodriguez, T. E. (2014). Comparing face-to-face, synchronous, Li, B., Cheng, L., & Wang, H. (2022). Challenges and Opportunities for Dental Education from COVID-19. *Dentistry Journal*, *10*(10), 188. doi:10.3390/dj10100188

Kuo, Y. C., Walker, A. E., Schroder, K. E., & Belland, B. R. (2014). Interaction, Internet self-efficacy, and self-regulated learning as predictors of student satisfaction in online education courses. *The Internet and Higher Education*, *20*, 35–50. doi:10.1016/j.iheduc.2013.10.001

Lacelle, N., Boutin, J.-F., & Lebrun, M. (2017). *La littératie médiatique multimodale appliquée en contexte numérique - LMM@: outils conceptuels et didactiques*. Presses de l'Université du Québec.

Laferrière, T. (2003). Apprendre ensemble: choisir nos mots pour discourir sur des pratiques émergentes. In C. Deaudelin & T. Nault (Eds.), *Apprendre avec des pairs et des TIC: Quels environnements pour quels impacts?* (pp. 11–18). Presses de l'Université du Québec. doi:10.2307/j.ctv18pgvgg.2

Lafleur, F., & Samson, G. (2019). *Formation et apprentissage en ligne*. PUQ. doi:10.1353/book65750

Lai, Y., Xie, M., & Chen, Y. (2020). The application of the teaching mode for "ideological and political education" in college English teaching. *International Journal of New Developments in Education*, *2*(7), 48–51. doi:10.25236/IJNDE.2020.020710

Lambert, J. (2013). *Digital storytelling: Capturing lives, creating community* (4th ed.). Routledge. doi:10.4324/9780203102329

Lamya, A., Mohamed, E., & Mohamed, K. (2021). Adaptive E-learning and scenarization tools: The case of personalization. *International Journal of Computer Trends and Technology*, *69*(6), 28–35. doi:10.14445/22312803/IJCTT-V69I6P105

Lamya, A., Mohamed, K., & Mohamed, E. (2022). Personalization between pedagogy and adaptive hypermedia system. In *Proceedings of the 5th International Conference on Big Data and Internet of Things* (pp. 223–234). Cham: Springer International Publishing. 10.1007/978-3-031-07969-6_17

Lando, P. (2003). *Progetto: a method for designing scenario templates for remote collective project-based educational activities* [DEA dissertation, University of Picardie].

LaRose, R., Gregg, J., & Eastin, M. (1998). Audio graphic tele-courses for the Web: An experiment. *Journal of Computer-Mediated Communication*, *4*(2), 0. doi:10.1111/j.1083-6101.1998.tb00093.x

Lazăr, A., Langa, C., Loredana, T. S., Magdalena, S. M., & Luiza, V. S. (2023). Using CLIL in cross-curricular education to develop European citizenship. In E. Soare, & C. Langa (Eds.), Education Facing Contemporary World Issues - EDU WORLD 2022, (pp. 25–35). European Publisher. doi:10.15405/epes.23045.4

Le Boterf, G. (1994). *On competence. Essai sur un attractor estrange*. Paris, Les Éditions d'organisation.

LearnDash Collaborator. (2021). *4 Learning Theories Every Online Educator Should Know*. LearnDash. https://www.learndash.com/4-learning-theories-every-online-educator-should-know/

Lebrun, N., & Berthelot, S. (1994). *Plan pédagogique: une démarche systématique de planification de l'enseignement*. Editions Nouvelles/De Boeck.

Lee, K. (2017). Rethinking the accessibility of online higher education: A historical review. *The Internet and Higher Education, 33*, 15–23. doi:10.1016/j.iheduc.2017.01.001

Lee, M. J., & McLoughlin, C. (Eds.). (2010). *Web 2.0-based e-learning: Applying social informatics for tertiary teaching: Applying social informatics for tertiary teaching*. IGI Global.

Legendre, R. (2005). *Dictionary of Education* (3rd ed.). Guérin.

Legendre, R. (2005). Summative evaluation. In *Current Dictionary of Education*. Guérin.

Legros. D. & Crinon, J. (dir.). (2002). Psychologie des apprentissages et multimédia. Paris: Armand Colin.

Lemke, J. (1990). *Talking science*. Ablex.

Lémonie, Y., & Grosstephan, V. (2021). Le laboratoire du changement. Une méthodologie d'intervention au service de la transformation du travailPerspectives méthodologiques pour une ergonomie développementale. *Revue d'anthropologie des connaissances, 15*(15-2).

Lenoir, Y. (2016). *School disciplines and life outside of school. The case of "education to" in Quebec. Health education, environmental education and citizenship education*. Saint-Lambert: Group- éditions Editeurs.

Leplat, J. (1992). *Work analysis in ergonomic psychology* (Vols. 1–2). Octares.

Leplat, J. (1997). *Insights into activity in a work situation*. PUF.

Li, L., & Zhang, G. (2023). 中国式现代化视域下的思想政治教育新形态研究 [Research on the new form of ideological and political education from the perspective of Chinese modernization]. 西南政法大学学报 *[Journal of Southwest University of Political Science & Law], 25*(1), 3–15. doi:10.3969/j.issn.1008-4355.2023.01.01

Li, L., Xiang, Y., & Ding, Q. (2020). 思政反哺课程:我国高校课程思政深入发展的实现路径 [Ideological and political back-feeding curriculum: the path of in-depth development of curriculum ideology and politics in college and universities in China]. 大理大学学报 *[Journal of Dali University], 5*(11), 75–80. doi:10.3969/j.issn.2096-2266.2020.11.012

Li, Q., & Zeng, R. (2019). Implementation of ideological and political education in China's foreign language teaching. In J. Guo, X. Xiao, & J. Liu (Eds.), *Proceedings of the 2019 3rd International Conference on Education, Economics and Management Research* (pp. 549–552). Atlantis Press. 10.2991/assehr.k.191221.133

Li, Y., & Wang, C. (2020). 科研生产力与中文首发制度 [Scientific research productivity and 'Chinese First' publishing system]. 语言战略研究 *[Chinese Journal of Language Policy and Planning], 26*(2), 10–11. https://doi.org/CNKI:SUN:YZLY.0.2020-02-006

Lieury, A., & De La Haye, F. (2009). *Psychologie cognitive de l'éducation*. Dunod.

Li, F., & Fu, H. (2020). Study on college English teaching based on the concept of ideological and political education in all courses. *Creative Education, 11*(7), 997–1007. doi:10.4236/ce.2020.117072

Li, F., Jin, T., Edirisingha, P., & Zhang, X. (2021). School-aged students' sustainable online learning engagement during covid-19: Community of inquiry in a chinese secondary education context. *Sustainability (Basel)*, *13*(18), 10147. doi:10.3390u131810147

Li, L., Pan, Q., Chen, T., & Huang, X. (2021). Curriculum ideological and political construction: Essence, connotation and realization path. *Advances in Soil Science*, *10*(2), 378–383. doi:10.12677/ASS.2021.102055

Lim, E. J., Kim, Y. S., Im, J. E., & Lee, J. G. (2023). Mobile educational tool based on augmented reality technology for tooth carving: Results of a prospective cohort study. *BMC Medical Education*, *23*(1), 1–10. doi:10.118612909-023-04443-6 PMID:37344879

Lim, F. P. (2017). An analysis of synchronous and asynchronous communication tools in e-learning. *Advanced Science and Technology Letters*, *143*(46), 230–234. doi:10.14257/astl.2017.143.46

Linard, M. (1996). Des machines et des hommes. Paris: L'Harmattan.

Lin, C., & Lu, M. (2010). The study of teachers' task values and self-efficacy on their commitment and effectiveness for technology-instruction integration. *US-China Education Review*, *7*(5), 1–11.

Lin, G. S. S., Goh, S. M., & Halil, M. H. M. (2023). Unravelling the impact of dental workforce training and education programmes on policy evolution: A mixed-method study protocol. *Health Research Policy and Systems*, *21*(1), 95. doi:10.118612961-023-01048-9 PMID:37700266

Li, R. (2018). The current situation and thinking of ideological and political education in college students. *KnE Social Sciences*, *3*(10), 1378–1387. doi:10.18502/kss.v3i10.3477

Liu, S. (2023). *Talent training model for music education majors based on the ADDIE model.* Applied Mathematics and Nonlinear Sciences. doi:10.2478/amns.2023.1.00266

Li, Y., & Li, A. (2023). Research on teaching quality improvement path of ideological and political course in universities. *Teacher Education and Curriculum Studies*, *8*(3), 117–120. doi:10.11648/j.tecs.20230803.11

Lombardi, M. M., & Oblinger, D. G. (2018). Competency-Based Education in Three Paradigms: Creators, Facilitators, and Teachers. *EDUCAUSE Review*.

Lonchamp, J. (2007). Un cadre conceptuel et logiciel pour la construction d'environnements d'apprentissage collaboratifs. *Sciences et technologies de l'information et de la communication pour l'éducation et la formation, 14*. https://www.persee.fr/doc/stice_1952-8302_2007_num_14_1_950

Lone, S. A., Puju, J. A., & Mir, M. T. (2023). *Invigoration of e-learning in Education: Challenges and Opportunities.*

Lorrain, M. (2007). Strategies to Engage Online Students and Reduce Attrition Rates. *The Journal of Educators Online*.

Louis, R. (1999). *The Assessment of Learning in the Classroom.* Théorie et pratique, Laval, Études vivantes.

Lou, L. (2021). Practice of curriculum ideological and political education in specialized courses of English school under the guidance of optimization theory. *Journal of Critical Studies in Language and Literature*, *2*(4), 14–19. doi:10.46809/jcsll.v2i4.71

Ludwig, C., & Van de Poel, K. (2013). University of Education Karlsruhe, Germany University of Antwerp, Belgium. Collaborative Learning and New Media, 63, 315.

Ludy, M. J., Brackenbury, T., Folkins, J. W., Peet, S. H., Langendorfer, S. J., & Beining, K. (2016). Student impressions of syllabus design: Engaging versus contractual syllabus. *International Journal for the Scholarship of Teaching and Learning*, *10*(2), n2. doi:10.20429/ijsotl.2016.100206

Lyon, L. J. (2014). Development of teaching expertise viewed through the Dreyfus Model of Skill Acquisition. *The Journal of Scholarship of Teaching and Learning, 15*(1), 88–105. doi:10.14434/josotl.v15i1.12866

Ma, R., & Liu, Y. (2021). 我国外语教学研究的热点、前沿及演进——基于中国知网学术期刊文献的共词可视化分析 [Hotspots, frontiers and evolution of foreign language teaching research in China — co-word visualization analysis based on CNKI academic journal articles]. 北京第二外国语学院学报 *[Journal of Beijing International Studies University], (4)*, 19–32. http://www.cnki.com.cn/Article/CJFDTOTAL-JDEW202104002.htm

Macaro, E., Hultgren, A. K., Kirkpatrick, A., & Lasagabaster, D. (2019). English medium instruction: Global views and countries in focus. *Language Teaching, 52*(3), 231–232. doi:10.1017/S0261444816000380

Macedo-Rouet, M., & Perron, J.-M. (2007). Content and usefulness of the educational scenarios in the PrimTICE database. In T. Nodenot, J. Wallet, and E. Fernandes, *Proceedings of the Computing Environment for Human Learning Conference (EIAH 2007)* (pp. 101-112). Paris/Lyon: Association of Information Technologies for Education and Training [ATIEF] and National Institute of Educational Research [INRP].

Maha, K., Jamal, B., Mohamed, E., & Mohamed, K. (2020). The educational scenario architecture of a learning situation. *Global Journal of Engineering and Technology Advances (GJETA). 03*(01), 027–040.

Maha, K., Omar, E., Mohamed, E., & Mohamed, K. (2021). Design of educational scenarios of activities in a learning situation for online teaching. *GSC Advanced Engineering and Technology, 1*(1), 049-064.

Maha, K., & Mohamed, E. (2020). Design and Development of an e-Learning Project Management System: Modeling and Prototyping. *International Journal Emerging Technologies in Learning, IJET, 15*(19), 2020.

Maier, R., & Thalmann, S. (2007). Describing learning objects for situationoriented knowledge management applications. In: N Gronau (ed) *4th Conference on Professional Konwledge Management Experiences and Visions.* GITO.

Malinowski, D., & Kramsch, C. (2014). The ambiguous world of heteroglossic computer-mediated language learning. *Heteroglossia as practice and pedagogy*, 155-178.

Maltz, L., & Deblois, P.The EDUCAUSE Current Issues Committee. (2005). Top Ten IT Issues. *EDUCAUSE Review, 40*(1), 15–28.

Mandell, S., Sorge, D. H., & Russell, J. D. (2002). TIPS for technology integration. *TechTrends for Leaders in Education and Training, 46*(5), 39–43.

Mapuva, J. (2009). Confronting challenges to e-learning in higher education institutions. *International Journal of Education and Development Using ICT, 5*(3), 101–114.

Marcel Lebrun et Julie Lecoq. (2015). *Classes inversées: enseigner et apprendre à l'endroit.* Canopé.

Marchand, L. (2003). e-learning en entreprise: Un aperçu de l'état des lieux au Canada et au Québec. *Distances et Savoirs, 4*(4), 501–516. doi:10.3166/ds.1.501-516

Marcoccia, M. (2010). Adolescent discussion forums: Writing practices and communicative competences. *Revue Française de Linguistique Appliquée, 15*(2), 139–154. doi:10.3917/rfla.152.0139

Marina. (n.d.). *4 Ways To Apply Behaviorism Principles to Your ELearning Materials.* Your eLearning World. https://yourelearningworld.com/how-to-apply-behaviorism-principles-to-elearning/.

Marisa, C. (2005). *Education bilingue et plurilingue. Le cas du Val d'Aoste.* Editions Didier.

Martín-Gutiérrez, J., Fabiani, P., Benesova, W., Meneses, M. D., & Mora, C. E. (2015). Augmented reality to promote collaborative and autonomous learning in higher education. *Computers in Human Behavior, 51,* 752–761. doi:10.1016/j.chb.2014.11.093

Marzano, R. J. (2011). Art & science of teaching: It's how you use a strategy. *Educational Leadership, 69*(4), 88–89.

Massacret, M. (1993). Français, langue maternelle, langue étrangère: une double culture? *L'Ecole des lettres, 9* (mars), 17-24.

Masseron, C. (2003). *Reading practices: what ways to promote the expression of the reading subject?* Review number 117/118.

Matejka, K., & Kurke, L. B. (1994). Designing a great syllabus. *College Teaching, 42*(3), 115–117. doi:10.1080/8756 7555.1994.9926838

Mayer, R. E. (2017). Using multimedia for e-learning. *Journal of Computer Assisted Learning, 33*(5), 403–423. doi:10.1111/jcal.12197

Mayes, T., de Freitas, S. (2004). *JISC e-Learning Models Desk Study, Stage 2: Review of e-learning theories frameworks and models.*

McBrien, J. L., Cheng, R., & Jones, P. (2009). Virtual spaces: Employing a synchronous online classroom to facilitate student engagement in online learning. *International review of research in open and distributed learning, 10*(3).

McCarthy, J., Minsky, M.L., Rochester, N. et Shannon, C.E. (1955). *A Proposal for the Dartmouth Summer Research Project on Artificial Intelligence* [Proposition pour le projet de recherche d'été de Dartmouth sur l'intelligence artificielle].

McClelland, G. & Hinton, G.E. (1987). *Le Débat Émergence du Cognitif.*

McConnell, D. (1994). What is Cooperative Learning. In *Implementing Computer Supported Cooperative Learning?* Kogan Page Limited.

McCulloh, W.S. & Pitts, W. (1943). A logical calculus of the ideas immanent in nervous activity. *The Bulletin of Mathematical Biophysics, 4,* 115-133.

McGrath, C., & Bolander Laksov, K. (2014). Laying bare educational crosstalk: A study of discursive repertoires in the wake of educational reform. *The International Journal for Academic Development, 19*(2), 139–149. doi:10.1080/1360 144X.2012.716760

McHaney, R. (2023). *The new digital shoreline: How Web 2.0 and millennials are revolutionizing higher education.* Taylor & Francis. doi:10.4324/9781003447979

McQuail, D. (2010). The future of communication studies: A contribution to the debate. *Media and communication studies interventions and intersections, 27.*

Mead, M. (2003). *Cooperation and competition Among the Primitive Peoples,* Transaction Publishers.

Meadows, D. (2003). Digital storytelling-research-based practice in new media. *Visual Communication, 2*(2), 189–193. doi:10.1177/1470357203002002004

Meerhoff, M., Audet, J., Davidson, T. A., De Meester, L., Hilt, S., Kosten, S., Liu, Z., Mazzeo, N., Paerl, H., Scheffer, M., & Jeppesen, E. (2022). Feedback between climate change and eutrophication: Revisiting the allied attack concept and how to strike back. *Inland Waters, 12*(2), 187–204. doi:10.1080/20442041.2022.2029317

Mehrabian, A. (1972). Some subtleties of communication. *Language, Speech, and Hearing Services in Schools, 3*(4), 62–67. doi:10.1044/0161-1461.0304.62

Mels. (2006). *Curriculum of the Quebecois School. Secondary education 2nd cycle.* Quebec: government of Quebec.

Merle, P. (1996). *Student Evaluation, Survey of Professorial Judgment.* Paris, PUF.

Merle, P. (1998). *Sociologie de l'évaluation scolaire.* Paris, PUF.

Merle, P. (2007). *La note, secret de fabrication, Coll.* Éducation et société, Presses Universitaires de France .

Merrill, M.D. (*2013*). *First Principles of Instruction: Identifying and Designing Effective, Efficient, and Engaging Instruction.* San Francisco, CA: Pfeiffer.

Merrill, D. (2002). First principles of instruction. *Educational Technology Research and Development, 50*(3), 43–59. doi:10.1007/BF02505024

Merrill, M. D. & ID2 Expert Group. (1996). Instructional transaction theory: Instructional design based on knowledge objects. *Educational Technology, 36*(3), 30–37.

Merrill, M. D. (2001). Components of instruction toward a theoretical tool for instructional design. *Instructional Science, 29*(4-5), 291–310. doi:10.1023/A:1011943808888

Merrill, M. D., Barclay, M., & van Schaak, A. (2007). Prescriptive Principles for Instructional Design. In J. M. Spector, M. D. Merrill, J. J. G. van Merriënboer, & M. P. Driscoll (Eds.), *Handbook of Research on Educational Communications and Technology* (pp. 173–184). Routledge, Taylor & Francis Group.

Messick, S. (1989). Validity. In R. L. Linn (Ed.), *Educational Measurement* (3rd ed.). American Council on Education/Macmillan.

Messick, S. (1995). Validity of Psychological Assessment: Validation of Inferences from Persons' Responses and Performances as Scientific Inquiry into Score Meaning. *The American Psychologist, 50*(9), 741–749. doi:10.1037/0003-066X.50.9.741

Meyer, H. (2004). Novice and expert teachers' conceptions of learners' prior knowledge. *Science Education, 88*(6), 970–983. doi:10.1002ce.20006

Michael, H. (1991). There life of the teachers: Evolution And balance sheet of a occupation. *Revue Française de Pédagogie, 95*, 146–198.

Michaelsen, L. K., Knight, A. B., & Fink, L. D. (2004). *Team-Based Learning: A Transformative Use of Small Groups.* Greenwood Publishing Group.

Michinov, N., & Michinov, E. (2009). Investigating the relationship between transactive memory and performance in collaborative learning. *Learning and Instruction, 19*(1), 43–54. doi:10.1016/j.learninstruc.2008.01.003

Miller, G. R. (1966). On Defining Communication: Another Stab. *Journal of Communication, 16*(2), 92. doi:10.1111/j.1460-2466.1966.tb00020.x PMID:5941548

Mills, J. D. (2020). Challenges of traditional assessment methods in competency-based education. *Journal of Education and Learning, 9*(4), 100–109.

Mingasson, M. (2002). *Le guide du e-learning: L'organisation apprenante.* Éditions d'Organisation.

Ministère du développement économique et régional et Recherche. (2004). *Industrie de la formation virtuelle: Profil industriel.* Québec: Direction générale des communications et des services à la clientèle.

Ministerial Decision No. 33127/D2/2023, Government Gazette 1948/B/24-3-2023.

Ministry of Education of The People's Republic of China. (2017, December 6). 中共教育部党组关于印发《高校思想政治工作质量提升工程实施纲要》的通知 [*Notice of the Ministry of Education of the Communist Party of China on issuing the "Implementation Outline of the Project to Improve the Quality of Ideological and Political Work in Colleges and Universities"*]. MoE. http://www.moe.gov.cn/srcsite/A12/s7060/201712/t20171206_320698.html

Minsky, M., & Papert, S. (1969). *Perceptrons: An Introduction to Computational Geometry*. MIT Press.

Moazami, F., Bahrampour, E., Azar, M. R., Jahedi, F., & Moattari, M. (2014). Comparing two methods of education (virtual versus traditional) on learning of Iranian dental students: A post-test only design study. *BMC Medical Education*, *14*(1), 45. doi:10.1186/1472-6920-14-45 PMID:24597923

Mödritscher, F., Garcia-Barrios, V. M., & Gütl, C. (2004). The Past, the Present and the Future of adaptive E-Learning. *Proceedings of ICL 2004*. ICL.

Mohammadi, N., Ghorbani, V., & Hamidi, F. (2011). Effects of elearning on language learning. *Procedia Computer Science*, *3*, 464–468. doi:10.1016/j.procs.2010.12.078

Mohammed, Z. E. A., Amel, N., & Mohamed, K. (2023). *Literature and the Teaching of French as a Foreign Language in Morocco: Rethinking the importance of the literary text using new approaches*.

Mohammed, K. (2016). Khalil and Ihsan A. Elkhider. Applying learning theories and instructional design models for effective instruction. *Advances in Physiology Education*, *40*(2), 147–156. doi:10.1152/advan.00138.2015 PMID:27068989

Mohammed, Z. E. A., Amel, N., & Mohamed, K. (2022). Reflection on E-Learning and Adaptability in the Teaching and Learning of French as Foreign Language. *RA Journal Of Applied Research*, *8*(5), 408–411. doi:10.47191/rajar/v8i5.17

Moje, E. B., Collazo, T., Carrillo, R., & Marx, R. (2001). "Maestro, what is 'quality'?" Language, literacy and discourse in project-based science. *Journal of Research in Science Teaching*, *38*(4), 469–498. doi:10.1002/tea.1014

Monge, P. R., & Contractor, N. S. (2003). *Theories of communication networks*. Oxford University Press. doi:10.1093/oso/9780195160369.001.0001

Moore, J. L., Dickson-Deane, C., & Galyen, K. (2011). e-Learning, online learning, and distance learning environments: Are they the same? *ScienceDirect*, 1-4.

Moore. (1990). Recent contributions to the theory of distance education. *Open Learning*, 11-14.

Moore, J., Dickson-Deane, C., & Galyen, K. (2011). E-learning, online learning and distance learning environments: Are they the same? *The Internet and Higher Education*, *14*(2), 129135. doi:10.1016/j.iheduc.2010.10.001

Moore, M. G., & Kearsley, G. (2012). *Distance education: A systems view of online learning*. Cengage Learning.

Moore, M., & Kearsley, G. (1996). *Distance education: A systems view*. Wadsworth.

Morales, A., & Gray, K. (n.d.). Cognitive Learning Theory in the Classroom [Théorie de l'apprentissage cognitif en classe]. Study.com. https://study.com/learn/lesson/cognitivism-education-learning-theory.html.

Morgado, M., Mendes, J. J., & Proença, L. (2021). Online Problem-Based Learning in Clinical Dental Education: Students' Self-Perception and Motivation. *Healthcare, 9*(4), 420. MDPI AG. doi:10.3390/healthcare9040420

Morgil, İ., Temel, S., Seyhan, H. G., & Alşan, E. U. (2009). The effect of project based laboratory application on pre-service teachers' understanding of nature of science. *Journal of Turkish Science Education*, *6*(2), 92–109.

Morin, E., & Viveret, P. (2010). *Comment vivre en temps de crise? Collection: Le temps d'une question. Editeur: Montrouge*. Bayard.

Mottier Lopez, L. (2013). From Measurement to Collaborative Evaluation in Education. *Revue française d'administration publique, 4*(148), 939-952.

Mottier Lopez, L., & Figari, G. (Eds.). (2012). *Modelling Evaluation in Education*. De Boeck.

Moulton, S., Strickland, J., Strickland, A., White, J., & Zimmerly, L. (2010, October). Online course development using the ADDIE model of instruction design: The need to establish validity in the analysis phase. In *ELearn: World Conference on ELearning in Corporate, Government, Healthcare, and Higher Education* (pp. 20462054). Association for the Advancement of Computing in Education (AACE).

Moulton, S. T., Türkay, S., & Kosslyn, S. M. (2017). Does a presentation's medium affect its message? PowerPoint, Prezi, and oral presentations. *PLoS One, 12*(7), e0178774. doi:10.1371/journal.pone.0178774 PMID:28678855

Moursund, D. G. (2003). *Project-based learning using information technology* (2nd ed.). International Society for Technology in Education.

Muilenburg, L. Y., & Berge, Z. L. (2005). Student barriers to online learning: A factor analytic study. *Distance Education, 26*(1), 29–48. doi:10.1080/01587910500081269

Mulder, M., Weigel, T., Collins, K., & Eby, L. T. (2017). Models of Competency-Based Education and Training: What Are They and How Do They Compare? *Journal of Vocational Education and Training, 69*(3), 347–366.

Murat, M. E., & Rudman, A. J. (1992). Automated first arrival picking: A neural network approach. *Geophysical Prospecting, 40*(6), 587–604. doi:10.1111/j.1365-2478.1992.tb00543.x

Murbay, S., Neelakantan, P., Chang, J. W. W., & Yeung, S. (2020). Evaluation of the introduction of a dental virtual simulator on the performance of undergraduate dental students in the pre-clinical operative dentistry course. *European Journal of Dental Education, 24*(1), 5–16. doi:10.1111/eje.12453 PMID:31278815

Muruganantham, G. (2015). Developing of E-content package by using ADDIE model. *International Journal of Applied Research, 1*(3), 52–54.

Mutambik, I. (2018). The Role of eLearning in Studying English as a Foreign Language in Saudi Arabia: Students' and Teachers' Perspectives. *English Language Teaching, 11*(5), 74–83. doi:10.5539/elt.v11n5p74

Nachmias, R., Mioduser, D., Oren, A., & Ram, J. (2000). Web-supported emergent collaboration in higher education courses. *Journal of Educational Technology & Society, 3*(3), 94–104.

Nagrale, P. (2013). *Advantages and disadvantages of distance education*. Sure Job.https://surejob.in/advantages-anddisadvantages-of-distance-education.html

Nam, C. W. (2017). The effects of digital storytelling on student achievement, social presence, and attitude in online collaborative learning environments. *Interactive Learning Environments, 25*(3), 412–427. doi:10.1080/10494820.2015.1135173

Nasseripour, M., Turner, J., Rajadurai, S., San Diego, J., Quinn, B., Bartlett, A., & Volponi, A. A. (2021). COVID 19 and dental education: Transitioning from a well-established synchronous format and face to face teaching to an asynchronous format of dental clinical teaching and learning. *Journal of Medical Education and Curricular Development, 8*, 2382120521999667. doi:10.1177/2382120521999667 PMID:33796791

Naturel, M. (1995). *Pour la littérature: de l'extrait à l'oeuvre*. FeniXX.

Nawrot-Lis, B. (2019). *The challenges of content acquisition in a CLIL course: a CLIL-based chemistry course at the lower secondary school level*. Springer. doi:10.1007/978-3-476-05139-4

Neelands, J. (2002). *Making sense of Drama: A guide to classroom practice*. Heinemann Educational Publishers.

Newton, P., Driver, R., & Osborne, J. (1999). The place of argumentation in the pedagogy of school science. *International Journal of Science Education, 21*(5), 553–576. doi:10.1080/095006999290570

Ng, K. C. (2007). Replacing face-to-face tutorials by synchronous online technologies: Challenges and pedagogical implications. *International Review of Research in Open and Distance Learning, 8*(1). Advance online publication. doi:10.19173/irrodl.v8i1.335

Nguyen, D. K., & Okatani, T. (2018). Improved fusion of visual and language representations by dense symmetric co-attention for visual question answering. In *Proceedings of the IEEE conference on computer vision and pattern recognition* (pp. 6087-6096). IEEE. 10.1109/CVPR.2018.00637

Nguyen, P. M., Elliott, J. G., Terlouw, C., & Pilot, A. (2009). Neocolonialism in education: Cooperative learning in an Asian context. *Comparative Education, 45*(1), 109–130. doi:10.1080/03050060802661428

Nguyên, P., & Daïd, G. (2014). *Practical guide to MOOCs*. Éditions Eyrolles.

Nichols, M. (2003). A Theory for E-Learning. *Journal of Educational Technology & Society, 6*(2), 1–10.

Nicoll, P., MacRury, S., Van Woerden, H. C., & Smyth, K. (2018). Evaluation of technology-enhanced learning programs for health care professionals: Systematic review. *Journal of Medical Internet Research, 20*(4), e9085. doi:10.2196/jmir.9085 PMID:29643049

Nikolić, D. (2017). Intelligibility within a modified CLIL framework. Glottodidactica. *International Journal of Applied Linguistics, 44*(1), 119–130. doi:10.14746/gl.2017.44.1.07

Nonaka, I., & Takeuchi, H. (1995). *The knowledge creatign company: how Japanese companies create the dynamics of innovation*. Oxford University Press. doi:10.1093/oso/9780195092691.001.0001

Núñez, M., Quirós, R., Núñez, I., Carda, J. B., Camahort, E., & Mauri, J. L. (2008, July). Collaborative augmented reality for inorganic chemistry education. In *WSEAS international conference. Proceedings. Mathematics and computers in science and engineering* (Vol. 5, pp. 271–277). WSEAS.

Nunziati, G. (1990, January). To build a formative evaluation system. Cahiers Pédagogiques. *Learning*, (280), 48–64.

Nuroh, E. Z., Kusumawardana, M. D., & Destiana, E. (2022). Developing digital literacy skill for initial teacher education through digital storytelling. *KnE Social Sciences, 7*(10), 475–496. doi:10.18502/kss.v7i10.11250

Nusbaum, A. T., Swindell, S., & Plemons, A. (2021). Kindness at First Sight: The Role of Syllabi in Impression Formation. *Teaching of Psychology, 48*(2), 130–143. doi:10.1177/0098628320959953

Nystrand, M., Wu, L. L., Gamoran, A., Zeiser, S., & Long, D. A. (2003). Questions in Time: Investigating the Structure and Dynamics of Unfolding Classroom Discourse. *Discourse Processes, 35*(2), 135–198. doi:10.1207/S15326950DP3502_3

O'Flaherty, J., & Phillips, C. (2015). The use of flipped classrooms in higher education: A scoping review. *The Internet and Higher Education, 25*, 85–95. doi:10.1016/j.iheduc.2015.02.002

Obasa, A. I., Eludire, A. A., & Ajao, T. A. (2013). A comparative study of synchronous and asynchronous e-learning resources. *International Journal of Innovative Research in Science, Engineering and Technology, 2*(11), 5938-5946.

Oblinger, D. G., & Hawkins, B. L. (2005). The myth about E-learning. *EDUCAUSE Review*.

OECD. (2002). *Glossary of key terms related to evaluation and results-based management*. OECD.

Ollivier, C. (2012). The interaction-based approach and invisible didactics-Two concepts for the design and practice of tasks on the social web. *Alsic-Apprentissage Des Langues Et Systems D Information Et De Communication, 15*(1).

Olson, J. D. (2003). *Beyond the Podium: Delivering Training and Performance to a Digital World.*

Organization for Economic Co-operation and Development (OECD). (2008). *The major changes that are transforming education*. OECD.

Othmane, Z., Derouich, A., & Talbi, A. (2019). A comparative study of the Most influential learning styles used in adaptive educational environments. *International Journal of Advanced Computer Science and Applications, 10*(11).

Otto, A., & Estrada, J. L. (2019). Towards an understanding of CLIL in a European context: Main assessment tools and the role of language in content subjects. *CLIL Journal of Innovation and Research in Plurilingual and Pluricultural Education, 2*(1), 31–42. doi:10.5565/rev/clil.11

Ouadoud, M., Nejjari, A., Chkouri, M. Y., & El-Kadiri, K. E. (2017, October). Learning management system and the underlying learning theories. In *Proceedings of the mediterranean symposium on smart city applications* (pp. 732-744). Cham: Springer International Publishing.

Ouariach, S., Khaldi, M., Mohamed, E., & Khaldi, M. (2023). From the Choice of a Learning Management System to the Installation of a Platform in a Server. In M. Khaldi (Ed.), *Handbook of Research on Scripting, Media Coverage, and Implementation of E-Learning Training in LMS Platforms* (pp. 330–375). IGI Global. doi:10.4018/978-1-6684-7634-5. ch015

Ouariach, S., Khaldi, M., Mohamed, E., & Khaldi, M. (2023). The Flipped Classroom: From Passive Information Absorption to Active Learning. In S. Karpava (Ed.), *Handbook of Research on Language Teacher Identity* (pp. 269–293). IGI Global. doi:10.4018/978-1-6684-7275-0.ch015

Ozan, O., & Ozarslan, Y. (2016). Video lecture watching behaviors of learners in online courses. *Educational Media International, 53*(1), 27–41. doi:10.1080/09523987.2016.1189255

Öztuna Kaplan, A., & Diker Coşkun, Y. (2012). Proje tabanlı öğretim uygulamalarında karşılaşılan güçlükler ve çözüm önerilerine yönelik bir eylem araştırması [An action research on the difficulties encountered in project-based teaching practices and solution suggestions]. *Mersin University Journal of the Faculty of Education, 8*(1), 137–159.

Pallant, J. (2007). *SPSS Survival Manual* (3rd ed.). Mcgrath Hill.

Panigrahi, R., Ranjan, P., & Sharma, D. (2018). Online learning: Adoption, continuance, and learning outcome—A review of literature. *International Journal of Information Management, 43*, 1–14. doi:10.1016/j.ijinfomgt.2018.05.005

Papanastasiou, G., Drigas, A., Skianis, C., Lytras, M., & Papanastasiou, E. (2019). Virtual and augmented reality effects on K-12, higher and tertiary education students' twenty-first century skills. *Virtual Reality (Waltham Cross), 23*(4), 425–436. doi:10.100710055-018-0363-2

Pappas, C. (2023, May 1). *Everything You Need To Know About The Connectivism Learning Theory*. eLearning Industry. https://elearningindustry.com/everything-you-need-to-know-about-the-connectivism-learning-theory.

Paquette, G. (2002). *L'ingénierie du téléapprentissage: pour construire l'apprentissage en réseaux*. Sainte-Foy: Presses de l'Université du Québec.

Paquette, G. (2002). The engineering of tele-learning, to build learning in networks. Presses de l'Université du Québec.

Paquette, G., & Léonard, M. Lundgren -Cayrol, K., Mihaila, S. & Gareau, D. (2006). Learning Design based on Graphical Knowledge-Modeling. *Journal of Educational technology and Society ET&S.*

Paquette, G. (2004). Instructional engineering for learning object repositories networks. *2nd International Conference on Computer Aided Learning in Engineering Education*, Grenoble, France.

Paquette, G., Bourdeau, J., Basque, J., Leonard, M., Henri, F., & Maina, M. (2003). *Construction of a knowledge base and a resource bank for the field of tele-learning.* Educational Sciences and Techniques.

Parikh, N., Risinger, D., Holland, J. N., Molony, D. A., & van der Hoeven, D. (2022). Evaluating dental students' perspectives on the concurrent teaching of didactic and case-based courses. *Journal of Dental Education, 86*(12), 1643–1652. doi:10.1002/jdd.13081 PMID:35994207

Parizeau, M. (2006). *Réseaux de Neurones. GIF-21140 et GIF-64326.* Université Laval.

Parkes, J. (2001). The Role of Transfer in the Variability of Performance Assessment Scores. *Educational Assessment, 7*(2), 143–164. doi:10.1207/S15326977EA0702_3

Parola, A., Simonsen, A., Bliksted, V., & Fusaroli, R. (2020). Voice patterns in schizophrenia: A systematic review and Bayesian meta-analysis. *Schizophrenia Research, 216*, 24–40. doi:10.1016/j.schres.2019.11.031 PMID:31839552

Parolia, A., Mohan, M., Kundabala, M., & Shenoy, R. (2012). Indian dental students' preferences regarding lecture courses. *Journal of Dental Education, 76*(3), 366–371. doi:10.1002/j.0022-0337.2012.76.3.tb05268.x PMID:22383607

Patel, H. (2019). Learning-space compass framework. *Higher Education Design Quality Forum.*

Patton, M. Q. (1997). Utilization-focused evaluation: The new century text. *The American Journal of Evaluation, 18*(3), 320–321.

Patton, M. Q. (2008). *Utilization-focused evaluation.* Sage Publications.

Patton, M. Q. (2010). *Developmental evaluation: Applying complexity concepts to enhance innovation and use.* Guilford Press.

Paudel, P. (2021). Online education: Benefits, challenges and strategies during and after COVID-19 in higher education. [IJonSE]. *International Journal on Studies in Education, 3*(2), 70–85. doi:10.46328/ijonse.32

Pavitt, C. (1998). *Small group communication: a theoretical approach* (3rd ed.). University of Delaware. https://www.uky.edu/~drlane/teams/pavitt/

Pernin, J. P. (2003). Educational objects: learning units, activities or resources? Revue Sciences et Techniques Educatives.

Pernin, J.-P., & Lejeune, A. (2004). Learning devices instrumented by technologies: towards scenario-centered engineering. In: TICE conference, Compiègne France.

Perraton, H. (1992). Une théorie de l'enseignement à distance. In A.-J. Deschênes (Ed.), *La formation à distance maintenant.* Presses de la Télé-Université du Québec.

Perraton, H. (2002). *Open and Distance Learning in the Developing World.* Routledge.

Perrenoud, P. (1991). Pour une approche pragmatique de l'évaluation formative. *Mesure et évaluation en éducation, 4*(13), 49-81.

Perrenoud, P. (1995). From knowledge to skills. What are we talking about when we talk about skills? *Pédagogie collégiale, 9*(1).

Perrenoud, P. (1998). *Student assessment. From the manufacture of excellence to the regulation of learning.* Brussels, De Boeck.

Perrenoud. (1999). *Teach: act in a hurry, decide in uncertainty. Knowledge and skills in an obscure profession* (2nd ed.). ESF.

Perret-Clermont, A., Perret, J.-F., & Bell, N. (1991). The social construction of meaning and cognitive activity in elementary school children. In L. Resnick, J. Levine. & S. Teasley (Eds.), Perspectives on socially shared cognition (p. 41- 62). Washington, DC: American Psychological association. doi:10.1037/10096-002

Peters, O. (1973). Distance teaching and industrial production: a comparative international outline. In D. Sewart, D. Keegan, & B. Holmberg (Eds.), *Distance education: International perspectives* (pp. 95–113). Routledge.

Petitjean, G. (2009). *Introduction aux réseaux de neurones.*

Petrosky, S. N. (2022). *Interprofessional education activities and new practitioner competence: Implications for practice in nutrition and dietetics education.* University of North Florida.

Petty, R. E., Cacioppo, J. T., Petty, R. E., & Cacioppo, J. T. (1986). *The elaboration likelihood model of persuasion.* Springer New York.

Peytard J. (1988). Des usages de la littérature en classe de langue. *Le Français dans le monde, Littérature et enseignement, la Perspective du lecteur,* 8-17.

Peytard, J. & Moirand, S. (1992). Discours et enseignement du français. Les lieux d'une rencontre, Paris, Hachette.

Piaget, J. (1967). *Biology and knowledge: An essay on the relation between organic regulations and cognitive processes.* University of Chicago Press.

Piaget, J. (1967). *The Psychology of Intelligence.* Armand Colin.

Pintrich, P. R., & De Groot, E. V. (1990). Motivational and self-regulated learning components of classroom academic performance. *Journal of Educational Psychology, 82*(1), 33–40. doi:10.1037/0022-0663.82.1.33

Pintrich, P. R., Smith, D., Garcia, T., & McKeachie, W. (1991). *A Manual for the Use of the Motivated Strategies for Learning Questionnaire (MSLQ).* The University of Michigan.

Pittaway, S. M. (2012). Student and staff engagement: Developing an engagement framework in a faculty of education. *The Australian Journal of Teacher Education, 37*(4), 37–45. doi:10.14221/ajte.2012v37n4.8

Poellhuber, B., Laferrière, T., & Breuleux, A. (2017). *Des outils numériques pour soutenir une approche pédagogique inclusive.* Profweb. https://www.profweb.ca/publications/dossiers/des-outils-numeriques-pour-soutenir-une-approche-pedagogique-inclusive

Porto, M. (2021). Intercultural citizenship in foreign language education: An opportunity to broaden CLIL's theoretical outlook and pedagogy. *International Journal of Bilingual Education and Bilingualism, 24*(7), 927–947. doi:10.1080/13670050.2018.1526886

Pretceille, M.-A. (2010). Literature as a Learning Space for Otherness and Diversity. *Synergies Brazil, 2.*

Puren, C. (1988). *Histoire des méthodologies de l'enseignement des langues.* Nathan - Clé International.

Puren, C. (1999). De l'approche communicative à la perspective actionnelle. *Contact+, 44,* 50-54.

Puren, C. (2004). Quels modèles didactiques pour la conception de dispositifs d'enseignement/apprentissage en environnement numérique? In Études de linguistique appliquée, 134.

Puren, C. (2009). Nouvelle perspective actionnelle et (nouvelles) technologies éducatives: Quelles convergences... et quelles divergences? *Cyber-Langues*. http://www.aplvlanguesmodernes.org/spip.php?article2673

Puren, C. (2012). *Perspectives actionnelles sur la littérature dans l'enseignement scolaire et universitaire des langues-cultures: des tâches scolaires sur les textes aux actions sociales par les textes.* Christian Puren. https://www.christian-puren.com/mestravaux/2012d/

Qodad, A., Benyoussef, A., & El Kenz, A. (2020). Toward an Adaptive Educational Hypermedia System (AEHS-JS) based on the Overlay Modeling and Felder and Silverman's Learning Styles Model for Job Seekers. International Journal Emerging Technologies in Learning, iJET, 15(8).

Querol Julián, M., & Crawford Camiciottoli, B. (2019). The impact of online technologies and English medium instruction on university lectures in international learning contexts. *Systematic Reviews.*

Quinn, B. F. A. (2022). Challenges and opportunities of online education in dentistry post-COVID-19. *British Dental Journal, 233*(6), 491. doi:10.103841415-022-4979-y PMID:36151177

Quintin, J., Depover, C., & Degache, C. (2005). *The role of the educational scenario in the analysis of distance training: Analysis of an educational scenario based on defined characterization elements.* HAL.

Rabat, H. E. C. (n.d.). *Le E-Learning et son importance pour le développement de compétences avancées.* HEC. https://hec.ac.ma/blog/le-e-learning-et-son-importance-pour-le-developpement-de-competences-avancees/

Rafferty, A. N., Riggio, R. E., & Dziobek, C. A. (2011). The role of real-time feedback in the training of a mental rotation task. *Computers in Human Behavior, 27*(4), 1357–1365.

Rao, G. K. L., & Mokhtar, N. (2023). Dental Education in the Information Age: Teaching Dentistry to Generation Z Learners Using an Autonomous Smart Learning Environment. In Handbook of Research on Instructional Technologies in Health Education and Allied Disciplines (pp. 243-264). IGI Global.

Rao, G. K. L., Iskandar, Y. H. P., & Mokhtar, N. (2020). Understanding the nuances of E-learning in orthodontic education. *Education and Information Technologies, 25*(1), 307–328. doi:10.100710639-019-09976-2

Rao, G. K., Iskandar, Y. H., & Mokhtar, N. (2020). Enabling Training in Orthodontics Through Mobile Augmented Reality: A Novel Perspective. In Y. Qian (Ed.), *Teaching, Learning, and Leading With Computer Simulations* (pp. 68–103). IGI Global. doi:10.4018/978-1-7998-0004-0.ch003

Rao, G. K., Iskandar, Y. H., & Mokhtar, N. (2022). Bolstering the Pedagogies of Orthodontic Education Using Smart Technologies. In A. Lopes & F. Soares (Eds.), *Online Distance Learning Course Design and Multimedia in E-Learning* (pp. 225–253). IGI Global. doi:10.4018/978-1-7998-9706-4.ch010

Redecker, C. (2008). *Review of Learning 2.0 Practices: Study on the Impact of Web 2.0 Innovations on Education and Training in Europe Seville.* European Commission - Joint Research Center - Institute for Prospective Technological Studies., Retrieved from http://ftp.jrc.es/EURdoc/JRC49108.pdf

Reigeluth, C. M. (1999). What Is Instructional-Design Theory and How Is It Changing? In C. M. Reigeluth (Ed.), Instructional-Design Theories and Models, Vol. II: A New Paradigm of Instructional Theory (pp. 1-29). Mahwah, NJ: Lawrence Erlbaum Associates.

Reigeluth, C. M. (1983). Instructional design: What it is and why is it? In C. M. Reigeluth (Ed.), *Instructional design theories and models* (pp. 3–36). Lawrence Erlbaum Associates. doi:10.4324/9780203824283

Reigeluth, C. M. (2012). *Instructional-Design Theories and Models: A New Paradigm of Instructional Theory* (Vol. II). Routledge.

Reigeluth, C. M. (Ed.). (1999). Instructional-Design Theories and Models: Vol. II. *A New Paradigm of Instructional Theory.* Lawrence Erlbaum Assoc.

Reigeluth, C. M., & Keller, J. B. (2009). Understanding Instruction. In C. M. Reigeluth & A. A. Carr-Chellman (Eds.), *Instructional-Design Theories and Models* (pp. 27–39). Routledge, Taylor and Francis Publishers Group.

Reissmann, D. R., Sierwald, I., Berger, F., & Heydecke, G. (2015). A model of blended learning in a pre-clinical course in prosthetic dentistry. *Journal of Dental Education, 79*(2), 157–165. doi:10.1002/j.0022-0337.2015.79.2.tb05870.x PMID:25640620

Ren, J. (2022). "课程思政"内涵的演进及其体用的发展 [The evolution of the connotation of "ideological and political education of curriculum" and the development of its application]. 创新教育研究 *[Creative Educaton Studies], 10*(1), 78–85. doi:10.12677/CES.2022.101015

Ren, N. (2020). A proposal for teaching MTI courses in China through a CLIL approach: Using the lesson on "Intellectual Property Law" as an example. *Journal of Education and Teaching Management Research, 1*(1), 24–26. doi:10.33969/twjournals.jetmr.2020.010107

Reuter Y. (1999). L'Enseignement de la littérature en question. *Enjeux,* (43), 191–203.

Richard, S., Gay, P., & Gentaz, É. (2021). Pourquoi et comment soutenir le développement des compétences émotionnelles chez les élèves âgés de 4 à 7 ans et chez leur enseignant. e? Apports des sciences cognitives. *Raisons éducatives, 25*(1), 261-287.

Richey, R. C., Klein, J. D., & Tracey, M. W. (2011). Conditions-based theory. In R. C. Richey, J. D. Klein, & M. W. Tracey (Eds.), *The Instructional Design Knowledge Base: Theory, Research and Practice* (pp. 104–128). Routledge.

Richmond, A. S., Morgan, R. K., Slattery, J. M., Mitchell, N. G., & Cooper, A. G. (2019). Project syllabus: An exploratory study of learner-centered syllabi. *Teaching of Psychology, 46*(1), 6–15. https://doi-org/ doi:10.1177/009862831881612

Richmond, A. S., Slattery, J., Morgan, R. K., Mitchell, N., & Becknell, J. (2016). Can a learner-centered syllabus change student's perceptions of student-professor rapport and master teacher behaviors? *Scholarship of Teaching and Learning in Psychology, 2*, 159–168. https://doi-org/ doi:10.1037/stl0000066

Rickabaugh, J. (2015). *Tapping the power of personalized learning: A roadmap for school leaders.* ASCD.

Robin, B. R. (2008). Digital storytelling: A powerful technology tool for the 21st century classroom. *Theory into Practice, 47*(3), 220–228. doi:10.1080/00405840802153916

Robinson, P., & Cole, R. A. (2000). *Issues in web-based pedagogy: A critical primer.*

Roediger, H. L. III. (2013). Applying Cognitive Psychology to Education: Translational Educational Science. *Psychological Science in the Public Interest, 14*(1), 1–3. doi:10.1177/1529100612454415 PMID:26173287

Roegiers. (2000). *Une pédagogie de l'intégration: compétences et intégration des acquis dans l'enseignement.* De Boeck Université.

Rogalski, J. (2005). Professional didactics: an alternative to "situated cognition" and "cognitivist" approaches in the psychology of acquisitions. *@ctivities, 1*(2), 103-120. http://www.activites.org/v1n2/Rogalski.pdfDOI: doi:10.4000/activites.1259

Rogers, E.M. & Shoemaker, F.F. (1971). *Communication of Innovation: A Cross-Cultural Approach.* (2nd Edition) The Free Press, New York.

Rogers, E. M., & Kincaid, D. L. (1981). *Communication networks: Toward a new paradigm for research.* No Title.

Rogers, P. J. (1995). Using programme theory to evaluate complicated and complex aspects of interventions. *Evaluation*, *1*(4), 404–420.

Rokeach, P. (1973). *The Nature of Human Values*. UK: Free Press. A division of Macmillan.

Romero, P. (1984). *English for Business: Developing Communication Skills*. Katha Publishing Co., Inc.

Romiszowski, A. J. (1981). *Designing Instructional systems*. Kogan Page et Nochols Publishing.

Ronny, C. (2019). Student Satisfaction and Learning Outcomes in Asynchronous Online Lecture Videos. *CBE Life Sciences Education*, *18*, 4.

Roschelle, J., & Teasley, S. (1995). The construction of shared knowledge in collaborative problem solving. In C. O'Malley (Ed.), Computer-Supported Collaborative Learning (p. 69-197). Berlin, Allemagne: Springer-Verlag. doi:10.1007/978-3-642-85098-1_5

Rosé, C. P., Wang, Y. C., Cui, Y., Arguello, J., Stegmann, K., Weinberger, A., & Fischer, F. (2008). Analyzing Collaborative Learning Processes Automatically: Exploiting the Advances of Computational Linguistics in Computer-Supported Collaborative Learning. *International Journal of Computer-Supported Collaborative Learning*, *3*(3), 237–271. doi:10.100711412-007-9034-0

Rosen, E. (2010). Practical Dictionary of the CEFR. Paris: Ophrys.

Rosenblatt, F. (1957). *Le perceptron: Un automate de perception et de reconnaissance*. No 85-460-1.

Rosenblatt, F. (1961). *Principes de la neurodynamique: Perceptrons and the Theory of Brain Mechanisms*. Semantic Scholar.

Rosenshine, B., & Meister, C. (1994). Reciprocal Teaching: A Review of the Research. *Review of Educational Research*, *64*(4), 479–530. doi:10.3102/00346543064004479

Rossi, P. H., Lipsey, M. W., & Freeman, H. E. (2004). *Evaluation: A systematic approach*. Sage Publications.

Röth, G., & Tarantola, A. (1994). Neural networks and inversion of seismic data. *Journal of Geophysical Research*, *99*(B4), 6753–6768. doi:10.1029/93JB01563

Rougier, B. (2009) *Construction of an educational sequence*. Academy of Versailles – Biological Sciences and Applied Social Sciences. http://sbssa.spip.ac-rouen.fr/?TERMINOLOGIE-BO-no35-du-17-09-92

Rouse, M. (2011, March). *Computer-Based Training (CBT)*.

Ruesch, J. (1957). Technology and Social Communication. In L. Thayer (Ed.), *Communication Theory and Research* (p. 462).

Ryan, S., Kaufman, J., Greenhouse, J., She, R., & Shi, J. (2016). The effectiveness of blended online learning courses at the Community College level. *Community College Journal of Research and Practice*, *40*(4), 285–298. doi:10.1080/10668926.2015.1044584

Saadé, R. G., Morin, D., & Thomas, J. D. (2012). Critical thinking in E-learning environments. *Computers in Human Behavior*, *28*(5), 1608–1617. doi:10.1016/j.chb.2012.03.025

Sabari, N. A. S., & Hashim, H. (2023). Sustaining education with digital storytelling in the English language teaching and learning: A systematic review. *International Journal of Academic Research in Business & Social Sciences*, *13*(4), 214–231. doi:10.6007/IJARBSS/v13-i4/16860

Sabeima, M., Lamolle, M., & Nanne, M. F. (2021). *Overview of adaptive and collaborative learning systems*.

Sabeima, M., Lamolle, M., Anghour, A., & Nanne, M. F. (2022). *Towards a semantic platform for adaptive and collaborative e-learning.*

Sadik, A. (2008). Digital storytelling: A meaningful technology-integrated approach for engaged student learning. *Educational Technology Research and Development*, *56*(4), 487–506. doi:10.100711423-008-9091-8

Saeedipour, B., Masoomifard, M., & Masoomifard, M. (2013). Survey of Relation between Control Resource, Learning Styles and Self-regulated Learning and Academic Success of Online Course Students. *Teaching and Learning Research*, *10*(1), 19–38.

Saemmer, A. (2017). Interpréter l'hyperlien en contexte pédagogique: éléments d'une sémiotique sociale. *Le français aujourd'hui*, *196*(1), 25-34.

Saemmer, A. (2015). *Rhétorique du texte numérique: figures de la lecture, anticipations de pratiques.* Presses de l'Enssib. doi:10.4000/books.pressesenssib.3870

Sakka, Z. I., & Zualkernan, I. A. (2005). Digital storytelling in higher education: a case study in a civil engineering laboratory. *Fifth IEEE International Conference on Advanced Learning Technologies (ICALT'05)*, (pp. 365-367). IEEE. 10.1109/ICALT.2005.124

Salamat, L., Ahmad, G., Bakht, M. I., & Saifi, I. L. (2018). Effects of elearning on students' academic learning at university level. *Asian Innovative Journal of Social Sciences and Humanities*, *2*(2), 1–12.

Saleem, F., AlNasrallah, W., Malik, M. I., & Rehman, S. U. (2022, April). Factors affecting the quality of online learning during COVID-19: Evidence from a developing economy. In Frontiers in Education (Vol. 7). Frontiers Media SA.

Salimzadeh, R., Hall, N. C., & Saroyan, A. (2021, September). Examining academics' strategies for coping with stress and emotions: A review of research. [). Frontiers Media SA.]. *Frontiers in Education*, *6*, 660676. doi:10.3389/feduc.2021.660676

Sanabria, J. C., & Arámburo-Lizárraga, J. (2016). Enhancing 21st century skills with AR: Using the gradual immersion method to develop collaborative creativity. *Eurasia Journal of Mathematics, Science and Technology Education*, *13*(2), 487–501. doi:10.12973/eurasia.2017.00627a

Sancar-Tokmak, H., Surmeli, H., & Ozgelen, S. (2014). Preservice science teachers' perceptions of their tpack development after creating digital stories. *International Journal of Environmental and Science Education*, *9*(3), 247–264. doi:10.12973/ijese.2014.214a

Sangrà, A., Vlachopoulos, D., & Cabrera, N. (2012). Building an inclusive definition of e-learning: An approach to the conceptual framework. *International Review of Research in Open and Distance Learning*, *13*(2), 145–159. doi:10.19173/irrodl.v13i2.1161

Sangra, A., Vlachopoulos, D., & Cabrera, N. (2012). *Building an Inclusive Definition of E-Learning: An Approach to the Conceptual Framework.* IRRODL.

Sartre. J.-P. (1970). Existentialism is a Humanism (1947). Paris: Éditions Nagel.

Sarwar, S., Qayyum, Z. U., García-Castro, R., Safyan, M., & Munir, R. F. (2019). Ontology based E-learning framework: A personalized, adaptive and context aware model. *Multimedia Tools and Applications*, *78*(24), 34745–34771. doi:10.100711042-019-08125-8

Sattar, E. (2017, October 20). *Cognitive Learning and Its Relationship With Online Education.* ATD. https://www.td.org/insights/cognitive-learning-and-its-relationship-with-online-education

Sattar, E. (2017, October 20). *Cognitive Learning and Its Relationship With Online Education*. ATD. https://www.td.org/insights/cognitive-learning-and-its-relationship-with-online-education..

Sawyer, K. (Ed.). (2009). *The Cambridge Handbook of Learning Science*. Cambridge University Press.

Scallon, G. (1999). *L'évaluation formative*. Éditions du Renouveau Pédagogique Inc.

Scallon, G. (2004). *L'évaluation des apprentissages dans une approche par competences*. Saint-Laurent, Éditions du Renouveau Pédagogique Inc.

Schank, R. C. (2000). A Vision of Education for the 21st Century. *T.H.E. Journal, 27*(6), 43–45.

Schellens, T., Van Keer, H., Valcke, M., & De Wever, B. (2007). Learning in asynchronous discussion groups: A multilevel approach to study the influence of student, group and task characteristics. *Behaviour & Information Technology, 26*(1), 55–71. doi:10.1080/01449290600811578

Schement, J. R. (2017). Communication and information. *Between communication and information*, 3-33.

Scherman, R., Islam, M. S., Dikaya, L. A., Dumulescu, D., Pop-Păcurar, I., & Necula, C. V. (2023). Learning Design for Future Higher Education–Insights From the Time of COVID-19. *Covid-19 and beyond: From (forced) remote teaching and learning to 'the new normal' in higher education*, 16648714.

Schleicher, A. (2018). Educating learners for their future, not our past. *ECNU Review of Education, 1*(1), 58–75. doi:10.30926/ecnuroe2018010104

Schneider, D. (2003). Design and implementation of rich educational scenarios with community portals. *Guéret conference*. Springer.

Schonenberg, M. H., Mans, R. S., Russell, N. C., Mulyar, N. A., & van der Aalst, W. M. P. (2007). Towards a Taxonomy of Process Flexibility (Extended Version). *BPM Center Report BPM-07-11*. BPMcenter.org.

Schonenberg, H., Mans, R., Russell, N., Mulyar, N., & Aalst, W. (2008). Process flexibility: A survey of contemporary approaches. *Lecture Notes in Business Information Processing, I*, 16–30. doi:10.1007/978-3-540-68644-6_2

Schönwetter, D. J., Gareau-Wilson, N., Cunha, R. S., & Mello, I. (2016). Assessing the Impact of Voice-Over Screen-Captured Presentations Delivered Online on Dental Students' Learning. *Journal of Dental Education, 80*(2), 141–148. doi:10.1002/j.0022-0337.2016.80.2.tb06069.x PMID:26834131

Schunk, D. H., & Pajares, F. (2004). Self-efficacy in education revisited: Empirical and applied evidence. In D. M. McInerney & S. Van Etten (Eds.), *Big theories revisited* (pp. 115–138). Information Age Publishing.

Schwartz. S. (2006). *The basic values of the person: theory, measures and applications*. Cairn. www.cairn.info/revue-francaise-de-sociologie-2006-4-page-929.htm

Scriven, M. (1967). The methodology of evaluation. In *Perspectives of curriculum evaluation* (pp. 39–83). Rand McNally.

Scriven, M. (1967). *The Methodology of Evaluation*. Social Science Education Consortium.

Scriven, M. (1991). *Thesaurus Evaluation*. Sage Publications.

Scriven, M. (1996). *Beyond formative and summative evaluation*. ERIC Digest.

Seels, B. B., & Richey, R. C. (2012). *Instructional technology: The definition and domains of the field*. IAP.

Şen, Ş. (2011). *Effect of conceptual change texts and dual situated learning model on students' achievement and motivation in the concepts of melting and dissolving* [Master's thesis, Hacettepe University]. Council of Higher Education Thesis Center. https://tez.yok.gov.tr/UlusalTezMerkezi/giris.jsp

Séoud, A. (1994, January-March). « Document authentique ou texte littéraire », Littérature et cultures en situation didactique. *ELA*, (93), 8–24.

Seoud, A. (1997). *Pour une didactique de la littérature, Paris.* Hatier-Didier, (LAL).

Shadish, W. R., Cook, T. D., & Leviton, L. C. (1991). *Foundations of program evaluation: Theories of practice.* Sage Publications.

Sharma, N., & Patnaik, S. (2018). Is jargon deterrent to effective communication in dental practice? the budding dentists' outlook. *The Journal of the Indian Association of Public Health Dentistry, 16*(1), 48–53. doi:10.4103/jiaphd.jiaphd_123_17

Sharma, R., Ekundayo, M. S., & Ng, E. (2009). Beyond the digital divide: Policy analysis for knowledge societies. *Journal of Knowledge Management, 13*(5), 373–386. doi:10.1108/13673270910988178

Shaw, M. (1981). *Group dynamics: the psychology of small group behaviour.* McGraw-Hill.

Shelton, C. C., Archambault, L. M., & Hale, A. E. (2017). Bringing digital storytelling to the elementary classroom: Video production for preservice teachers. *Journal of Digital Learning in Teacher Education, 33*(2), 58–68. doi:10.108 0/21532974.2016.1276871

Shen, Y. (2023). 一流课程建设背景下大学英语课程思政的内涵和实施路径 [The connotation and implementation path of values education in college English courses under the background of first-class course construction]. 教育进展 *[Advances in Education], 13*(3), 1047–1055. doi:10.12677/AE.2023.133166

Shibley, I., Amaral, K. E., Shank, J. D., & Shibley, L. R. (2011). Designing a blended course: Using ADDIE to guide instructional design. *Journal of College Science Teaching, 40*(6).

Shih, Y.-C., & Yang, M. T. (2008). A Collaborative Virtual Environment for Situated Language Learning Using VEC3D. *Journal of Educational Technology & Society, 11*, 56–68.

Shimura, K. (2006). *Computer-based learning and web-based training: A review.* Research Gate.

Shin, W. S., Han, I., & Kim, I. (2014). Teachers' technology use and the change of their pedagogical beliefs in Korean educational context. *International Education Studies, 7*(8), 11–22. doi:10.5539/ies.v7n8p11

Shorey, S., Pereira, T. L. B., Teo, W. Z., Ang, E., Lau, T. C., & Samarasekera, D. D. (2022). Navigating nursing curriculum change during COVID-19 pandemic: A systematic review and meta-synthesis. *Nurse Education in Practice, 65*, 103483. doi:10.1016/j.nepr.2022.103483 PMID:36327596

Shrivastava, A. (2018). Using connectivism theory and technology for knowledge creation in cross-cultural communication. *Research in Learning Technology, 26*(0), 26. doi:10.25304/rlt.v26.2061

Shulman, L. S. (1986). Paradigms and research programs in the study of teaching: a contemporary perspective. In C. Wittrock Merlin (Ed.), *Handbook of research on teaching* (pp. 3–36). Macmillan.

Shute, V. J., & Psotka, J. (1994). *Intelligent Tutoring Systems: Past, Present, and Future (No. AL/HR-TP-1994-0005).* ARMSTRONG LAB BROOKS AFB TX HUMAN RESOURCES DIRECTORATE.

Siemens, G., & Yurkiw, S. (2003). The roles of the learner and the instructor in elearning. *Preparing learners for elearning*, 123138.

Siemens, G. (2005). Connectivism: A learning theory for the digital age. *International Journal of Instructional Technology and Distance Learning, 2*(1), 3–10.

Siemens, G., & Long, P. (2011). Penetrating the Fog: Analytics in Learning and Education. *EDUCAUSE Review, 46*(5), 30–32.

Simamora, R. M. (2020). Les défis de l'apprentissage en ligne pendant la pandémie de COVID-19: An Essay Analysis of Performing Arts Education Students (Analyse d'un essai d'apprenants en arts du spectacle). *Studies in Learning and Teaching, 1*(2), 86–103. doi:10.46627ilet.v1i2.38

Simon, H. (1969). The science of the artificial, (trans. Jean-Louis Le Moigne). MIT Press.

Simonson, M., Smaldino, S., Albright, M., & Zvacek, S. (2000). *Teaching and Learning at a Distance: Foundations of Distance Education.* Merrill.

Singham, M. (2007). Death to the syllabus. *Liberal Education, 93*(4), 52–56. https://freethoughtblogs.com/singham/files/2022/01/Death-to-the-Syllabus.pdf

Singh, J., Steele, K., & Singh, L. (2021). Combining the best of online and face-to-face learning: Hybrid and blended learning approach for COVID-19, post vaccine, & post-pandemic world. *Journal of Educational Technology Systems, 50*(2), 140–171. doi:10.1177/00472395211047865

Sintawati, M., Yuli Erviana, V., Bhattacharyya, E., Habil, H., & Fatmawati, L. (2022). The effect of project-based learning on technological pedagogical content knowledge among elementary school pre-service teacher. *Pegem Journal of Education and Instruction, 12*(2), 151–156. doi:10.47750/pegegog.12.02.15

Slavin, R. E. (2015). Cooperative Learning in Elementary Schools. *Education 3-13, 43*(1), 5-14.

Smeby, J.-C., & Vågan, A. (2008). Recontextualising professional knowledge – newly qualified nurses and physicians. *Journal of Education and Work, 21*(2), 159–173. doi:10.1080/13639080802018014

Smeda, N., Dakich, E., & Sharda, N. (2014). The effectiveness of digital storytelling in the classrooms: A comprehensive study. *Smart Learning Environments, 1*(6), 1–21. doi:10.118640561-014-0006-3

Smith, G. A., & Harris, M. A. (2017). The importance of assessment in competency-based education. *The Journal of Competency-Based Education, 2*(3), 143–152.

Smith, P. L., & Ragan, T. J. (2005). *Instructional Design* (3rd ed.). Wiley & Sons.

Soller, A., Lesgold, A., Linton, F., & Goodman, B. (1999). *What Makes Peer Interaction Effective? Modeling Effective Communication in an Intelligent CSCL.* Proceedings of the 1999 AAAI Fall Symposium: Psychological Models of Communication in Collaborative Systems, Cape Cod, MA. https://www.researchgate.net/publication/2279217_What_Makes_Peer_Interaction_Effective_Modeling_Effective_Communication_in_an_Intelligent_CSCL

Soller, A. (2001). Supporting Social Interaction in an Intelligent Collaborative Learning System. *International Journal of Artificial Intelligence in Education, 12*(1), 40–62.

Song, Q., & Xiao, W. (1992). 当代思想政治教育热点问题思考 [Reflections on hot issues in contemporary ideological and political education]. China Procurational Press.

Song, Y. (2018). Improving primary students' collaborative problem solving competency in project-based science learning with productive failure instructional design in a seamless learning environment. *Educational Technology Research and Development, 66*(4), 979–1008. doi:10.100711423-018-9600-3

Sorin, N. (2005). Vers une didactique de l'écriture littéraire du récit de fiction au primaire. Nouveaux cahiers de la recherche en éducation, 65-78.

Souchier, E., Jeanneret, Y. et Le Marec, J. (dir.). (2003). *Lire, écrire, récrire*. Bibliothèque publique d'information.

Spitzer, L. (1970). *Etudes de style*. Gallimard.

Spring, J. (2012). *Education networks: Power, wealth, cyberspace, and the digital mind*. Routledge. doi:10.4324/9780203156803

Sreedevi, P. S., & Kapilas, P. (2022). Impact of Effective E-content Modules for Improving Science Process Skills. *Emerging Trends of ICT in Teaching and Learning, 266*.

Srithar, U., & Selvaraj, D. (2015). Learning at your own pace: M-learning solution for school students. *International Journal of Information and Electronics Engineering, 5*(3), 216. doi:10.7763/IJIEE.2015.V5.533

Stahl, G., Koschmann, T., & Suthers, D. (2006). Computer-supported collaborative learning: an historical perspective. In R. Sawyer (Ed.), *Cambridge handbook of the learning sciences* (pp. 409–426). Cambridge University Press.

Stake, R. E. (2004). *Standards-based & responsive evaluation*. Sage Publications. doi:10.4135/9781412985932

Stamou, G. A., Politis, P., & Archakis, A. (Eds.). (2016). *Linguistic Diversity and Critical Literacies in the Discourse of Mass Culture: Educational Proposals for Language Education. Kavala*. Saita Publications.

Stern, H. H. (1983). *Fundamental concepts of language teaching: Historical and interdisciplinary perspectives on applied linguistic research*. Oxford university press.

Stevens, D. D., & Levi, A. J. (2013). *Introduction to Rubrics: An Assessment Tool to Save Grading Time, Convey Effective Feedback, and Promote Student Learning* (2nd ed.). Stylus Publishing.

Strijbos, J. W. (2004). *The effect of roles on computer-supported collaborative learning*. [Doctoral Thesis, Open Universiteit: faculties and services]. https://research.ou.nl/en/publications/the-effect-of-roles-on-computer-supported-collaborative-learning

Stufflebeam, D. L. (2001). Evaluation models. *New Directions for Evaluation, 89*(89), 7–98. doi:10.1002/ev.3

Stufflebeam, D. L., & Shinkfield, A. J. (2007). *Evaluation theory, models, and applications*. Jossey-Bass.

Sun, A., & Chen, X. (2016). Online education and its effective practice: A research review. *Journal of Information Technology Education, 15*.

Sun, B. (2021). Reflection on ideological and political education in foreign language teaching. In Y. Zhang (Ed.), *Proceedings of the 2nd International Conference on Education Studies: Experience and Innovation* (pp. 307–311). Atlantis Press. 10.2991/assehr.k.211217.049

Sunzuma, G., & Maharaj, A. (2019). In-service teachers' geometry content knowledge: Implications for how geometry is taught in teacher training institutions. *International Electronic Journal of Mathematics Education, 14*(3), 633–646. doi:10.29333/iejme/5776

Swan, K. (2001). Virtual interaction: Design factors affecting student satisfaction and perceived learning in asynchronous online courses. *Distance Education, 22*(2), 306–331. doi:10.1080/0158791010220208

Sword, H. (2012). *Stylish Academic Writing*. Harvard University Press.

Tadlaoui, M. A., & Khaldi, M. (2020). Concepts and Interactions of Personalization, Collaboration, and Adaptation in Digital Learning. In M. Tadlaoui & M. Khaldi (Eds.), *Personalization and Collaboration in Adaptive E-Learning* (pp. 1–33). IGI Global. doi:10.4018/978-1-7998-1492-4.ch001

Taylor, J. C. (2001). *Fifth generation distance education*. Paper presented at the 20th ICDE World Conference, Düsseldorf, Germany. USQ. http://www.usq.edu.au/users/ taylorj/conferences.htm

Team F. M. E. (2013). *Effective communication*. FME. www. free-management-ebooks. com/dldebkpdf/fme-effective-communication. pdf

Tendero, E. (2009). *Fundamentals of Effective Speech and Oral Communication*. Mutya Publishing House, Inc.

Tennyson, R. D. (2010). Historical reflection on learning theories and instructional design. *Contemporary Educational Technology*, *1*(1), 1–16. doi:10.30935/cedtech/5958

Tentolouris, F., & Chatzisavvidis, S. (2014). Discourses of Critical Literacies and Their 'Placement' in School Practice: Towards a Reflective Language Teaching. *Studies on the Greek Language*, *34*, 411–421.

Theelen, H., & van Breukelen, D. H. (2022). The didactic and pedagogical design of e-learning in higher education: A systematic literature review. *Journal of Computer Assisted Learning*, *38*(5), 1286–1303. doi:10.1111/jcal.12705

Thomson, J. R., & Cooke, J. (2000). Generating Instructional Hypermedia with APHID. In Hypertext, 2000. doi:10.1145/336296.336492

Tobias, S., & Duffy, T.M. (Eds.). (2009). *Constructivist instruction: Success or failure?* Routledge/Taylor & Francis Group. Abstract.

Toffler, A. (1970). *Future shock*. Sydney.

Toulmin, S. E. (1958). *The Uses of Argument*. Cambridge University Press.

Touzet, C. (1992). *Les Réseaux de Neurones Artificiels: Introduction au Connexionnisme.*

Training Magazine. (2019). 2019 Training Industry Report. *Training Magazine*. https://trainingmag.com/2019-training-industry-report/ ↗

Trestini, M. (2018). *Modeling of Next Generation Digital Learning Environments: Complex Systems Theory.* John Wiley & Sons. doi:10.1002/9781119513728

Triantafyllou, S. A. (2019). *The Effects of Constructivism Theory in the Environment of E-learning*. GRIN Verlag.

Tricot, A. (2017). *Myths and realities. Educational innovation*, Paris: ed. Retz.

Trilling, B., & Fadel, C. (2009). *21st century skills: Learning for life in our times*. John Wiley & Sons.

Trumbull, E. (2000). *Grading and Reporting Student Progress in an Age of Standards*. Christopher-Gordon.

Tsybulsky, D., Gatenio-Kalush, M., Abu Ganem, M., & Grobgeld, E. (2020). Experiences of preservice teachers exposed to project-based learning. *European Journal of Teacher Education*, *43*(3), 368–383. doi:10.1080/02619768.2019.1711052

Tsybulsky, D., & Muchnik-Rozanov, Y. (2023). The contribution of a project-based learning course, designed as a pedagogy of practice, to the development of preservice teachers' professional identity. *Teaching and Teacher Education*, *124*, 104020. doi:10.1016/j.tate.2023.104020

Tuncay, N., & Uzunboylu, H. (2012). English language teachers' success in blended and online elearning. *Procedia: Social and Behavioral Sciences*, *47*, 131–137. doi:10.1016/j.sbspro.2012.06.626

Ulum, H. (2022). The effects of online education on academic success: A meta-analysis study. *Education and Information Technologies, 27*(1), 429–450. doi:10.100710639-021-10740-8 PMID:34512101

United Nations Development Programme Evaluation Office. (2019). *Impact Evaluation of the United Nations Development Programme.* UN.

United Nations Evaluation Group. (2016). *UNEG Standards for Evaluation in the Development Sector.* UN.

United Nations Evaluation Group. (2018). *Evaluation Standards for Effective Planning and Management for Results.* UN.

Uzunboylu, H., & Koşucu, E. (2017). Comparison and evaluation of seels &glasgow and addie instructional design model. *International Journal of Scientific Research, 73*(6), 98.

Valamis. (n.d.). *Cognitive Learning Theory: Benefits, Strategies and Examples.* Valamis HUB. https://www.valamis.com/hub/cognitive-learning ↗

Valérie Bardot. (2014). Educational scripting in all its debates. *International journal of technologies in university teaching, 4*(2).

Van den Berghe, R., Wopereis, I., & Van der Linden, J. (2019). The interplay between assessment criteria and cognitive processes in technology-enhanced formative assessment. *Computers & Education, 138*, 122–132.

Van der Maren, J.-M. (1996). *Search methods for education* (2nd ed.). PUM and de Boeck.

Van Dinther, M., Dochy, F., & Segers, M. (2011). Factors affecting students' self-efficacy in higher education. *Educational Research Review, 6*(2), 95–108. doi:10.1016/j.edurev.2010.10.003

Van Merriënboer. (1997). Training complex cognitive skills: A four-component instructional design model for technical training. JJG.

Van Rosmalen, P., Vogten, H., Van Es, R., Passier, H., Poelmans, P., & Koper, R. (2006). Authoring a full life cycle model in standards-based, adaptive e-learning. *Journal of Educational Technology & Society, 9*(1).

VanLehn, K. (2006). The Behavior of Tutoring Systems. *International Journal of Artificial Intelligence in Education, 16*(3), 227–265.

VanLehn, K. (2011). The relative effectiveness of human tutoring, intelligent tutoring systems, and other tutoring systems. *Educational Psychologist, 46*(4), 197–221. doi:10.1080/00461520.2011.611369

Vantroys, T., & Peter, Y. (2005). COW, an educational scenario execution support service. *STICEF Review, 12.* ISSN: 1764-7223.

Vial, M. (2012). *Finding your way around the evaluation models.* De Boeck.

Viau, R. (1997). *La motivation en contexte scolaire.* De Boeck.

Vikas, S., & Mathur, A. (2022). An empirical study of student perception towards pedagogy, teaching style and effectiveness of online classes. *Education and Information Technologies, 27*(1), 1–22. doi:10.100710639-021-10793-9 PMID:34720659

Villiot-Leclercq, E. (2007). Genèse, réception, orientation et explicitation des scénarios pédagogiques: vers un modèle de conception des scénarios par contraintes. *Distances et savoirs, 54*(4), 507-526.

Vourdanou, K. (2019). Challenging curricular boundaries and identities through CLIL: an e-learning professional development program for CLIL teachers. In A. Kostoulas (Ed.), *Challenging boundaries in language education: second language learning and teaching* (pp. 89–106). Springer. doi:10.1007/978-3-030-17057-8_6

Vygotsky, L. S. (1986). Thought and language (rev. ed.) A. Kozulin (ed.). Cambridge, M.A.: The MIT Press.

Vygotsky, L. S. (1978). *Mind in society: The development of higher mental processes Cambridge.* Harvard University Press.

Vygotsky, L. S. (1978). *Mind in Society: The Development of Higher Psychological Processes.* Harvard University Press.

Wachira, P., & Keengwe, J. (2011). Technology Integration in K-12: Teachers' Perceptions and Use of Digital Media in the Classroom. *International Journal of Education and Development Using Information and Communication Technology*, 7(2), 136–149.

Wagner, J. L., Smith, K. J., Johnson, C., Hilaire, M. L., & Medina, M. S. (2023). Best practices in syllabus design. *American Journal of Pharmaceutical Education*, 87(3), 432–437. doi:10.5688/ajpe8995 PMID:35487683

Walkington, C., & Bernacki, M. L. (2020). *Appraising research on personalized learning: Definitions, theoretical alignment, advancements, and future directions.*

Wang, S., & Xing, J. (2021). 国内 CLIL 教学研究回顾与展望 [Retrospect and prospect of CLIL teaching research in China]. 考试与评价·大学英语教研版 *[Testing and Evaluation (College English Teaching & Research)]*, (2), 90–95. doi:10.16830/j.cnki.22-1387/g4.2021.02.018

Wang, X. (2019). 中国优秀传统文化融入大学英语教学路径研究——以江苏食品药品职业技术学院为例 [Research on the paths of integrating Chinese excellent traditional culture into college English teaching — take the Jiangsu Food and Pharmaceutical Science College as an example]. 湖州职业技术学院学报 *[Journal of Huzhou Vocational and Technological College]*, (4), 53–56. doi:10.13690/j.cnki.hzyxb.issn.1672-2388.2019.04.15

Wang, Z., Lu, Y., Guang, Y., & Zhou, E. (2022). 医学人文教育视角下的医学英语课程思政教学探索 [Teaching medical English combined with ideological and political education from the perspective of medical humanities education]. 中华医学教育杂志 *[Chinese Journal of Medical Education]*, 42(1), 11–15. doi:10.3760/cma.j.cn115259-20210513-00629

Wang, F., Leary, K. A., Taylor, L. C., & Derosier, M. E. (2016). Peer and teacher preference, student–teacher relationships, student ethnicity, and peer victimization in elementary school. *Psychology in the Schools*, 53(5), 488–501. doi:10.1002/pits.21922

Wang, H., Xuan, J., Liu, L., Shen, X., & Xiong, Y. (2021). Problem-based learning and case-based learning in dental education. *Annals of Translational Medicine*, 9(14), 1137. doi:10.21037/atm-21-165 PMID:34430578

Wang, P., Ma, T., Liu, L. B., Shang, C., An, P., & Xue, Y. X. (2021). A comparison of the effectiveness of online instructional strategies optimized with smart interactive tools versus traditional teaching for postgraduate students. *Frontiers in Psychology*, 12, 747719. doi:10.3389/fpsyg.2021.747719 PMID:35002844

Wang, Y., & Sun, C. (2001). Internetbased real time language education: Towards a fourth generation distance education. *CALICO Journal*, 539–561.

Weaver, W. (1949). *The mathematical theory of communication, by CE Shannon (and recent contributions to the mathematical theory of communication).* University of Illinois Press.

Webb, N. (1991). Task related verbal interaction and mathematics learning in small groups. *Journal for Research in Mathematics Education*, 22(5), 366–389. doi:10.2307/749186

Webley, K. (2013). The adaptive learning revolution. *Time Magazine*, 6.

Weibelzahl, S., Paramythis, A., & Masthoff, J. (2020, July). Evaluation of adaptive systems. In *Proceedings of the 28th ACM Conference on User Modeling, Adaptation and personalization* (pp. 394-395). ACM. 10.1145/3340631.3398668

Weinstein, C. E., & Mayer, R. E. (1986). The teaching of learning strategies. In M. C. Wittrock (Ed.), *Handbook of Research on Teaching* (pp. 315–327). Macmilian Publishing Company.

Weiss, C. H. (1995). Nothing as practical as good theory: Exploring theory-based evaluation for comprehensive community initiatives for children and families. *New Approaches to Evaluating Community Initiatives: Concepts, Methods, and Contexts*, 65-92.

Weiss, C. H. (1998). *Evaluation: Methods for studying programs and policies.* Prentice Hall.

Wen, Q. (2019). 新中国外语教学理论70年发展历程 [Foreign language teaching theories in China in the past 70 years]. 中国外语 *[Journal of the Foreign Languages in China], 16*(5), 14–22. doi:10.13564/j.cnki.issn.1672-9382.2019.05.003

Wen, Q. (2021). 大学外语课程思政的内涵和实施框架 [A framework of integrating moral education into college foreign language teaching]. 中国外语 *[Journal of the Foreign Languages in China], 18*(2), 47–52. doi:10.13564/j.cnki.issn.1672-9382.2021.02.008

Wentling, T. L., Waight, C., Gallagher, J., La Fleur, J., Wang, C., & Kanfer, A. (2000). E-learning - a review of literature. *Knowledge and Learning Systems Group NCSA, 9*, 1–73.

WGU. (n.d.). *Connectivism Learning Theory.* WGU. https://www.wgu.edu/blog/connectivism-learning-theory2105.html ↗

Whitehead, J. C., & Limniou, M. (2010). Online general prelaboratory training course for facilitating first year chemical laboratory. *Cypriot Journal of Educational Sciences, 5*, 39–55.

Willingham, D. T. (2010). *Why children don't like school!* La Librairie des Écoles. doi:10.1002/9781118269527

Willis, K. (2011). *Theories and Practices of Development* (2nd ed.). Routledge., doi:10.4324/9780203844182

Wintergerst, A. C., DeCapua, A., & Itzen, R. C. (2001). The construct validity of one learning styles instrument. *System, 29*(3), 385–403. doi:10.1016/S0346-251X(01)00027-6

Wittrock, M. C. (1986). Studens thought processes. In M. C. Wittrock (Ed.), *Handbook of Research on Teaching* (pp. 255–296). Macmilian Publishing Company.

Wong, L.H., SingChai, C., & PohAw, G. (2017). Seamless language learning: Second language learning with social media. *Comunicar: Revista Científica de Comunicacíon y Educacíon, 25*(50), 9–21. doi:10.3916/C50-2017-01

Xiao, Q., & Huang, G. (2020). 关于外语课程思政建设的思考 [On the ideological-political construction of foreign language courses]. 中国外语 *[Journal of the Foreign Languages in China], 17*(5), 10–14. doi:10.13564/j.cnki.issn.1672-9382.2020.05.001

Xin, P., & Yin, X. (2016). 打造精彩优秀的思政课程——以"大国方略"系列课程为例 [To forge high-quality curriculum of ideological and political education—a case study of "What Matters to Rising China" series]. 青年学报 *[Youth Research], (4),* 19–24. doi:10.3969/j.issn.2095-7947.2016.04.004

Xu, Y., Wang, L., Li, P., Xu, H., Liu, Z., Ji, M., & Luo, Z. (2023). Exploring the impact of online and offline teaching methods on the cognitive abilities of medical students: A comparative study. *BMC Medical Education, 23*(1), 557. doi:10.118612909-023-04549-x PMID:37553632

Yang, Y. (2019). "一带一路"建设与高校语言人才培养 [A research on the development of "Belt and Road Initiatives" and language human resources]. 兴义民族师范学院学报 *[Journal of Xingyi Normal University for Nationalities], (2),* 106–110. doi:10.3969/j.issn.1009-0673.2019.02.023

Yarbro, J., McKnight, K., Elliott, S., Kurz, A., & Wardlow, L. (2016). Digital instructional strategies and their role in classroom learning. *Journal of Research on Technology in Education, 48*(4), 274–289. doi:10.1080/15391523.2016.1212632

Yildiz, E. P. (2021). Augmented reality research and applications in education. In *Augmented Reality and Its Application*. IntechOpen.

Yılmaz, Y., Üstündağ, M. T., & Güneş, E. (2017b). Investigation of digital story development stages and tools as teaching materials. *Abant İzzet Baysal Üniversitesi Eğitim Fakültesi Dergisi, 17*(3), 1621–1640. doi:10.17240/aibuefd.2017.17.31178-338851

Yılmaz, Y., Üstündağ, M. T., Güneş, E., & Çalişkan, G. (2017a). Utilizing digital storytelling method for effective Turkish language teaching. *Educational Technology Theory and Practice, 7*(2), 254–275.

Young, S. (2006). Student views of effective online teaching in higher education. *American Journal of Distance Education, 20*(2), 65–77. doi:10.120715389286ajde2002_2

Yu, X. (2021). Exploration on the university curriculum ideological and political innovation system. *E3S Web of Conferences, 295*(2021), Article 05028. doi:10.1051/e3sconf/202129505028

Yüce, E. (2019). Possible problems in online foreign language teaching at a university context. *International Journal of Curriculum and Instruction, 11*(2), 75–86.

Yumnam, R. (2021). Elearning: An effective mode of teaching English as a Second Language. *Journal of Translation and Language Studies, 2*(2), 1–9. doi:10.48185/jtls.v2i2.275

Yu, Z. (2021). The effects of gender, educational level, and personality on online learning outcomes during the COVID-19 pandemic. *International Journal of Educational Technology in Higher Education, 18*(1), 14. doi:10.118641239-021-00252-3 PMID:34778520

Yüzer, T. V., & Kılınç, A. G. H. (2015). Benefit from the digital storytelling in the open learning system. *Journal of Research in Education and Teaching, 4*(1), 243–250.

Zahra, O. F., Amel, N., & Mohamed, K. (2023). *Communication Tools and E-Learning: A Revolution in the Research Methodology of Communication for a Pedagogical Scenario.*

Zahra, O. F., Amel, N., & Mohamed, K. (2023). Communication Tools and E-Learning: A Revolution in the Research Methodology of Communication for a Pedagogical Scenario. *RA Journal of Applied Research, 9*(4), 170–177. doi:10.47191/rajar/v9i4.03

Zakarneh, B. M. (2018). Effectiveness of Elearning mode for teaching English language in Arab Universities. *International Journal of Applied Linguistics and English Literature, 7*(7), 171–181. doi:10.7575/aiac.ijalel.v.7n.7p.171

Zargane, K., Erradi, M., & Khaldi, M. (2023). Design and Implementation of Collaborative Pedagogical Scenarios for Adaptive Learning. In Handbook of Research on Scripting, Media Coverage, and Implementation of E-Learning Training in LMS Platforms (pp. 242-250). IGI Global. doi:10.4018/978-1-6684-7634-5.ch010

Zarouk, M. Y., Olivera, E., Peres, P., & Khaldi, M. (2020). The Impact of Flipped Project-Based Learning on Self-Regulation in Higher Education. International Journal Emerging Technologies in Learning, iJET, 15. doi:10.3991/ijet.v15i17.14135

Zarraonandia, T. (2007). *Adaptations of Learning Units at Runtime*. [Doctoral Thesis, Department of Computer Science, Higher Polytechnic School, Carlos III University of Madrid, Leganes, Madrid].

Zeitoun, H. (2008). *E-learning: Concept, Issues, Application, Evaluation, Riyadh*. Dar Alsolateah publication.

Zengin, B., Arikan, A., & Dogan, D. (2011). Opinions of English major students about their departments' websites. *Contemporary Educational Technology, 2*(4), 294–307. doi:10.30935/cedtech/6060

Zhang, X. (2021). 我国高校德语专业本土化的内容—语言融合教学策略探究——以跨文化交际课程为例 [The localisation of CLIL teaching strategies in the German language major programmes at Chinese universities: a study of intercultural communication course]. 外语教育研究前沿 *[Foreign Language Education in China], 4*(3), 57–64. http://www.cnki.com.cn/Article/CJFDTotal-WYQY202103008.htm

Zhang, C., & Fagan, C. (2016). Examining the role of ideological and political education on university students' civic perceptions and civic participation in Mainland China: Some hints from contemporary citizenship theory. Citizenship. *Social and Economics Education, 15*(2), 117–142. doi:10.1177/2047173416681170

Zhang, Y., & Paulson, K. V. (1997). Enhancement of Signal-to-noise Ratio in Natural-source Transient Magnetotelluric Data with Wavelet Transform. *Pure and Applied Geophysics, 149*(2), 405–419. doi:10.1007000240050033

Zhang, Y., & Paulson, K. V. (1997). Magnetotelluric inversion using regularized Hopfield neural networks. *Geophysical Prospecting, 45*(5), 725–743. doi:10.1046/j.1365-2478.1997.660299.x

Zhetpisbayeva, B. A., Kitibayeva, A. K., Kazimova, D. A., Akbayeva, G. N., & Zatyneiko, M. A. (2018). Assessment issues in content and language integrated learning (CLIL). *Journal of Advanced Pharmacy Education and Research, 8*(4), 32–38. https://japer.in/article/assessment-issues-in-content-and-language-integrated-learning-clil

Zhou, D. (2004). 双语教学与语言-内容融合学习教学法 [Bilingual teaching and content language integrated learning approach]. 比较教育研究. *Comparative Education Review*, (6), 28–32. doi:10.3969/j.issn.1003-7667.2004.06.006

Zhou, X. (2021). Global citizenship education in school curricula: A Chinese perspective. *Journal of Liberal Arts and Social Science, 9*(4), 40–60. https://ijlass.org/articles/9.4.6.40-60.pdf

Zimmerman, B. J., & Martinez-Pons, M. (1990). Student differences in self-regulated learning: Relating grade, sex, and giftedness to self-efficacy and strategy use. *Journal of Educational Psychology, 82*(1), 51–59. doi:10.1037/0022-0663.82.1.51

About the Contributors

Lamya Anoir is a PhD candidate in Computer sciences, and member of Research team in Computer Science and University Pedagogical Engineering Higher Normal School, Abdelmalek Essaadi University, Tetouan, Morocco. She has a Master degree in Instructional design Multimedia engineering at Higher Normal School of Martil, Morocco in 2019. The current research focuses on: Personnalized E-learning, Adaptive Hypermedia Systems, Artificial Intelligence.

Joan Bailey graduated from Hunter College of The City University of New York and received a Ph.D. in Social and Personality Psychology from the Graduate School and University Center of the City University of New York. Dr. Bailey has been a textbook reviewer for several publishing houses including Allyn & Bacon, Erlbaum Publishers, and Sage Publications. She was elected to studying psychology at New Jersey City University 25 the National Cancer Institute's Consumer Advocates in Research and Related Activities Program where she has helped to develop accessible patient-education materials. She is also a First Connections Trainer for The Leukemia and Lymphoma Society where she provides patient information and facilitates patient communication with physicians. She has received awards for her work with the Leukemia and Lymphoma Society. Dr. Bailey's major academic interests have focused on Social Cognition, The Social Psychology of Prejudice, Multicultural Issues, Behavioral Genetics and the Neurobiology of Personality, and Adjustment to Chronic Illness.

Mohammad Erradi is a professor at ENS Tetouan Morocco and a member of the Laboratory of Computer Science and University Pedagogical Engineering.

Harwati Hashim is a senior lecturer at the Faculty of Education, Universiti Kebangsaan Malaysia. Her research interest is in Teaching English as a Second Language and Mobile-assisted Language Learning.

Hengzhi Hu is a PhD candidate at the Faculty of Education, Universiti Kebangsaan Malaysia. His research interest is in Second Language Acquisition and Bilingual Education.

Ahmed Ibrahimi is a teacher-researcher at Abdelmalek Essaadi University. He is coordinator of the Specialized Master in Didactics of French as a Foreign Language and coordinator of the Didactic, Literacy and Mediation Research Team within the Humanities and Education Laboratory at the ENS of Tétouan.

Gururajaprasad Kaggal Lakshmana Rao holds a master's in orthodontics from Nizhny Novgorod State Medical Academy, Russia, and holds a Ph.D. in Orthodontics from Universiti Sains Malaysia. His research focus is on smart learning environments. His research interests are centered around orthodontic education, clinical education, and smart learning environments with special interests in augmented reality and its educational applications. He has won the best research student award on two occasions and has published in several peer-reviewed indexed journals both locally and internationally. He is also an inventor and holds a patent from India.

Maha Khaldi, a lecturer and e-learning engineer at Rabat business school, international university of Rabat, Morocco, specializes in cumputer science and has a keen interest in pedagogy and e-learning methodologies. Her work reflects a dedication to advancing education through innovative technology and teaching practices

Nur Ehsan Mohd Said is a lecturer and the head of Higher Education English Test at Universiti Kebangsaan Malaysia. His research interest is in Teaching English as a Second Language and applied linguistics.

Amel Nejjari is a Professor at National School of Applied Sciences-Tetuan, Morocco since 2008. Currently, she is a member of the research team: Didactics, Literacies and Mediation, ENS of Tetuan. Her research focuses on innovative pedagogies and digital in language learning and teaching.

Fatima Zahra Ouariach is a Doctoral Researcher specializing in Educational Technologies at Abdelmalek Essaadi University. She is currently working on her doctorate, which focuses on the management of communication tools in e-learning via an LMS platform. Her research aims to design an efficient architecture for communication tools in the specific context of e-learning using an LMS platform. In addition to her academic work, she has gained experience as a reviewer for prestigious publishing houses such as Hindawi ... In addition, she has made valuable contributions as a member of the jury for oral interviews at Abdelmalek Essaadi University, highlighting her dedication and contribution to the advancement of research and higher education.

Soufiane Ouariach is a budding fourth-year Ph.D. student with a passion for computer science and university pedagogical engineering. He's currently carrying out research under the tutelage of the esteemed Professor Khadi Mohamed at Abdel Malek Essaadi University. His research focuses on the exciting new frontier of flipped classroom models, using the innovative approach of SPOC (Small Private Online Courses) as well as distance learning design and implementation. His academic prowess extends to distance learning design and implementation, where he's keen on breaking new ground.

Mohammed Saleh received his Master of Science degree in Software Quality from Abdelmalek Essaâdi University, Morocco. His research interests include data science, logistics, management, machine learning, artificial intelligence, and data mining.

Şenol Şen is currently an associated professor in the Department of Mathematics and Science Education at Hacettepe University, Ankara, Türkiye. He received B.Sc., M.Sc., and Ph.D. degree from the Faculty of Education at Hacettepe University in 2009, 2011 and 2015. His research interests include self-regulated learning, chemistry education, inquiry-based learning, problem-based learning, and technology integration.

Peri Yuksel is a tenured associate professor of psychology at NJCU. Dr. Yuksel's research concerns bilingual language development, parenting across cultures, trauma-informed pedagogy, and effective teaching and learning environments that facilitate student success and engagement in psychological literacy and global citizenship. Dr. Yuksel published in the field of psycholinguistics, scholarship of teaching and learning, and international education. She always encourages her students to conduct research for peer review. Among others, Dr. Yuksel chairs the Annual NJCU Pedagogy Day and serves in the NJCU's Institutional Review Board. She is the co-advisor to the NJCU Psychology Society and Chapter of Psi Chi- International Honor Society to Psychology. She received the Isenberg Award in recognition of her endangered language documentation, which helped in the publication and distribution of two children's books in the endangered Laz language.

Kawtar Zargane PhD candidate in Computer Sciences, and member of research team in Computer Science and University Pedagogical Engineering Higher Normal School, Abdelmalek Essaadi University, Tetouan, Morocco. She has a Master degree in Instructional design Multimedia engineering at Higher Normal School of Martil, Morocco in 2019. The current research focuses on: Collaboration E-learning, Adaptive Hypermedia Systems, Artificial Intelligence.

Mohammed Zine El Abidine is a PHD student at Abdelmalek Essaadi University. He is also a member of the research team: educational sciences, language didactics, humanities and social sciences faculty of letters and humanities of tetouan. His research focus on Adaptive E-learning and development of training devices: integral works.

Index

Recommended Reference Books

IGI Global's reference books are available in three unique pricing formats:
Print Only, E-Book Only, or Print + E-Book.

Order direct through IGI Global's Online Bookstore at
www.igi-global.com or through your preferred provider.

Premier Reference Source

Online Distance Learning Course Design and Multimedia in E-Learning

ISBN: 9781799897064
EISBN: 9781799897088
© 2022; 302 pp.
List Price: US$ 215

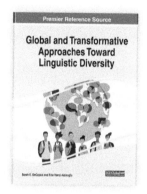

Premier Reference Source

Global and Transformative Approaches Toward Linguistic Diversity

ISBN: 9781799889854
EISBN: 9781799889878
© 2022; 383 pp.
List Price: US$ 215

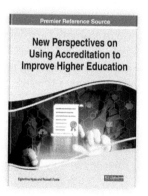

Premier Reference Source

New Perspectives on Using Accreditation to Improve Higher Education

ISBN: 9781668451953
EISBN: 9781668451960
© 2022; 300 pp.
List Price: US$ 195

Premier Reference Source

Impact of School Shootings on Classroom Culture, Curriculum, and Learning

ISBN: 9781799852001
EISBN: 9781799852018
© 2022; 355 pp.
List Price: US$ 215

Premier Reference Source

Modern Reading Practices and Collaboration Between Schools, Family, and Community

ISBN: 9781799897507
EISBN: 9781799897521
© 2022; 304 pp.
List Price: US$ 215

Premier Reference Source

Designing Effective Distance and Blended Learning Environments in K-12

ISBN: 9781799868293
EISBN: 9781799868316
© 2022; 389 pp.
List Price: US$ 215

Do you want to stay current on the latest research trends, product announcements, news, and special offers?
Join IGI Global's mailing list to receive customized recommendations, exclusive discounts, and more.
Sign up at: **www.igi-global.com/newsletters**.

Publisher of Timely, Peer-Reviewed Inclusive Research Since 1988

IGI Global
PUBLISHER of TIMELY KNOWLEDGE

www.igi-global.com  Sign up at www.igi-global.com/newsletters   f facebook.com/igiglobal   t twitter.com/igiglobal   in linkedin.com/igiglobal

Ensure Quality Research is Introduced
to the Academic Community

Become an Evaluator
for IGI Global Authored
Book Projects

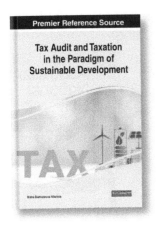

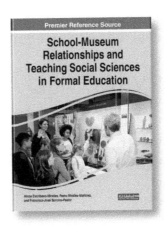

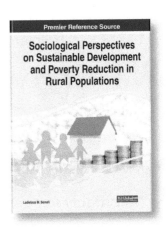

The overall success of an authored book project is dependent on quality and timely manuscript evaluations.

Applications and Inquiries may be sent to:
development@igi-global.com

Applicants must have a doctorate (or equivalent degree) as well as publishing, research, and reviewing experience. Authored Book Evaluators are appointed for one-year terms and are expected to complete at least three evaluations per term. Upon successful completion of this term, evaluators can be considered for an additional term.

If you have a colleague that may be interested in this opportunity, we encourage you to share this information with them.

Easily Identify, Acquire, and Utilize Published Peer-Reviewed Findings in Support of Your Current Research

IGI Global OnDemand

Purchase Individual IGI Global OnDemand Book Chapters and Journal Articles

For More Information:

www.igi-global.com/e-resources/ondemand/

Browse through 150,000+ Articles and Chapters!

Find specific research related to your current studies and projects that have been contributed by international researchers from prestigious institutions, including:

- Accurate and Advanced Search

- Affordably Acquire Research

- Instantly Access Your Content

- Benefit from the InfoSci Platform Features

It really provides an excellent entry into the research literature of the field. It presents a manageable number of highly relevant sources on topics of interest to a wide range of researchers. The sources are scholarly, but also accessible to 'practitioners'.

- Ms. Lisa Stimatz, MLS, University of North Carolina at Chapel Hill, USA

Interested in Additional Savings?

Subscribe to

IGI Global OnDemand *Plus*

Learn More

Acquire content from over 128,000+ research-focused book chapters and 33,000+ scholarly journal articles for as low as US$ 5 per article/chapter (original retail price for an article/chapter: US$ 37.50).

7,300+ E-BOOKS.
ADVANCED RESEARCH.
INCLUSIVE & AFFORDABLE.

IGI Global e-Book Collection

- **Flexible Purchasing Options** (Perpetual, Subscription, EBA, etc.)
- Multi-Year Agreements with **No Price Increases** Guaranteed
- **No Additional Charge** for Multi-User Licensing
- No Maintenance, Hosting, or Archiving Fees
- Continually Enhanced & Innovated **Accessibility Compliance Features** (WCAG)

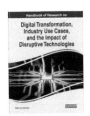

Handbook of Research on Digital Transformation, Industry Use Cases, and the Impact of Disruptive Technologies
ISBN: 9781799877127
EISBN: 9781799877141

Handbook of Research on New Investigations in Artificial Life, AI, and Machine Learning
ISBN: 9781799886860
EISBN: 9781799886877

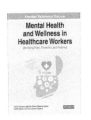

Handbook of Research on Future of Work and Education
ISBN: 9781799882756
EISBN: 9781799882770

Research Anthology on Physical and Intellectual Disabilities in an Inclusive Society (4 Vols.)
ISBN: 9781668435427
EISBN: 9781668435434

Innovative Economic, Social, and Environmental Practices for Progressing Future Sustainability
ISBN: 9781799895909
EISBN: 9781799895923

Applied Guide for Event Study Research in Supply Chain Management
ISBN: 9781799889694
EISBN: 9781799889717

Mental Health and Wellness in Healthcare Workers
ISBN: 9781799888130
EISBN: 9781799888147

Clean Technologies and Sustainable Development in Civil Engineering
ISBN: 9781799898108
EISBN: 9781799898122

Request More Information, or Recommend the IGI Global e-Book Collection to Your Institution's Librarian

For More Information or to Request a Free Trial, Contact IGI Global's e-Collections Team: eresources@igi-global.com | 1-866-342-6657 ext. 100 | 717-533-8845 ext. 100

Milton Keynes UK
Ingram Content Group UK Ltd.
UKHW050408260224
438397UK00020B/55

9 798369 331286